WEST KENT STREET ATLAS

Ordnance Survey

WEST KENT STREET ATLAS

3½ INCHES TO 1 MILE

GEORGE PHILIP

WEST KENT STREET ATLAS

First published 1989 by

Ordnance Survey and George Philip Ltd

Ordnance Survey
Romsey Road
Maybush
Southampton SO9 4DH

George Philip Ltd
59 Grosvenor Street
London W1X 9DA

British Library Cataloguing in Publication Data

West Kent street atlas.
1. Kent. Maps, atlases
1. Ordnance Survey
912'.4223
ISBN 0-319-00189-X (Ordnance Survey)
ISBN 0-540-05560-3 (George Philip)

To the best of the Publishers' knowledge, the information in this atlas was correct at the time of going to press. No responsibility can be accepted for any errors or their consequences.

The representation in this atlas of a road, track or path is no evidence of the existence of a right of way.

contents

Key map	vi–vii
Administrative map	viii
Street maps	1-197
Index explanation and abbreviations	199
List of towns, villages and rural localities	200
Index	201

key to map symbols

British Rail Station

Private Railway Station

Bus or Coach Station

Police Station
(may not be open 24hrs)

Hospital with Casualty Facilities
(may not be open 24hrs)

Post Office

Place of Worship

Important Building

P Parking

120 Adjoining page indicator

Motorway and Dual Carriageway

Main or through road

A 27(T) Road numbers (Dept of Transport)

Gate and obstruction to traffic
(restrictions may not apply at all times and to all vehicles)

Footpath
Bridleway
The representation in this atlas of a road, track or path is no evidence of the existence of a right of way.

Amb Sta	Ambulance Station
Coll	College
FB	Foot Bridge
F Sta	Fire Station
LC	Level Crossing
Liby	Library
Mus	Museum
Sch	School
TH	Town Hall

The large letters and numbers around the edge of the maps are the referencing system.
An explanation of how to use the system for locating the position of street names appears on page **199**

The small numbers identify the 1 kilometre National Grid lines.

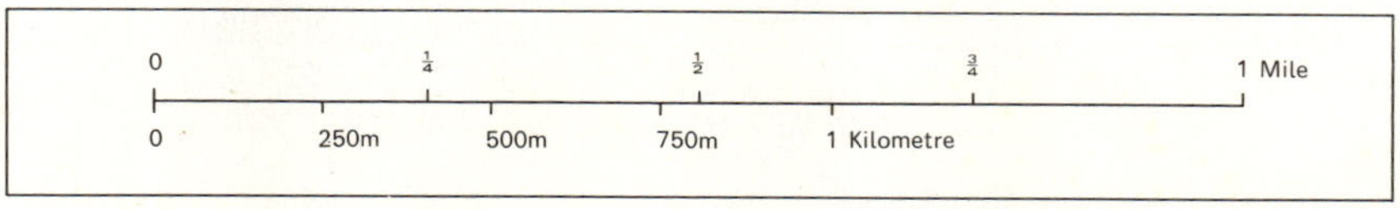

Scale of Maps is $3\frac{1}{2}$ inches to 1 mile (1:18103)

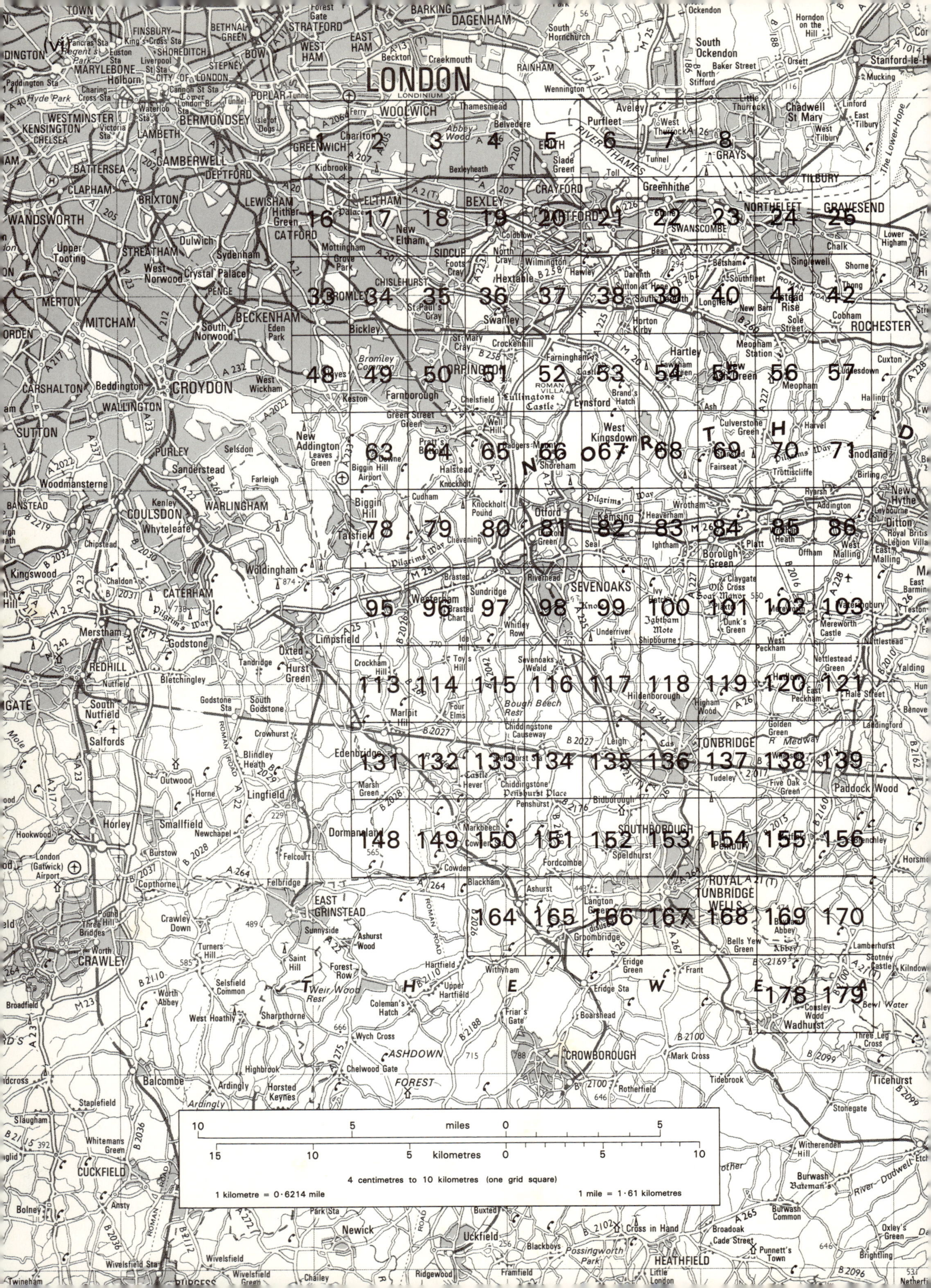
(vi)
LONDON
LONDINIUM
STRATFORD
DAGENHAM
BARKING
WEST HAM
EAST HAM
RAINHAM
WOOLWICH
GREENWICH
BERMONDSEY
WESTMINSTER
KENSINGTON
CHELSEA
LAMBETH
CAMBERWELL
DEPTFORD
BATTERSEA
CLAPHAM
BRIXTON
LEWISHAM
CATFORD
WANDSWORTH
STREATHAM
Dulwich
Sydenham
Crystal Palace
MERTON
MITCHAM
BECKENHAM
BROMLEY
CROYDON
CARSHALTON
WALLINGTON
SUTTON
PURLEY
COULSDON
WARLINGHAM
CATERHAM
REDHILL
Godstone
Oxted
Limpsfield
Lingfield
Horley
Smallfield
CRAWLEY
EAST GRINSTEAD
Forest Row
CROWBOROUGH
ASHDOWN
FOREST
Uckfield
Heathfield
Wadhurst
Ticehurst
ROYAL TUNBRIDGE WELLS
SOUTHBOROUGH
TONBRIDGE
SEVENOAKS
Westerham
Otford
Kemsing
Wrotham
Edenbridge
Hever
Penshurst
Chiddingstone
ERITH
CRAYFORD
DARTFORD
BEXLEY
ELTHAM
SIDCUP
CHISLEHURST
Swanley
ORPINGTON
Farnborough
Eynsford
Lullingstone Castle
Greenhithe
SWANSCOMBE
NORTHFLEET
GRAVESEND
TILBURY
GRAYS
Purfleet
South Ockendon
Chadwell St Mary
Stanford-le-Hope
Cobham
ROCHESTER
Meopham
Snodland
West Malling
Borough Green
Ightham
Plaxtol
Hadlow
Paddock Wood
Pembury
Bewl Water
Groombridge
Cuckfield
Balcombe
Ardingly
Crowhurst
Felbridge
Dormansland
RIVER THAMES
Pilgrims' Way
1
2
3
4
5
6
7
8
16
17
18
19
20
21
22
23
24
26
33
34
35
36
37
38
39
40
41
42
48
49
50
51
52
53
54
55
56
57
63
64
65
66
67
68
69
70
71
78
79
80
81
82
83
84
85
86
95
96
97
98
99
100
101
102
103
113
114
115
116
117
118
119
120
121
131
132
133
134
135
136
137
138
139
148
149
150
151
152
153
154
155
156
164
165
166
167
168
169
170
178
179
10 5 miles 0 5
15 10 5 kilometres 0 5 10
4 centimetres to 10 kilometres (one grid square)
1 kilometre = 0·6214 mile
1 mile = 1·61 kilometres

KEY TO MAP PAGES

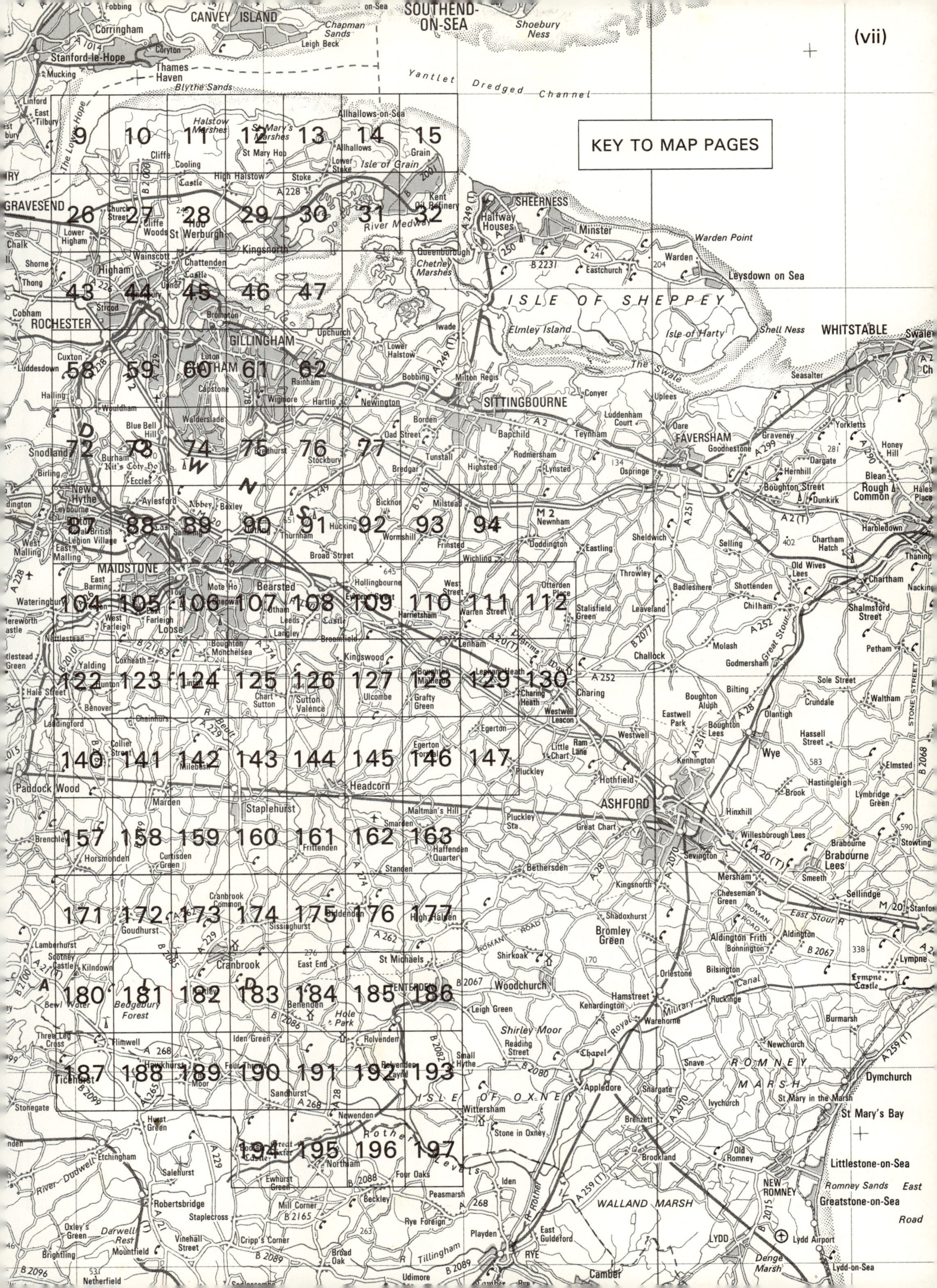

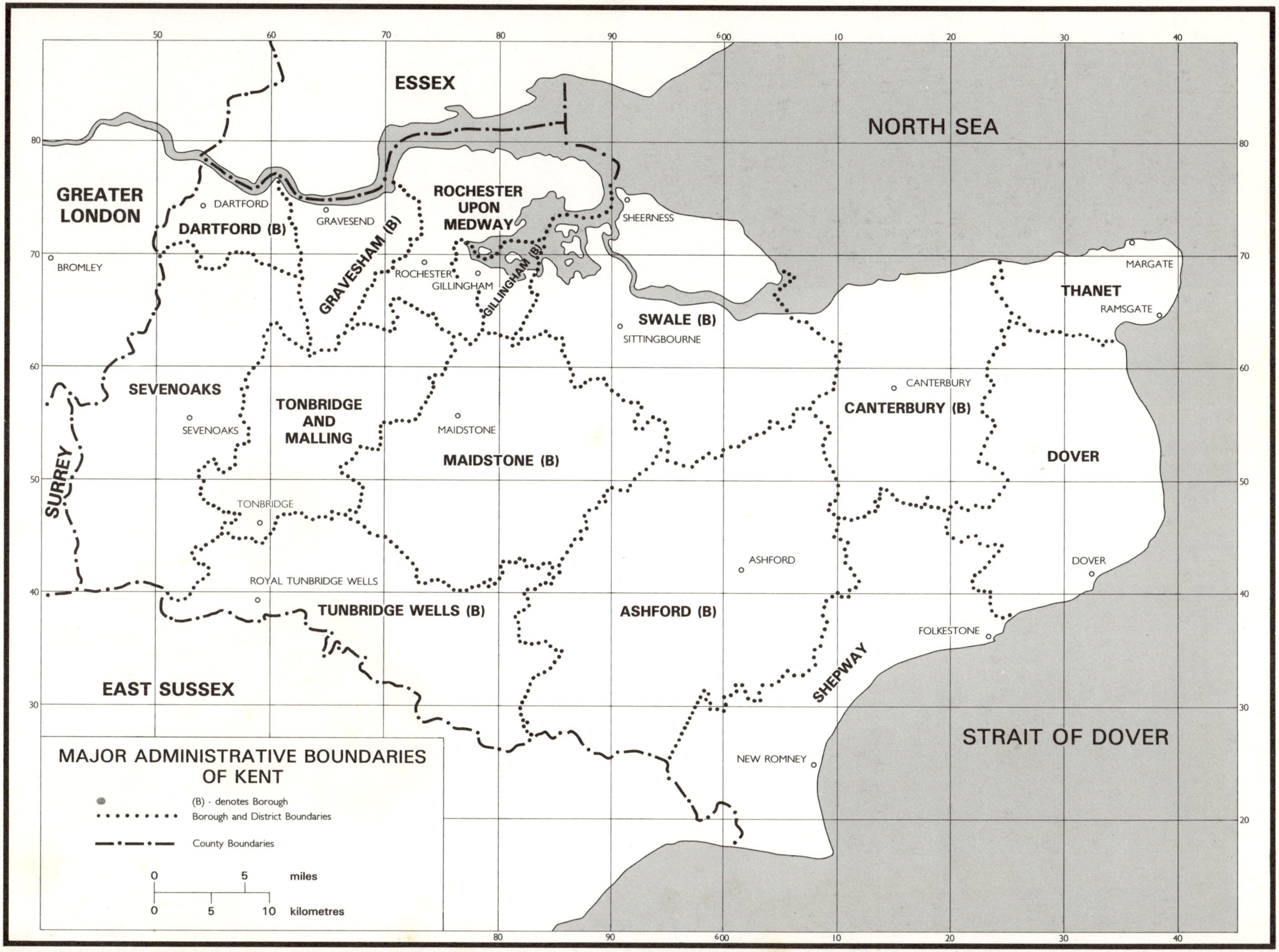
MAJOR ADMINISTRATIVE BOUNDARIES OF KENT
(B) - denotes Borough
Borough and District Boundaries
County Boundaries
miles
kilometres
NORTH SEA
STRAIT OF DOVER
ESSEX
GREATER LONDON
SURREY
EAST SUSSEX
DARTFORD (B)
GRAVESHAM (B)
ROCHESTER UPON MEDWAY
GILLINGHAM (B)
SWALE (B)
THANET
DOVER
CANTERBURY (B)
SEVENOAKS
TONBRIDGE AND MALLING
MAIDSTONE (B)
TUNBRIDGE WELLS (B)
ASHFORD (B)
SHEPWAY
BROMLEY
DARTFORD
GRAVESEND
ROCHESTER
GILLINGHAM
SHEERNESS
SITTINGBOURNE
MARGATE
RAMSGATE
CANTERBURY
DOVER
FOLKESTONE
NEW ROMNEY
ASHFORD
MAIDSTONE
SEVENOAKS
TONBRIDGE
ROYAL TUNBRIDGE WELLS

not continued, see key diagram

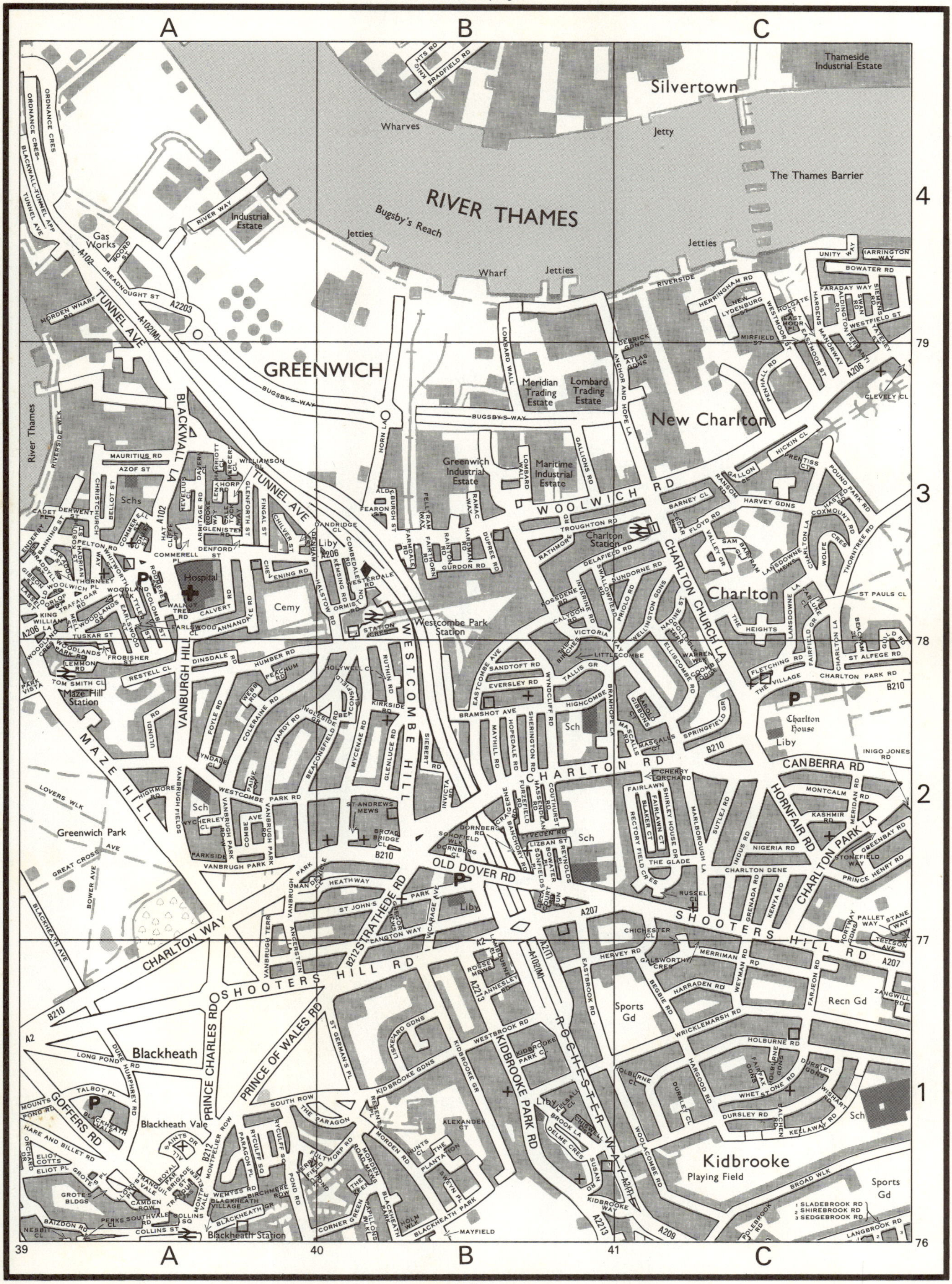

2

16

not continued, see key diagram

1

17

not continued, see key diagram

4

18

not continued, see key diagram

3

19

not continued, see key diagram

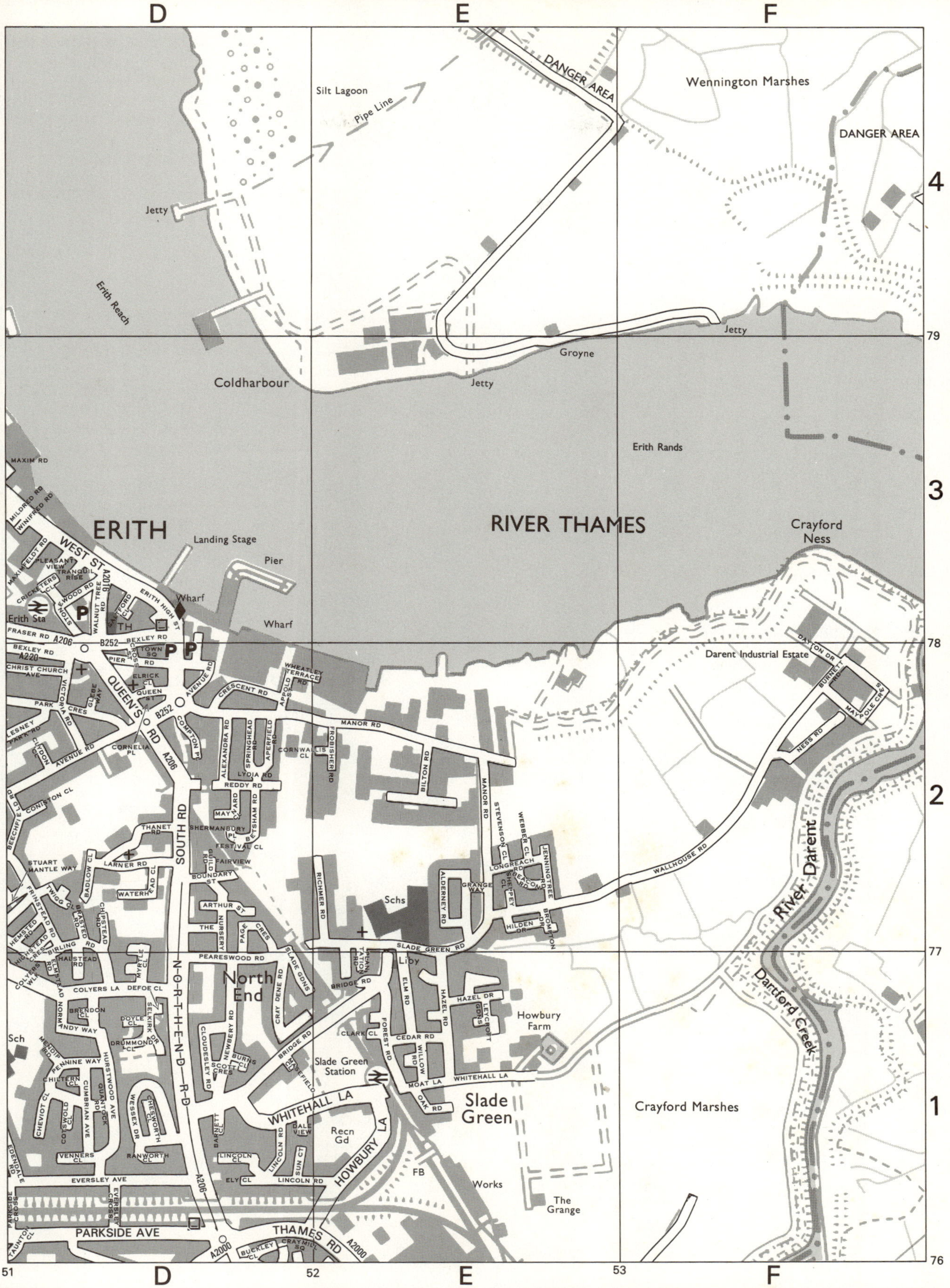

6

20

not continued, see key diagram

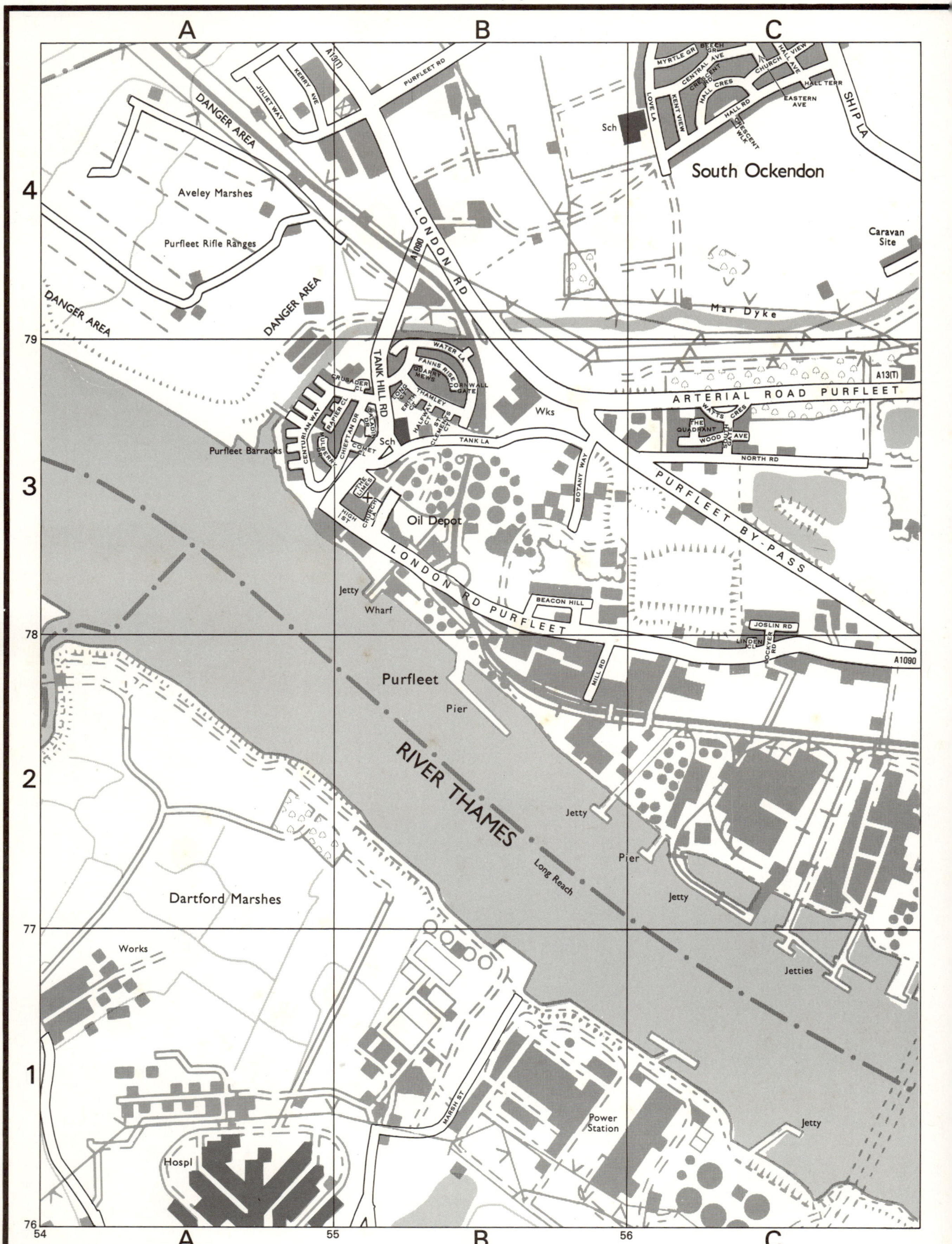

5

not continued, see key diagram

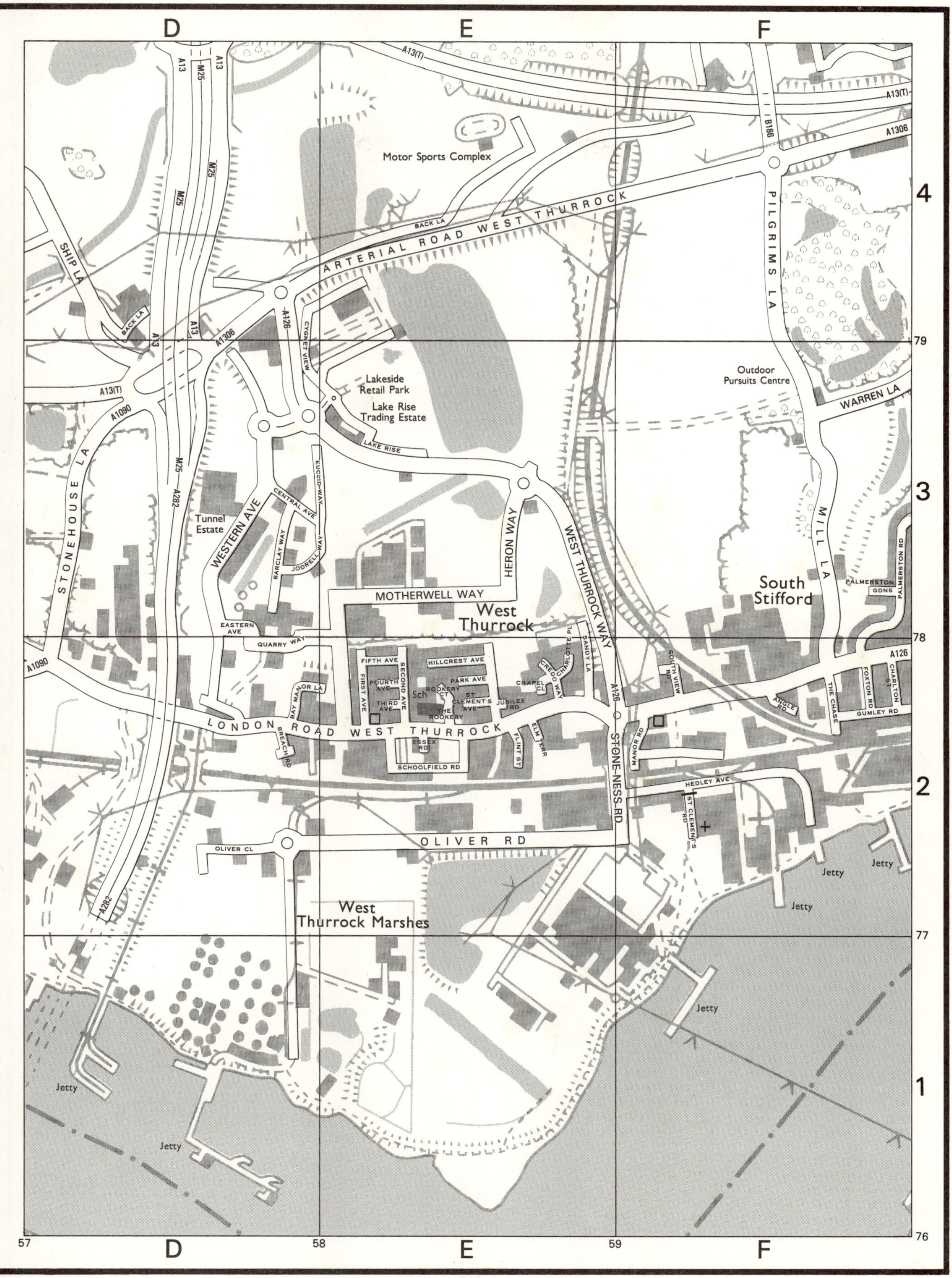

22

not continued, see key diagram

7

23

not continued, see key diagram

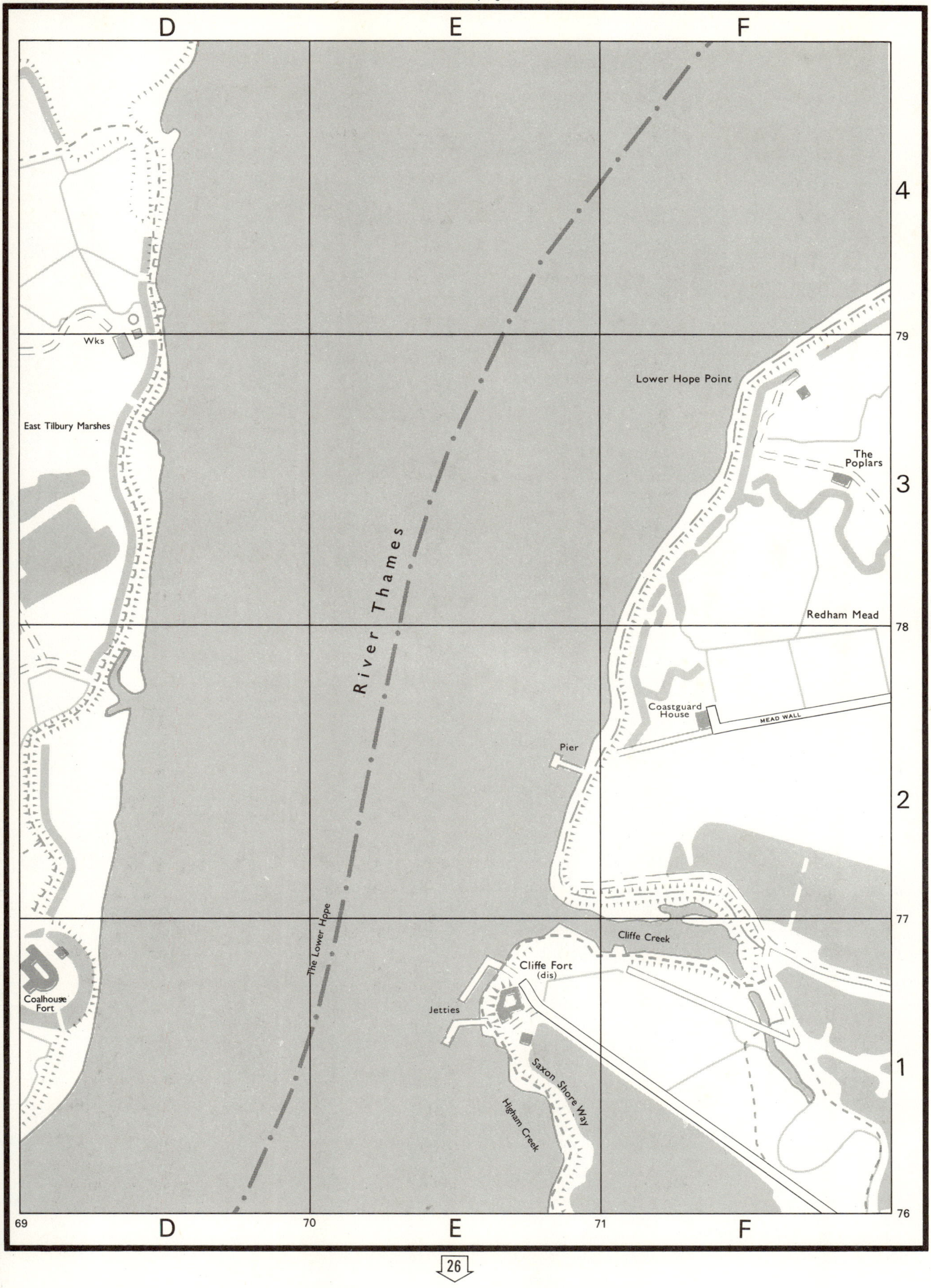

10

26

not continued, see key diagram

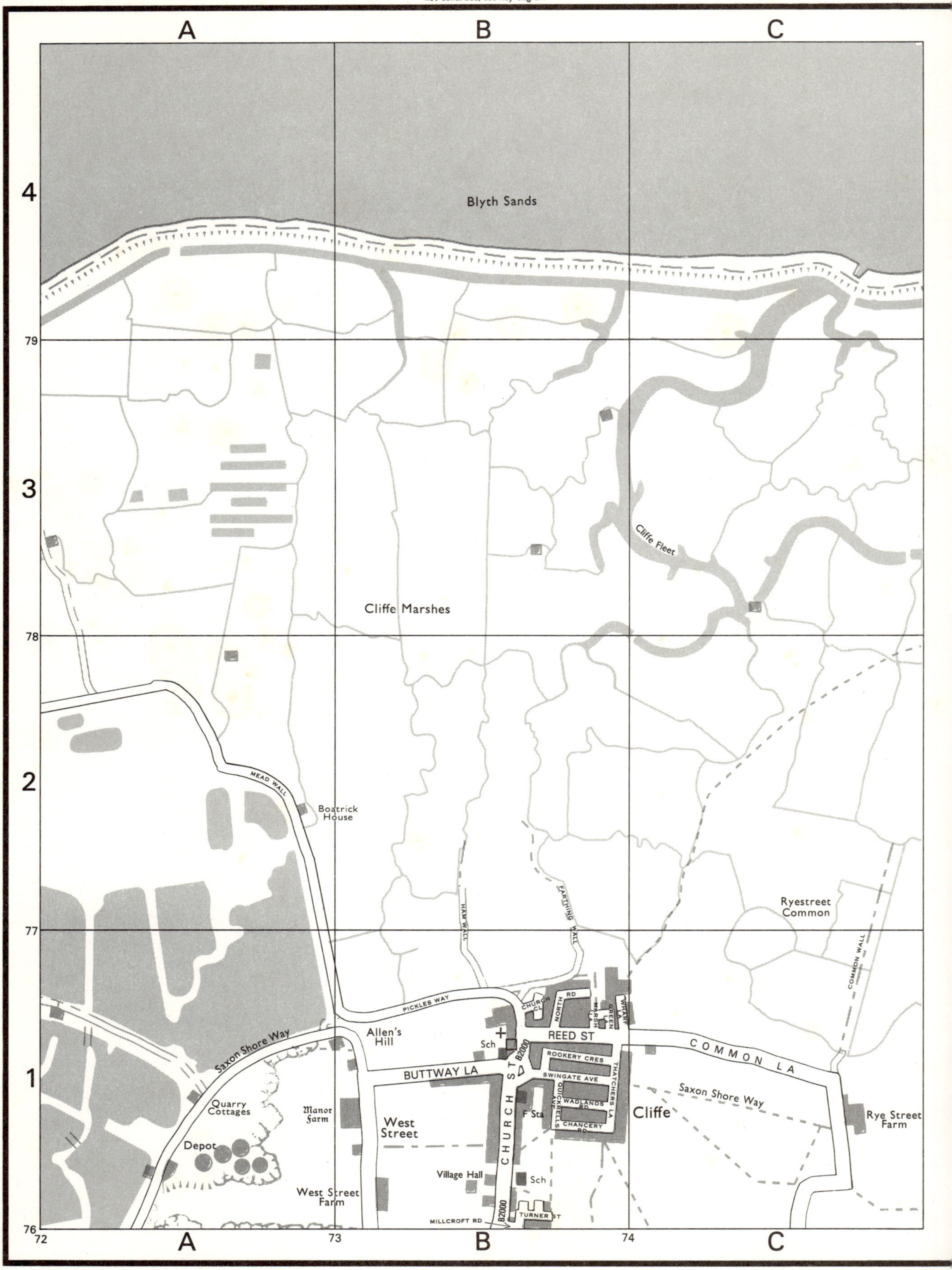

9

27

not continued, see key diagram

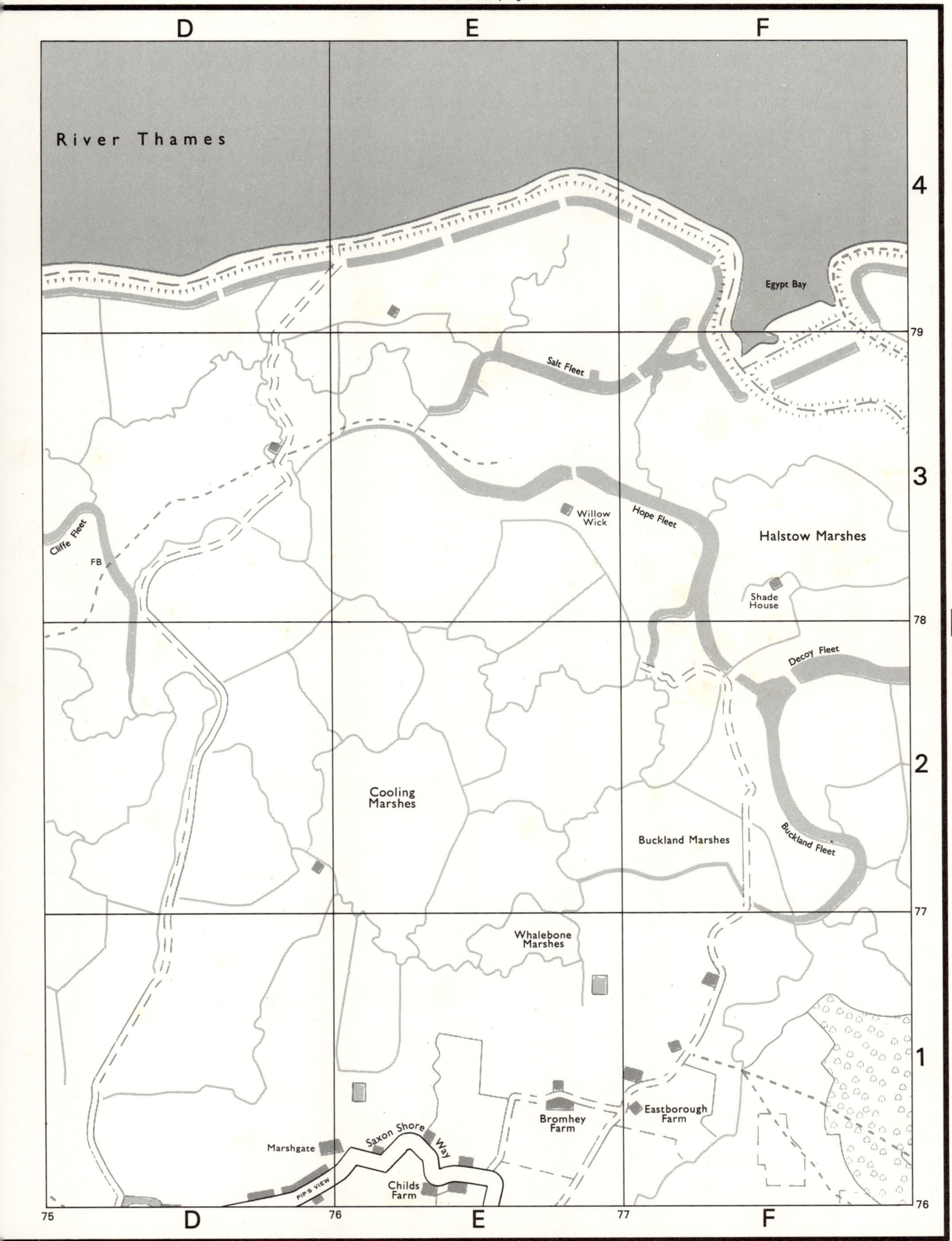

12

28

not continued, see key diagram

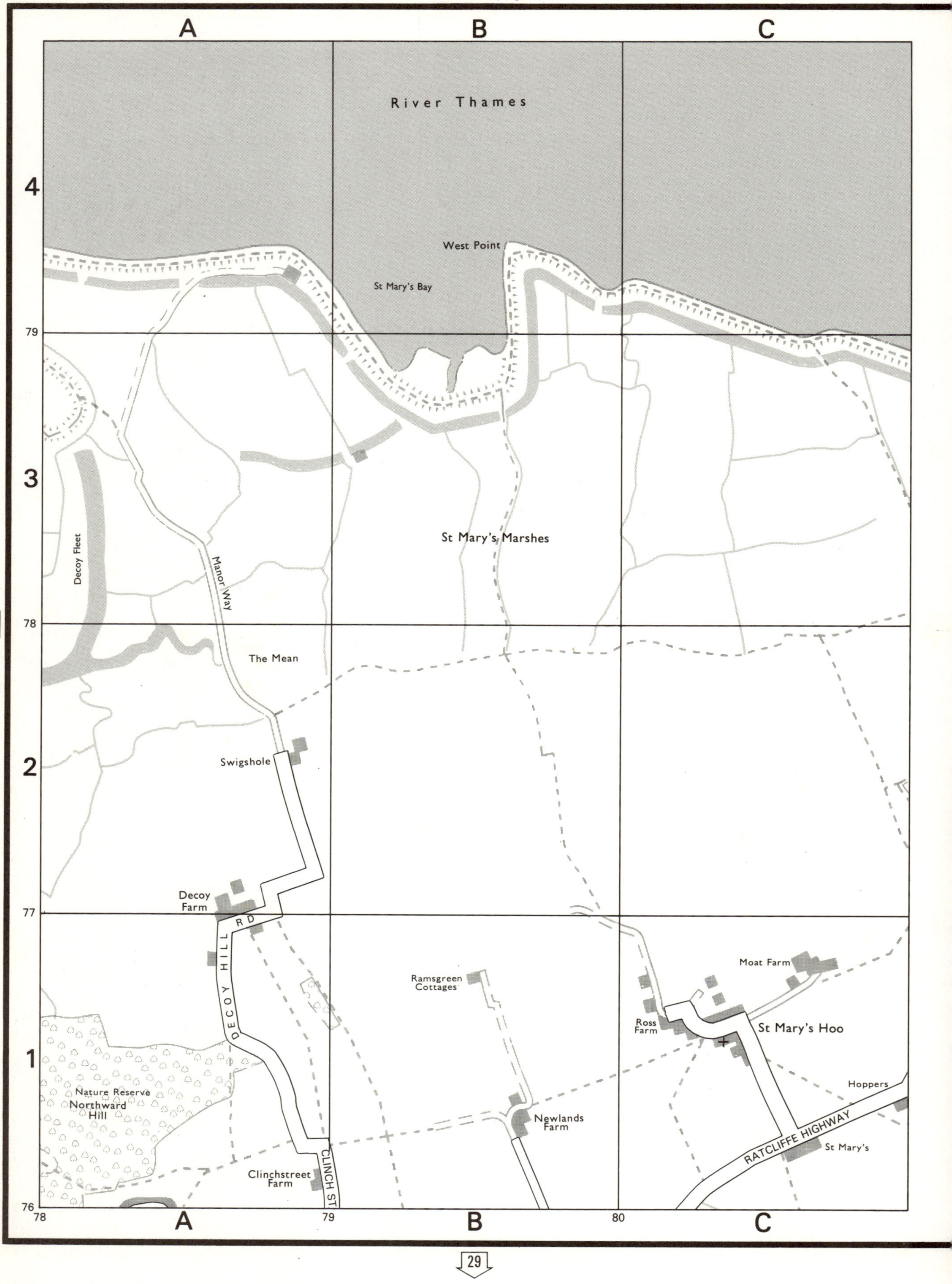

11

29

not continued, see key diagram

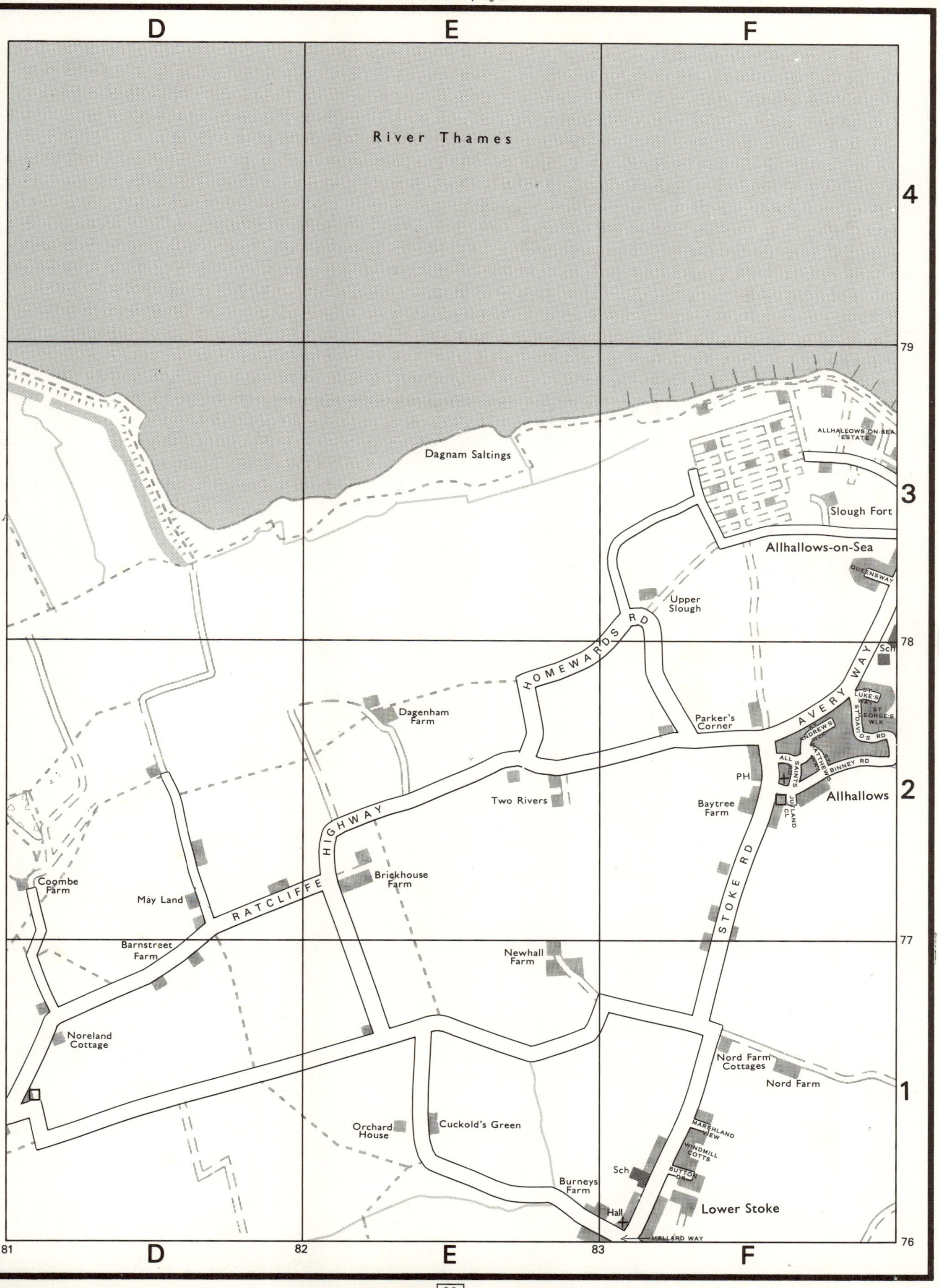

14

30

not continued, see key diagram

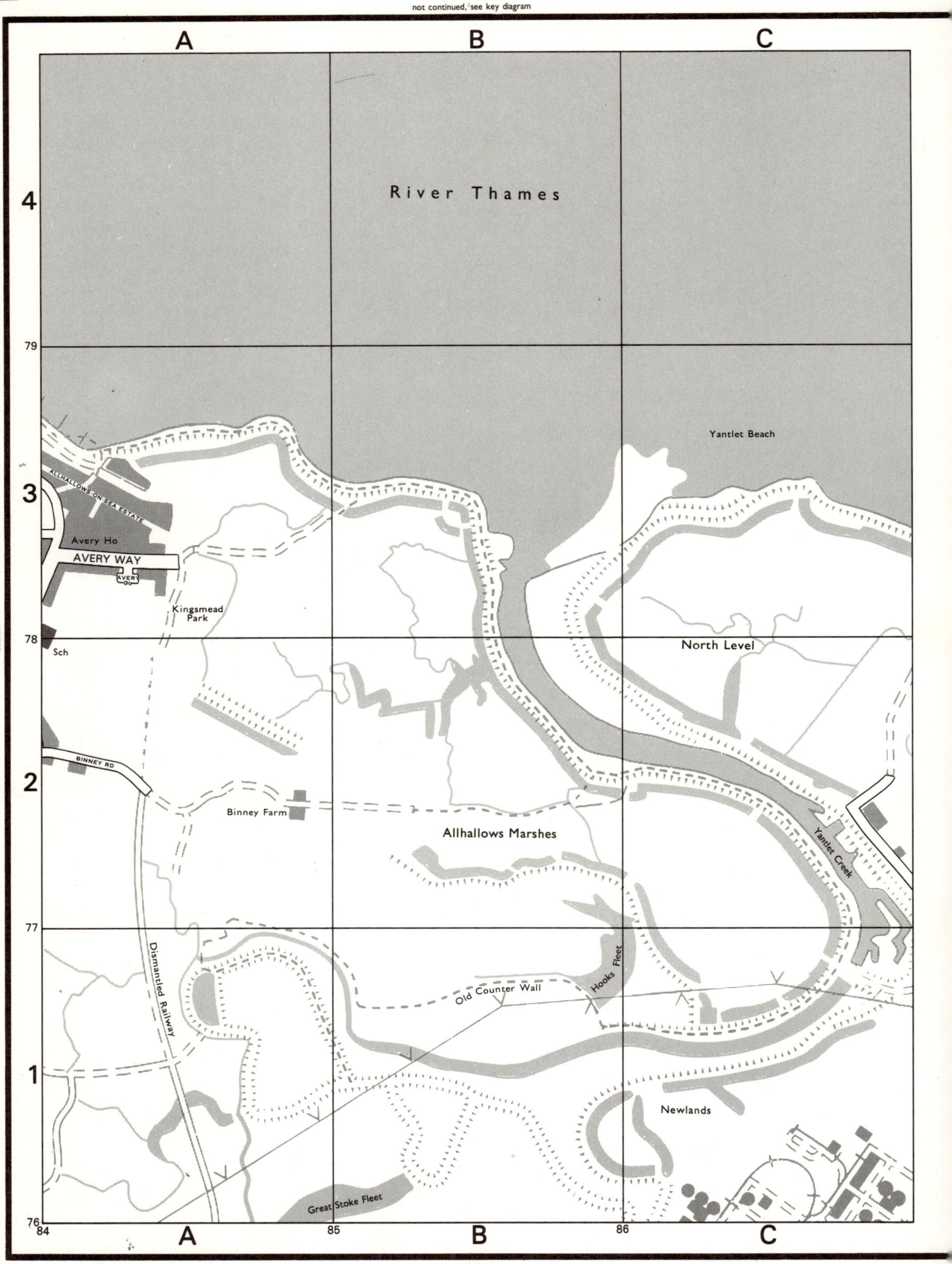

13

31

not continued, see key diagram

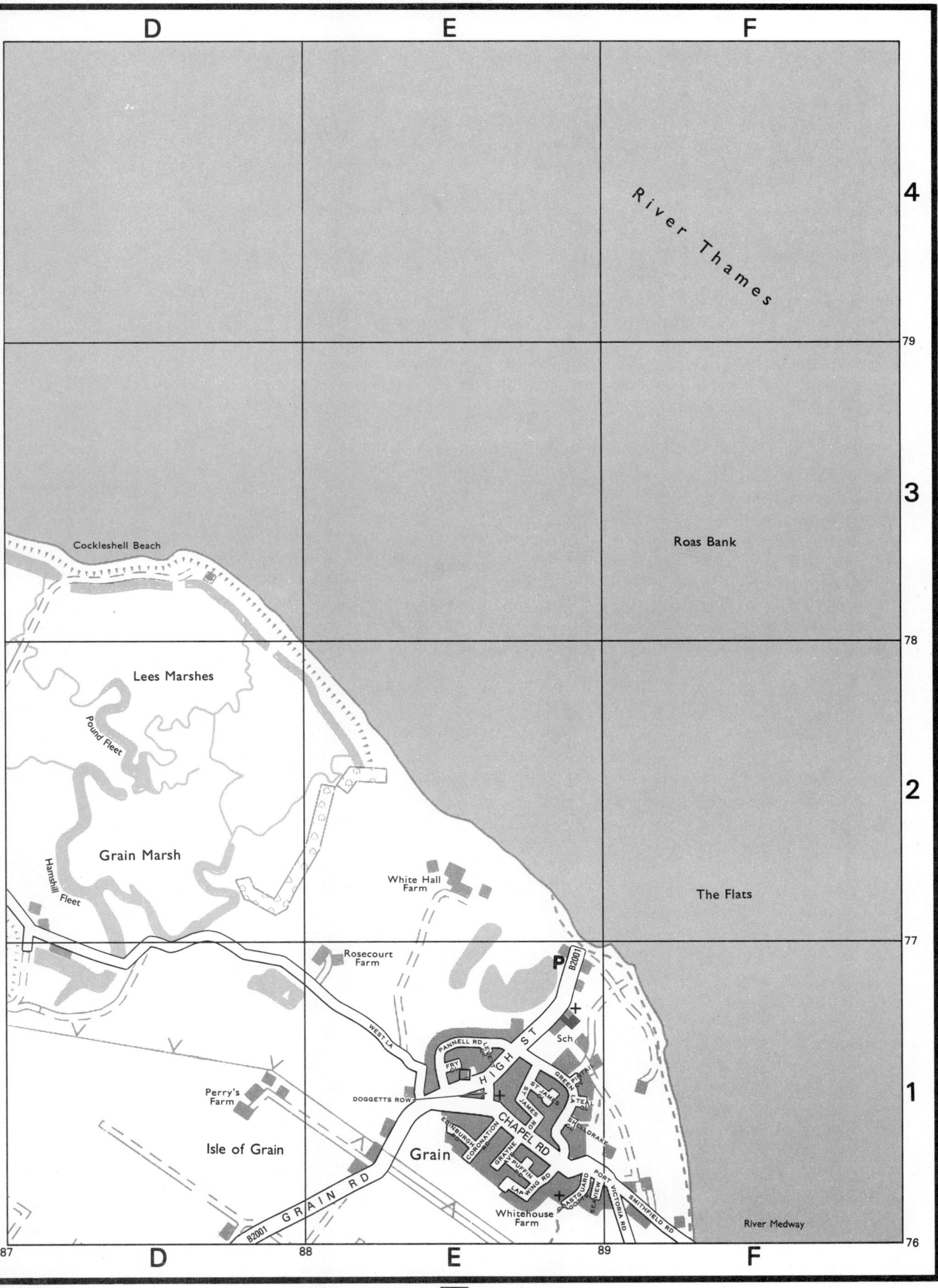

not continued, see key diagram

1

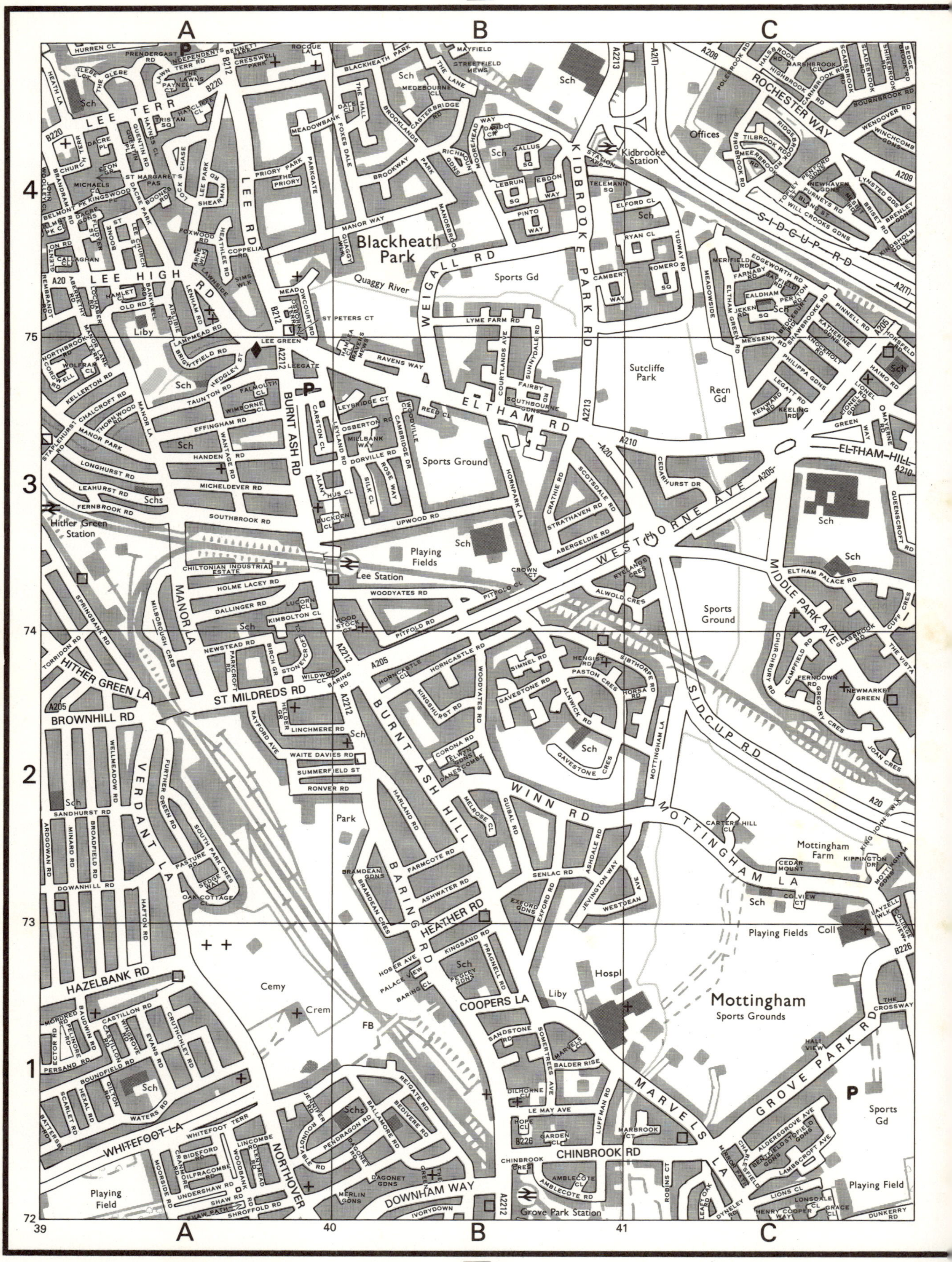

not continued, see key diagram

33

2

D
E
F
Oxleas Wood
Welling Way
Falconwood Field
Falconwood Station
Eltham Park
Rochester Way
Westmount Rd
Well Hall Rd
Sports Ground
Eltham Station
Golf Course
Cemy
Rifield Rd
Crown Woods Way
Bexley Rd
Eltham High St
Eltham Hill
Eltham
Coll
Avery Hill
College Halls
Eltham Palace
Playing Fields
Golf Course
Court Rd
Middle Park Ave
Mottingham Station
The Tarn
Footscray Rd
Sports Grounds
Avery Hill Rd
Sports Ground
New Eltham
West Park
Sidcup Rd
Green La
Southwood Rd
Mottingham Rd
William Barefoot Dr
Dunkerry Rd
Longlands
Sports Ground
1
2
3
4
42
43
44
72
73
74
75

18

34

3

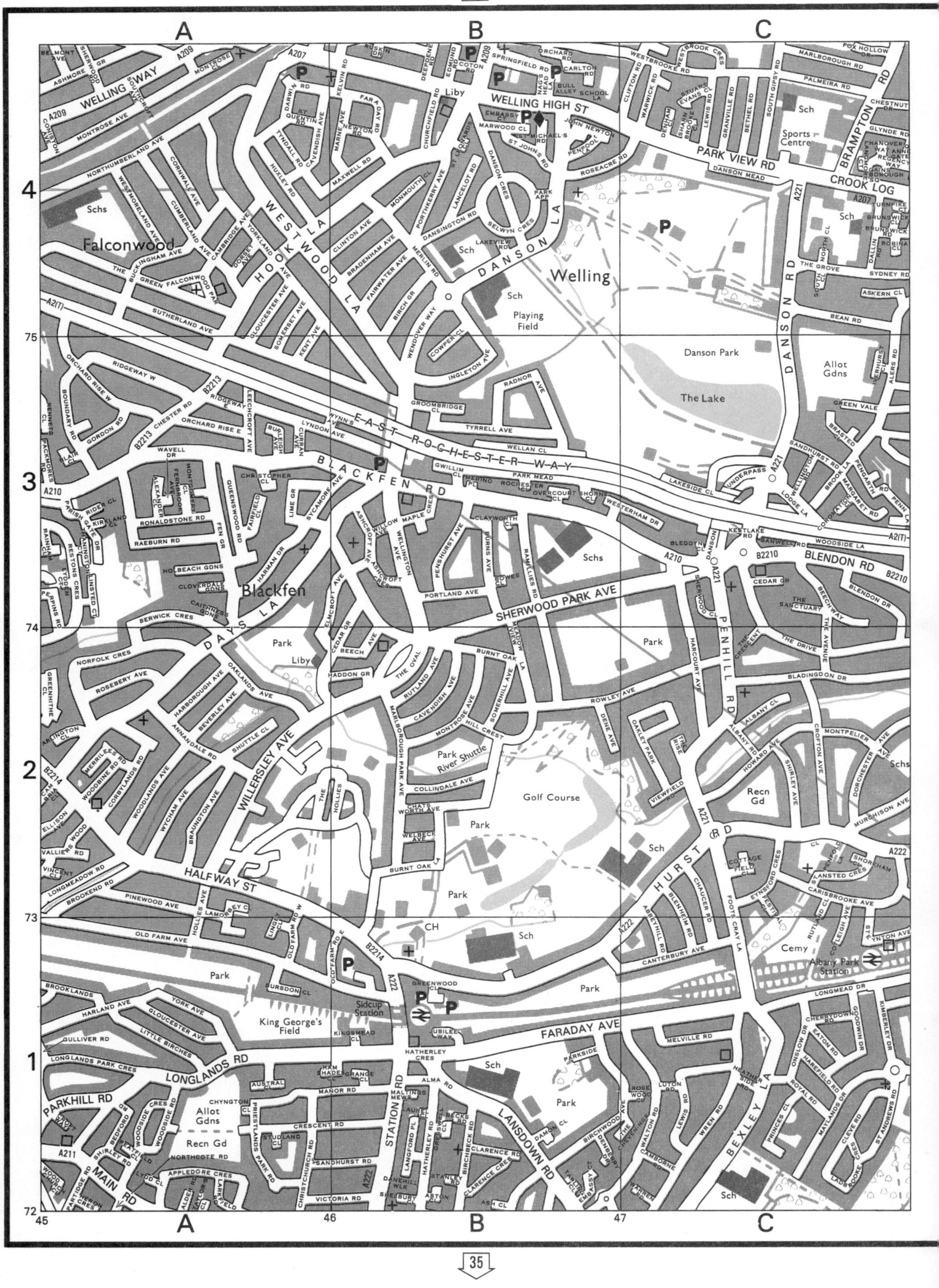
A
B
C
4
3
2
1
75
74
73
72
45
46
47
Falconwood
Welling
Blackfen
Schs
Sch
Liby
Playing Field
Danson Park
The Lake
Allot Gdns
Park
Golf Course
Park River Shuttle
Recn Gd
CH
Cemy
Albany Park Station
Sidcup Station
King George's Field
Sports Centre
WELLING WAY
WELLING HIGH ST
PARK VIEW RD
DANSON MEAD
CROOK LOG
BRAMPTON RD
DANSON RD
DANSON LA
WESTWOOD LA
HOOK LA
EAST ROCHESTER WAY
BLACKFEN RD
SHERWOOD PARK AVE
DAYS LA
BLENDON RD
PENHILL RD
HURST RD
HALFWAY ST
WILLERSLEY AVE
FARADAY AVE
LONGLANDS RD
PARKHILL RD
MAIN RD
STATION RD
LANSDOWN RD
BEXLEY LA
FOOTS CRAY LA
MARLBOROUGH PARK AVE
OLD FARM AVE
SUTHERLAND AVE
NORTHUMBERLAND AVE
MONTROSE AVE
RIDGEWAY W
ORCHARD RISE W
CHESTER RD
BUCKINGHAM AVE
WOODSIDE LA
ROWLEY AVE
BURNT OAK LA
MARLBOROUGH RD
PALMEIRA RD
A2(T)
A207
A209
A210
A211
A221
A222
B2210
B2213
B2214

17

35

4

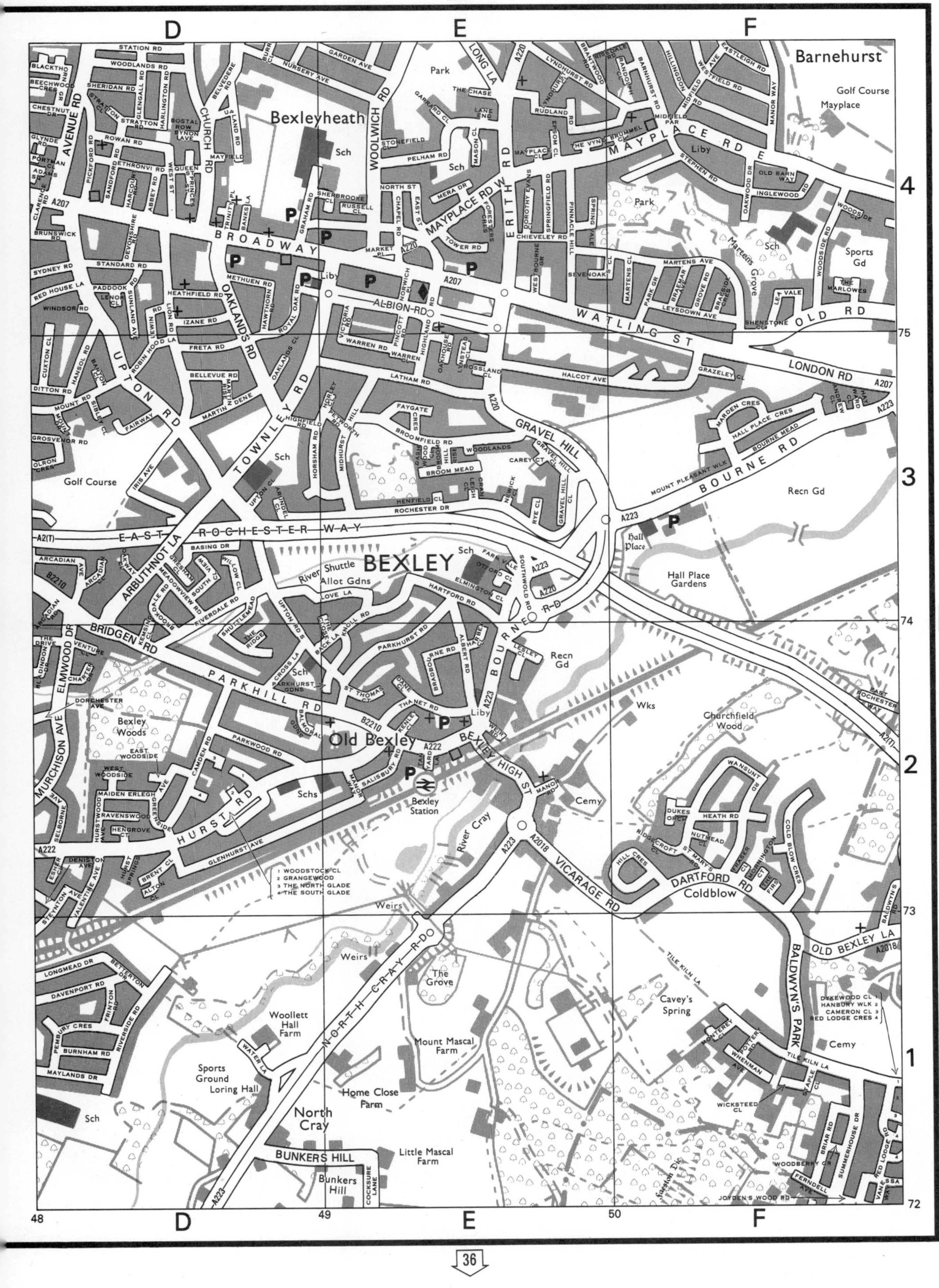
D
E
F
Barnehurst
Golf Course
Mayplace
Bexleyheath
Park
Sch
Liby
BROADWAY
STATION RD
WOODLANDS RD
NURSERY AVE
GARDEN AVE
LONG LA
A220
CHURCH RD
WOOLWICH RD
AVENUE RD
MAYPLACE RD W
MAYPLACE RD E
ERITH RD
BRANTWOOD RD
LYNDHURST RD
BARNEHURST RD
HILLINGDON RD
EASTLEIGH RD
WESTFIELD RD
MANOR WAY
MIDFIELD AVE
STEPHEN RD
OLD BARN WAY
INGLEWOOD RD
OAKWOOD DR
WOODSIDE RD
Martens Grove
Sports Gd
THE MARLOWES
MARTENS AVE
LEYSDOWN AVE
SHENSTONE CL
LEA VALE
OLD RD
WATLING ST
LONDON RD
A207
A223
ALBION RD
HALCOT AVE
GRAZELEY CL
MARDEN CRES
HALL PLACE CRES
BOURNE MEAD
BOURNE RD
MOUNT PLEASANT WLK
Recn Gd
GRAVEL HILL
ROCHESTER DR
EAST ROCHESTER WAY
A2(T)
OAKLANDS RD
TOWNLEY RD
UPTON RD
Golf Course
BEXLEY
River Shuttle
Allot Gdns
Hall Place
Hall Place Gardens
ARBUTHNOT LA
BRIDGEN RD
PARKHILL RD
PARKHURST RD
Old Bexley
BEXLEY HIGH ST
Bexley Station
Schs
HURST RD
Bexley Woods
MURCHISON AVE
ELMWOOD DR
GLENHURST AVE
River Cray
Cemy
Wks
Churchfield Wood
VICARAGE RD
DARTFORD RD
Coldblow
A2018
A222
1 WOODSTOCK CL
2 GRANGEWOOD
3 THE NORTH GLADE
4 THE SOUTH GLADE
Weirs
NORTH CRAY RD
The Grove
TILE KILN LA
Cavey's Spring
BALDWYN'S PARK
OLD BEXLEY LA
DYKEWOOD CL 1
HANBURY WLK 2
CAMERON CL 3
RED LODGE CRES 4
Cemy
Woollett Hall Farm
Mount Mascal Farm
Sports Ground
Loring Hall
Home Close Farm
North Cray
BUNKERS HILL
Bunkers Hill
Little Mascal Farm
COCKSURE LANE
Sch
WICKSTEED CL
JOYDEN'S WOOD RD
A223
1
2
3
4
75
74
73
72
48
49
50
D
E
F

20

36

5

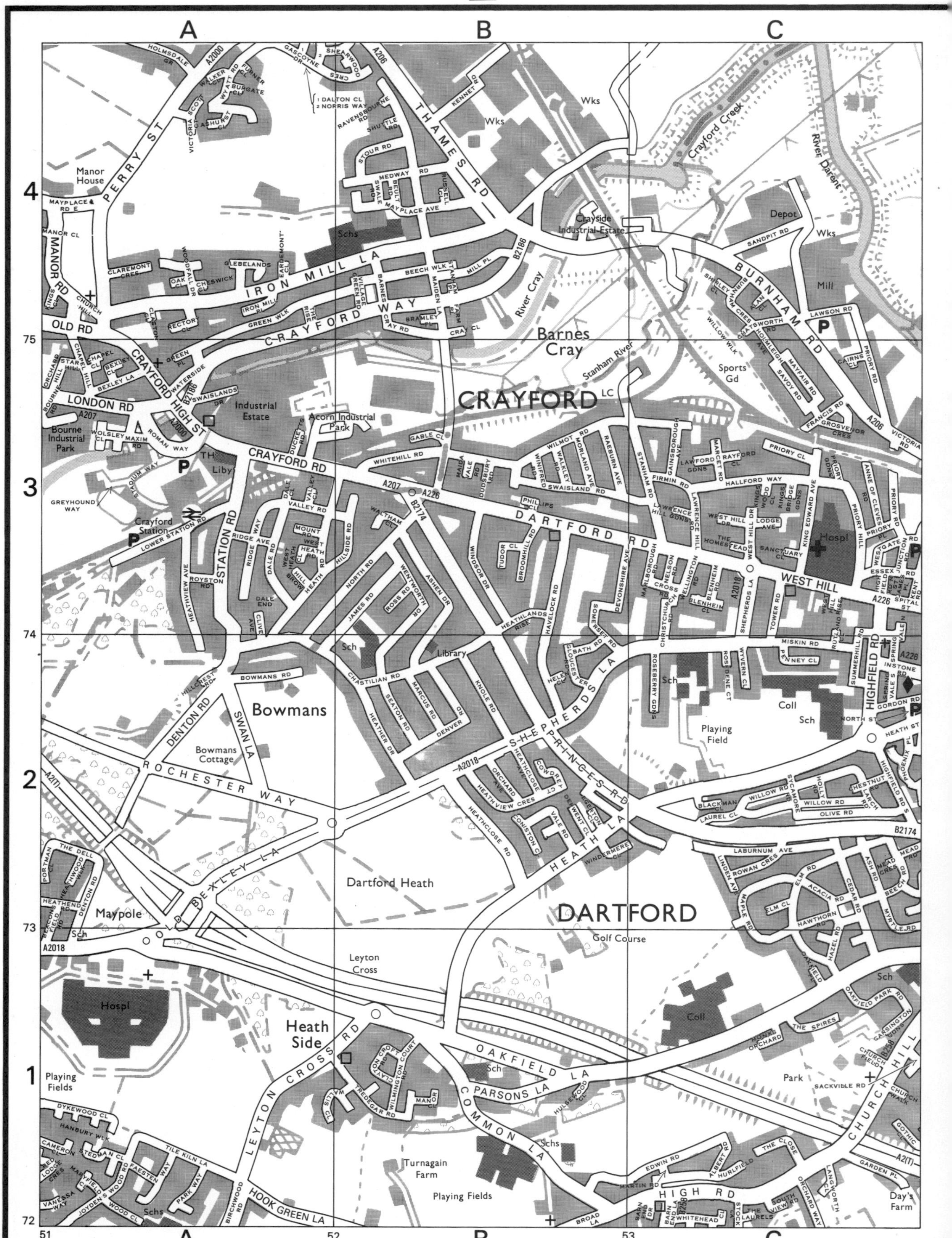

A
B
C
4
3
2
1
75
74
73
72
51
52
53
CRAYFORD
DARTFORD
Barnes Cray
Bowmans
Bowmans Cottage
Dartford Heath
Maypole
Heath Side
Leyton Cross
Manor House
Bourne Industrial Park
Industrial Estate
Acorn Industrial Park
Crayside Industrial Estate
Crayford Station
Sports Gd
Golf Course
Turnagain Farm
Playing Fields
Playing Field
Day's Farm
Park
Depot
Wks
Mill
Hospl
Coll
Sch
Schs
Library
Liby
River Cray
River Darent
Crayford Creek
Stanham River
PERRY ST
THAMES RD
IRON MILL LA
CRAYFORD WAY
CRAYFORD HIGH ST
LONDON RD
OLD RD
MANOR RD
CRAYFORD RD
DARTFORD RD
WEST HILL
BURNHAM RD
STATION RD
ROCHESTER WAY
BEXLEY LA
SHEPHERDS LA
PRINCES RD
HEATH LA
OAKFIELD LA
PARSONS LA
COMMON LA
LEYTON CROSS RD
HOOK GREEN LA
HIGH RD
CHURCH HILL
HIGHFIELD RD
DENTON RD
SWAN LA
BOWMANS RD
A2000
A206
A207
A226
A2018
A2(T)
B2186
B2174

19

37

6

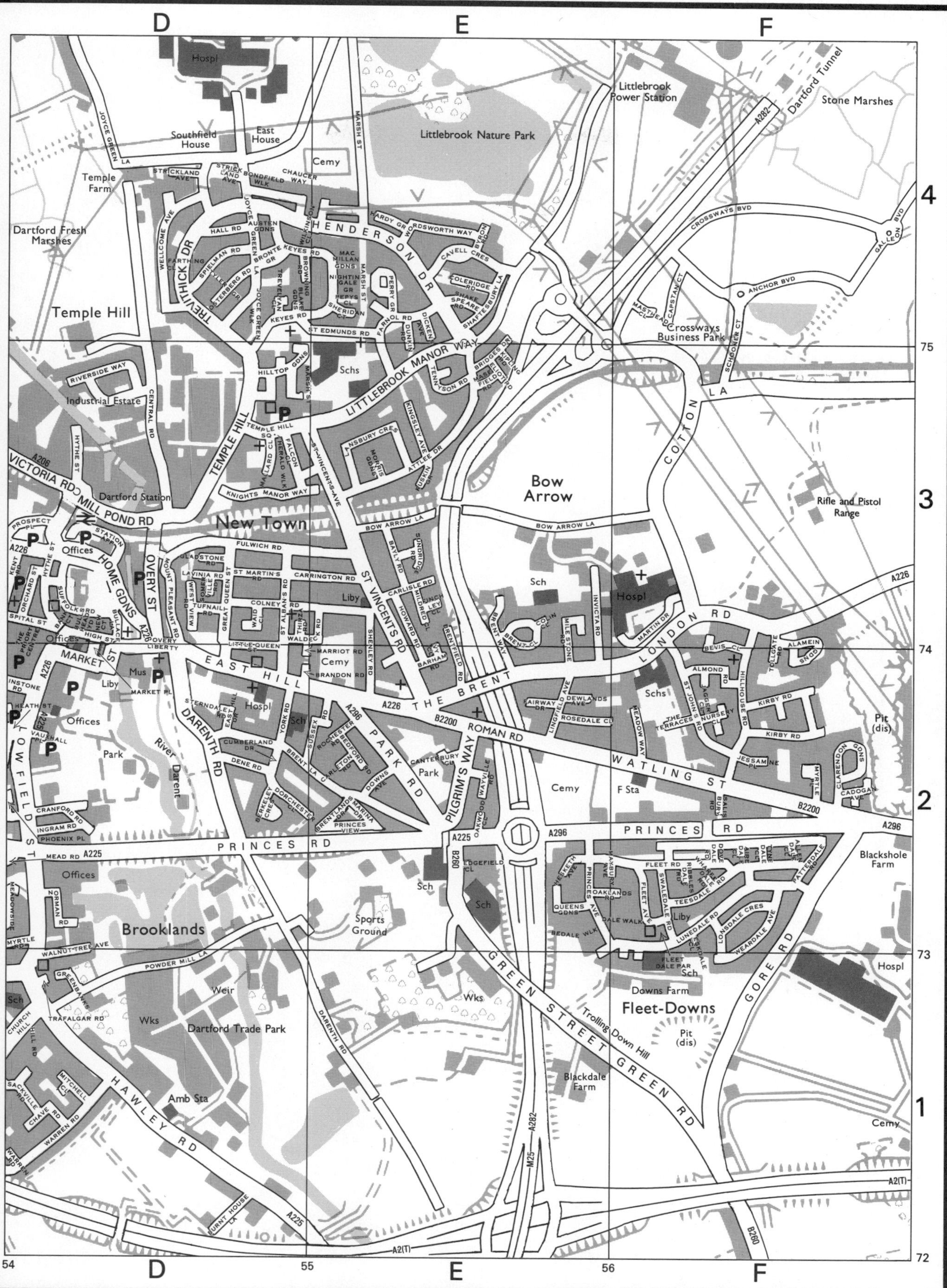
D
E
F
4
3
2
1
75
74
73
72
54
55
56
Hospl
Southfield House
East House
Cemy
Littlebrook Nature Park
Littlebrook Power Station
Dartford Tunnel
Stone Marshes
Temple Farm
Dartford Fresh Marshes
Temple Hill
JOYCE GREEN LA
STRICKLAND AVE
BONDFIELD WLK
CHAUCER WAY
MARSH ST
HENDERSON DR
HARDY GR
WORDSWORTH WAY
CAVELL CRES
COLERIDGE RD
SHAKESPEARE RD
SHAFTESBURY LA
BYRON RD
HALL RD
AUSTEN GDNS
BRONTE GR
KEYES RD
SPIELMAN RD
FARTHING CL
WELLCOME AVE
TREVITHICK DR
OSTERBERG RD
TREVELYAN CL
JOYCE GREEN WLK
MACMILLAN GDNS
NIGHTINGALE GR
PEPYS CL
SHERIDAN CT
PERRY GR
FARNOL RD
DICKENS AVE
DUNKIN RD
ST EDMUNDS RD
CROSSWAYS BVD
GALLEON BVD
ANCHOR BVD
MASTHEAD CL
CAPSTAN CT
Crossways Business Park
SCHOONER CT
COTTON LA
Riverside Way
Industrial Estate
CENTRAL RD
HILLTOP GDNS
Schs
LITTLEBROOK MANOR WAY
TENNYSON RD
BRIDGES DR
KIPLING RD
MASEFIELD RD
TEMPLE HILL
TEMPLE HILL SQ
LANSBURY CRES
KINGSLEY AVE
MORRIS GDNS
ATTLEE DR
RUSKIN GR
FALCON
HERALD WLK
MALLARD CL
ST VINCENTS AVE
KNIGHTS MANOR WAY
HYTHE ST
A206
VICTORIA RD
MILL POND RD
Dartford Station
Bow Arrow
BOW ARROW LA
Rifle and Pistol Range
New Town
PROSPECT PL
STATION APP
Offices
A226
HOME GDNS
OVERY ST
FULWICH RD
GLADSTONE RD
LAVINIA RD
ST MARTIN'S RD
CARRINGTON RD
BAYLY RD
SANDRIDGE RD
CARLISLE RD
MILDRED CL
LINCOLN RD
Liby
Sch
Hospl
INVICTA RD
MILESTONE RD
COLIN CL
BRENT CL
BRENT WAY
MARTIN DR
LONDON RD
A226
BEVIS CL
ALAMEIN GDNS
TOLLGATE RD
ALMOND RD
HILLHOUSE RD
ST JOHN'S RD
ACORN RD
NURSERY RD
THE TERRACES
KIRBY RD
JESSAMINE PL
Pit (dis)
MOUNT PLEASANT RD
WEST VIEW
TUFNAIL RD
GREAT QUEEN ST
COLNEY RD
WAID CL
ST ALBAN'S RD
THIRZA RD
WALDECK RD
HOWARD RD
SHENLEY RD
ST VINCENTS RD
BRENTFIELD RD
BARHAM RD
SPITAL ST
HIGH ST
Offices
LITTLE QUEEN ST
MARRIOT RD
Cemy
BRANDON RD
MARKET ST
Mus
Liby
MARKET PL
INSTONE RD
HEATH ST
VAUXHALL
Offices
Park
EAST HILL
STERNDALE RD
Hospl
Sch
YORK RD
SUSSEX RD
ROCHESTER RD
BEDFORD RD
A296
PARK RD
CANTERBURY CL
A226
THE BRENT
B2200
ROMAN RD
FAIRWAY DR
DEWLANDS AVE
ROSEDALE CL
LINGFIELD AVE
MEADOW WAY
Schs
WATLING ST
B2200
MYRTLE RD
CLARENDON GDNS
CADOGAN AVE
River Darent
DARENTH RD
CUMBERLAND DR
DENE RD
BRENT LA
CARLETON RD
DOWNS AVE
Park
PILGRIM'S WAY
WAYVILLE RD
OAKWOOD CL
BERKELEY CRES
DORCHESTER CL
BRENTLANDS DR
MARINA DR
PRINCES VIEW
Cemy
F Sta
SALISBURY RD
CRANFORD RD
INGRAM RD
PHOENIX PL
LOWFIELD ST
PRINCES RD
A225
A296
PRINCES RD
A296
Blackshole Farm
MEAD RD
Offices
NORMAN RD
MEADOWSIDE
B260
EDGEFIELD CL
Sch
Sch
HESKETH AVE
PRINCES AVE
MARKHAM RD
OAKLANDS RD
QUEENS GDNS
FLEET AVE
FLEET RD
SWALEDALE RD
TEESDALE RD
Liby
BEDALE WLK
DALE WALK
LUNEDALE RD
LONSDALE CRES
WEARDALE AVE
ESKDALE
PATTERDALE RD
GORE RD
Sports Ground
Brooklands
MYRTLE RD
WALNUT TREE AVE
POWDER MILL LA
GREENBANKS
TRAFALGAR RD
CHURCH HILL
HILL RD
Weir
Wks
Wks
Dartford Trade Park
GREEN STREET GREEN RD
Trolling Down Hill
Fleetdale Par
Sch
Downs Farm
Fleet-Downs
Pit (dis)
Hospl
Blackdale Farm
Cemy
SACKVILLE CL
MITCHELL CL
CHAVE RD
WARREN RD
Amb Sta
HAWLEY RD
A282
M25
A2(T)
B260
BURNT HOUSE LA
A225
A2(T)

22

38

7

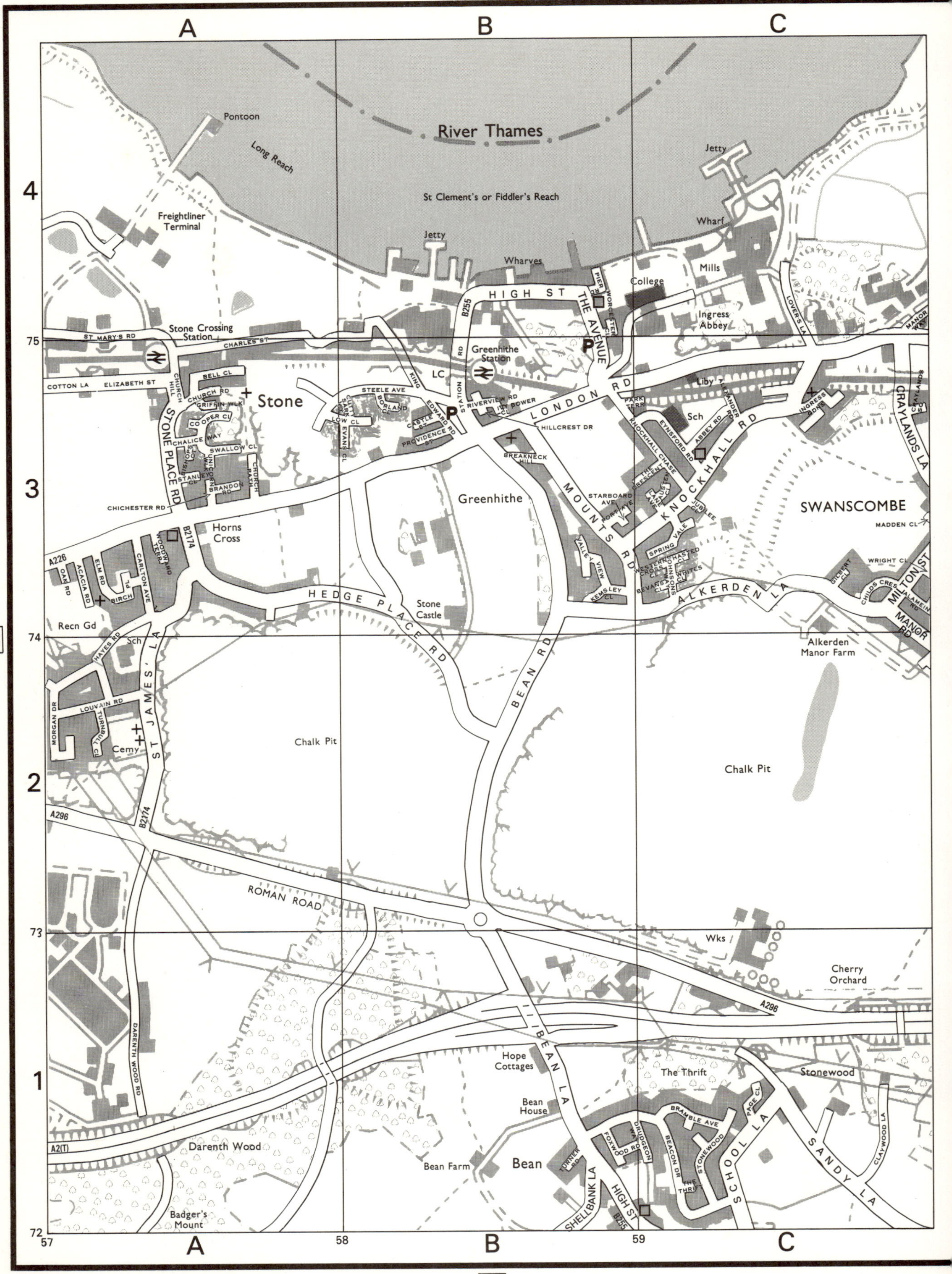

A
B
C
4
3
2
1
75
74
73
72
57
58
59
River Thames
Pontoon
Long Reach
St Clement's or Fiddler's Reach
Jetty
Wharves
Wharf
Mills
College
Ingress Abbey
Freightliner Terminal
Stone Crossing Station
ST MARY'S RD
CHARLES ST
COTTON LA
ELIZABETH ST
HIGH ST
B255
THE AVENUE
PIER RD
WORCESTER CL
LOVERS LA
MANOR WAY
Greenhithe Station
LC
KING
STATION RD
STEELE AVE
BORLAND
LOW CL
EVANS CL
CASTLE ST
EDWARD RD
PROVIDENCE ST
RIVERVIEW RD
IVY BOWER CL
LONDON RD
PARK TERR
Liby
Sch
ALEXANDER RD
INGRESS GDNS
CRAYLANDS LA
Stone
BELL CL
CHURCH RD
GRIFFIN WLK
COOPER CL
CHALICE WAY
SWALLOW CL
STANLEY CL
BRANDON RD
CHURCH RD
CHURCH HILL
STONE PLACE RD
CHICHESTER RD
HILLCREST DR
BREAKNECK HILL
EYNSFORD RD
ABBEY RD
KNOCKHALL CHASE
KNOCKHALL RD
THE CRESCENT
STARBOARD AVE
PORT AVE
JUBILEE CL
SPRING VALE
Greenhithe
SWANSCOMBE
MADDEN CL
WRIGHT CL
GILBERT CL
CHILDS CRES
MILTON ST
MANOR RD
Horns Cross
B2174
WOODLAND TERR
A226
OAK RD
ACACIA RD
ELM RD
BIRCH PL
CARLTON AVE
HEDGE PLACE RD
Stone Castle
MOUNTS RD
VALLEY VIEW
KEMSLEY CL
WESTERN CROSS CL
HASTED CL
BEVANS CL
WHITES CL
ALKERDEN LA
Recn Gd
HAYES RD
Sch
Alkerden Manor Farm
LOUVAIN RD
MORGAN DR
TURNBULL CL
Cemy
ST JAMES' LA
BEAN RD
Chalk Pit
Chalk Pit
A296
B2174
ROMAN ROAD
Wks
Cherry Orchard
A296
DARENTH WOOD RD
Hope Cottages
BEAN LA
The Thrift
Stonewood
Bean House
BRAMBLE AVE
PAGE CL
DRUDGEON WAY
FOXWOOD RD
BEACON DR
STONEWOOD
THE THRIFT
SCHOOL LA
SANDY LA
CLAYWOOD LA
A2(T)
Darenth Wood
Bean Farm
Bean
TURNER RD
SHELLBANK LA
HIGH ST
B255
Badger's Mount

21
39

8

D
E
F
4
3
2
1
75
74
73
72
60
61
62
Botany Marshes
GREEN MANOR WAY
MANOR WAY
Pier
Northfleet Hope
River Thames
Wks
Tower Wharf
Pier
Tilbury Ness
Gravesend Reach
LOWER RD
PILGRIM RD
Wks
LONDON RD
KENT KRAFT INDUSTRIAL ESTATE
GALLEY HILL RD
GALLEY HILL TRADING ESTATE
B259
ALL SAINTS
Sports Ground
Swanscombe Station
TAUNTON RD
Jetty
GROVE RD
THE CREEK
THE SHORE
Wharf
EBBSFLEET INDUSTRIAL ESTATE
STONEBRIDGE RD
WALLIS PARK
HUGGENS'S COLLEGE
COLLEGE RD
HIVE LA
P
Wks
Mill
CRETE HALL ROAD
PORTLAND RD
GRANBY RD
Recn Gd
HIGH ST
BROOMFIELD RD
CRAYLANDS LA
MILTON RD
MILTON ST
CHAPEL CT
LEWIS RD
GASSON RD
STANLEY RD
Liby
HOPE RD
HARMER RD
ALBERT RD
CHURCH
HERBERT RD
STANHOPE RD
AMES RD
MOORE RD
BROAD RD
ARK RD
EGLINTON RD
CASTLE RD
VERNON RD
SUN RD
SWANSCOMBE ST
MANOR RD
Council Offices
Schs
Sch
LEONARD AVE
CURRANT WAY
MUNFORD DR
KEARY RD
BETSHAM RD
Northfleet Station
RAILWAY ST
STATION RD
EBBSFLEET WLK
ROSE ST
Ebbsfleet
Sports Gd
HIGH ST
WEST KENT AVE
COUNCIL AVE
Coun Off
VICARAGE DR
THE HILL
LONDON RD A226
Liby
B2175
B261
SALEM PL
HARTFIELD PL
LABURNAM GR
LIME AVE
ROBINIA AVE
PLANE AVE
DOVER RD B261
YORK RD
SHEPHERD ST
TOOLEY ST
BUCKINGHAM RD
Sch
Sch
VALE ROAD
Works
SOUTHFLEET RD
SPRINGHEAD RD
THAMES WAY
SPRINGHEAD ENTERPRISE PARK
Cemy
Schs
WATERDALES
MEADOW RD
MITCHELL AVE
GWYNN RD
COLYER RD
HALL RD B262
Spring Head
WATLING ST
ROMAN ROAD (course of)
PARK CORNER RD
STATION ROAD
B259
B262
NEW BARN RD
PEPPERHILL LA
FLEET RD
VIKING
BOTOLPH RD
PEPPER HILL
SAXON CL
ROMAN RD
PAINTERS ASH LA
MASEFIELD RD
TENNYSON WLK
MARCONI RD
ASPDIN RD
JOHNSON CL
DENE HOLM RD
PICKWICK GDNS
GAINSBOROUGH DR
LANDSEER AVE
REMBRANDT DR
A2(T)
Sch
Sch
P
24

40

not continued, see key diagram

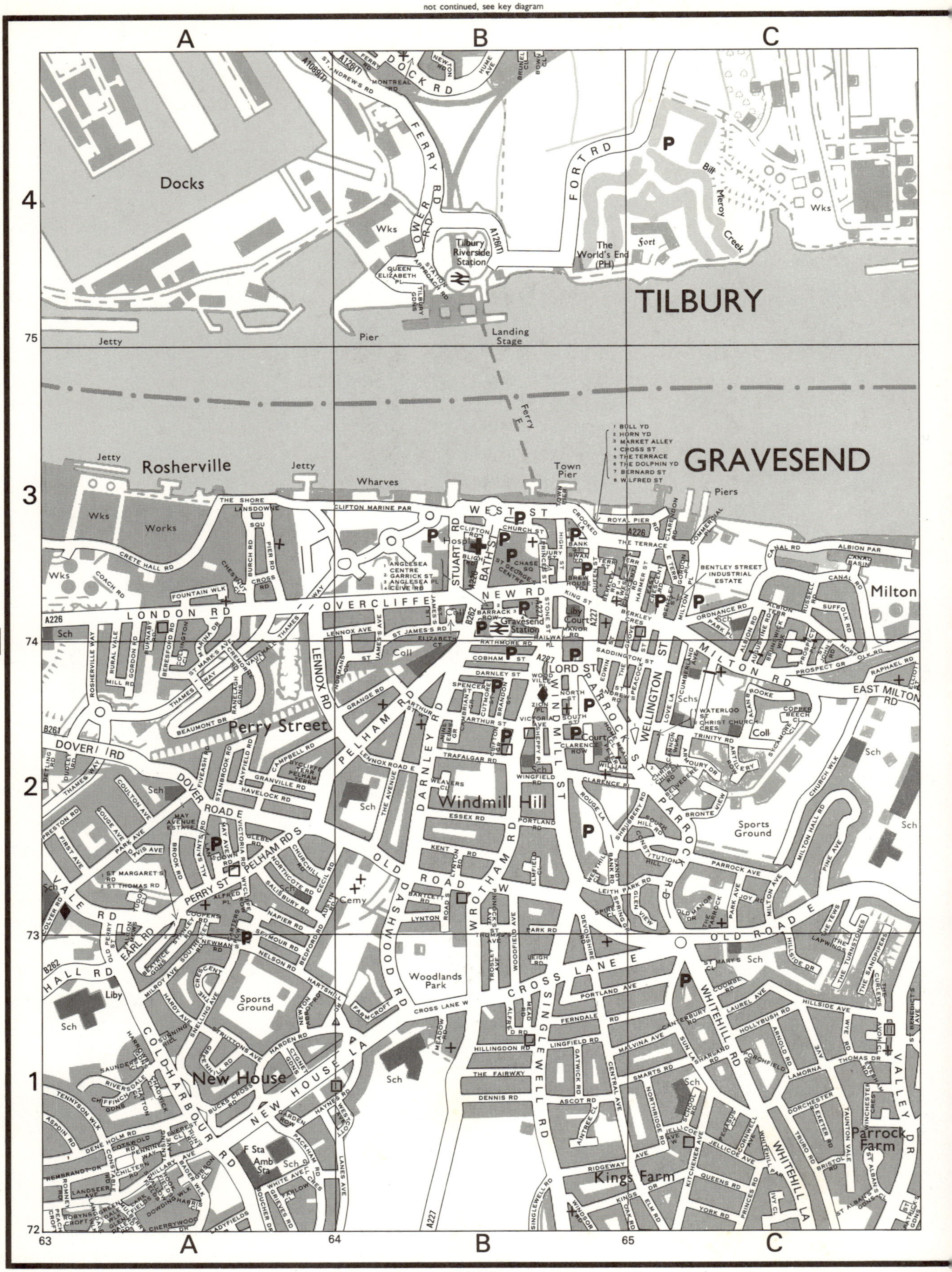

23

41

not continued, see key diagram

26

42

9

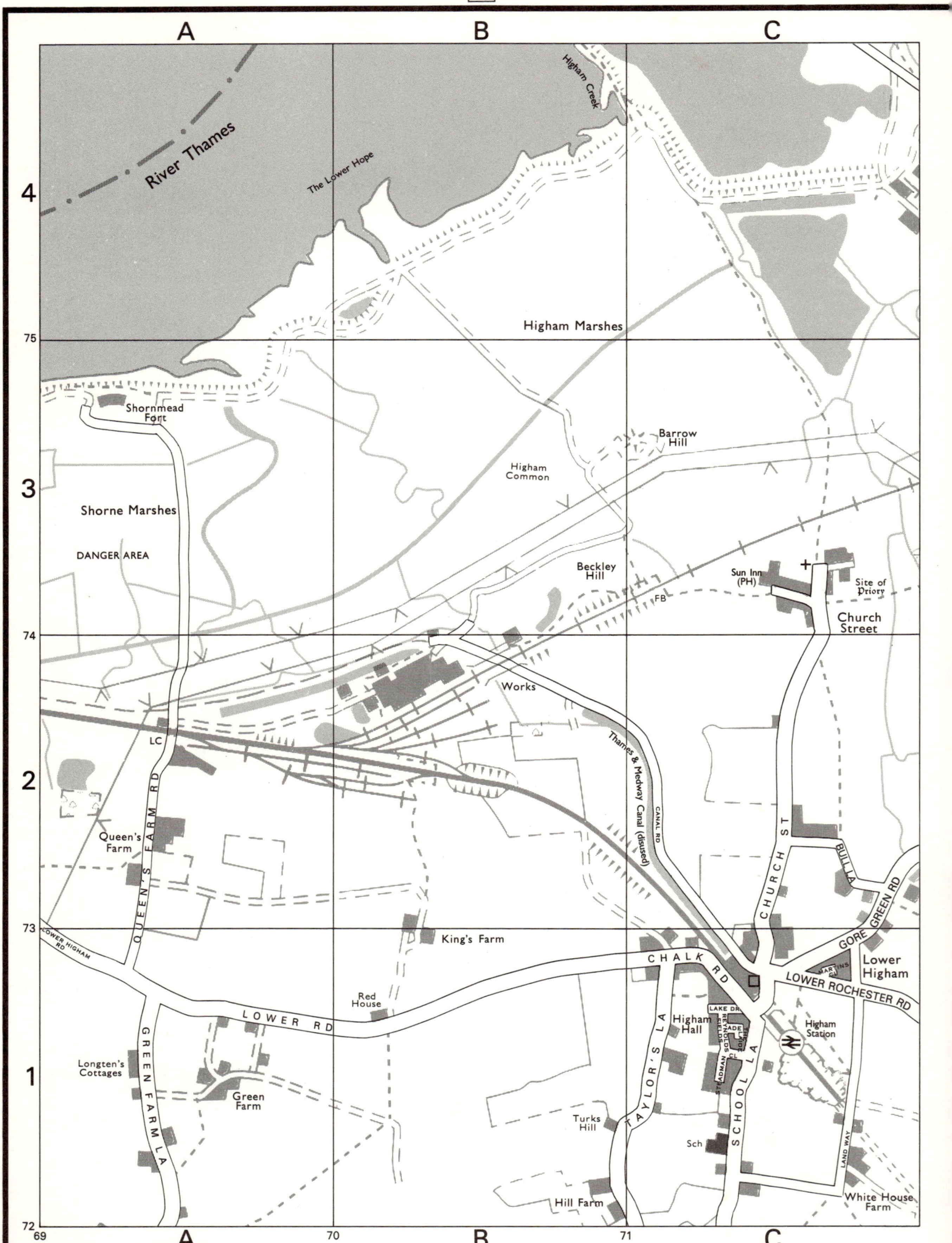
A
B
C
4
75
3
74
2
73
1
72
69
70
71
River Thames
The Lower Hope
Higham Creek
Higham Marshes
Shornmead Fort
Barrow Hill
Higham Common
Shorne Marshes
DANGER AREA
Beckley Hill
Sun Inn (PH)
Site of Priory
FB
Church Street
Works
LC
Thames & Medway Canal (disused)
CANAL RD
Queen's Farm
QUEEN'S FARM RD
CHURCH ST
BULL LA
GORE GREEN RD
LOWER HIGHAM RD
King's Farm
CHALK RD
Lower Higham
LOWER ROCHESTER RD
Red House
LOWER RD
LAKE DR
REYNOLDS
Higham Hall
Higham Station
Longten's Cottages
GREEN FARM LA
Green Farm
TAYLOR'S LA
SCHOOL LA
Turks Hill
Sch
LAND WAY
Hill Farm
White House Farm

25

43

10

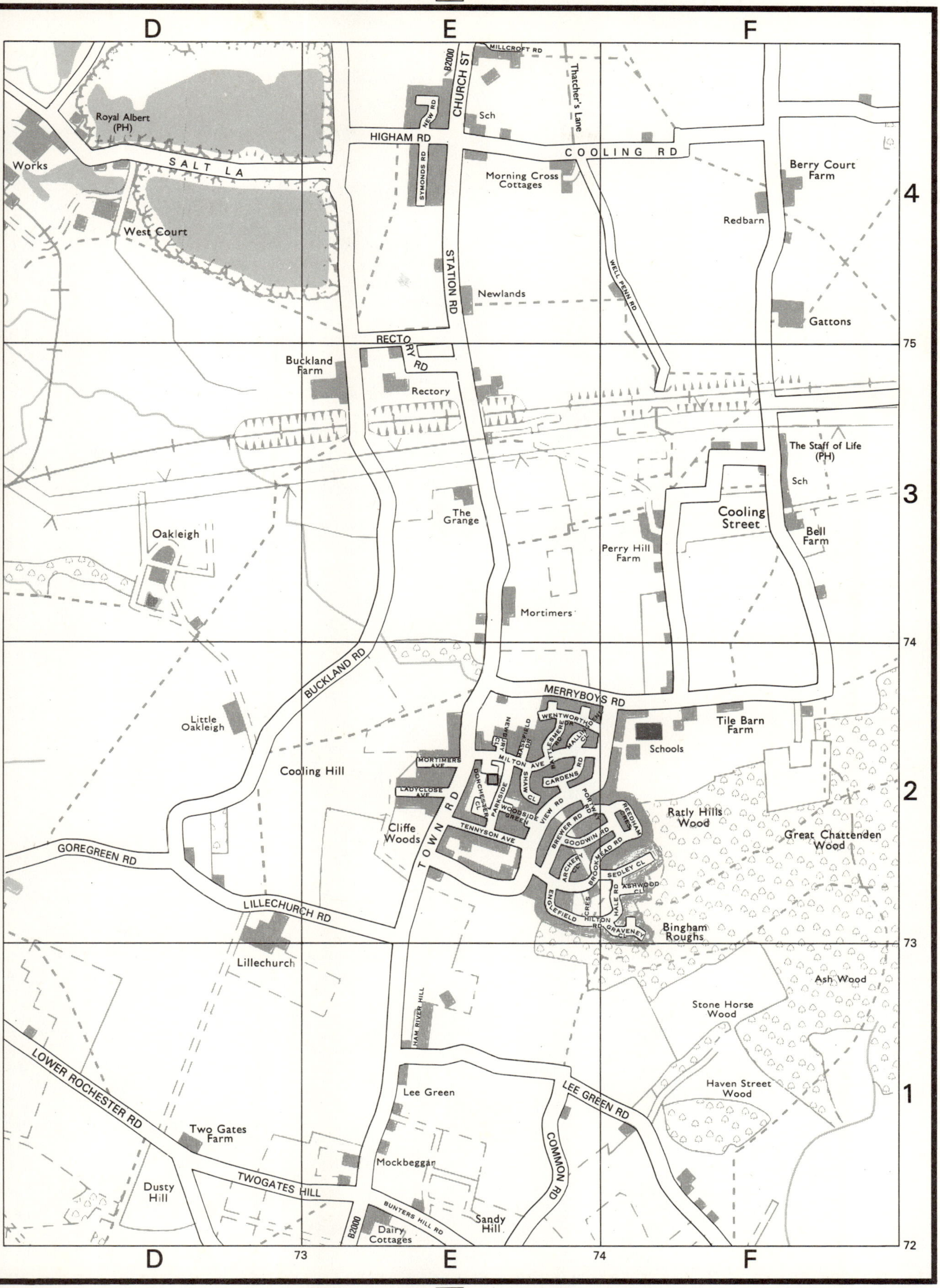
D
E
F
Royal Albert (PH)
Works
SALT LA
West Court
HIGHAM RD
B2000
CHURCH ST
NEW RD
MILLCROFT RD
Sch
Thatcher's Lane
COOLING RD
SYMONDS RD
Morning Cross Cottages
Berry Court Farm
Redbarn
STATION RD
WELL PENN RD
Newlands
Gattons
RECTORY RD
Buckland Farm
Rectory
The Staff of Life (PH)
Sch
The Grange
Cooling Street
Bell Farm
Oakleigh
Perry Hill Farm
Mortimers
BUCKLAND RD
MERRYBOYS RD
WENTWORTH DR
Little Oakleigh
Tile Barn Farm
Schools
Cooling Hill
MORTIMERS AVE
MILTON AVE
CARDENS RD
LADYCLOSE AVE
DORCHESTER CL
PARKSIDE
SHAW CL
WOODSIDE GREEN
VIEW RD
BREWER RD
REEDHAM CRES
Ratly Hills Wood
Great Chattenden Wood
Cliffe Woods
TENNYSON AVE
GOODWIN RD
TOWN RD
GOREGREEN RD
ARCHERY CL
BROOKMEAD RD
SEDLEY CL
ASHWOOD CL
HALE RD
LILLECHURCH RD
ENGLEFIELD CRES
HILTON RD
GRAVENEY CL
Bingham Roughs
Lillechurch
Ash Wood
Stone Horse Wood
HAM RIVER HILL
LOWER ROCHESTER RD
Lee Green
LEE GREEN RD
Haven Street Wood
Two Gates Farm
COMMON RD
Mockbeggar
Dusty Hill
TWOGATES HILL
BUNTERS HILL RD
Sandy Hill
B2000
Dairy Cottages
4
3
2
1
75
74
73
72
73
74
D
E
F

28

44

11

27

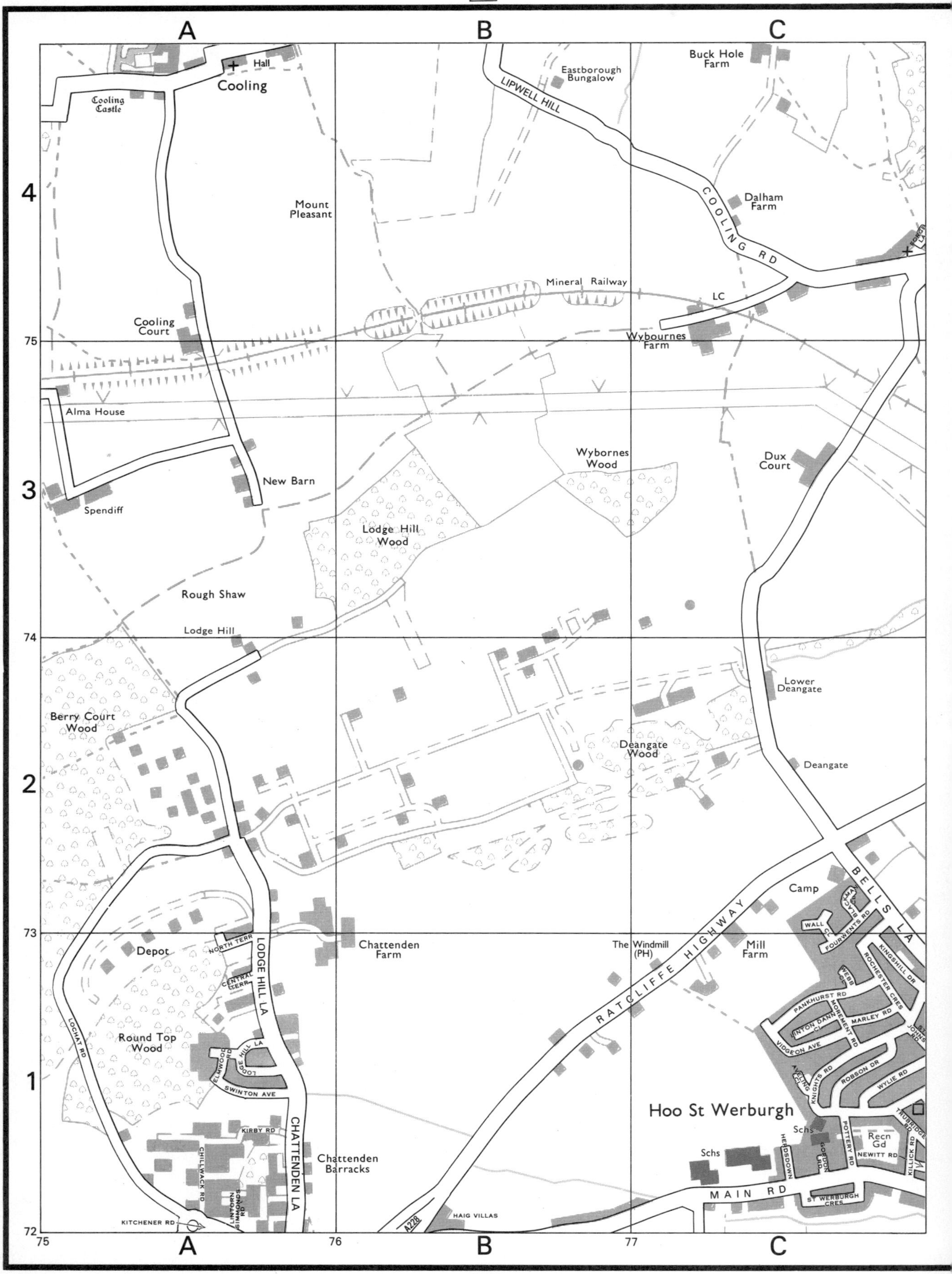

A
B
C
4
3
2
1
75
74
73
72
76
77
Hall
Cooling
Cooling Castle
Eastborough Bungalow
Buck Hole Farm
LIPWELL HILL
Mount Pleasant
Dalham Farm
COOLING RD
FORGE LA
Mineral Railway
LC
Cooling Court
Wybournes Farm
Alma House
Wybornes Wood
Dux Court
New Barn
Spendiff
Lodge Hill Wood
Rough Shaw
Lodge Hill
Lower Deangate
Berry Court Wood
Deangate Wood
Deangate
Camp
BELLS LA
WALL CL
FOURWENTS RD
RATCLIFFE HIGHWAY
Depot
NORTH TERR
LODGE HILL LA
Chattenden Farm
The Windmill (PH)
Mill Farm
CENTRAL TERR
WEBB CL
KINGSHILL DR
ROCHESTER CRES
PANKHURST RD
MOVEMENT RD
MARLEY RD
LINTON DANN CL
VIDGEON AVE
ST JOHNS RD
Round Top Wood
LOCHAT RD
LODGE HILL LA
ELMWOOD RD
SWINTON AVE
AVELING CL
KNIGHTS RD
ROBSON DR
WYLIE RD
Hoo St Werburgh
Schs
KIRBY RD
CHATTENDEN LA
CHILLWACK RD
Chattenden Barracks
HERDSDOWN
GORDON RD
POTTERY RD
Recn Gd
NEWITT RD
KILLICK RD
TRUBRIDGE RD
MAIN RD
ST WERBURGH CRES
LINTORN SIMMONDS RD
KITCHENER RD
A228
HAIG VILLAS

45

12

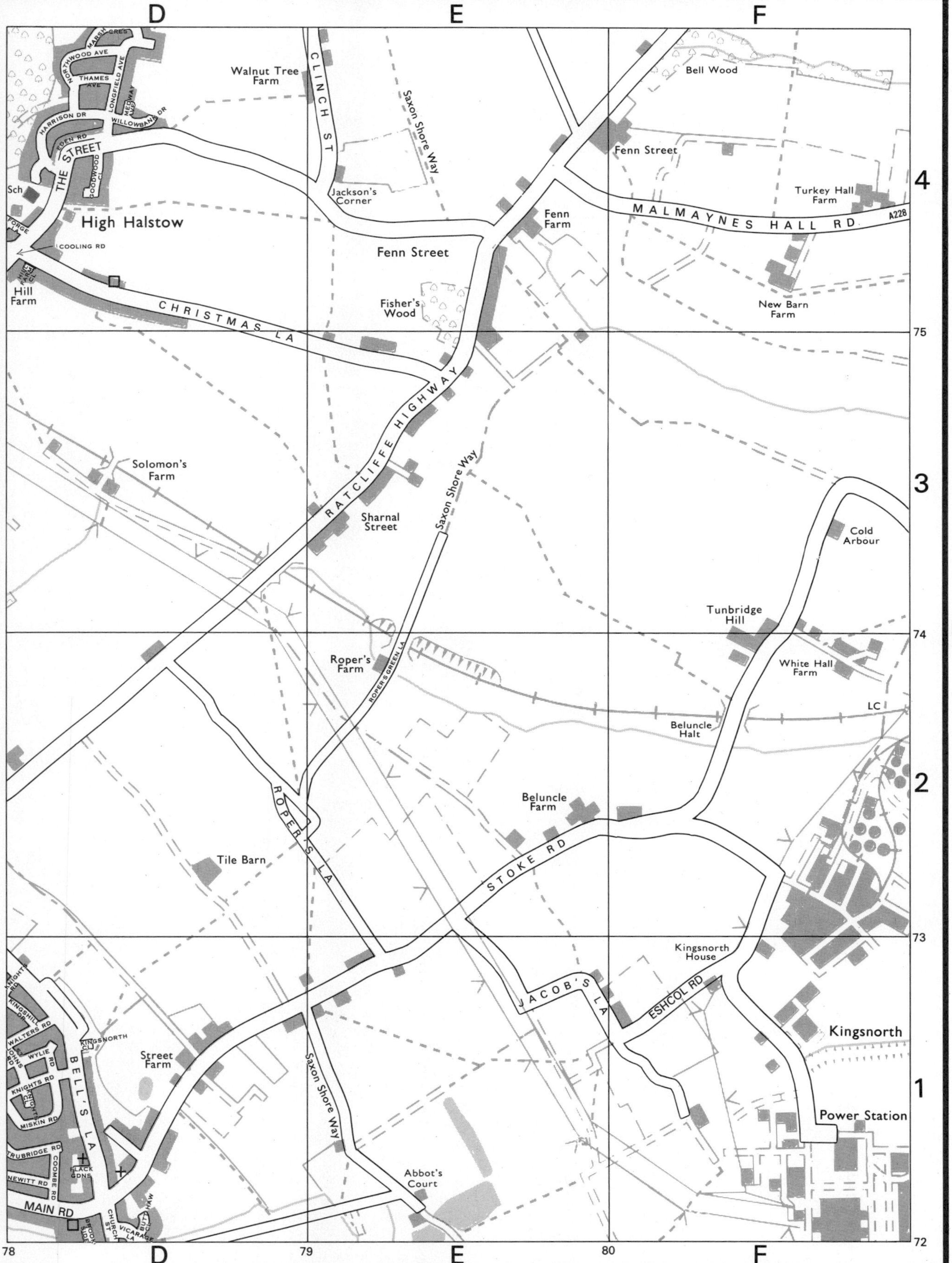
D
E
F
Walnut Tree Farm
CLINCH ST
Saxon Shore Way
Bell Wood
NORTHWOOD AVE
THAMES AVE
LONGFIELD AVE
MEADWAY
HARRISON DR
EDEN RD
WILLOWBANK DR
THE STREET
GOODWOOD CL
Sch
High Halstow
FORGE
COOLING RD
Hill Farm
Jackson's Corner
Fenn Street
Fenn Farm
Fenn Street
MALMAYNES HALL RD
A228
Turkey Hall Farm
New Barn Farm
CHRISTMAS LA
Fisher's Wood
4
75
RATCLIFFE HIGHWAY
Solomon's Farm
Sharnal Street
Saxon Shore Way
3
Cold Arbour
Tunbridge Hill
74
White Hall Farm
Roper's Farm
ROPERS GREEN LA
LC
Beluncle Halt
2
Beluncle Farm
ROPER'S LA
STOKE RD
Tile Barn
73
Kingsnorth House
JACOB'S LA
ESHCOL RD
Kingsnorth
KNIGHTS RD
KINGSHILL DR
WALTERS RD
KINGSNORTH CL
WYLIE RD
BELL'S LA
KNIGHTS RD
MISKIN RD
TRUBRIDGE RD
COOMBE RD
FLACK GDNS
NEWITT RD
MAIN RD
CHURCH ST
VICARAGE LA
BROOKSIDE
BUTTSHAW
Street Farm
Saxon Shore Way
1
Power Station
Abbot's Court
78
79
80
72
D
E
F

30

46

13

A
B
C
4
3
2
1
75
74
73
72
81
82
83
A228
MALMAYNES HALL RD
Malmaynes Hall Farm
The White Horse (PH)
VICARAGE CL
CORONATION COTTS
Stoke
Walnut Tree Farm
MALLARD WAY
GREBE
HERON WAY
SHEPHERDS WAY
Mackay's Court Farm
Middle Stoke
GRAIN RD
ANCHORAGE
BURROWS LA
Tudor Farm
Stoke Creek Crossing
Wharf
Stoke Saltings
North Street Farm
North Street
STOKE RD
Oil Refinery
Stoke Creek
Humble Bee Creek
Damhead Creek
Bee Ness Jetty
Slede Creek
East Hoo Creek
Oakham Ness Jetty
Oakham Marsh
Power Station
Slede Ooze

29

47

14

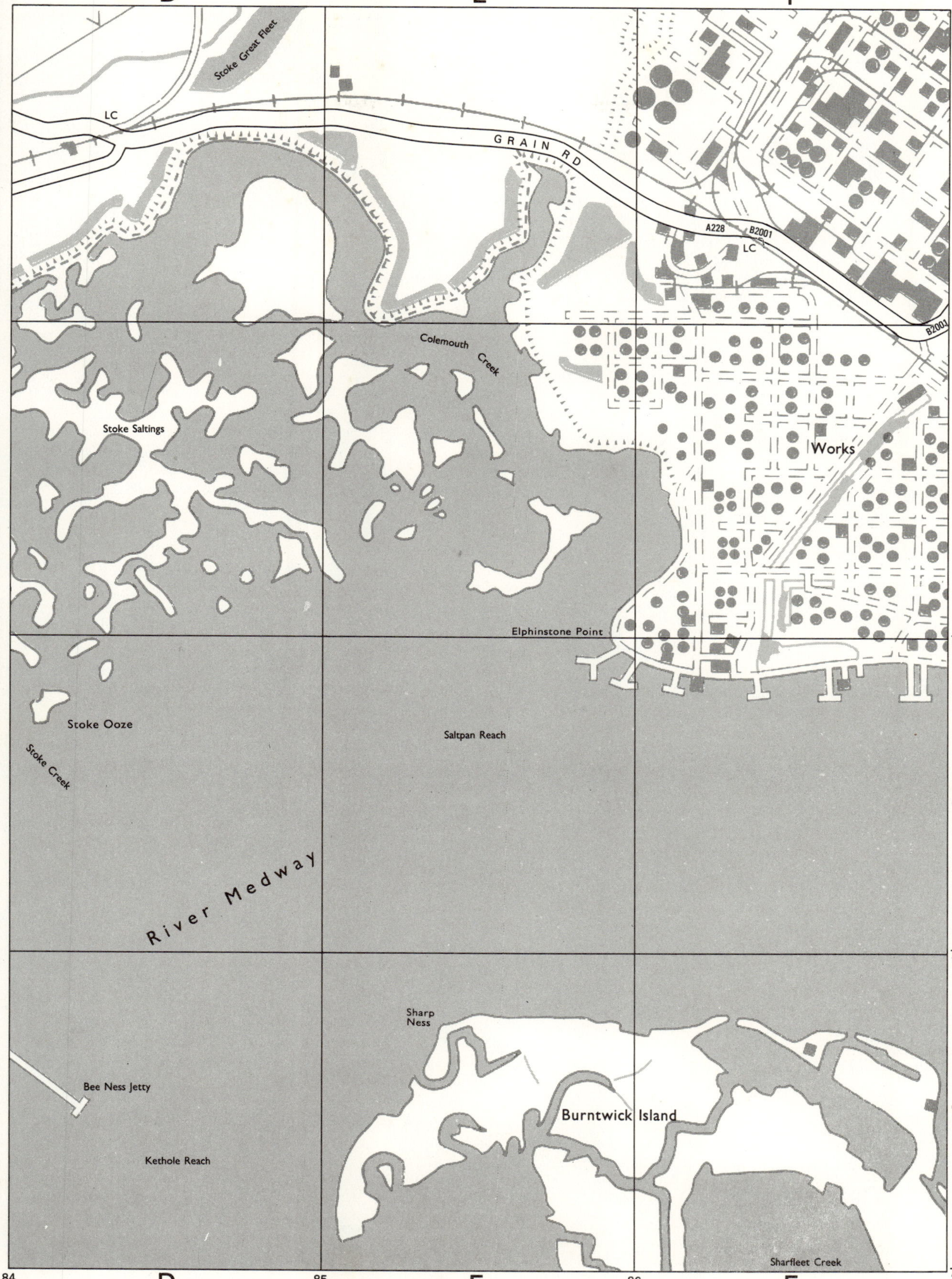
D
E
F
Stoke Great Fleet
LC
GRAIN RD
A228
B2001
LC
B2001
Colemouth
Creek
Stoke Saltings
Works
Elphinstone Point
Stoke Ooze
Stoke Creek
Saltpan Reach
River Medway
Sharp
Ness
Bee Ness Jetty
Burntwick Island
Kethole Reach
Sharfleet Creek
4
3
2
1
75
74
73
72
84
85
86
D
E
F

32

15

A
B
C
Smithfield Marshes
Home Farm
Wallend
GRAIN ROAD
B2001
PORT VICTORIA RD
Kent Oil Refinery
House Fleet
Cockleshell Hard
Jetty
Horseshoe Point
Jetties
River Medway
Saltpan Reach
Deadmans Island
The Swale
Shepherds Creek
Stangate Creek
Tailness Marshes
4
75
3
74
2
73
1
72
87
88
89

31

16

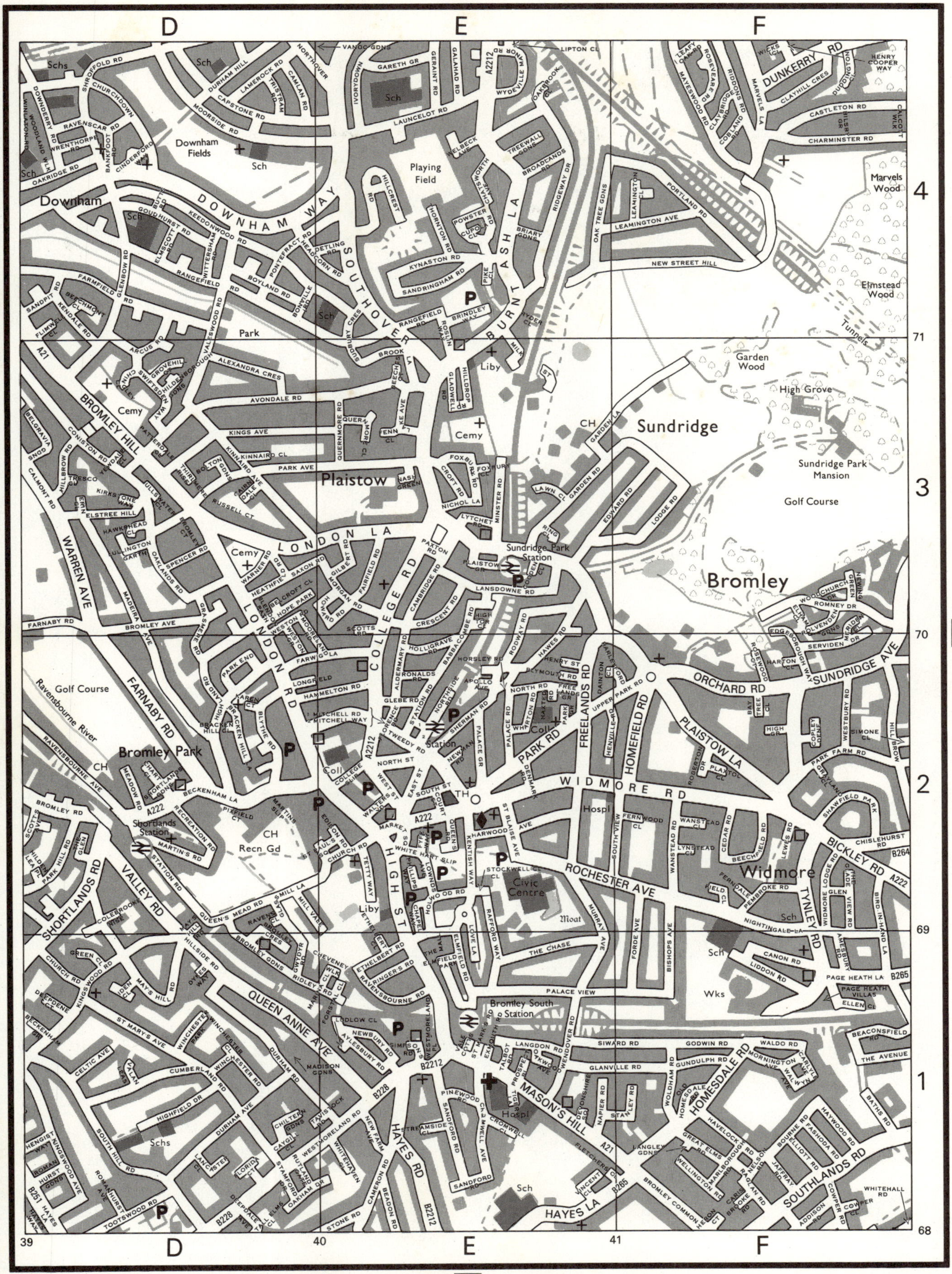
D
E
F
4
3
2
1
71
70
69
68
39
40
41
Downham
Downham Fields
DOWNHAM WAY
SOUTHOVER
BURNT ASH LA
Playing Field
Park
Cemy
Plaistow
LONDON LA
COLLEGE RD
LONDON RD
BROMLEY HILL
WARREN AVE
FARNABY RD
Golf Course
Ravensbourne River
Bromley Park
Shortlands Station
Recn Gd
HIGH ST
Station
Sundridge Park Station
Sundridge
Garden Wood
High Grove
Sundridge Park Mansion
Golf Course
Bromley
Marvels Wood
Elmstead Wood
Tunnels
WIDMORE RD
ROCHESTER AVE
Civic Centre
Moat
Widmore
Bromley South Station
MASON'S HILL
QUEEN ANNE AVE
HAYES RD
HAYES LA
SOUTHLANDS RD
HOMESDALE RD
BICKLEY RD
SUNDRIDGE AVE
ORCHARD RD
PLAISTOW LA
FREELANDS RD
HOMEFIELD RD
SHORTLANDS RD
VALLEY RD
Hospl
Coll
Liby
Sch
Schs
Wks
DUNKERRY RD
NEW STREET HILL
LEAMINGTON AVE

34

48

17

33

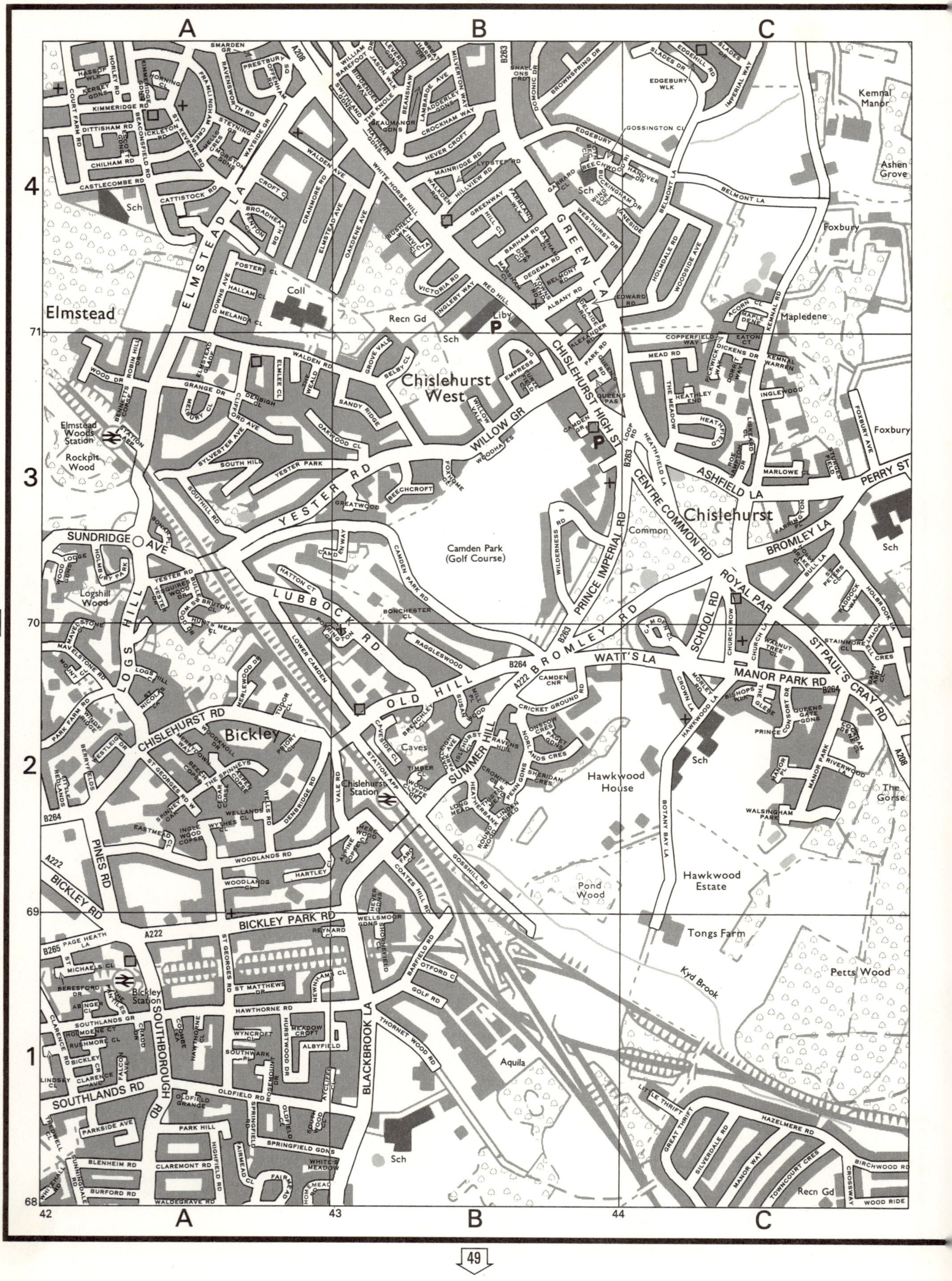
A
B
C
4
3
2
1
71
70
69
68
42
43
44
Elmstead
Chislehurst West
Chislehurst
Bickley
Kemnal Manor
Ashen Grove
Foxbury
Mapledene
Coll
Recn Gd
Sch
Liby
Elmstead Woods Station
Rockpit Wood
Logshill Wood
Camden Park (Golf Course)
Common
Caves
Chislehurst Station
Hawkwood House
Hawkwood Estate
Pond Wood
Tongs Farm
Kyd Brook
Petts Wood
The Gorse
Aquila
Bickley Station
ELMSTEAD LA
SUNDRIDGE AVE
LOGS HILL
CHISLEHURST RD
PINES RD
BICKLEY RD
BICKLEY PARK RD
SOUTHBOROUGH RD
SOUTHLANDS RD
BLACKBROOK LA
YESTER RD
LUBBOCK RD
OLD HILL
WILLOW GR
CHISLEHURST HIGH ST
PRINCE IMPERIAL RD
BROMLEY RD
WATT'S LA
CENTRE COMMON RD
ASHFIELD LA
BROMLEY LA
ROYAL PAR
SCHOOL RD
MANOR PARK RD
ST PAUL'S CRAY RD
PERRY ST
GREEN LA
BELMONT LA
WHITE HORSE HILL
SUMMER HILL
BOTANY BAY LA
CAMDEN PARK RD
GOSSHILL RD
HAZELMERE RD
WOODLANDS RD
OLDFIELD RD
A208
A222
B264
B263
B265

49

18

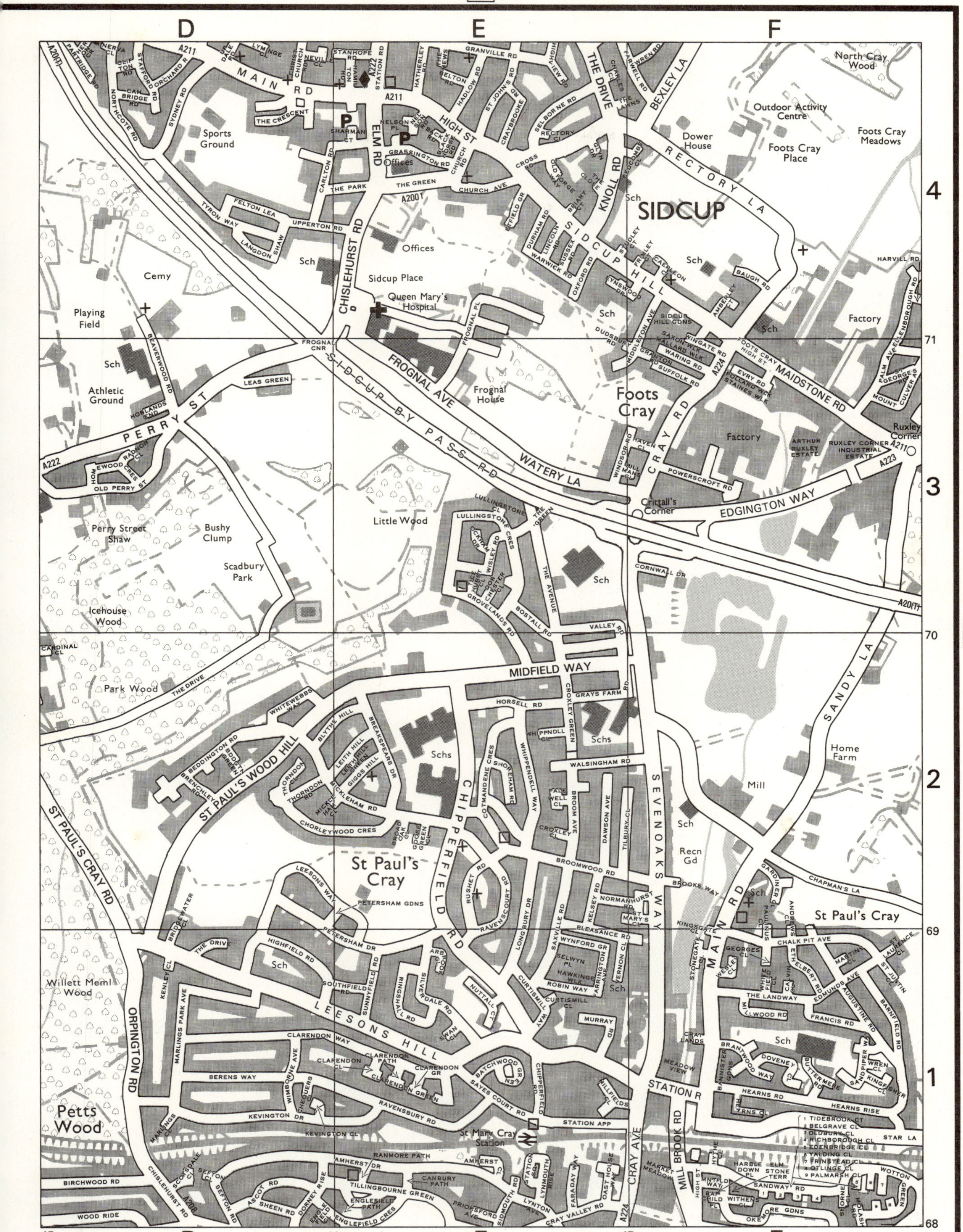
D
E
F
4
3
2
1
71
70
69
68
45
46
47
SIDCUP
Foots Cray
St Paul's Cray
St Paul's Cray
Petts Wood
MAIN RD
HIGH ST
ELM RD
STATION RD
CHISLEHURST RD
THE GREEN
THE PARK
CHURCH AVE
RECTORY LA
BEXLEY LA
THE DRIVE
KNOLL RD
SIDCUP HILL
SIDCUP BY PASS RD
FROGNAL AVE
FROGNAL CNR
WATERY LA
PERRY ST
LEAS GREEN
OLD PERRY ST
MAIDSTONE RD
CRAY RD
FOOTS CRAY HIGH ST
EDGINGTON WAY
POWERSCROFT RD
RUXLEY CORNER INDUSTRIAL ESTATE
ARTHUR RUXLEY ESTATE
Ruxley Corner
Crittall's Corner
CORNWALL DR
SANDY LA
A20(T)
A211
A222
A223
A224
A2001
A208
MIDFIELD WAY
THE AVENUE
VALLEY RD
GRAYS FARM RD
CROXLEY GREEN
HORSELL RD
WALSINGHAM RD
SEVENOAKS WAY
CHIPPERFIELD RD
ST PAUL'S WOOD HILL
ST PAUL'S CRAY RD
ORPINGTON RD
LEESONS HILL
CHORLEYWOOD CRES
BROOMWOOD RD
CHAPMAN'S LA
MAIN RD
CHALK PIT AVE
STATION R
STATION APP
CRAY AVE
MILL BROOK RD
RAVENSBURY RD
KEVINGTON DR
CLARENDON WAY
BERENS WAY
MARLINGS PARK AVE
BIRCHWOOD RD
WOOD RIDE
CHISLEHURST RD
HEARNS RD
HEARNS RISE
STAR LA
CRAY VALLEY RD
1 TIDEBROOK CT
2 BELGRAVE CL
3 OLDBURY CL
4 RICHBOROUGH CL
5 EDENBRIDGE CL
6 YALDING CL
7 FRINSTEAD CL
8 OTLINGE CL
9 PALMARSH CL
Sports Ground
Offices
Sidcup Place
Queen Mary's Hospital
Dower House
Foots Cray Place
Outdoor Activity Centre
North Cray Wood
Foots Cray Meadows
Factory
Frognal House
Cemy
Playing Field
Athletic Ground
Perry Street Shaw
Bushy Clump
Scadbury Park
Little Wood
Icehouse Wood
Park Wood
Willett Meml Wood
Home Farm
Mill
Recn Gd
Sch
Schs
St Mary Cray Station

36

50

19

35

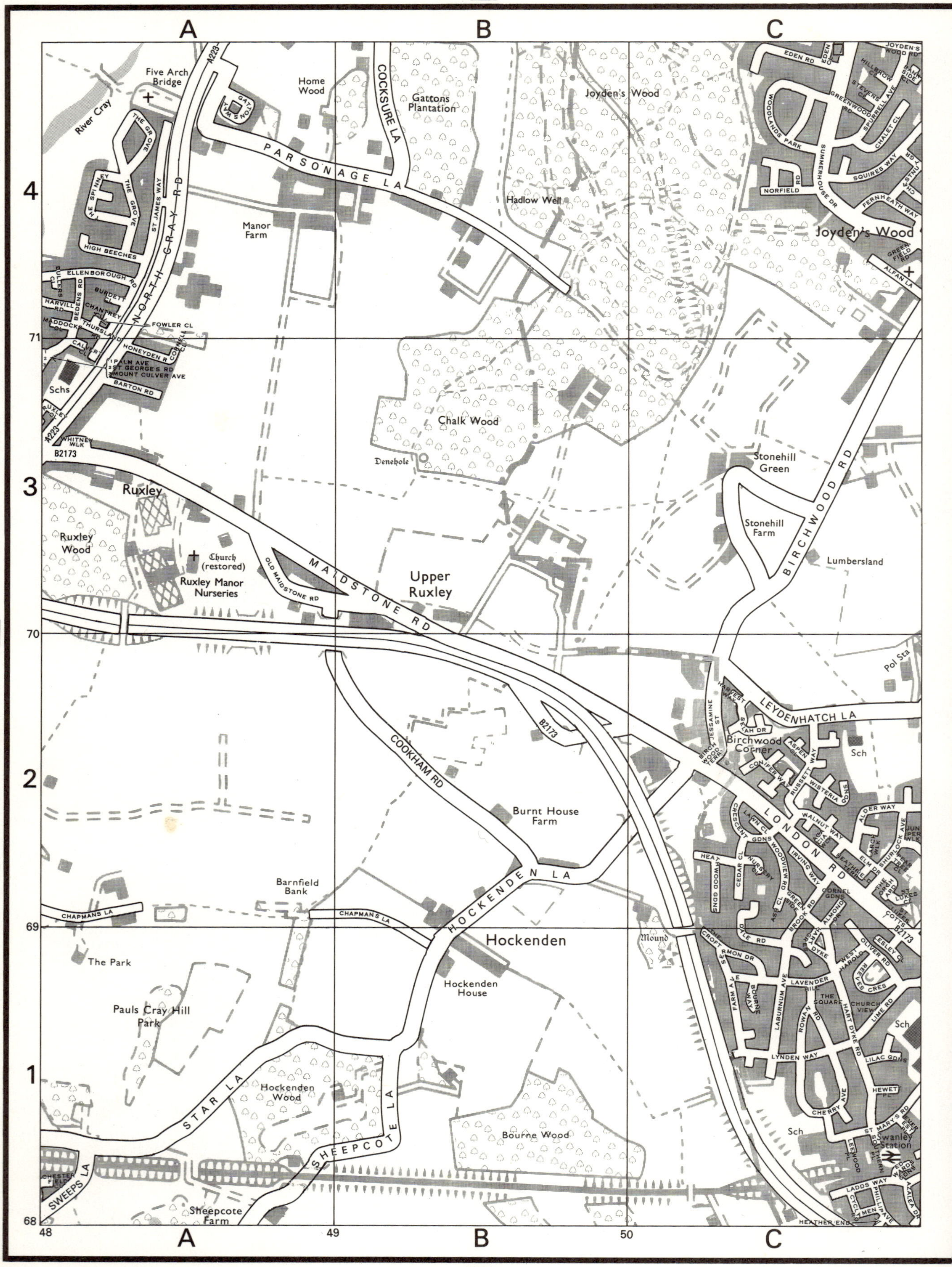
A
B
C
4
3
2
1
71
70
69
68
48
49
50
Five Arch Bridge
River Cray
A223
Home Wood
COCKSURE LA
Gattons Plantation
Joyden's Wood
PARSONAGE LA
Hadlow Well
Manor Farm
THE GROVE
THE SPINNEY
ST JAMES WAY
NORTH GRAY RD
HIGH BEECHES
ELLENBOROUGH RD
BURDETT CL
CHANTREY CL
HARVILL RD
BEDENS RD
THURSLAND
FOWLER CL
HONEYDEN RD
CORNELL CL
CALVERT CL
1 PALM AVE
2 ST GEORGES RD
3 MOUNT CULVER AVE
BARTON RD
Schs
WHITNEY WLK
B2173
Ruxley
Ruxley Wood
Church (restored)
Ruxley Manor Nurseries
OLD MAIDSTONE RD
MAIDSTONE RD
Upper Ruxley
Chalk Wood
Denehole
Stonehill Green
Stonehill Farm
BIRCHWOOD RD
Lumbersland
EDEN RD
HILLCROW
STEVENS CL
GREENWOOD RD
SPURRELL AVE
WOODLANDS PARK
CHALET CL
SUMMERHOUSE DR
NORFIELD RD
SQUIRES WAY
FERNHEATH WAY
Joyden's Wood
ALFAN LA
Pol Sta
LEYDENHATCH LA
JESSAMINE ST
BIRCH WOOD TERR
Birchwood Corner
Sch
CONIFER WAY
RUSSETT WAY
WISTERIA GDNS
ALDER WAY
WALNUT WAY
LONDON RD
CRESCENT GDNS
LAWN CL
WOODVIEW RD
HEATH GDNS
CEDAR CL
NURSERY CL
IRVING WAY
GREEN CT
CORNEL GDNS
BROOK RD
DALE RD
ALMOND DR
OLIVER RD
HART DYKE RD
REEVES CRES
LAVENDER HILL
THE SQUARE
CHURCH VIEW
LIME RD
FARM AVE
BOURNE WAY
LABURNUM AVE
ROWAN RD
LYNDEN WAY
LILAC GDNS
HEWETT PL
CHERRY AVE
ST MARY'S RD
Swanley Station
LADDS WAY
HEATHER END
COOKHAM RD
B2173
Burnt House Farm
HOCKENDEN LA
Barnfield Bank
CHAPMANS LA
CHAPMANS LA
Hockenden
Mound
Hockenden House
The Park
Pauls Cray Hill Park
STAR LA
Hockenden Wood
SHEEPCOTE LA
Bourne Wood
Sch
SWEEPS LA
Sheepcote Farm

51

20

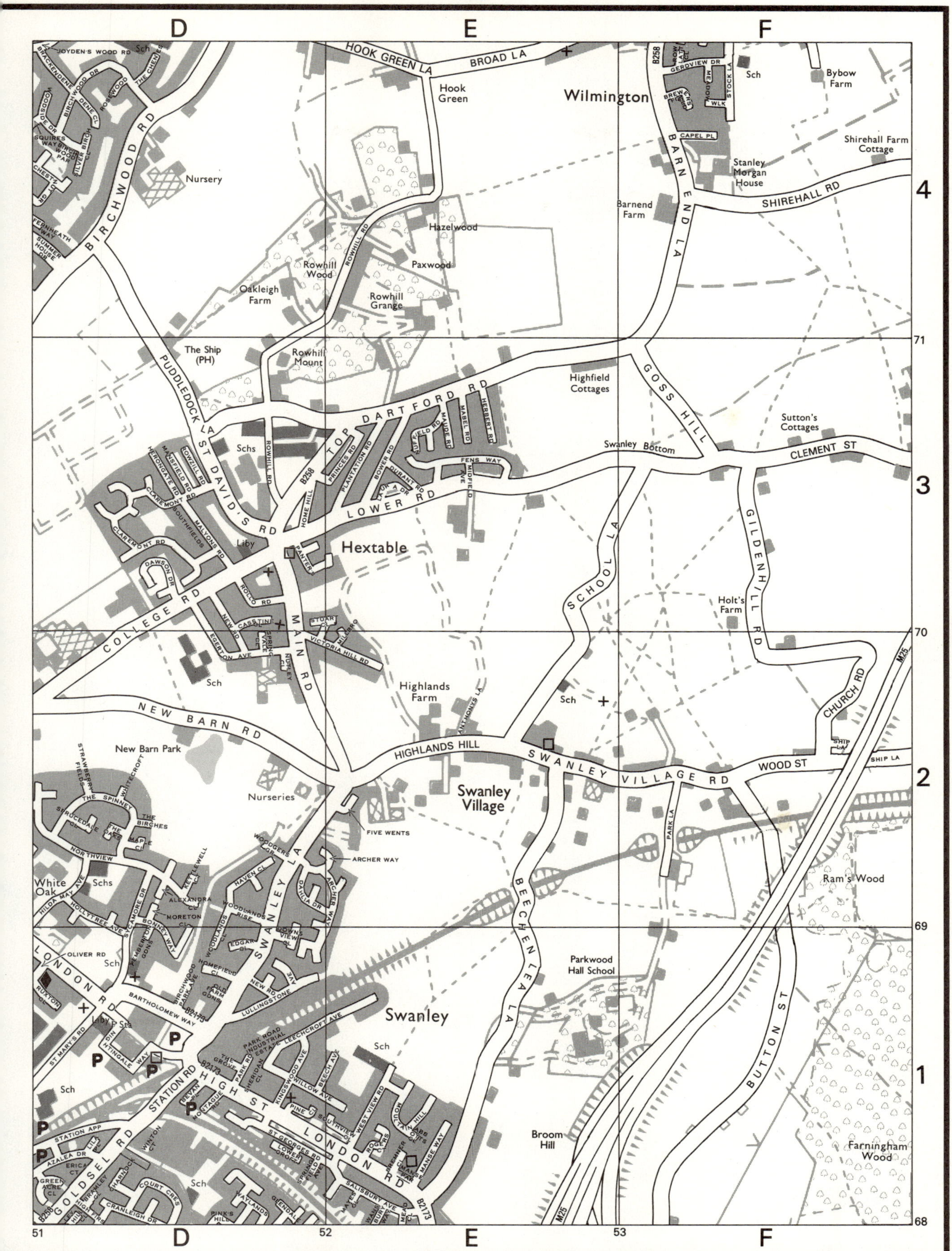
D
E
F
Wilmington
Hook Green
HOOK GREEN LA
BROAD LA
Sch
Bybow Farm
Shirehall Farm Cottage
Stanley Morgan House
SHIREHALL RD
BARN END LA
Barnend Farm
CAPEL PL
GERDVIEW DR
STOCK LA
B258
Nursery
BIRCHWOOD RD
JOYDEN'S WOOD RD
Hazelwood
Paxwood
Rowhill Wood
ROWHILL RD
Rowhill Grange
Oakleigh Farm
The Ship (PH)
Rowhill Mount
PUDDLEDOCK LA
TOP DARTFORD RD
Highfield Cottages
GOSS HILL
Sutton's Cottages
CLEMENT ST
Swanley Bottom
Schs
ST DAVID'S RD
LOWER RD
FENS WAY
Hextable
Liby
COLLEGE RD
MAIN RD
SCHOOL LA
GILDENHILL RD
Holt's Farm
Highlands Farm
Sch
NEW BARN RD
New Barn Park
HIGHLANDS HILL
SWANLEY VILLAGE RD
WOOD ST
SHIP LA
CHURCH RD
M25
Swanley Village
Nurseries
FIVE WENTS
ARCHER WAY
SWANLEY LA
Ram's Wood
White Oak
Schs
BEECHENLEA LA
PARK LA
Parkwood Hall School
LONDON RD
Swanley
Sta
HIGH ST
STATION RD
B2173
BUTTON ST
Broom Hill
Farningham Wood
GOLDSEL RD
1
2
3
4
71
70
69
68
51
52
53

38

52

21

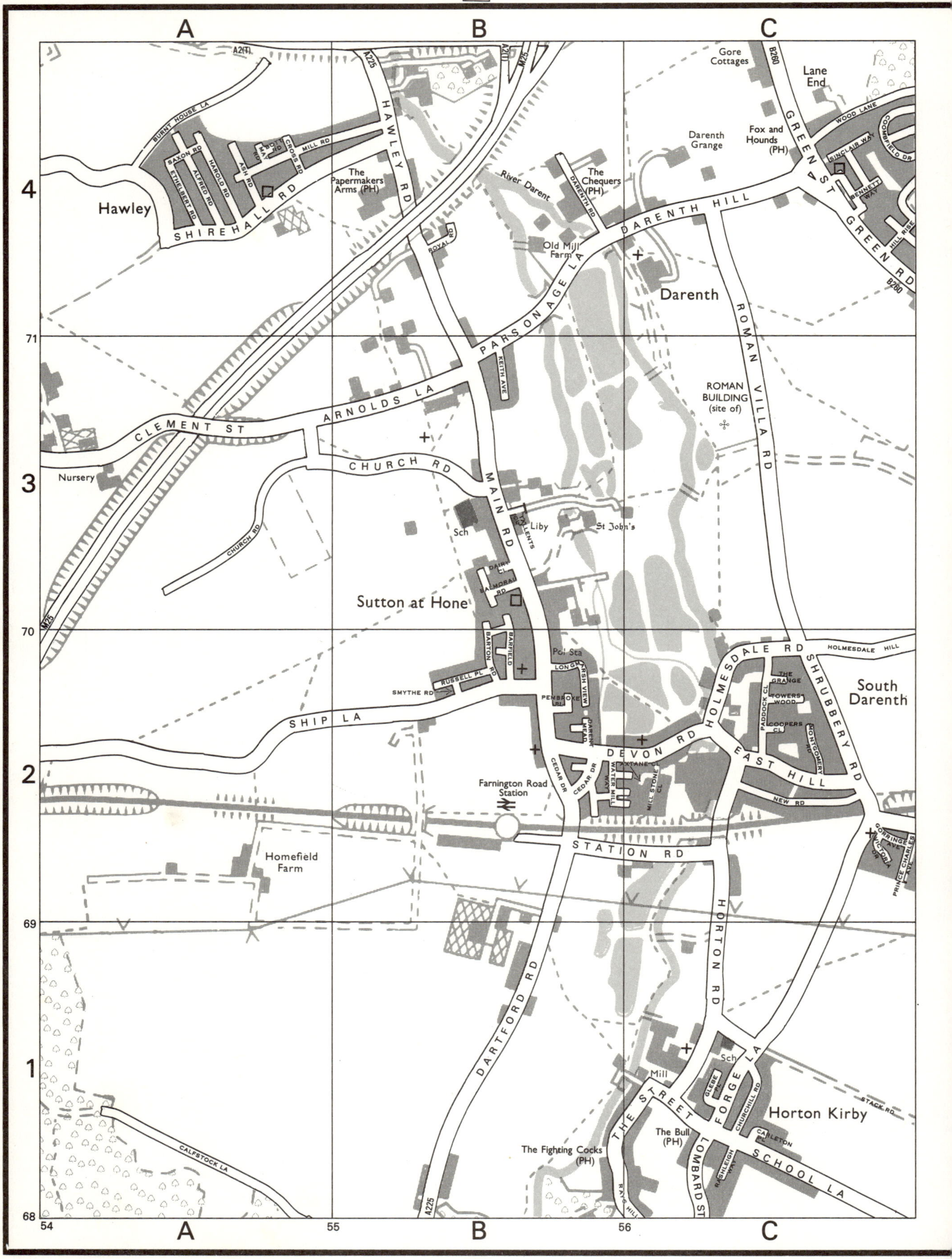
A
B
C
4
3
2
1
71
70
69
68
54
55
56
Hawley
SHIREHALL RD
BURNT HOUSE LA
SAXON RD
ETHELBERT RD
ALFRED RD
HAROLD RD
ASH RD
MILL RD
CROSS RD
HAWLEY RD
A2(T)
A225
M25
The Papermakers Arms (PH)
River Darent
The Chequers (PH)
DARENTH RD
Darenth Grange
Gore Cottages
Lane End
Fox and Hounds (PH)
B260
WOOD LANE
GREEN ST GREEN RD
SINCLAIR WAY
BENNETT WAY
HILL RISE
DARENTH HILL
Old Mill Farm
PARSONAGE LA
ROYAL RD
Darenth
ROMAN VILLA RD
ROMAN BUILDING (site of)
KEITH AVE
ARNOLDS LA
CLEMENT ST
Nursery
CHURCH RD
MAIN RD
Sch
Liby
St John's
Sutton at Hone
BALMORAL RD
BARTON RD
BARFIELD
RUSSELL PL
SMYTHE RD
SHIP LA
Pol Sta
PEMBROKE
HOLMESDALE RD
HOLMESDALE HILL
SHRUBBERY RD
South Darenth
PADDOCK CL
THE GRANGE
TOWERS WOOD
COOPERS CL
MONTGOMERY RD
DEVON RD
EAST HILL
NEW RD
CEDAR DR
WATER MILL WAY
MILL STONE CL
Farnington Road Station
STATION RD
Homefield Farm
GOWRINGE AVE
VICTORIA DR
PRINCE CHARLES AVE
DARTFORD RD
HORTON RD
CALFSTOCK LA
Mill
Sch
THE STREET
FORGE LA
GLEBE
CHURCHILL RD
STACK RD
Horton Kirby
The Bull (PH)
The Fighting Cocks (PH)
LOMBARD ST
SCHOOL LA
CARLETON
RAY'S HILL

37

53

22

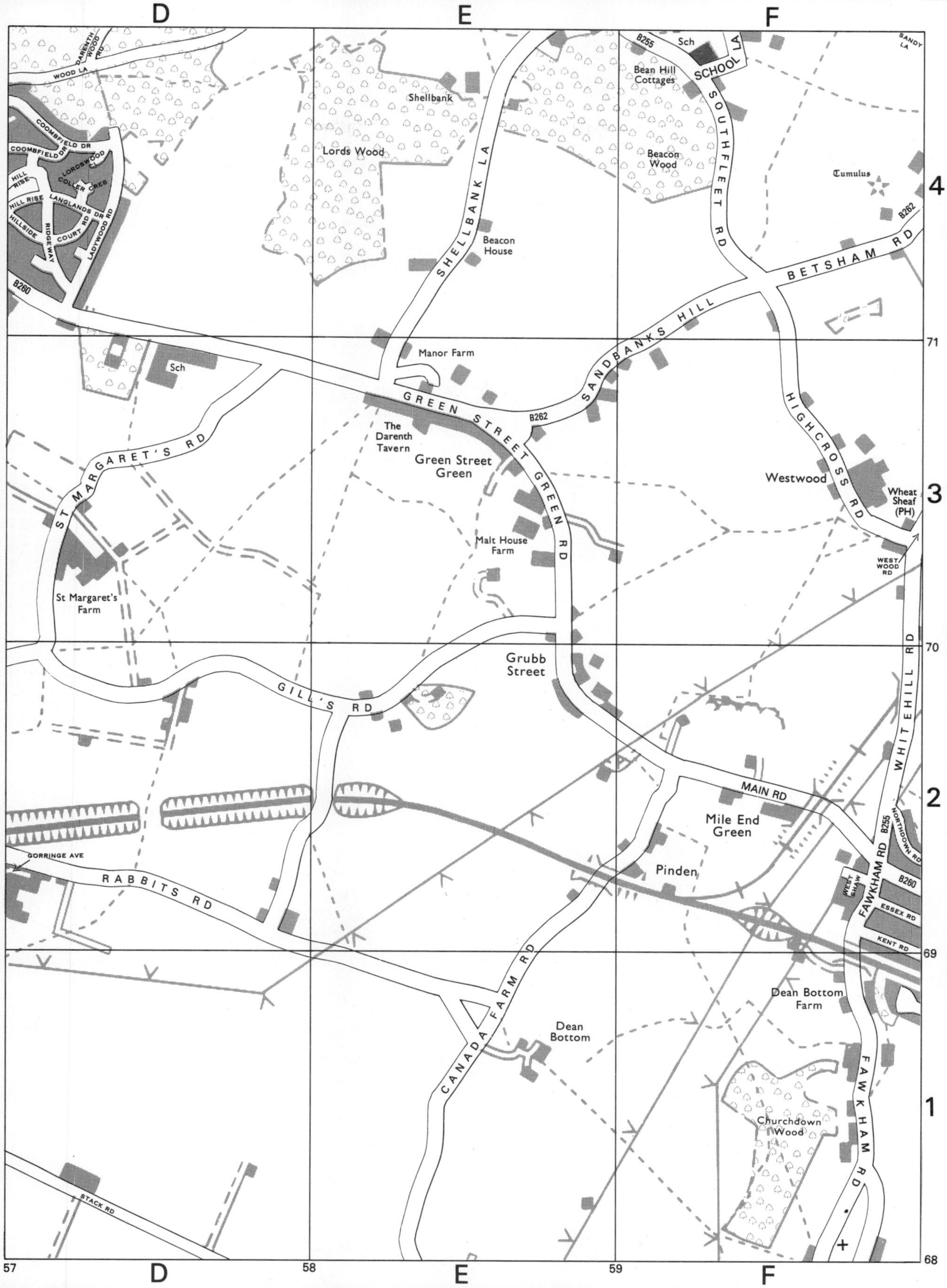
D
E
F
WOOD LA
DARENTH WOOD RD
COOMBFIELD DR
LORDSWOOD CL
HILL RISE
COLLER CRES
LANGLANDS DR
HILLSIDE
RIDGEWAY
COURT RD
LADYWOOD RD
B260
Lords Wood
Shellbank
SHELLBANK LA
Beacon House
B255
Sch
SCHOOL LA
Bean Hill Cottages
SOUTHFLEET RD
Beacon Wood
SANDY LA
Tumulus
B262
BETSHAM RD
SANDBANKS HILL
Manor Farm
Sch
GREEN STREET
B262
The Darenth Tavern
Green Street Green
GREEN ST GREEN RD
HIGHCROSS RD
Westwood
Wheat Sheaf (PH)
WEST WOOD RD
ST MARGARET'S RD
Malt House Farm
St Margaret's Farm
Grubb Street
GILL'S RD
WHITEHILL RD
MAIN RD
Mile End Green
B255
NORTHDOWN RD
FAWKHAM RD
WEST SHAW
B260
Pinden
ESSEX RD
KENT RD
GORRINGE AVE
RABBITS RD
CANADA FARM RD
Dean Bottom Farm
Dean Bottom
Churchdown Wood
FAWKHAM RD
STACK RD
1
2
3
4
57
58
59
68
69
70
71

40

54

23

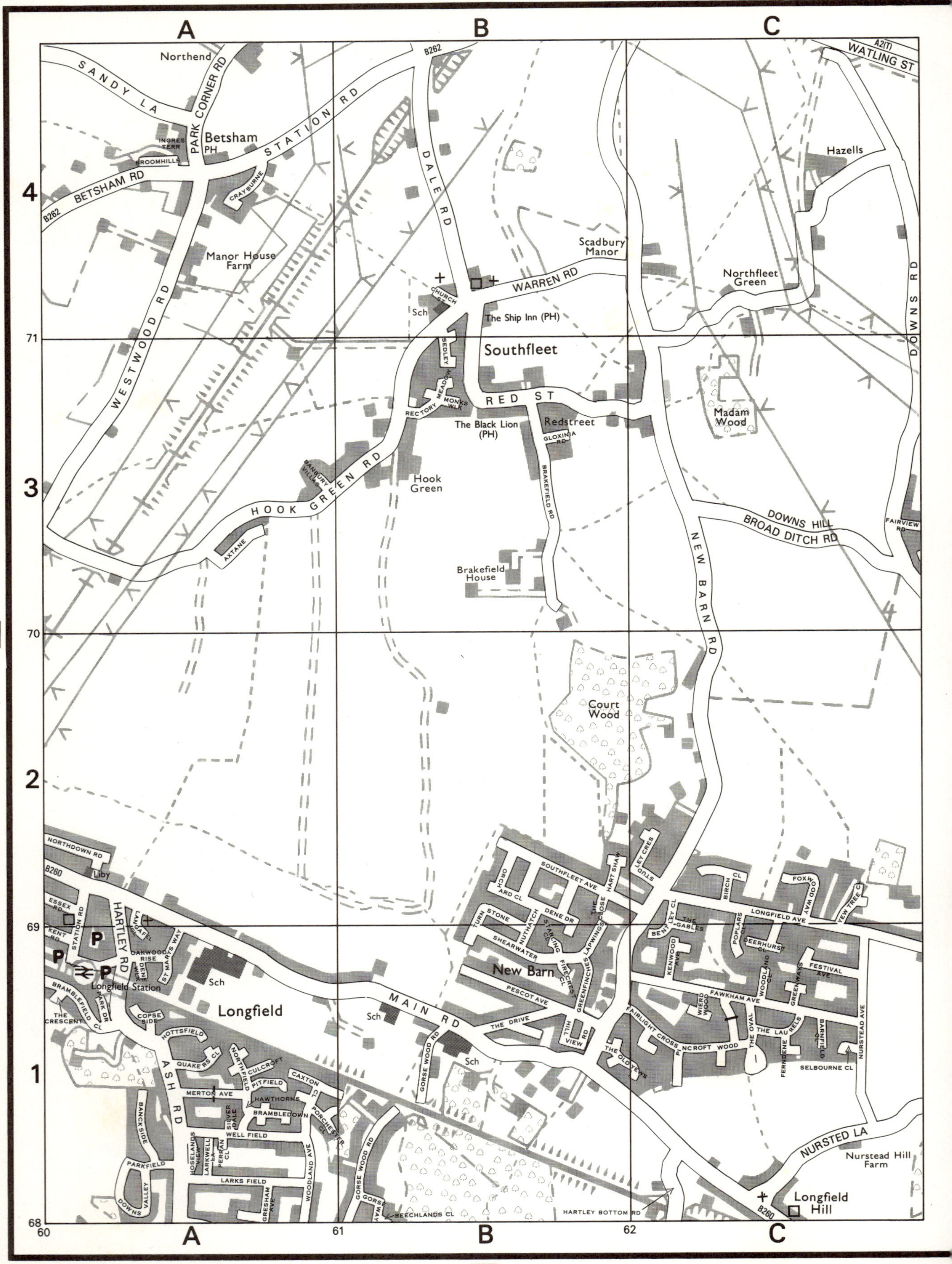
A
B
C
Northend
SANDY LA
PARK CORNER RD
B262
STATION RD
Betsham
PH
INGRES TERR
BROOMHILLS
BETSHAM RD
B262
CRAYBURNE
DALE RD
Manor House Farm
WESTWOOD RD
Scadbury Manor
WARREN RD
CHURCH
Sch
The Ship Inn (PH)
Southfleet
SEDLEY
MEADOW
MONKS WLK
RECTORY
RED ST
The Black Lion (PH)
Redstreet
GLOXINIA RD
BANBURY VILLAS
HOOK GREEN RD
Hook Green
BRAKEFIELD RD
AXTANE
Brakefield House
Hazells
WATLING ST
A2(T)
Northfleet Green
DOWNS RD
Madam Wood
DOWNS HILL
BROAD DITCH RD
FAIRVIEW RD
NEW BARN RD
Court Wood
NORTHDOWN RD
B260
Liby
ESSEX RD
KENT RD
STATION RD
HARTLEY RD
LANGAFEL
OAKWOOD RISE
ST MARYS WAY
Longfield Station
Sch
Longfield
BRAMBLEFIELD CL
THE CRESCENT
PARK DR
COPSE SIDE
HOTTSFIELD
QUAKERS CL
NORTHFIELD
CULCROFT
PITFIELD
CAXTON CL
MERTON AVE
HAWTHORNS
BRAMBLEDOWN
SILVER DALE
PORCHESTER CL
WELL FIELD
ASH RD
BANCKSIDE
PARKFIELD
DOWNS VALLEY
HOSELANDS VIEW
LARKWELL
FERRAN CL
LARKS FIELD
GRESHAM AVE
WOODLAND AVE
GORSE WOOD RD
GORSE WAY
BEECHLANDS CL
MAIN RD
Sch
GORSE WOOD RD
Sch
ORCHARD CL
SOUTHFLEET AVE
HART SHAW
STUDLEY CRES
TURNSTONE
NUTHATCH
DENE DR
THE CLOSE
STARLING CL
SHEARWATER
LAPWINGS
FIRECREST
GREENFINCHES
New Barn
PESCOT AVE
THE DRIVE
HILL VIEW RD
THE OLD YEWS
FAIRLIGHT CROSS
PINCROFT WOOD
BEWLEY CL
THE GABLES
KENWOOD AVE
BIRCH CL
POPLARS
DEERHURST CL
LONGFIELD AVE
FOXWOOD WAY
YEW TREE CL
WOODLANDS CL
GREENWAYS
FESTIVAL AVE
FAWKHAM AVE
WIERD WOOD
THE OVAL
THE LAURELS
FERNDENE
BARNFIELD
SELBOURNE CL
NURSTEAD AVE
NURSTED LA
Nurstead Hill Farm
HARTLEY BOTTOM RD
B260
Longfield Hill
4
3
2
1
71
70
69
68
60
61
62

39

55

24

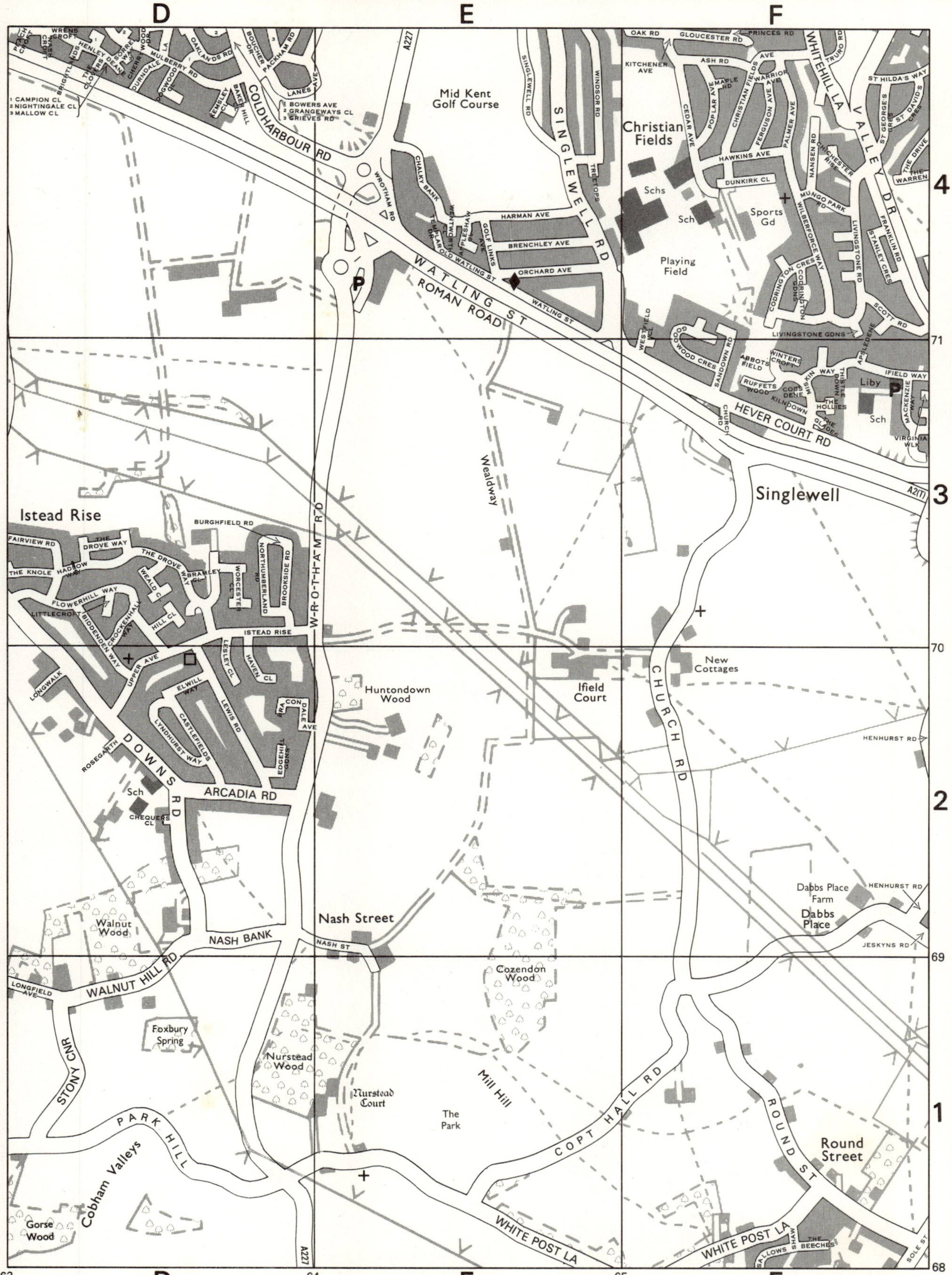
D
E
F
Mid Kent Golf Course
Christian Fields
Schs
Sch
Sports Gd
Playing Field
COLDHARBOUR RD
WATLING ST
ROMAN ROAD
SINGLEWELL RD
HEVER COURT RD
Singlewell
Liby
Wealdway
Istead Rise
ISTEAD RISE
W-R-O-T-H-A-M RD
DOWNS RD
ARCADIA RD
Huntondown Wood
Ifield Court
New Cottages
CHURCH RD
HENHURST RD
Dabbs Place Farm
Dabbs Place
JESKYNS RD
Nash Street
NASH BANK
NASH ST
Walnut Wood
WALNUT HILL RD
Cozendon Wood
Foxbury Spring
STONY CNR
Nurstead Wood
Nurstead Court
Mill Hill
The Park
COPT HALL RD
ROUND ST
Round Street
PARK HILL
Cobham Valleys
Gorse Wood
WHITE POST LA
A227
A2(T)
1 CAMPION CL
2 NIGHTINGALE CL
3 MALLOW CL
1 BOWERS AVE
2 GRANGEWAYS CL
3 GRIEVES RD
4
3
2
1
71
70
69
68
63
64
65

42

56

25

A
B
C
4
3
2
1
71
70
69
68
66
67
68
Sports Ground
Sports Centre
Riverview Park
Sch
Liby
P
LEANDER DR
VIGILANT WAY
CAMBRIA CRES
CLIPPER CRES
KELSO DR
BELTANIA DR
CERNE RD
DORSET CRES
THE DRIVE
THE RISE
ST FRANCIS AVE
WHINFELL WAY
IMPERIAL DR
BRITANNIA DR
SIRDAR STRAND
LAYONA DR
CHALLENGE CL
HOPEWELL DR
ASTRA DR
FROBISHER WAY
MARLING WAY
DOBSON RD
STACEY CL
FRANKLIN RD
IFIELD WAY
VIRGINIA WLK
MACKENZIE WAY
HEVER COURT RD
THE WARREN
VALLEY DR
DAVY'S PL
A2(T)
A226
MUGGINS LA
Shorne Hill
MILL HILL LA
Harts Hill
Upper Ifield
Ifield Place
SHORNE IFIELD RD
GREEN LA
Westwood Farm
THONG LA
Thong
Brummelhill Wood
Cheneys Farm
Claylane Wood
Randall Heath
Randall Wood
WOODLANDS LA
Shorne Wood (Country Park)
The Burnett
HENHURST RD
Henhurst Dale
ROMAN ROAD
WATLING ST
BREWERS RD
Brewers Wood
Scalers Hill
Henhurst
Winstead Hill
The Mount
Resr
Cumulus
Ashenbank Wood
Golf Course
Peggy Taylor's Hill
Jeskyns Court
West Park
HALFPENCE LA
Cobham Hall
JESKYNS RD
Scotland Lane
Owletts
Jeskyns Farm
The Avenue
Cobham Park
BATTLE ST
SARSENS CL
Battle Street
Sch
THE STREET
Cobham
LAWRENCE DR
College
COBHAM BURY RD
Cobhambury Farm
LODGE LA
Lodge Farm
Lodge Wood
BATT'S RD
Winterham Hill

41

57

26

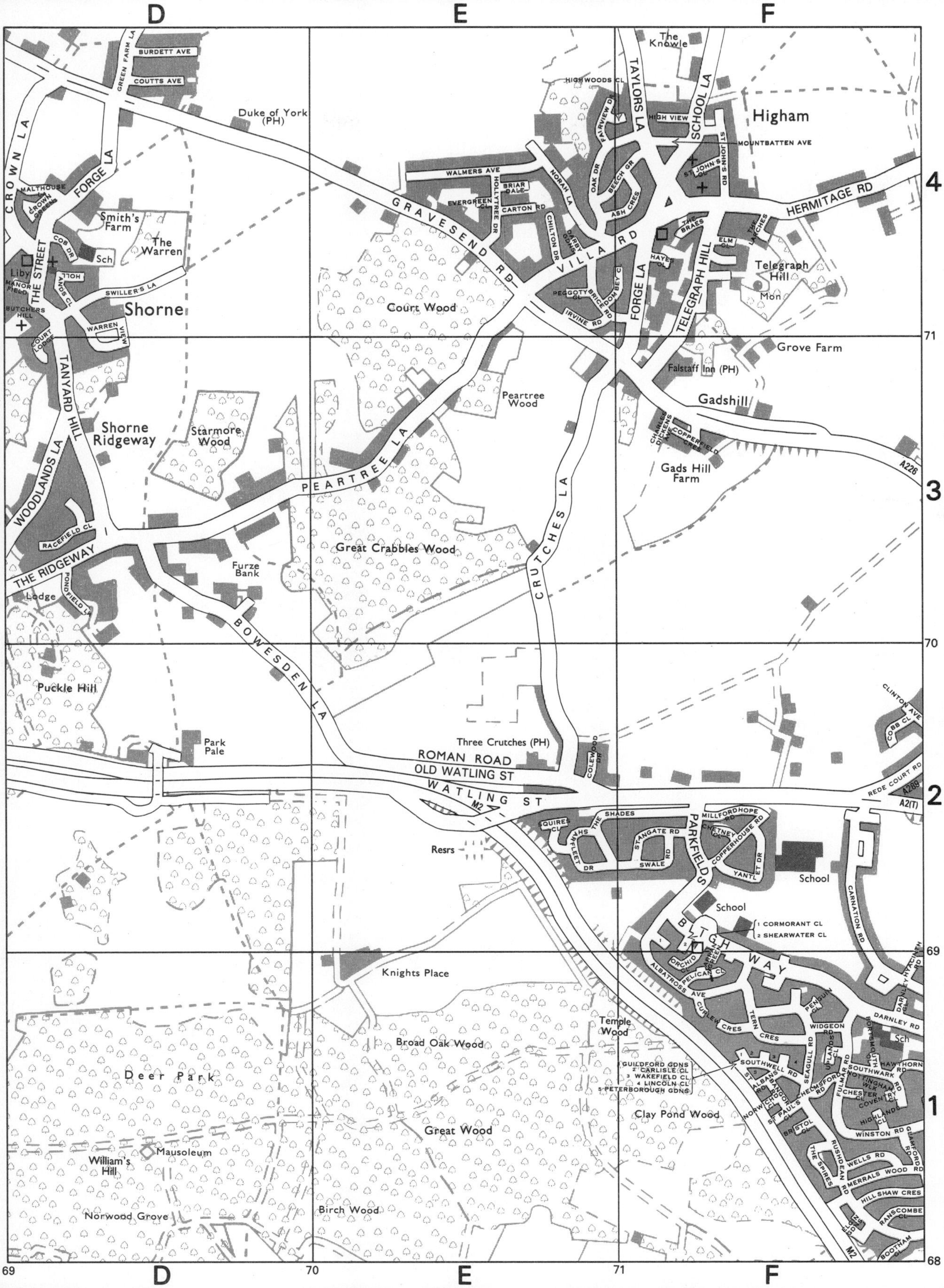

D
E
F
Shorne
Shorne Ridgeway
Higham
Gadshill
Telegraph Hill
Mon
Grove Farm
Falstaff Inn (PH)
Gads Hill Farm
The Knowle
Duke of York (PH)
Smith's Farm
The Warren
Sch
Liby
Court Wood
Peartree Wood
Starmore Wood
Great Crabbles Wood
Furze Bank
Lodge
Puckle Hill
Park Pale
Three Crutches (PH)
Resrs
School
Knights Place
Temple Wood
Broad Oak Wood
Deer Park
Mausoleum
William's Hill
Norwood Grove
Great Wood
Birch Wood
Clay Pond Wood
BURDETT AVE
COUTTS AVE
GREEN FARM LA
CROWN LA
FORGE LA
MALTHOUSE LA
THE STREET
COB DR
SWILLER'S LA
WARREN VIEW
COURT LODGE
BUTCHERS HILL
MANOR FIELD
TANYARD HILL
WOODLANDS LA
RACEFIELD CL
THE RIDGEWAY
PONDFIELD LA
GRAVESEND RD
WALMERS AVE
HOLLYTREE DR
BRIAR DALE
EVERGREEN CL
CARTON RD
CHILTON DR
NORAH LA
DARBY GDNS
VILLA RD
PEGGOTTY CL
BRICE RD
DOMBEY CL
IRVINE RD
HIGHWOODS CL
FAIRVIEW DR
OAK DR
BEECH GR
ASH CRES
TAYLORS LA
HIGH VIEW
SCHOOL LA
ST JOHN'S RD
MOUNTBATTEN AVE
HERMITAGE RD
THE BRAES
HAYES CL
ELM CL
THE LARCHES
TELEGRAPH HILL
CHARLES DICKENS AVE
COPPERFIELD CRES
A226
PEARTREE LA
CRUTCHES LA
BOWESDEN LA
ROMAN ROAD
OLD WATLING ST
WATLING ST
M2
COLEWOOD DR
CLINTON AVE
COBB CL
REDE COURT RD
A289
A2(T)
SQUIRES CL
THE SHADES
SHARFLEET DR
STANGATE RD
SWALE RD
PARKFIELDS
MILLFORDHOPE RD
CHETNEY CL
COPPERHOUSE RD
YANTLET DR
CARNATION RD
1 CORMORANT CL
2 SHEARWATER CL
BLIGH WAY
ORCHID CL
PELICAN CL
ALBATROSS AVE
CURLEW CRES
TERN CRES
PENGUIN CL
WIDGEON RD
SEAGULL RD
UPLANDS CL
HYACINTH RD
DARNLEY RD
PORTSMOUTH CL
HAWTHORN RD
1 GUILDFORD GDNS
2 CARLISLE CL
3 WAKEFIELD CL
4 LINCOLN CL
5 PETERBOROUGH GDNS
SOUTHWELL RD
ST ALBANS RD
NORWICH CL
ST PAUL'S CRES
CHELMSFORD RD
FULMAR RD
SOUTHWARK RD
NOTTINGHAM WLK
CHESTER CL
COVENTRY CL
HIGHLANDS CL
WINSTON RD
BRISTOL CL
THE SPIRES
RUSHDEAN RD
WELLS RD
MERRALS WOOD RD
HILLSHAW CRES
RANSCOMBE CL
BOOTHAM CL
4
3
2
1
71
70
69
68
69
70
71

44

58

27

43

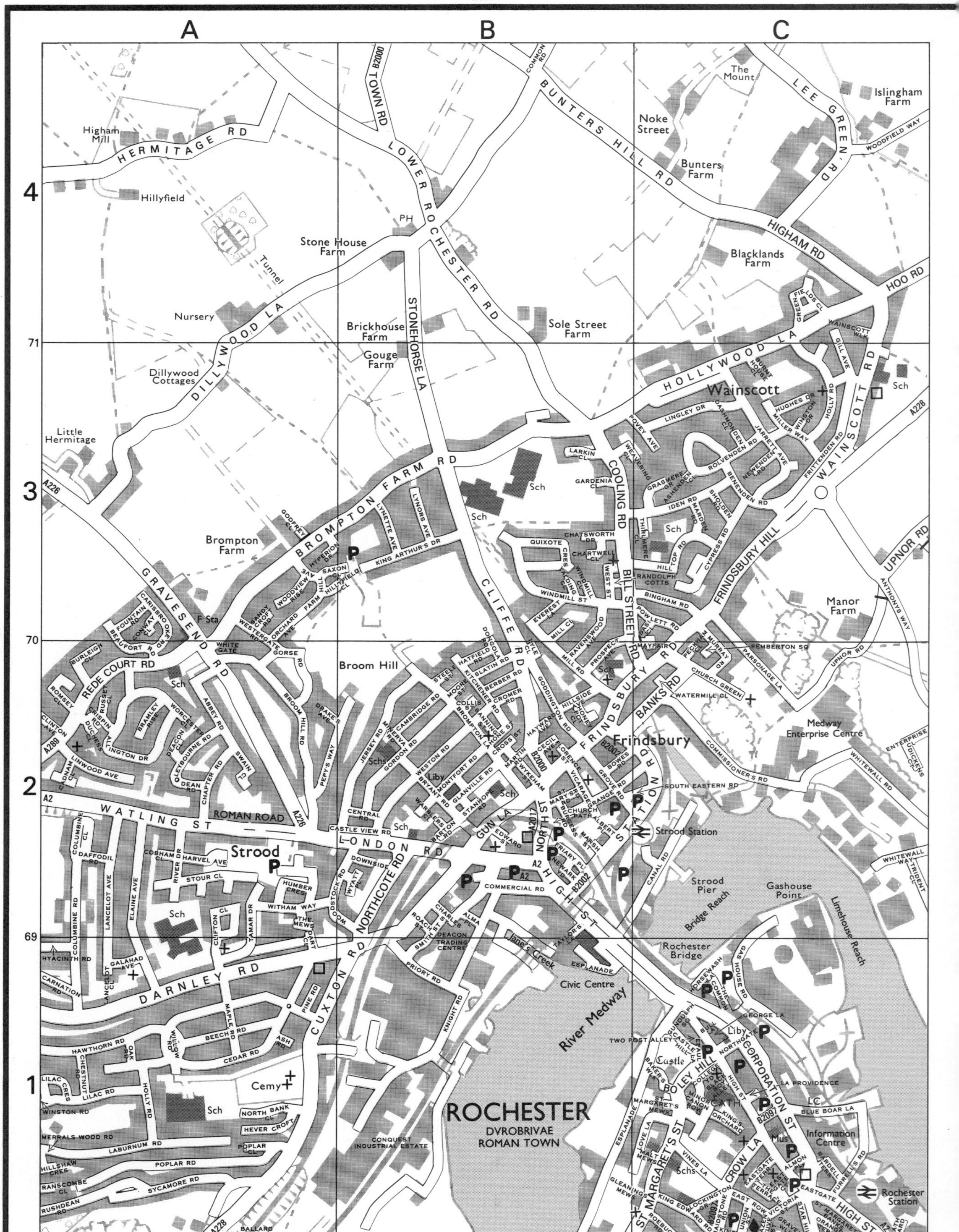

A
B
C
4
3
2
1
71
70
69
68
72
73
74
Higham Mill
HERMITAGE RD
Hillyfield
TOWN RD
B2000
LOWER ROCHESTER RD
COMMON RD
BUNTERS HILL RD
Noke Street
The Mount
LEE GREEN RD
Islingham Farm
WOODFIELD WAY
Bunters Farm
HIGHAM RD
Blacklands Farm
HOO RD
PH
Stone House Farm
Tunnel
Nursery
DILLYWOOD LA
Brickhouse Farm
STONEHORSE LA
Sole Street Farm
Gouge Farm
Dillywood Cottages
HOLLYWOOD LA
Wainscott
WAINSCOTT RD
Sch
A228
Little Hermitage
A226
BROMPTON FARM RD
COOLING RD
BILL STREET RD
FRINDSBURY HILL
UPNOR RD
Brompton Farm
GRAVESEND RD
KING ARTHUR'S DR
CLIFFE RD
Manor Farm
F Sta
WHITE GATE
Broom Hill
REDE COURT RD
FRINDSBURY RD
BANKS RD
Frindsbury
Medway Enterprise Centre
COMMISSIONER'S RD
A289
A2
WATLING ST
ROMAN ROAD
A226
LONDON RD
Strood
Strood Station
SOUTH EASTERN RD
Strood Pier
Bridge Reach
Gashouse Point
Limehouse Reach
Rochester Bridge
HIGH ST
COMMERCIAL RD
NORTHCOTE RD
DARNLEY RD
CUXTON RD
Jane's Creek
ESPLANADE
Civic Centre
River Medway
Castle
BOLEY HILL
CORPORATION ST
Cemy
ROCHESTER
DVROBRIVAE
ROMAN TOWN
CONQUEST INDUSTRIAL ESTATE
BALLARD BUSINESS PARK
Information Centre
Rochester Station
Mus
Liby
Schs
ST MARGARET'S ST
CROW LA
EASTGATE
KING EDWARD RD

59

28

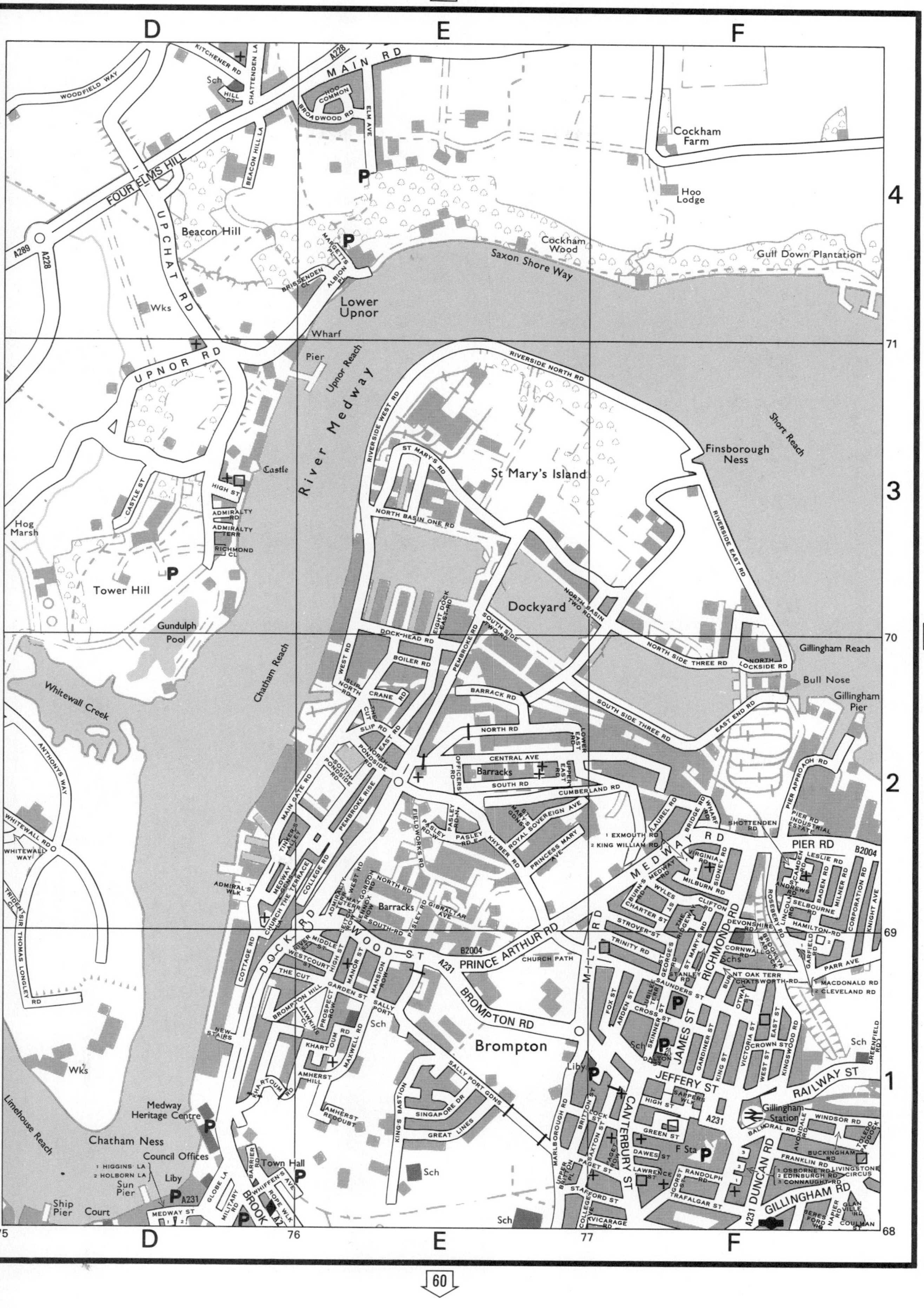
D
E
F
4
3
2
1
71
70
69
68
75
76
77
A228
MAIN RD
KITCHENER RD
CHATTENDEN LA
WOODFIELD WAY
Sch
HILL CT
HOO COMMON
BROADWOOD RD
ELM AVE
BEACON HILL LA
FOUR ELMS HILL
A289
UPCHAT RD
Beacon Hill
Cockham Farm
Hoo Lodge
Cockham Wood
Saxon Shore Way
Gull Down Plantation
MARGETTS PL
BRISSENDEN CL
ALBION PL
Lower Upnor
Wks
Wharf
Pier
Upnor Reach
UPNOR RD
River Medway
RIVERSIDE NORTH RD
RIVERSIDE WEST RD
Short Reach
Finsborough Ness
ST MARY'S RD
St Mary's Island
Castle
HIGH ST
CASTLE ST
ADMIRALTY RD
ADMIRALTY TERR
RICHMOND CL
Hog Marsh
Tower Hill
NORTH BASIN ONE RD
RIVERSIDE EAST RD
Dockyard
NORTH BASIN TWO RD
EIGHT DOCK EAST RD
SOUTH SIDE TWO RD
PEMBROKE RD
Gundulph Pool
DOCK-HEAD RD
BOILER RD
WEST RD
NORTH SIDE THREE RD
NORTH LOCKSIDE RD
Gillingham Reach
Bull Nose
Gillingham Pier
Chatham Reach
Whitewall Creek
SLIP NORTH
CRANE RD
BARRACK RD
SOUTH SIDE THREE RD
EAST END RD
SLIP RD
NORTH RD
LOWER EAST RD
ANTHONY'S WAY
SOUTH PONDSIDE RD
NORTH PONDSIDE RD
EAST RD
CENTRAL AVE
Barracks
OFFICERS RD
UPPER EAST RD
SOUTH RD
CUMBERLAND RD
PIER APPROACH RD
MAIN GATE RD
PEMBROKE RISE
PASLEY ROW
FIELDWORKS RD
PASLEY RD
PASLEY RD E
KHYBER RD
ROYAL SOVEREIGN AVE
PRINCESS MARY AVE
LAUREL RD
BRIDGE RD
WHARF RD
SHOTTENDEN RD
PIER RD INDUSTRIAL ESTATE
PIER RD
B2004
WHITEWALL RD
WHITEWALL WAY
TINKER'S ALLEY
MEDWAY RD
1 EXMOUTH RD
2 KING WILLIAM RD
VIRGINIA RD
SIDNEY RD
MILBURN RD
LESLIE RD
CAMDEN RD
BADEN RD
MILNER RD
LINCOLN RD
ANDREWS
SELBOURNE RD
CORPORATION RD
KNIGHT AVE
ADMIRAL'S WLK
MEDWAY GDNS
CHURCH THE TERRACE
COLLEGE RD
NORTH RD
GIBRALTAR AVE
Barracks
SOUTH RD
WYLES
CHARTER ST
CLIFTON RD
DEVONSHIRE RD
HAMILTON RD
ROSEBERY RD
TRIDENT CL
SIR THOMAS LONGLEY RD
DOCK RD
WOOD ST
MIDDLE ST
WESTCOURT ST
HIGH ST
MANOR ST
MANSION ROW
PRINCE ARTHUR RD
B2004
A231
CHURCH PATH
MILL RD
STROVER ST
TRINITY RD
THE RIDGEWAY
ST MARY'S RD
RICHMOND RD
CORNWALL RD
BROOKLYN PADDOCK
Schs
GARFIELD RD
PARR AVE
COTTAGE RD
THE CUT
BROMPTON HILL
GARDEN ST
SALLY PORT
BROMPTON RD
ST GEORGE'S RD
JUBILEE TERR
STANLEY RD
SAUNDERS ST
BURNT OAK TERR
CHATSWORTH RD
1 MACDONALD RD
2 CLEVELAND RD
FOX ST
ARDEN ST
CROSS ST
SKINNER ST
OTWAY ST
EAST ST
JAMES ST
GARDINER ST
KING ST
VICTORIA ST
WEST ST
CROWN ST
STOPFORD RD
KINGSWOOD RD
GREENFIELD RD
NEW STAIRS
HAWKINS CL
PROSPECT ROW
KHARTOUM RD
MAXWELL RD
Sch
Brompton
Sch
DALTON ST
Liby
JEFFERY ST
RAILWAY ST
Wks
AMHERST HILL
SALLY PORT GDNS
KHARTOUM RD
HIGH ST
SAPPERS WLK
Gillingham Station
A231
Limehouse Reach
Medway Heritage Centre
KING'S BASTION
SINGAPORE DR
AMHERST REDOUBT
GREAT LINES
MARLBOROUGH RD
BRITTON ST
CANTERBURY ST
GREEN ST
WINDSOR RD
BALMORAL RD
AVONDALE RD
TOLEDO PADDOCK
Chatham Ness
Council Offices
1 HIGGINS LA
2 HOLBORN LA
Sun Pier
Liby
A231
Town Hall
BARRIER RD
Sch
F Sta
DAWES ST
LAWRENCE ST
RANDOLPH RD
DUNCAN RD
BUCKINGHAM RD
FRANKLIN RD
1 OSBORNE RD
2 EDINBURGH RD
3 CONNAUGHT RD
LIVINGSTONE CIRCUS
GILLINGHAM RD
Ship Pier
Court
MEDWAY ST
GLOBE LA
MILITARY RD
BROOK
WHIFFEN'S AVE
ROPE WLK
UPPER BRITTON PL
PAGET ST
SAXTON ST
GORST ST
STAFFORD ST
TRAFALGAR ST
COLLEGE AVE
VICARAGE RD
Sch
BERESFORD RD
NAPIER RD
GLANVILLE RD
COULMAN ST
A231

46
60

29

45

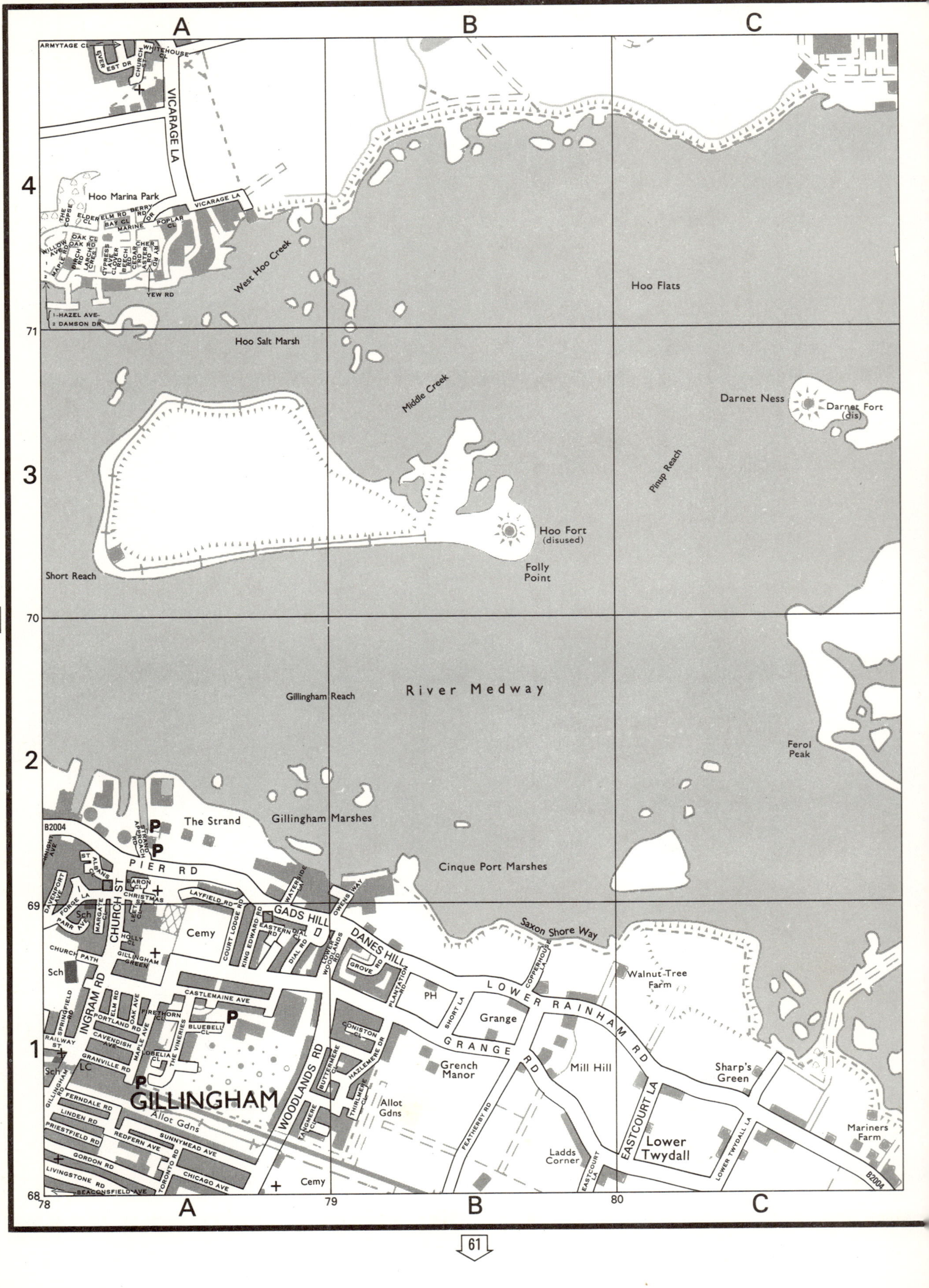
A
B
C
4
3
2
1
71
70
69
68
78
79
80
ARMYTAGE CL
WHITEHOUSE CL
CHURCH ST
VICARAGE LA
Hoo Marina Park
THE COPSE
ELDER CL
ELM RD
BERRY RD
BAY CL
MARINE DR
POPLAR CL
WILLOW AVE
MAPLE RD
BIRCH RD
OAK RD
LARCH CRES
CYPRESS CL
CLOVER
BEECH RD
CEDAR RD
YEW RD
1-HAZEL AVE
2 DAMSON DR
West Hoo Creek
Hoo Flats
Hoo Salt Marsh
Middle Creek
Darnet Ness
Darnet Fort (dis)
Pinup Reach
Hoo Fort (disused)
Folly Point
Short Reach
River Medway
Gillingham Reach
Ferol Peak
The Strand
Gillingham Marshes
Cinque Port Marshes
B2004
STRAND APPROACH RD
PIER RD
DAVENPORT AVE
ST ALBANS CL
BARON CL
CHRISTMAS ST
LAYFIELD RD
WATERSIDE LA
OWENS WAY
FORGE LA
Sch
PARR AVE
MARGATE CL
CHURCH ST
HOLLY CL
GILLINGHAM GREEN
Cemy
COURT LODGE RD
KING EDWARD RD
EASTERN RD
DIAL CL
DIAL RD
GADS HILL
DANES HILL
Saxon Shore Way
COPPERHOUSE LA
Walnut Tree Farm
CHURCH PATH
INGRAM RD
SPRINGFIELD RD
RAILWAY ST
CASTLEMAINE AVE
PORTLAND RD
ELM RD
OAK AVE
FIRETHORN CL
BLUEBELL CL
CAVENDISH AVE
MAPLE AVE
LOBELIA CL
THE VINERIES
GRANVILLE RD
LC
GILLINGHAM RD
FERNDALE RD
LINDEN RD
PRIESTFIELD RD
REDFERN AVE
SUNNYMEAD AVE
GORDON RD
LIVINGSTONE RD
TORONTO RD
CHICAGO AVE
BEACONSFIELD AVE
GILLINGHAM
Allot Gdns
P
WOODLANDS RD
LOWER WOODLANDS RD
GROVE RD
PLANTATION RD
CONISTON CL
BUTTERMERE CL
HAZLEMERE DR
THIRLMERE CL
TANGMERE CL
PH
SHORT LA
Grange
LOWER RAINHAM RD
GRANGE RD
Grench Manor
Allot Gdns
FEATHERBY RD
Mill Hill
Ladds Corner
EASTCOURT LA
Lower Twydall
Sharp's Green
LOWER TWYDALL LA
Mariners Farm
B2004
Cemy

61

30

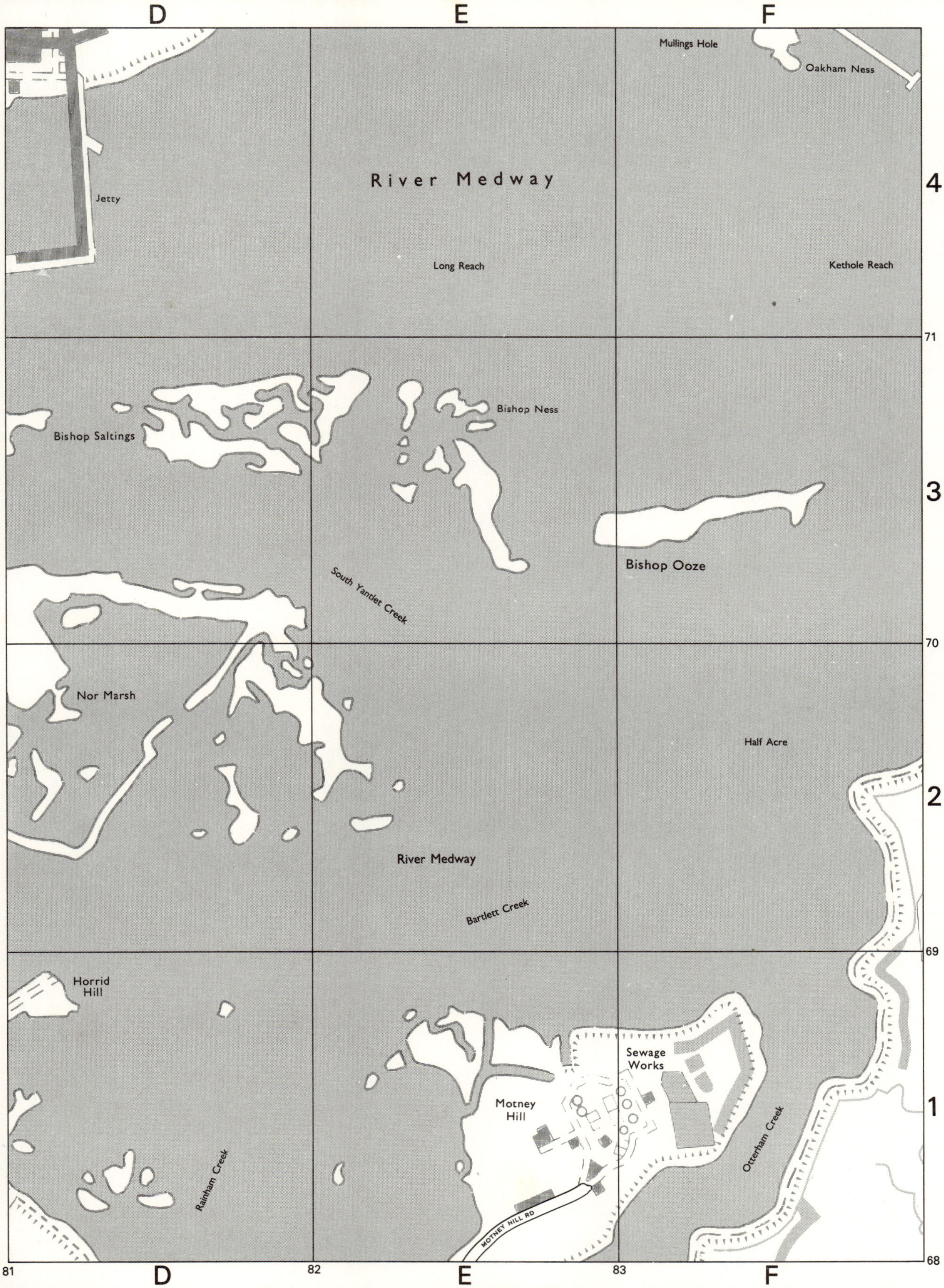

not continued, see key diagram

62

33

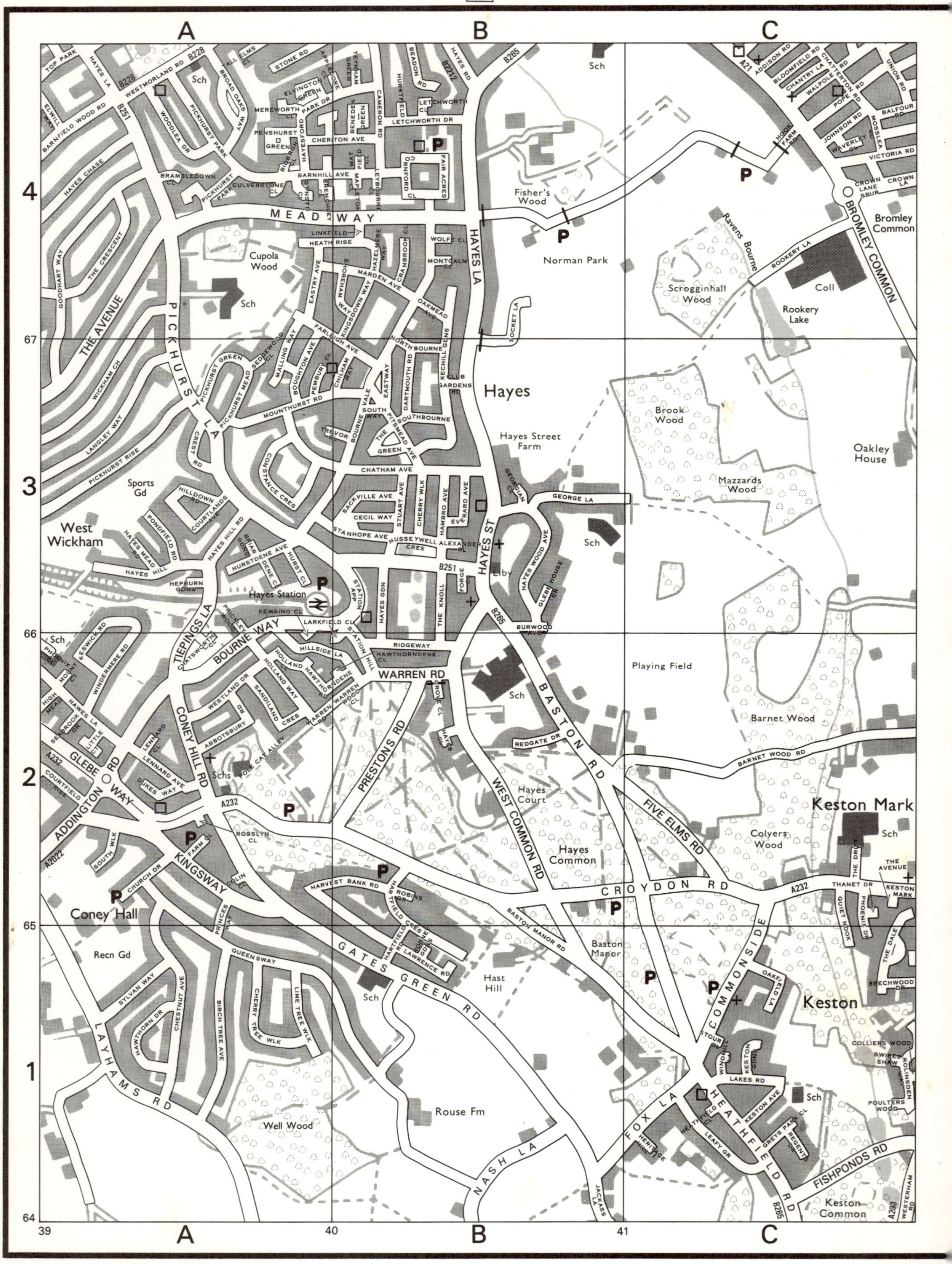

not continued, see key diagram

not continued, see key diagram

34

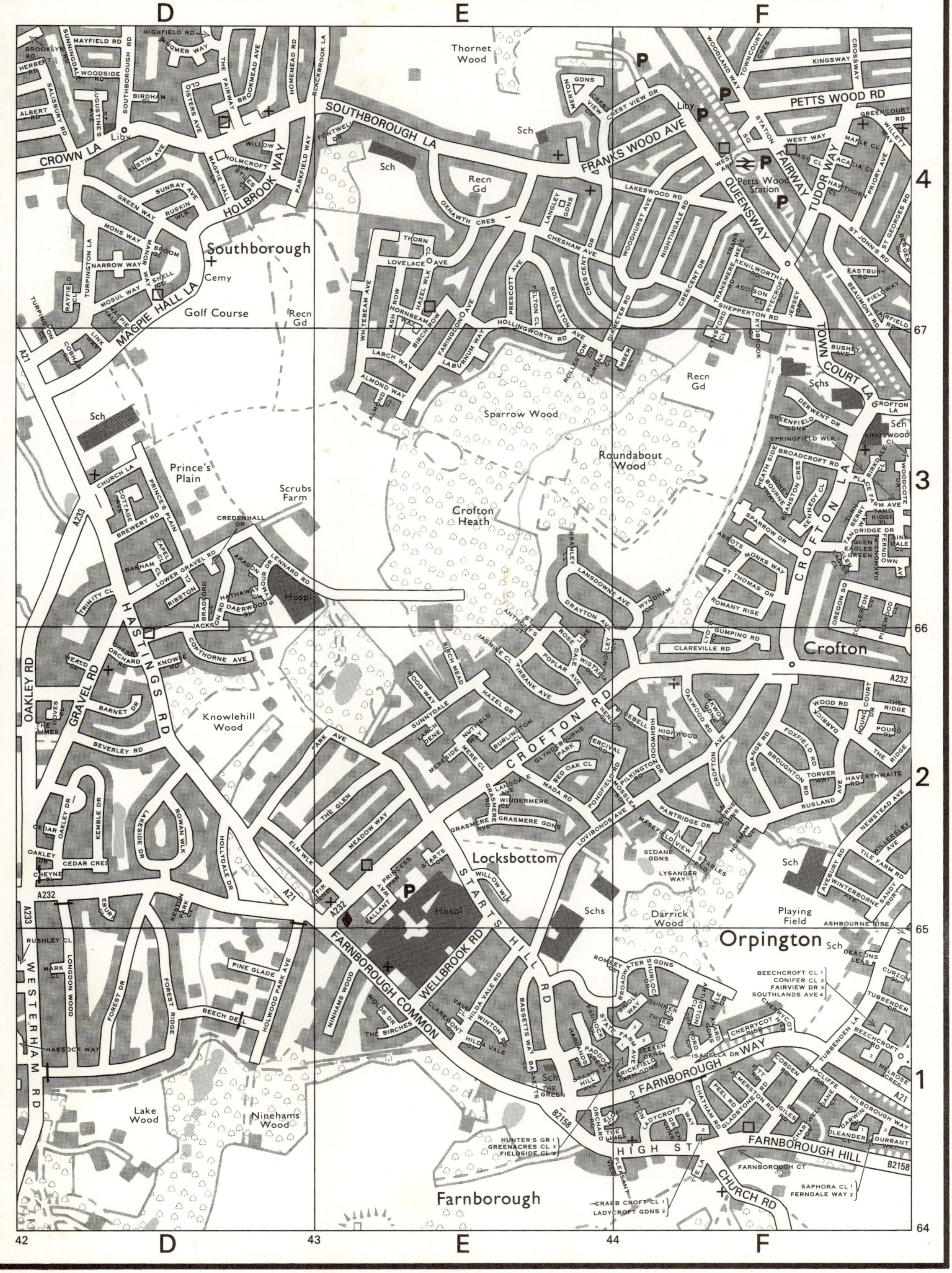
D
E
F
Thornet Wood
Southborough
Golf Course
Recn Gd
Sch
Prince's Plain
Scrubs Farm
Hospl
Knowlehill Wood
Sparrow Wood
Roundabout Wood
Crofton Heath
Locksbottom
Crofton
Orpington
Darrick Wood
Playing Field
Petts Wood Station
Lake Wood
Ninehams Wood
Farnborough
SOUTHBOROUGH LA
FRANKS WOOD AVE
PETTS WOOD RD
QUEENSWAY
TUDOR WAY
FAIRWAY
CROWN LA
HOLBROOK WAY
MAGPIE HALL LA
HASTINGS RD
OAKLEY RD
GRAVEL RD
CROFTON RD
CROFTON LA
TOWN COURT LA
STARTS HILL RD
FARNBOROUGH COMMON
WELLBROOK RD
FARNBOROUGH WAY
FARNBOROUGH HILL
HIGH ST
CHURCH RD
WESTERHAM RD
A21
A232
A233
B2158
BEECHCROFT CL 1
CONIFER CL 2
FAIRVIEW DR 3
SOUTHLANDS AVE 4
HUNTER'S GR 1
GREENACRES CL 2
FIELDSIDE CL 3
SAPHORA CL 1
FERNDALE WAY 2
CRABB CROFT CL 1
LADYCROFT GDNS 2
4
3
2
1
67
66
65
64
42
43
44

50

63

35

49

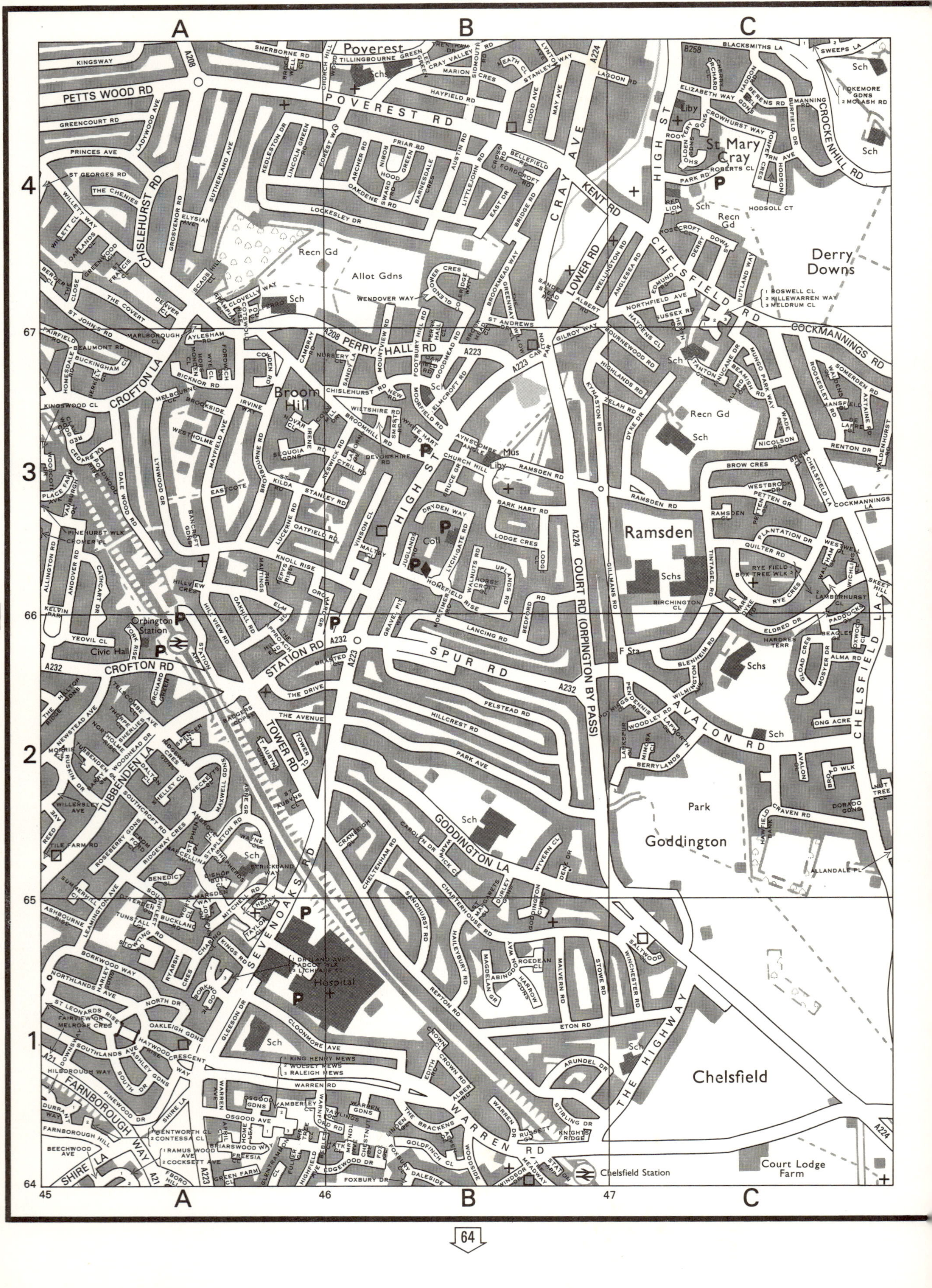
A
B
C
Poverest
St Mary Cray
Derry Downs
Broom Hill
Ramsden
Goddington
Park
Chelsfield
Orpington Station
Civic Hall
Chelsfield Station
Court Lodge Farm
Hospital
Recn Gd
Allot Gdns
Sch
Schs
Coll
Liby
Mus
F Sta
PETTS WOOD RD
KINGSWAY
GREENCOURT RD
PRINCES AVE
ST GEORGES RD
THE CHENIES
CHISLEHURST RD
SUTHERLAND AVE
GROSVENOR RD
LADYWOOD AVE
SHERBORNE RD
TILLINGBOURNE GREEN
POVEREST RD
HAYFIELD RD
MARION CRES
LAGOON RD
BLACKSMITHS LA
SWEEPS LA
CROCKENHILL RD
ELIZABETH WAY
CROWHURST WAY
HIGH ST
CRAY AVE
KENT RD
LOWER RD
CHELSFIELD RD
COCKMANNINGS RD
LOCKESLEY DR
KEDLESTON DR
LINCOLN GREEN RD
FOREST WAY
ARCHER RD
FRIAR RD
AUSTIN RD
BELLEFIELD RD
FORDCROFT RD
BRIDGE RD
EAST DR
LITTLEJOHN RD
BROOKMEAD WAY
WENDOVER WAY
CLOVELLY WAY
ST ANDREWS
PERRY HALL RD
A208
A223
A224
A232
A21
B258
CROFTON LA
CROFTON RD
AYLESHAM RD
BICKNOR RD
MARLBOROUGH CL
THE COVERT
ST JOHNS RD
FAIRFIELD RD
BEAUMONT RD
BUCKINGHAM CL
KINGSWOOD CL
LYNWOOD GR
DALE WOOD RD
MAYFIELD AVE
WESTHOLME
BROOKSIDE
IRVINE WAY
EASTCOTE
CHISLEHURST RD
WILTSHIRE RD
BROOMHILL RD
STANLEY RD
OATFIELD RD
LUCERNE RD
KNOLL RISE
VINSON CL
CHURCH HILL
RAMSDEN RD
BARK HART RD
LODGE CRES
DRYDEN WAY
LYCHGATE RD
HOMEFIELD RISE
LANCING RD
BEDFORD RD
COURT RD (ORPINGTON BY PASS)
GILLMANS RD
HIGHLANDS RD
KYNASTON RD
ZELAH RD
DYKE DR
BROW CRES
WESTBROOK DR
PLANTATION DR
QUILTER RD
TINTAGEL RD
BIRCHINGTON CL
RYE CRES
ELDRED DR
CHELSFIELD LA
NICOLSON RD
RENTON DR
SPUR RD
STATION RD
THE DRIVE
THE AVENUE
TOWER RD
FELSTEAD RD
HILLCREST RD
PARK AVE
GODDINGTON LA
AVALON RD
BLENHEIM RD
WOODLEY RD
BERRYLANDS
CRAVEN RD
ALLANDALE PL
TUBBENDEN LA
SOUTHCROFT RD
RIDGEWAY CRES
WILLERSLEY AVE
TILE FARM RD
ASHBOURNE RISE
LEAMINGTON AVE
BORKWOOD WAY
NORTHLANDS AVE
NORTH DR
OAKLEIGH GDNS
SEVENOAKS RD
CLOONMORE AVE
KINGS RD
CHARTERHOUSE RD
CHELTENHAM RD
SANDHURST RD
HAILEYBURY RD
REPTON RD
ETON RD
MALVERN RD
STOWE RD
WINCHESTER RD
SALTWOOD
ARUNDEL DR
THE HIGHWAY
WARREN RD
STIRLING DR
KNIGHTS RIDGE
WOODSIDE
THE BRACKENS
GOLDFINCH CL
FOXBURY DR
OSGOOD AVE
BRIARSWOOD WAY
FARNBOROUGH WAY
FARNBOROUGH HILL
BEECHWOOD AVE
SHIRE LA
PINEWOOD DR
HILBOROUGH WAY
SOUTHLANDS AVE
CRESCENT WAY
1 BOSWELL CL
2 KILLEWARREN WAY
3 MELDRUM CL
1 KING HENRY MEWS
2 WOLSEY MEWS
3 RALEIGH MEWS
1 WENTWORTH CL
2 CONTESSA CL
1 RAMUS WOOD AVE
2 COCKSETT AVE
45
46
47
64
65
66
67
1
2
3
4

64

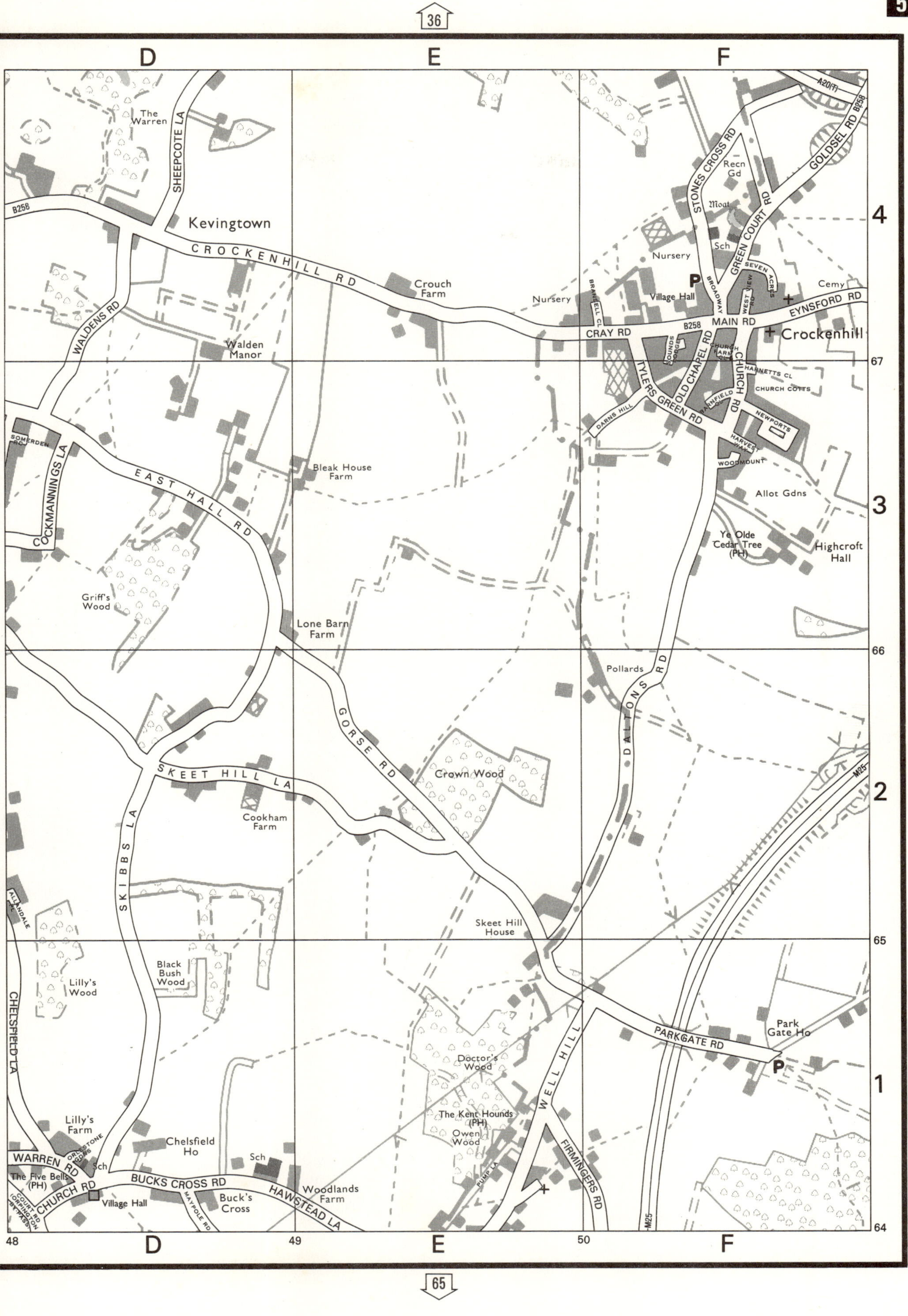
36
D
E
F
The Warren
SHEEPCOTE LA
B258
Kevingtown
CROCKENHILL RD
Crouch Farm
WALDENS RD
Walden Manor
STONES CROSS RD
Recn Gd
Moat
GREEN COURT RD
GOLDSEL RD B258
A20(T)
Sch
Nursery
SEVEN ACRES
WEST VIEW RD
BROADWAY
Village Hall
Nursery
BRANELL CL
Cemy
EYNSFORD RD
MAIN RD
B258
CRAY RD
Crockenhill
4
67
TYLERS GREEN RD
OLD CHAPEL RD
CHURCH RD
CHURCH FARM CL
HARNETTS CL
CHURCH COTTS
DARNS HILL
BARNFIELD
NEWPORTS
HARVEST WAY
WOODMOUNT
SOMERDEN RD
COCKMANNINGS LA
EAST HALL RD
Bleak House Farm
Allot Gdns
3
Ye Olde Cedar Tree (PH)
Highcroft Hall
Griff's Wood
Lone Barn Farm
66
52
Pollards
DALTONS RD
GORSE RD
SKEET HILL LA
Crown Wood
M25
2
Cookham Farm
SKIBBS LA
ALLENDALE CL
Skeet Hill House
65
Lilly's Wood
Black Bush Wood
CHELSFIELD LA
PARKGATE RD
Park Gate Ho
WELL HILL
Doctor's Wood
1
The Kent Hounds (PH)
Owen Wood
FIRMINGERS RD
Lilly's Farm
ORLESTONE GDNS
Chelsfield Ho
WARREN RD
Sch
Sch
The Five Bells (PH)
BUCKS CROSS RD
HAWSTEAD LA
Woodlands Farm
CHURCH RD
Village Hall
MAYPOLE RD
Buck's Cross
PUMP LA
COURT RD (ORPINGTON BY-PASS)
M25
64
48
49
50
D
E
F
65

37

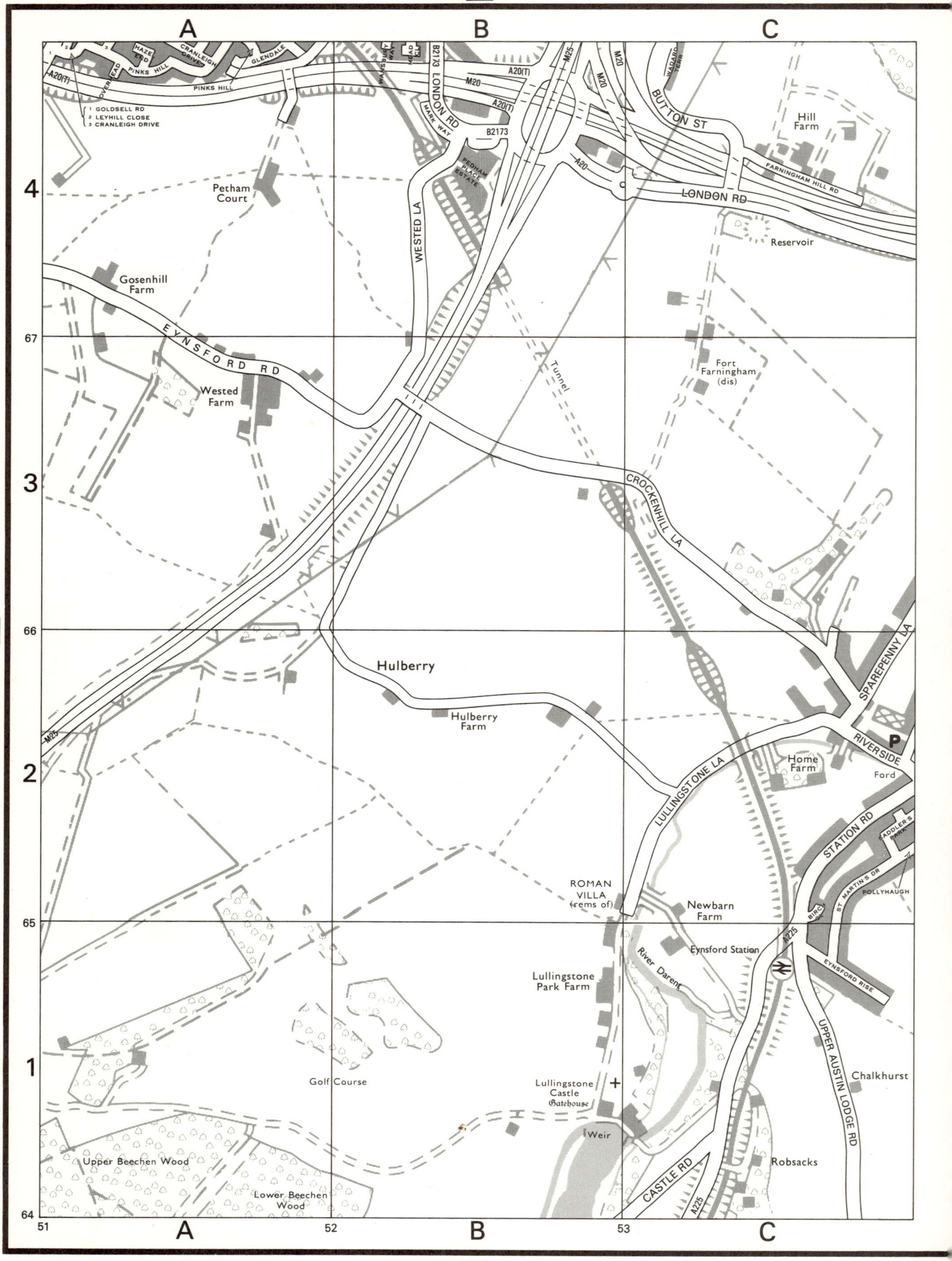

A
B
C
4
3
2
1
67
66
65
64
51
52
53
1 GOLDSELL RD
2 LEYHILL CLOSE
3 CRANLEIGH DRIVE
HAZE END
CRANLEIGH DRIVE
PINKS HILL
GLENDALE
OVERHEAD
A20(T)
M20
B2173
LONDON RD
MARK WAY
M25
BUTTON ST
Hill Farm
FARNINGHAM HILL RD
LONDON RD
A20
Reservoir
Petham Court
PEDHAM PLACE ESTATE
WESTED LA
Gosenhill Farm
EYNSFORD RD
Wested Farm
Tunnel
Fort Farningham (dis)
CROCKENHILL LA
SPAREPENNY LA
Hulberry
Hulberry Farm
RIVERSIDE
P
Home Farm
Ford
LULLINGSTONE LA
STATION RD
ST MARTIN'S DR
POLLYHAUGH
ROMAN VILLA (rems of)
Newbarn Farm
Eynsford Station
A225
EYNSFORD RISE
River Darent
Lullingstone Park Farm
UPPER AUSTIN LODGE RD
Chalkhurst
Golf Course
Lullingstone Castle Gatehouse
Weir
Robsacks
Upper Beechen Wood
Lower Beechen Wood
CASTLE RD

51

66

38

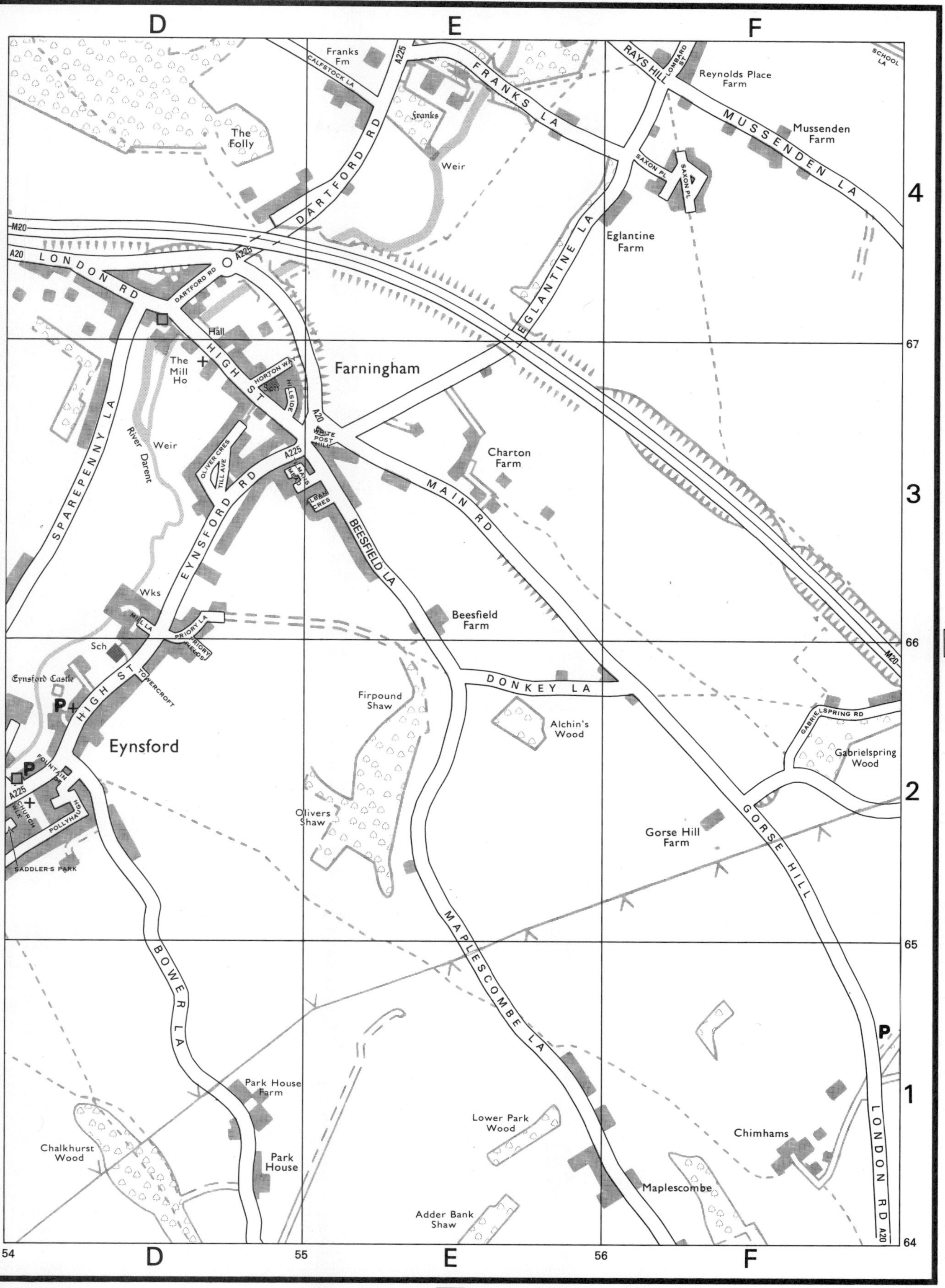
D
E
F
Franks Fm
Franks
Reynolds Place Farm
Mussenden Farm
The Folly
Weir
Eglantine Farm
Farningham
Hall
The Mill Ho
Sch
Charton Farm
Weir
River Darent
Wks
Beesfield Farm
Sch
Eynsford Castle
Eynsford
Firpound Shaw
Alchin's Wood
Gabrielspring Wood
Olivers Shaw
Gorse Hill Farm
Park House Farm
Lower Park Wood
Chimhams
Chalkhurst Wood
Park House
Maplescombe
Adder Bank Shaw
CALFSTOCK LA
A225
DARTFORD RD
FRANKS LA
RAYS HILL
LOMBARD ST
SCHOOL LA
MUSSENDEN LA
SAXON PL
EGLANTINE LA
M20
A20
LONDON RD
HIGH ST
HORTON WAY
HILLSIDE
WHITE POST HILL
SPAREPENNY LA
OLIVER CRES
TILL AVE
EYNSFORD RD
MAIN RD
ALBAN CRES
BEESFIELD LA
MILL LA
PRIORY LA
PRIORY FIELDS
TOWERCROFT
DONKEY LA
GABRIELSPRING RD
FOUNTAIN
CHURCH WLK
POLLYHAUGH
SADDLER'S PARK
GORSE HILL
MAPLESCOMBE LA
BOWER LA
LONDON RD
4
67
3
66
2
65
1
64
54
55
56

54

67

39

53

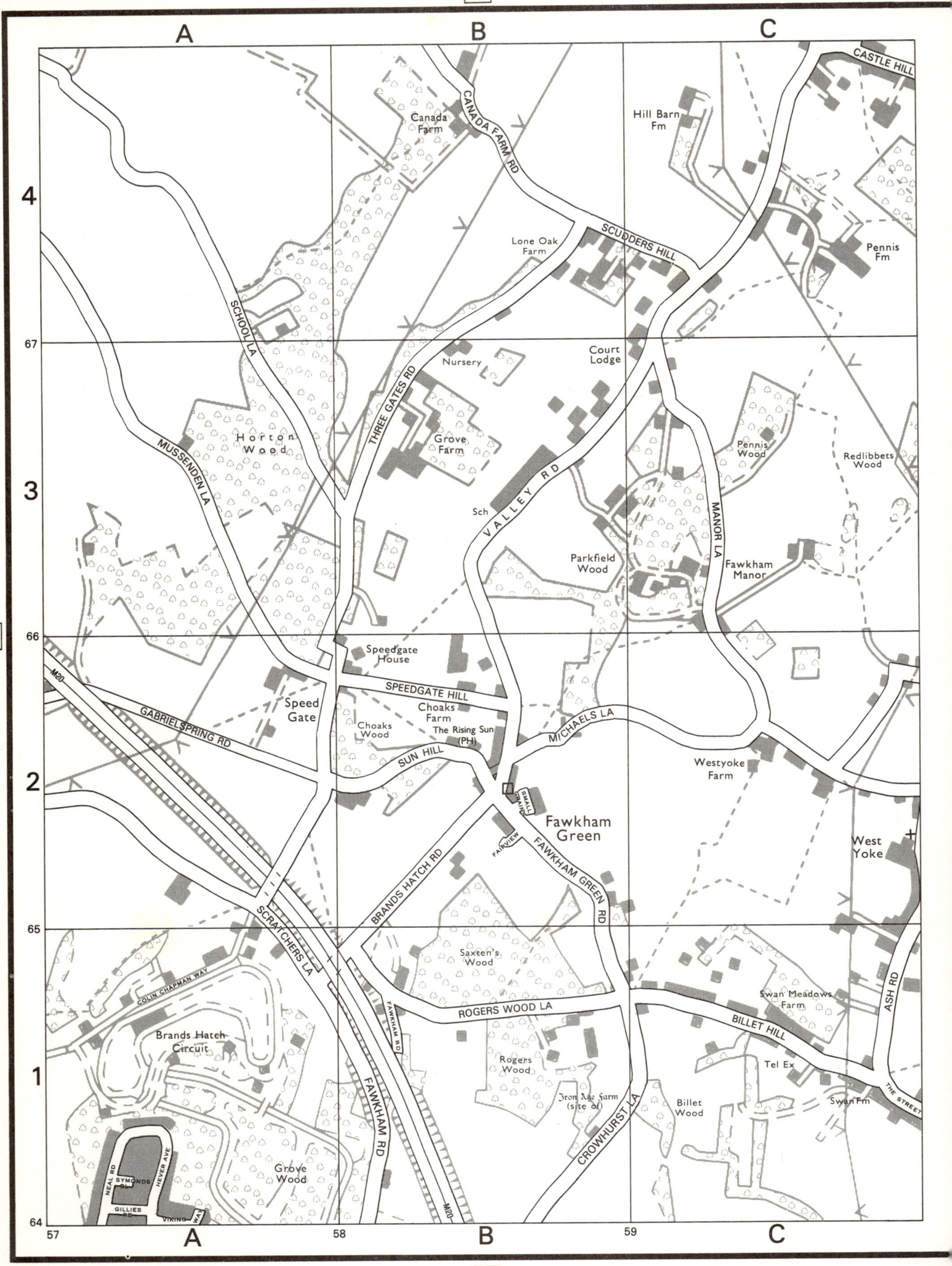
A
B
C
4
3
2
1
67
66
65
64
57
58
59
CASTLE HILL
Canada Farm
CANADA FARM RD
Hill Barn Fm
Lone Oak Farm
SCUDDERS HILL
Pennis Fm
SCHOOL LA
THREE GATES RD
Nursery
Court Lodge
Horton Wood
MUSSENDEN LA
Grove Farm
Pennis Wood
Redlibbets Wood
Sch
VALLEY RD
MANOR LA
Parkfield Wood
Fawkham Manor
Speedgate House
M20
SPEEDGATE HILL
GABRIELSPRING RD
Speed Gate
Choaks Farm
Choaks Wood
The Rising Sun (PH)
MICHAELS LA
SUN HILL
Westyoke Farm
SMALL GRAINS
Fawkham Green
FAIRVIEW
West Yoke
BRANDS HATCH RD
FAWKHAM GREEN RD
SCRATCHERS LA
Saxten's Wood
COLIN CHAPMAN WAY
ROGERS WOOD LA
ASH RD
Swan Meadows Farm
FAWKHAM RD
BILLET HILL
Brands Hatch Circuit
Tel Ex
Rogers Wood
Iron Age Farm (site of)
Billet Wood
Swan Fm
THE STREET
CROWHURST LA
FAWKHAM RD
Grove Wood
NEAL RD
SYMONDS CL
HEVER AVE
GILLIES RD
VIKING WAY

68

40

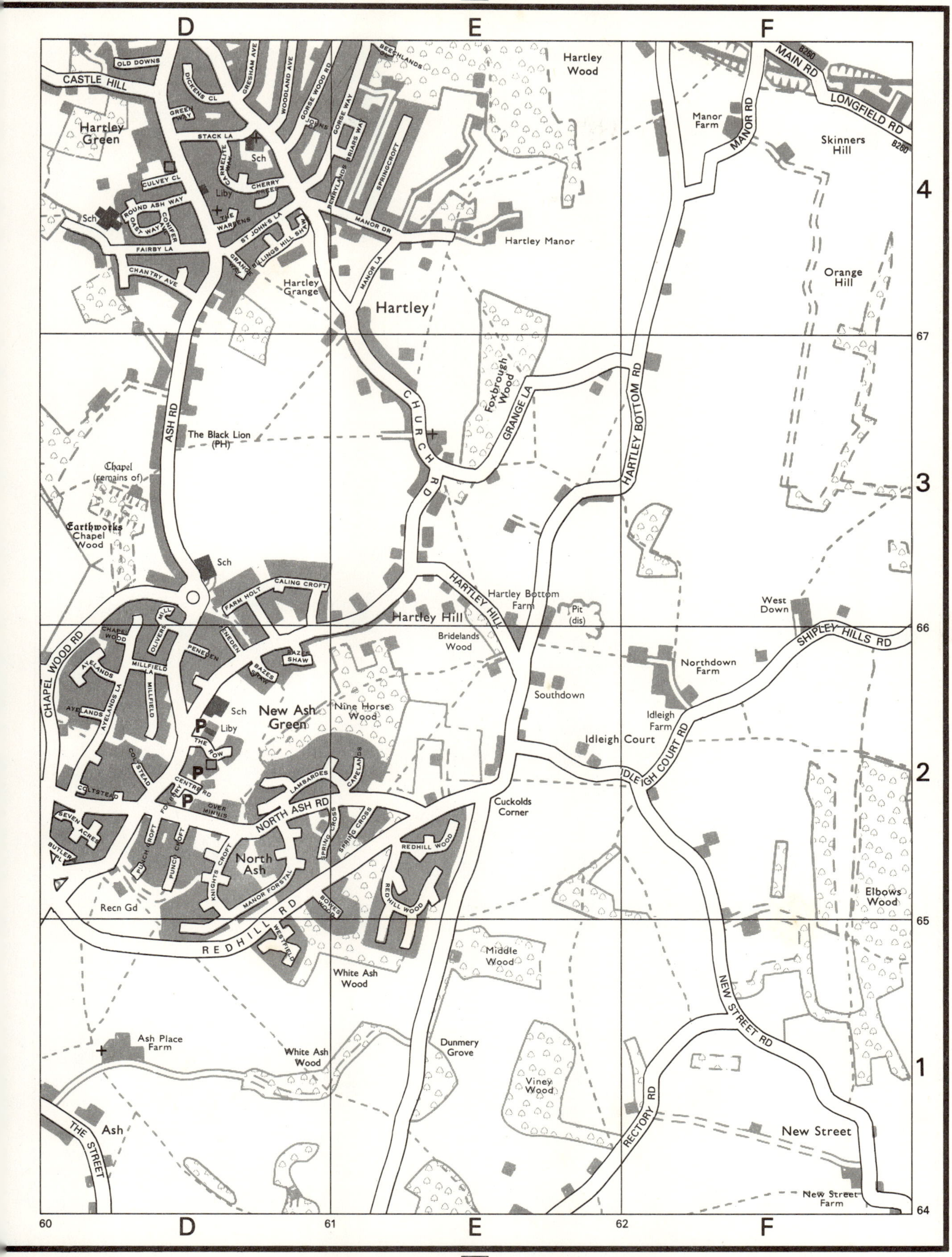
D
E
F
Hartley Wood
CASTLE HILL
OLD DOWNS
DICKENS CL
GRESHAM AVE
WOODLAND AVE
GORSE WOOD RD
BEECHLANDS CL
GORSE WAY
BRIARS WAY
SPRINGCROFT
PERRYLANDS
B260
MAIN RD
LONGFIELD RD
Manor Farm
MANOR RD
Skinners Hill
Hartley Green
GREEN WAY
STACK LA
CARMELITE WAY
Sch
CULVEY CL
Liby
CHERRY TREES
ROUND ASH WAY
OAST WAY
CONIFER
THE WARRENS
ST JOHN'S LA
BILLINGS HILL SHAW
MANOR DR
Hartley Manor
FAIRBY LA
GRANGE WAY
CHANTRY AVE
Hartley Grange
MANOR LA
Hartley
Orange Hill
4
67
ASH RD
Foxbrough Wood
GRANGE LA
HARTLEY BOTTOM RD
CHURCH RD
The Black Lion (PH)
Chapel (remains of)
Earthworks
Chapel Wood
3
CALING CROFT
FARM HOLT
MILL
CHAPEL WOOD
OLIVERS
PENEDEN
FENEDEN
BAZES SHAW
HARTLEY HILL
Hartley Bottom Farm
Hartley Hill
Pit (dis)
West Down
SHIPLEY HILLS RD
66
Bridelands Wood
Northdown Farm
CHAPEL WOOD RD
AYELANDS
MILLFIELD
AYELANDS LA
Southdown
Idleigh Farm
New Ash Green
Nine Horse Wood
THE ROW
Idleigh Court
IDLEIGH COURT RD
COLTSTEAD
CENTRE RD
CAPELANDS
LAMBARDES
2
OVER MINNIS
NORTH ASH RD
Cuckolds Corner
SEVEN ACRES
SPRING CROSS
REDHILL WOOD
BUTLERS PL
PUNCH CROFT
KNIGHTS CROFT
North Ash
Recn Gd
MANOR FORSTAL
BOKES WOOD
Elbows Wood
65
REDHILL RD
WESTFIELD
Middle Wood
White Ash Wood
NEW STREET RD
Ash Place Farm
White Ash Wood
Dunmery Grove
1
Viney Wood
Ash
THE STREET
RECTORY RD
New Street
New Street Farm
64
60
61
62

56

69

41

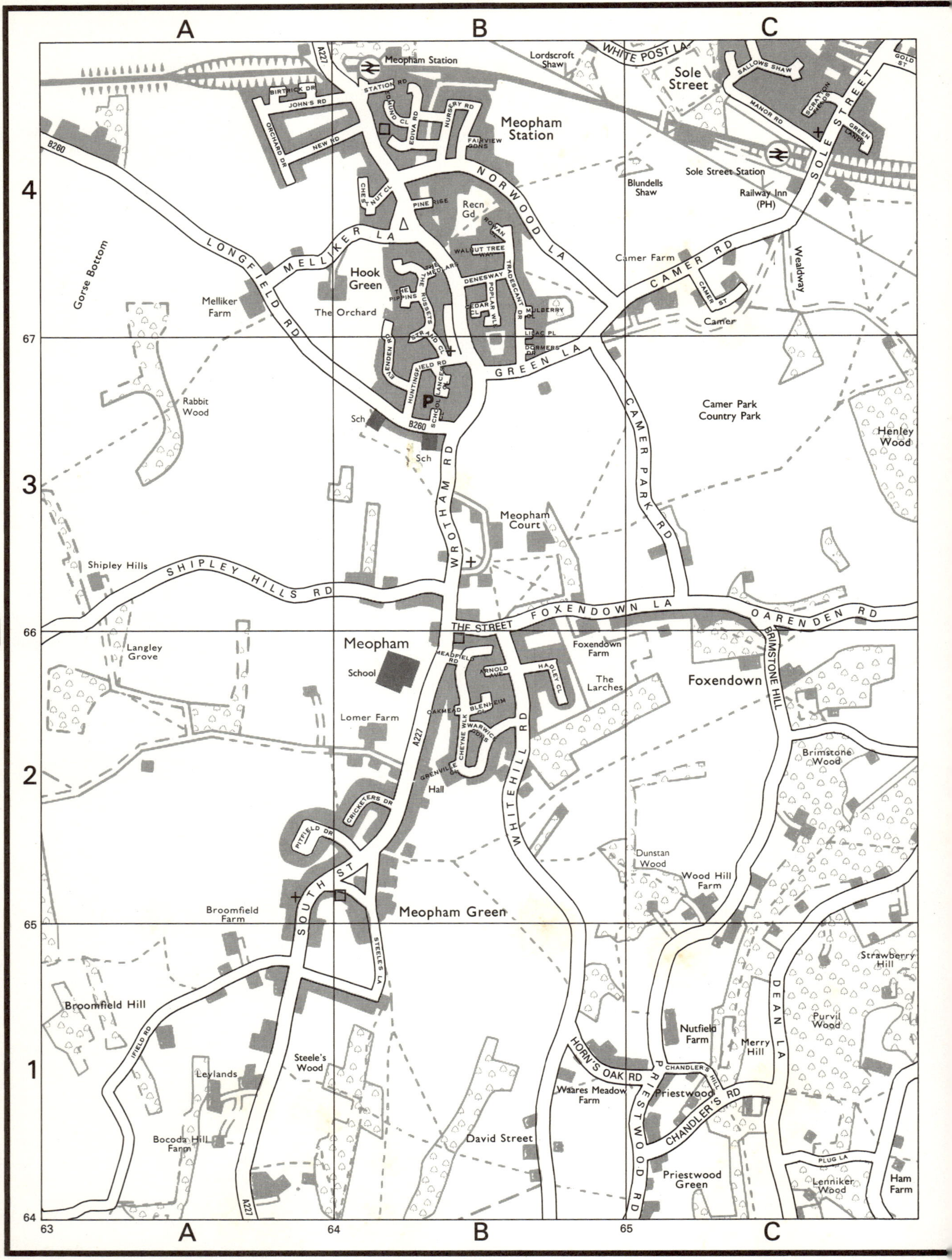
A
B
C
4
3
2
1
67
66
65
64
63
64
65
Meopham Station
Lordscroft Shaw
WHITE POST LA
Sole Street
SALLOWS SHAW
GOLD ST
MANOR RD
SCRATTON FIELDS
GREEN LANDS
SOLE STREET
Sole Street Station
Railway Inn (PH)
Blundells Shaw
A227
BIRTRICK DR
JOHN'S RD
ORCHARD DR
NEW RD
STATION RD
EDMUND CL
EDIVA RD
NURSERY RD
FAIRVIEW GDNS
Meopham Station
B260
NORWOOD LA
CHESTNUT CL
PINE RISE
Recn Gd
ROWAN
WALNUT TREE WAY
MELLIKER LA
Hook Green
THE MEADLARS
THE PIPPINS
THE RUSSETS
DENESWAY
TRADESCANT DR
POPLAR WLK
CEDAR CL
MULBERRY CL
LILAC PL
DORMERS DR
STRAND CL
GREEN LA
The Orchard
Melliker Farm
LONGFIELD RD
Gorse Bottom
Camer Farm
CAMER RD
CAMER ST
Camer
Wealdway
ELLENDEN RD
HUNTINGFIELD RD
SCHOOL LANE
LANCE CL
P
Sch
B260
Sch
Rabbit Wood
Camer Park Country Park
Henley Wood
CAMER PARK RD
WROTHAM RD
Meopham Court
Shipley Hills
SHIPLEY HILLS RD
FOXENDOWN LA
OARENDEN RD
THE STREET
Meopham
Langley Grove
School
MEADFIELD RD
ARNOLD AVE
HADLEY CL
Foxendown Farm
The Larches
Foxendown
BRIMSTONE HILL
OAKMEAD
BLENHEIM CL
WARWICK GDNS
CHEYNE WLK
GRENVILLE CL
Lomer Farm
A227
WHITEHILL RD
Brimstone Wood
Hall
CRICKETERS DR
PITFIELD DR
SOUTH ST
Dunstan Wood
Wood Hill Farm
Broomfield Farm
Meopham Green
STEELE'S LA
Strawberry Hill
DEAN LA
Broomfield Hill
IFIELD RD
Nutfield Farm
Merry Hill
Purvil Wood
Leylands
Steele's Wood
HORN'S OAK RD
CHANDLER'S HILL
Priestwood
CHANDLER'S RD
Waares Meadow Farm
PRIESTWOOD RD
Bocoda Hill Farm
David Street
PLUG LA
Priestwood Green
Lenniker Wood
Ham Farm
A227

55

70

42

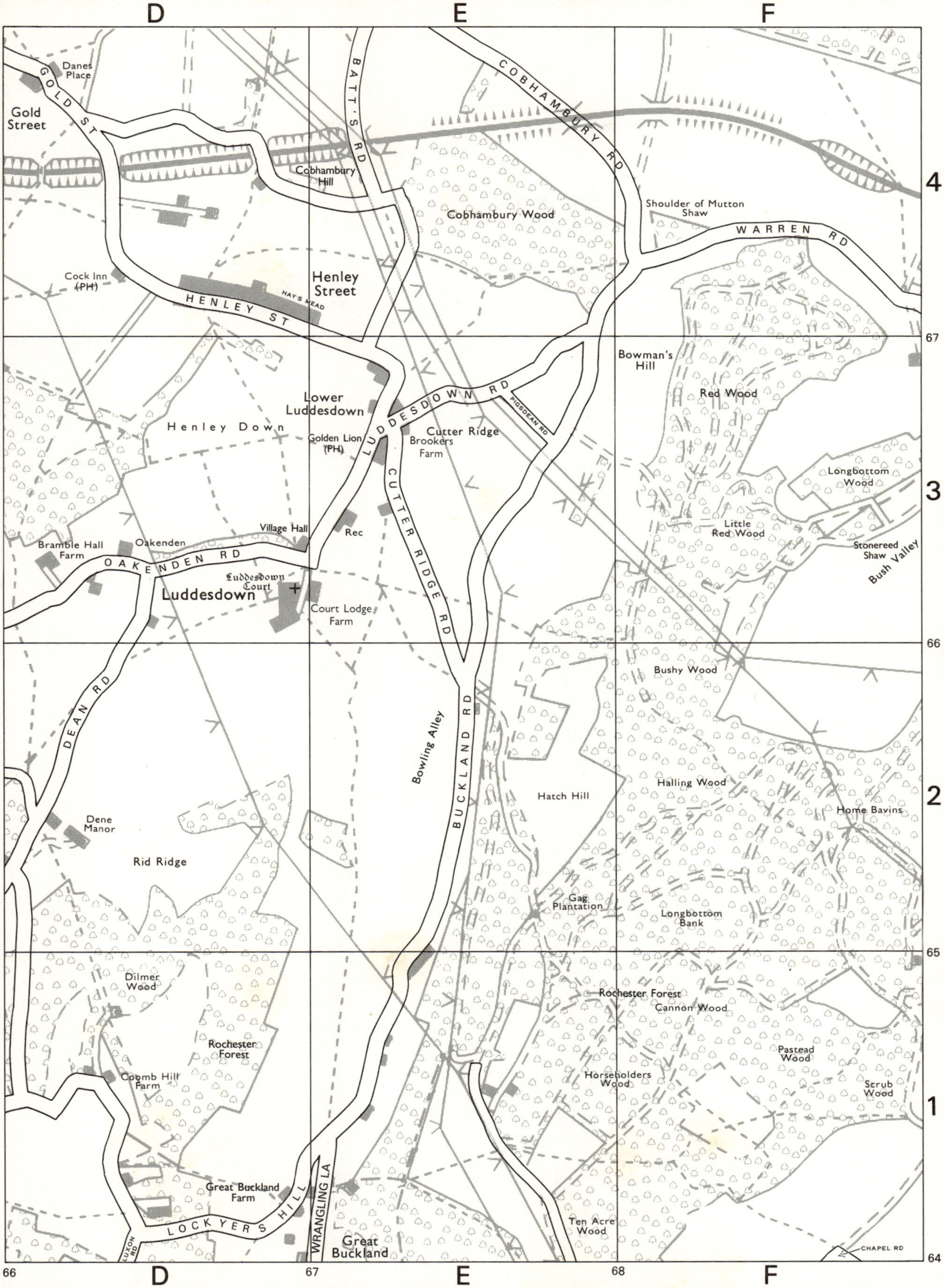
D
E
F
Danes Place
Gold Street
GOLD ST
Cobhambury Hill
BATT'S RD
COBHAMBURY RD
Cobhambury Wood
Shoulder of Mutton Shaw
WARREN RD
4
Cock Inn (PH)
Henley Street
HENLEY ST
HAY'S MEAD
67
Bowman's Hill
Red Wood
Lower Luddesdown
LUDDESDOWN RD
PIGSDEAN RD
Henley Down
Golden Lion (PH)
Cutter Ridge
Brookers Farm
Longbottom Wood
3
CUTTER RIDGE RD
Village Hall
Rec
Little Red Wood
Bramble Hall Farm
Oakenden
OAKENDEN RD
Luddesdown Court
Luddesdown
Court Lodge Farm
Stonereed Shaw
Bush Valley
66
Bushy Wood
DEAN RD
Bowling Alley
BUCKLAND RD
Halling Wood
Hatch Hill
2
Home Bavins
Dene Manor
Rid Ridge
Gag Plantation
Longbottom Bank
65
Dilmer Wood
Rochester Forest
Cannon Wood
Rochester Forest
Pastead Wood
Coomb Hill Farm
Horseholders Wood
Scrub Wood
1
Great Buckland Farm
LOCKYERS HILL
WRANGLING LA
LUXON RD
Great Buckland
Ten Acre Wood
CHAPEL RD
64
66
67
68
D
E
F

58

71

43

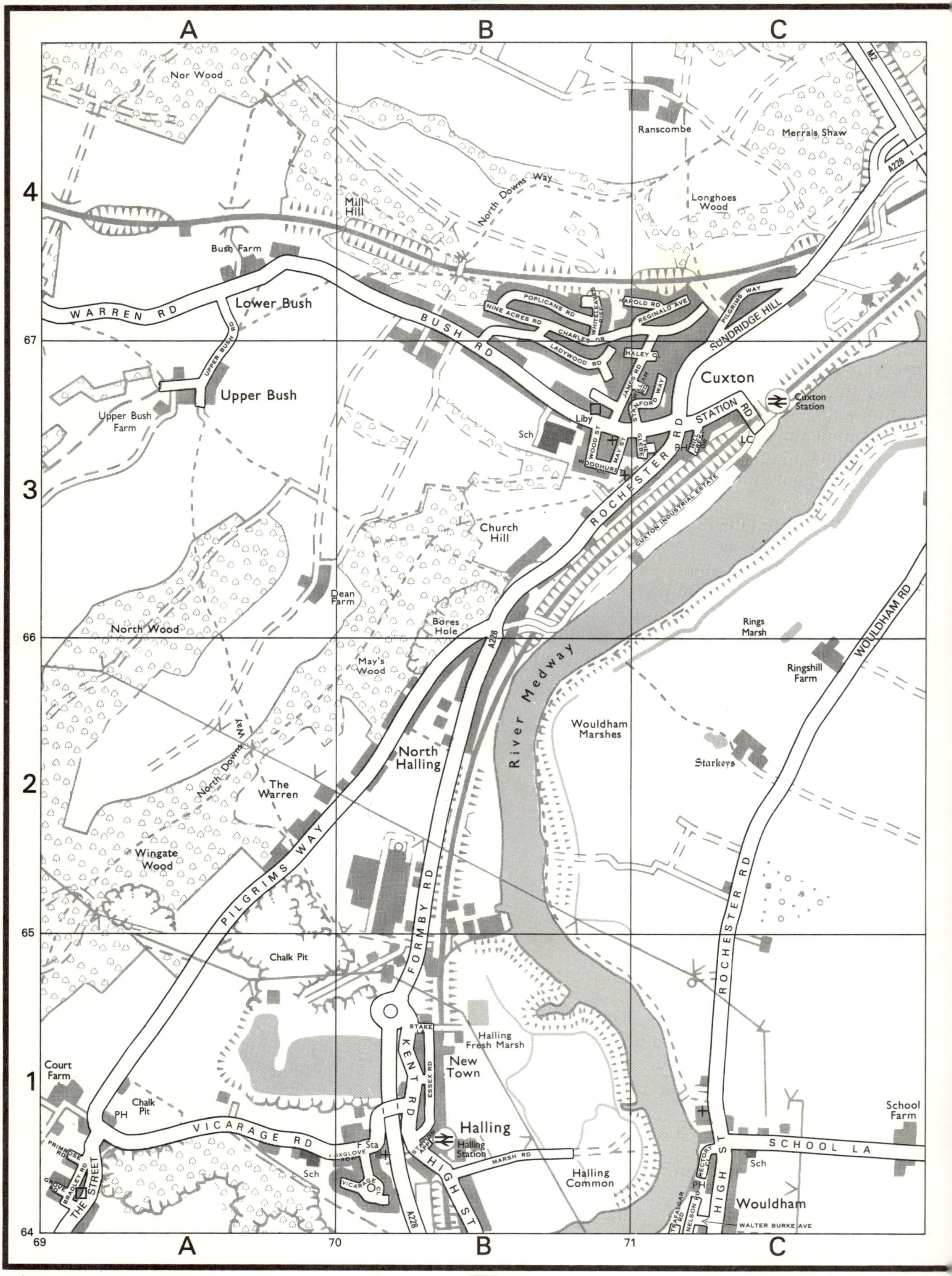
A
B
C
4
3
2
1
67
66
65
64
69
70
71
Nor Wood
Ranscombe
Merrals Shaw
M2
A228
North Downs Way
Mill Hill
Longhoes Wood
Bush Farm
Lower Bush
WARREN RD
BUSH RD
POPLICANS RD
NINE ACRES RD
WHITELEAVES RISE
HAROLD RD
REGINALD AVE
CHARLES DR
LADYWOOD RD
PILGRIMS WAY
SUNDRIDGE HILL
HALEY C
JAMES RD
STAFFORD WAY
UPPER BUSH RD
Upper Bush
Upper Bush Farm
Cuxton
Cuxton Station
STATION RD
Liby
Sch
WOOD ST
MAY ST
THE GLEBE
WOODHURST CL
PH
LC
ROCHESTER RD
CUXTON INDUSTRIAL ESTATE
Church Hill
Dean Farm
Bores Hole
North Wood
May's Wood
Rings Marsh
Ringshill Farm
WOULDHAM RD
River Medway
Wouldham Marshes
Starkeys
North Halling
North Downs Way
The Warren
PILGRIMS WAY
Wingate Wood
FORMBY RD
ROCHESTER RD
Chalk Pit
STAKE
KENT RD
ESSEX RD
Halling Fresh Marsh
New Town
Court Farm
Chalk Pit
PH
Halling
Halling Station
STATION APP
VICARAGE RD
F Sta
FOXGLOVE ROW
PRIMROSE RD
BRADLEY RD
GROVE RD
THE STREET
Sch
VICARAGE CL
MARSH RD
HIGH ST
A228
Halling Common
School Farm
SCHOOL LA
Sch
RECTORY CL
PH
TRAFALGAR RD
NELSON RD
HIGH ST
Wouldham
WALTER BURKE AVE

57

72

44

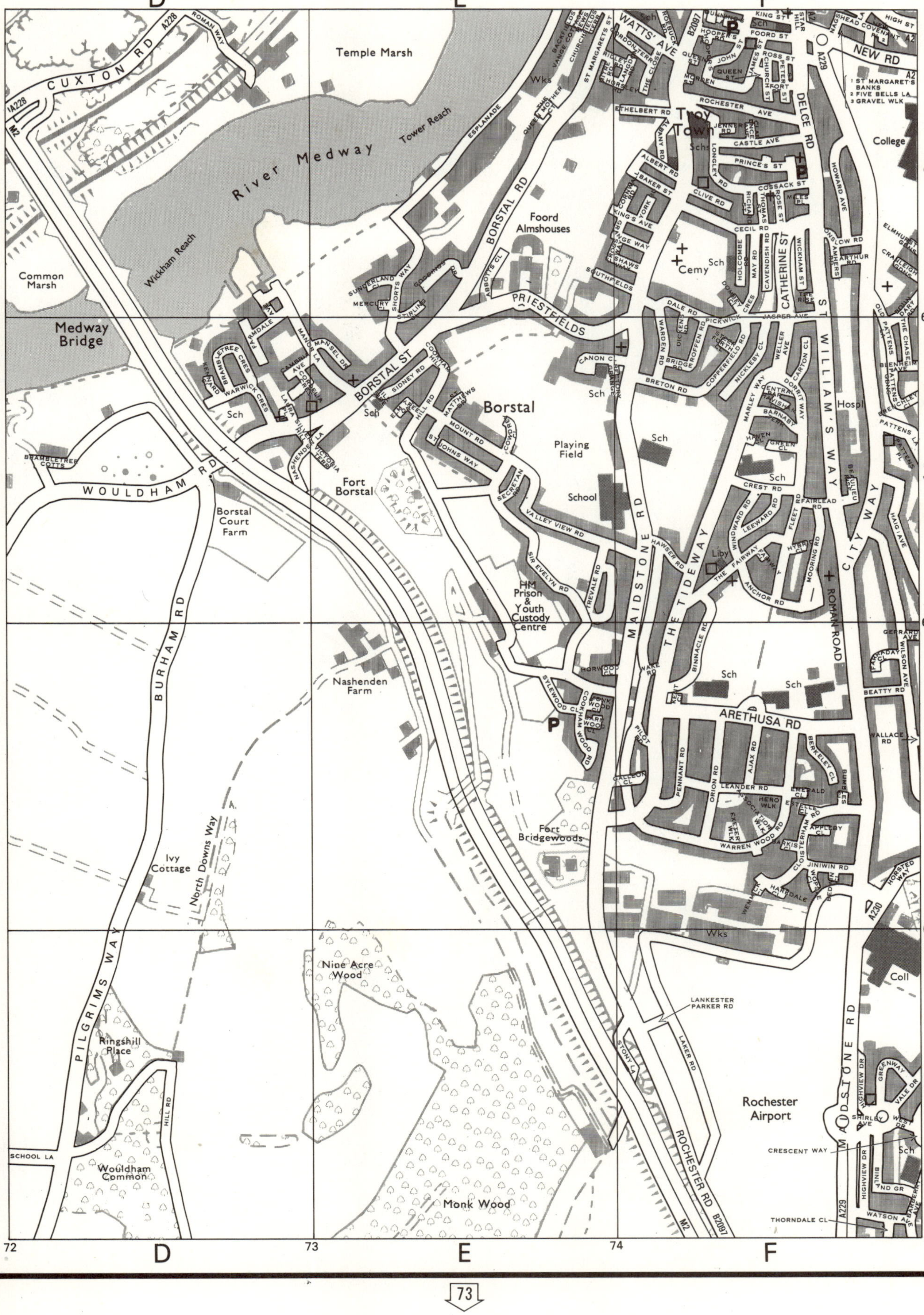
D
E
F
Temple Marsh
River Medway
Tower Reach
Wickham Reach
Common Marsh
Medway Bridge
CUXTON RD
A228
ROMAN WAY
M2
ESPLANADE
BORSTAL RD
Foord Almshouses
PRIESTFIELDS
BORSTAL ST
Borstal
Playing Field
School
Sch
Fort Borstal
WOULDHAM RD
Borstal Court Farm
BRAMBLETREE COTTS
BURHAM RD
Nashenden Farm
HM Prison & Youth Custody Centre
VALLEY VIEW RD
MAIDSTONE RD
THE TIDEWAY
ROMAN ROAD
CITY WAY
ST WILLIAM'S WAY
Hospl
College
Troy Town
Cemy
WATTS' AVE
DELCE RD
NEW RD
ROCHESTER AVE
CASTLE AVE
PRINCE'S ST
CATHERINE ST
ARETHUSA RD
LEANDER RD
WARREN WOOD RD
Fort Bridgewoods
Wks
Ivy Cottage
North Downs Way
PILGRIMS WAY
Nine Acre Wood
Ringshill Place
HILL RD
SCHOOL LA
Wouldham Common
Monk Wood
ROCHESTER RD
B2097
LANKESTER PARKER RD
LAKER RD
Rochester Airport
Coll
A229
A230
CRESCENT WAY
THORNDALE CL
1 ST MARGARET'S BANKS
2 FIVE BELLS LA
3 GRAVEL WLK
72
73
74
64
65
66
67
1
2
3
4

60

73

45

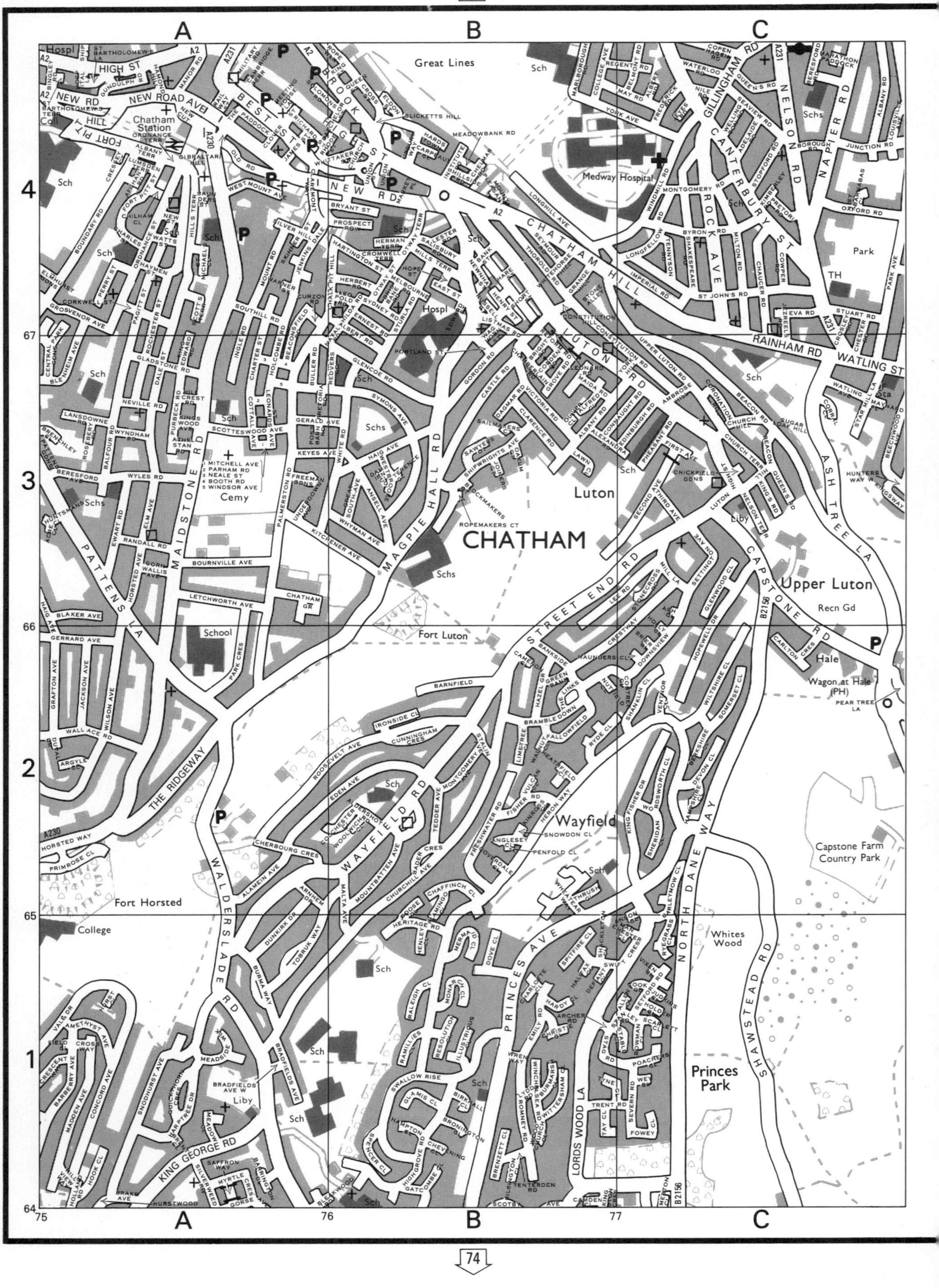
A
B
C
4
3
2
1
67
66
65
64
75
76
77
Great Lines
Medway Hospital
Chatham Station
CHATHAM HILL
NEW RD
HIGH ST
NEW ROAD AVE
FORT PITT HILL
GILLINGHAM RD
NELSON RD
CANTERBURY ST
RAINHAM RD
WATLING ST
LUTON RD
MAIDSTONE RD
PATTENS LA
MAGPIE HALL RD
STREET END RD
CAPSTONE RD
THE RIDGEWAY
WALDERSLADE RD
WAYFIELD RD
PRINCES AVE
NORTH DANE WAY
SHAWSTEAD RD
LORDS WOOD LA
KING GEORGE RD
ASH TREE LA
CHATHAM
Luton
Upper Luton
Recn Gd
Hale
Wagon at Hale (PH)
Cemy
School
Fort Luton
Wayfield
Capstone Farm Country Park
Fort Horsted
College
Whites Wood
Princes Park
Park
TH
Liby
Hospl
Schs
Sch
1 MITCHELL AVE
2 PARHAM RD
3 NEALE ST
4 BOOTH RD
5 WINDSOR AVE
A2
A230
A231
B2156

59

74

07887850941

46

62

75

47

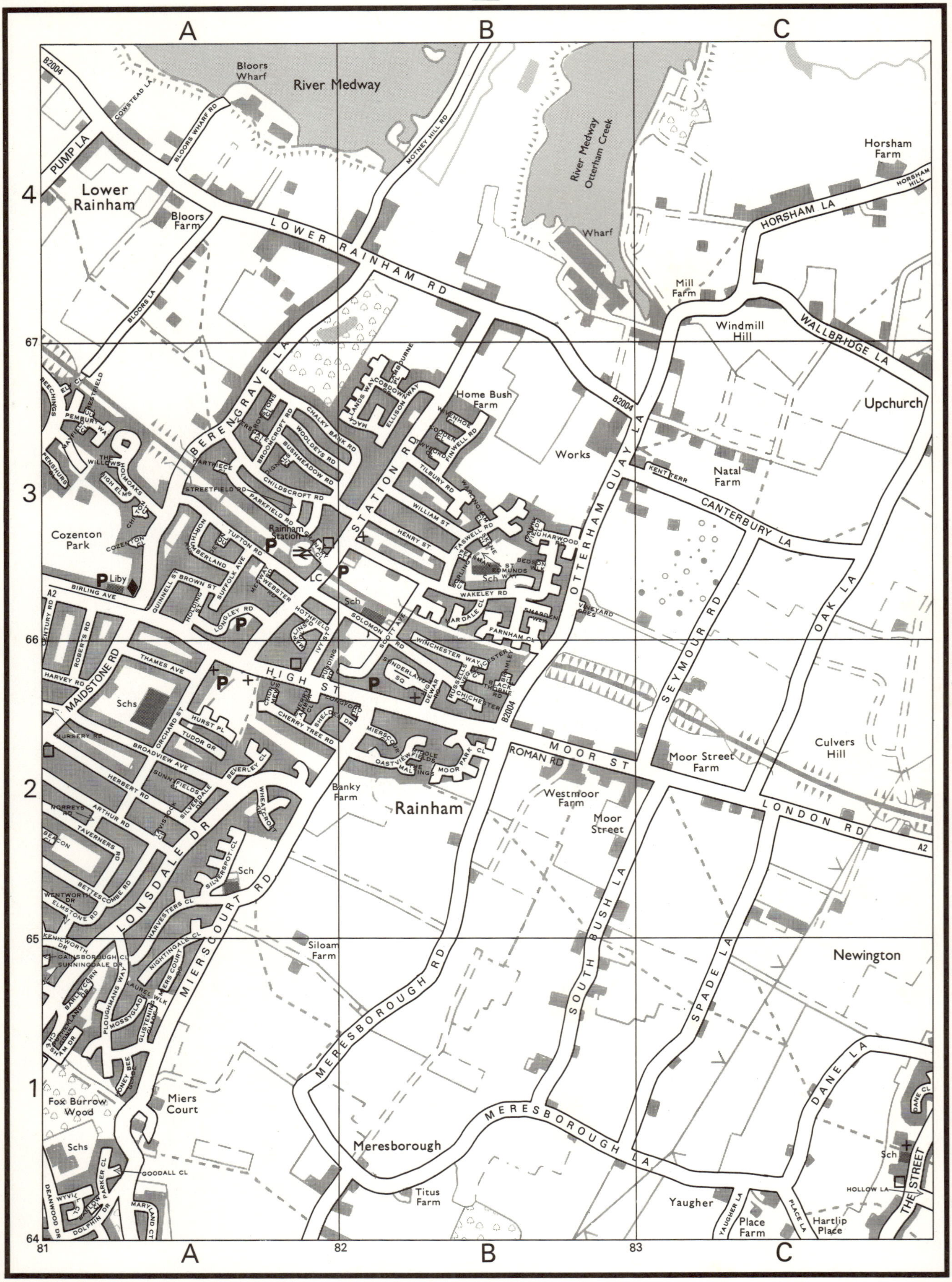

61

not continued, see key diagram

76

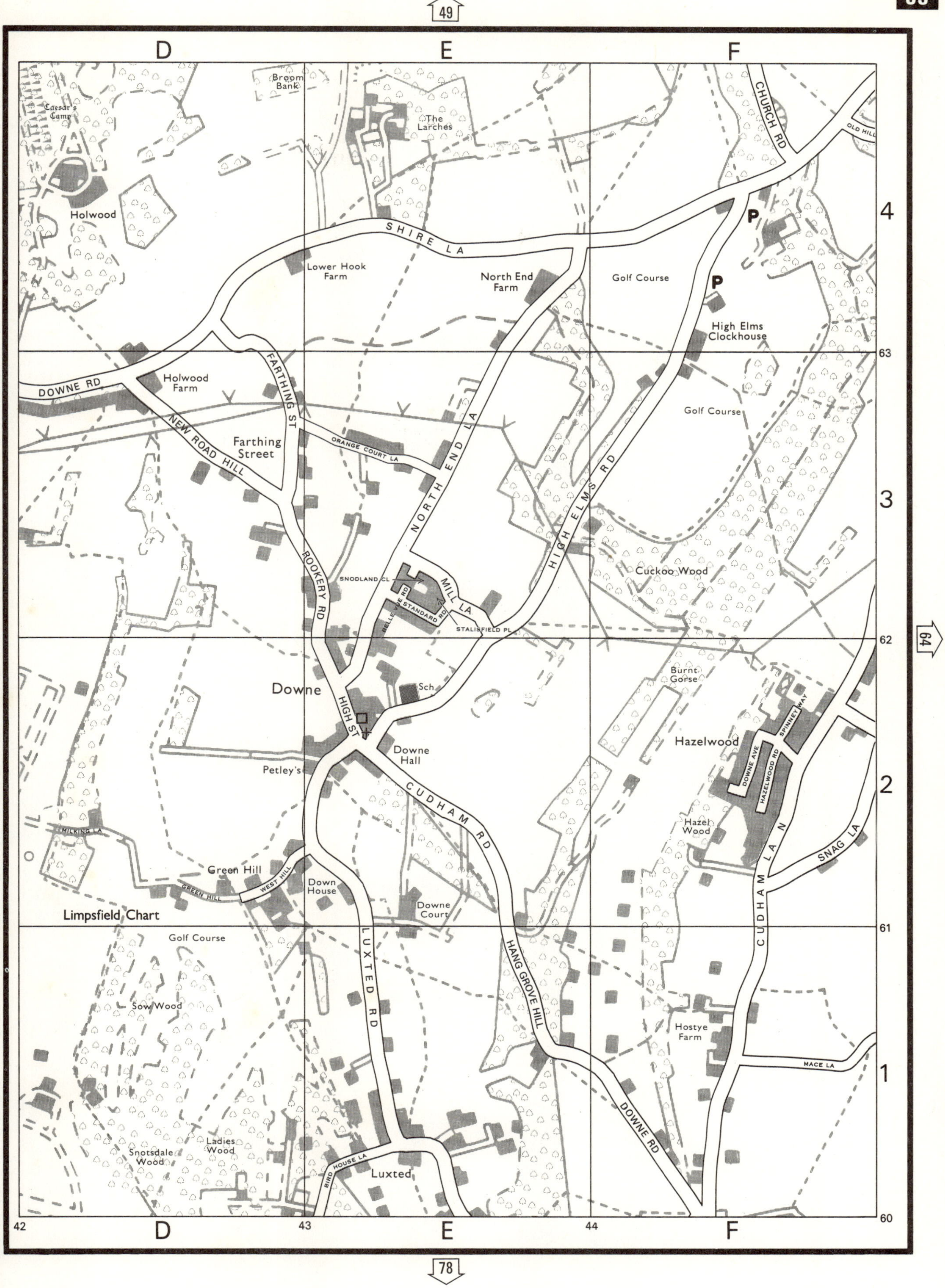
49
D
E
F
Broom Bank
Caesar's Camp
The Larches
CHURCH RD
OLD HILL
Holwood
SHIRE LA
Lower Hook Farm
North End Farm
Golf Course
High Elms Clockhouse
DOWNE RD
Holwood Farm
FARTHING ST
NEW ROAD HILL
Farthing Street
ORANGE COURT LA
NORTH END LA
HIGH ELMS RD
Golf Course
ROOKERY RD
SNODLAND CL
BELLE VUE RD
STANDARD RD
MILL LA
STALISFIELD PL
Cuckoo Wood
Downe
HIGH ST
Sch
Burnt Gorse
Hazelwood
SPINNEY WAY
DOWNE AVE
HAZELWOOD RD
Downe Hall
Petley's
CUDHAM RD
Hazel Wood
SNAG LA
CUDHAM LA N
MILKING LA
Green Hill
WEST HILL
GREEN HILL
Down House
Downe Court
Limpsfield Chart
Golf Course
LUXTED RD
HANG GROVE HILL
Sow Wood
Hostye Farm
MACE LA
DOWNE RD
Snotsdale Wood
Ladies Wood
BIRD HOUSE LA
Luxted
4
3
2
1
63
62
61
60
64
42
43
44
78

50

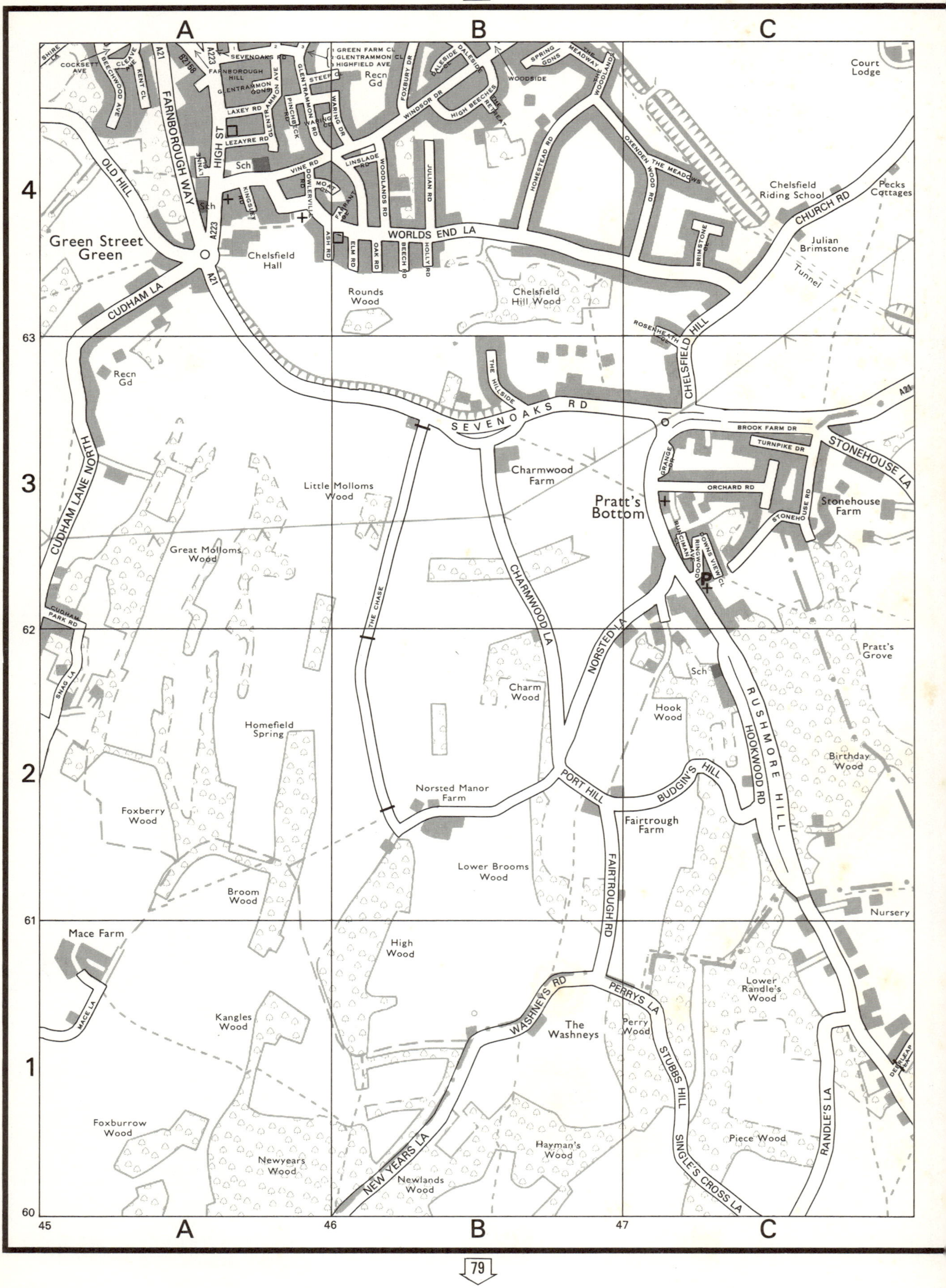

A
B
C
Green Street Green
Chelsfield Hall
Rounds Wood
Chelsfield Hill Wood
Chelsfield Riding School
Julian Brimstone
Pecks Cottages
Court Lodge
Recn Gd
Little Molloms Wood
Great Molloms Wood
Charmwood Farm
Pratt's Bottom
Stonehouse Farm
Pratt's Grove
Charm Wood
Hook Wood
Homefield Spring
Birthday Wood
Norsted Manor Farm
Fairtrough Farm
Foxberry Wood
Lower Brooms Wood
Broom Wood
Nursery
Mace Farm
High Wood
Lower Randle's Wood
Kangles Wood
The Washneys
Perry Wood
Foxburrow Wood
Newyears Wood
Hayman's Wood
Piece Wood
Newlands Wood
FARNBOROUGH WAY
HIGH ST
OLD HILL
CUDHAM LA
CUDHAM LANE NORTH
WORLDS END LA
SEVENOAKS RD
CHELSFIELD HILL
CHURCH RD
STONEHOUSE LA
BROOK FARM DR
TURNPIKE DR
ORCHARD RD
THE CHASE
CHARMWOOD LA
NORSTED LA
PORT HILL
BUDGIN'S HILL
HOOKWOOD RD
RUSHMORE HILL
FAIRTROUGH RD
WASHNEYS RD
PERRYS LA
STUBBS HILL
SINGLE'S CROSS LA
NEW YEARS LA
RANDLE'S LA
MACE LA
SNAG LA
A21
A223
4
3
2
1
63
62
61
60
45
46
47

63

51

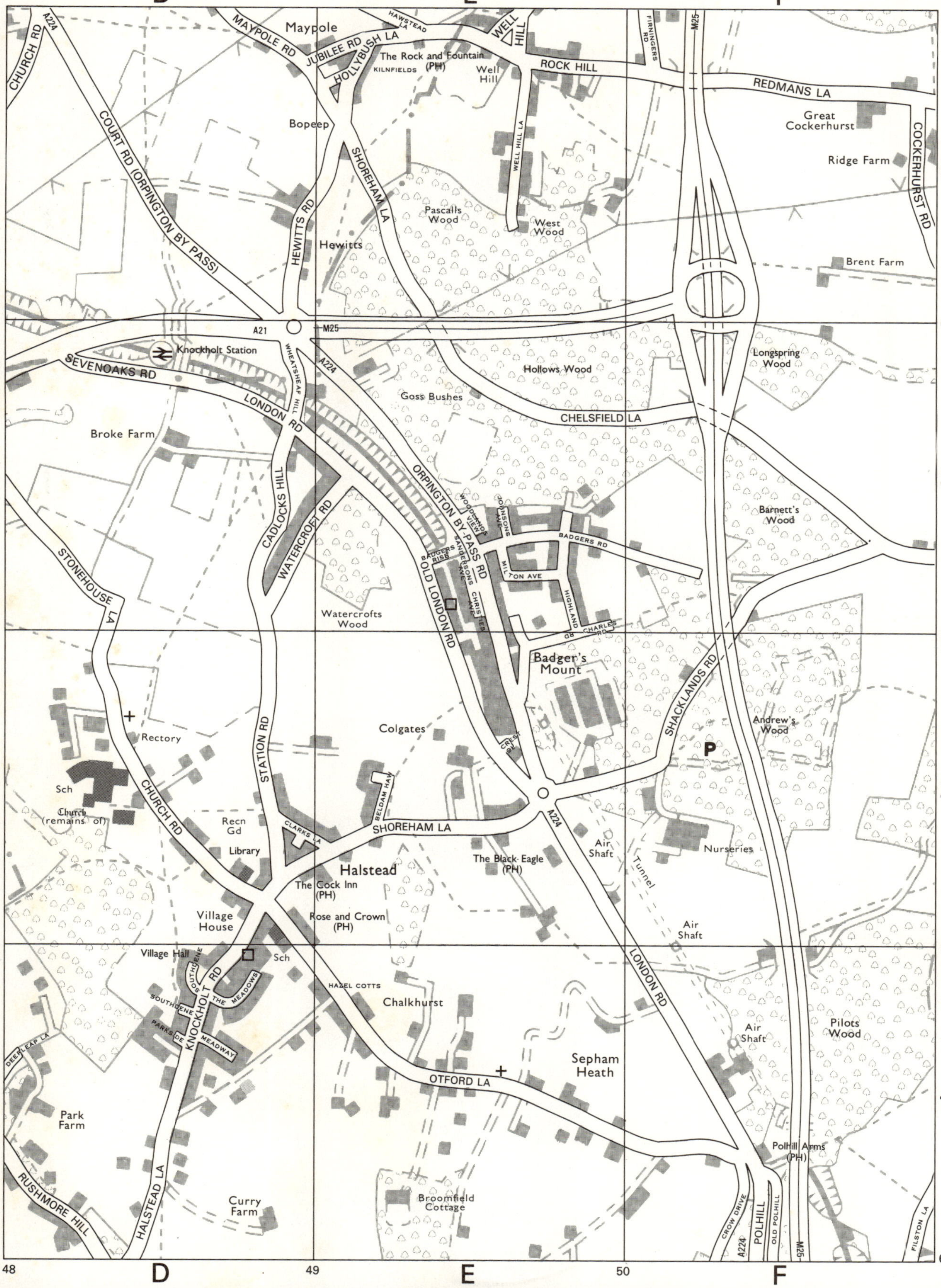
D
E
F
Maypole
MAYPOLE RD
JUBILEE RD
HOLLYBUSH LA
HAWSTEAD LA
WELL HILL
The Rock and Fountain (PH)
KILNFIELDS
Well Hill
ROCK HILL
FIRNINGERS RD
M25
REDMANS LA
Great Cockerhurst
COCKERHURST RD
Ridge Farm
CHURCH RD
A224
COURT RD (ORPINGTON BY PASS)
Bopeep
SHOREHAM LA
WELL HILL LA
Pascalls Wood
West Wood
HEWITTS RD
Hewitts
Brent Farm
4
A21
M25
63
Knockholt Station
SEVENOAKS RD
WHEATSHEAF HILL
A224
Hollows Wood
Longspring Wood
Goss Bushes
LONDON RD
CHELSFIELD LA
Broke Farm
3
CADLOCKS HILL
WATERCROFT RD
ORPINGTON BY-PASS RD
WOODLANDS VIEW
JOHNSONS AVE
BADGERS RD
Barnett's Wood
BADGERS RISE
SANDERSONS AVE
MILTON AVE
STONEHOUSE LA
OLD LONDON RD
CHRISTIES AVE
HIGHLAND RD
Watercrofts Wood
CHARLES RD
62
Badger's Mount
SHACKLANDS RD
Andrew's Wood
Rectory
Colgates
CREST RD
P
STATION RD
Sch
BELDAM HAW
2
Church (remains of)
CHURCH RD
Recn Gd
SHOREHAM LA
CLARKS LA
A224
Library
Air Shaft
Nurseries
Tunnel
Halstead
The Black Eagle (PH)
The Cock Inn (PH)
Village House
Rose and Crown (PH)
Air Shaft
Village Hall
SOUTHDENE
Sch
61
KNOCKHOLT RD
THE MEADOWS
HAZEL COTTS
Chalkhurst
LONDON RD
SOUTHDENE
PARKSIDE
MEADWAY
Air Shaft
Pilots Wood
DEERLEAP LA
Sepham Heath
OTFORD LA
1
Park Farm
Polhill Arms (PH)
RUSHMORE HILL
HALSTEAD LA
Curry Farm
Broomfield Cottage
CROW DRIVE
POLHILL
OLD POLHILL
A224
M25
FILSTON LA
60
48
D
49
E
50
F

66

80

52

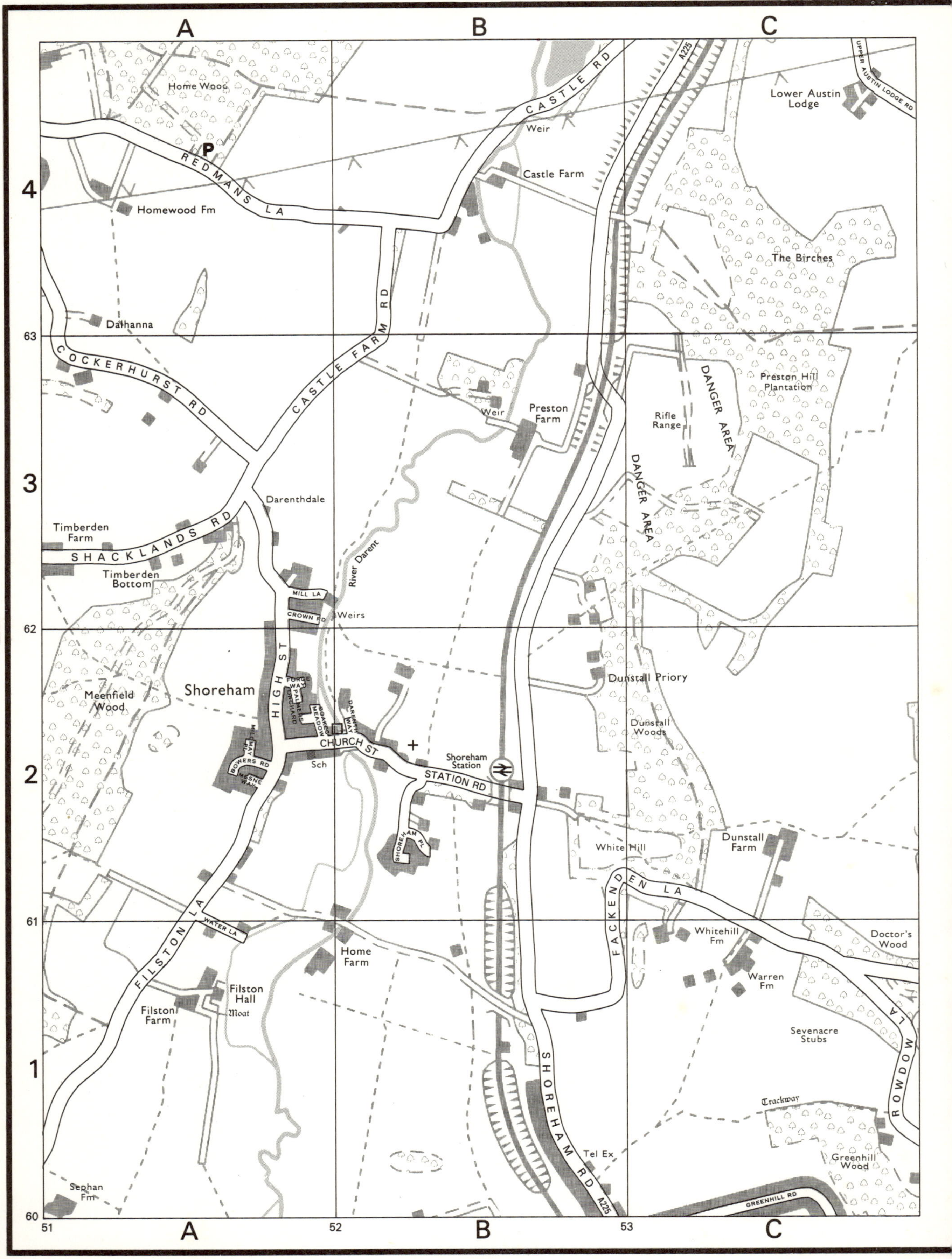

A
B
C
Home Wood
Lower Austin Lodge
UPPER AUSTIN LODGE RD
CASTLE RD
A225
Weir
REDMANS LA
Castle Farm
Homewood Fm
The Birches
CASTLE FARM RD
Dalhanna
COCKERHURST RD
Preston Hill Plantation
DANGER AREA
Rifle Range
Weir
Preston Farm
Darenthdale
Timberden Farm
SHACKLANDS RD
Timberden Bottom
River Darent
MILL LA
CROWN RD
Weirs
HIGH ST
Dunstall Priory
Meenfield Wood
Shoreham
FORGE WAY
PALMERS ORCHARD
DARENTH WAY
Dunstall Woods
CHURCH ST
Shoreham Station
Sch
STATION RD
BOWERS RD
MESNE WAY
SHOREHAM PL
White Hill
Dunstall Farm
FACKENDEN LA
WATER LA
FILSTON LA
Whitehill Fm
Doctor's Wood
Home Farm
Warren Fm
Filston Hall
Filston Farm
Moat
Sevenacre Stubs
SHOREHAM RD
ROWDOW LA
Trackway
Greenhill Wood
Tel Ex
Sephan Fm
GREENHILL RD
4
63
3
62
2
61
1
60
51
52
53

65

81

53

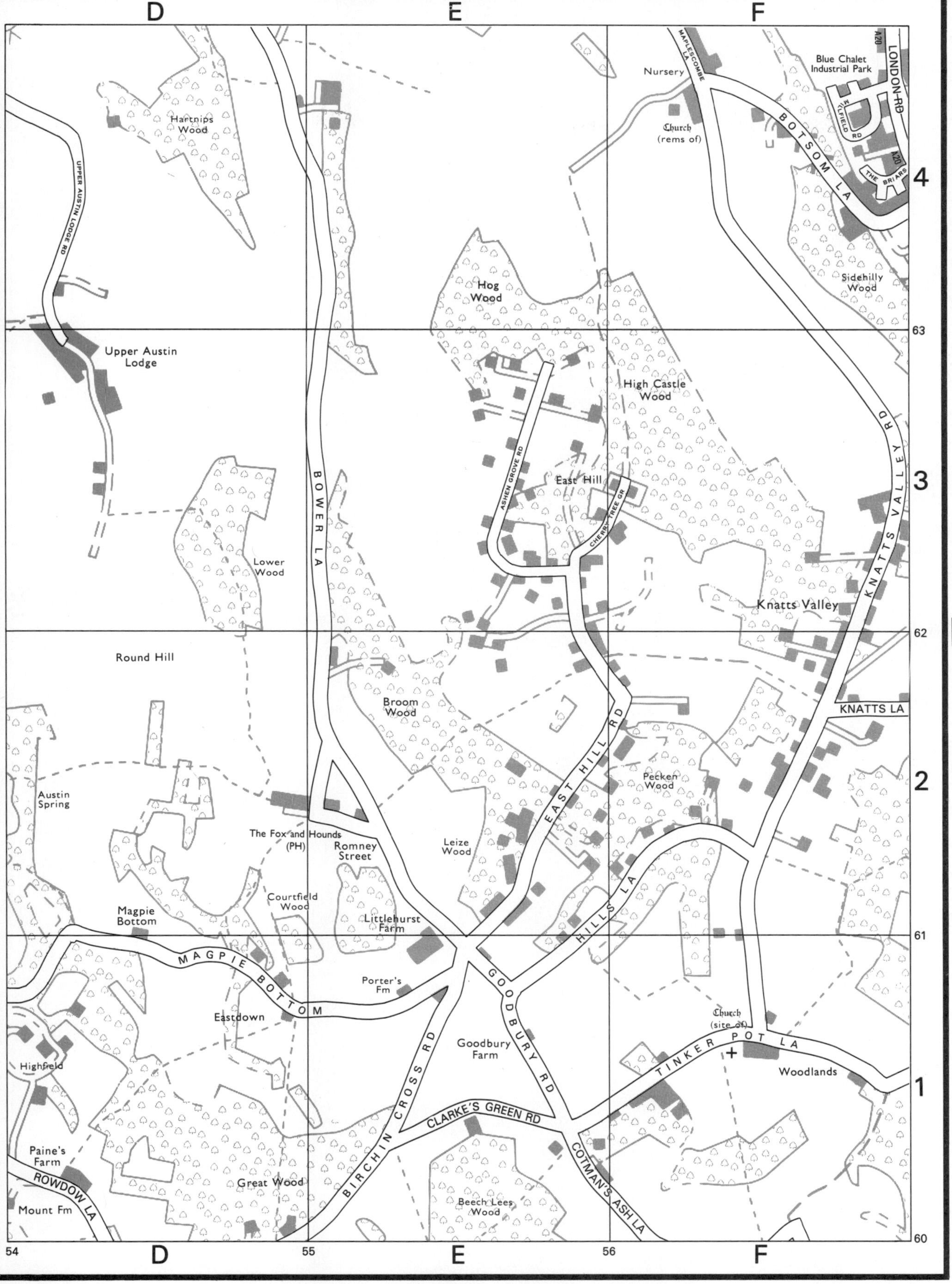
D
E
F
Nursery
Blue Chalet
Industrial Park
LONDON RD
A20
MAPLESCOMBE LA
Church
(rems of)
BOTSOM LA
THE BRIARS
Hartnips
Wood
UPPER AUSTIN LODGE RD
4
Hog
Wood
Sidehilly
Wood
63
Upper Austin
Lodge
High Castle
Wood
KNATTS VALLEY RD
ASHEN GROVE RD
East Hill
CHERRY TREE GR
BOWER LA
3
Lower
Wood
Knatts Valley
62
Round Hill
Broom
Wood
KNATTS LA
EAST HILL RD
2
Austin
Spring
Pecken
Wood
The Fox and Hounds
(PH)
Romney
Street
Leize
Wood
Courtfield
Wood
HILLS LA
Magpie
Bottom
Littlehurst
Farm
61
MAGPIE BOTTOM
Porter's
Fm
GOODBURY RD
Eastdown
Church
(site of)
TINKER POT LA
Goodbury
Farm
Highfield
Woodlands
1
BIRCHIN CROSS RD
CLARKE'S GREEN RD
Paine's
Farm
COTMAN'S ASH LA
ROWDOW LA
Great Wood
Beech Lees
Wood
Mount Fm
60
54
55
56

68

82

54

67

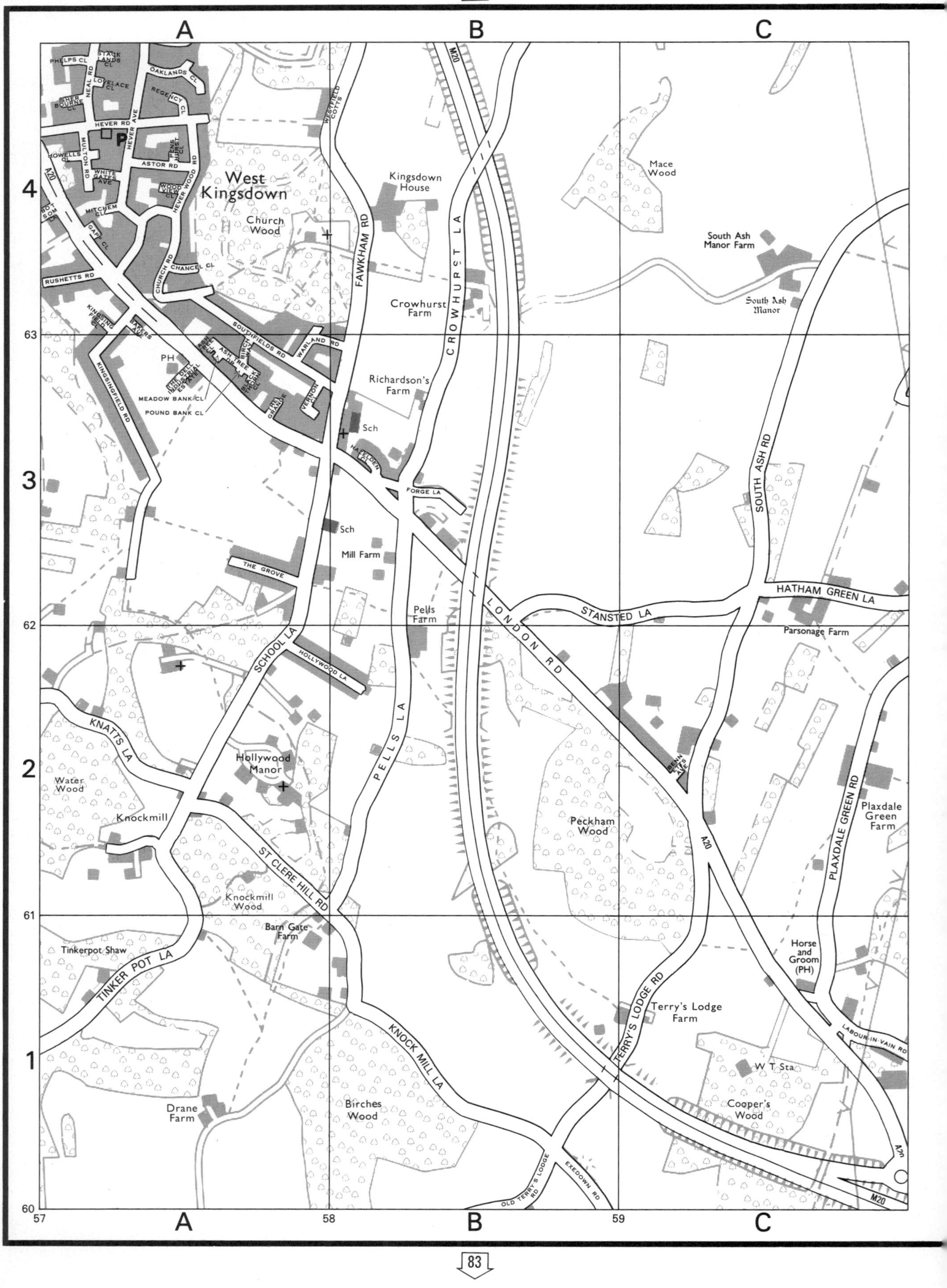
A
B
C
4
3
2
1
63
62
61
60
57
58
59
West Kingsdown
Church Wood
Kingsdown House
Mace Wood
South Ash Manor Farm
South Ash Manor
Crowhurst Farm
Richardson's Farm
Sch
Mill Farm
Pells Farm
Parsonage Farm
Hollywood Manor
Water Wood
Knockmill
Knockmill Wood
Barn Gate Farm
Tinkerpot Shaw
Peckham Wood
Plaxdale Green Farm
Horse and Groom (PH)
Terry's Lodge Farm
W T Sta
Cooper's Wood
Birches Wood
Drane Farm
PH
PHELPS CL
STACKLANDS CL
NEAL RD
LOVELACE CL
OAKLANDS CL
REGENCY CL
SHERBOURNE CL
HEVER RD
HEVER AVE
MULTON RD
HOWELLS CL
ASTOR RD
WHITE GATES AVE
FENS HURST CL
WOODVIEW CL
HEVER WOOD RD
MITCHEM CL
CAPEL CL
CHURCH RD
CHANCEL CL
RUSHETTS RD
KINGSING FIELD CL
BAKERS AVE
KINGSINGFIELD RD
SOUTHFIELDS RD
WARLAND RD
ASH TREE CL
THE DELL INDUSTRIAL ESTATE
MEADOW BANK CL
POUND BANK CL
THE GRANGE
VERNON PL
WESTFIELD COTTS
FAWKHAM RD
CROWHURST LA
M20
A20
HAZELDEN CL
FORGE LA
THE GROVE
SCHOOL LA
HOLLYWOOD LA
PELLS LA
LONDON RD
STANSTED LA
HATHAM GREEN LA
SOUTH ASH RD
PLAXDALE GREEN RD
KNATTS LA
ST CLERE HILL RD
TINKER POT LA
KNOCK MILL LA
TERRY'S LODGE RD
OLD TERRY'S LODGE RD
EXEDOWN RD
LABOUR-IN-VAIN RD

83

55

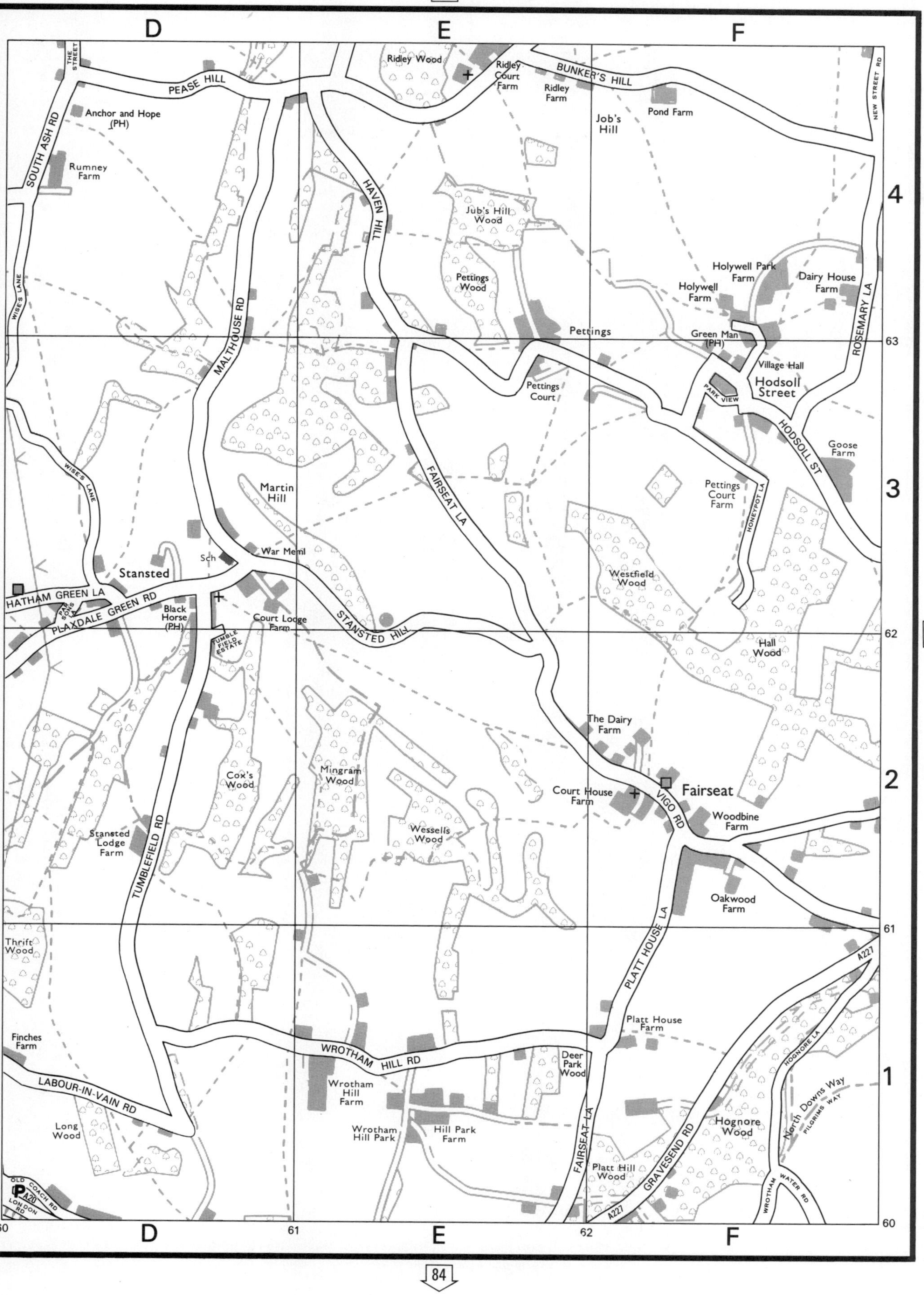

D
E
F
Ridley Wood
Ridley Court Farm
Ridley Farm
BUNKER'S HILL
Pond Farm
Job's Hill
NEW STREET RD
THE STREET
PEASE HILL
Anchor and Hope (PH)
SOUTH ASH RD
Rumney Farm
HAVEN HILL
Jub's Hill Wood
Pettings Wood
Holywell Park Farm
Dairy House Farm
Holywell Farm
ROSEMARY LA
WISE'S LANE
MALTHOUSE RD
Pettings
Green Man (PH)
Village Hall
Hodsoll Street
PARK VIEW
Pettings Court
HODSOLL ST
Goose Farm
WISE'S LANE
FAIRSEAT LA
Martin Hill
Pettings Court Farm
HONEYPOT LA
Sch
War Meml
Westfield Wood
Stansted
HATHAM GREEN LA
PLAXDALE GREEN RD
Black Horse (PH)
Court Lodge Farm
STANSTED HILL
TUMBLEFIELD ESTATE
Hall Wood
The Dairy Farm
Cox's Wood
Mingram Wood
Court House Farm
Fairseat
VIGO RD
Woodbine Farm
Wessells Wood
Stansted Lodge Farm
TUMBLEFIELD RD
Oakwood Farm
PLATT HOUSE LA
Thrift Wood
A227
Platt House Farm
Finches Farm
WROTHAM HILL RD
Deer Park Wood
LABOUR-IN-VAIN RD
Wrotham Hill Farm
HOGNORE LA
North Downs Way
PILGRIMS WAY
Long Wood
Wrotham Hill Park
Hill Park Farm
Hognore Wood
FAIRSEAT LA
GRAVESEND RD
Platt Hill Wood
OLD COACH RD
A20
LONDON RD
A227
WROTHAM WATER RD
4
3
2
1
63
62
61
60
60
61
62
D
E
F

70

84

56

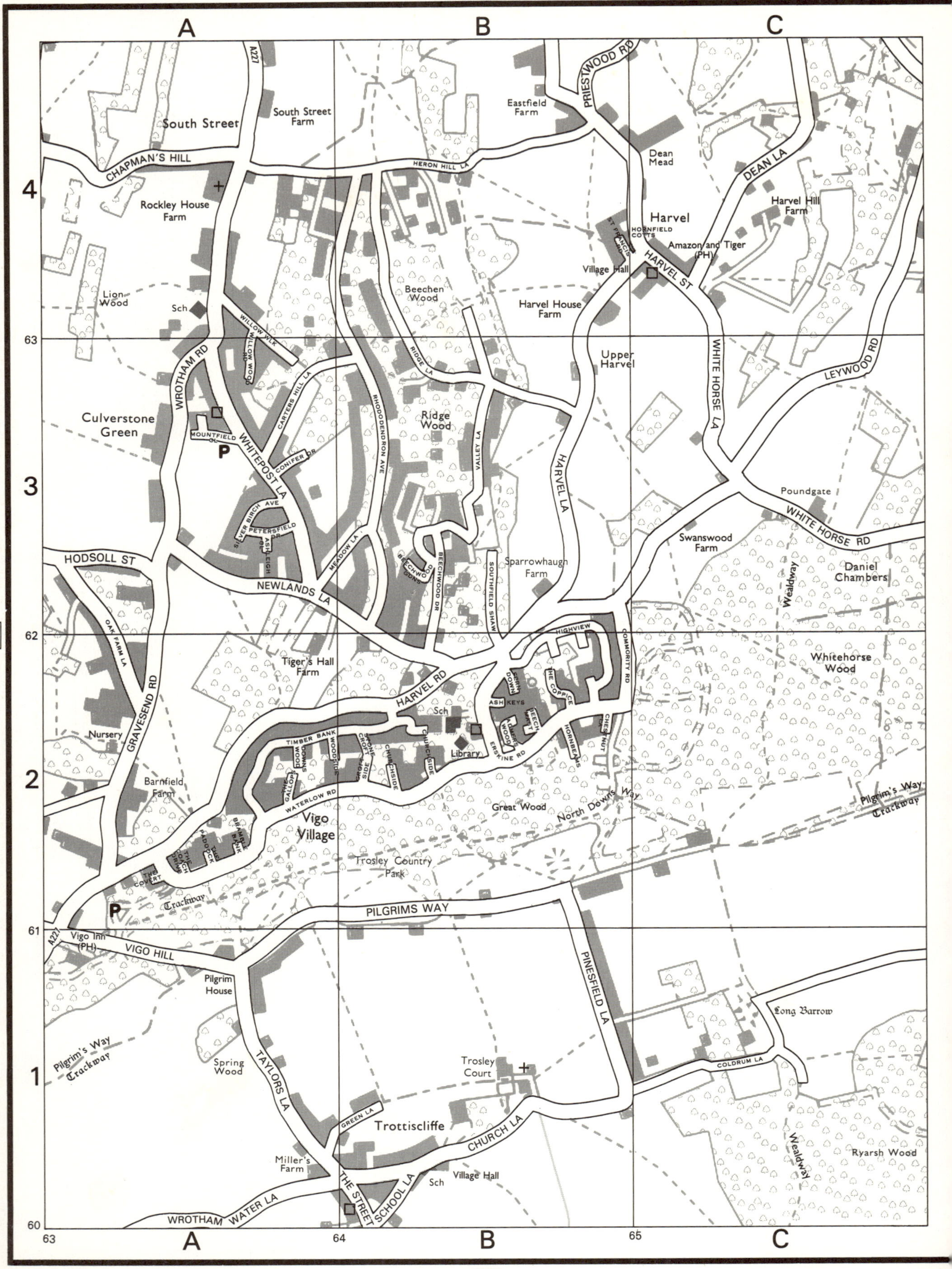
A
B
C
4
3
2
1
63
62
61
60
64
65
A227
South Street
South Street Farm
Eastfield Farm
PRIESTWOOD RD
CHAPMAN'S HILL
HERON HILL LA
Dean Mead
DEAN LA
Rockley House Farm
Harvel
Harvel Hill Farm
ST FRANCIS
HORNFIELD COTTS
Amazon and Tiger (PH)
Village Hall
HARVEL ST
Lion Wood
Sch
Beechen Wood
Harvel House Farm
WILLOW WLK
WILLOW WOOD RD
RIDGE LA
Upper Harvel
WHITE HORSE LA
LEYWOOD RD
WROTHAM RD
CARTERS HILL LA
RHODODENDRON AVE
Ridge Wood
VALLEY LA
Culverstone Green
MOUNTFIELD CL
P
WHITEPOST LA
CONIFER DR
HARVEL LA
Poundgate
SILVER BIRCH AVE
PETERSFIELD DR
ASHLEIGH
MEADOW LA
BEECHWOOD GDNS
BEECHWOOD DR
WHITE HORSE RD
Swanswood Farm
HODSOLL ST
SOUTHFIELD SHAW
Sparrowhaugh Farm
Wealdway
Daniel Chambers
NEWLANDS LA
HIGHVIEW
COMMORITY RD
OAK FARM LA
Tiger's Hall Farm
FERN DOWN
THE COPPICE
Whitehorse Wood
HARVEL RD
ASH KEYS
BEECH HURST
Sch
GRAVESEND RD
Nursery
TIMBER BANK
WOODSIDE
STONE CROFT
CHURCHSIDE
HORNBEAMS
CHESTNUT
Library
ERSKINE RD
DOWNS WOOD
THE GALLOPS
HILLSIDE
Barnfield Farm
WATERLOW RD
Great Wood
North Downs Way
Pilgrim's Way
Trackway
Vigo Village
PADDOCK
BRAMBLE BANK
THE COACH DRIVE
Trosley Country Park
THE COVERT
P
Trackway
PILGRIMS WAY
A227
Vigo Inn (PH)
VIGO HILL
Pilgrim House
PINESFIELD LA
Long Barrow
Pilgrim's Way
Trackway
Spring Wood
TAYLORS LA
Trosley Court
COLDRUM LA
GREEN LA
Trottiscliffe
CHURCH LA
Wealdway
Ryarsh Wood
Miller's Farm
THE STREET
SCHOOL LA
Sch
Village Hall
WROTHAM WATER LA

69

85

57

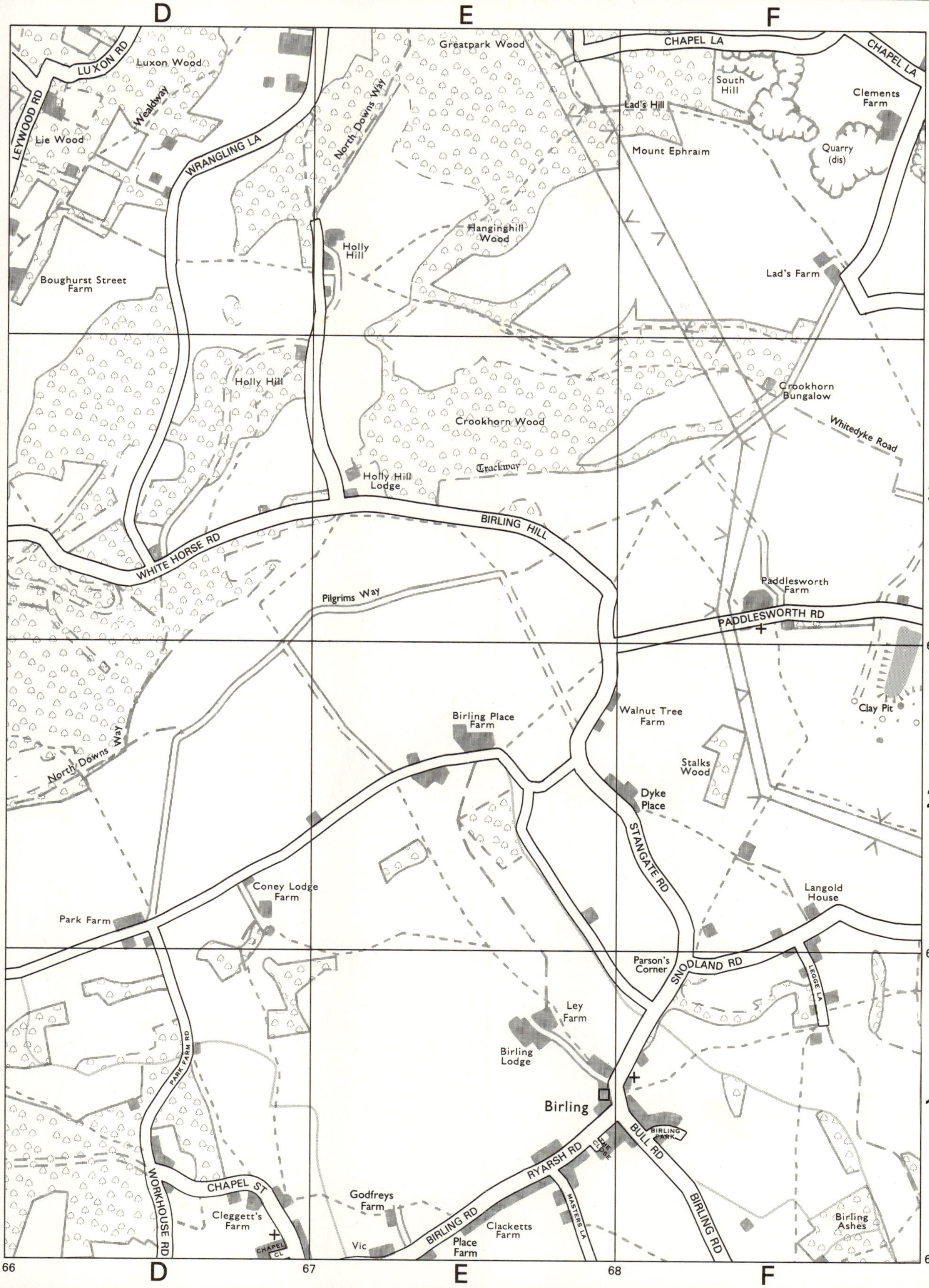
D
E
F
CHAPEL LA
Greatpark Wood
LUXON RD
Luxon Wood
LEYWOOD RD
Lie Wood
Wealdway
WRANGLING LA
North Downs Way
South Hill
Clements Farm
Lad's Hill
Mount Ephraim
Quarry (dis)
Hanginghill Wood
Holly Hill
Boughurst Street Farm
Lad's Farm
Holly Hill
Crookhorn Bungalow
Crookhorn Wood
Whitedyke Road
Trackway
Holly Hill Lodge
BIRLING HILL
WHITE HORSE RD
Pilgrims Way
Paddlesworth Farm
PADDLESWORTH RD
Birling Place Farm
Walnut Tree Farm
Clay Pit
North Downs Way
Stalks Wood
Dyke Place
STANGATE RD
Coney Lodge Farm
Park Farm
Langold House
Parson's Corner
SNODLAND RD
LEGGE LA
Ley Farm
PARK FARM RD
Birling Lodge
Birling
BIRLING PARK
BULL RD
RYARSH RD
WORKHOUSE RD
CHAPEL ST
Godfreys Farm
MASTERS LA
BIRLING RD
Cleggett's Farm
Clacketts Farm
Birling Ashes
CHAPEL CL
Vic
Place Farm
BIRLING RD
4
3
2
1
63
62
61
60
66
67
68

72

86

58

71

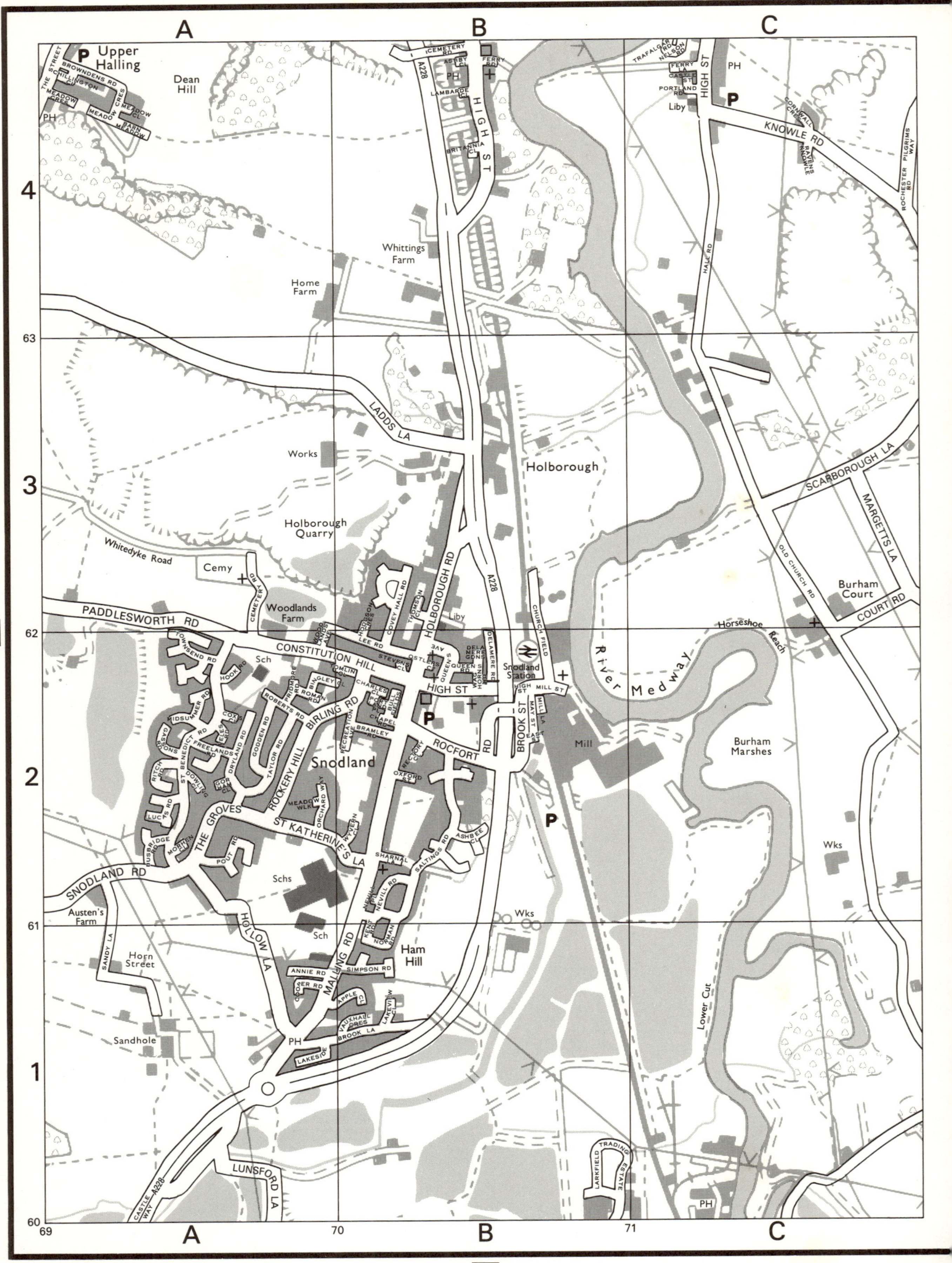
A
B
C
4
3
2
1
63
62
61
60
69
70
71
Upper Halling
Dean Hill
PH
THE STREET
BROWNDENS RD
CHILLINGTON
MEADOW CRES
MEADOW CL
BARN MEADOW
CEMETERY RD
A228
ASHBY CL
FERRY RD
LAMBARDE CL
BRITANNIA CL
HIGH ST
TRAFALGAR RD
NELSON RD
FERRY LA
CASTLE ST
PORTLAND RD
Liby
KNOWLE RD
CORNWALL CRES
RAVEN KNOWLE
ROCHESTER RD
PILGRIMS WAY
Whittings Farm
Home Farm
HALL RD
LADDS LA
Works
Holborough
SCARBOROUGH LA
MARGETTS LA
Holborough Quarry
Whitedyke Road
Cemy
Woodlands Farm
HOLBOROUGH RD
COVEY HALL RD
THOMSON CL
HODGSON CRES
LEE RD
OLD CHURCH RD
Burham Court
COURT RD
CHURCH FIELD
PADDLESWORTH RD
CONSTITUTION HILL
TOWNSEND RD
HOOK RD
Sch
STEVENS CL
OSTLERS
QUEEN'S AVE
QUEEN ST
DELAMERE GDNS
DELAMERE RD
Snodland Station
Horseshoe Reach
River Medway
HIGH ST
MILL ST
BINGLEY CL
TOMLIN CL
ROMAN RD
CHARLES CL
ROBERTS RD
PRIMROSE
BIRLING RD
CHAPEL
MIDSUMMER RD
COX'S CL
GODDEN RD
RECREATION AVE
BRAMLEY
ROCFORT RD
BROOK ST
MILL LA
MAY ST
EAST
Mill
Burham Marshes
FREELANDS RD
DRYLAND RD
TAYLOR RD
ROCKERY HILL
Snodland
RECTORY CL
OXFORD ST
ST BENEDICT RD
ST DOWLING
MEADOW WLK
ORCHARD WAY
LUCKS RD
THE GROVES
ST KATHERINE'S LA
ASHBEE CL
SALTINGS RD
SHARNAL LA
NEVILL RD
POUT RD
Wks
SNODLAND RD
Schs
Austen's Farm
Sch
KENT RD
NORMAN
Ham Hill
SANDY LA
Horn Street
HOLLOW LA
MALLING RD
ANNIE RD
SIMPSON RD
APPLE CL
VAUXHALL CRES
LAKEVIEW
BROOK LA
LAKESIDE
Lower Cut
Sandhole
PH
LUNSFORD LA
CASTLE WAY
LARKFIELD TRADING ESTATE
P

87

59

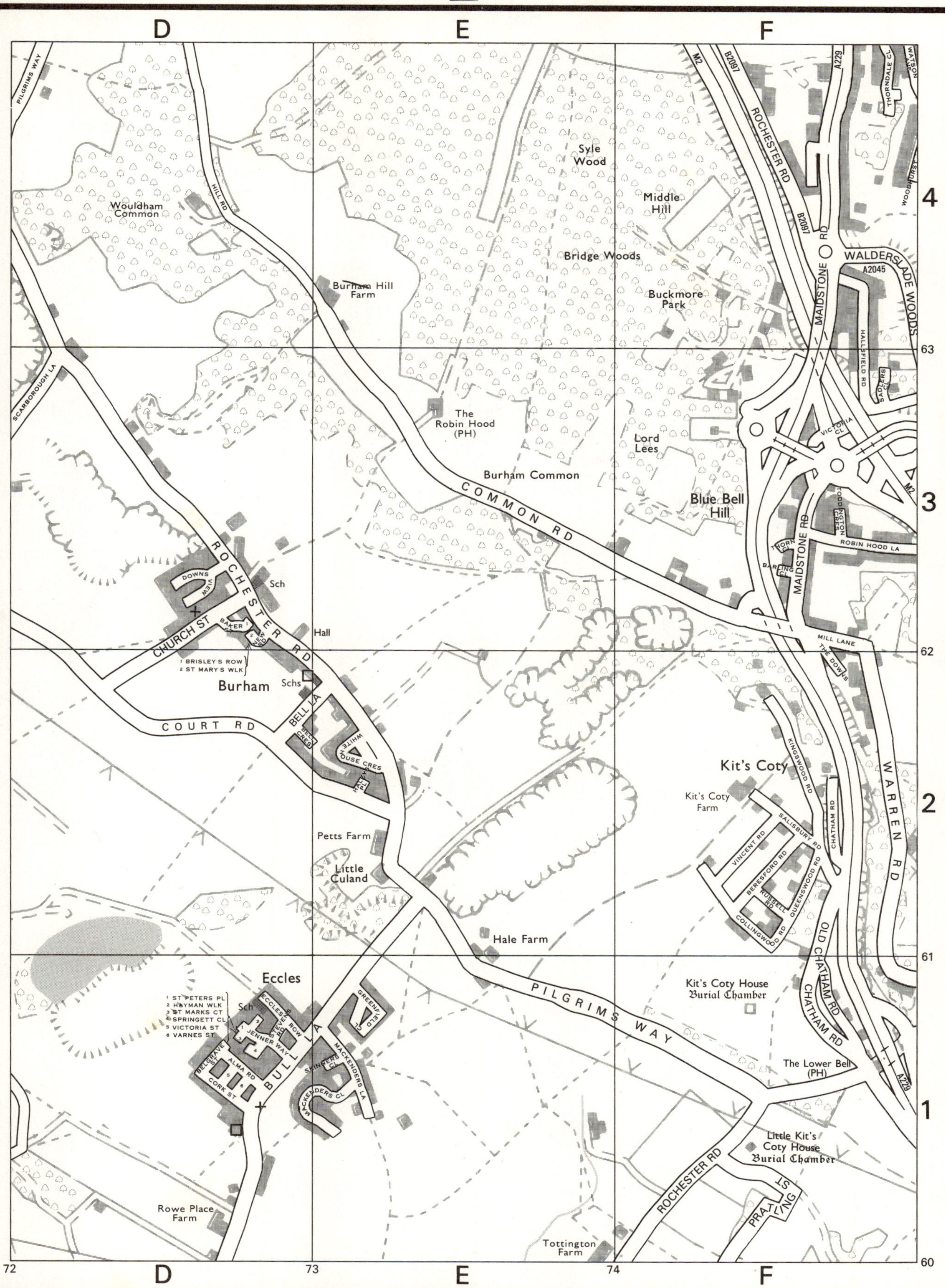
D
E
F
Wouldham Common
Syle Wood
Middle Hill
Bridge Woods
Buckmore Park
Burham Hill Farm
The Robin Hood (PH)
Lord Lees
Burham Common
Blue Bell Hill
COMMON RD
ROCHESTER RD
HILL RD
PILGRIMS WAY
SCARBOROUGH LA
DOWNS VIEW
CHURCH ST
BAKER
Sch
Hall
Schs
1 BRISLEY'S ROW
2 ST MARY'S WLK
Burham
COURT RD
BELL LA
BELL CRES
WHITE HOUSE CRES
Petts Farm
Little Culand
Hale Farm
Eccles
1 ST PETERS PL
2 HAYMAN WLK
3 ST MARKS CT
4 SPRINGETT CL
5 VICTORIA ST
6 VARNES ST
ECCLES ROW
STEVENS
JENNER WAY
GREENFIELD
BELGRAVE ST
ALMA RD
CORK ST
BULL LA
SPINDERS CL
MACKENDERS LA
MACKENDERS CL
Rowe Place Farm
Tottington Farm
M2
B2097
A229
ROCHESTER RD
THORNDALE CL
WATSON
WOODHURST
MAIDSTONE RD
WALDERSLADE WOODS
A2045
HALLSFIELD RD
SADLERS CL
VICTORIA CL
TODDINGTON CRES
THORN
BARLING CL
MAIDSTONE RD
ROBIN HOOD LA
MILL LANE
THE DOWNS
Kit's Coty
Kit's Coty Farm
KINGSWOOD RD
CHATHAM RD
SALISBURY RD
VINCENT RD
BERESFORD RD
RUSSELL RD
QUEENSWOOD RD
COLLINGWOOD RD
WARREN RD
OLD CHATHAM RD
CHATHAM RD
Kit's Coty House Burial Chamber
The Lower Bell (PH)
Little Kit's Coty House Burial Chamber
ROCHESTER RD
PRATLING ST
4
3
2
1
63
62
61
60
72
73
74

74

88

60

A
B
C
4
3
2
1
63
62
61
60
75
76
77
Walderslade
Sharsted Farm
Hook Wood
Lords Wood
Gibraltar Farm
Kit Hill
Taddington Wood
Walderslade Bottom
Impton Wood
Crematorium
Round Wood
Beechen Bank
Hall Wood
Lordswood Industrial Estate
Cowbeck Wood
Frith Wood
WT Station
Cossington Fields
Malling Wood
Resr
Westfield Sole
Westfield Sole Farm
Westfield Wood
North Downs Way
White Horse Stone
Pilgrims Way
Black Cottages
CHESTNUT AVE
KING GEORGE RD
WALDERSLADE RD
PRINCES AVE
DARGETS RD
LORDS WOOD LA
NORTH DANE WAY
SHAWSTEAD RD
HAM LA
ALBERMARLE RD
CLANDON RD
BOXLEY RD
BEECHEN BANK RD
ROBIN HOOD LA (LOWER)
ROBIN HOOD LA (UPPER)
FOSTINGTON WAY
TADDINGTON WOOD LA
TUNBURY AVE
WALDERSLADE WOODS
GLEAMING WOOD DR
WESTFIELD SOLE RD
YELSTED LA
HARP FARM RD
BELL LA
LOWER WARREN RD
WARREN RD
CHATHAM RD
LIDSING RD
M2
A229
Sch
Schs
Liby

73

89

61

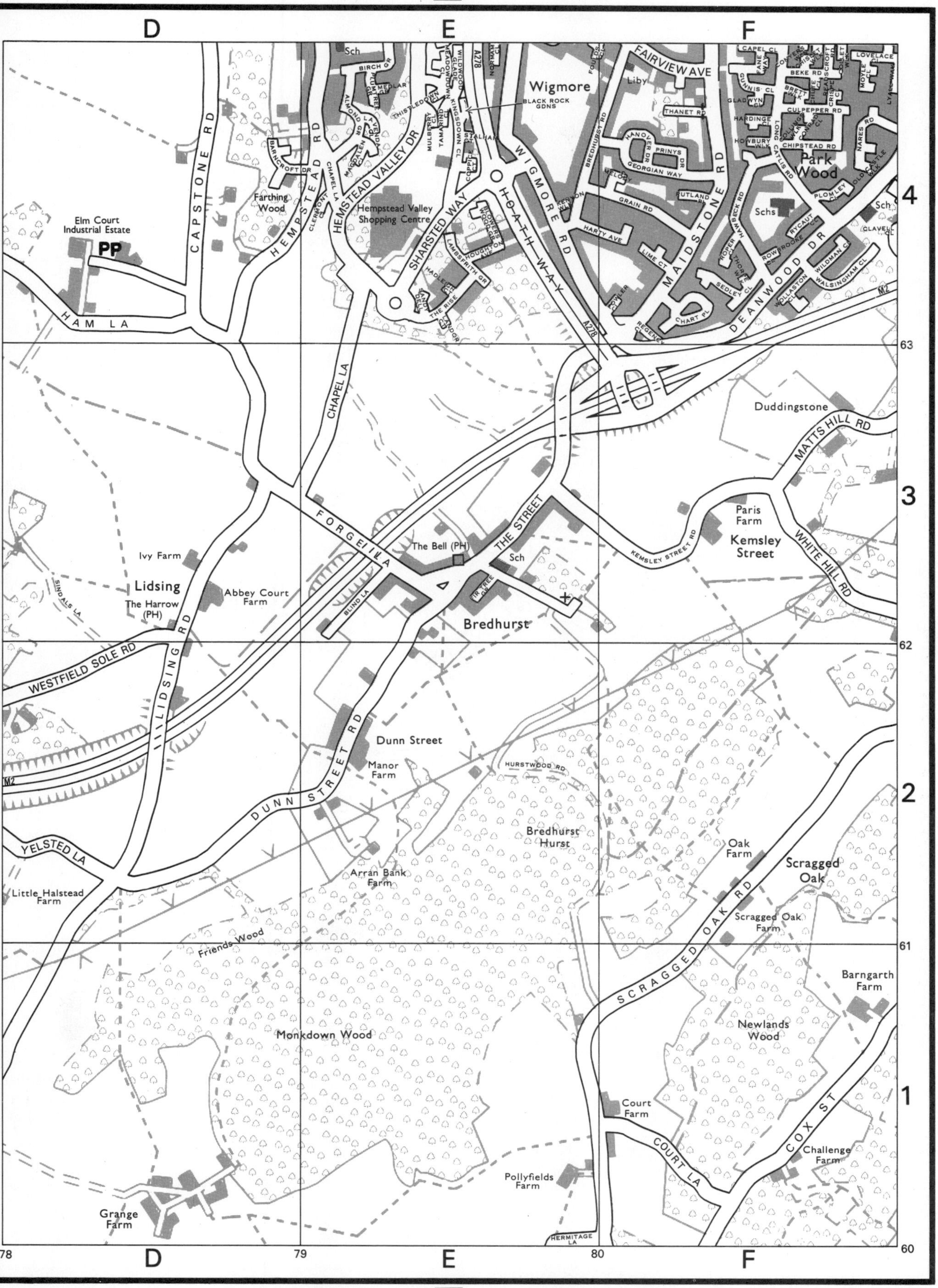
D
E
F
Sch
BIRCH GR
MEDLAR
Wigmore
FAIRVIEW AVE
Liby
BLACK ROCK GDNS
THANET RD
CAPEL CL
BEKE RD
LOVELACE
GUNNIS CL
GLADWYN CL
CULPEPPER RD
HARDINGE CL
HOWBURY WK
CHIPSTEAD RD
Park Wood
A278
HEMSTEAD VALLEY DR
THISTLEDOWN
MULBERRY CL
KINGSDOWN CL
STALHAM
COPPICE
WIGMORE RD
BREDHURST RD
HANOVER DR
PRINYS DR
GEORGIAN WAY
RUTLAND PL
GRAIN RD
HARTY AVE
MAIDSTONE RD
LIME CT
HAWBECK RD
ROPER
THORNE WK
ROWBROOKE
RYCAUT
PLOMLEY CL
NARES RD
Schs
Sch
CLAVELL CL
4
CAPSTONE RD
HEMPSTEAD RD
BARNCROFT DR
CHAPEL LA
CLERMONT CL
Farthing Wood
Hempstead Valley Shopping Centre
SHARSTED WAY
HOATH WAY
LAMBSFRITH GR
HOUGHTON AVE
HADLEIGH CT
THE RISE
CONDOR
Elm Court Industrial Estate
PP
HAM LA
SEDLEY CL
CHART PL
DEANWOOD DR
WALSINGHAM CL
WILDMAN CL
REGENCY
M2
63
CHAPEL LA
Duddingstone
MATTS HILL RD
3
FORGE LA
THE STREET
The Bell (PH)
Sch
Paris Farm
Kemsley Street
KEMSLEY STREET RD
WHITE HILL RD
Ivy Farm
Lidsing
The Harrow (PH)
Abbey Court Farm
SINDALS LA
BLIND LA
FIR TREE GR
Bredhurst
62
WESTFIELD SOLE RD
LIDSING RD
Dunn Street
Manor Farm
DUNN STREET RD
HURSTWOOD RD
M2
2
Bredhurst Hurst
Oak Farm
Scragged Oak
YELSTED LA
Arran Bank Farm
Little Halstead Farm
Scragged Oak Farm
SCRAGGED OAK RD
Friends Wood
61
Barngarth Farm
Newlands Wood
Monkdown Wood
1
Court Farm
COURT LA
COX ST
Challenge Farm
Pollyfields Farm
Grange Farm
HERMITAGE LA
78
79
80
60
D
E
F

76

90

62

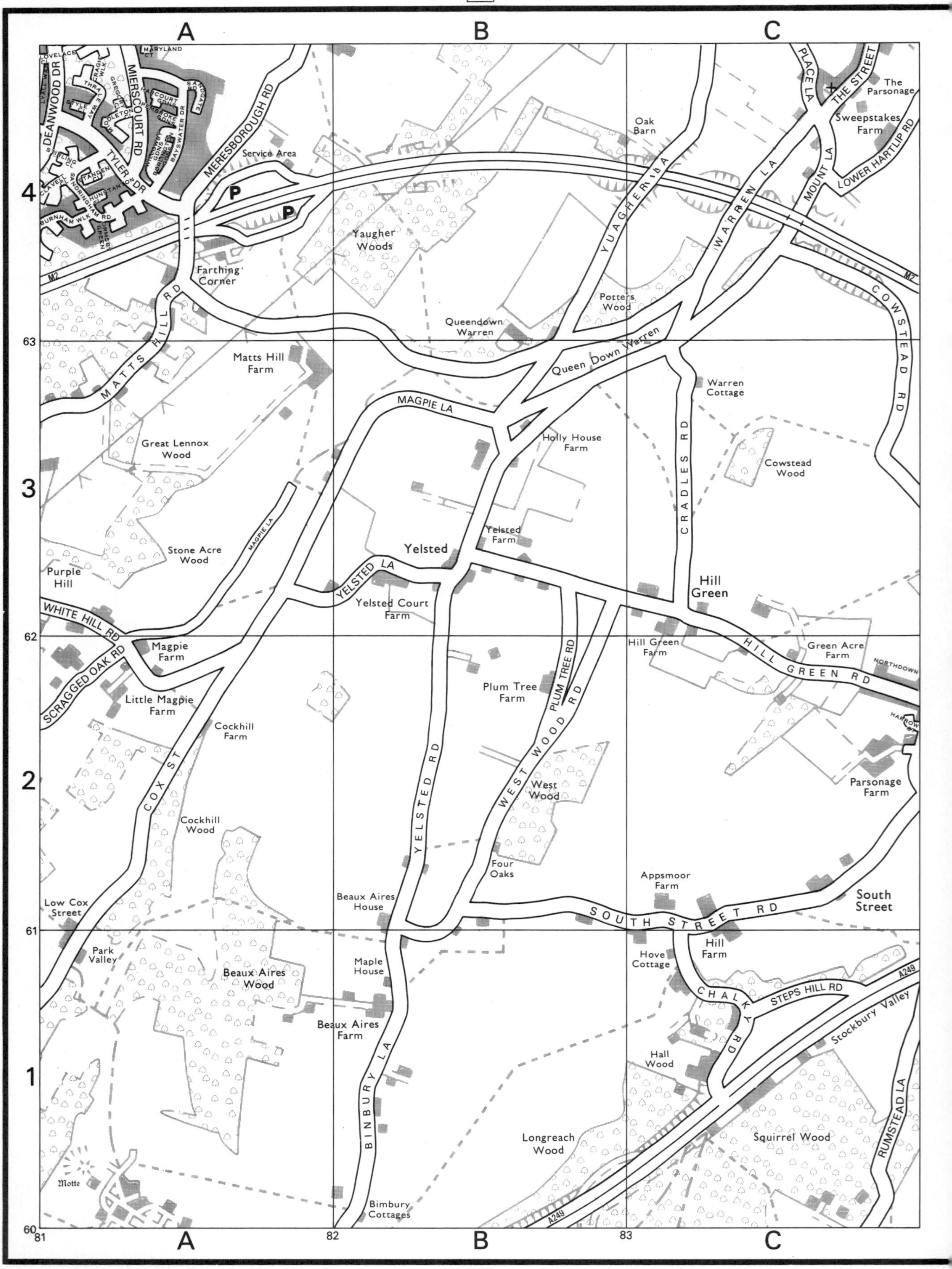
A
B
C
4
3
2
1
63
62
61
60
81
82
83
MERESBOROUGH RD
MIERSCOURT RD
DEANWOOD DR
TYLER DR
Service Area
P
P
M2
Farthing Corner
Yaugher Woods
Oak Barn
YUAGHER LA
WARREN LA
MOUNT LA
PLACE LA
THE STREET
The Parsonage
Sweepstakes Farm
LOWER HARTLIP RD
COWSTEAD RD
Potters Wood
Queendown Warren
Queen Down Warren
MATTS HILL RD
Matts Hill Farm
MAGPIE LA
Warren Cottage
Holly House Farm
Great Lennox Wood
Cowstead Wood
CRADLES RD
Yelsted Farm
Yelsted
Stone Acre Wood
MAGPIE LA
Purple Hill
YELSTED LA
Yelsted Court Farm
Hill Green
WHITE HILL RD
Magpie Farm
SCRAGGED OAK RD
Hill Green Farm
HILL GREEN RD
Green Acre Farm
NORTHDOWN
Little Magpie Farm
Plum Tree Farm
PLUM TREE RD
Cockhill Farm
COX ST
YELSTED RD
WEST WOOD RD
West Wood
Parsonage Farm
Cockhill Wood
Four Oaks
Appsmoor Farm
South Street
Low Cox Street
Beaux Aires House
SOUTH STREET RD
Park Valley
Maple House
Hill Farm
Hove Cottage
Beaux Aires Wood
CHALKY RD
STEPS HILL RD
A249
Beaux Aires Farm
Stockbury Valley
Hall Wood
BINBURY LA
RUMSTEAD LA
Longreach Wood
Squirrel Wood
Motte
Bimbury Cottages
A249

75

91

not continued, see key diagram

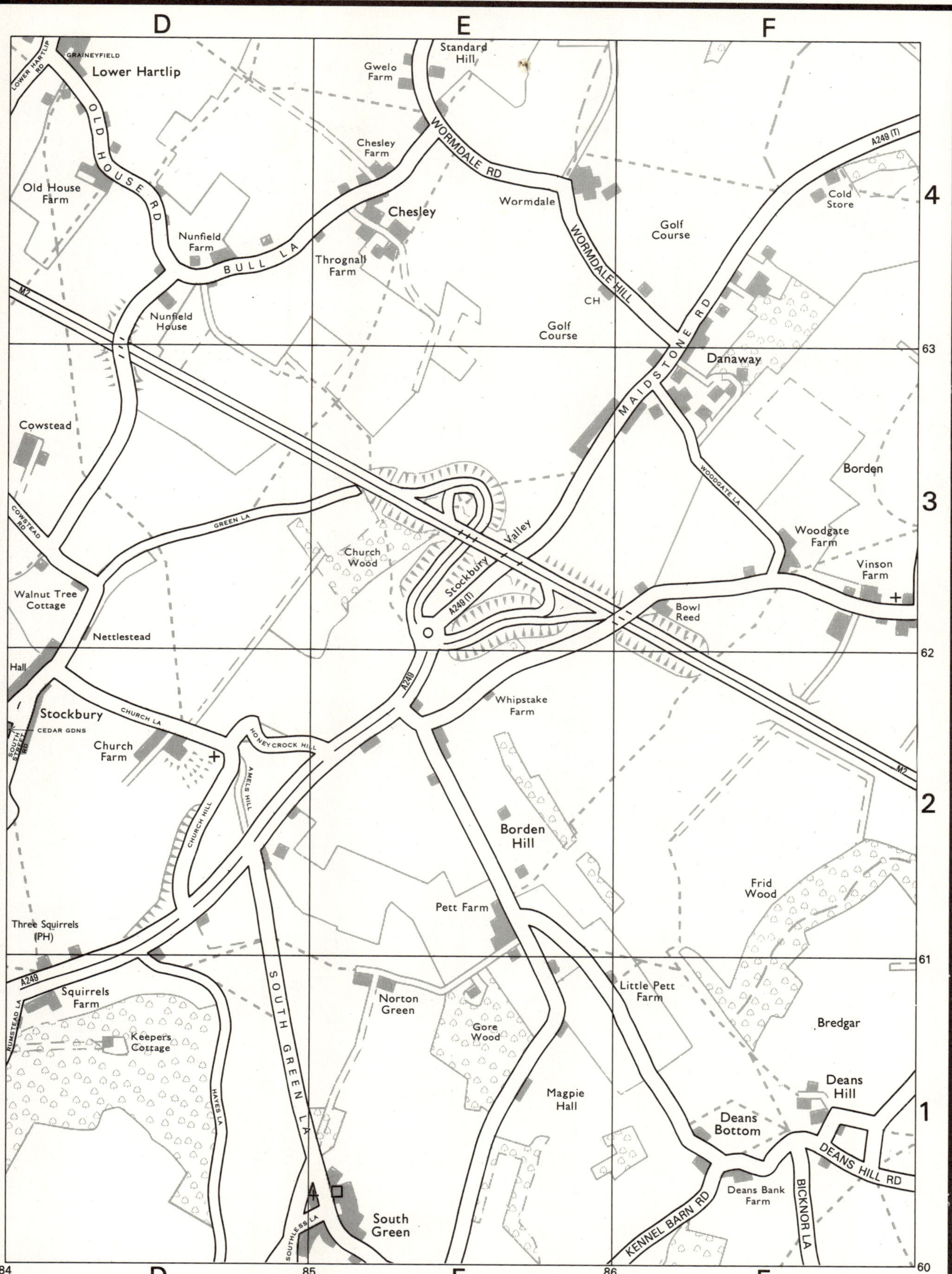

not continued, see key diagram

92

63
not continued, see key diagram

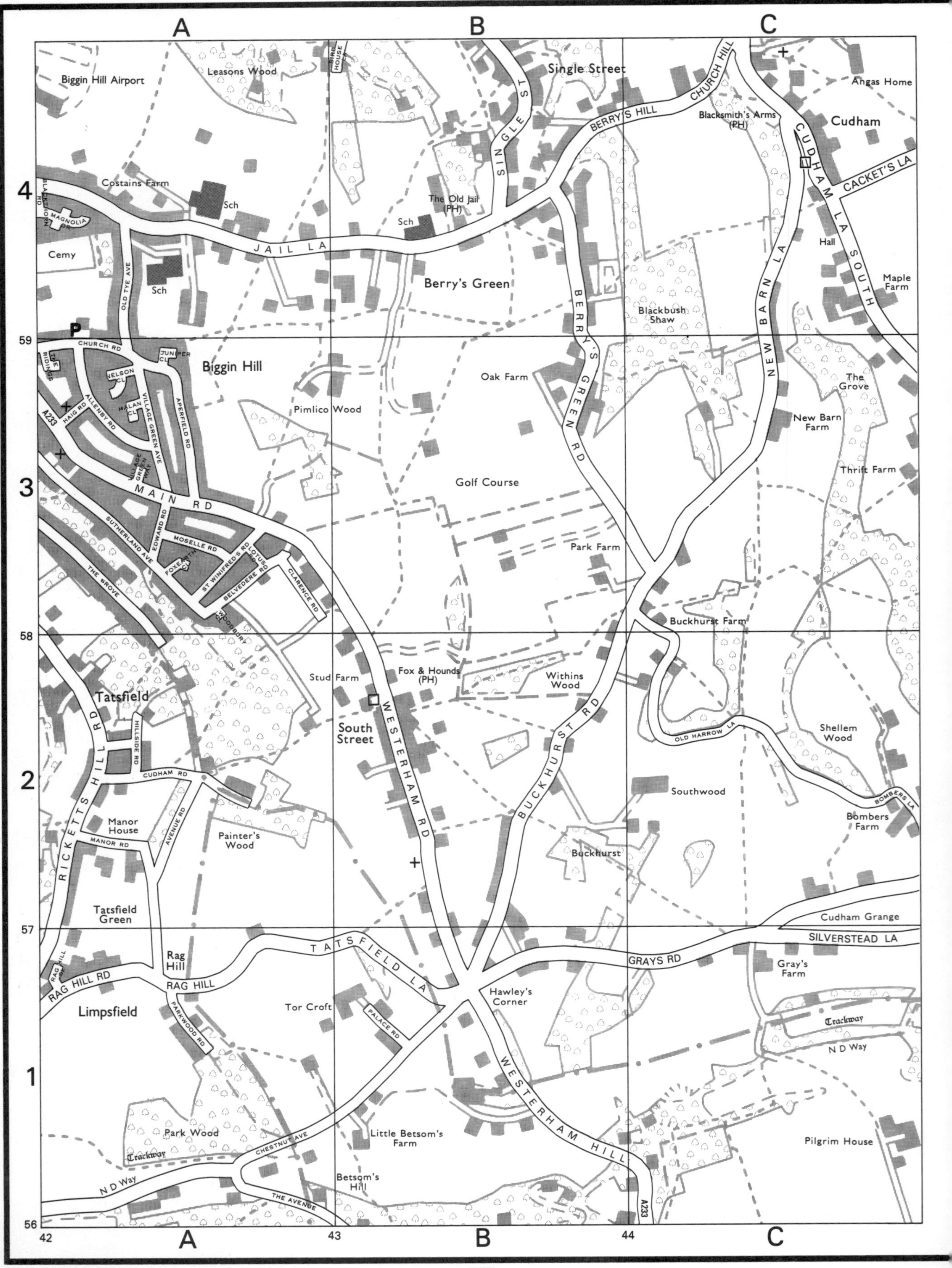

95

64

D
E
F
Single's Cross
RANDLES LA
SINGLE'S CROSS LA
POUND LA
Birches Croft
Cacket's Farm
Jockey's Wood
Blueberry Farm
Nurseries
BOND
CACKET'S LA
NEW YEARS LA
BLUEBERRY LA
ELMTREE COTTS
P
4
Lett's Green
Shelleys
Chine Farm
Broom Wood
SHELLEYS LA
Mitchell House
59
North Downs Way
Burlings
Baston Wood
Knockholt
Sch
N D Way
The Crown (Inn)
Lord Chatham's Ride
Ash Platt
BURLINGS LA
MAIN RD
SUNDRIDGE LA
Horns Green
WT Sta
3
Sand Banks
CUDHAM LA S
Portlands
Tally-Ho (PH)
The Mount
BRASTED LA
Trackway
Sundridge Hill Farm
Park Wood
58
STONEINGS LA
Roughfields Wood
SUNDRIDGE HILL
Hagbush Wood
North Downs Way
Cudham Frith
Scott's Lodge
Stoneings
Shootfield
THE NOWER
Home Farm
2
GRAYS RD
VIEWLANDS AVE
Brasted Hill Farm
Shootfield Wood
BOMBERS LA
BRASTED HILL
Joeland's Wood
OVENDEN RD
SILVERSTEAD LA
57
HOGTROUGH HILL
Oveny Green Farm
N D Way
Pilgrims' Way
BRASTED HILL RD
Combe Bank Farm
Chalk Pit
Hogtrough Hill
1
Court Lodge Farm
M25
Combe Wood
M25
56
45
D
46
E
47
F

80

96

65

79

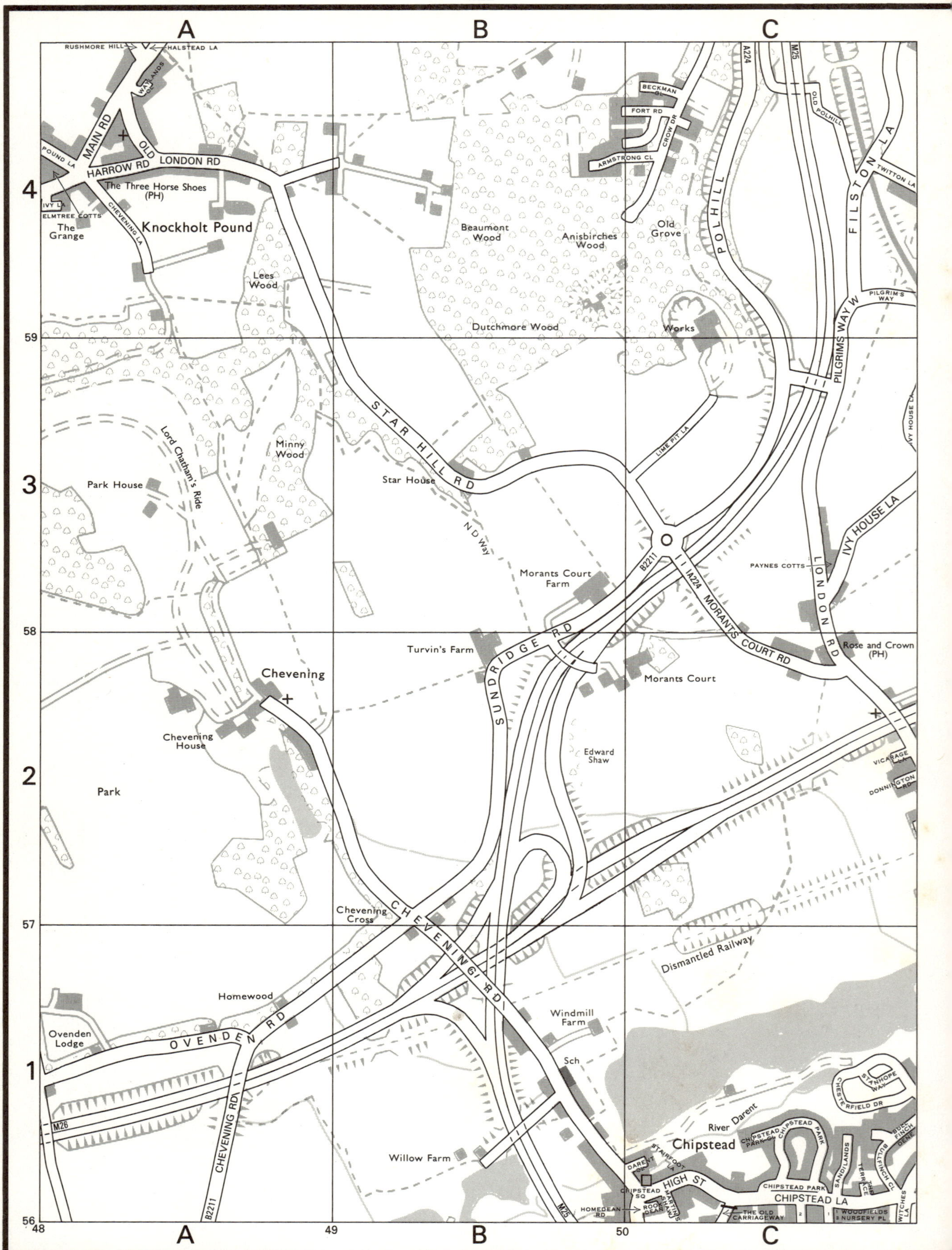
A
B
C
RUSHMORE HILL
HALSTEAD LA
WAYLANDS CL
MAIN RD
OLD LONDON RD
HARROW RD
POUND LA
IVY LA
ELMTREE COTTS
The Three Horse Shoes (PH)
CHEVENING LA
The Grange
Knockholt Pound
Lees Wood
BECKMAN CL
FORT RD
CROW DR
ARMSTRONG CL
A224
M25
OLD POLHILL
FILSTON LA
TWITTON LA
POLHILL
Beaumont Wood
Anisbirches Wood
Old Grove
PILGRIMS WAY
PILGRIMS WAY W
Dutchmore Wood
Works
4
59
STAR HILL RD
LIME PIT LA
IVY HOUSE LA
Lord Chatham's Ride
Minny Wood
Park House
Star House
3
N D Way
B2211
A224
Morants Court Farm
PAYNES COTTS
LONDON RD
MORANTS COURT RD
58
Turvin's Farm
SUNDRIDGE RD
Rose and Crown (PH)
Chevening
Morants Court
Chevening House
Edward Shaw
VICARAGE LA
DONNINGTON RD
2
Park
Chevening Cross
CHEVENING RD
57
Dismantled Railway
Homewood
Windmill Farm
Ovenden Lodge
OVENDEN RD
1
Sch
STANHOPE WAY
CHESTERFIELD DR
M26
River Darent
CHEVENING RD
Chipstead
CHIPSTEAD PARK CL
CHIPSTEAD PARK
BULLFINCH DENE
BULLFINCH CL
SANDLANDS
TERRACE
Willow Farm
DARENT CL
STAIRFOOT LA
HIGH ST
B2211
CHIPSTEAD SQ
ROOKDEAN
MARTINS SHAW
M25
HOMEDEAN RD
THE OLD CARRIAGEWAY
CHIPSTEAD LA
1 WOODFIELDS
2 NURSERY PL
WITCHES LA
56
48
49
50
A
B
C

97

66

D
E
F
Lower Barn
GREENHILL RD
SHOREHAM RD
A225
HILLYDEAL RD
Hillydeal Wood
Otford Mount
Tumulus
North Downs Way
COOMBE RD
Twitton Brook
TWITTON LA
The Rising Sun (PH)
WICKHAM FIELD
Park Farm
Liby
P
LEONARD AVE
HIGH ST
STATION RD
Otford Station
PILGRIM'S WAY E
ROWDOW
ST MICHAELS DR
PILGRIMS WAY W
PILGRIMS WAY
PICKMOSS LA
Sch
WARHAM RD
COLETS ORCHARD
Palace (rems of)
TUDOR DR
TUDOR CRES
IVY HOUSE LA
ORCHARD RD
KNIGHTON RD
HALE LA
DANE RD
DARNETS FIELD
WILLOW PARK
RYECROFT RD
BROUGHTON RD
THE CHARNE
Otford
SEVENOAKS RD
BUBBLESTONE RD
THE BUTTS
THE OLD WLK
SIDNEY GDNS
WELL RD
EVELYN RD
New Barn Farm
TELSTON LA
FLOWERFIELD
Homestead Farm
DYNES RD
NORMAN RD
NIGHTINGALE RD
Oxenhill Shaw
N D Way
M26
RYE LA
Broughton House
Ladds House
OLD OTFORD RD
Rye House Farm
River Darent
Bartram Farm
Rye Cottage
WICKENS MEADOW
VESTRY RD
OTFORD RD
Dunton Green Station
Sch
Dunton Green
Rye Wood
Amb Sta
BARRETTS RD
LENNARD RD
LUSTED RD
LONDON RD
HILLFIELD RD
Longford
CRESCENT RD
STATION RD
Wks
THE MOOR RD
SWANZY RD
CRAMPTON'S RD
WATERCRESS CL
WATERCRESS DR
ORCHARD CL
FARM RD
QUEEN'S DR
COOMBE AVE
BERWICK WAY
ANTHONY CL
KINGSWOOD
MILL RD
MILTON RD
POUNSLEY RD
SEVENOAKS BUSINESS CENTRE
Bat and Ball Station
GREATNESS LA
WEAVERS LA
MILL LA
Greatness
Cemy
Longford Bridges
DARENTH
CHATHAM HILL RD
GREATNESS RD
CROVE
A25
SEAL RD
NORTH VIEW RD
PINEWOOD AVE
Works
HOSPITAL RD
Hospl
Liby
THE CRESCENT
B2019
HAMLIN RD
Bradbourne Farm
Sch
WEALDEN PL
HILLINGDON AVE
CHESTERFIELD DR
BADEN POWELL RD
BULLFINCH CNR
THE PATCH
HEATHFIELD RD
HAWTHORN CL
BRADBOURNE VALE RD
SACKVILLE CL
St John's
ST JAMES'S RD
ST JOHN'S RD
GOLDING RD
LITTLE WOOD
GARDEN RD
THE GREEN
HILLINGDON RISE
BULLFINCH LA
ELMSTEAD CL
SCOTTS WAY
DEN
ORCHARD RD
A25
MAIDSTONE RD
BROOMFIELD RD
ROBYNS WAY
ST GEORGE'S RD
ST JOHN'S HILL
SWAFFIELD RD
WICKENDEN RD
WEST FIELD
NICOLSON WAY
WILDERNESSE MOUNT
SEAL HOLLOW RD
Riverhead
HOMEFIELD RD
BETENSON AVE
CAVENDISH AVE
HARRISON WAY
BRADBOURNE PARK RD
BRADBOURNE RD
CAMDEN RD
NURSERY PL
CHIPSTEAD LA
THE SQUARE
WORSHIPS HILL
AMHERST HILL
CHURCH RD
Sch
A224
SHOREHAM LA
PONTOISE CL
MEADWAY
LAKE VIEW RD
LAMBARDE RD
HILL CREST
OAKDENE RD
CHANCELLOR WAY
Schs
AMHERST RD
A225
PROSPECT RD
KENNEDY GDNS
HILLBOROUGH AVE
BARNFIELD RD
WESTWOOD WAY
CLOCK HOUSE LA
LINDEN CHASE
Sch
QUAKER'S HALL LA
4
3
2
1
59
58
57
56
51
52
53

82

98

67

81

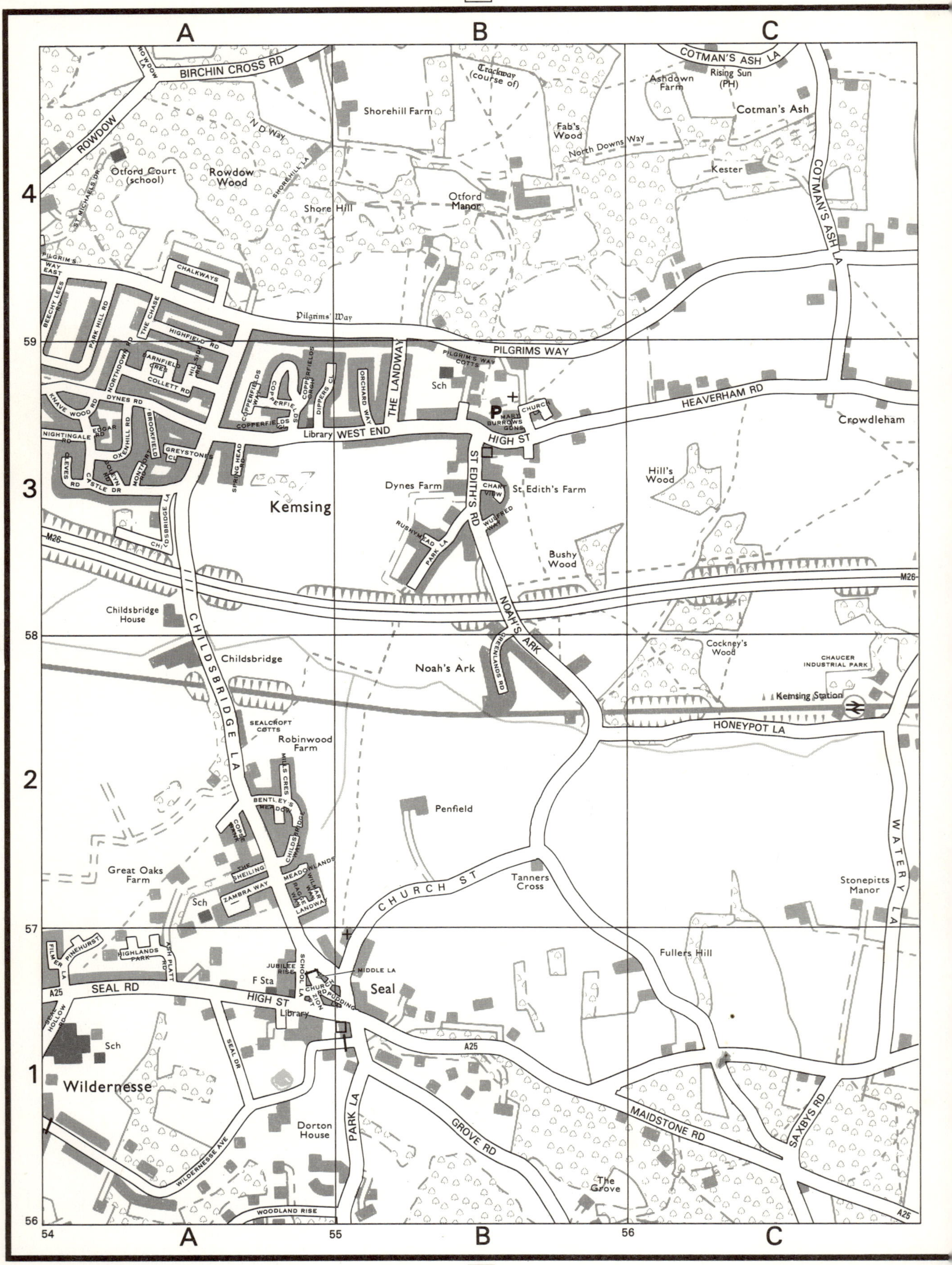
A
B
C
4
3
2
1
59
58
57
56
54
55
56
BIRCHIN CROSS RD
ROWDOW
Otford Court
(school)
Rowdow
Wood
N D Way
SHOREHILL LA
Shorehill Farm
Shore Hill
Trackway
(course of)
Fab's
Wood
North Downs Way
Otford
Manor
COTMAN'S ASH LA
Ashdown
Farm
Rising Sun
(PH)
Cotman's Ash
Kester
ST MICHAELS DR
PILGRIMS WAY EAST
CHALKWAYS
BEECHY LEES RD
PARK HILL RD
THE CHASE
HIGHFIELD RD
NORTHDOWN RD
BARNFIELD CRES
COLLETT RD
DYNES RD
KNAVE WOOD RD
EDGAR RD
NIGHTINGALE RD
OXENHILL RD
BROOKFIELD
GREYSTONES CL
CLEVES RD
CASTLE DR
MONTFORT RD
SPRING HEAD RD
CHILDSBRIDGE LA
Pilgrims' Way
PILGRIMS WAY
COPPERFIELDS WALK
COPPERFIELDS
COPPERFIELDS ORCH
DIPPERS CL
ORCHARD WAY
THE LANDWAY
COPPERFIELDS
Library
WEST END
PILGRIMS WAY COTTS
Sch
P
CHURCH
MARY BURROWS GDNS
HIGH ST
HEAVERHAM RD
Crowdleham
ST EDITH'S RD
Dynes Farm
St Edith's Farm
CHART VIEW
WULFRED WAY
Kemsing
RUSHYMEAD
PARK LA
Hill's
Wood
Bushy
Wood
M26
Childsbridge
House
CHILDSBRIDGE LA
NOAH'S ARK
GREENLANDS RD
Childsbridge
Noah's Ark
Cockney's
Wood
CHAUCER
INDUSTRIAL PARK
Kemsing Station
HONEYPOT LA
SEALCROFT
COTTS
Robinwood
Farm
MILLS CRES
BENTLEY'S MEADOW
COPSE BANK
CHILDSBRIDGE WAY
Penfield
Great Oaks
Farm
THE SHEILING
MEADOWLANDS
ZAMBRA WAY
WILMAR WAY
LANDWAY
Sch
CHURCH ST
Tanners
Cross
WATERY LA
Stonepitts
Manor
FILMER LA
PINEHURST
HIGHLANDS PARK
ASH PLATT RD
JUBILEE RISE
SCHOOL LA
MIDDLE LA
F Sta
Seal
A25
SEAL RD
HIGH ST
Library
Fullers Hill
Sch
SEAL DR
A25
Wildernesse
PARK LA
Dorton
House
GROVE RD
MAIDSTONE RD
SAXBYS RD
WILDERNESSE AVE
WOODLAND RISE
The
Grove
A25
A
B
C

99

68

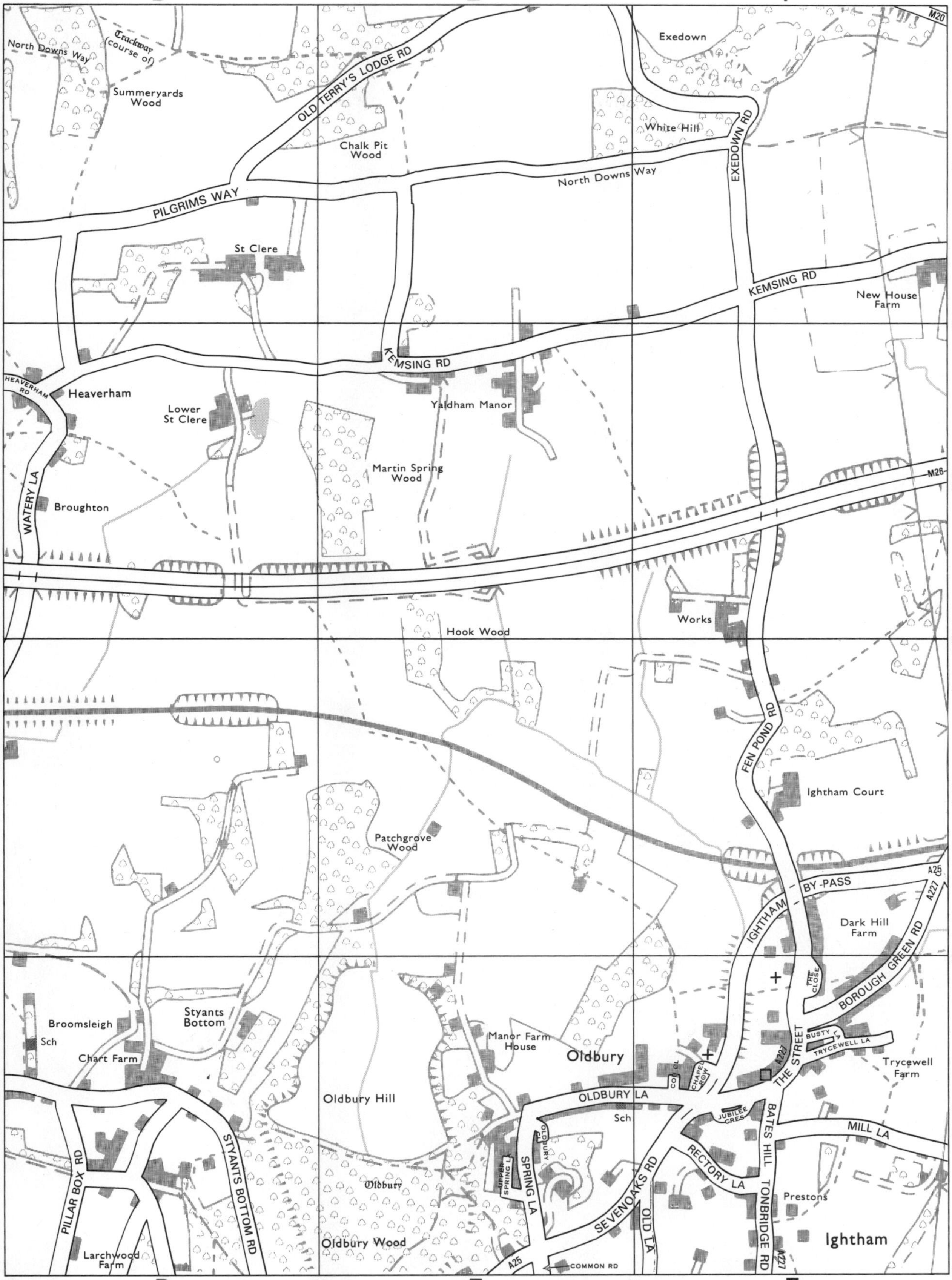
D
E
F
North Downs Way
Trackway (course of)
Summeryards Wood
OLD TERRY'S LODGE RD
Chalk Pit Wood
Exedown
White Hill
EXEDOWN RD
M20
PILGRIMS WAY
North Downs Way
St Clere
KEMSING RD
New House Farm
KEMSING RD
HEAVERHAM RD
Heaverham
Lower St Clere
Yaldham Manor
Martin Spring Wood
WATERY LA
Broughton
M26
Works
Hook Wood
FEN POND RD
Ightham Court
Patchgrove Wood
IGHTHAM BY-PASS
A25
A227
Dark Hill Farm
THE CLOSE
BOROUGH GREEN RD
Broomsleigh
Sch
Styants Bottom
Chart Farm
Manor Farm House
Oldbury
COB CL
CHAPEL ROW
A227
THE STREET
BUSTY LA
TRYCEWELL LA
Trycewell Farm
OLDBURY LA
JUBILEE CRES
Oldbury Hill
Sch
BATES HILL
MILL LA
PILLAR BOX RD
STYANTS BOTTOM RD
UPPER SPRING LA
SPRING LA
OLDBURY
Oldbury
RECTORY LA
SEVENOAKS RD
OLD LA
TONBRIDGE RD
A227
Prestons
Ightham
Larchwood Farm
Oldbury Wood
A25
COMMON RD
4
3
2
1
59
58
57
56
57
58
59
D
E
F

84

100

69

83

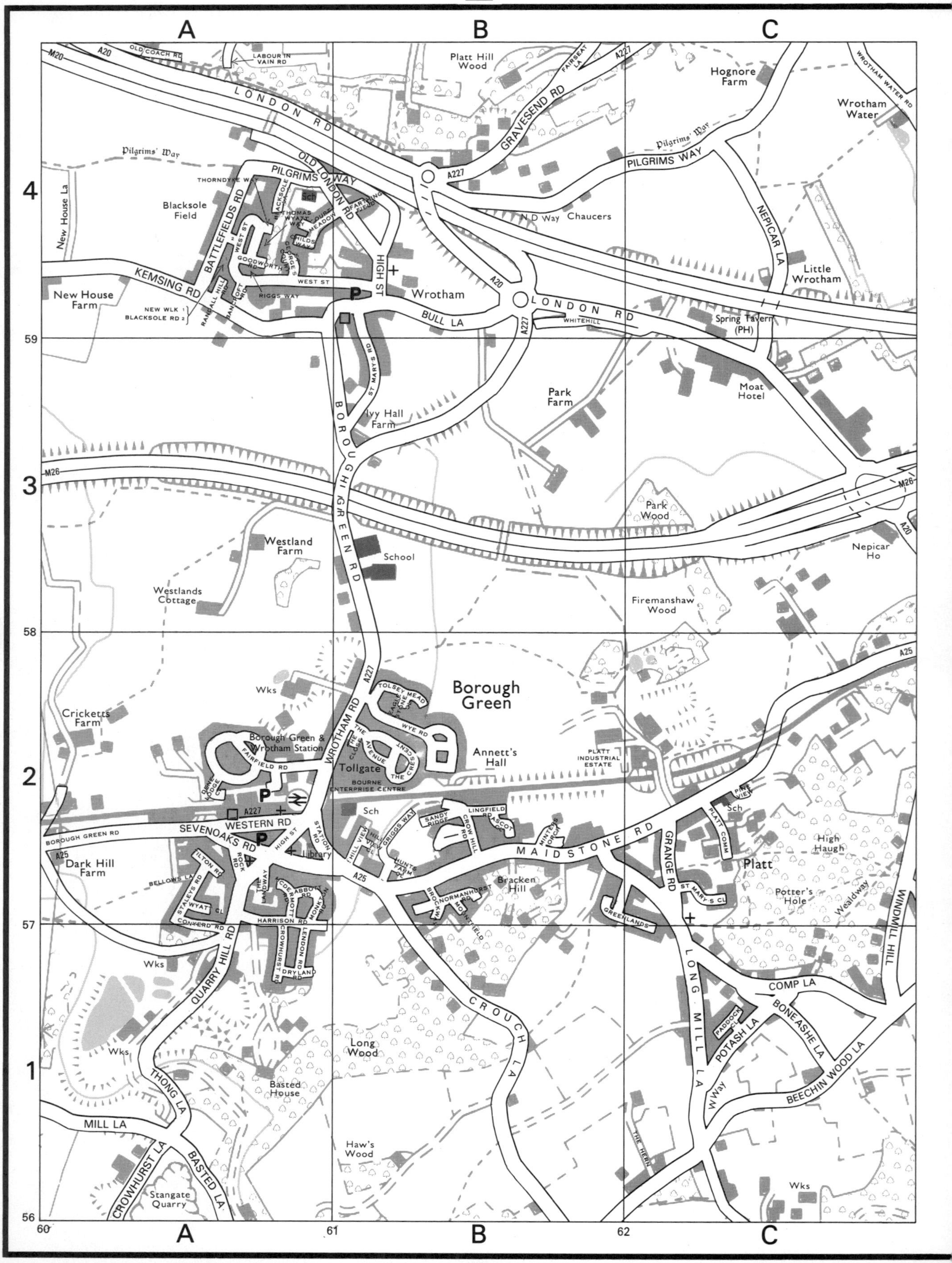
A
B
C
4
3
2
1
59
58
57
56
60
61
62
M20
A20
OLD COACH RD
LABOUR IN VAIN RD
Platt Hill Wood
FAIRSEAT LA
A227
Hognore Farm
WROTHAM WATER RD
Wrotham Water
LONDON RD
GRAVESEND RD
Pilgrims' Way
PILGRIMS WAY
OLD LONDON RD
PILGRIMS WAY
THORNDYKE WAY
Blacksole Field
BATTLEFIELDS RD
BLACKSOLE RD
Sch
THOMAS WYATT WAY
MEADOW
FARTHING FIELD
CHILDS WAY
GEORGES
WEST ST
GOODWORTH RD
New House La
KEMSING RD
New House Farm
RANDALL HILL RD
BANCROFT
RIGGS WAY
NEW WLK
BLACKSOLE RD
HIGH ST
Wrotham
N D Way
Chaucers
NEPICAR LA
Little Wrotham
A20
LONDON RD
WHITEHILL
BULL LA
A227
Spring Tavern (PH)
ST MARY'S RD
Moat Hotel
Park Farm
Ivy Hall Farm
BOROUGH GREEN RD
M26
Park Wood
Nepicar Ho
Westland Farm
School
Westlands Cottage
Firemanshaw Wood
Wks
Borough Green
TOLSEY MEAD
EAGLE STONE
WYE RD
Cricketts Farm
Borough Green & Wrotham Station
WROTHAM RD
THE CLOSE
THE AVENUE
THE CRESCENT
Annett's Hall
PLATT INDUSTRIAL ESTATE
FAIRFIELD RD
Tollgate
BOURNE ENTERPRISE CENTRE
DENE LODGE
A227
WESTERN RD
Sch
PINE VIEW
SANDY RIDGE
LINGFIELD RD
ASCOT
CROW HILL
MINTERS ORCH
PLATT COMM
GRANGE RD
Sch
SEVENOAKS RD
BOROUGH GREEN RD
ROCK RD
HIGH ST
STATION RD
HILL VIEW
HILLVIEW CL
GRIGGS WAY
Library
HUNTS FARM CL
MAIDSTONE RD
High Haugh
A25
Dark Hill Farm
HILTON RD
BELLOWS LA
A25
BRACKWOOD
NORMANHURST RD
Bracken Hill
Platt
ST MARY'S CL
Potter's Hole
Wealdway
WINDMILL HILL
STALEYS RD
WYATT CL
THE LANDWAY
COERMOTT RD
ABBOTT RD
MONKTON RD
MONTFIELD
GREENLANDS
CONYERD RD
HARRISON RD
CROWHURST RD
LONDON RD
DRYLAND RD
Wks
QUARRY HILL RD
CROUCH LA
LONG MILL LA
COMP LA
PADDOCK CL
BONEASHE LA
POTASH LA
Long Wood
Wks
BEECHIN WOOD LA
THONG LA
Basted House
W Way
MILL LA
THE HERN
Haw's Wood
CROWHURST LA
BASTED LA
Stangate Quarry
Wks

101

70

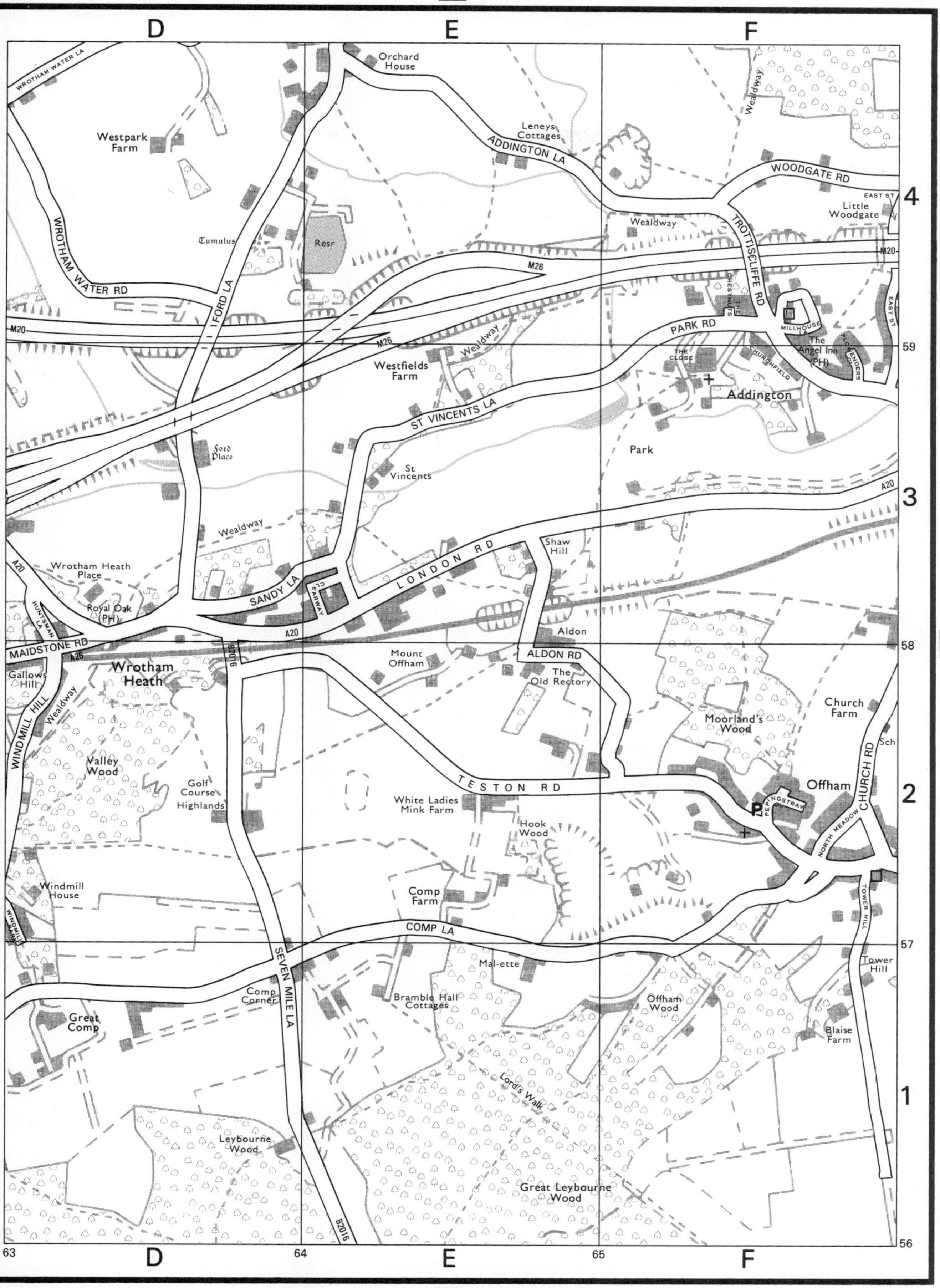

D
E
F
WROTHAM WATER LA
Westpark Farm
Orchard House
Leneys Cottages
ADDINGTON LA
Wealdway
WOODGATE RD
EAST ST
Little Woodgate
4
WROTHAM WATER RD
Tumulus
Resr
FORD LA
M26
M20
TROTTISCLIFFE RD
THE CHESTNUTS
MILLHOUSE LA
EAST ST
PARK RD
The Angel Inn (PH)
PLOVENDERS
THE CLOSE
CHURCHFIELD
Westfields Farm
Addington
59
ST VINCENTS LA
Ford Place
St Vincents
Park
A20
3
Wrotham Heath Place
Royal Oak (PH)
SANDY LA
CLEARWAY
LONDON RD
Shaw Hill
HUNTSMAN LA
Aldon
MAIDSTONE RD
A25
B2016
ALDON RD
58
Mount Offham
The Old Rectory
Gallows Hill
Wrotham Heath
WINDMILL HILL
Valley Wood
Church Farm
Moorland's Wood
Sch
Golf Course
Highlands
TESTON RD
Offham
2
White Ladies Mink Farm
PEPINGSTRAW CL
CHURCH RD
NORTH MEADOW
Hook Wood
Windmill House
Comp Farm
TOWER HILL
WINDMILL BANK
COMP LA
57
SEVEN MILE LA
Mal-ette
Tower Hill
Comp Corner
Bramble Hall Cottages
Offham Wood
Great Comp
Blaise Farm
Lord's Walk
1
Leybourne Wood
Great Leybourne Wood
56
63
64
65

86

102

71

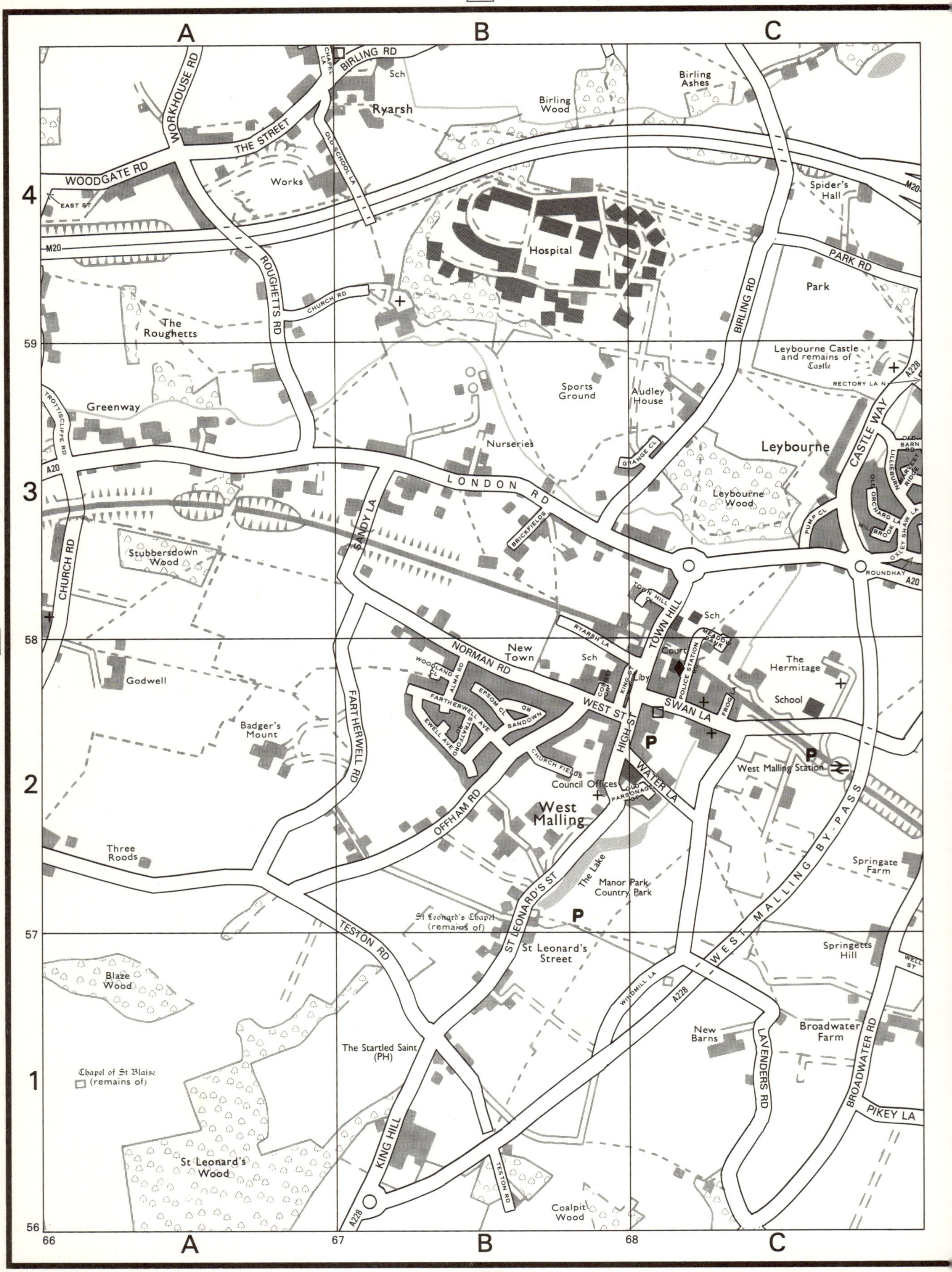
A
B
C
4
3
2
1
59
58
57
56
66
67
68
Birling Rd
Chapel La
Sch
Ryarsh
Birling Wood
Birling Ashes
Workhouse Rd
The Street
Woodgate Rd
East St
Works
Old School La
M20
Hospital
Spider's Hall
Park Rd
Park
Roughetts Rd
Church Rd
The Roughetts
Leybourne Castle and remains of Castle
Rectory La N
A228
Castle Way
Trottiscliffe Rd
Greenway
Sports Ground
Audley House
Nurseries
Grange Cl
Leybourne
A20
London Rd
Sandy La
Brickfields
Leybourne Wood
Pump Cl
Orchard La
Millbrook
Oxley Shaw La
Lillieburn
Old Barn Rd
Roundhay
Stubbersdown Wood
Church Rd
Town Hill Cl
Town Hill
Sch
Meadow Bank
Ryarsh La
New Town
Norman Rd
Court
Police Station
Godwell
Woodland Cl
Alma Rd
Sch
Court
Liby
King St
The Hermitage
School
Fartherwell Ave
Epsom Cl
Sandown Rd
West St
Swan La
Frog La
Badger's Mount
Ewell Ave
Stratford
High St
Church Fields
Water La
P
P
West Malling Station
Fartherwell Rd
Offham Rd
Council Offices
Old Parsonage
West Malling
Three Roods
The Lake
Manor Park Country Park
Springate Farm
St Leonard's St
St Leonard's Chapel (remains of)
P
Teston Rd
St Leonard's Street
West Malling By-Pass
Springetts Hill
Well St
Blaze Wood
Windmill La
A228
New Barns
Lavenders Rd
Broadwater Farm
Broadwater Rd
The Startled Saint (PH)
Chapel of St Blaise (remains of)
Pikey La
King Hill
St Leonard's Wood
Teston Rd
Coalpit Wood
A228

85

103

72

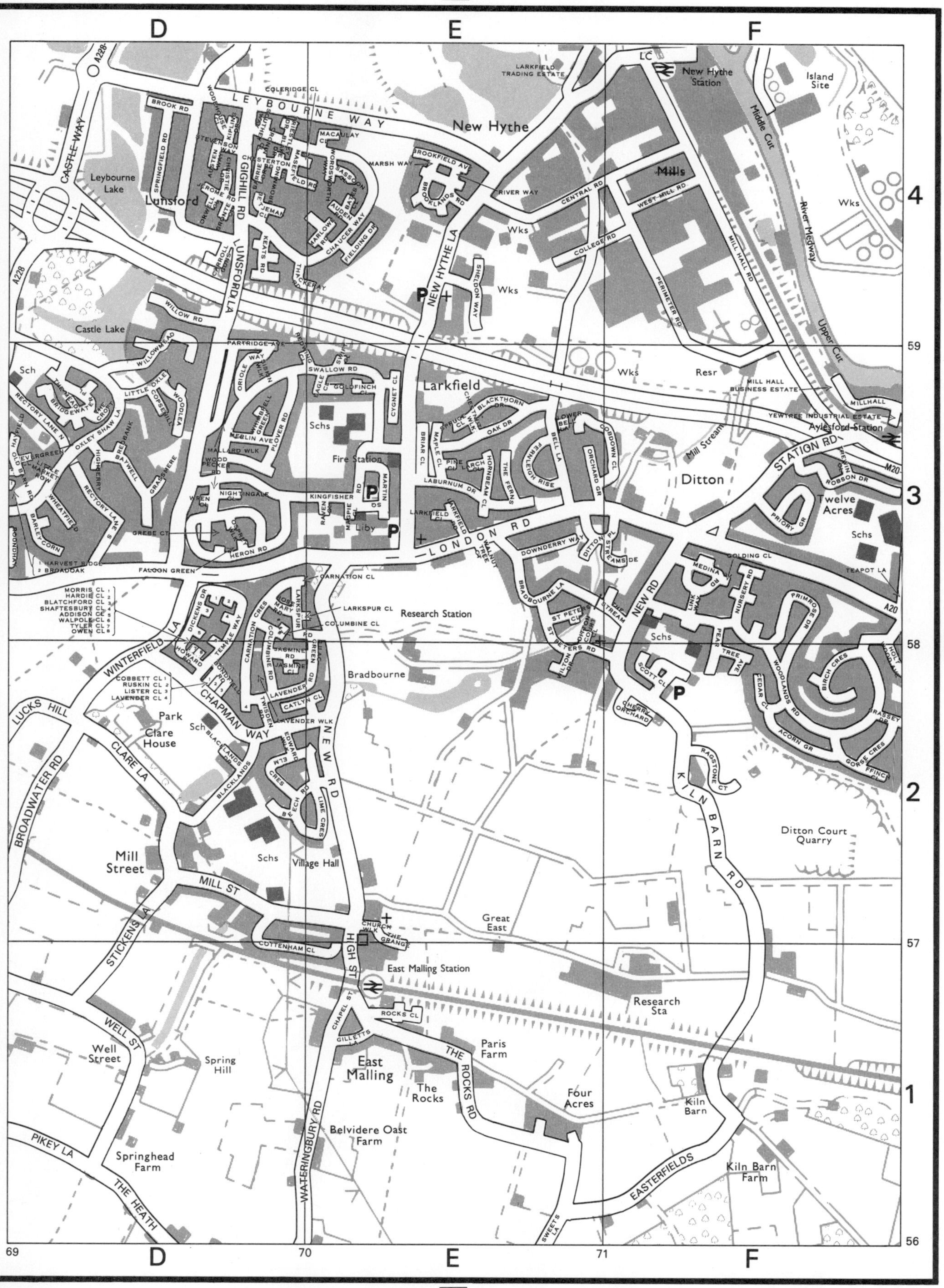
D
E
F
4
3
2
1
59
58
57
56
69
70
71
Leybourne Way
New Hythe
New Hythe Station
Larkfield Trading Estate
Island Site
Middle Cut
River Medway
Upper Cut
Mills
Wks
Leybourne Lake
Lunsford
Castle Way
Castle Lake
Lunsford La
Gighill Rd
Springfield Rd
Brook Rd
Coleridge Cl
Macaulay Cl
Wordsworth
Marsh Way
Brookfield Ave
Brooklands Rd
River Way
Central Rd
West Mill Rd
College Rd
Mill Hall Rd
Perimeter Rd
New Hythe La
Sheldon Way
Keats Rd
Chaucer Way
Fielding Dr
Thackeray
Willow Rd
Partridge Ave
Swallow Rd
Goldfinch Cl
Cygnet Cl
Larkfield
Resr
Mill Hall Business Estate
Millhall
Yewtree Industrial Estate
Aylesford Station
Station Rd
M20
Robson Dr
Twelve Acres
Schs
Sch
Fire Station
Kingfisher
Martin
Liby
London Rd
Oak Dr
Blackthorn Dr
Laburnum Dr
Hornbeam Cl
The Ferns
Fernleigh Rise
Bell La
Orchard Gr
Cobdown Cl
Mill Stream
Ditton
Priory Gr
Golding Cl
Teapot La
A20
Downderry Way
Ditton Pl
Streamside
Bradbourne La
New Rd
Medina
Nursery Rd
Primrose Dr
Link Way
Pear Tree Ave
Woodlands Rd
Cedar Cl
Birch Cres
Brassey Dr
Acorn Gr
Gorse Cres
Finch Cl
Scott Cl
Cherry Orchard
Ragstone Ct
Kiln Barn Rd
Ditton Court Quarry
Research Station
Carnation Cl
Larkspur Cl
Columbine Cl
Bradbourne
Falcon Green
Heron Rd
Grebe Ct
Nightingale Cl
Mallard Wlk
Merlin Ave
Plover Rd
Oxley Shaw La
Rectory Lane N
Rectory Lane S
Highberry
Wheatfield
Barleycorn
Little Oxle
Woodlea
Willowmead
1 Harvest Ridge
2 Broadoak
Morris Cl 1
Hardie Cl 2
Blatchford Cl 3
Shaftesbury Cl 4
Addison Cl 5
Walpole Cl 6
Tyler Cl 7
Owen Cl 8
Cobbett Cl 1
Ruskin Cl 2
Lister Cl 3
Lavender Cl 4
Winterfield La
Dickens Dr
Temple Way
Howard
Carnation Cres
Columbine Rd
Jasmine Rd
Lavender Rd
Catlyn Cl
Lavender Wlk
Chapman Way
Blacklands
Park
Clare House
Lucks Hill
Clare La
Broadwater Rd
Elm Cres
Beech Rd
Lime Cres
New Rd
Village Hall
Mill Street
Mill St
Stickens La
Cottenham Cl
High St
Church Wlk
The Grange
Great East
East Malling Station
Research Sta
Rocks Cl
Chapel St
Gilletts La
East Malling
The Rocks Rd
Paris Farm
The Rocks
Four Acres
Kiln Barn
Well St
Well Street
Spring Hill
Wateringbury Rd
Belvidere Oast Farm
Springhead Farm
Pikey La
The Heath
Easterfields
Sweets La
Kiln Barn Farm

88

104

73

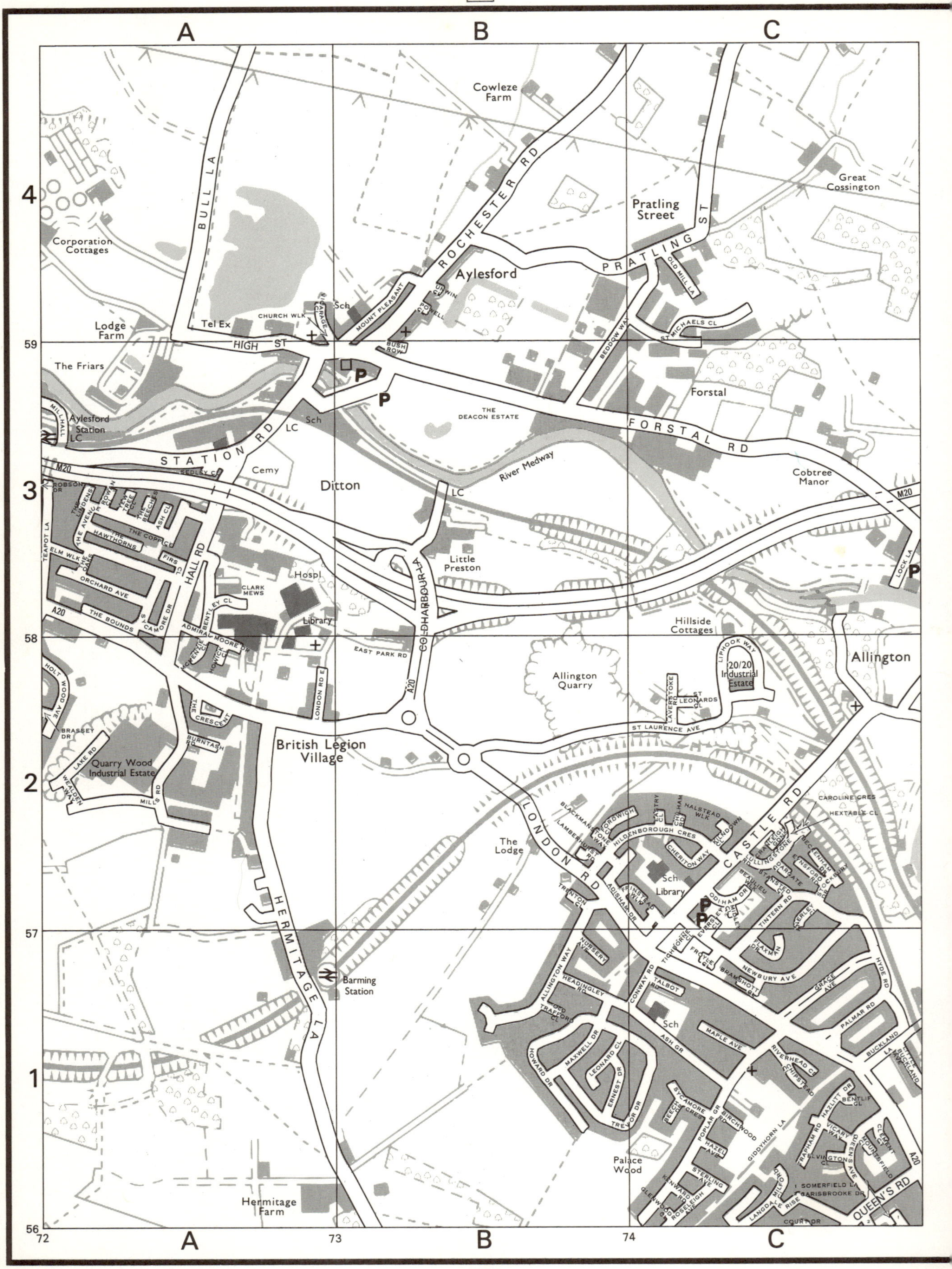
A
B
C
4
3
2
1
59
58
57
56
72
73
74
Cowleze Farm
Great Cossington
Pratling Street
PRATLING ST
BULL LA
ROCHESTER RD
Corporation Cottages
Aylesford
Lodge Farm
Tel Ex
CHURCH WLK
Sch
MOUNT PLEASANT
HIGH ST
BUSH ROW
ST MICHAELS CL
OLD MILL LA
BEDDOW WAY
The Friars
Aylesford Station
LC
MILL HALL
STATION RD
THE DEACON ESTATE
Forstal
FORSTAL RD
River Medway
Cemy
Ditton
M20
Cobtree Manor
SEDLEY CL
ROBSON DR
THE LINDENS
THE AVENUE
ROWAN
ASH CL
THE COPPICE
THE HAWTHORNS
FIRS CL
HALL RD
TEAPOT LA
ELM WLK
ORCHARD AVE
THE OAKS
Little Preston
Hospl
CLARK MEWS
BENTLEY CL
COLDHARBOUR LA
LOCK LA
P
A20
THE BOUNDS
SYCAMORE DR
ADMIRAL MOORE DR
Library
EAST PARK RD
Hillside Cottages
LIPHOOK WAY
20/20 Industrial Estate
Allington
Allington Quarry
LAVERSTOKE RD
ST LEONARDS CL
ST LAURENCE AVE
HOLTWOOD AVE
BRASSEY DR
THE CRESCENT
BURNTASH RD
LONDON RD E
British Legion Village
Quarry Wood Industrial Estate
LAKE RD
WEALDEN WAY
MILLS RD
LONDON RD
CASTLE RD
BLACKMANSTONE WAY
FORDWICH
EASTRY CL
HALSTEAD WLK
KILNDOWN
LAMBERHURST WAY
HILDENBOROUGH CRES
CHERITON WAY
CAROLINE CRES
HEXTABLE CL
The Lodge
Sch
Library
FRINSTEAD WLK
ADISHAM DR
ODIHAM DR
BEAULIEU
LULLINGSTONE
STANSTED
DARGATE
EYNSFORD
BECKENHAM
TRENTON CL
TINTERN RD
HERMITAGE LA
NURSERY AVE
TICHBORNE CL
EVERSLEY CL
FLAXMAN DR
BRAMSHOTT CL
NEWBURY AVE
HYDE RD
Barming Station
ALLINGTON WAY
HEADINGLEY RD
TALBOT RD
CONWAY RD
GRACE AVE
OLD TRAFFORD CL
PALMAR RD
MAPLE AVE
BUCKLAND LA
ASH GR
RIVERHEAD CL
CHIPSTEAD
HOWARD DR
MAXWELL DR
LEONARD CL
ERNEST DR
TREVOR DR
SYCAMORE CRES
BEECH
POPLAR GR
BIRCHWOOD RD
GIDDYHORN LA
HAZLITT DR
BENTLIF CL
RAPHAM RD
VICARY QUEENS AVE
ELVINGTON CL
HAZEL AVE
STERLING AVE
A20
Palace Wood
SOMERFIELD LA
GARISBROOKE DR
QUEEN'S RD
Hermitage Farm
KENWARD RD
GLENWOOD
ROSELEIGH AVE
MILFORD
LANGDALE RISE
COURT DR

87

105

74

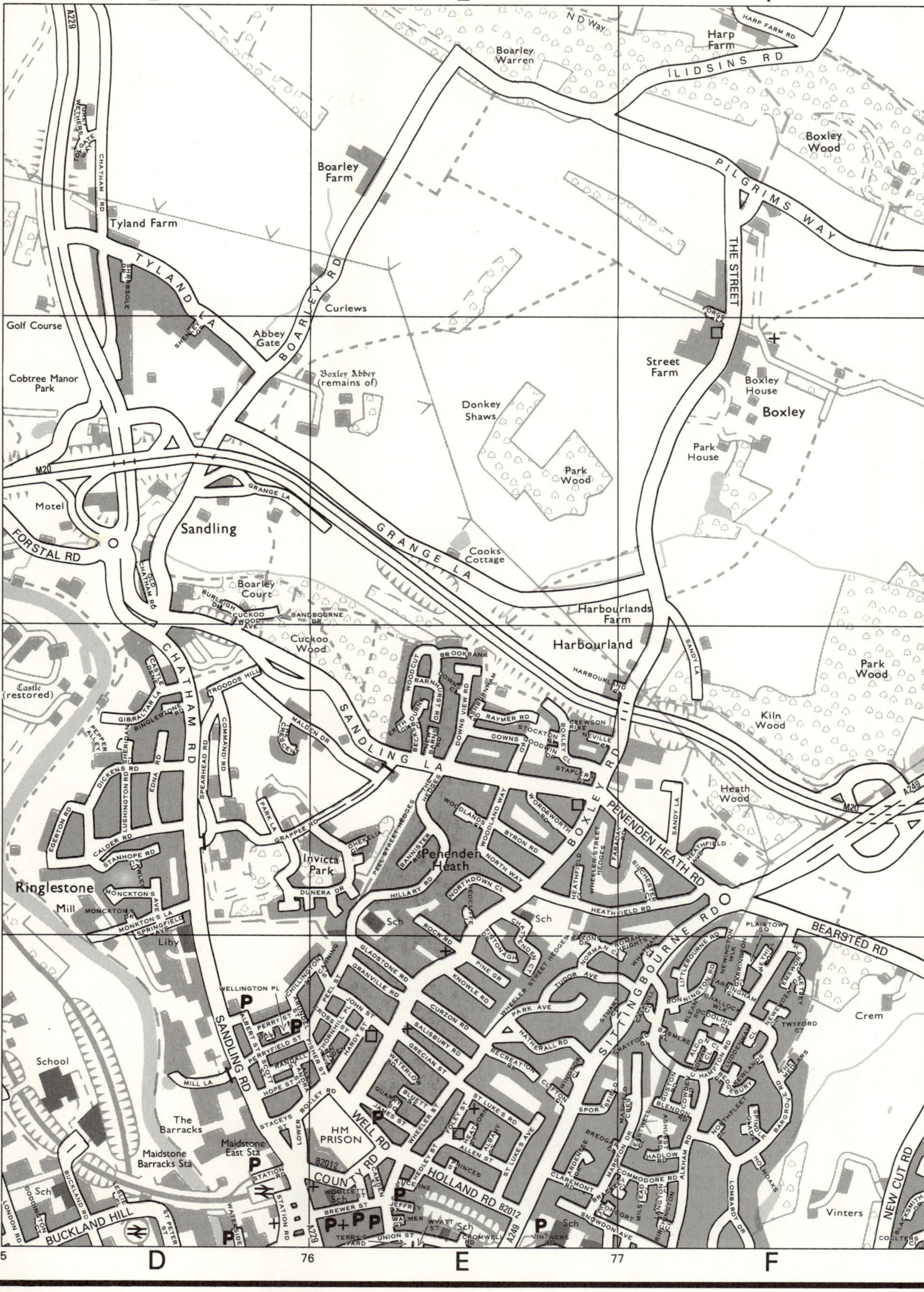
D
E
F
4
3
2
1
59
58
57
56
75
76
77
A229
Harp Farm
HARP FARM RD
ILIDSINS RD
N D Way
Boarley Warren
Boxley Wood
PILGRIMS WAY
Boarley Farm
CHATHAM RD
Tyland Farm
TYLAND LA
BOARLEY RD
Curlews
THE STREET
FORGE LA
Golf Course
Abbey Gate
Boxley Abbey (remains of)
Street Farm
Boxley House
Boxley
Cobtree Manor Park
Donkey Shaws
Park House
M20
Park Wood
Motel
GRANGE LA
Sandling
FORSTAL RD
Cooks Cottage
Boarley Court
OLD CHATHAM RD
BURLEIGH DR
CUCKOO WOOD AVE
SANDBOURNE DR
Harbourlands Farm
Harbourland
HARBOURLAND CL
SANDY LA
Cuckoo Wood
Castle (restored)
TROODOS HILL
BROOKBANK
Park Wood
CASTLE DENE
GIBRALTAR LA
RINGLESTONE RD
COMMANDO RD
MALDEN DR
SANDLING LA
WOODCUT
BARNHURST RD
DOWNS VIEW RD
RAYMER RD
STOCKTON CL
DOWNS CL
GOODWIN DR
BOXLEY RD
NEVILLE CL
STAPLERS CT
Kiln Wood
PEPPER ALLEY
SHERIDAN CL
DICKENS RD
EDNA RD
SPEARHEAD RD
THE CRESCENT
DHEKELIA CL
Heath Wood
A249
LUSHINGTON RD
EGERTON RD
CALDER RD
PARK LA
GRAPPEE RD
PEEL STREET HEDGES
THE HEDGES
WOODLANDS
WOODLAND WAY
WORDSWORTH RD
BYRON RD
NORTH WAY
PENENDEN HEATH RD
HEATHFIELD AVE
HEATHFIELD RD
FARADAY
SILCHESTER CT
Ringlestone
STANHOPE RD
MONCKTON'S AVE
MONCKTON'S LA
MONCKTON'S DR
SPRINGFIELD AVE
Mill
Invicta Park
DUNERA DR
Penenden Heath
BANNISTER RD
HILLARY RD
NORTHDOWN CL
HEDCLIFFE
Sch
BEARSTED RD
PLAISTOW SQ
Liby
ROCK RD
PINE GR
CHATTENDEN CT
WHEELER STREET HEDGES
TUDOR AVE
SITTINGBOURNE RD
LITTLEBOURNE RD
BONNINGTON RD
WELLINGTON PL
GLADSTONE RD
GRANVILLE RD
KNOWLE RD
CURZON RD
PARK AVE
HATHERALL RD
Crem
TWYFORD CT
P
SANDLING RD
ALBERT ST
PERRY ST
PERRYFIELD ST
RANDALL ST
HOPE ST
MILL LA
JOHN ST
HARDY ST
SALISBURY RD
GRECIAN ST
WATERLOO ST
RECREATION CL
CLIFTON CL
BASMERE CL
School
BOXLEY RD
QUARRY ST
BLUETT ST
ST LUKE'S RD
ST LUKE'S AVE
The Barracks
STACEYS ST
HM PRISON
WELL RD
JAMES ST
WHEELER ST
ALBANY ST
ALLEN ST
Maidstone East Sta
Maidstone Barracks Sta
STATION RD
B2012
COUNTY RD
HOLLAND RD
PRINCES ST
CLAREMONT RD
COMMODORE RD
HADLOW RD
ALKHAM RD
LOMBARDY DR
HOLMOAKS
NEW CUT RD
Sch
BUCKLAND RD
BUCKLAND HILL
LONDON RD
ST PETER ST
WATERSIDE
WOOLLETT ST
BREWER ST
JEFFREY ST
UNION ST
WYATT ST
CROMWELL RD
VINTNERS RD
SNOWDON AVE
TERRY'S YARD
Vinters
BLACKSMITH DR
COULTERS CL

90

106

75

89

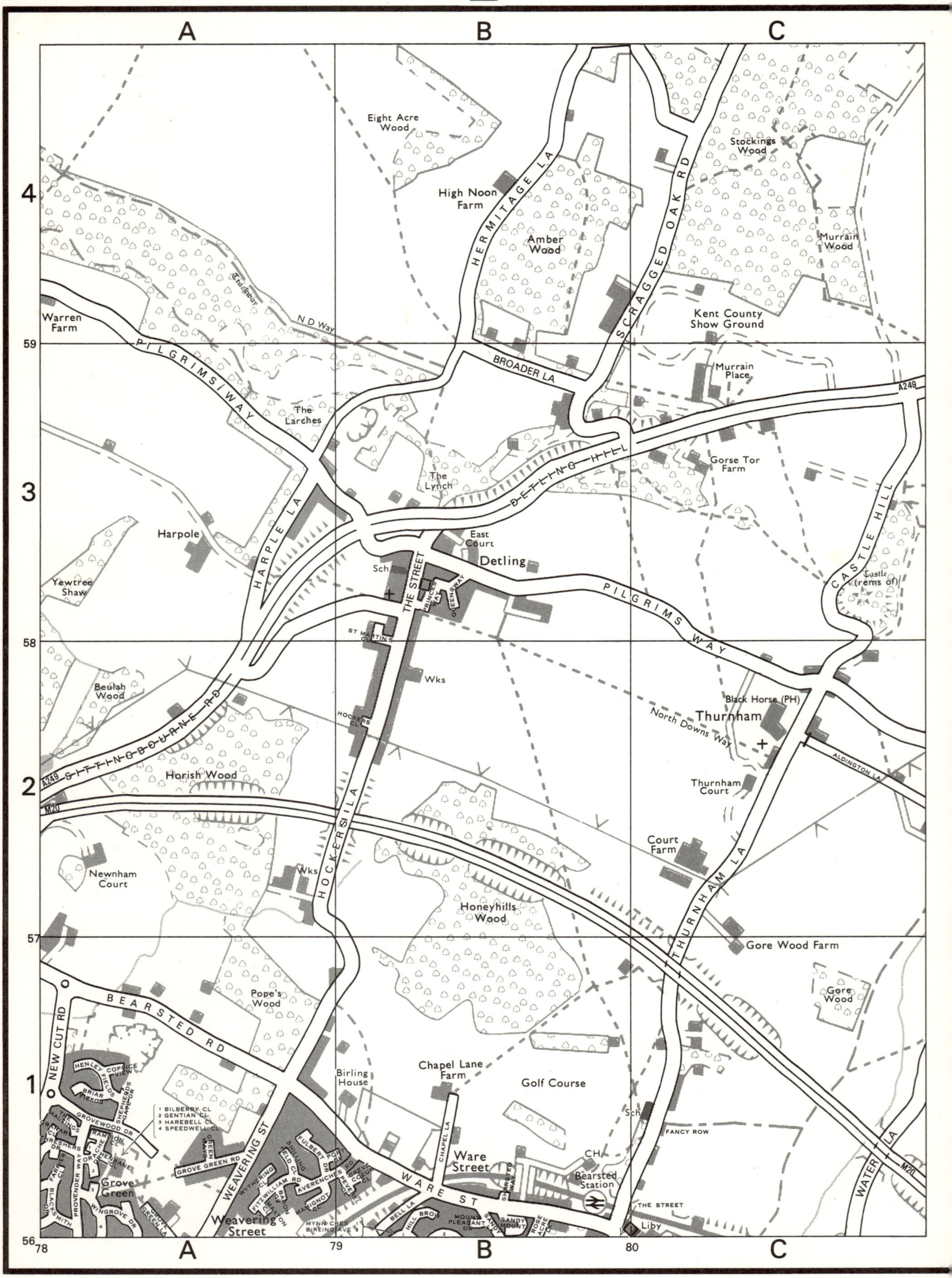

A
B
C
4
3
2
1
59
58
57
56
78
79
80
Eight Acre Wood
High Noon Farm
HERMITAGE LA
Amber Wood
SCRAGGED OAK RD
Stockings Wood
Murrain Wood
Kent County Show Ground
Warren Farm
PILGRIMS WAY
N D Way
BROADER LA
Murrain Place
A249
The Larches
The Lynch
DETLING HILL
Gorse Tor Farm
Harpole
HARPLE LA
East Court
Detling
Sch
THE STREET
PILGRIMS WAY
CASTLE HILL
Castle (rems of)
Yewtree Shaw
ST MARTINS CL
Wks
Beulah Wood
HOCKERS CL
Black Horse (PH)
Thurnham
North Downs Way
SITTINGBOURNE RD
Horish Wood
ALDINGTON LA
Thurnham Court
M20
Court Farm
Newnham Court
Wks
HOCKERS LA
THURNHAM LA
Honeyhills Wood
Gore Wood Farm
Gore Wood
BEARSTED RD
Pope's Wood
NEW CUT RD
Birling House
Chapel Lane Farm
Golf Course
HENLEY FIELDS
COPPICE VIEW
BRIAR FIELDS
SHEPHERDS GATE DR
1 BILBERRY CL
2 GENTIAN CL
3 HAREBELL CL
4 SPEEDWELL CL
GROVEWOOD DR
Sch
FANCY ROW
CHAPEL LA
GROVE GREEN RD
WEAVERING ST
Ware Street
CH
Bearsted Station
WATER LA
Grove Green
WARE ST
THE STREET
Weavering Street
BELL LA
Liby
A
B
C

107

76

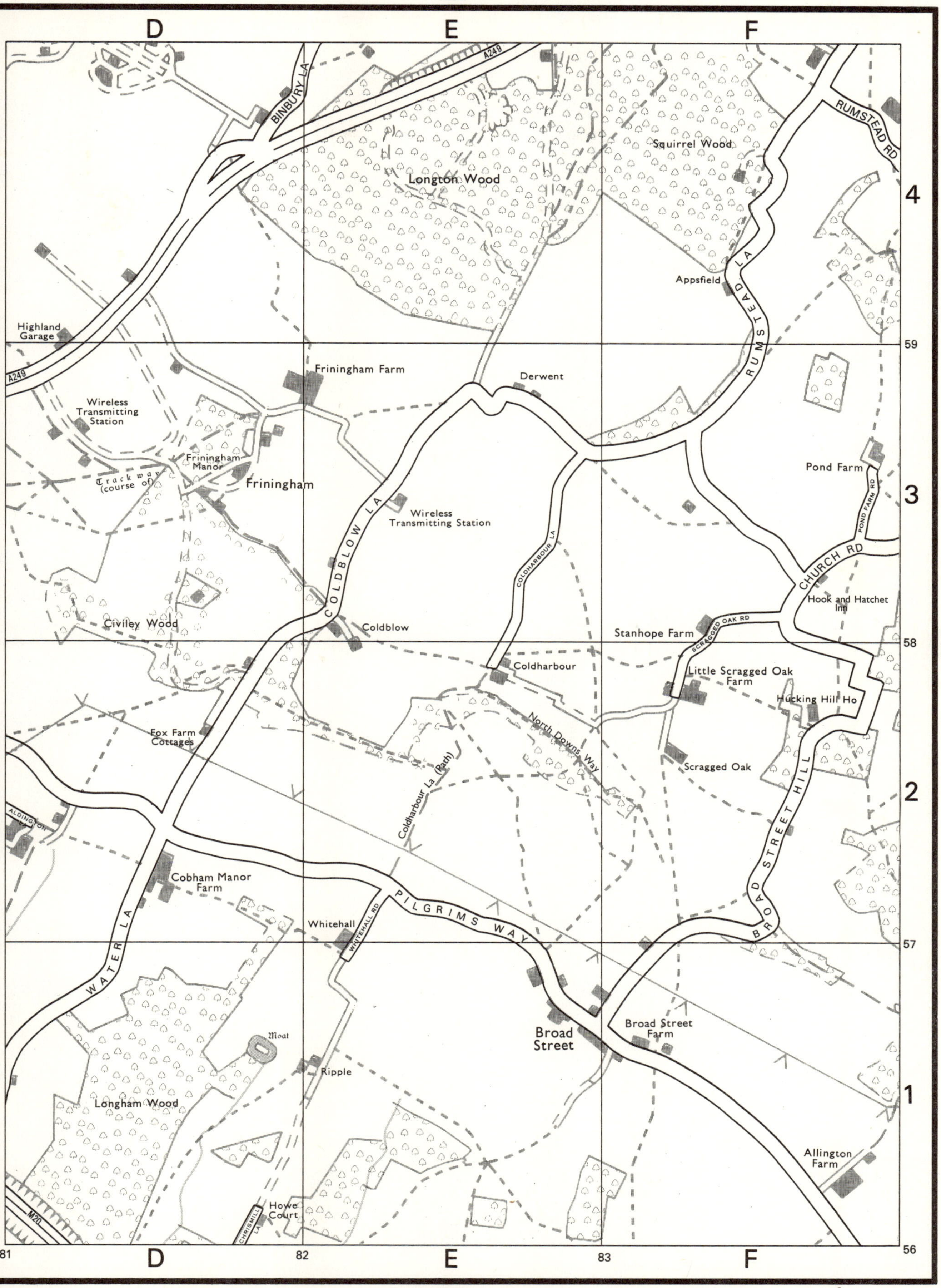
D
E
F
BINBURY LA
A249
Longton Wood
Squirrel Wood
RUMSTEAD RD
4
Appsfield
RUMSTEAD LA
Highland Garage
A249
59
Frinigham Farm
Derwent
Wireless Transmitting Station
Friningham Manor
Friningham
Trackway (course of)
Pond Farm
POND FARM RD
3
COLDBLOW LA
Wireless Transmitting Station
COLDHARBOUR LA
CHURCH RD
Hook and Hatchet Inn
Civiley Wood
Coldblow
Stanhope Farm
SCRAGGED OAK RD
58
Coldharbour
Little Scragged Oak Farm
Hucking Hill Ho
North Downs Way
Fox Farm Cottages
Scragged Oak
Coldharbour La (Path)
BROAD STREET HILL
ALDINGTON LA
2
Cobham Manor Farm
Whitehall
WHITEHALL RD
PILGRIMS WAY
WATER LA
57
Moat
Broad Street
Broad Street Farm
Ripple
Longham Wood
1
Allington Farm
M20
Howe Court
CHRISMILL LA
81
82
83
56
D
E
F

92

108

77

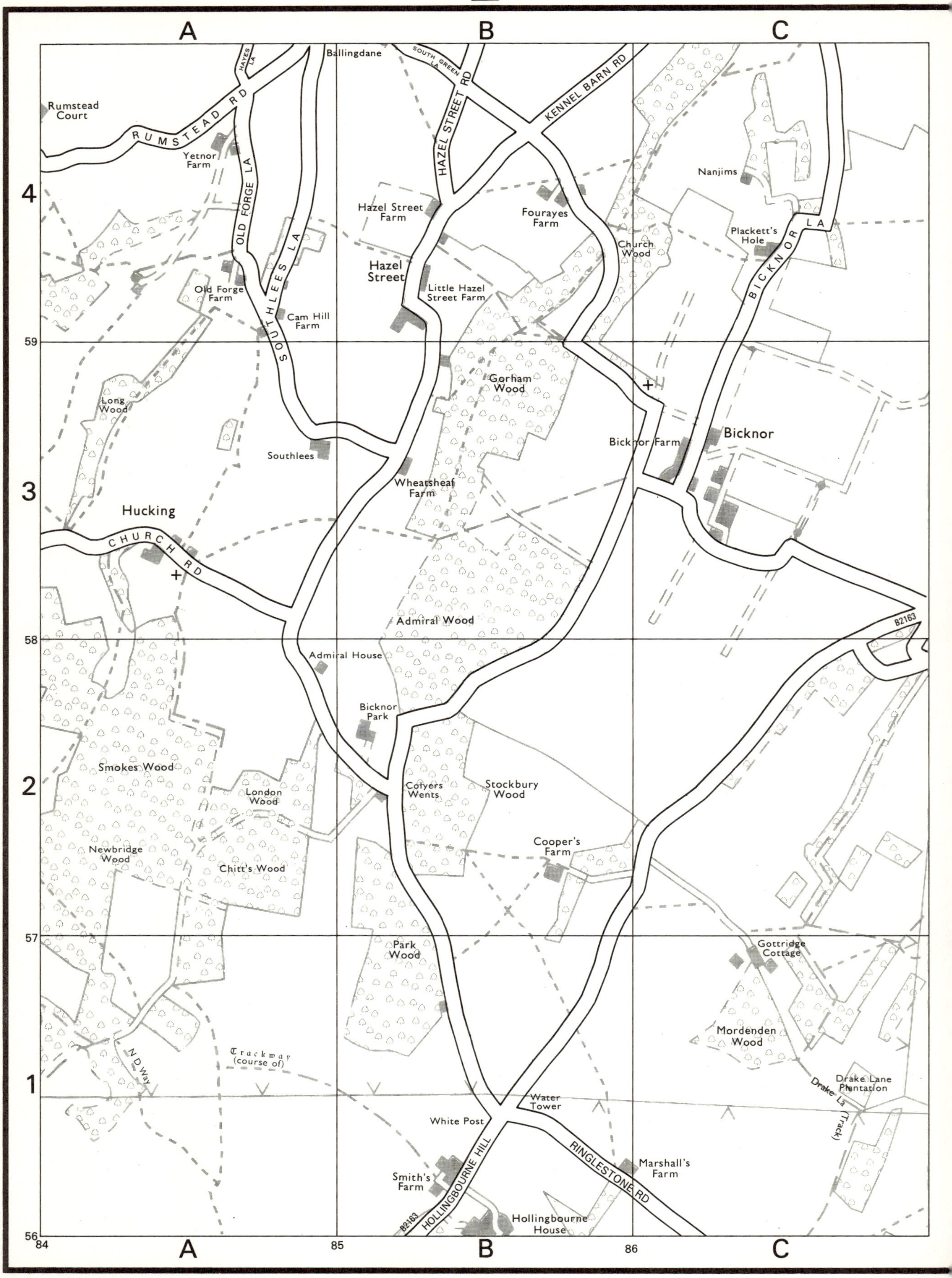
A
B
C
Ballingdane
HAYES LA
SOUTH GREEN LA
KENNEL BARN RD
Rumstead Court
RUMSTEAD RD
Yetnor Farm
HAZEL STREET RD
OLD FORGE LA
Nanjims
Hazel Street Farm
Fourayes Farm
Plackett's Hole
Church Wood
BICKNOR LA
Hazel Street
Little Hazel Street Farm
Old Forge Farm
SOUTHLEES LA
Cam Hill Farm
4
59
Gorham Wood
Long Wood
Bicknor
Bicknor Farm
Southlees
3
Wheatsheaf Farm
Hucking
CHURCH RD
Admiral Wood
58
B2163
Admiral House
Bicknor Park
Smokes Wood
2
London Wood
Colyers Wents
Stockbury Wood
Newbridge Wood
Cooper's Farm
Chitt's Wood
57
Park Wood
Gottridge Cottage
Mordenden Wood
N D Way
Trackway (course of)
1
Drake Lane Plantation
Drake La (Track)
Water Tower
White Post
RINGLESTONE RD
Marshall's Farm
Smith's Farm
HOLLINGBOURNE HILL
B2163
Hollingbourne House
56
84
85
86
A
B
C
91

109

not continued, see key diagram

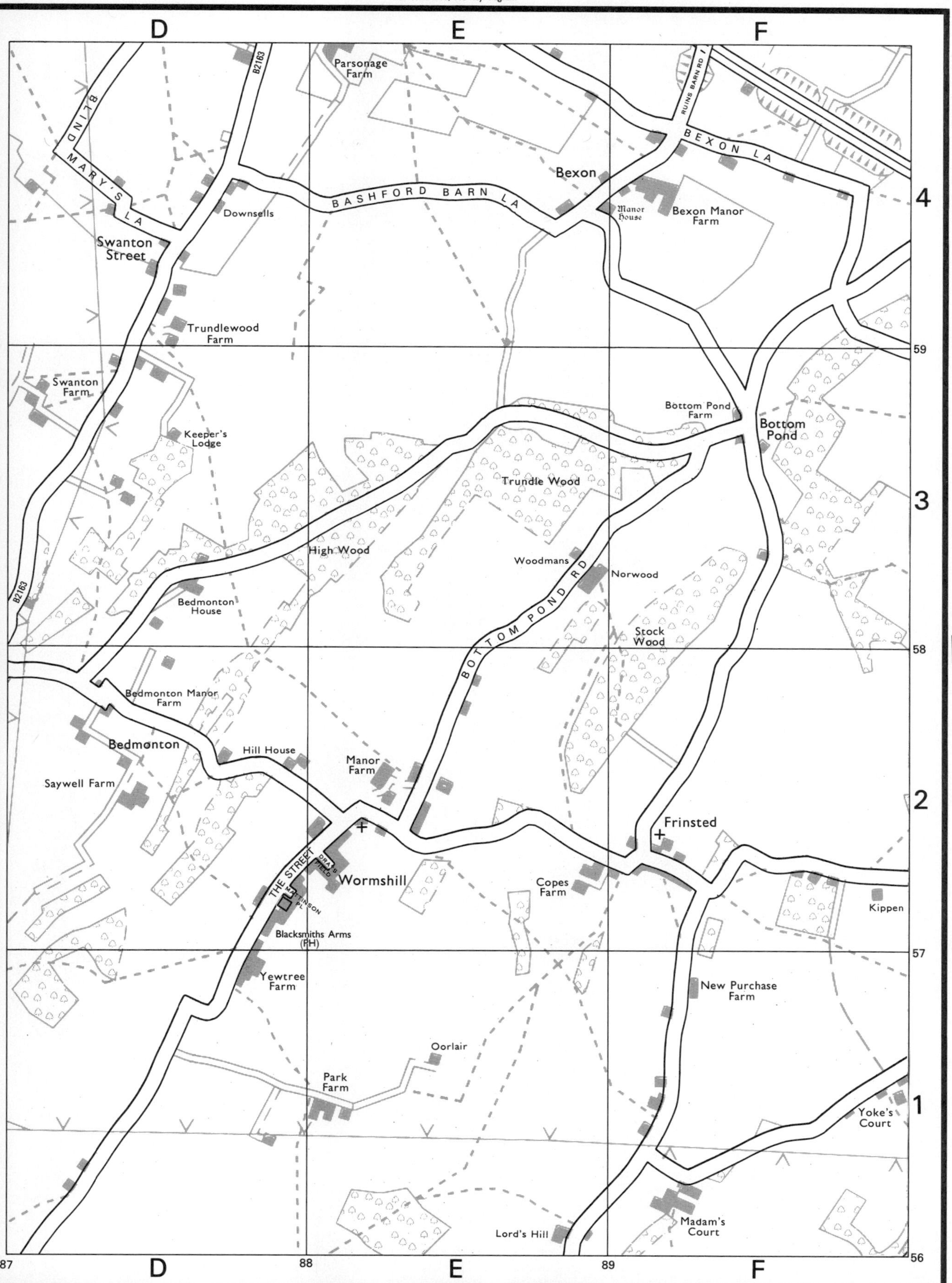

94

110

not continued, see key diagram

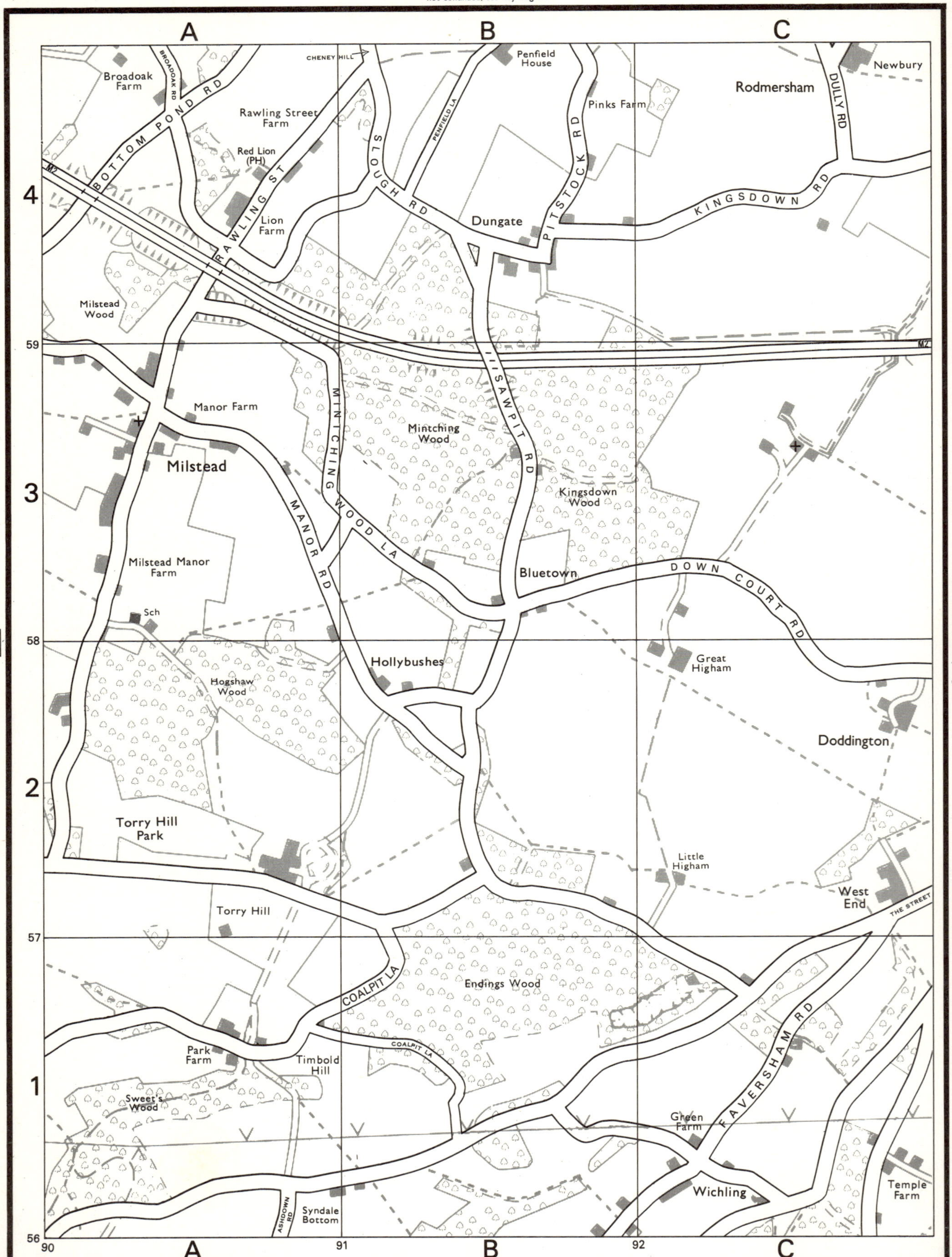

not continued, see key diagram

93

111

78

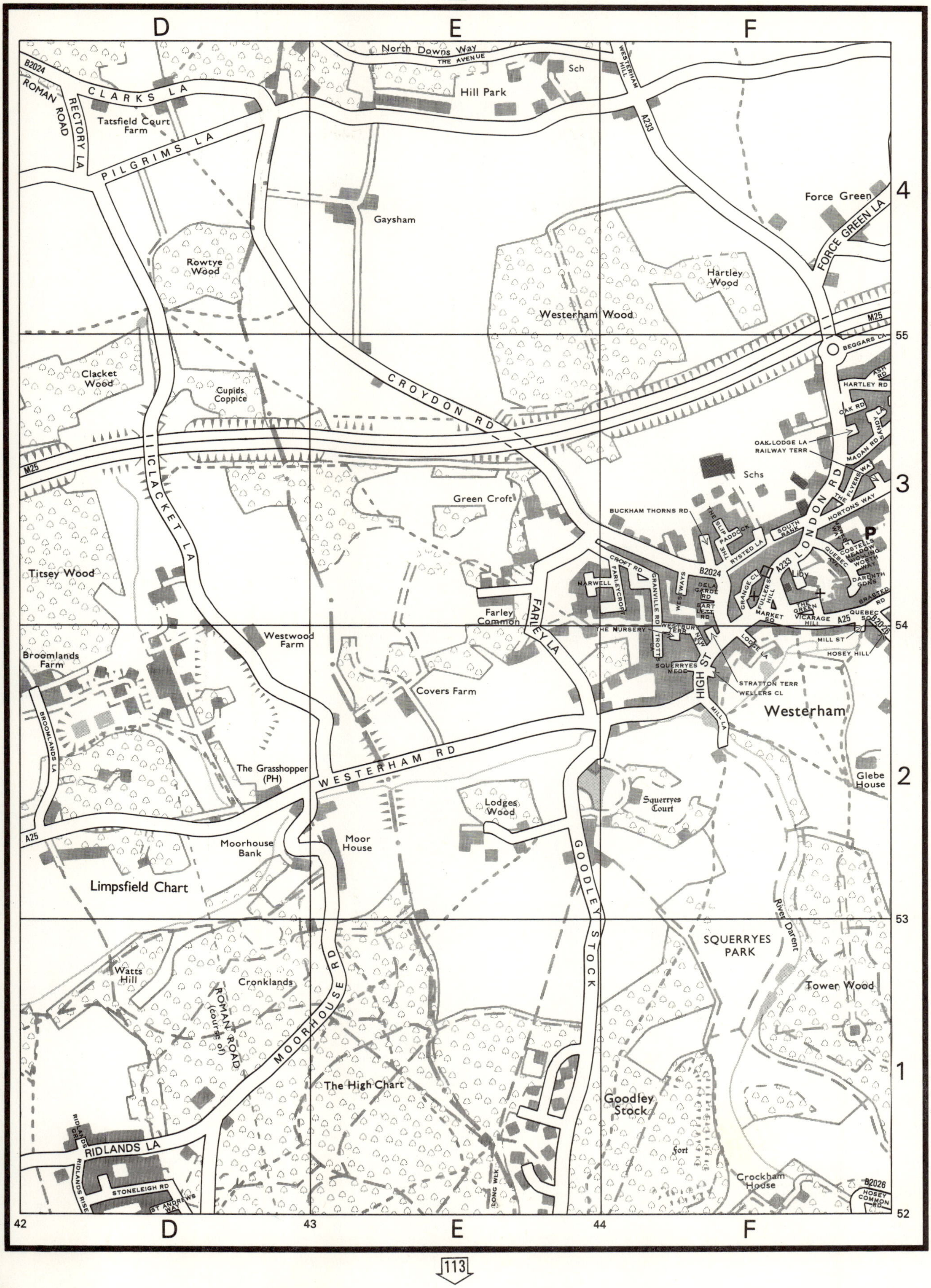

D
E
F
North Downs Way
THE AVENUE
B2024
ROMAN ROAD
RECTORY LA
CLARKS LA
Tatsfield Court Farm
PILGRIMS LA
Hill Park
Sch
WESTERHAM HILL
A233
Gaysham
Force Green
FORCE GREEN LA
4
Rowtye Wood
Hartley Wood
Westerham Wood
M25
55
BEGGARS LA
ASH RD
HARTLEY RD
Clacket Wood
Cupids Coppice
CROYDON RD
OAK RD
SANDY LA
OAK LODGE LA
RAILWAY TERR
MADAN RD
THE FLYERS WAY
Schs
3
CLACKET LA
Green Croft
BUCKHAM THORNS RD
THE SLIP
PADDOCK
RYSTED LA
SOUTH BANK
HORTONS WAY
LONDON RD
MARKET WAY
COSTELLS MEADOW
WOOLLING WORTH WAY
QUEBEC AVE
DARENTH GDNS
P
Titsey Wood
CROFT RD
FARLEYCROFT
MARWELL
GRANVILLE RD
WESTWAYS
DELA GARDE RD
BARTLETT RD
B2024
GRANGE CL
FULLERS HILL
A233
Liby
BRASTED RD
THE GREEN
MARKET SQ
VICARAGE HILL
A25
QUEBEC SQ
B2026
Farley Common
FARLEY LA
54
MILL ST
HOSEY HILL
THE NURSERY
WESTBURY TERR
TROTTS LA
Westwood Farm
Broomlands Farm
SQUERRYES MEDE
HIGH ST
LODGE LA
STRATTON TERR
WELLERS CL
Covers Farm
Westerham
MILL LA
BROOMLANDS LA
WESTERHAM RD
The Grasshopper (PH)
Squerryes Court
Glebe House
2
Lodges Wood
A25
Moorhouse Bank
Moor House
GOODLEY STOCK
Limpsfield Chart
River Darent
53
SQUERRYES PARK
Watts Hill
Cronklands
ROMAN ROAD (course of)
MOORHOUSE RD
Tower Wood
1
The High Chart
Goodley Stock
RIDLANDS GR
RIDLANDS LA
RIDLANDS RISE
Fort
Crockham House
STONELEIGH RD
ST ANDREWS WAY
LONG WLK
B2026
HOSEY COMMON RD
52
42
43
44
D
E
F

96

113

79

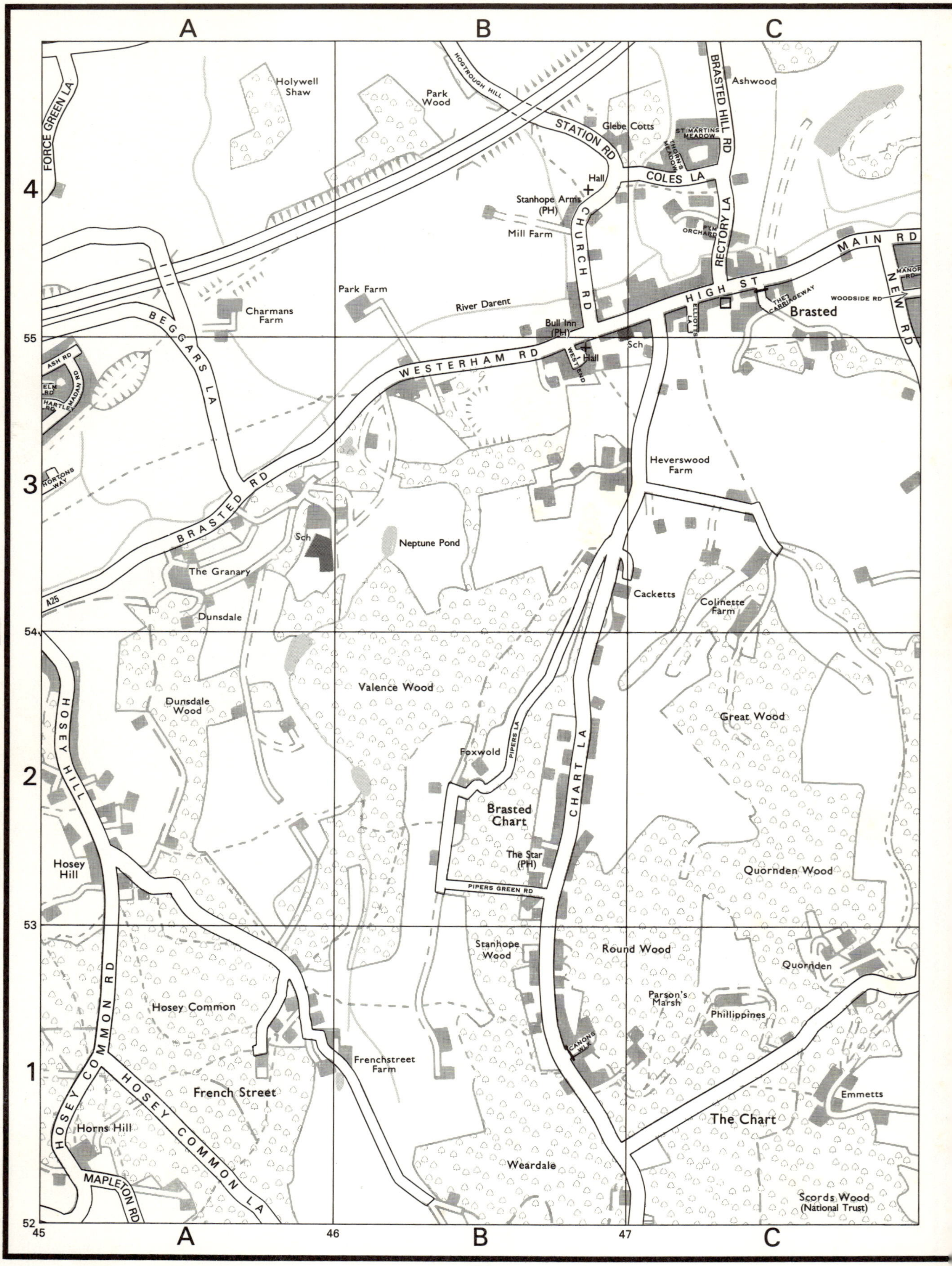
A
B
C
Holywell Shaw
Park Wood
HOGTROUGH HILL
STATION RD
Glebe Cotts
Ashwood
BRASTED HILL RD
ST MARTINS MEADOW
THORNS MEADOW
FORCE GREEN LA
COLES LA
Hall
Stanhope Arms (PH)
CHURCH RD
Mill Farm
PYM ORCHARD
RECTORY LA
MAIN RD
MANOR RD
NEW RD
HIGH ST
THE CARRIAGEWAY
WOODSIDE RD
Brasted
ELLIOTTS LA
Park Farm
Charmans Farm
River Darent
Bull Inn (PH)
Sch
Hall
WEST END
WESTERHAM RD
BEGGARS LA
ASH RD
ELM RD
MADAN RD
HARTLEY RD
HORTONS WAY
Heverswood Farm
BRASTED RD
Sch
Neptune Pond
The Granary
A25
Cacketts
Colinette Farm
Dunsdale
Valence Wood
Dunsdale Wood
HOSEY HILL
Great Wood
Foxwold
PIPERS LA
Brasted Chart
CHART LA
The Star (PH)
Hosey Hill
Quornden Wood
PIPERS GREEN RD
Stanhope Wood
Round Wood
Quornden
Hosey Common
Parson's Marsh
Phillippines
HOSEY COMMON RD
CANONS WLK
Frenchstreet Farm
French Street
Emmetts
The Chart
Horns Hill
HOSEY COMMON LA
Weardale
MAPLETON RD
Scords Wood (National Trust)
4
3
2
1
55
54
53
52
45
46
47

95

114

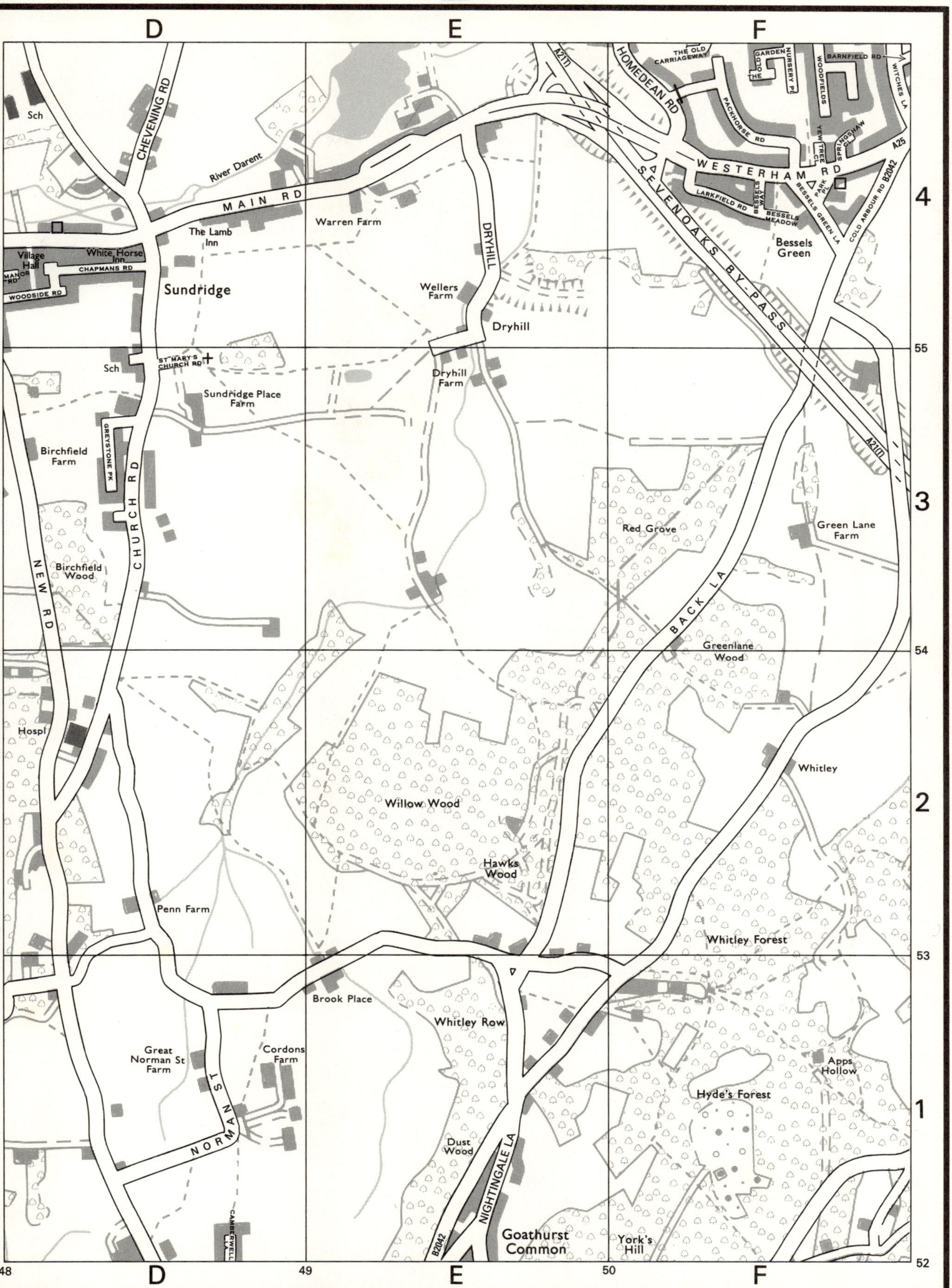
D
E
F
Sch
CHEVENING RD
River Darent
MAIN RD
Warren Farm
The Lamb Inn
Village Hall
White Horse Inn
CHAPMANS RD
MANOR RD
WOODSIDE RD
Sundridge
DRYHILL
Wellers Farm
Dryhill
Dryhill Farm
ST MARY'S CHURCH RD
Sch
Sundridge Place Farm
Birchfield Farm
GREYSTONE PK
CHURCH RD
NEW RD
Birchfield Wood
Hospl
Penn Farm
Willow Wood
Hawks Wood
Brook Place
Whitley Row
Great Norman St Farm
Cordons Farm
NORMAN ST
Dust Wood
NIGHTINGALE LA
B2042
Goathurst Common
CAMBERWELL LA
York's Hill
Hyde's Forest
Apps Hollow
Whitley Forest
Whitley
Greenlane Wood
BACK LA
Red Grove
Green Lane Farm
A21(T)
SEVENOAKS BY-PASS
Bessels Green
HOMEDEAN RD
THE OLD CARRIAGEWAY
THE OLD GARDEN
NURSERY PL
WOODFIELDS
BARNFIELD RD
WITCHES LA
PACKHORSE RD
WESTERHAM RD
YEW TREE CL
SPRINGSHAW CL
PARK PL
A25
B2042
COLD ARBOUR RD
LARKFIELD RD
BESSELS WAY
BESSELS MEADOW
BESSELS GREEN LA
4
3
2
1
55
54
53
52
48
49
50

81

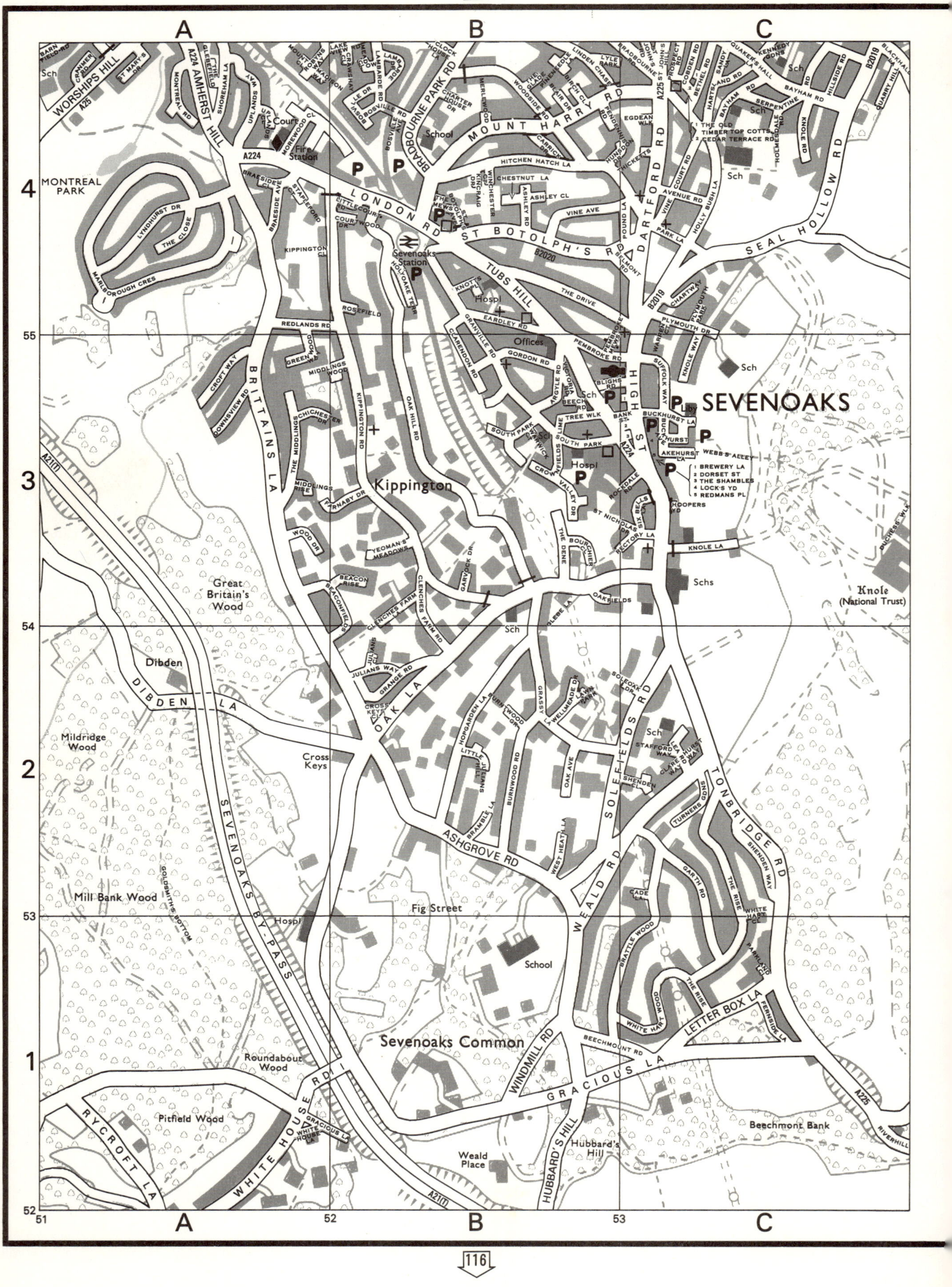

A
B
C
4
3
2
1
55
54
53
52
51
52
53
SEVENOAKS
Kippington
Sevenoaks Common
Montreal Park
Great Britain's Wood
Dibden
Dibden La
Mildridge Wood
Mill Bank Wood
Cross Keys
Roundabout Wood
Pitfield Wood
Fig Street
School
Weald Place
Hubbard's Hill
Beechmont Bank
Knole
(National Trust)
Sevenoaks Station
Worships Hill
A224 Amherst Hill
London Rd
St Botolph's Rd
Tubs Hill
Mount Harry Rd
Bradbourne Park Rd
Dartford Rd
Seal Hollow Rd
High St
Brittains La
Kippington Rd
Oak Hill Rd
Oak La
Ashgrove Rd
Solefields Rd
Weald Rd
Tonbridge Rd
Sevenoaks By-Pass
White House Rd
Rycroft La
Gracious La
Letter Box La
Windmill Rd
Hubbard's Hill
Knole La
Hitchen Hatch La
Redlands Rd
Beaconfields
Clenches Farm Rd
Grange Rd
Julians Way
Hopgarden La
Burnwood Rd
West Heath La
Garth Rd
Shenden Way
Beechmount Rd
Goldsmith's Bottom
A25
A224
A225
A21(T)
B2019
B2020
1 Brewery La
2 Dorset St
3 The Shambles
4 Lock's Yd
5 Redmans Pl
1 The Old Timber Top Cotts
2 Cedar Terrace Rd

97

116

82

D E F

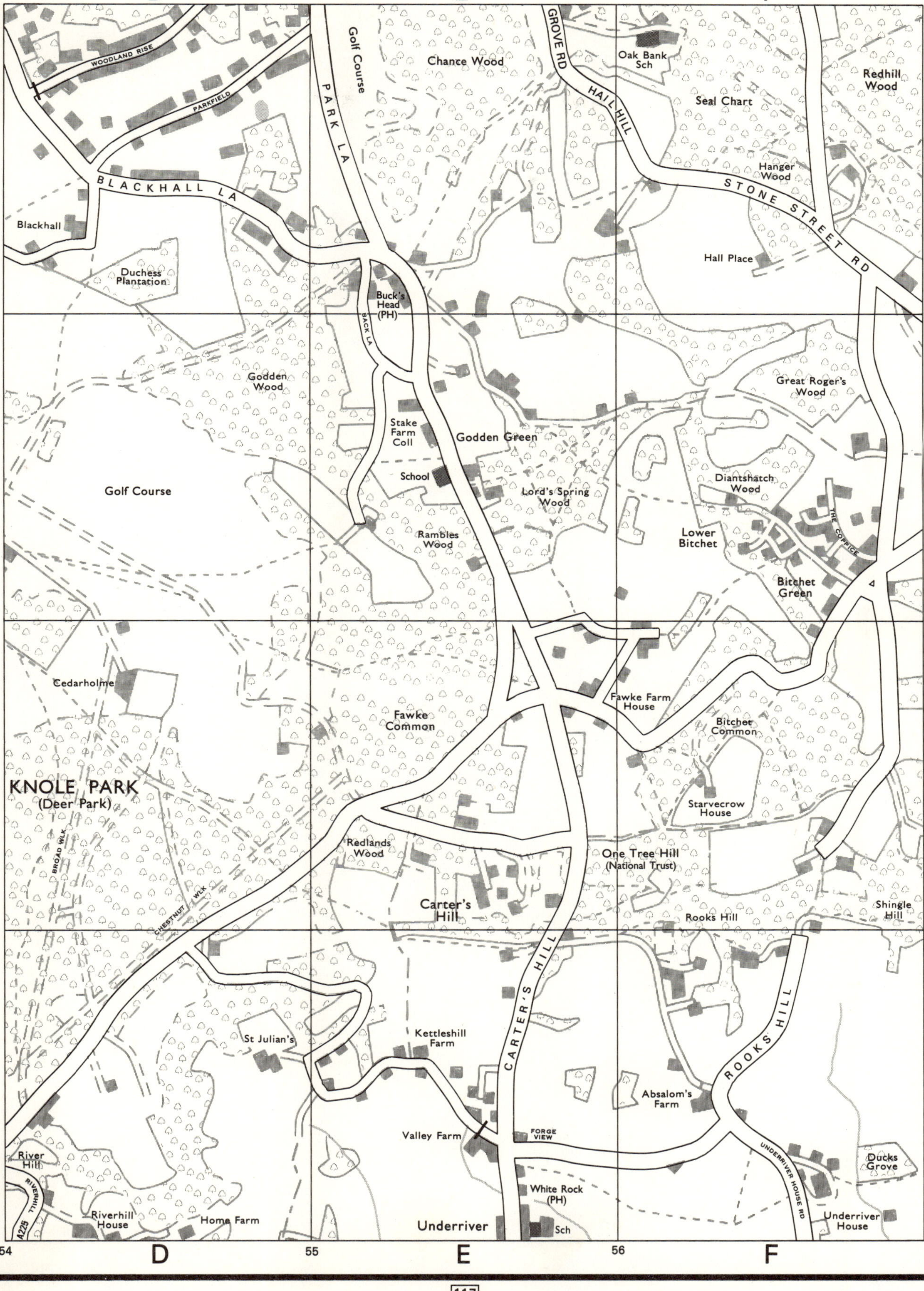

D E F

100

117

83

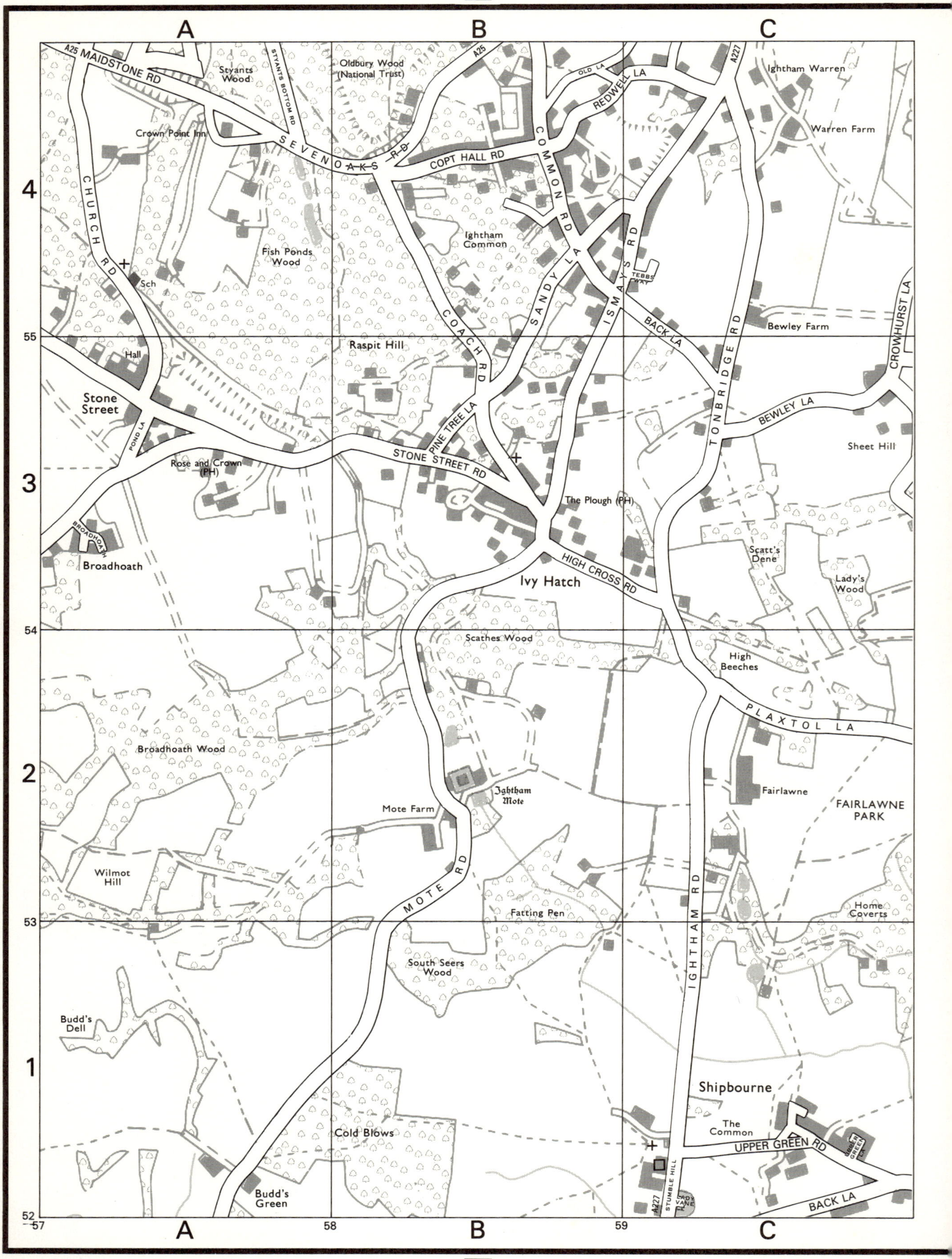
A
B
C
A25 MAIDSTONE RD
Styants Wood
STYANTS BOTTOM RD
Oldbury Wood (National Trust)
A25
OLD LA
REDWELL LA
A227
Ightham Warren
Warren Farm
Crown Point Inn
SEVENOAKS RD
COPT HALL RD
COMMON RD
CHURCH RD
Ightham Common
Fish Ponds Wood
Sch
SANDY LA
ISMAYS RD
TEBBS WAY
BACK LA
TONBRIDGE RD
Bewley Farm
CROWHURST LA
COACH RD
Raspit Hill
Hall
Stone Street
PINE TREE LA
BEWLEY LA
POND LA
Sheet Hill
STONE STREET RD
Rose and Crown (PH)
The Plough (PH)
BROADHOATH
Broadhoath
Scatt's Dene
Lady's Wood
HIGH CROSS RD
Ivy Hatch
Scathes Wood
High Beeches
PLAXTOL LA
Broadhoath Wood
Ightham Mote
Fairlawne
FAIRLAWNE PARK
Mote Farm
MOTE RD
Wilmot Hill
Fatting Pen
IGHTHAM RD
Home Coverts
South Seers Wood
Budd's Dell
Shipbourne
The Common
UPPER GREEN RD
Cold Blows
A227
STUMBLE HILL
BACK LA
Budd's Green
4
3
2
1
55
54
53
52
57
58
59

99

118

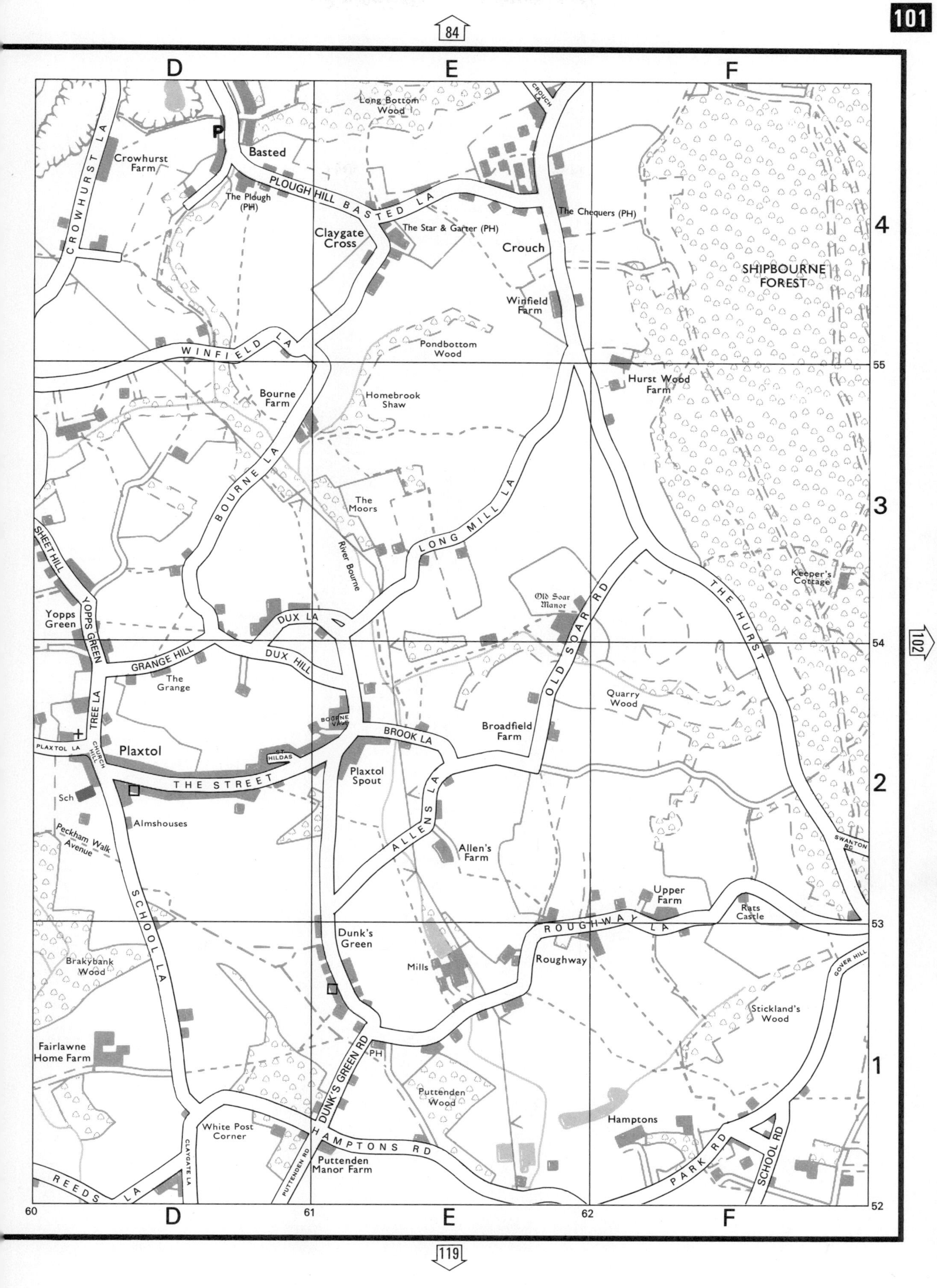
84
D
E
F
Long Bottom Wood
Basted
Crowhurst Farm
CROWHURST LA
CROUCH LA
PLOUGH HILL
BASTED LA
The Plough (PH)
The Chequers (PH)
The Star & Garter (PH)
Claygate Cross
Crouch
SHIPBOURNE FOREST
Winfield Farm
WINFIELD LA
Pondbottom Wood
Hurst Wood Farm
Bourne Farm
Homebrook Shaw
BOURNE LA
The Moors
LONG MILL LA
River Bourne
SHEET HILL
YOPPS GREEN
Yopps Green
DUX LA
Old Soar Manor
OLD SOAR RD
THE HURST
Keeper's Cottage
GRANGE HILL
DUX HILL
The Grange
Quarry Wood
TREE LA
BOURNE VALE
BROOK LA
Broadfield Farm
PLAXTOL LA
CHURCH HILL
Plaxtol
ST HILDAS
THE STREET
Plaxtol Spout
Sch
Almshouses
ALLENS LA
Peckham Walk Avenue
Allen's Farm
SWANTON RD
SCHOOL LA
Upper Farm
Rats Castle
ROUGHWAY LA
Dunk's Green
Brakybank Wood
Mills
Roughway
GOVER HILL
Stickland's Wood
DUNK'S GREEN RD
PH
Fairlawne Home Farm
Puttenden Wood
Hamptons
White Post Corner
HAMPTONS RD
PARK RD
SCHOOL RD
CLAYGATE LA
PUTTENDEN RD
Puttenden Manor Farm
REEDS LA
4
3
2
1
55
54
53
52
60
61
62
102
119

85

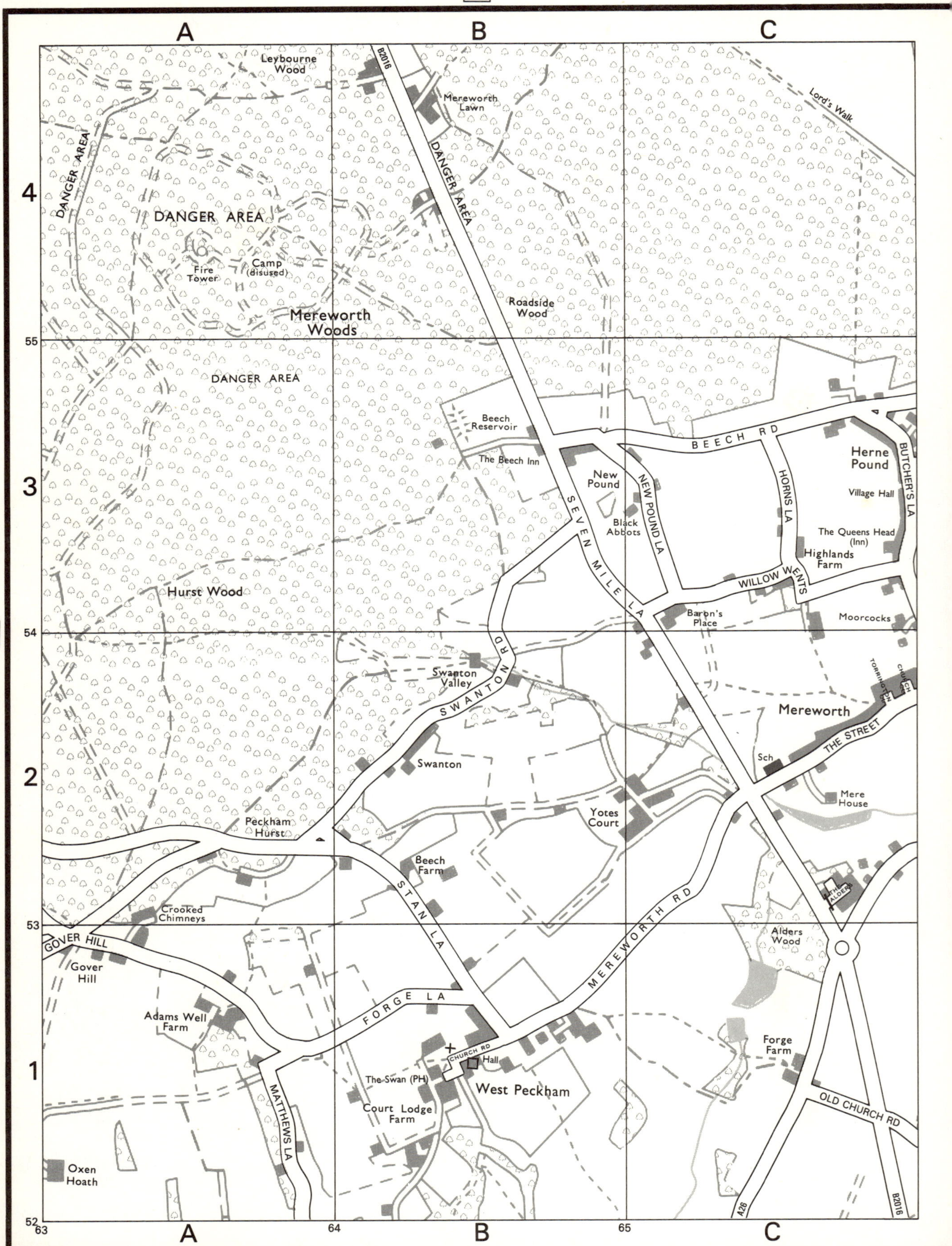
A
B
C
4
3
2
1
55
54
53
52
63
64
65
B2016
Leybourne Wood
Mereworth Lawn
Lord's Walk
DANGER AREA
DANGER AREA
DANGER AREA
Fire Tower
Camp (disused)
Mereworth Woods
Roadside Wood
DANGER AREA
Beech Reservoir
The Beech Inn
BEECH RD
Herne Pound
BUTCHER'S LA
New Pound
NEW POUND LA
HORNS LA
Village Hall
SEVEN MILE LA
Black Abbots
The Queens Head (Inn)
Highlands Farm
WILLOW WENTS
Hurst Wood
Baron's Place
Moorcocks
SWANTON RD
Swanton Valley
TORRINGTON
CHURCH
Mereworth
THE STREET
Swanton
Sch
Mere House
Yotes Court
Peckham Hurst
Beech Farm
STAN LA
THE ALDERS
Crooked Chimneys
GOVER HILL
Alders Wood
MEREWORTH RD
Gover Hill
FORGE LA
Adams Well Farm
Forge Farm
CHURCH RD
Hall
The Swan (PH)
West Peckham
OLD CHURCH RD
MATTHEWS LA
Court Lodge Farm
Oxen Hoath
A26
B2016

101

120

86

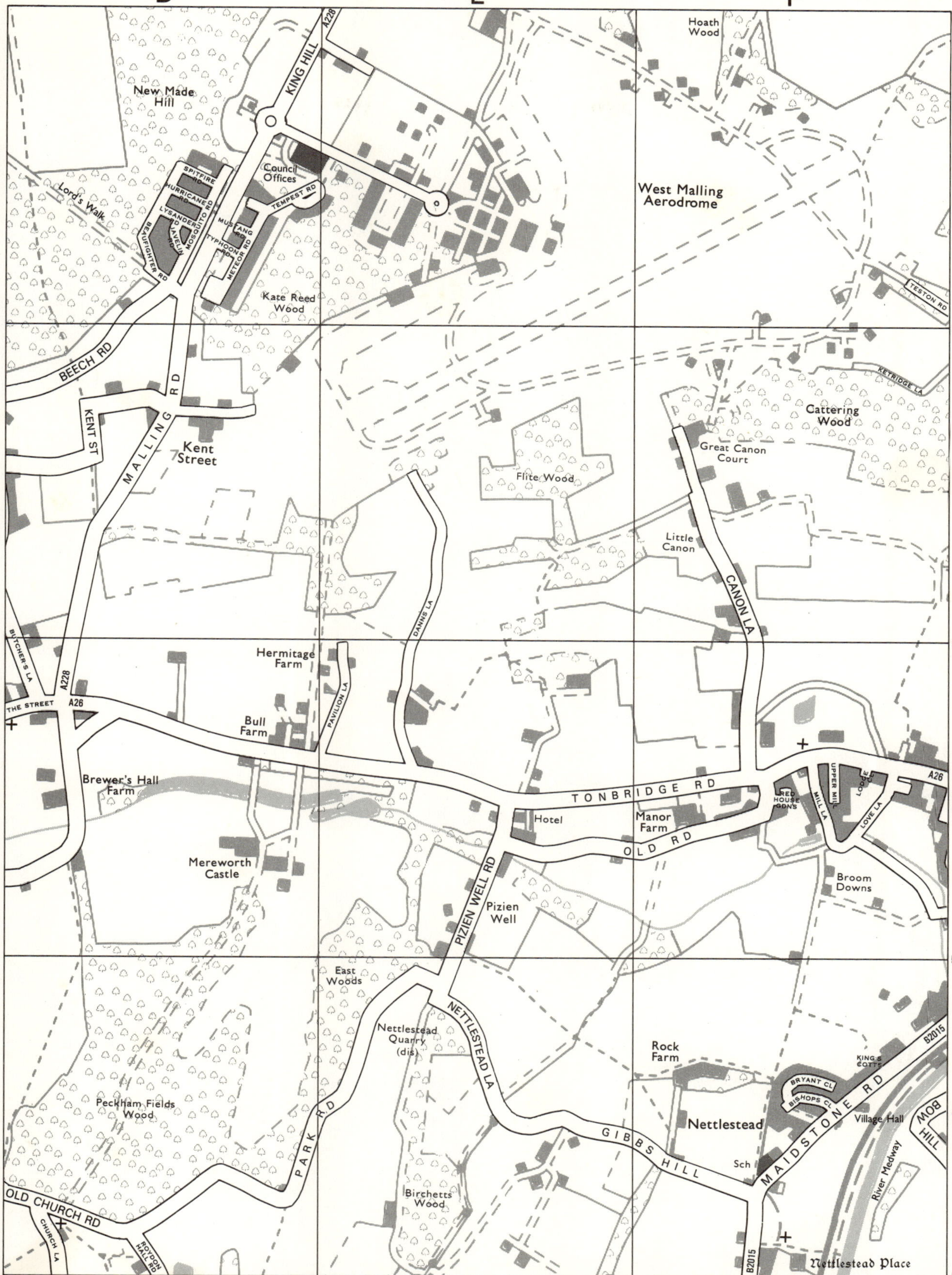
D
E
F
4
3
2
1
55
54
53
52
66
67
68
New Made Hill
KING HILL
A228
Council Offices
TEMPEST RD
SPITFIRE RD
HURRICANE RD
LYSANDER RD
JAVELIN RD
MOSQUITO RD
MUSTANG RD
TYPHOON RD
METEOR RD
BEAUFIGHTER RD
Lord's Walk
Kate Reed Wood
Hoath Wood
West Malling Aerodrome
TESTON RD
KETRIDGE LA
Cattering Wood
BEECH RD
MALLING RD
KENT ST
Kent Street
Great Canon Court
Flite Wood
Little Canon
CANON LA
DANNS LA
BUTCHER'S LA
Hermitage Farm
PAVILION LA
Bull Farm
THE STREET
A26
Brewer's Hall Farm
TONBRIDGE RD
RED HOUSE GDNS
UPPER MILL
MILL LA
LODGE
LOVE LA
Hotel
Manor Farm
OLD RD
Mereworth Castle
PIZIEN WELL RD
Pizien Well
Broom Downs
East Woods
NETTLESTEAD LA
Nettlestead Quarry (dis)
Rock Farm
B2015
KING'S COTTS
BRYANT CL
BISHOPS CL
MAIDSTONE RD
Village Hall
BOW HILL
Nettlestead
Peckham Fields Wood
PARK RD
GIBBS HILL
Sch
River Medway
Birchetts Wood
OLD CHURCH RD
CHURCH LA
ROYDON HALL RD
Nettlestead Place

104

121

87

A
B
C
4
3
2
1
55
54
53
52
69
70
71
THE HEATH
SWEETS LA
Upper Paris Farm
Manor Farm
Luckhurst Farm
Oaken Wood
Heath Farm
East Malling Heath
WATERINGBURY RD
Seven Wents
KETRIDGE LA
North Pole (PH)
BARMING RD
TESTON RD
NORTH POLE RD
Hall Place
Hoath Wood
Teston Corner
Hall Place Farm
Redhill Farm
LIVESEY ST
Livesey Street
A26
Red Hill
MALLING RD
RED HILL
FAIRLAWN CL
Wateringbury
COURTLANDS
NESTOR CT
WOODLANDS
COURTLANDS CL
Barham Court
Court Lodge Farm
Teston
CHURCH ST
THE STREET
TONBRIDGE RD
THE ORPINES
Court Lodge
B2010
CHARLTON LA
CHURCH LA
B2015
B2163
LC
P
FIELDS LA
GLEBE MEADOW
COBBS CL
THE BRUCKS
LENEY RD
WARDEN MILL CL
PHOENIX DR
BOW RD
TESTON LA
LOWER RD
River Medway
Sch
Wateringbury Station
Bow Bridge
Waregrave's Wood
West Farleigh
Tutsham Hall
EWELL LA
Ewell Manor
SMITH HILL
BOW HILL
HUNT ST
SMALL PROFITS

103

122

88

D
E
F
Ditton Common
Fullingpits Wood
Barming Heath
Hospital
Mills
HERMITAGE LA
QUEEN'S RD
Playing Field
Sch
Oakwood Park
Cherry Orchard
Coll
Schs
OAKWOOD RD
BOWER MOUNT RD
CORNWALLIS RD
A26
NORTH POLE RD
ST ANDREW'S RD
HEATH RD
TONBRIDGE RD
FANT LA
HACKNEY RD
UPPER FANT RD
GATLAND LA
GLEBE LA
NORTH ST
SOUTH ST
East Barming
Glebe Farm
RECTORY LA
FARLEIGH LA
St Helen's Corner
Bydews Wood
B2010
Barming Bridge
Half Yoke Farm
The Priory
East Farleigh Station
River Medway
ST HELENS LA
STATION RD
LOWER RD
Dean Farm
Court Lodge Farm
Gallants Court
Liby
Hall
FORGE LA
NEW CUT
DEAN ST
East Farleigh
Dean Street
VICARAGE LA
Sch
Gallants Farm
GALLANTS LA
CHARLTON LA
Farleigh Green
Good Intent (PH)
EWELL LA
HEATH RD
WILSONS LA
STOCKETT LA
Hamlet Wood
Horse Shoe Inn (PH)
WORKHOUSE LA
Cuckoo Farm
55
54
53
52
4
3
2
1
72
73
74

106

123

89

105

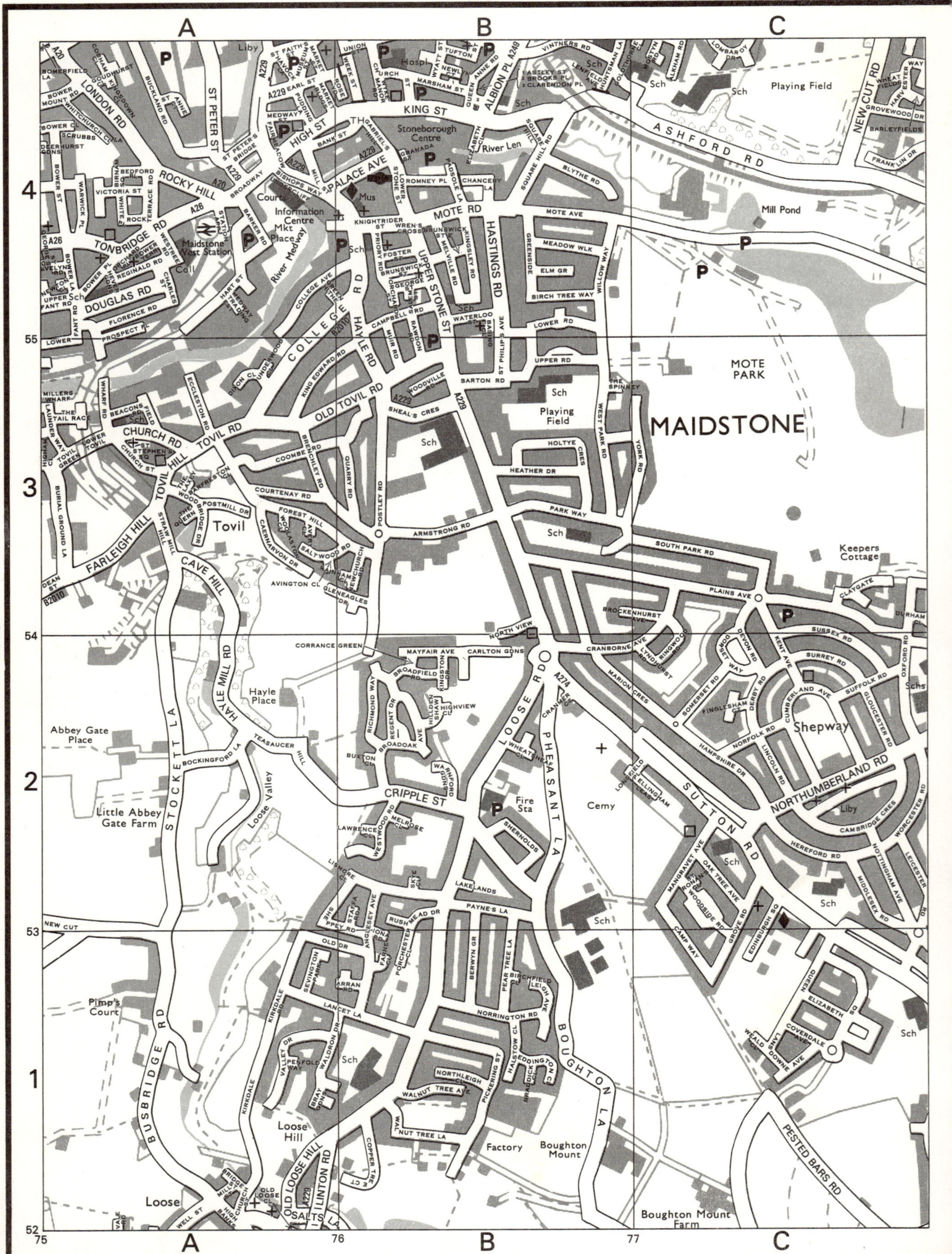
A
B
C
4
3
2
1
55
54
53
52
75
76
77
MAIDSTONE
MOTE PARK
Mill Pond
Playing Field
Keepers Cottage
Shepway
Tovil
Hayle Place
Abbey Gate Place
Little Abbey Gate Farm
Pimp's Court
Loose
Loose Hill
Loose Valley
Boughton Mount
Boughton Mount Farm
Factory
Cemy
Fire Sta
Stoneborough Centre
Information Centre
Mkt Place
Courts
Mus
Hospl
Maidstone West Station
Coll
River Medway
River Len
Liby
ASHFORD RD
KING ST
HIGH ST
PALACE AVE
MOTE RD
HASTINGS RD
UPPER STONE ST
COLLEGE RD
HAYLE RD
OLD TOVIL RD
TOVIL RD
TOVIL HILL
CHURCH RD
FARLEIGH HILL
ROCKY HILL
LONDON RD
TONBRIDGE RD
DOUGLAS RD
ST PETER ST
ALBION PL
ARMSTRONG RD
PARK WAY
SOUTH PARK RD
PLAINS AVE
CRANBORNE AVE
MARION CRES
SUTTON RD
NORTHUMBERLAND RD
LOOSE RD
PHEASANT LA
BOUGHTON LA
CRIPPLE ST
STOCKETT LA
BUSBRIDGE RD
CAVE HILL
HAYLE MILL RD
NEW CUT
NEW CUT RD
PESTED BARS RD
OLD LOOSE HILL
LINTON RD
NORRINGTON RD
WALNUT TREE LA
PAYNE'S LA
SHEAL'S CRES
BARTON RD
UPPER RD
LOWER RD
HOLTYE CRES
HEATHER DR
WEST PARK RD
YORK RD
MOTE AVE
MEADOW WLK
ELM GR
BIRCH TREE WAY
WILLOW WAY
BLYTHE RD
SQUARE HILL RD
MAYFAIR AVE
CARLTON GDNS
CORRANCE GREEN
NORTH VIEW
BROCKENHURST AVE
SUSSEX RD
SURREY RD
SUFFOLK RD
KENT AVE
DEVON RD
HEREFORD RD
CAMBRIDGE CRES
WORCESTER RD
LEICESTER RD
MIDDLESEX RD
NOTTINGHAM AVE
QUEEN ELIZABETH SQ
COVERDALE AVE
DOWNE AVE
CAMP WAY
GROVE RD
EDINBURGH SQ
MANGRAVET AVE
OAK TREE AVE
WOODSIDE RD
SOMERSET RD
HAMPSHIRE DR
NORFOLK RD
LINCOLN RD
CUMBERLAND AVE
GLOUCESTER RD
FINGLESHAM
DERBY RD
OXFORD RD
DURHAM
CLAYGATE
BUXTON CL
BROADOAK
REGENT DR
RICHMOND WAY
BROADFIELD RD
KINGSTON DR
HIGHVIEW CL
BOCKINGFORD LA
TEASAUCER HILL
LAWRENCE CL
WESTWOOD RD
MELROSE CL
LISMORE CL
SKYE CL
LAKELANDS
RUSHMEAD DR
SHEPPEY RD
STAFFA RD
ANGLESEY AVE
PORCHESTER CL
BERWYN GR
PEAR TREE LA
BIRCHFIELD CL
LEIGH AVE
OLD DR
SEVINGTON PARK
ARRAN
KIRKDALE RD
KIRKDALE
LANCET LA
VALLEY DR
PENFOLD WAY
WALDRON DR
BRAY GDNS
NORTHLEIGH CL
PICKERING ST
HALSTOW CL
BRADDICK CL
EDDINGTON CL
COPPER TREE CT
WELL ST
VALE RD
BRIDGE MILL WAY
CHURCH ST
HIGH BANKS
SALTS LA
COURTENAY RD
COOMBE RD
BRENCHLEY RD
QUARRY RD
POSTLEY RD
FOREST HILL
SALTWOOD RD
CAERNARVON DR
AVINGTON CL
GLENEAGLES DR
NEWCHURCH RD
STRAW MILL HILL
POSTMILL DR
WOODBRIDGE DR
BURIAL GROUND LA
DEAN ST
B2010
A20
A26
A229
A249
A274
MILLERS WHARF
WHARF RD
BEACONSFIELD RD
ECCLESTON RD
DIXON CL
UNDERWOOD CL
KING EDWARD RD
CAMPBELL RD
MUIR RD
RAWDON RD
WOODVILLE RD
WATERLOO ST
ST PHILIP'S AVE
THE SPINNEY
KNIGHTRIDER ST
ROMNEY PL
CHANCERY LA
MARSHAM ST
VINTNERS RD
LOMBARDY DR
GROVEWOOD DR
BARLEYFIELDS
FRANKLIN DR
FLORENCE RD
PROSPECT PL
BOWER ST
BOWER LA
VICTORIA ST
MEDWAY TRADING EST
BARKER RD
BROADWAY
EARL ST
WEEK ST
UNION ST
GRANADA
Sch
P

124

90

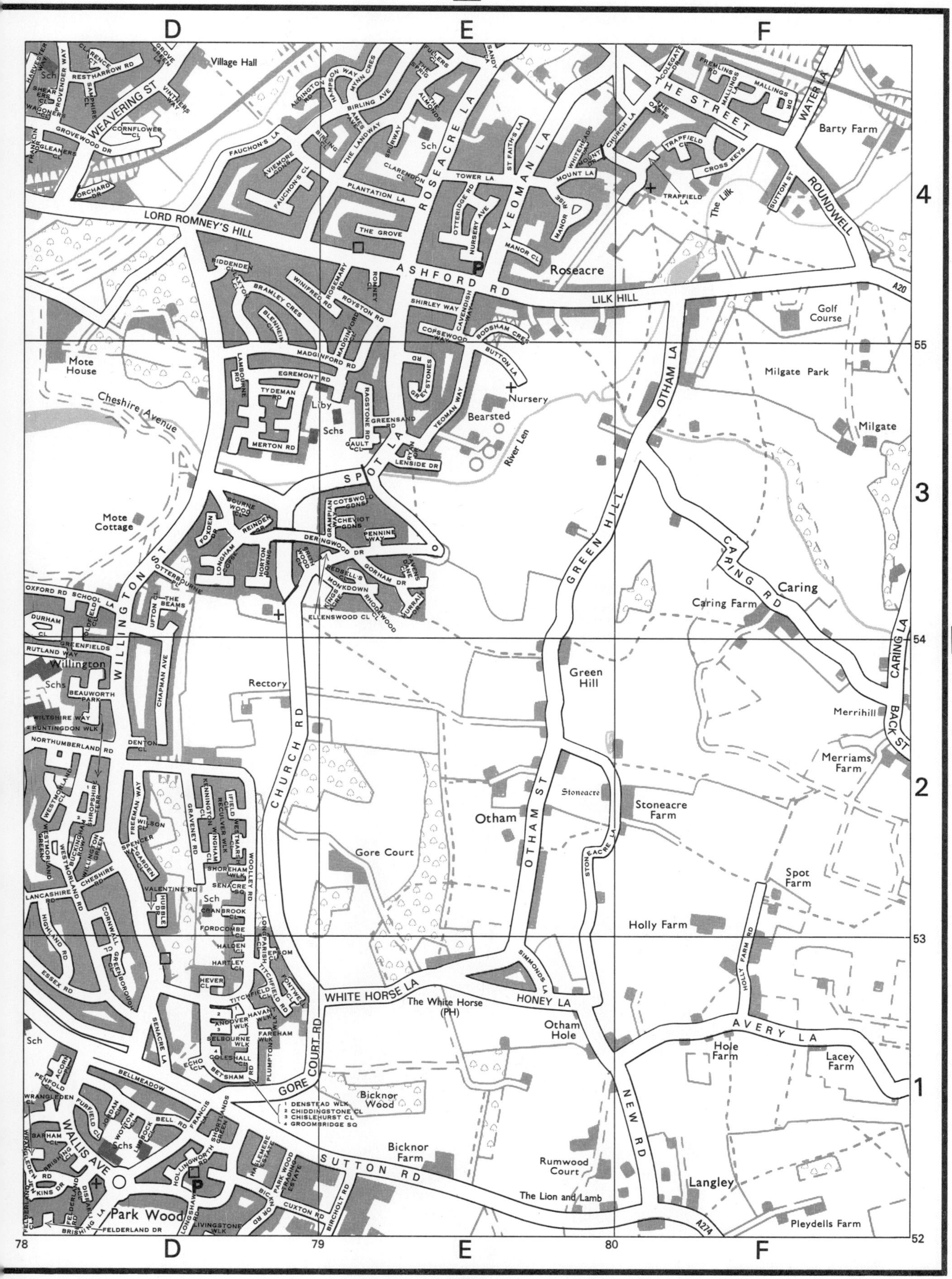
D
E
F
Village Hall
Sch
RESTHARROW RD
CLARENCE CL
GROVE GREEN
WEAVERING ST
VINTNERS WAY
SAMPHIRE
PROVENDER WAY
HARVESTER WAY
WAGONERS
CORNFLOWER CL
GROVEWOOD DR
GLEANERS
ORCHARD DR
LORD ROMNEY'S HILL
FAUCHON'S LA
FAUCHON'S CL
AVIEMORE GDNS
ALDINGTON RD
HAMPSON WAY
MYNN CRES
BIRLING AVE
BIRLING CL
THE LANDWAY
SPURWAY
Sch
CLARENDON CL
PLANTATION LA
THE GROVE
FULLERS CL
ALMONDS
SANDY LA
ROSEACRE LA
TOWER LA
OTTERIDGE RD
NURSERY AVE
ST FAITH'S LA
YEOMAN LA
WHITEHEADS
MOUNT LA
MANOR RISE
MANOR CL
Roseacre
ASHFORD RD
LILK HILL
A20
THE STREET
COLEGATES
FREMLINS RD
MALLINGS LA
MALLINGS DR
WATER LA
Barty Farm
CHURCH LA
TRAPFIELD CL
TRAPFIELD LA
CROSS KEYS
The Lilk
SUTTON ST
ROUNDWELL
Golf Course
Milgate Park
Milgate
BIDDENDEN CL
PAXTON
BRAMLEY CRES
BLENHEIM
WINIFRED RD
ROSEMARY RD
ROMNEY
ROYSTON RD
MADGINFORD CL
MADGINFORD RD
SHIRLEY WAY
CAVENDISH WAY
COPSEWOOD WAY
BODSHAM CRES
BUTTON LA
Mote House
Cheshire Avenue
LAMBOURNE RD
EGREMONT RD
TYDEMAN RD
Liby
Schs
MERTON RD
RAGSTONE RD
GREENSAND RD
GAULT CL
GREYSTONES RD
YEOMAN WAY
LENSIDE DR
Nursery
Bearsted
River Len
OTHAM LA
SPOT LA
Mote Cottage
BOURNE WOOD CL
REINDEN GR
FOXDEN DR
LONGHAM COPSE
HORTON DOWNS
COTSWOLD GDNS
GRAMPIAN WAY
CHEVIOT GDNS
PENNINE WAY
DERINGWOOD DR
GORHAM DR
REDSELL'S CL
MONKDOWN
RHODEWOOD CL
ELLENSWOOD CL
TURRAIN DR
GREEN HILL
CARING RD
Caring
Caring Farm
CARING LA
BACK ST
Merrihill
Merriams Farm
WILLINGTON ST
OTTERBOURNE
OXFORD RD
SCHOOL LA
DURHAM CL
OLDFIELD CL
UFTON CL
THE BEAMS
RUTLAND WAY
GREENFIELDS
Willington
Schs
BEAUWORTH PARK
CHAPMAN AVE
WILTSHIRE WAY
HUNTINGDON WLK
NORTHUMBERLAND RD
DENTON CL
Rectory
CHURCH RD
Green Hill
WESTMORLAND CL
SHROPSHIRE TERR
BUCKINGHAM ROW
WILLINGTON GREEN
WESTMORLAND GREEN
WESTMORLAND RD
FREEMAN WAY
WILSON CL
SPENCER WAY
GARDEN
KENNINGTON CL
IFIELD
RECULVER WLK
WESTMARSH CL
WINGHAM CL
GRAVENEY RD
SHOREHAM WLK
SENACRE SQ
WOOLLEY RD
CHESHIRE RD
LANCASHIRE RD
CORNWALL CL
VALENTINE RD
HUBBLE DR
Sch
CRANBROOK CL
FORDCOMBE CL
HALDEN CL
HARTLEY CL
HEVER CL
LONGPARISH CL
EPSOM CL
TITCHFIELD CL
FONTWELL CL
HIGHLAND RD
GREENBOROUGH CL
ESSEX RD
Gore Court
Otham
OTHAM ST
Stoneacre
Stoneacre Farm
STONEACRE LA
Spot Farm
Holly Farm
HOLLY FARM RD
SIMMONDS LA
WHITE HORSE LA
The White Horse (PH)
HONEY LA
Otham Hole
AVERY LA
Hole Farm
Lacey Farm
ANDOVER WLK
HAVANT WLK
SELBOURNE WLK
FAREHAM WLK
COLESHALL CL
PLUMPTON WLK
ECHO CL
BETSHAM RD
SENACRE LA
GORE COURT RD
Sch
BELLMEADOW
ACORN PL
PENFOLD
WRANGLEDEN RD
FURFIELD CL
JORDAN CL
WOLFE
BELL
FRANCIS LA
SHORTLANDS GREEN
Bicknor Wood
1 DENSTEAD WLK
2 CHIDDINGSTONE CL
3 CHISLEHURST CL
4 GROOMBRIDGE SQ
NEW RD
BARHAM CL
WALLIS AVE
Schs
HOLLINGWORTH RD
HASLEMERE ESTATE
PARK WOOD TRADING ESTATE
BICKNOR RD
SUTTON RD
Bicknor Farm
Rumwood Court
Langley
The Lion and Lamb
A274
Pleydells Farm
BIRCHOLT RD
CUXTON RD
LIVINGSTONE WLK
LONGSHAW RD
Park Wood
BRISHING LA
FELDERLAND DR
FELDERLAND RD
KINS DR
DISHLEY
4
3
2
1
55
54
53
52
78
79
80
D
E
F

108

125

91

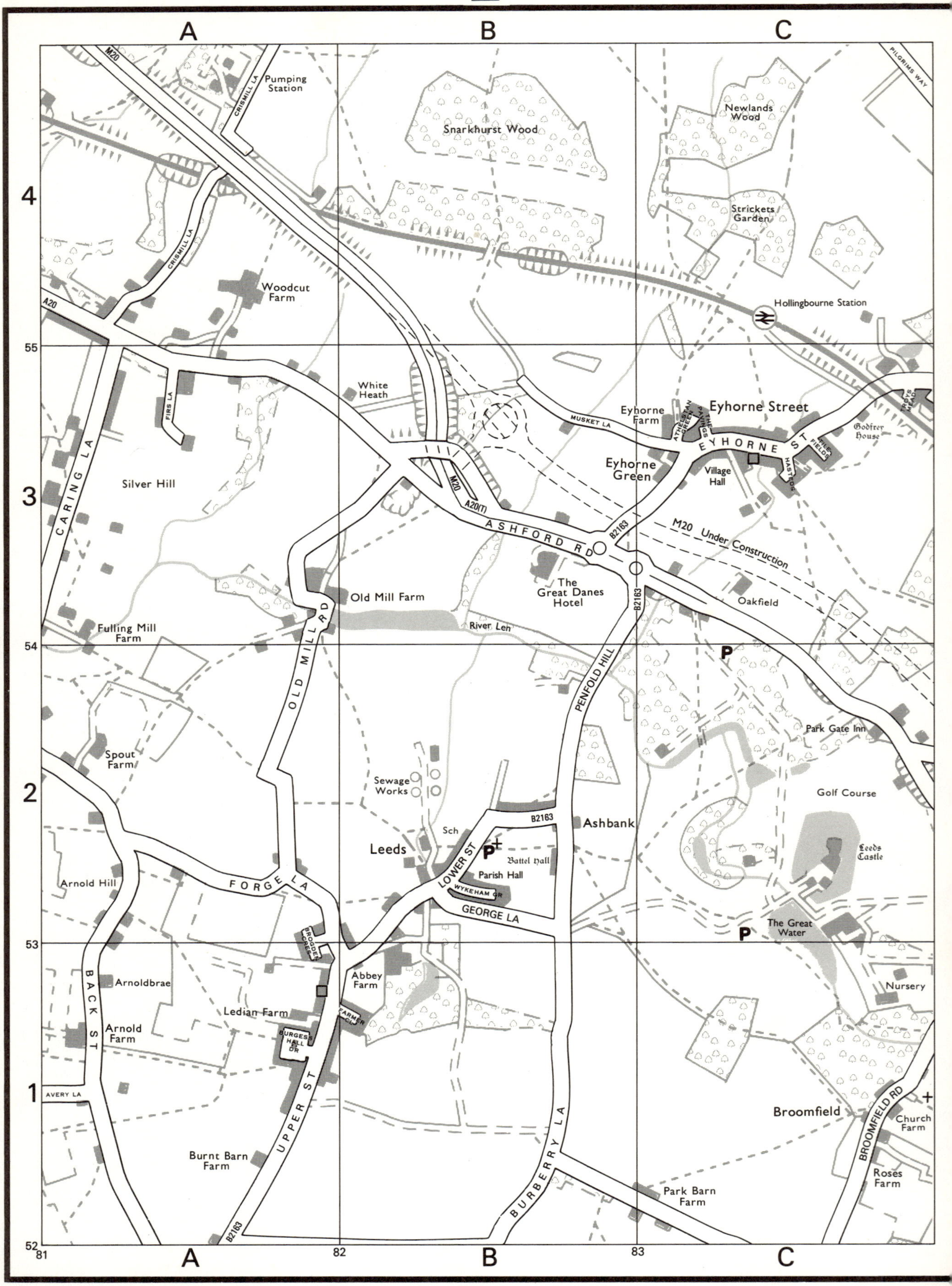
A
B
C
4
3
2
1
55
54
53
52
81
82
83
Pumping Station
CRISMILL LA
M20
Snarkhurst Wood
Newlands Wood
Strickets Garden
Hollingbourne Station
Woodcut Farm
A20
White Heath
FIRS LA
Silver Hill
CARING LA
Eyhorne Farm
Eyhorne Street
MUSKET LA
EYHORNE ST
Godfrey House
Eyhorne Green
Village Hall
A20(T)
ASHFORD RD
B2163
M20 Under Construction
The Great Danes Hotel
Oakfield
Old Mill Farm
OLD MILL RD
River Len
Fulling Mill Farm
PENFOLD HILL
P
Park Gate Inn
Spout Farm
Sewage Works
Golf Course
Ashbank
Sch
Leeds
LOWER ST
Battel Hall
Parish Hall
WYKEHAM GR
Leeds Castle
GEORGE LA
FORGE LA
Arnold Hill
The Great Water
Abbey Farm
Arnoldbrae
BACK ST
Nursery
Ledian Farm
Arnold Farm
UPPER ST
AVERY LA
BURBERRY LA
Broomfield
BROOMFIELD RD
Church Farm
Burnt Barn Farm
Roses Farm
Park Barn Farm

107

126

92

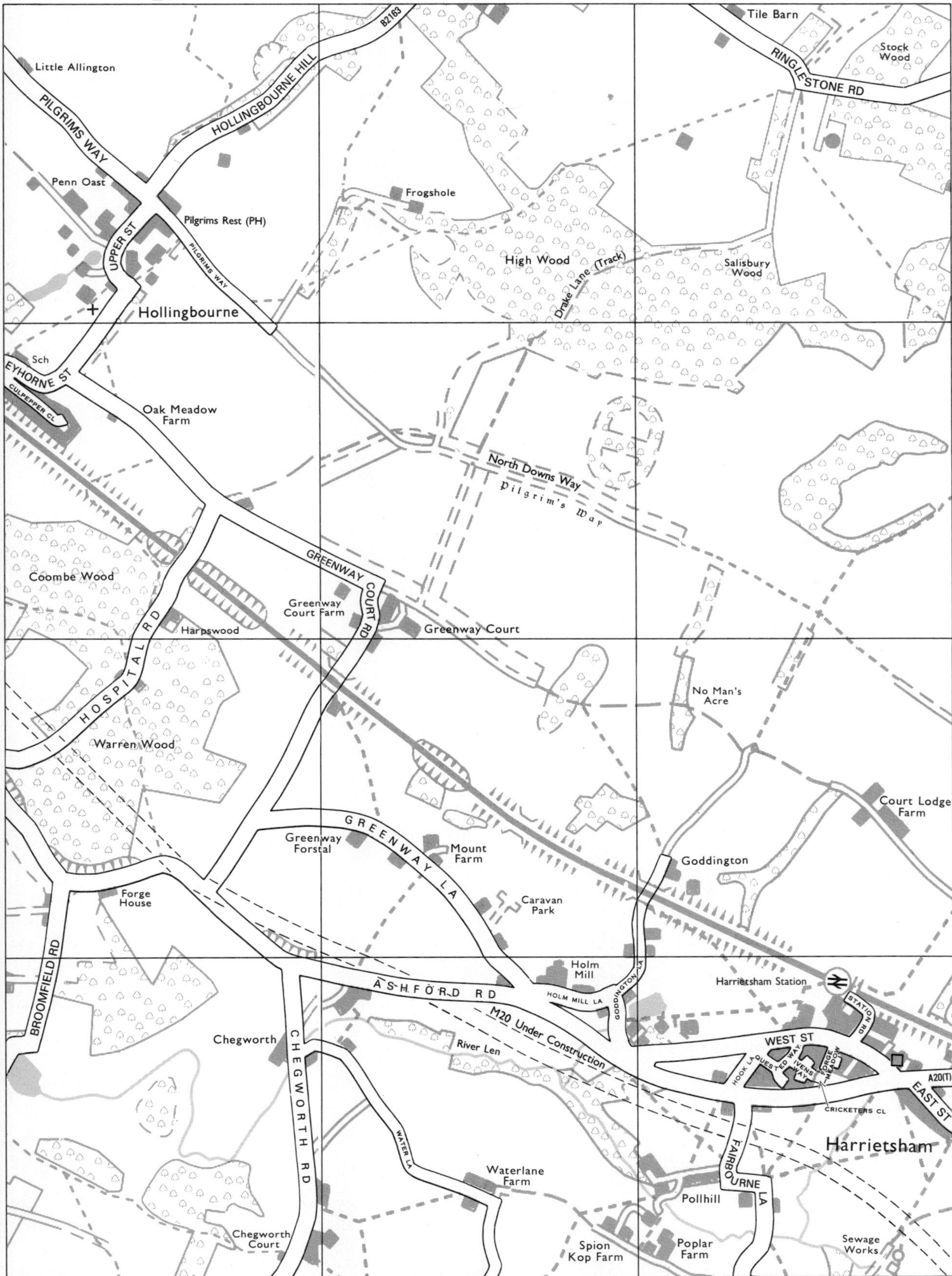

D
E
F
Little Allington
PILGRIMS WAY
HOLLINGBOURNE HILL
B2163
Tile Barn
RINGLESTONE RD
Stock Wood
Penn Oast
Frogshole
Pilgrims Rest (PH)
UPPER ST
PILGRIMS WAY
High Wood
Drake Lane (Track)
Salisbury Wood
Hollingbourne
Sch
EYHORNE ST
CULPEPPER CL
Oak Meadow Farm
North Downs Way
Pilgrim's Way
GREENWAY COURT RD
Coombe Wood
Greenway Court Farm
Greenway Court
Harpswood
HOSPITAL RD
No Man's Acre
Warren Wood
Court Lodge Farm
GREENWAY LA
Greenway Forstal
Mount Farm
Goddington
Forge House
Caravan Park
BROOMFIELD RD
Holm Mill
ASHFORD RD
HOLM MILL LA
GODDINGTON LA
Harrietsham Station
STATION RD
M20 Under Construction
Chegworth
River Len
WEST ST
HOOK LA
QUESTED WAY
IVENS WAY
FORGE MEADOW
A20(T)
EAST ST
CRICKETERS CL
CHEGWORTH RD
WATER LA
Harrietsham
FAIRBOURNE LA
Waterlane Farm
Pollhill
Chegworth Court
Spion Kop Farm
Poplar Farm
Sewage Works
4
55
3
54
2
53
1
52
84
85
86

110

127

93

A
B
C
West Leas
Ringlestone
RINGLESTONE RD
Black Post
Ringlestone Inn (PH)
4
Minnels
Lenniker
The Dell
Wrinsted Court
Butts Bank
Merlewood
HOGBARN LA
55
Dean's Hill
Horsalls
Hogbarn
Lower Deans Farm
STEDE HILL
3
Stedehill Wood
Harrietsham Manor
Newage Farm
Flint Barn Farm
54
Stede Hill
Coles Dane
Hillside Farm
2
Marlow Farm
Marley Court
PILGRIMS WAY
Lea Farm
Whitegates Poultry Farm
North Downs Way
53
MARLEY RD
LAKELANDS
CHURCH RD
ST WELCUME'S WAY
CHURCH LA
MERCER DR
NORTHDOWN VIEW
DICKLEY LA
Marley Works
ASHFORD RD
A20(T)
Sch
RECTORY LA
Mayfield
Dickley Wood
1
EAST ST
Westgate House
Bell Farm
Lenham
Cherry Tree Farm
MAIDSTONE RD
FAVERSHAM RD
NAPOLEON WLK
CHERRY CL
HAM LA
Schs
Liby
THE SQUARE
OLD ASHFORD RD
HATCH RD
BEACON RD
ROBINS AVE
MALTHOUSE CL
Depot
HONYWOOD RD
HIGH ST
CROFT GDNS
SANDWAY RD
52
87
88
89

109

128

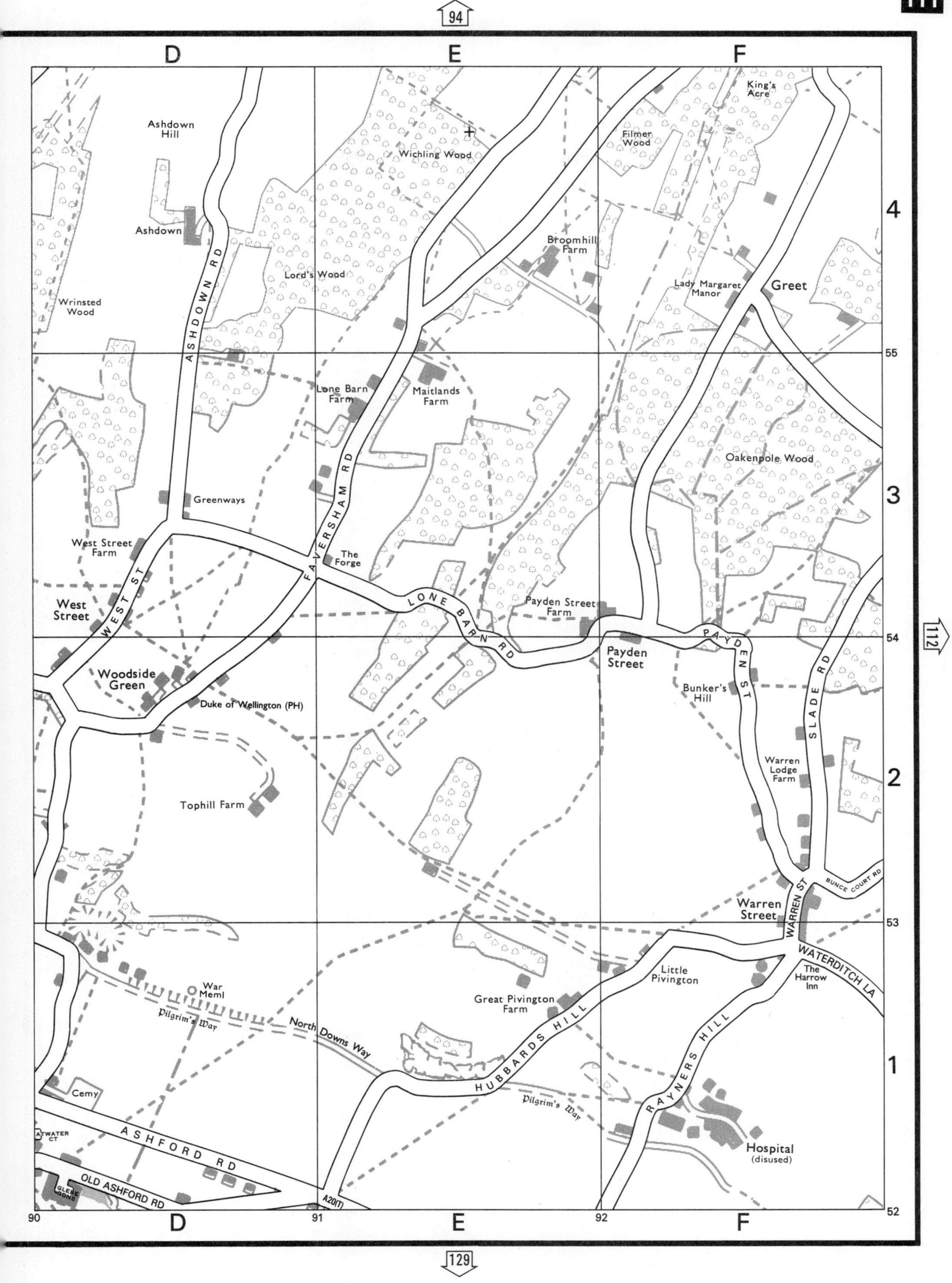
94
D
E
F
King's Acre
Ashdown Hill
Filmer Wood
Wichling Wood
4
Ashdown
Broomhill Farm
Lord's Wood
Lady Margaret Manor
Greet
Wrinsted Wood
ASHDOWN RD
55
Lone Barn Farm
Maitlands Farm
Oakenpole Wood
FAVERSHAM RD
3
Greenways
West Street Farm
The Forge
LONE BARN RD
Payden Street Farm
West Street
WEST ST
112
54
Payden Street
PAYDEN ST
Woodside Green
Bunker's Hill
Duke of Wellington (PH)
SLADE RD
Warren Lodge Farm
2
Tophill Farm
BUNCE COURT RD
Warren Street
WARREN ST
53
WATERDITCH LA
Little Pivington
The Harrow Inn
War Meml
Great Pivington Farm
HUBBARDS HILL
Pilgrim's Way
North Downs Way
RAYNERS HILL
1
Cemy
Pilgrim's Way
ATWATER CT
ASHFORD RD
Hospital (disused)
OLD ASHFORD RD
GLEBE GDNS
A20(T)
52
90
91
92
129

not continued, see key diagram

111

not continued, see key diagram

130

95

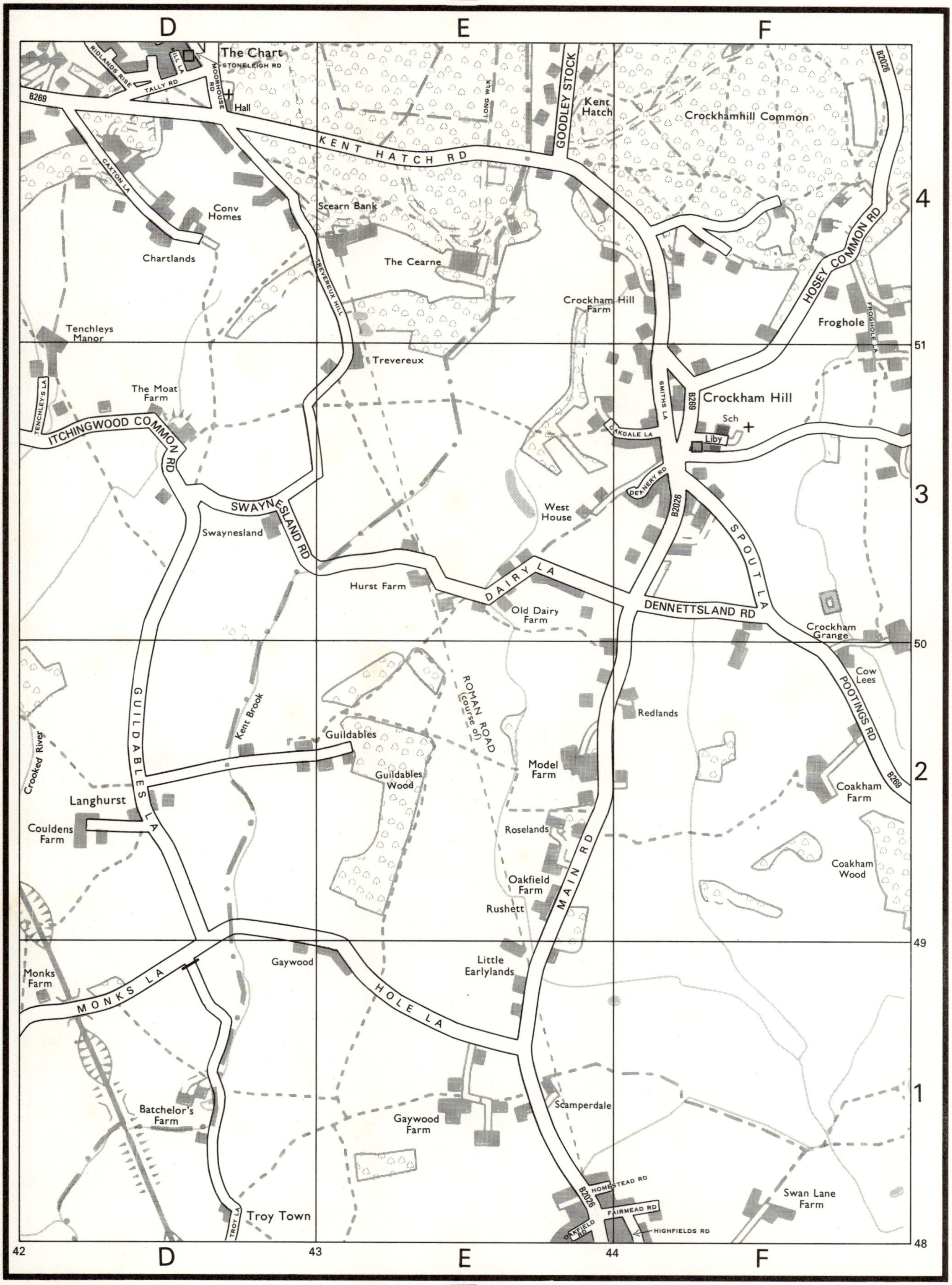

D
E
F
The Chart
STONELEIGH RD
RIDLANDS RISE
HILL LA
TALLY RD
MOORHOUSE RD
Hall
B269
KENT HATCH RD
LONG WLK
GOODLEY STOCK
Kent Hatch
Crockhamhill Common
B2026
CAXTON LA
Conv Homes
Scearn Bank
Chartlands
The Cearne
TREVEREUX HILL
Crockham Hill Farm
HOSEY COMMON RD
Froghole
FROGHOLE LA
Tenchleys Manor
Trevereux
51
TENCHLEY'S LA
The Moat Farm
SMITHS LA
B269
Crockham Hill
Sch
Liby
ITCHINGWOOD COMMON RD
OAKDALE LA
DEANERY RD
SWAYNESLAND RD
West House
B2026
SPOUT LA
3
4
Swaynesland
Hurst Farm
DAIRY LA
Old Dairy Farm
DENNETTSLAND RD
Crockham Grange
50
Cow Lees
POOTINGS RD
ROMAN ROAD (course of)
Redlands
GUILDABLES LA
Kent Brook
Guildables
Model Farm
Crooked River
Guildables Wood
Langhurst
Couldens Farm
Coakham Farm
B269
2
Roselands
Coakham Wood
Oakfield Farm
MAIN RD
Rushett
49
Gaywood
Little Earlylands
Monks Farm
MONKS LA
HOLE LA
1
Scamperdale
Batchelor's Farm
Gaywood Farm
HOMESTEAD RD
B2026
Swan Lane Farm
FAIRMEAD RD
TROY LA
Troy Town
OAKFIELD RD
HIGHFIELDS RD
42
43
44
48
D
E
F

114

131

96

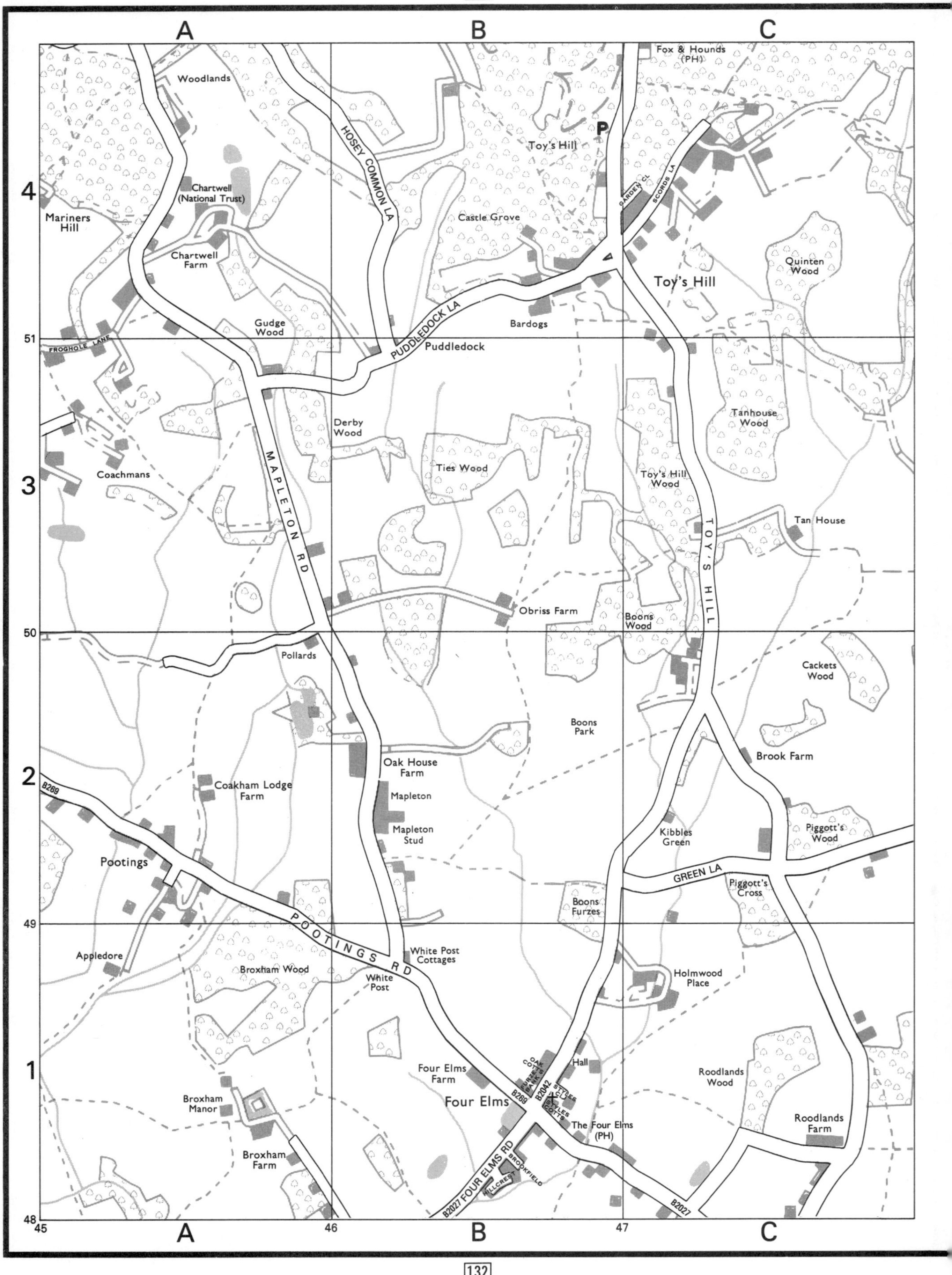
A
B
C
4
3
2
1
51
50
49
48
45
46
47
Woodlands
Fox & Hounds (PH)
HOSEY COMMON LA
Toy's Hill
Chartwell (National Trust)
Mariners Hill
Castle Grove
GARDEN CL
SCORDS LA
Chartwell Farm
Toy's Hill
Quinten Wood
Gudge Wood
PUDDLEDOCK LA
Bardogs
FROGHOLE LANE
Puddledock
Derby Wood
Tanhouse Wood
Ties Wood
Coachmans
MAPLETON RD
Toy's Hill Wood
Tan House
TOY'S HILL
Obriss Farm
Boons Wood
Pollards
Cackets Wood
Boons Park
Brook Farm
Oak House Farm
Coakham Lodge Farm
Mapleton
B269
Mapleton Stud
Kibbles Green
Piggott's Wood
Pootings
GREEN LA
Piggott's Cross
Boons Furzes
POOTINGS RD
White Post Cottages
Appledore
Broxham Wood
White Post
Holmwood Place
OAK COTTS
FURZE BANK
Hall
Four Elms Farm
Roodlands Wood
B2042
STYLES CL
STYLES COTTS
Broxham Manor
Four Elms
B269
The Four Elms (PH)
Roodlands Farm
Broxham Farm
FOUR ELMS RD
BROOKFIELD
HILLCREST
B2027
B2027
A
B
C

113

132

97

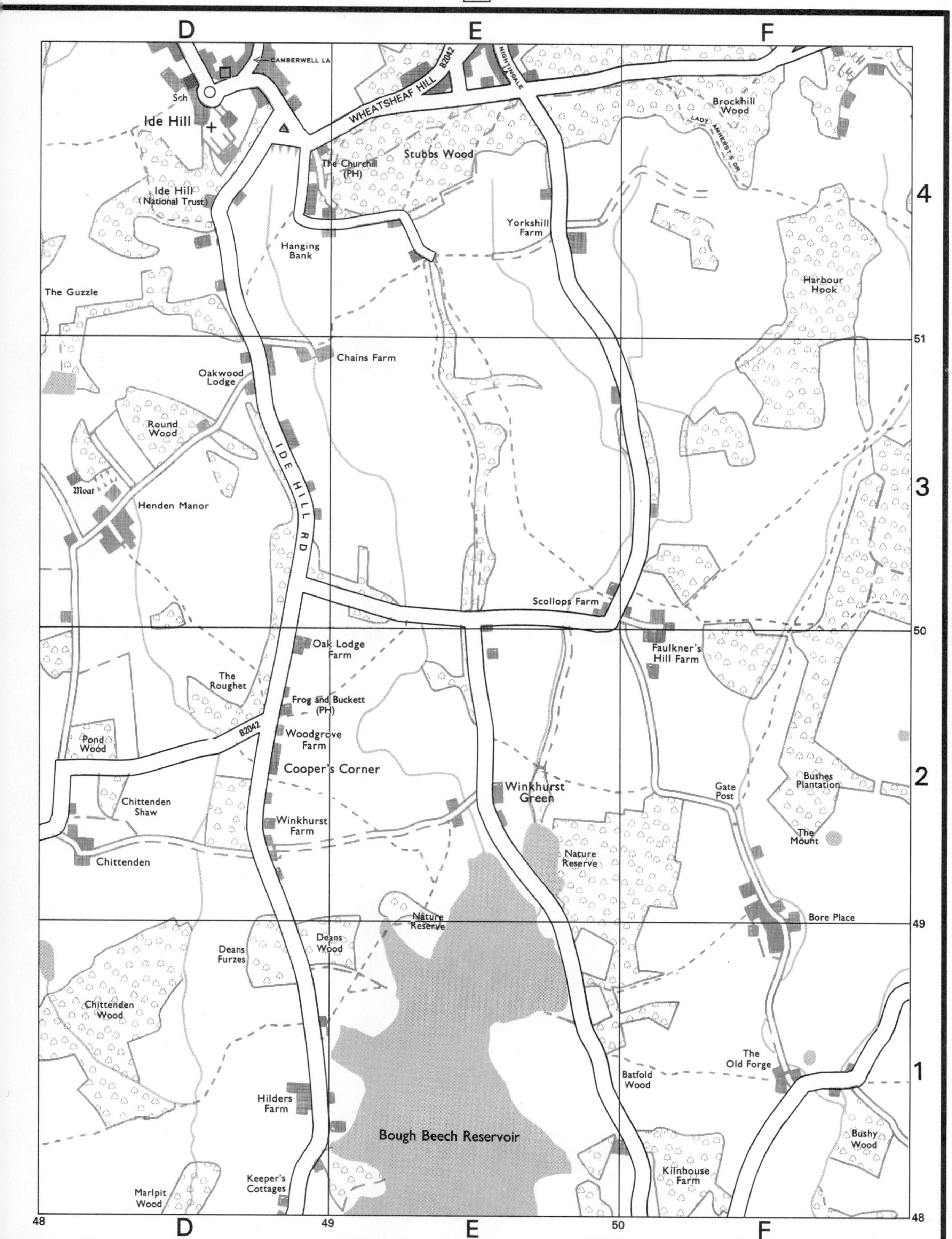
D
E
F
CAMBERWELL LA
Sch
Ide Hill
WHEATSHEAF HILL
B2042
NIGHTINGALE
Brockhill Wood
LADY AMHERST'S DR
The Churchill (PH)
Stubbs Wood
Ide Hill (National Trust)
Yorkshill Farm
Hanging Bank
The Guzzle
Harbour Hook
Chains Farm
Oakwood Lodge
Round Wood
IDE HILL RD
Moat
Henden Manor
Scollops Farm
Oak Lodge Farm
Faulkner's Hill Farm
The Roughet
Frog and Buckett (PH)
Woodgrove Farm
B2042
Pond Wood
Cooper's Corner
Chittenden Shaw
Winkhurst Green
Gate Post
Bushes Plantation
Winkhurst Farm
The Mount
Chittenden
Nature Reserve
Nature Reserve
Bore Place
Deans Wood
Deans Furzes
Chittenden Wood
The Old Forge
Batfold Wood
Hilders Farm
Bough Beech Reservoir
Bushy Wood
Keeper's Cottages
Kilnhouse Farm
Marlpit Wood
4
3
2
1
51
50
49
48
48
49
50

116

133

98

115

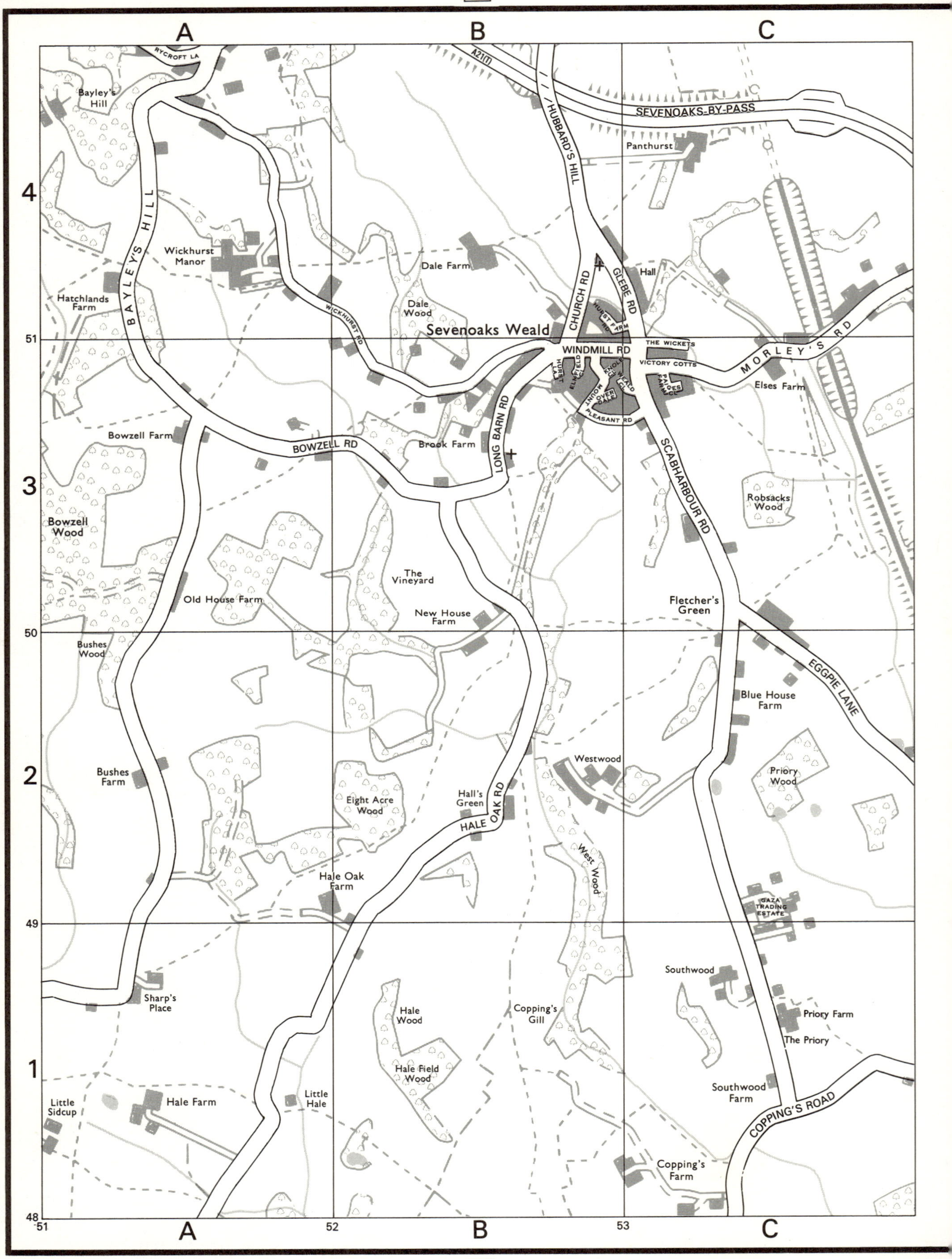
A
B
C
4
3
2
1
51
50
49
48
52
53
RYCROFT LA
A21(T)
SEVENOAKS-BY-PASS
HUBBARD'S HILL
Panthurst
Bayley's Hill
BAYLEY'S HILL
Wickhurst Manor
Hatchlands Farm
Dale Farm
Dale Wood
Hall
CHURCH RD
GLEBE RD
HURST FARM RD
Sevenoaks Weald
WICKHURST RD
WINDMILL RD
THE WICKETS
VICTORY COTTS
MORLEY'S RD
Elses Farm
HURST LA
ELMFIELD CL
KNOLE CL
WEALD CL
PAGES FARM CL
MOUNT PLEASANT RD
OVER DALE
Bowzell Farm
BOWZELL RD
Brook Farm
LONG BARN RD
SCABHARBOUR RD
Robsacks Wood
Bowzell Wood
The Vineyard
Old House Farm
New House Farm
Fletcher's Green
Bushes Wood
EGGPIE LANE
Blue House Farm
Westwood
Bushes Farm
Priory Wood
Eight Acre Wood
Hall's Green
HALE OAK RD
West Wood
Hale Oak Farm
GAZA TRADING ESTATE
Southwood
Sharp's Place
Hale Wood
Copping's Gill
Priory Farm
The Priory
Hale Field Wood
Southwood Farm
Little Sidcup
Hale Farm
Little Hale
COPPING'S ROAD
Copping's Farm

134

99

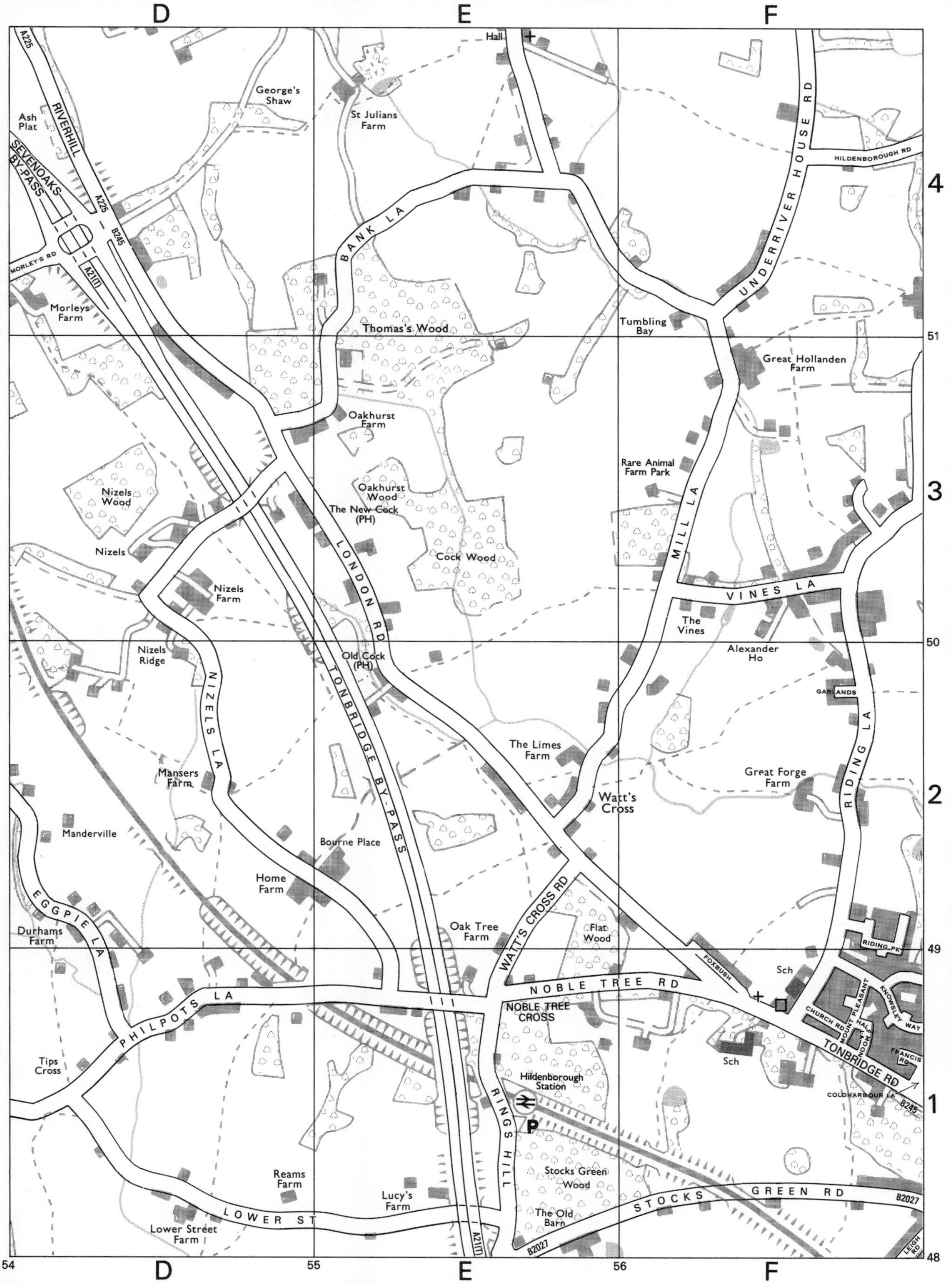
D
E
F
Hall
George's Shaw
St Julians Farm
Ash Plat
RIVERHILL
SEVENOAKS BY-PASS
A225
B245
A21(T)
MORLEY'S RD
Morleys Farm
BANK LA
Thomas's Wood
Tumbling Bay
UNDERRIVER HOUSE RD
HILDENBOROUGH RD
Great Hollanden Farm
Oakhurst Farm
Rare Animal Farm Park
Nizels Wood
Oakhurst Wood
The New Cock (PH)
Cock Wood
Nizels
MILL LA
VINES LA
Nizels Farm
LONDON RD
The Vines
Alexander Ho
Nizels Ridge
Old Cock (PH)
TONBRIDGE BY-PASS
NIZELS LA
GARLANDS
The Limes Farm
RIDING LA
Mansers Farm
Watt's Cross
Great Forge Farm
Manderville
Bourne Place
Home Farm
WATT'S CROSS RD
EGGPIE LA
Durhams Farm
Oak Tree Farm
Flat Wood
RIDING PK
FOXBUSH
Sch
NOBLE TREE RD
PHILPOTS LA
NOBLE TREE CROSS
CHURCH RD
MOUNT PLEASANT
HALF MOON
KNOWSLEY WAY
FRANCIS RD
TONBRIDGE RD
Sch
Tips Cross
Hildenborough Station
COLDHARBOUR LA
B245
RINGS HILL
P
Stocks Green Wood
Reams Farm
Lucy's Farm
STOCKS GREEN RD
B2027
The Old Barn
LOWER ST
Lower Street Farm
B2027
LEIGH RD
4
3
2
1
51
50
49
48
54
55
56

118

135

100

117

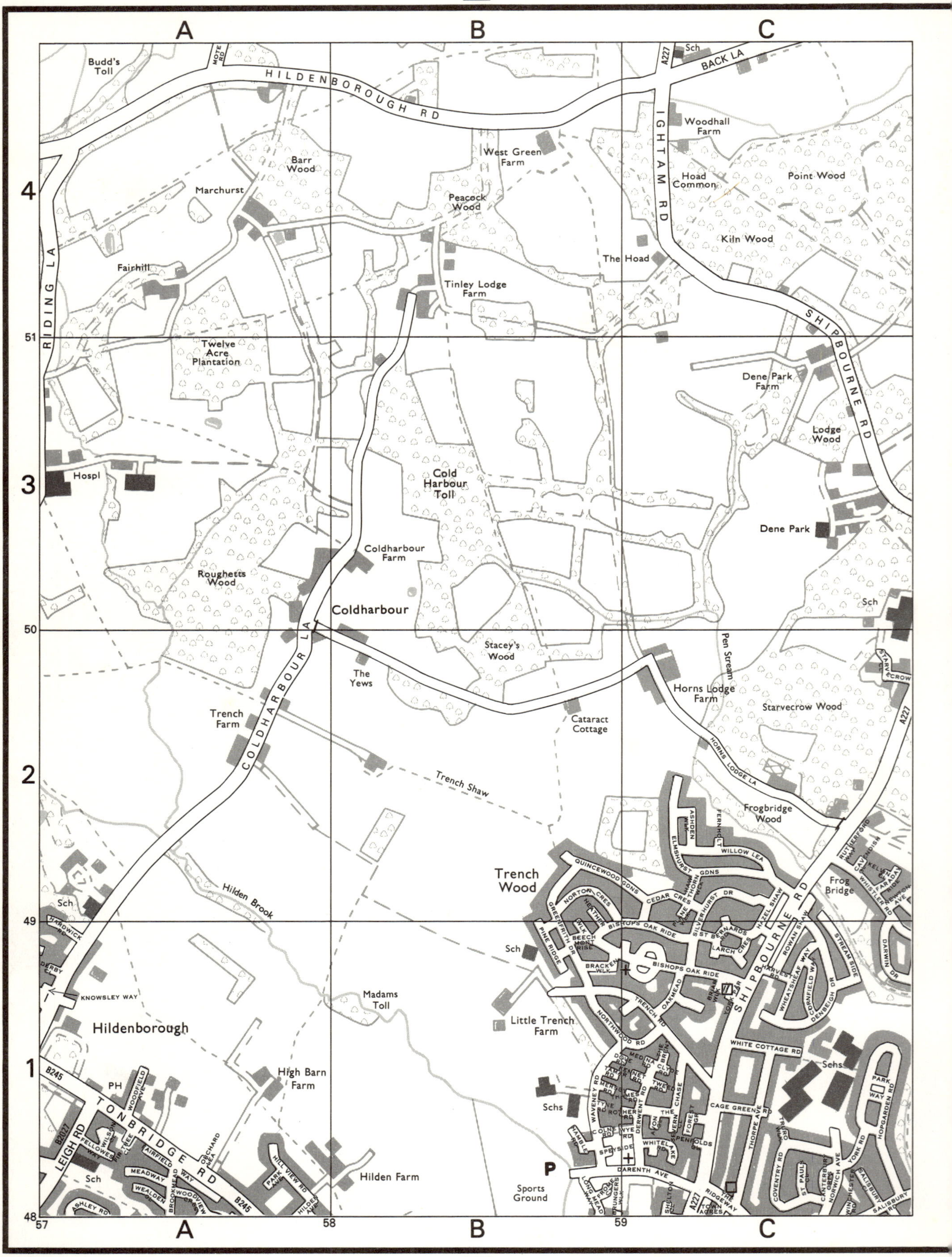

A
B
C
4
3
2
1
51
50
49
48
57
58
59
Budd's Toll
HILDENBOROUGH RD
MOTE RD
BACK LA
A227
Sch
Woodhall Farm
IGHTAM RD
West Green Farm
Barr Wood
Marchurst
Peacock Wood
Hoad Common
Point Wood
Kiln Wood
The Hoad
Fairhill
Tinley Lodge Farm
RIDING LA
SHIPBOURNE RD
Twelve Acre Plantation
Dene Park Farm
Lodge Wood
Hospl
Cold Harbour Toll
Dene Park
Coldharbour Farm
Roughetts Wood
Coldharbour
Sch
Stacey's Wood
COLDHARBOUR LA
The Yews
Pen Stream
Horns Lodge Farm
Starvecrow Wood
Trench Farm
Cataract Cottage
HORNS LODGE LA
Trench Shaw
Frogbridge Wood
Trench Wood
Hilden Brook
Frog Bridge
Sch
HARDWICK RD
DERBY RD
KNOWSLEY WAY
QUINCEWOOD GDNS
WILLOW LEA
CEDAR CRES
SILVERHURST DR
BISHOPS OAK RIDE
ST BERNARDS RD
LARCH CRES
HAZEL SHAW
ROWAN SHAW
STREAM SIDE
DARWIN DR
WHEATSHEAF WAY
CORNFIELD WAY
DENBEIGH DR
PINE RIDGE
GREENFRITH DR
NORTON CRES
BRACKEN WLK
OAKMEAD
TRENCH RD
NORTHWOOD RD
Madams Toll
Little Trench Farm
Hildenborough
WHITE COTTAGE RD
Schs
High Barn Farm
PH
B245
TONBRIDGE RD
WOODFIELD AVE
CAGE GREEN RD
THORPE AVE
PARK WAY
HOPGARDEN RD
Schs
WAVENEY RD
FOREST GR
PENFOLDS CL
WHITELAKE RD
SPEYSIDE
B2027
LEIGH RD
FELLOWES WAY
AIRFIELD WAY
MEADWAY
WEALDEN CL
ORCHARD LEA
HILL VIEW RD
PARK AVE
Hilden Farm
P
DARENTH AVE
Sports Ground
THE RIDGEWAY
TONK ACRES
COVENTRY RD
ST PAULS CT
CANTERBURY GDNS
NORWICH AVE
WINCHESTER RD
YORK RD
SALISBURY RD
Sch
ASHLEY RD
BROOKMEAD
WOODVIEW CRES
HILDEN AVE

136

101

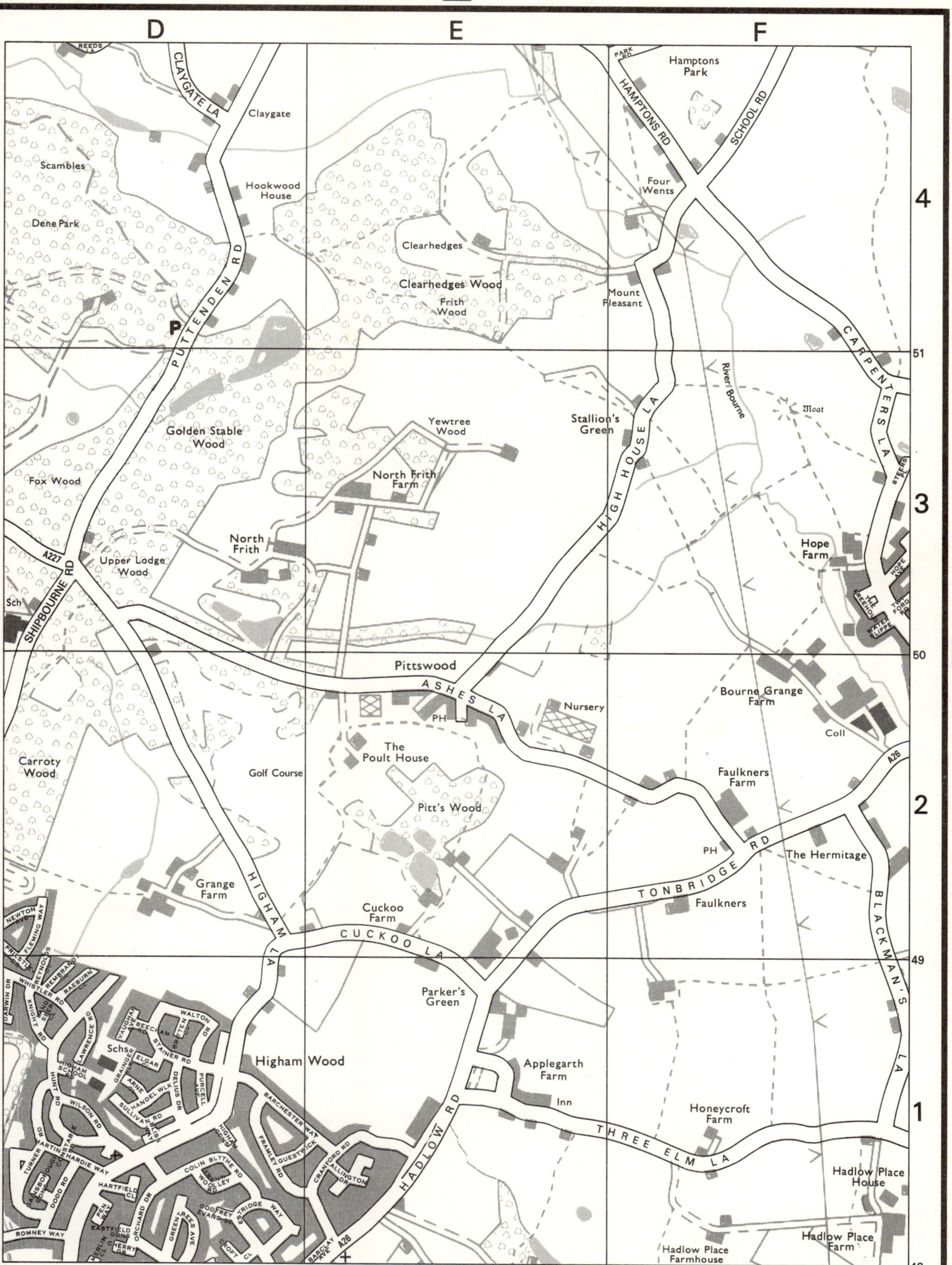
D
E
F
Reeds La
Claygate La
Claygate
Scambles
Hookwood House
Dene Park
Puttenden Rd
P
Clearhedges
Clearhedges Wood
Frith Wood
Park Rd
Hamptons Park
Hamptons Rd
School Rd
Four Wents
Mount Pleasant
Carpenters La
Golden Stable Wood
Yewtree Wood
North Frith Farm
Stallion's Green
High House La
River Bourne
Moat
Steers Pl
Fox Wood
North Frith
Upper Lodge Wood
A227
Shipbourne Rd
Sch
Hope Farm
Hope Ave
Pittswood
Ashes La
PH
Nursery
Bourne Grange Farm
Coll
Carroty Wood
The Poult House
Golf Course
Faulkners Farm
A26
Pitt's Wood
PH
The Hermitage
Tonbridge Rd
Grange Farm
Higham La
Cuckoo Farm
Faulkners
Blackman's La
Cuckoo La
Newton Ave
Fleming Way
Priestley Dr
Reynolds La
Rembrandt Cl
Whistler Rd
Raeburn Cl
Darwin Dr
Knight Rd
Parker's Green
Walton Rd
Lawrence Rd
Vaughan Ave
Beecham Rd
Britten Cl
Stainer Rd
Schs
Elgar Cl
Higham Wood
Applegarth Farm
Higham School Rd
Grainger Wlk
Arne Cl
Delius Dr
Purcell Ave
Hunt Rd
Wilson Rd
Handel Wlk
Sullivan Rd
Bliss Way
Inn
Hadlow Rd
Barchester Way
Framley Rd
Guestwick
Cranford Rd
Allington Dr
Honeycroft Farm
Three Elm La
Martin Hardie Way
Turner Rd
Gainsborough Gdns
Constable Rd
Dodd Rd
Hartfield Cl
Colin Blythe Rd
Woolley Rd
Orchard Dr
Godfrey Evans Cl
Estridge Way
Hadlow Place House
Pen Way
Eastfield Gdns
Greentrees Ave
Cherry Gr
Romney Way
Croft Cl
Barclay Ave
A26
Hadlow Place Farmhouse
Hadlow Place Farm
4
3
2
1
51
50
49
48
60
61
62

120

137

102

119

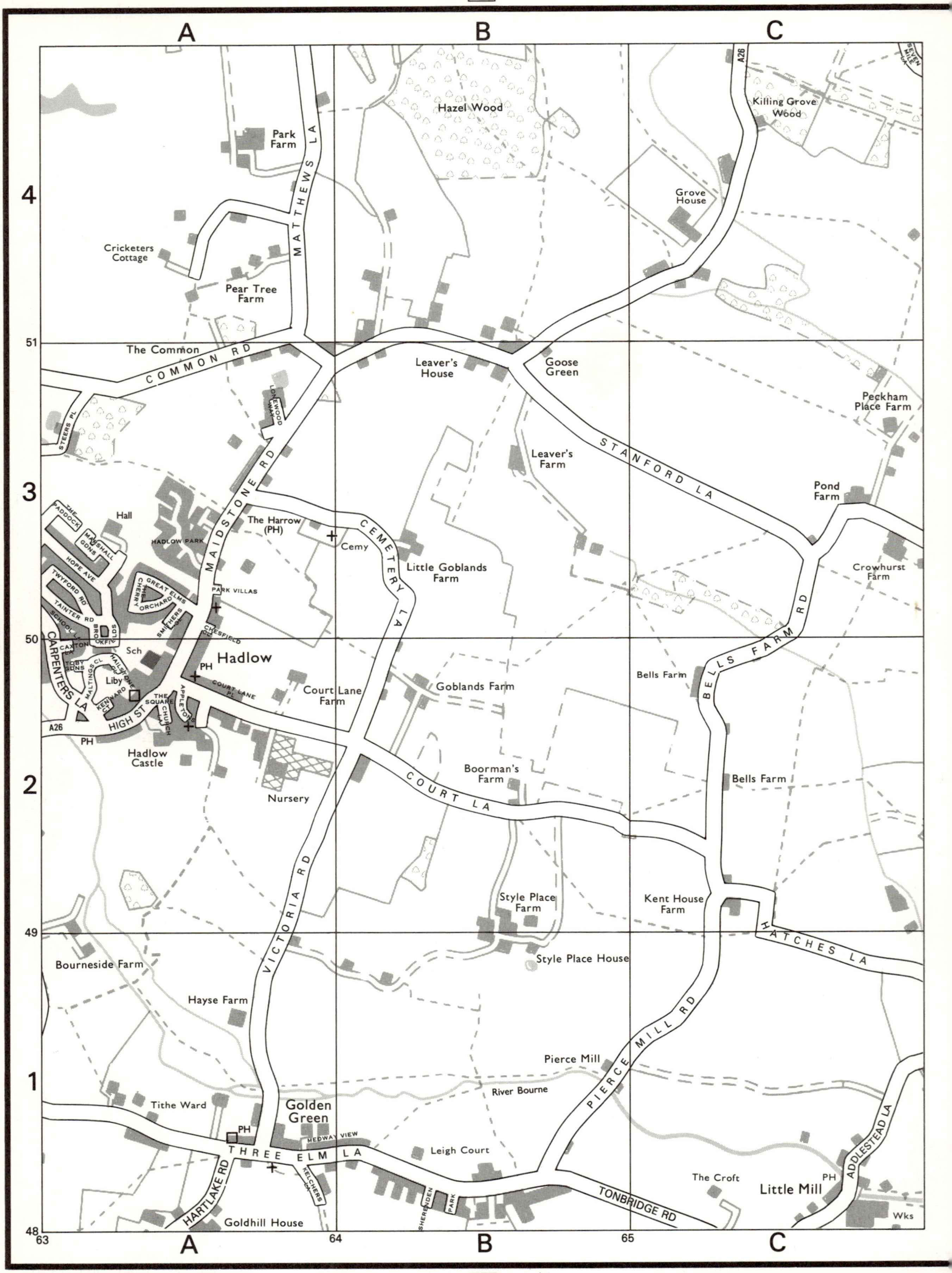
A
B
C
4
3
2
1
51
50
49
48
63
64
65
Hazel Wood
Killing Grove Wood
Park Farm
MATTHEWS LA
A26
Grove House
Cricketers Cottage
Pear Tree Farm
The Common
COMMON RD
Leaver's House
Goose Green
Peckham Place Farm
STEERS PL
LONEWOOD WAY
MAIDSTONE RD
Leaver's Farm
STANFORD LA
Pond Farm
THE PADDOCK
Hall
MARSHALL GDNS
HOPE AVE
HADLOW PARK
The Harrow (PH)
Cemy
CEMETERY LA
Little Goblands Farm
Crowhurst Farm
TWYFORD RD
GREAT ELMS
THE CHERRY ORCHARD
PARK VILLAS
TAINTER RD
SCHOOL LA
SMITHERS
CHESFIELD CL
BELLS FARM RD
CARPENTERS LA
CAXTON
TOBY GDNS
Sch
Hadlow
PH
MALTINGS CL
Liby
KENWARD CL
THE SQUARE
CHURCH
APPLETONS
COURT LANE PL
Court Lane Farm
Goblands Farm
Bells Farm
A26
HIGH ST
PH
Hadlow Castle
Nursery
Boorman's Farm
COURT LA
Bells Farm
VICTORIA RD
Style Place Farm
Kent House Farm
HATCHES LA
Style Place House
Bourneside Farm
Hayse Farm
PIERCE MILL RD
Pierce Mill
River Bourne
Tithe Ward
Golden Green
PH
MEDWAY VIEW
THREE ELM LA
Leigh Court
HARTLAKE RD
KELCHERS
SHERENDEN PARK
TONBRIDGE RD
The Croft
Little Mill
PH
ADDLESTEAD LA
Wks
Goldhill House

138

103

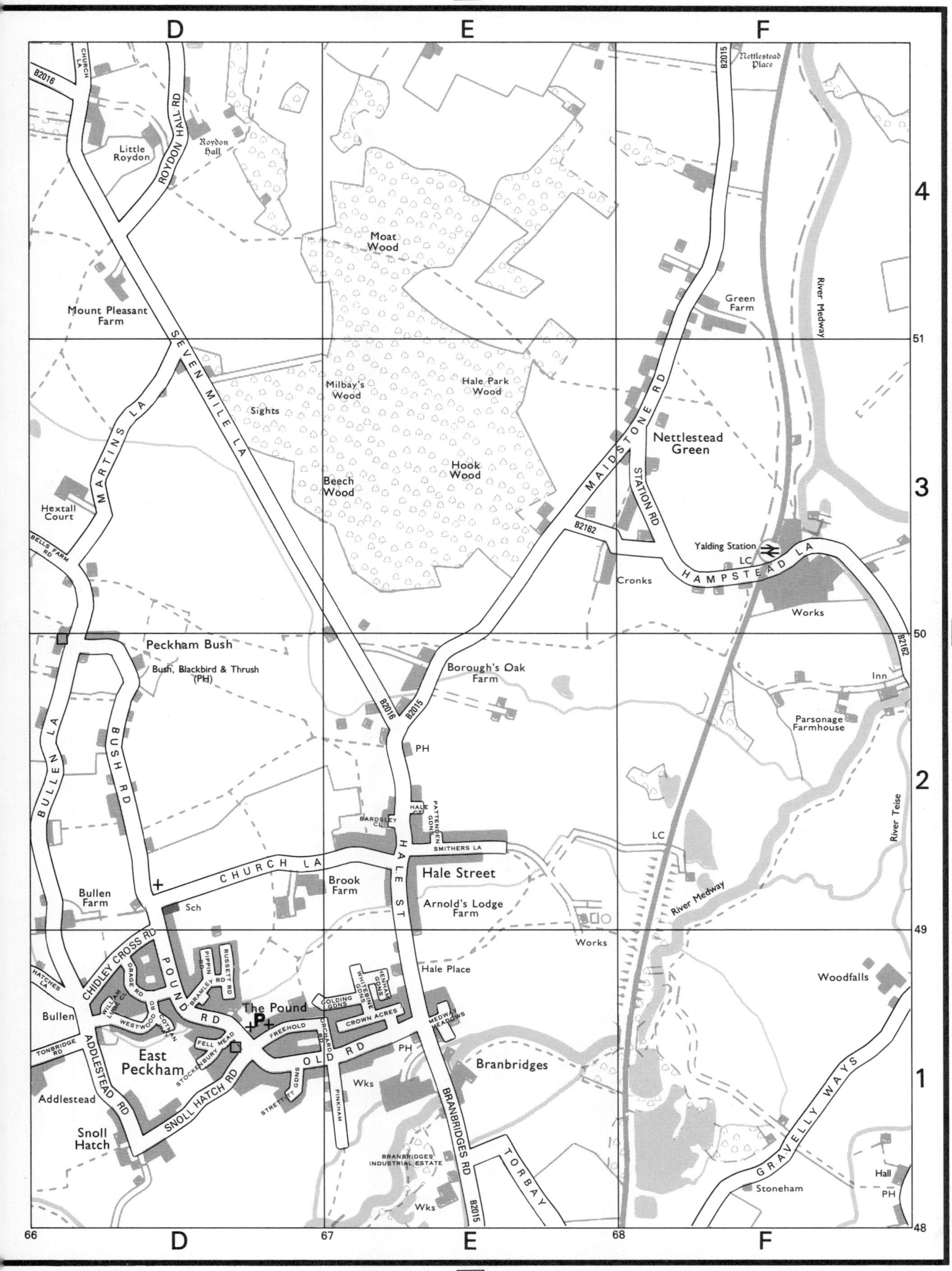
D
E
F
B2016
CHURCH LA
ROYDON HALL RD
Roydon Hall
Little Roydon
B2015
Nettlestead Place
Moat Wood
Mount Pleasant Farm
Green Farm
River Medway
SEVEN MILE LA
MARTINS LA
Sights
Milbay's Wood
Hale Park Wood
Beech Wood
Hook Wood
MAIDSTONE RD
Nettlestead Green
STATION RD
Hextall Court
BELLS FARM RD
B2162
Yalding Station
LC
HAMPSTEAD LA
Cronks
Works
Peckham Bush
Bush, Blackbird & Thrush (PH)
Borough's Oak Farm
Inn
B2016
B2015
BULLEN LA
BUSH RD
PH
Parsonage Farmhouse
HALE CT
PATTENDEN GDNS
BARDSLEY CL
SMITHERS LA
River Teise
CHURCH LA
HALE ST
Hale Street
Brook Farm
Arnold's Lodge Farm
River Medway
Bullen Farm
Sch
Works
CHIDLEY CROSS RD
POUND RD
PIPPIN RD
RUSSETT RD
BRAMLEY RD
DRAGE RD
WHITEBINE GDNS
HENHAM GDNS
Hale Place
Woodfalls
HATCHES LA
WILLIAM LUCK CL
WESTWOOD RD
COTMAN WAY
The Pound
GOLDING GDNS
CROWN ACRES
MEDWAY MEADOWS
Bullen
TONBRIDGE RD
ADDLESTEAD RD
FELL MEAD
STOCKENBURY
FREEHOLD
ORCHARD RD
OLD RD
PH
East Peckham
Branbridges
STRETTITT GDNS
Wks
PINKHAM
BRANBRIDGES RD
GRAVELLY WAYS
Addlestead
SNOLL HATCH RD
Snoll Hatch
BRANBRIDGES INDUSTRIAL ESTATE
TORBAY
Hall
Stoneham
PH
Wks
B2015
4
51
3
50
2
49
1
48
66
67
68
D
E
F

122

139

104

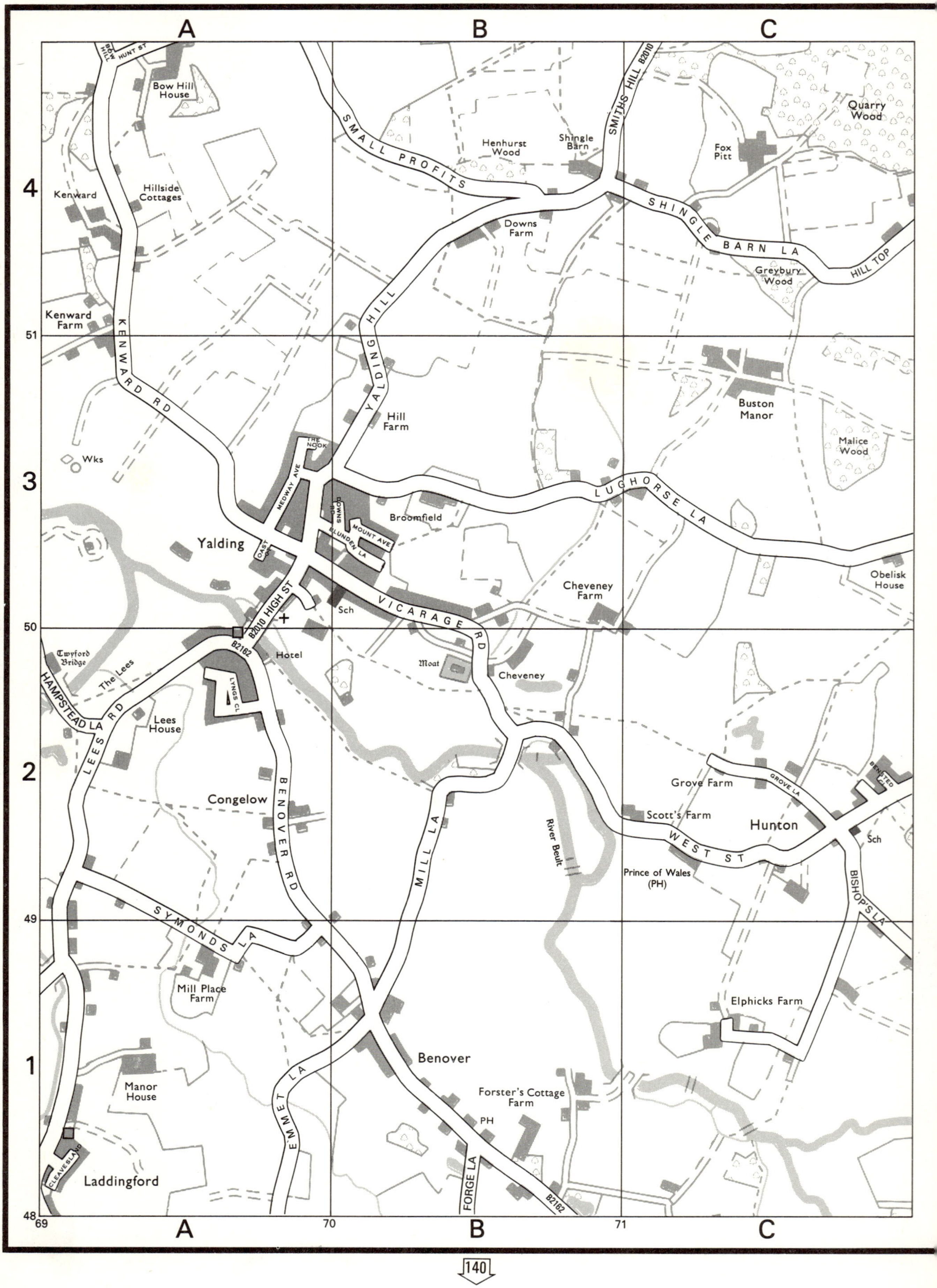
A
B
C
4
3
2
1
51
50
49
48
69
70
71
Bow Hill House
Kenward
Hillside Cottages
Kenward Farm
KENWARD RD
SMALL PROFITS
Henhurst Wood
Shingle Barn
SMITHS HILL B2010
Fox Pitt
Quarry Wood
SHINGLE BARN LA
HILL TOP
Greybury Wood
Downs Farm
YALDING HILL
Buston Manor
Malice Wood
Hill Farm
Wks
LUGHORSE LA
Broomfield
Yalding
MEDWAY AVE
MOUNT AVE
ELUNDEN LA
Obelisk House
Cheveney Farm
B2010 HIGH ST
VICARAGE RD
Sch
Hotel
B2162
Twyford Bridge
The Lees
HAMPSTEAD LA
Moat
Cheveney
LYNGS CL
LEES RD
Lees House
Congelow
BENOVER RD
MILL LA
River Beult
Grove Farm
GROVE LA
Scott's Farm
Hunton
WEST ST
Sch
Prince of Wales (PH)
BISHOPS LA
SYMONDS LA
Mill Place Farm
Elphicks Farm
Benover
EMMET LA
Manor House
Forster's Cottage Farm
PH
FORGE LA
B2162
Laddingford

121

140

105

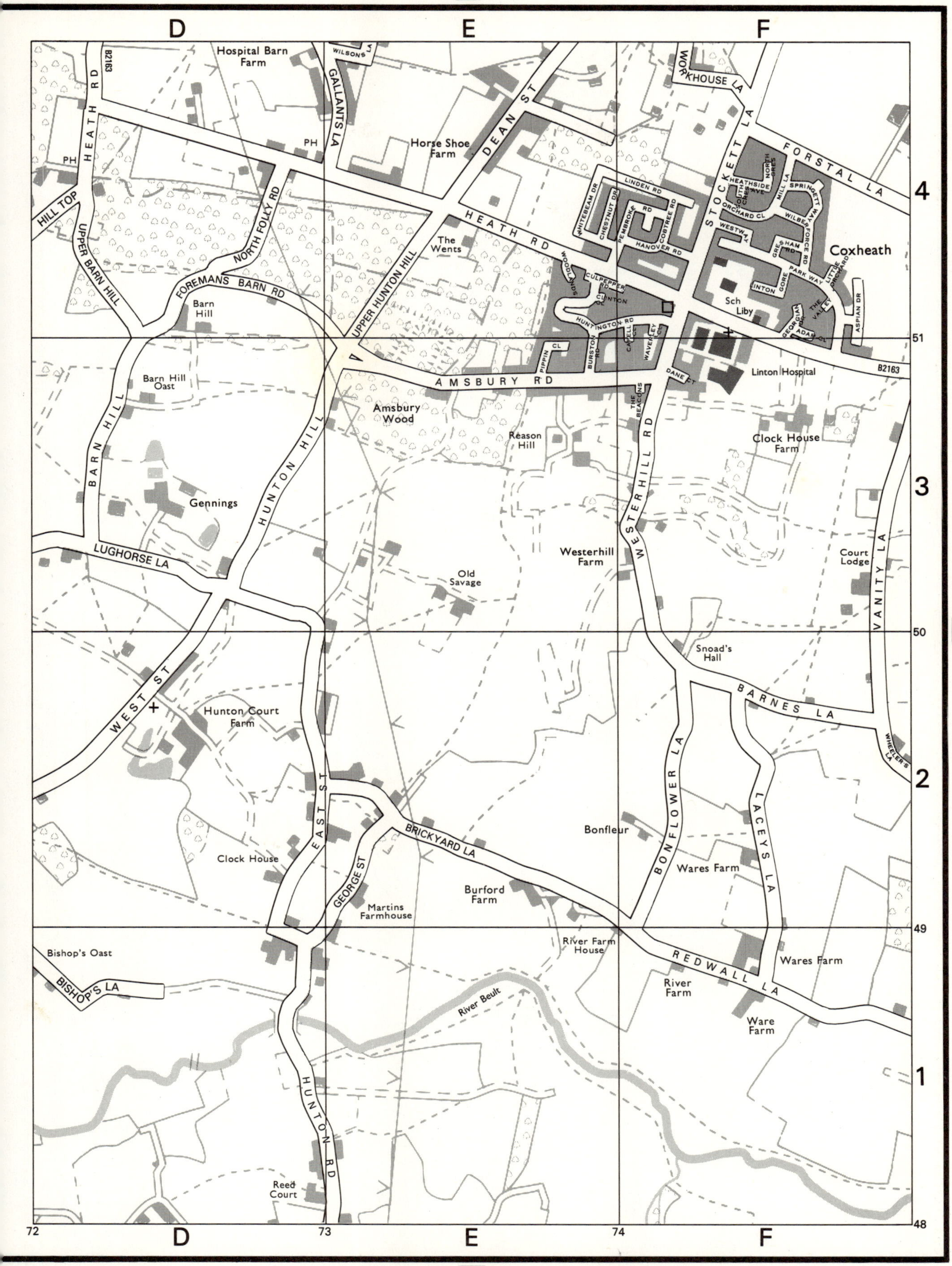
D
E
F
Hospital Barn Farm
WILSONS LA
GALLANTS LA
B2163
HEATH RD
PH
HILL TOP
UPPER BARN HILL
NORTH FOLLY RD
FOREMANS BARN RD
Barn Hill
Horse Shoe Farm
DEAN ST
UPPER HUNTON HILL
The Wents
HEATH RD
WORKHOUSE LA
STOCKETT LA
FORSTAL LA
LINDEN RD
WHITEBEAM DR
CHESTNUT DR
PEMBROKE RD
COBTREE RD
HANOVER RD
HEATHSIDE AVE
ORCHARD CL
WESTWAY
WILBERFORCE RD
SPRINGETT WAY
MILL LA
GRESHAM RD
PARK WAY
LITTLE ORCHARD
LINTON GORE
THE VALLEY
GEORGIAN DR
ADAM CL
ASPIAN DR
Coxheath
WOODLANDS
CULPEPPER RD
CLINTON CL
HUNTINGTON RD
BURSTON RD
CAPELL CL
WAVERLEY CL
PIPPIN CL
Sch
Liby
Linton Hospital
B2163
4
51
AMSBURY RD
DANE CT
THE BEACONS
Barn Hill Oast
BARN HILL
Amsbury Wood
Reason Hill
Clock House Farm
WESTERHILL RD
3
Gennings
HUNTON HILL
Westerhill Farm
Court Lodge
VANITY LA
LUGHORSE LA
Old Savage
50
Snoad's Hall
BARNES LA
WEST ST
Hunton Court Farm
WHEELER'S LA
2
EAST ST
BRICKYARD LA
Bonfleur
BONFLOWER LA
LACEYS LA
Clock House
Wares Farm
GEORGE ST
Burford Farm
Martins Farmhouse
49
Bishop's Oast
BISHOP'S LA
River Farm House
REDWALL LA
Wares Farm
River Farm
Ware Farm
River Beult
1
HUNTON RD
Reed Court
72
73
74
48
D
E
F

124

141

106

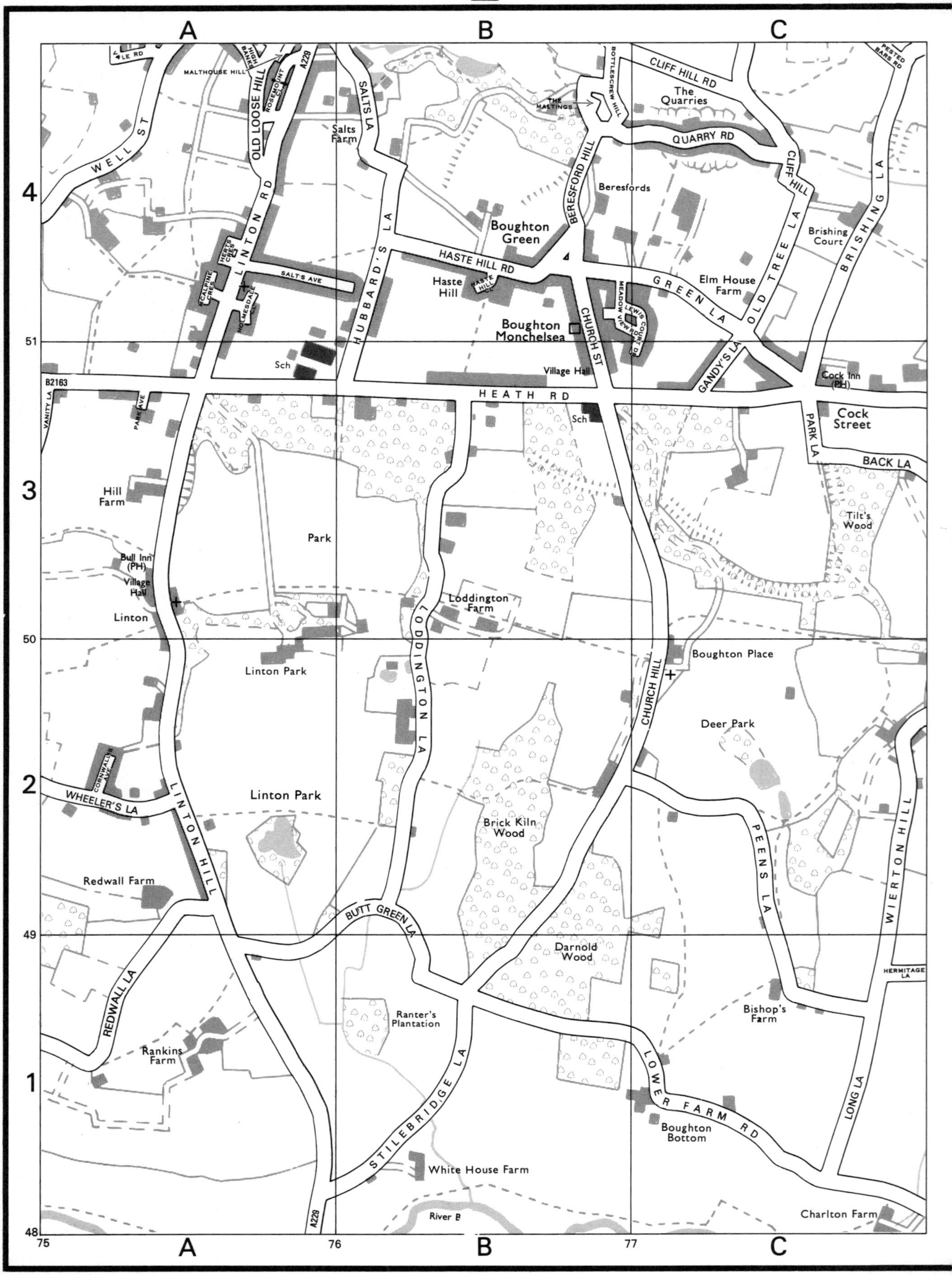
A
B
C
4
3
2
1
51
50
49
48
75
76
77
WELL ST
MALTHOUSE HILL
OLD LOOSE HILL
ROSEMOUNT CL
HIGH BANKS
A229
SALTS LA
Salts Farm
LINTON RD
HERTS CRES
MCALPINE CRES
HOLMESDALE CL
SALTS AVE
Sch
B2163
VANITY LA
PARK AVE
HUBBARD'S LA
HASTE HILL RD
Haste Hill
HASTE HILL CL
Boughton Green
Boughton Monchelsea
Village Hall
BERESFORD HILL
Beresfords
THE MALTINGS
BOTTLESCREW HILL
CLIFF HILL RD
The Quarries
QUARRY RD
CLIFF HILL
OLD TREE LA
BRISHING LA
Brishing Court
PESTED BARS RD
GREEN LA
Elm House Farm
CHURCH ST
MEADOW VIEW RD
LEWIS COURT DR
GANDY'S LA
Cock Inn (PH)
HEATH RD
Cock Street
PARK LA
BACK LA
Tilt's Wood
Hill Farm
Park
Bull Inn (PH)
Village Hall
Linton
Loddington Farm
LODDINGTON LA
Linton Park
CHURCH HILL
Boughton Place
Deer Park
CORNWALLIS AVE
WHEELER'S LA
LINTON HILL
Linton Park
Brick Kiln Wood
PEENS LA
WIERTON HILL
Redwall Farm
BUTT GREEN LA
Darnold Wood
HERMITAGE LA
REDWALL LA
Ranter's Plantation
Bishop's Farm
Rankins Farm
STILEBRIDGE LA
LOWER FARM RD
LONG LA
Boughton Bottom
White House Farm
A229
River B
Charlton Farm

123

142

107

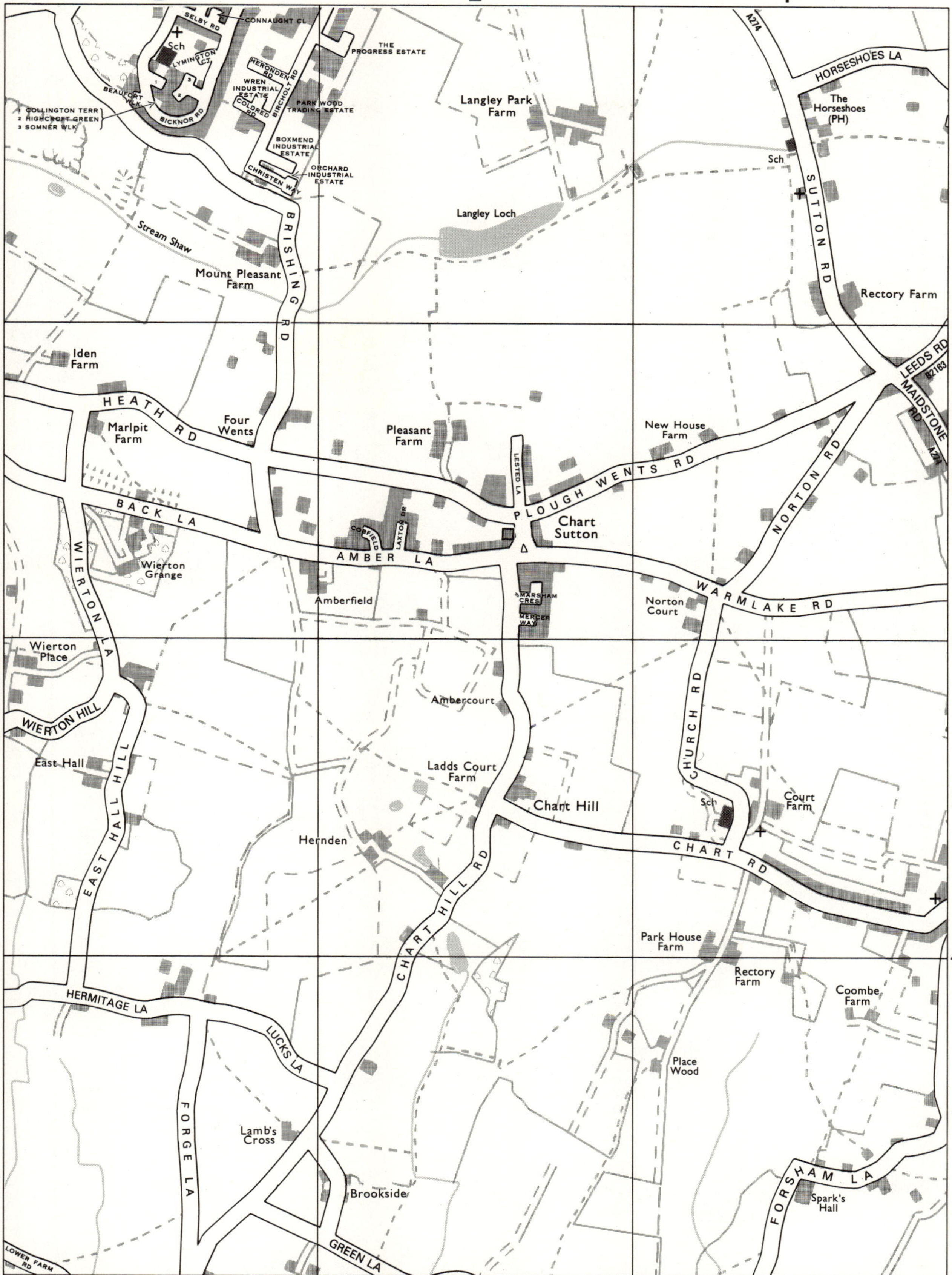
D
E
F
SELBY RD
CONNAUGHT CL
Sch
LYMINGTON CT
BEAUFORT WLK
BICKNOR RD
1 COLLINGTON TERR
2 HIGHCROFT GREEN
3 SOMNER WLK
HERONDEN RD
WREN INDUSTRIAL ESTATE
COLDRED RD
BIRCHOLT RD
PARK WOOD TRADING ESTATE
THE PROGRESS ESTATE
BOXMEND INDUSTRIAL ESTATE
ORCHARD INDUSTRIAL ESTATE
CHRISTEN WAY
Langley Park Farm
Langley Loch
Stream Shaw
Mount Pleasant Farm
BRISHING RD
A274
HORSESHOES LA
The Horseshoes (PH)
Sch
SUTTON RD
Rectory Farm
4
51
LEEDS RD
B2163
MAIDSTONE RD
A274
Iden Farm
HEATH RD
Marlpit Farm
Four Wents
Pleasant Farm
LESTED LA
New House Farm
PLOUGH WENTS RD
NORTON RD
3
BACK LA
COBFIELD
LAXTON DR
Chart Sutton
AMBER LA
WIERTON LA
Wierton Grange
Amberfield
MARSHAM CRES
MERCER WAY
Norton Court
WARMLAKE RD
50
Wierton Place
WIERTON HILL
Ambercourt
CHURCH RD
East Hall
EAST HALL HILL
Ladds Court Farm
Chart Hill
Sch
Court Farm
2
Hernden
CHART HILL RD
CHART RD
Park House Farm
49
Rectory Farm
Coombe Farm
HERMITAGE LA
LUCKS LA
Place Wood
FORGE LA
Lamb's Cross
1
FORSHAM LA
Spark's Hall
Brookside
GREEN LA
LOWER FARM RD
78
D
79
E
80
F

126

143

108

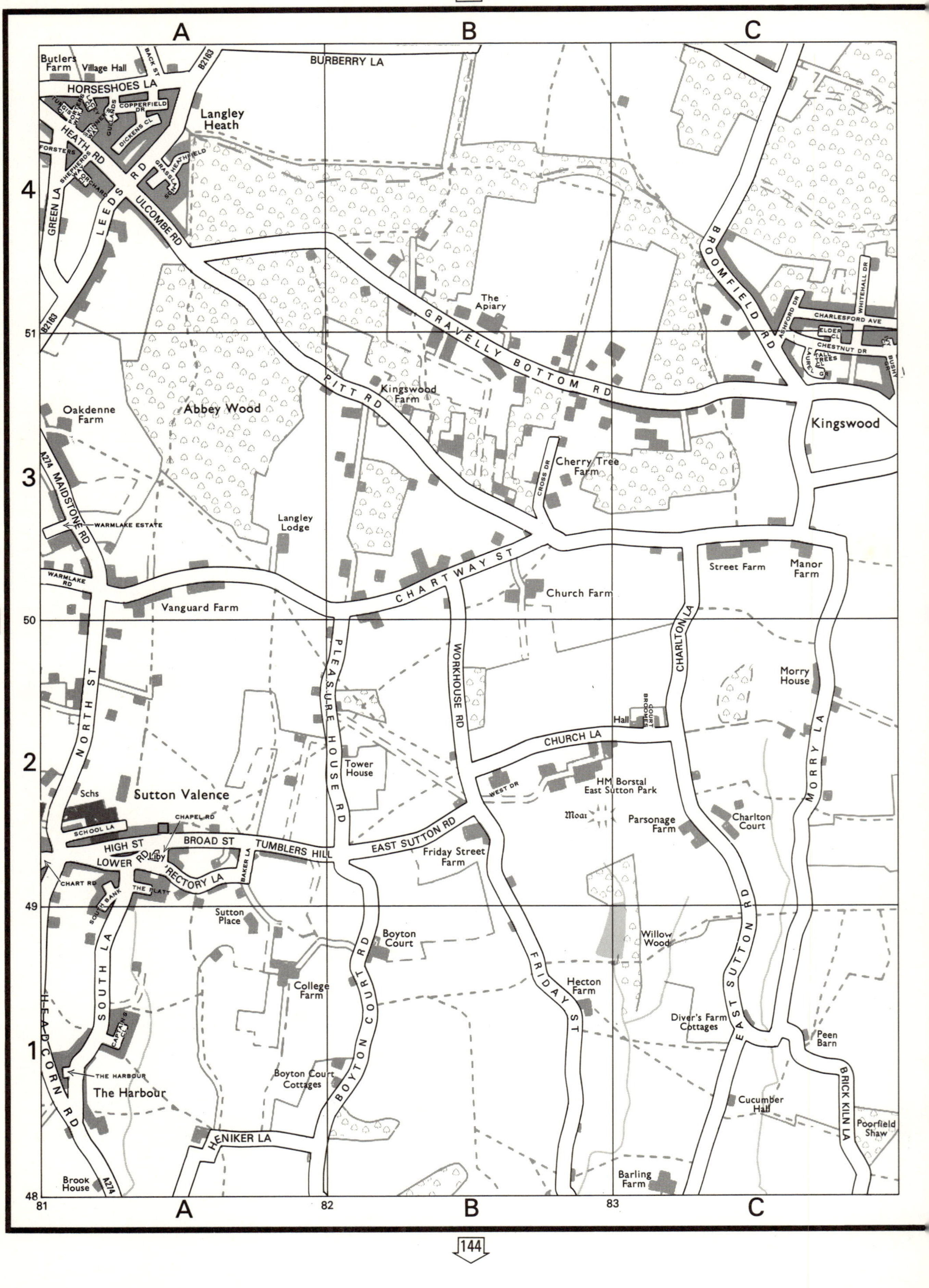
A
B
C
Butlers Farm
Village Hall
BACK ST
B2163
BURBERRY LA
HORSESHOES LA
COPPERFIELD DR
DICKENS CL
GUILDS
Langley Heath
HEATH RD
FORSTERS
SHEPHERDS WAY
ORCHARD
GRASSLANDS
HEATHFIELD
LEEDS RD
ULCOMBE RD
GREEN LA
B2163
4
3
2
1
51
50
49
48
81
82
83
BROOMFIELD RD
WHITEHALL DR
ASHFORD DR
CHARLESFORD AVE
ELDER CL
CHESTNUT DR
BUSH
The Apiary
GRAVELLY BOTTOM RD
PITT RD
Kingswood Farm
Kingswood
Oakdenne Farm
Abbey Wood
Cherry Tree Farm
CROSS DR
A274 MAIDSTONE RD
WARMLAKE ESTATE
Langley Lodge
WARMLAKE RD
CHARTWAY ST
Street Farm
Manor Farm
Church Farm
Vanguard Farm
CHARLTON LA
WORKHOUSE RD
PLEASURE HOUSE RD
Morry House
NORTH ST
COURT BROOMES
Hall
CHURCH LA
Tower House
HM Borstal East Sutton Park
Schs
Sutton Valence
WEST DR
Moat
Parsonage Farm
Charlton Court
MORRY LA
CHAPEL RD
SCHOOL LA
HIGH ST
BROAD ST
TUMBLERS HILL
EAST SUTTON RD
Friday Street Farm
LOWER RD
Liby
RECTORY LA
BAKER LA
CHART RD
THE PLATT
SOUTH BANK
Sutton Place
Boyton Court
BOYTON COURT RD
Willow Wood
EAST SUTTON RD
SOUTH LA
College Farm
FRIDAY ST
Hecton Farm
Diver's Farm Cottages
CAPTAINS CL
Peen Barn
HEADCORN RD
THE HARBOUR
The Harbour
Boyton Court Cottages
BRICK KILN LA
Cucumber Hall
Poorfield Shaw
HENIKER LA
Barling Farm
Brook House
A274

125

144

109

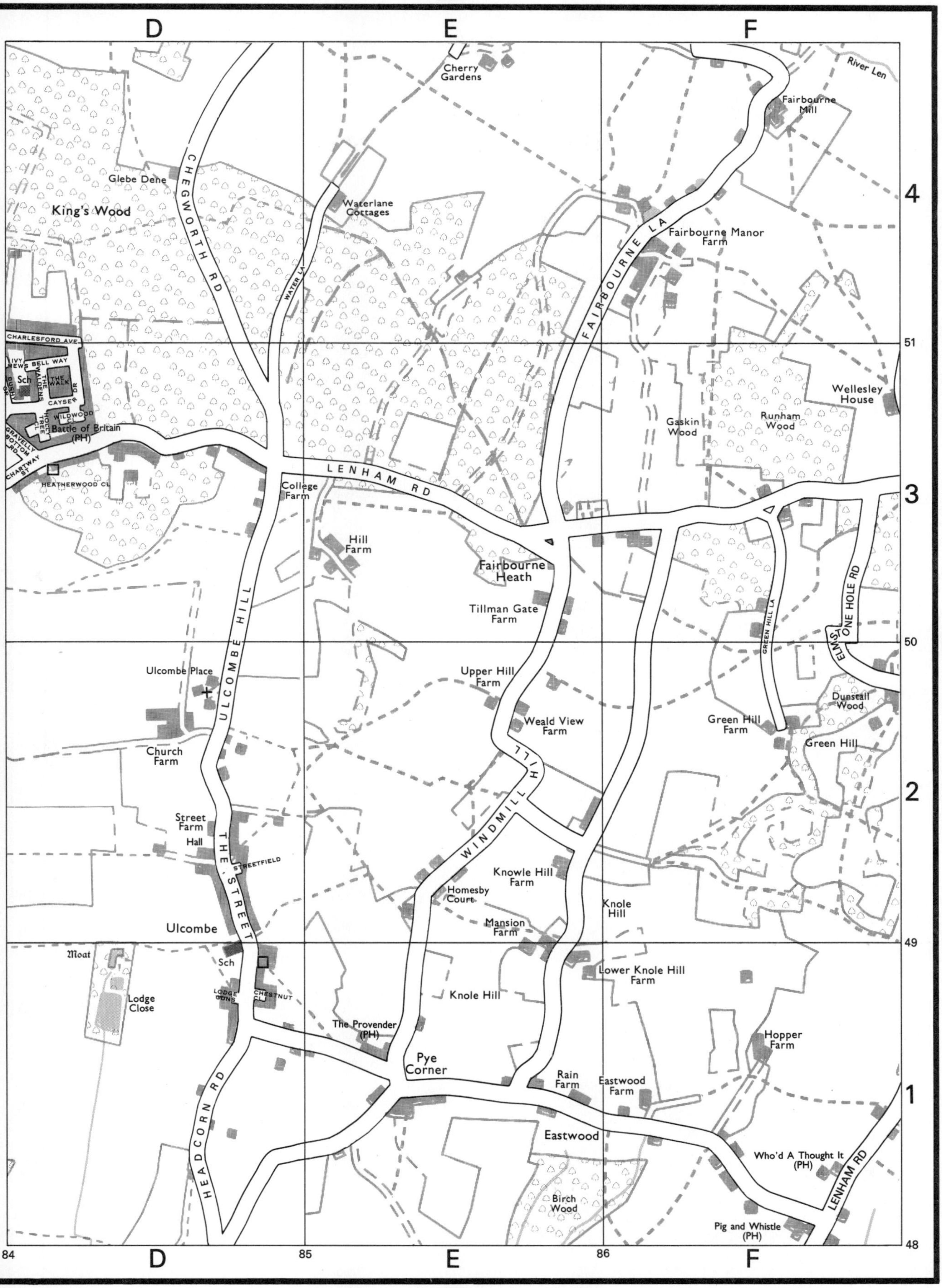
D
E
F
Cherry Gardens
River Len
Fairbourne Mill
Glebe Dene
King's Wood
CHEGWORTH RD
Waterlane Cottages
WATER LA
FAIRBOURNE LA
Fairbourne Manor Farm
CHARLESFORD AVE
IVY MEWS
BELL WAY
Sch
THE WALK
CAYSER DR
WILDWOOD
Battle of Britain (PH)
CHARTWAY ST
HEATHERWOOD CL
Wellesley House
Gaskin Wood
Runham Wood
LENHAM RD
College Farm
Hill Farm
Fairbourne Heath
Tillman Gate Farm
ULCOMBE HILL
GREEN HILL LA
ONE HOLE RD
ELMS
Ulcombe Place
Upper Hill Farm
Dunstall Wood
Weald View Farm
Green Hill Farm
Green Hill
Church Farm
WINDMILL HILL
Street Farm
Hall
THE STREET
STREETFIELD
Knowle Hill Farm
Homesby Court
Knole Hill
Ulcombe
Mansion Farm
Moat
Sch
Lower Knole Hill Farm
Lodge Close
LODGE GDNS
CHESTNUT CL
Knole Hill
The Provender (PH)
Hopper Farm
Pye Corner
Rain Farm
Eastwood Farm
HEADCORN RD
Eastwood
Who'd A Thought It (PH)
LENHAM RD
Birch Wood
Pig and Whistle (PH)
4
51
3
50
2
49
1
48
84
85
86

128

145

110

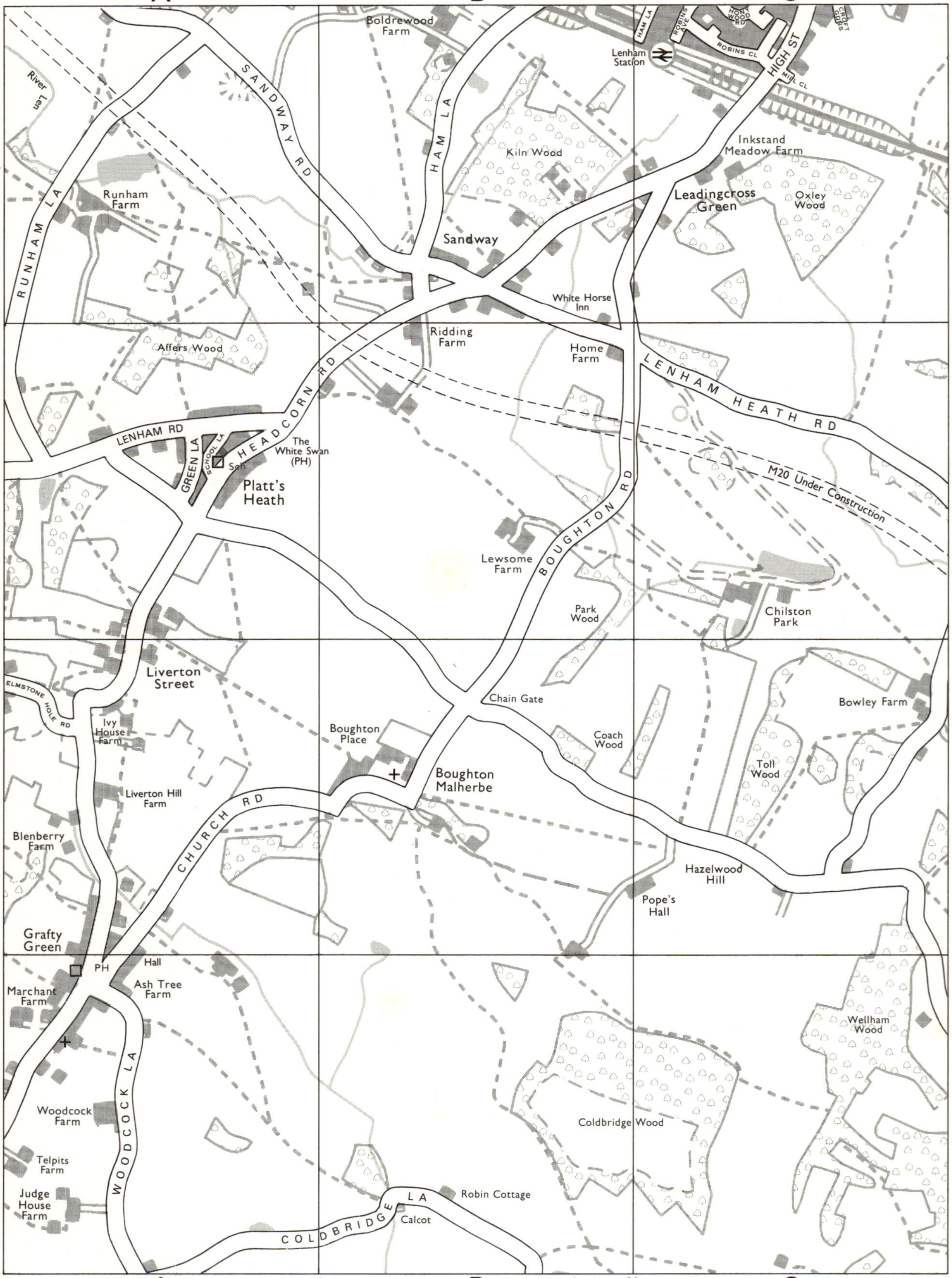
A
B
C
4
3
2
1
51
50
49
48
87
88
89
Boldrewood Farm
Lenham Station
HIGH ST
ROBINS CL
MILL CL
River Len
SANDWAY RD
HAM LA
Kiln Wood
Inkstand Meadow Farm
Runham Farm
RUNHAM LA
Leadingcross Green
Oxley Wood
Sandway
White Horse Inn
Ridding Farm
Home Farm
Affers Wood
LENHAM HEATH RD
HEADCORN RD
LENHAM RD
GREEN LA
SCHOOL LA
The White Swan (PH)
Sch
Platt's Heath
M20 Under Construction
BOUGHTON RD
Lewsome Farm
Park Wood
Chilston Park
Liverton Street
ELMSTONE HOLE RD
Chain Gate
Bowley Farm
Ivy House Farm
Boughton Place
Coach Wood
Boughton Malherbe
Toll Wood
Liverton Hill Farm
CHURCH RD
Blenberry Farm
Hazelwood Hill
Pope's Hall
Grafty Green
PH
Hall
Ash Tree Farm
Marchant Farm
Wellham Wood
WOODCOCK LA
Woodcock Farm
Coldbridge Wood
Telpits Farm
Judge House Farm
Robin Cottage
COLDBRIDGE LA
Calcot

127

146

111

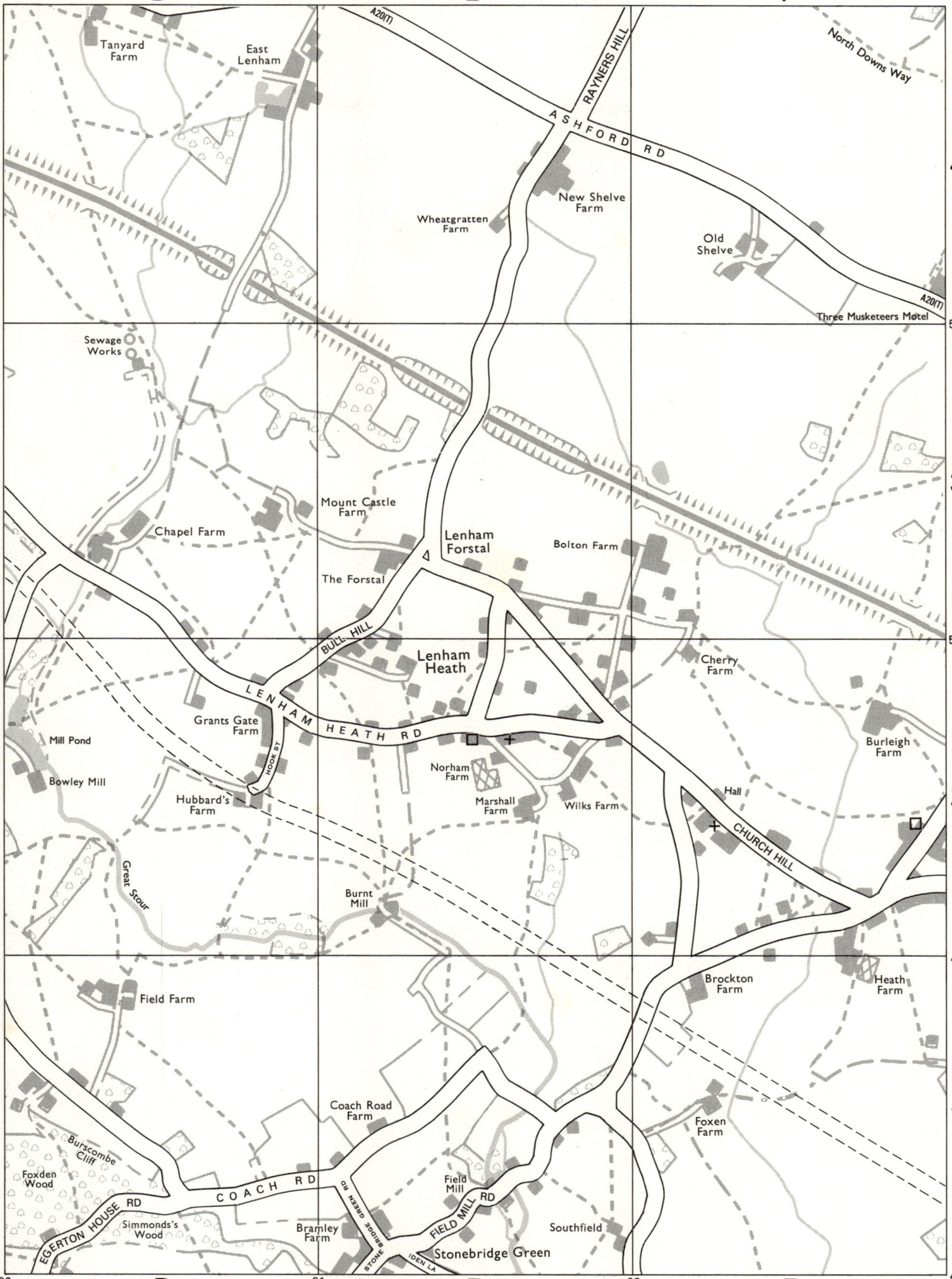
D
E
F
Tanyard Farm
East Lenham
A20(T)
RAYNERS HILL
North Downs Way
ASHFORD RD
4
New Shelve Farm
Wheatgratten Farm
Old Shelve
A20(T)
Three Musketeers Motel
51
Sewage Works
3
Mount Castle Farm
Chapel Farm
Lenham Forstal
Bolton Farm
The Forstal
BULL HILL
Lenham Heath
50
Cherry Farm
LENHAM HEATH RD
Grants Gate Farm
Mill Pond
HOOK ST
Burleigh Farm
Norham Farm
Bowley Mill
Hubbard's Farm
Marshall Farm
Wilks Farm
Hall
2
CHURCH HILL
Great Stour
Burnt Mill
49
Field Farm
Brockton Farm
Heath Farm
Coach Road Farm
1
Foxen Farm
Burscombe Cliff
Foxden Wood
COACH RD
Field Mill
FIELD MILL RD
STONEBRIDGE GREEN RD
EGERTON HOUSE RD
Simmonds's Wood
Bramley Farm
Southfield
Stonebridge Green
IDEN LA
90
91
92
48
D
E
F

130

147

112

129

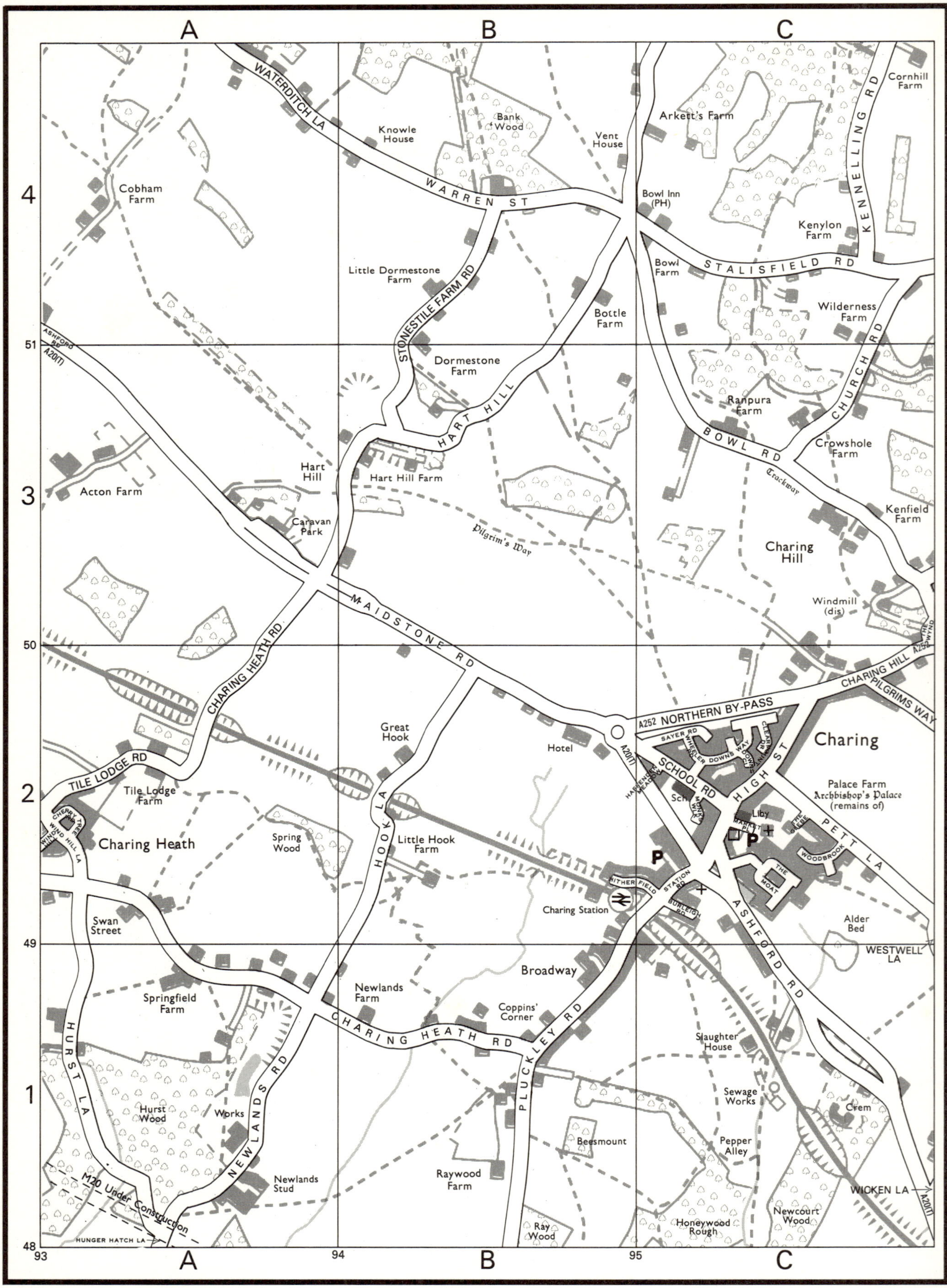

not continued, see key diagram

not continued, see key diagram

113

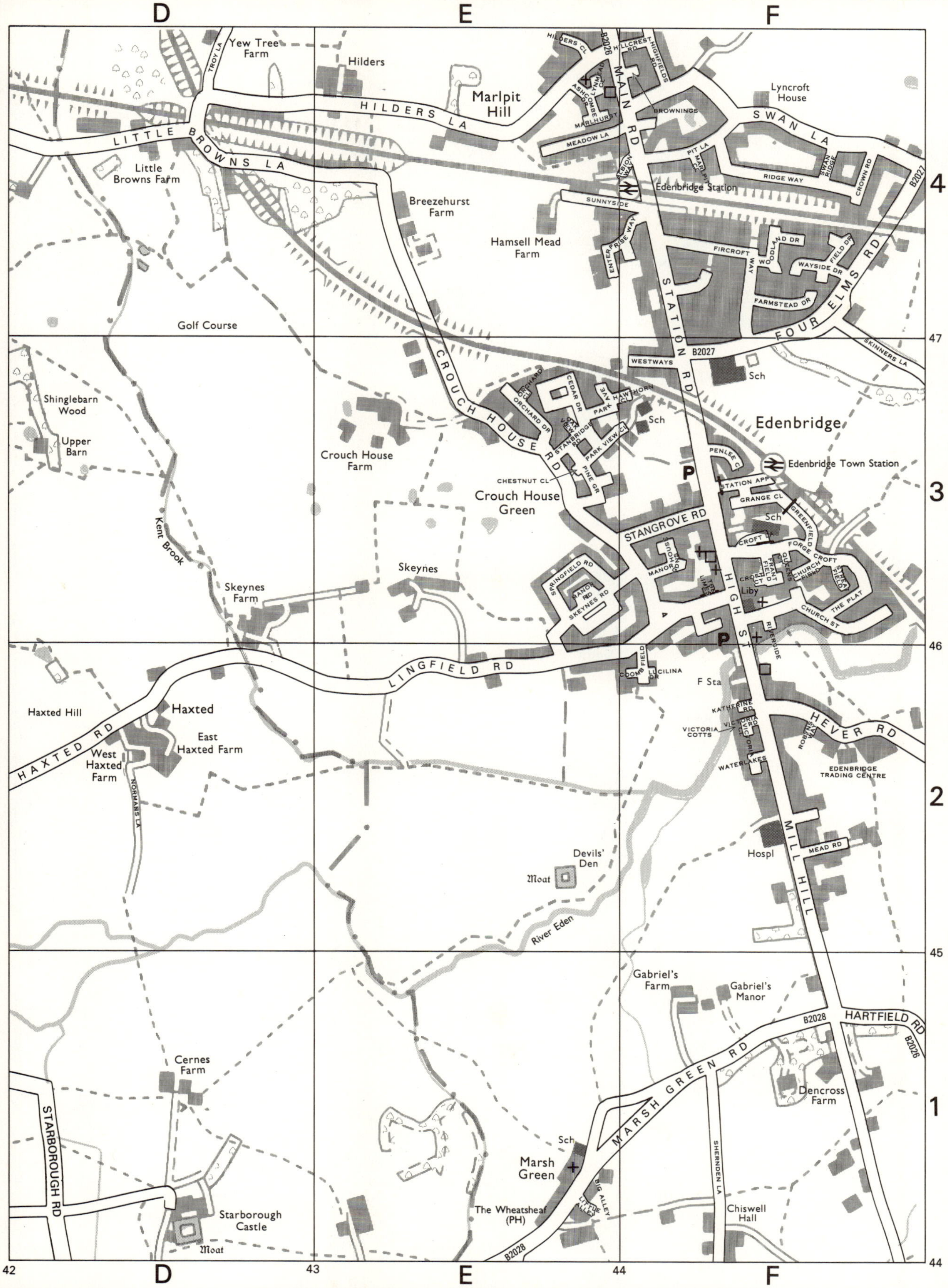
D
E
F
Yew Tree Farm
Hilders
Marlpit Hill
Lyncroft House
HILDERS LA
LITTLE BROWNS LA
SWAN LA
MEADOW LA
MAIN RD
B2026
B2027
Edenbridge Station
Little Browns Farm
Breezehurst Farm
Hamsell Mead Farm
SUNNYSIDE
ENTERPRISE WAY
FIRCROFT
FIRCROFT WAY
WOODLAND DR
WAYSIDE DR
FARMSTEAD DR
FOUR ELMS RD
RIDGE WAY
CROWN RD
PIT LA
BROWNINGS
STATION RD
WESTWAYS
SKINNERS LA
Golf Course
Sch
Shinglebarn Wood
Upper Barn
Crouch House Farm
CROUCH HOUSE RD
Edenbridge
Edenbridge Town Station
ORCHARD DR
CEDAR DR
STANBRIDGE RD
PARK VIEW CL
PINE GR
CHESTNUT CL
Crouch House Green
STATION APP
GRANGE CL
PENLEE CL
STANGROVE RD
CROFT LA
FORGE CROFT
GREENFIELD
CHURCH FIELD
THE PLAT
CHURCH ST
Kent Brook
Skeynes
Skeynes Farm
SPRINGFIELD RD
SKEYNES RD
MANOR RD
HIGH ST
Liby
RIVERSIDE
P
4
3
2
1
47
46
45
44
LINGFIELD RD
COOMBFIELD
LUCILINA DR
F Sta
KATHERINE RD
VICTORIA COTTS
VICTORIA RD
WATERLAKES
HEVER RD
EDENBRIDGE TRADING CENTRE
Haxted Hill
Haxted
HAXTED RD
East Haxted Farm
West Haxted Farm
NORMANS LA
MILL HILL
MEAD RD
Hospl
Devils' Den
Moat
River Eden
Gabriel's Farm
Gabriel's Manor
HARTFIELD RD
B2028
MARSH GREEN RD
Dencross Farm
Cernes Farm
STARBOROUGH RD
Marsh Green
SHERNDEN LA
BIG ALLEY
LITTLE ALLEY
The Wheatsheaf (PH)
Chiswell Hall
Starborough Castle
42
43
44

132

148

114

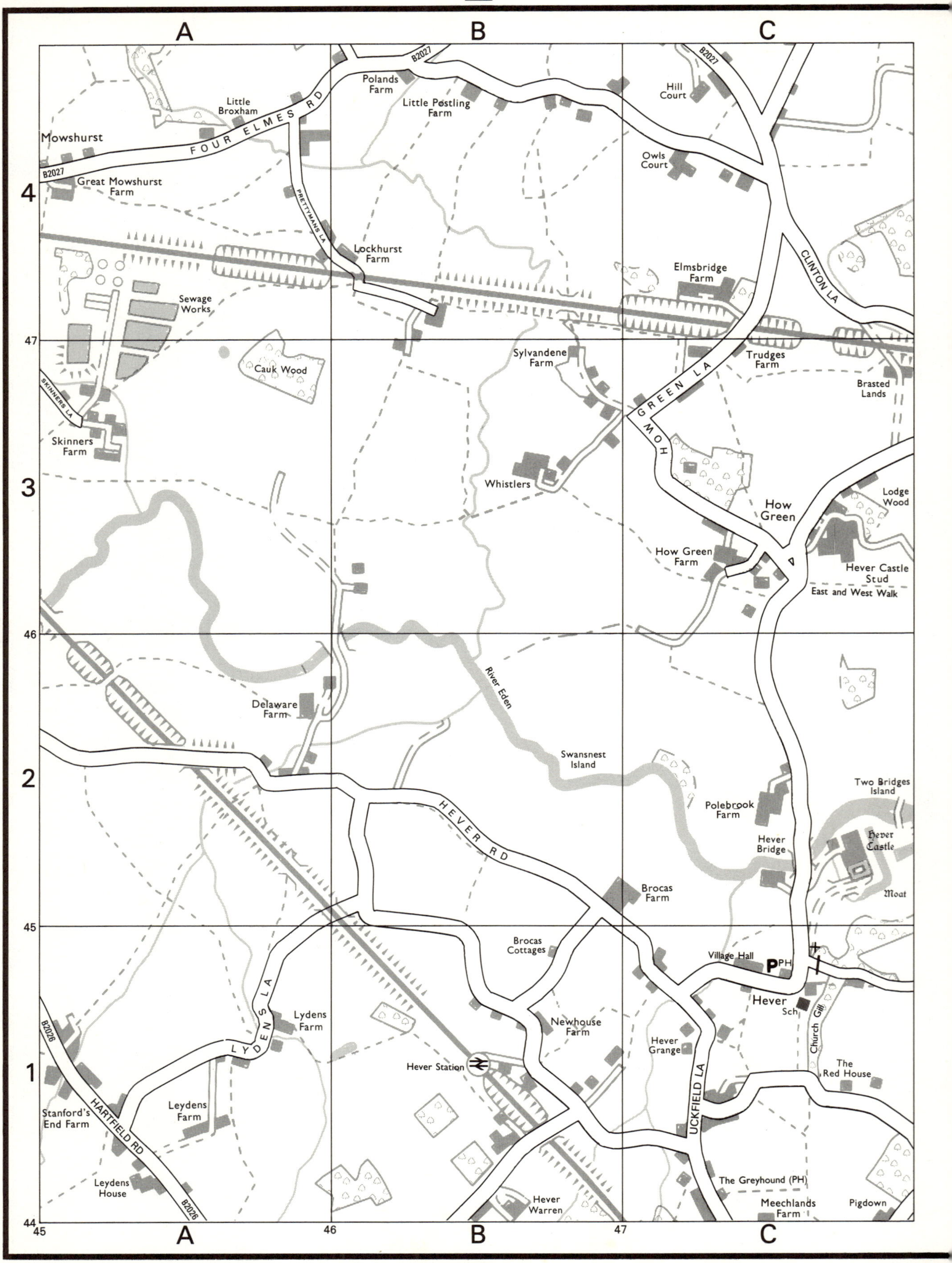
A
B
C
Mowshurst
Little Broxham
FOUR ELMES RD
B2027
Great Mowshurst Farm
Polands Farm
Little Postling Farm
Hill Court
Owls Court
PRETTYMANS LA
Lockhurst Farm
Elmsbridge Farm
CLINTON LA
Sewage Works
Cauk Wood
Sylvandene Farm
Trudges Farm
Brasted Lands
GREEN LA
HOW
SKINNERS LA
Skinners Farm
Whistlers
How Green
Lodge Wood
How Green Farm
Hever Castle Stud
East and West Walk
River Eden
Delaware Farm
Swansnest Island
Two Bridges Island
Polebrook Farm
HEVER RD
Hever Bridge
Hever Castle
Moat
Brocas Farm
Brocas Cottages
Village Hall
P
PH
Hever
Sch
LYDENS LA
Lydens Farm
Newhouse Farm
Hever Grange
Church Gill
Hever Station
The Red House
B2026
HARTFIELD RD
Stanford's End Farm
Leydens Farm
UCKFIELD LA
The Greyhound (PH)
Leydens House
Hever Warren
Meechlands Farm
Pigdown
4
3
2
1
47
46
45
44
45
46
47

131

149

115

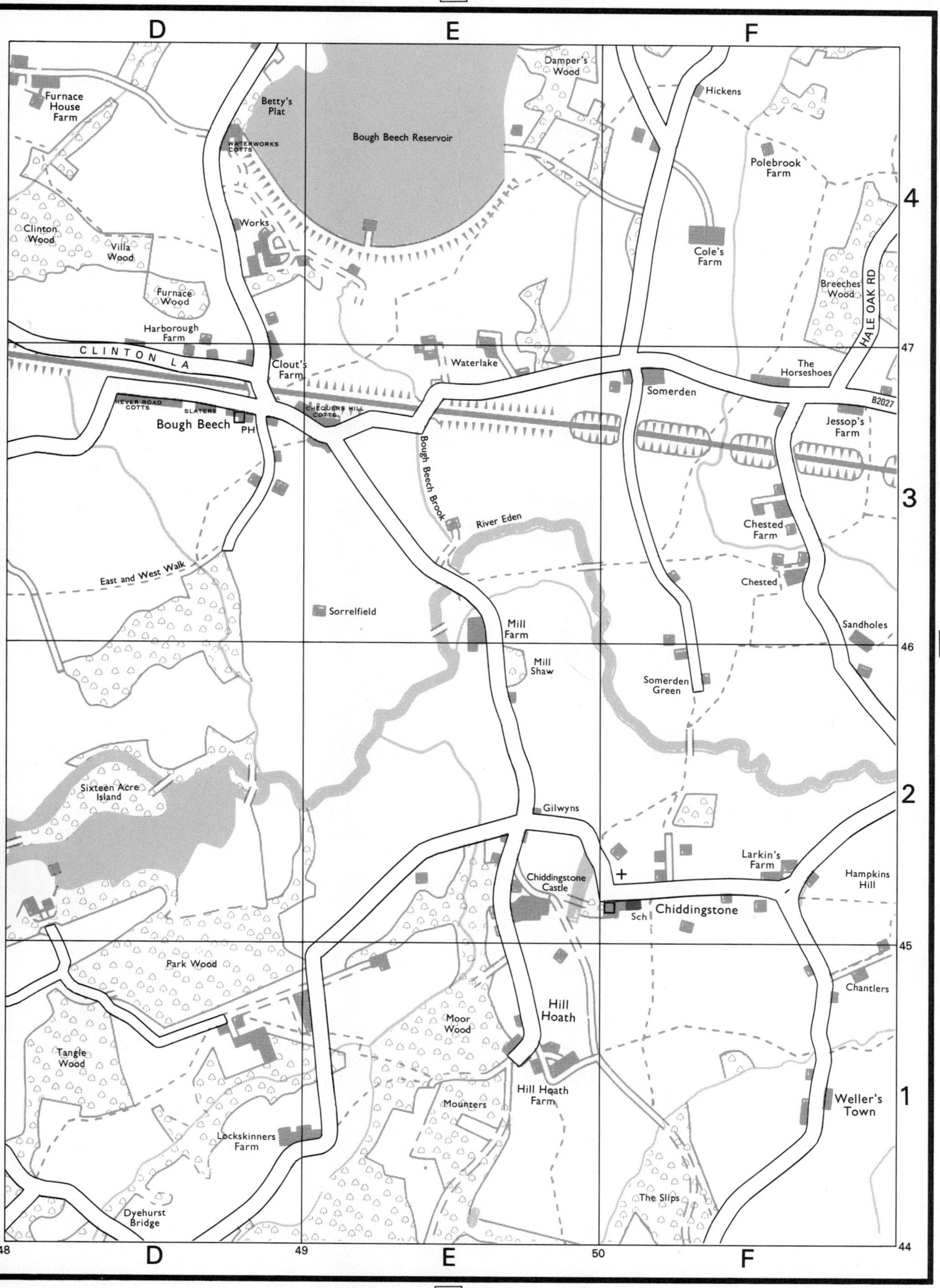
D
E
F
Furnace House Farm
Betty's Plat
Damper's Wood
Hickens
Bough Beech Reservoir
WATERWORKS COTTS
Polebrook Farm
Clinton Wood
Villa Wood
Works
Cole's Farm
Furnace Wood
Breeches Wood
HALE OAK RD
Harborough Farm
CLINTON LA
Clout's Farm
Waterlake
The Horseshoes
HEVER ROAD COTTS
SLATERS
CHEQUERS HILL COTTS
Somerden
B2027
Bough Beech
PH
Jessop's Farm
Bough Beech Brook
River Eden
Chested Farm
East and West Walk
Chested
Sorrelfield
Mill Farm
Sandholes
Mill Shaw
Somerden Green
Sixteen Acre Island
Gilwyns
Larkin's Farm
Hampkins Hill
Chiddingstone Castle
Sch
Chiddingstone
Park Wood
Chantlers
Hill Hoath
Moor Wood
Tangle Wood
Hill Hoath Farm
Mounters
Weller's Town
Lockskinners Farm
The Slips
Dyehurst Bridge
4
3
2
1
47
46
45
44
48
49
50

134

150

116

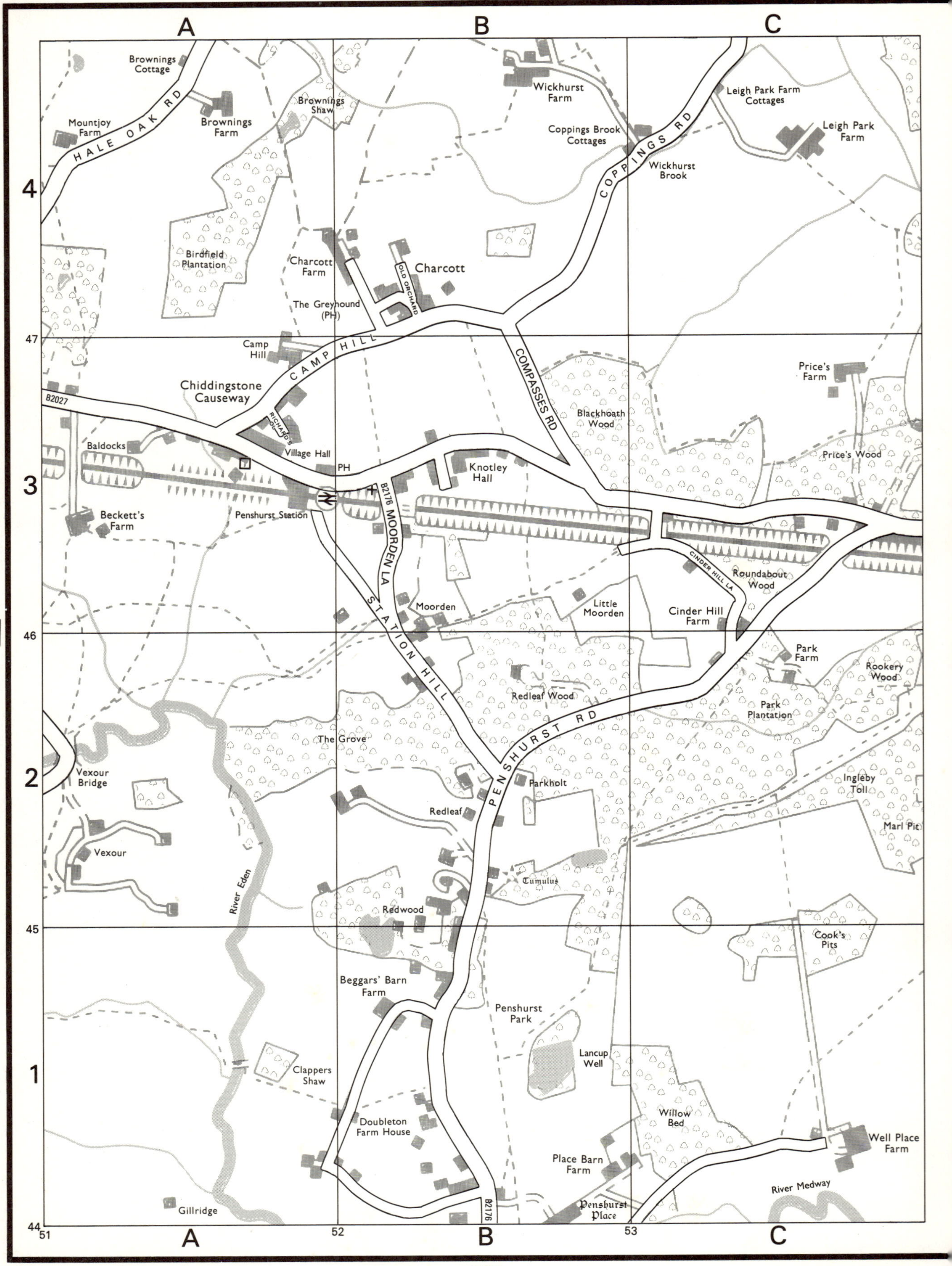
A
B
C
4
3
2
1
47
46
45
44
51
52
53
Brownings Cottage
Mountjoy Farm
HALE OAK RD
Brownings Farm
Brownings Shaw
Wickhurst Farm
Leigh Park Farm Cottages
Leigh Park Farm
Coppings Brook Cottages
COPPINGS RD
Wickhurst Brook
Birdfield Plantation
Charcott Farm
Charcott
OLD ORCHARD
The Greyhound (PH)
Camp Hill
CAMP HILL
Chiddingstone Causeway
B2027
RICHARDS CL
COMPASSES RD
Blackhoath Wood
Price's Farm
Price's Wood
Baldocks
Village Hall
PH
Knotley Hall
Beckett's Farm
Penshurst Station
B2176
MOORDEN LA
CINDER HILL LA
Roundabout Wood
Moorden
Little Moorden
Cinder Hill Farm
STATION HILL
Park Farm
Rookery Wood
Redleaf Wood
Park Plantation
PENSHURST RD
The Grove
Vexour Bridge
Parkholt
Ingleby Toll
Redleaf
Marl Pit
Vexour
Tumulus
River Eden
Redwood
Cook's Pits
Beggars' Barn Farm
Penshurst Park
Lancup Well
Clappers Shaw
Willow Bed
Doubleton Farm House
Well Place Farm
Place Barn Farm
River Medway
B2176
Gillridge
Penshurst Place

133

151

117

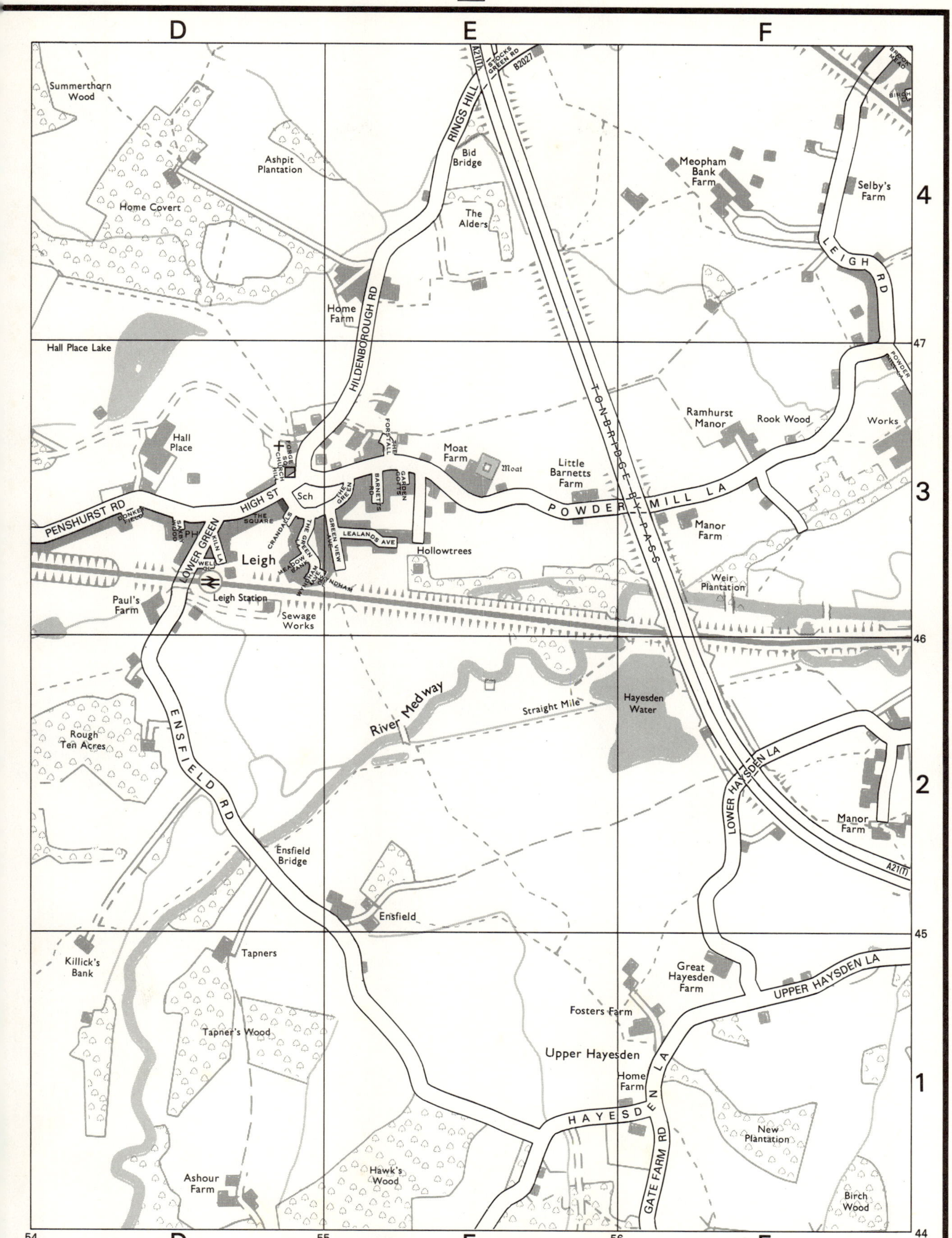
D
E
F
4
3
2
1
47
46
45
44
54
55
56
Summerthorn Wood
Ashpit Plantation
Home Covert
Rings Hill
Stocks Green Rd
A21(T)
B2027
Bid Bridge
The Alders
Home Farm
Hildenborough Rd
Meopham Bank Farm
Selby's Farm
Leigh Rd
Hall Place Lake
Hall Place
Forge Sq
Church Hill
The Forstall
Moat Farm
Moat
Little Barnetts Farm
Ramhurst Manor
Rook Wood
Works
Powder Mill La
Penshurst Rd
High St
Sch
The Square
Lower Green
Kiln La
Crandalls
The Green
Barnetts Rd
Garden Cotts
Green View Ave
Lealands Ave
Hollowtrees
Manor Farm
Tonbridge By-Pass
Leigh
PH
Well
Meadow Bank
Wyndham Ave
Wyndham Cl
Paul's Farm
Leigh Station
Sewage Works
Weir Plantation
River Medway
Straight Mile
Hayesden Water
Rough Ten Acres
Ensfield Rd
Lower Haysden La
Manor Farm
Ensfield Bridge
Ensfield
Killick's Bank
Tapners
Tapner's Wood
Great Hayesden Farm
Upper Haysden La
Fosters Farm
Upper Hayesden
Home Farm
Hayesden La
Gate Farm Rd
New Plantation
Ashour Farm
Hawk's Wood
Birch Wood

136

152

118

135

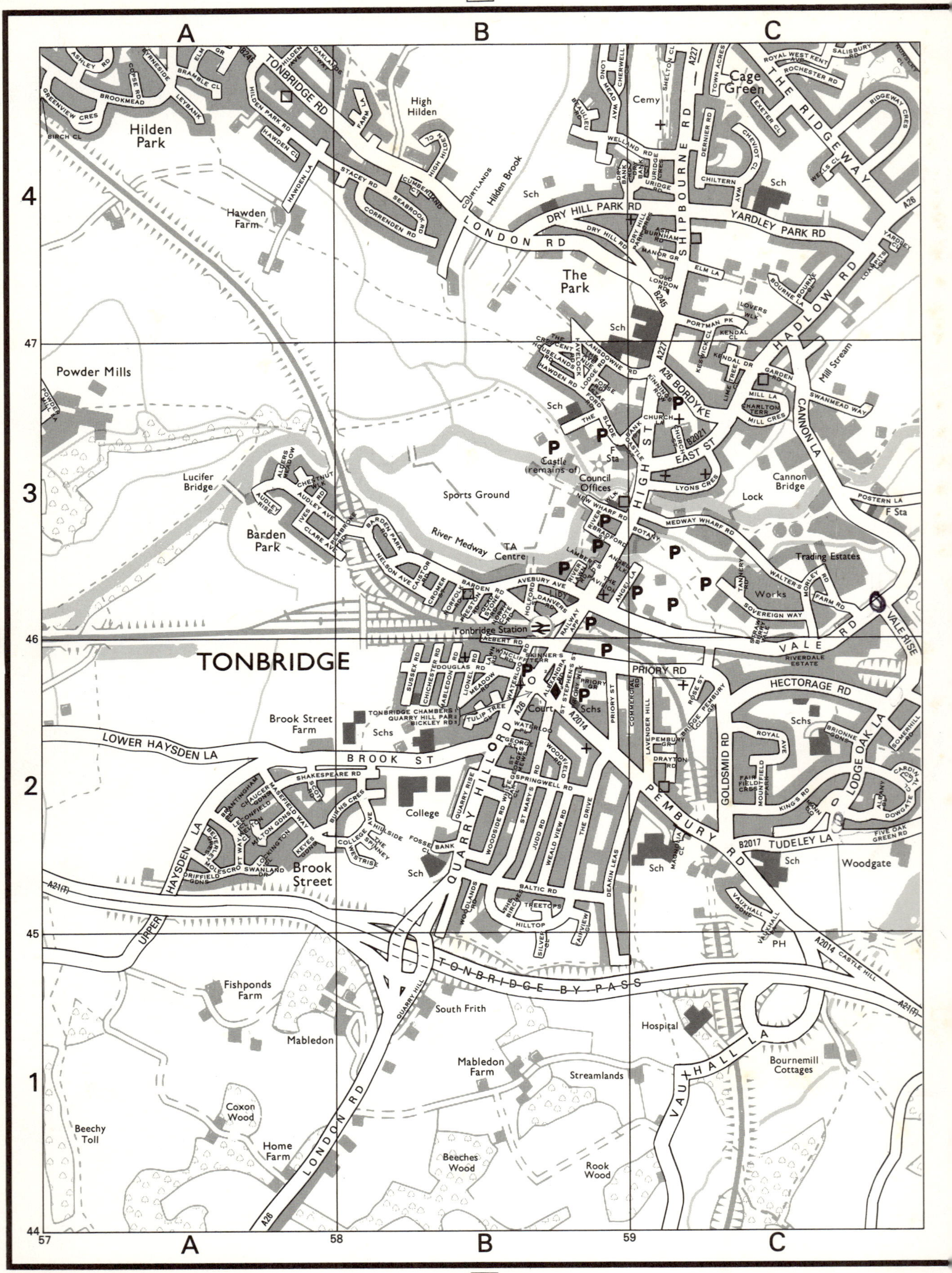
A
B
C
4
3
2
1
47
46
45
44
57
58
59
TONBRIDGE
Hilden Park
High Hilden
Hawden Farm
Powder Mills
Lucifer Bridge
Barden Park
The Park
Cage Green
Cemy
Sch
Schs
Castle (remains of)
Council Offices
Sports Ground
River Medway
TA Centre
Tonbridge Station
Court
Lock
Cannon Bridge
Trading Estates
Works
Mill Stream
Brook Street Farm
Brook Street
College
Woodgate
PH
Hospital
Fishponds Farm
South Frith
Mabledon
Mabledon Farm
Streamlands
Bournemill Cottages
Coxon Wood
Beechy Toll
Home Farm
Beeches Wood
Rook Wood
TONBRIDGE RD
LONDON RD
DRY HILL PARK RD
YARDLEY PARK RD
SHIPBOURNE RD
THE RIDGEWAY
HADLOW RD
HIGH ST
EAST ST
BORDYKE
CANNON LA
VALE RD
VALE RISE
MEDWAY WHARF RD
SOVEREIGN WAY
HECTORAGE RD
PRIORY RD
LODGE OAK LA
GOLDSMID RD
PEMBURY RD
TUDELEY LA
LOWER HAYSDEN LA
BROOK ST
HAYSDEN LA
UPPER HAYSDEN LA
QUARRY HILL RD
TONBRIDGE BY PASS
VAUXHALL LA
A21(T)
A26
A227
A2014
B2017
B245
B2021
CASTLE HILL
POSTERN LA
F Sta

153

119

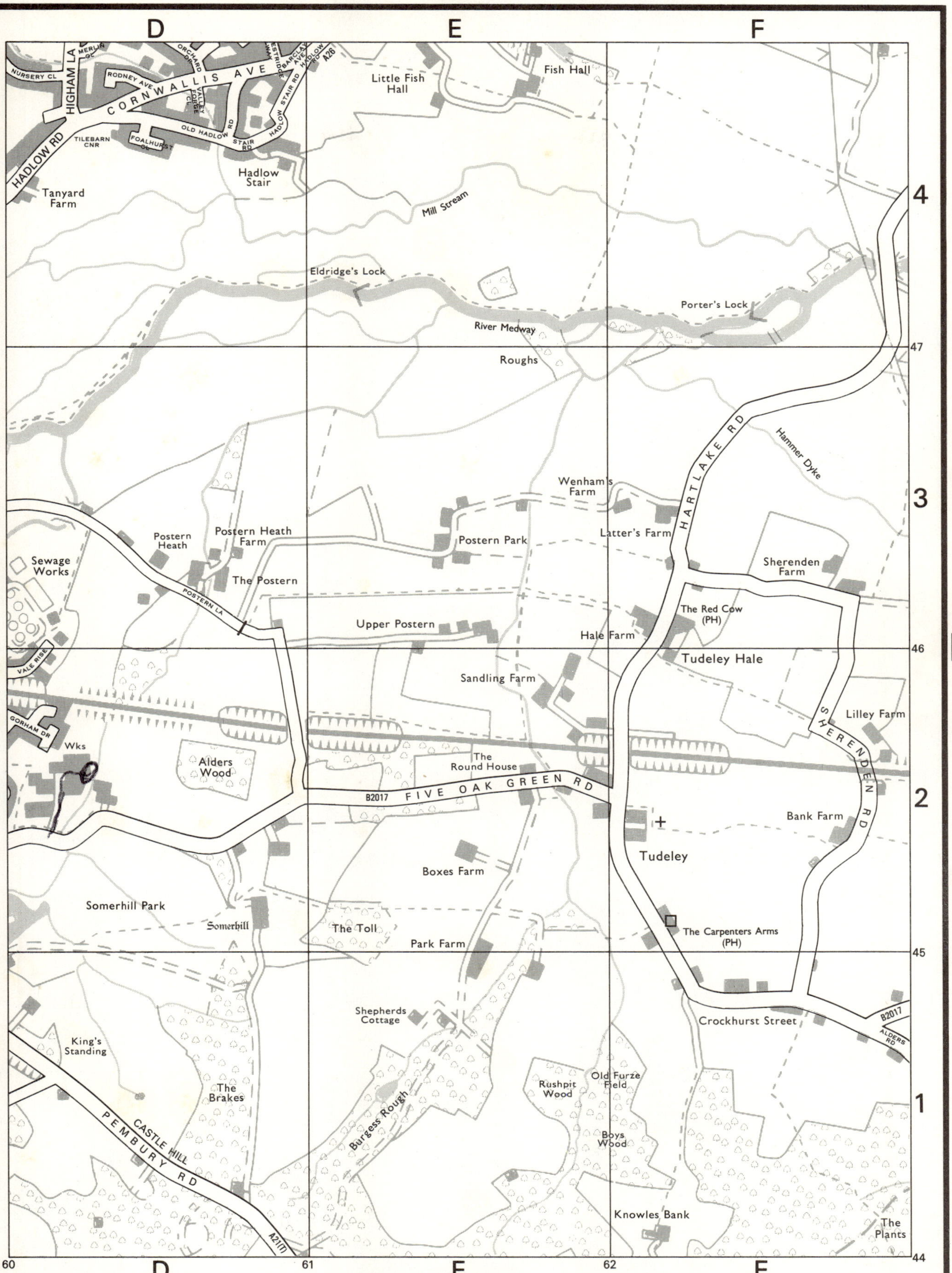
D
E
F
NURSERY CL
MERLIN CL
HIGHAM LA
RODNEY AVE
CORNWALLIS AVE
ORCHARD DR
VALLEY FORGE CL
BARCLAY AVE
HADLOW RD
A26
HADLOW STAIR RD
OLD HADLOW RD
STAIR RD
HADLOW RD
TILEBARN CNR
FOALHURST CL
Tanyard Farm
Hadlow Stair
Little Fish Hall
Fish Hall
Mill Stream
Eldridge's Lock
Porter's Lock
River Medway
Roughs
4
47
HARTLAKE RD
Hammer Dyke
Wenham's Farm
Latter's Farm
3
Postern Heath
Postern Heath Farm
Postern Park
Sewage Works
The Postern
Sherenden Farm
POSTERN LA
Upper Postern
The Red Cow (PH)
Hale Farm
Tudeley Hale
46
VALE RISE
Sandling Farm
GORHAM DR
SHERENDEN RD
Lilley Farm
Wks
Alders Wood
The Round House
B2017
FIVE OAK GREEN RD
2
Bank Farm
Tudeley
Boxes Farm
Somerhill Park
Somerhill
The Toll
Park Farm
The Carpenters Arms (PH)
45
Crockhurst Street
B2017
ALDERS RD
Shepherds Cottage
King's Standing
Old Furze Field
Rushpit Wood
The Brakes
1
Burgess Rough
Boys Wood
CASTLE HILL
PEMBURY RD
Knowles Bank
The Plants
A21(T)
60
61
62
44

138

154

120

137

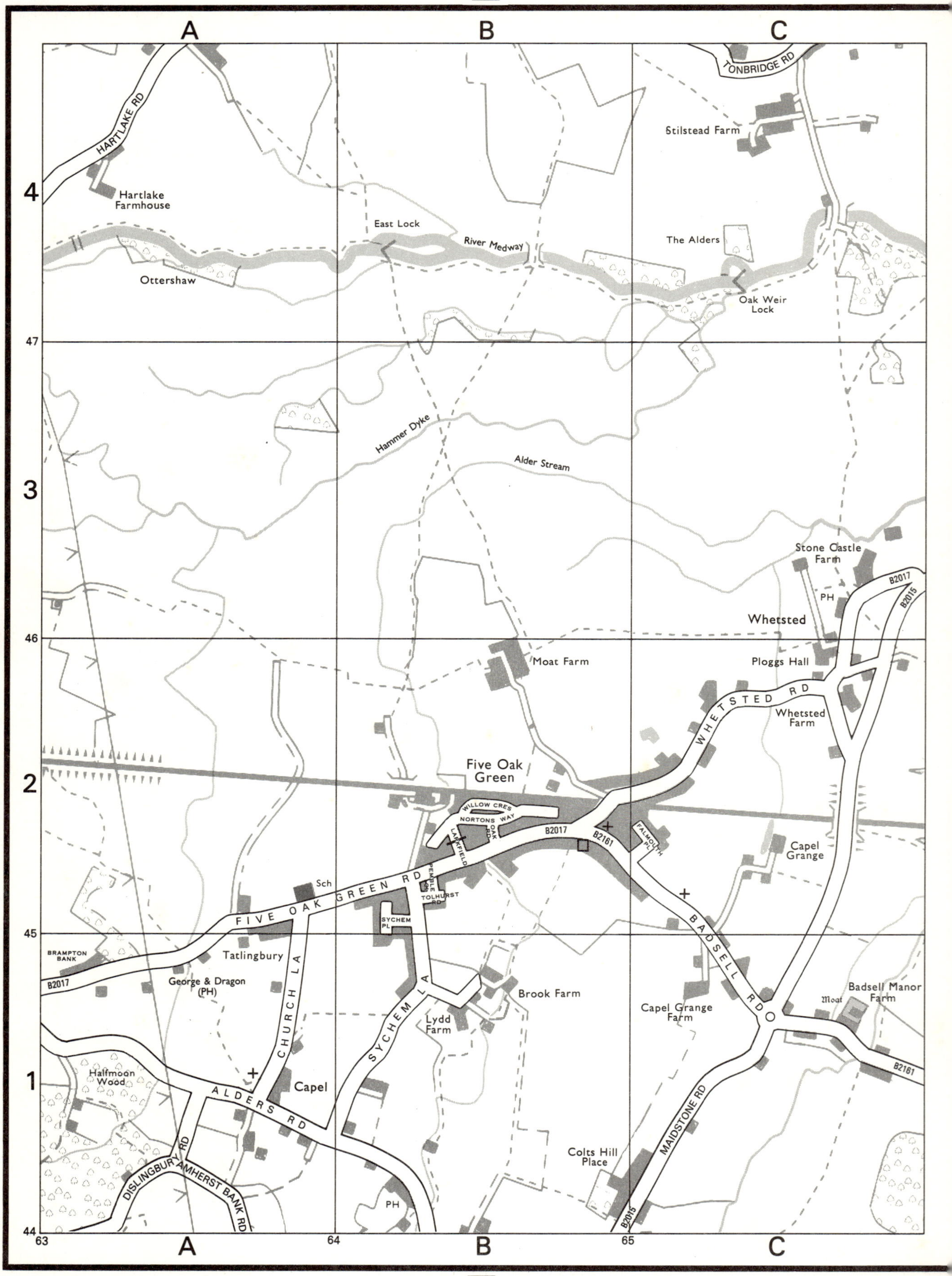
A
B
C
4
3
2
1
47
46
45
44
63
64
65
HARTLAKE RD
Hartlake Farmhouse
TONBRIDGE RD
Stilstead Farm
East Lock
River Medway
The Alders
Ottershaw
Oak Weir Lock
Hammer Dyke
Alder Stream
Stone Castle Farm
PH
Whetsted
B2017
B2015
Moat Farm
Ploggs Hall
WHETSTED RD
Whetsted Farm
Five Oak Green
WILLOW CRES
NORTONS WAY
OAK RD
LARKFIELD
B2017
B2161
FALMOUTH PL
Capel Grange
Sch
FIVE OAK GREEN RD
PEMBLE CL
TOLHURST RD
SYCHEM PL
BADSELL RD
BRAMPTON BANK
Tatlingbury
George & Dragon (PH)
CHURCH LA
SYCHEM LA
Brook Farm
Lydd Farm
Capel Grange Farm
Moat
Badsell Manor Farm
B2161
Halfmoon Wood
ALDERS RD
Capel
MAIDSTONE RD
DISLINGBURY RD
AMHERST BANK RD
PH
Colts Hill Place
B2015

155

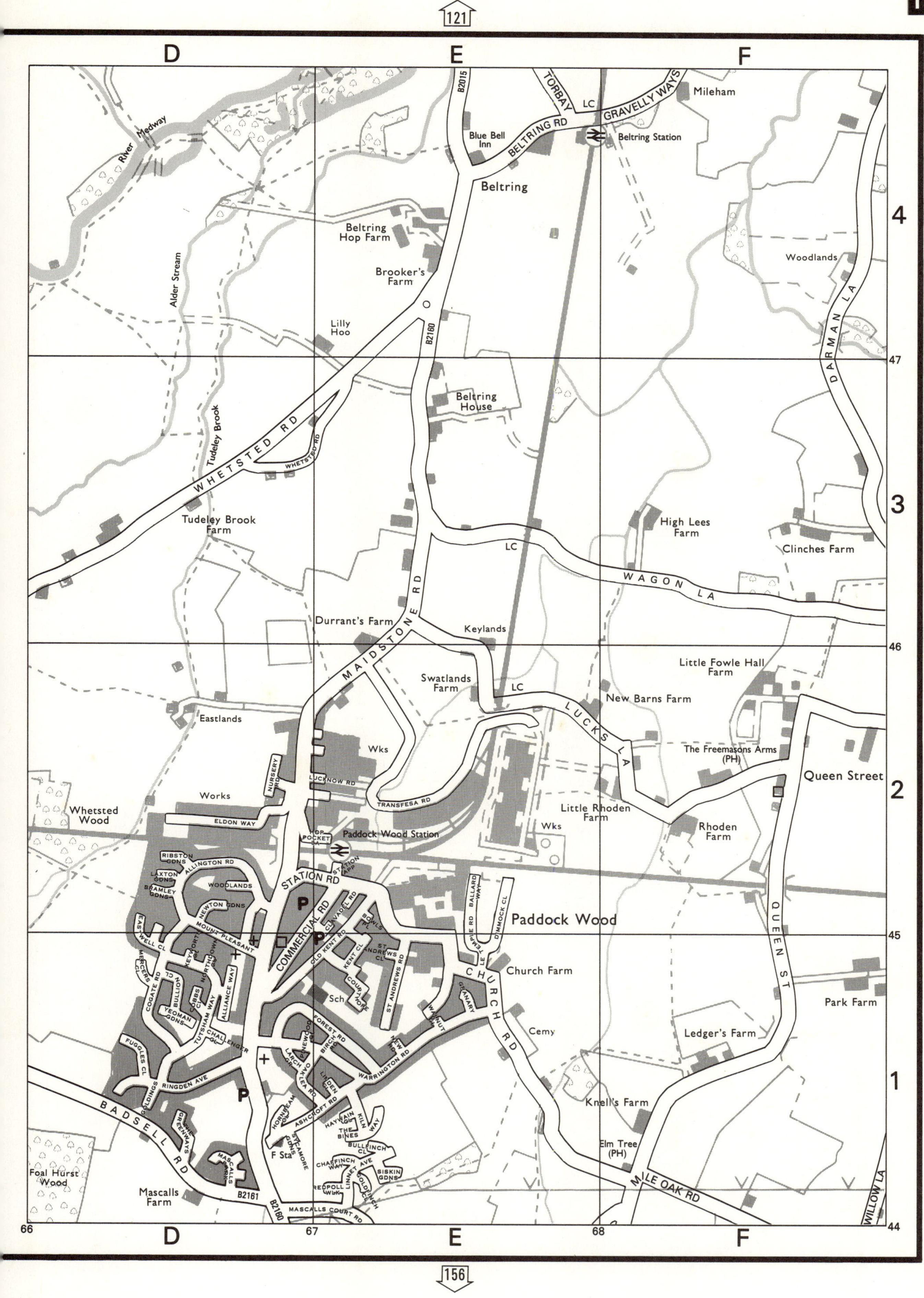
121
D
E
F
Beltring
Blue Bell Inn
Beltring Station
Mileham
TORBAY
GRAVELLY WAYS
BELTRING RD
LC
River Medway
Alder Stream
Beltring Hop Farm
Brooker's Farm
Lilly Hoo
Woodlands
DARMAN LA
Beltring House
Tudeley Brook
WHETSTED RD
Tudeley Brook Farm
High Lees Farm
Clinches Farm
WAGON LA
Durrant's Farm
Keylands
MAIDSTONE RD
B2160
B2015
Little Fowle Hall Farm
Swatlands Farm
New Barns Farm
LUCKS LA
Eastlands
Wks
The Freemasons Arms (PH)
Queen Street
Works
Whetsted Wood
Little Rhoden Farm
Rhoden Farm
Paddock Wood Station
TRANSFESA RD
LUCKNOW RD
ELDON WAY
NURSERY RD
STATION RD
Paddock Wood
Church Farm
QUEEN ST
Park Farm
CHURCH RD
Cemy
Ledger's Farm
COMMERCIAL RD
MOUNT PLEASANT
RINGDEN AVE
WARRINGTON RD
FOREST RD
Sch
Knell's Farm
Elm Tree (PH)
MILE OAK RD
BADSELL RD
B2161
F Sta
Foal Hurst Wood
Mascalls Farm
MASCALLS COURT RD
WILLOW LA
66
67
68
44
45
46
47
1
2
3
4
140
156

122

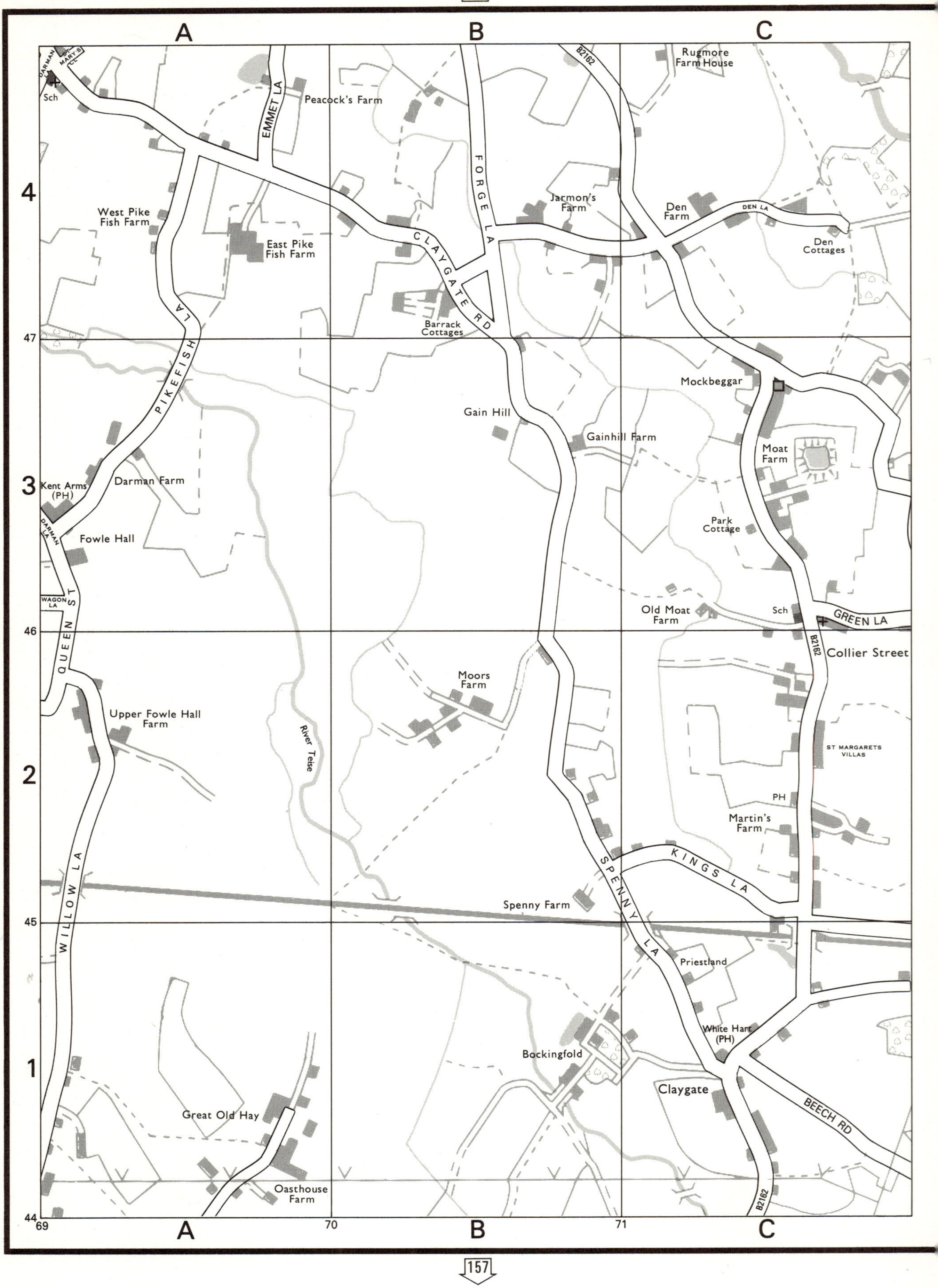
A
B
C
4
3
2
1
47
46
45
44
69
70
71
Rugmore Farm House
Peacock's Farm
EMMET LA
B2162
FORGE LA
Jarmon's Farm
Den Farm
DEN LA
Den Cottages
West Pike Fish Farm
East Pike Fish Farm
CLAYGATE RD
Barrack Cottages
PIKEFISH LA
Mockbeggar
Gain Hill
Gainhill Farm
Moat Farm
Kent Arms (PH)
Darman Farm
Park Cottage
Fowle Hall
DARMAN LA
WAGON LA
QUEEN ST
Old Moat Farm
Sch
GREEN LA
Collier Street
Moors Farm
Upper Fowle Hall Farm
River Teise
ST MARGARETS VILLAS
PH
Martin's Farm
KINGS LA
SPENNY LA
Spenny Farm
WILLOW LA
Priestland
White Hart (PH)
Bockingfold
Claygate
BEECH RD
Great Old Hay
Oasthouse Farm
ST MARY'S CL
Sch

139

157

123

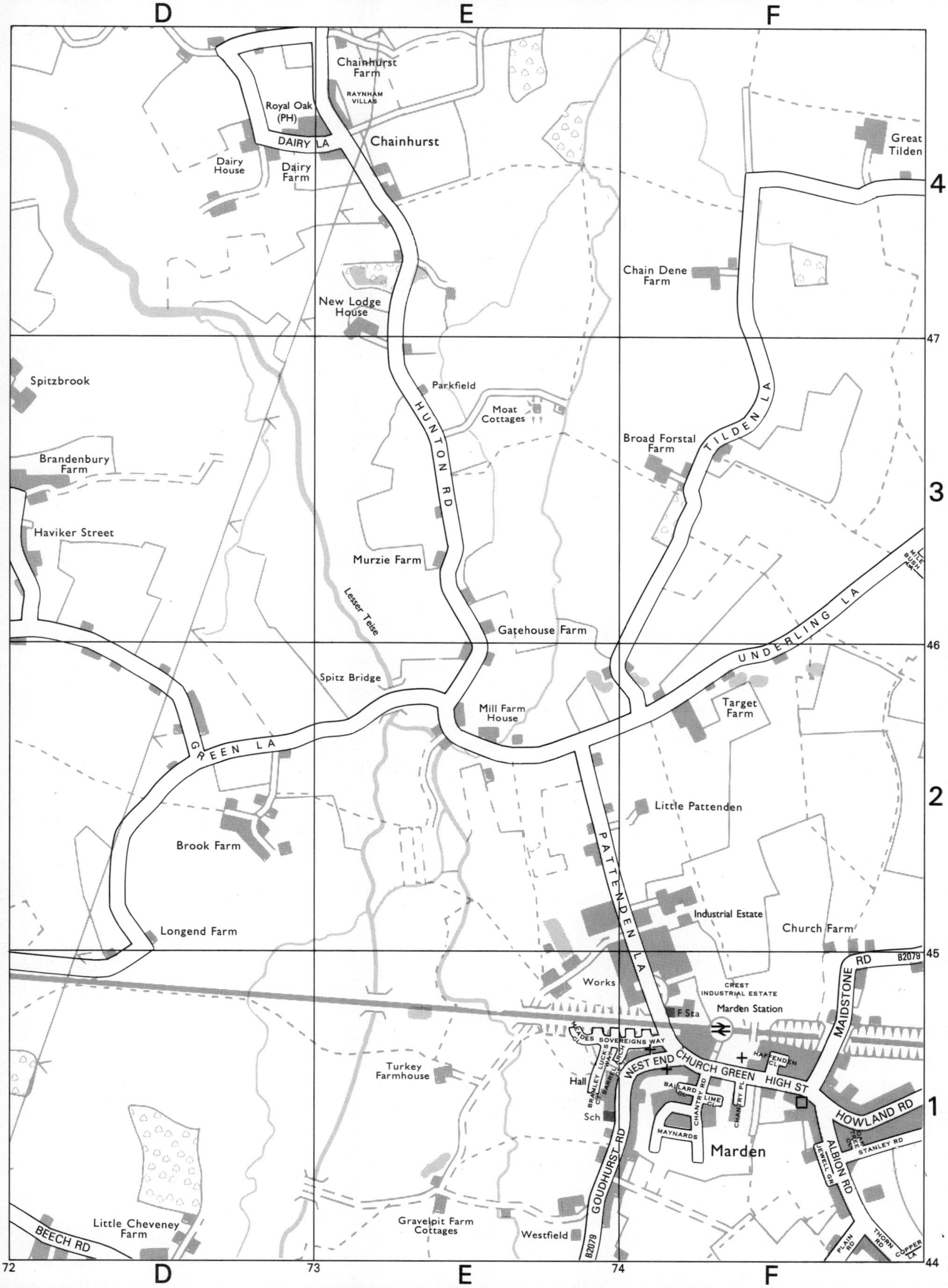
D
E
F
Chainhurst Farm
RAYNHAM VILLAS
Royal Oak (PH)
DAIRY LA
Chainhurst
Dairy House
Dairy Farm
Great Tilden
4
Chain Dene Farm
New Lodge House
47
Spitzbrook
Parkfield
Moat Cottages
HUNTON RD
Broad Forstal Farm
TILDEN LA
Brandenbury Farm
3
Haviker Street
Murzie Farm
MILE BUSH LA
Lesser Teise
UNDERLING LA
Gatehouse Farm
46
Spitz Bridge
Mill Farm House
Target Farm
GREEN LA
2
Little Pattenden
Brook Farm
PATTENDEN LA
Industrial Estate
Church Farm
Longend Farm
45
MAIDSTONE RD
B2079
Works
CREST INDUSTRIAL ESTATE
Marden Station
F Sta
SOVEREIGNS WAY
WEST END
CHURCH GREEN
HIGH ST
HAFFENDEN CL
Turkey Farmhouse
Hall
BRAMLEY CL
LUCKS WAY
BARREL
BALLARD CL
CHANTRY RD
LIME CL
CHANTRY PL
HOWLAND RD
1
Sch
MAYNARDS
Marden
STANLEY RD
ALBION RD
JEWELL GR
GOUDHURST RD
Little Cheveney Farm
Gravelpit Farm Cottages
Westfield
BEECH RD
B2079
PLAIN RD
THORN RD
COPPER LA
72
73
74
44
D
E
F

142

158

124

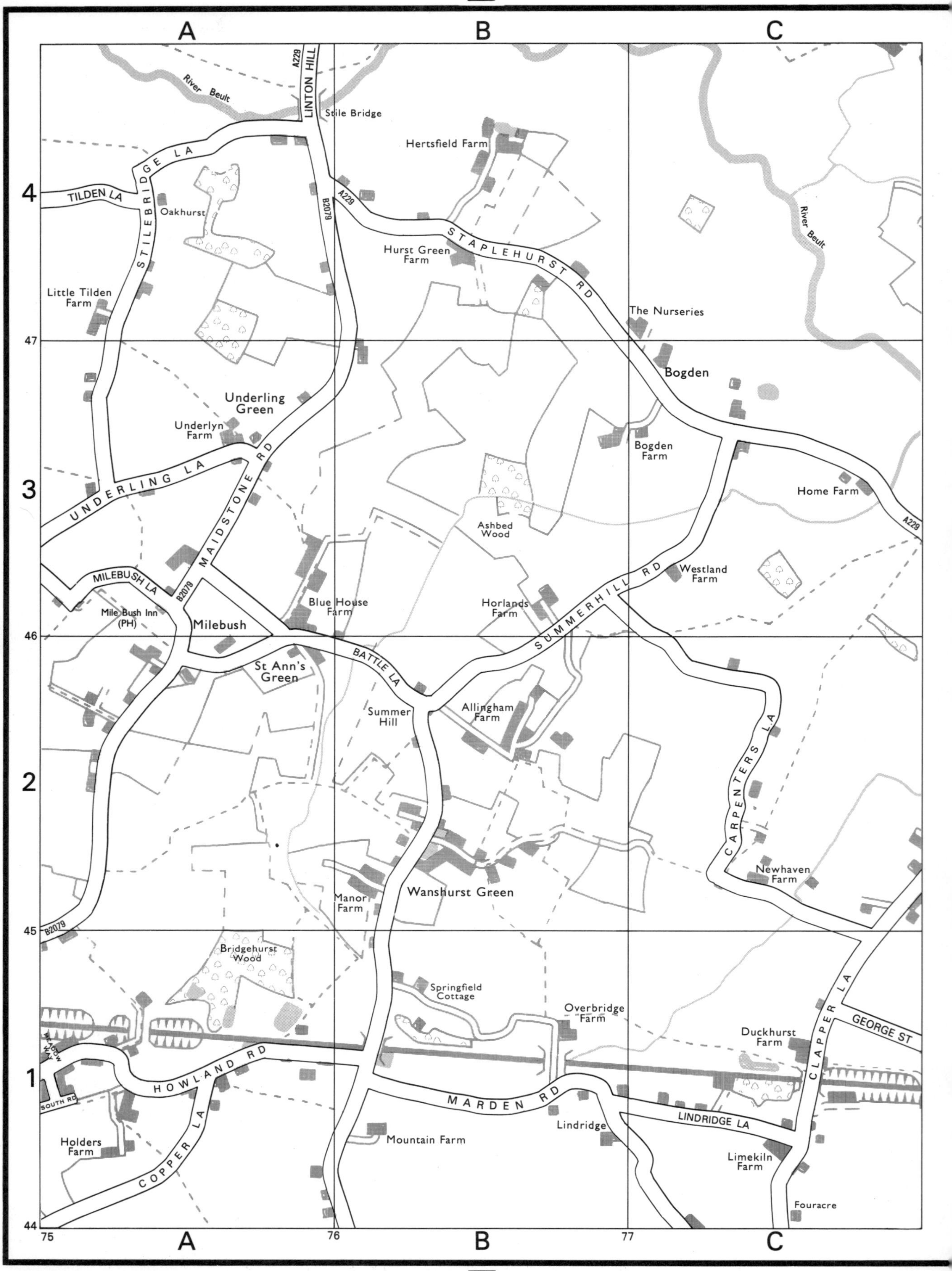
A
B
C
River Beult
LINTON HILL
A229
Stile Bridge
Hertsfield Farm
STILEBRIDGE LA
TILDEN LA
Oakhurst
B2079
A229
STAPLEHURST RD
Hurst Green Farm
Little Tilden Farm
The Nurseries
Bogden
Underling Green
Underlyn Farm
Bogden Farm
MAIDSTONE RD
UNDERLING LA
Home Farm
A229
Ashbed Wood
Westland Farm
MILEBUSH LA
B2079
Mile Bush Inn (PH)
Milebush
Blue House Farm
Horlands Farm
SUMMERHILL RD
St Ann's Green
BATTLE LA
Summer Hill
Allingham Farm
CARPENTERS LA
Newhaven Farm
Wanshurst Green
Manor Farm
B2079
Bridgehurst Wood
Springfield Cottage
Overbridge Farm
CLAPPER LA
GEORGE ST
Duckhurst Farm
HOWLAND RD
MARDEN RD
SOUTH RD
LINDRIDGE LA
Lindridge
Holders Farm
Mountain Farm
Limekiln Farm
COPPER LA
Fouracre
4
3
2
1
47
46
45
44
75
76
77

141

159

125

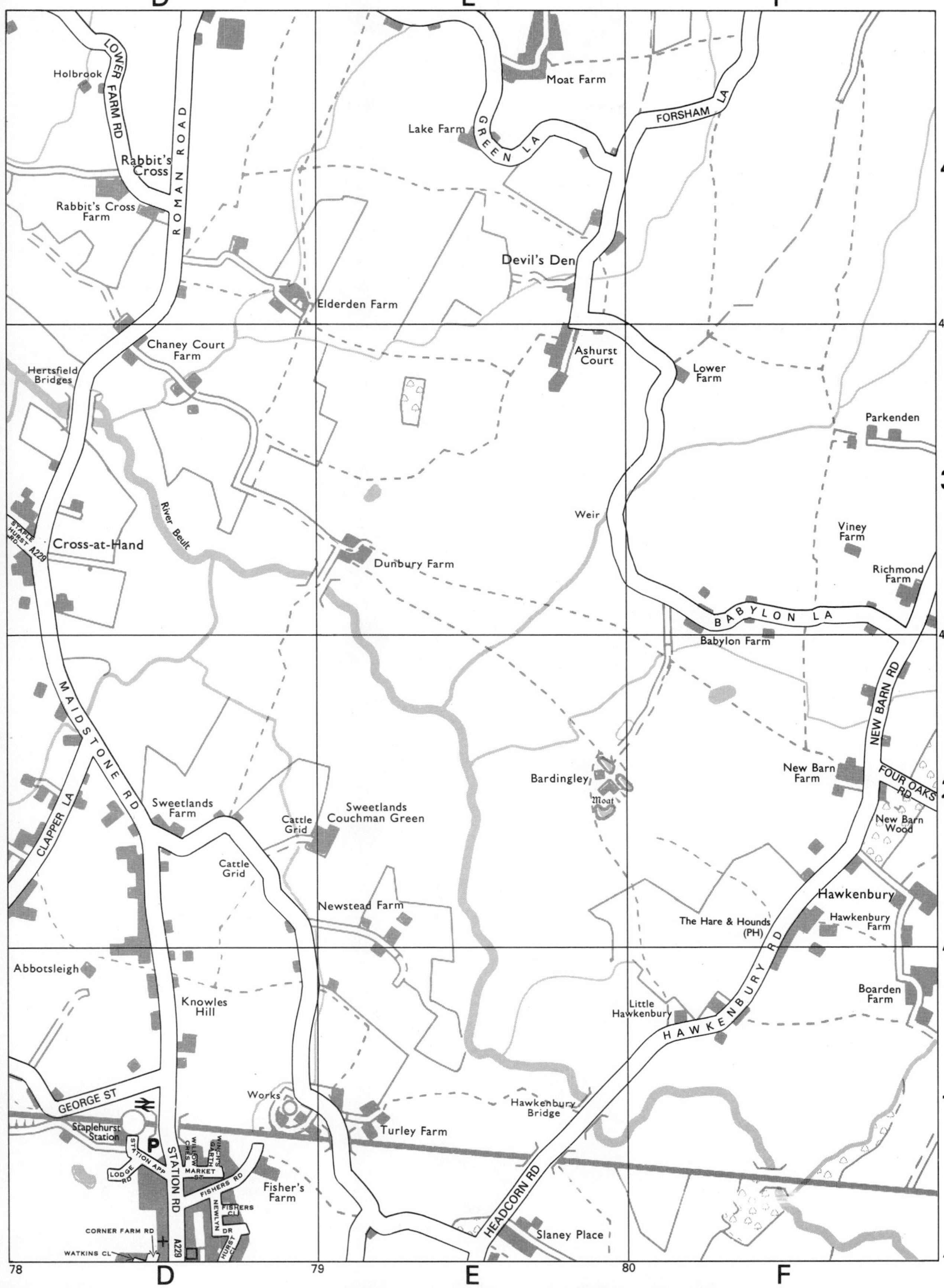
D
E
F
Holbrook
LOWER FARM RD
ROMAN ROAD
Rabbit's Cross
Rabbit's Cross Farm
Moat Farm
Lake Farm
GREEN LA
FORSHAM LA
Devil's Den
Elderden Farm
Chaney Court Farm
Ashurst Court
Lower Farm
Hertsfield Bridges
Parkenden
River Beult
Weir
STAPLEHURST RD. A229
Cross-at-Hand
Dunbury Farm
Viney Farm
Richmond Farm
BABYLON LA
Babylon Farm
MAIDSTONE RD
NEW BARN RD
Bardingley
Moat
New Barn Farm
FOUR OAKS RD
CLAPPER LA
Sweetlands Farm
Cattle Grid
Sweetlands Couchman Green
New Barn Wood
Cattle Grid
Hawkenbury
Newstead Farm
The Hare & Hounds (PH)
Hawkenbury Farm
HAWKENBURY RD
Abbotsleigh
Knowles Hill
Little Hawkenbury
Boarden Farm
HAWKENBURY
GEORGE ST
Works
Hawkenbury Bridge
Staplehurst Station
Turley Farm
P
STATION APP
WILLOW CRES
WINCHS GARTH
MARKET ST
LODGE RD
STATION RD
FISHERS RD
Fisher's Farm
NEWLYN DR
FISHERS CL
HEADCORN RD
CORNER FARM RD
A229
HURST CL
Slaney Place
WATKINS CL
4
3
2
1
47
46
45
44
78
79
80
D
E
F

144

160

126

143

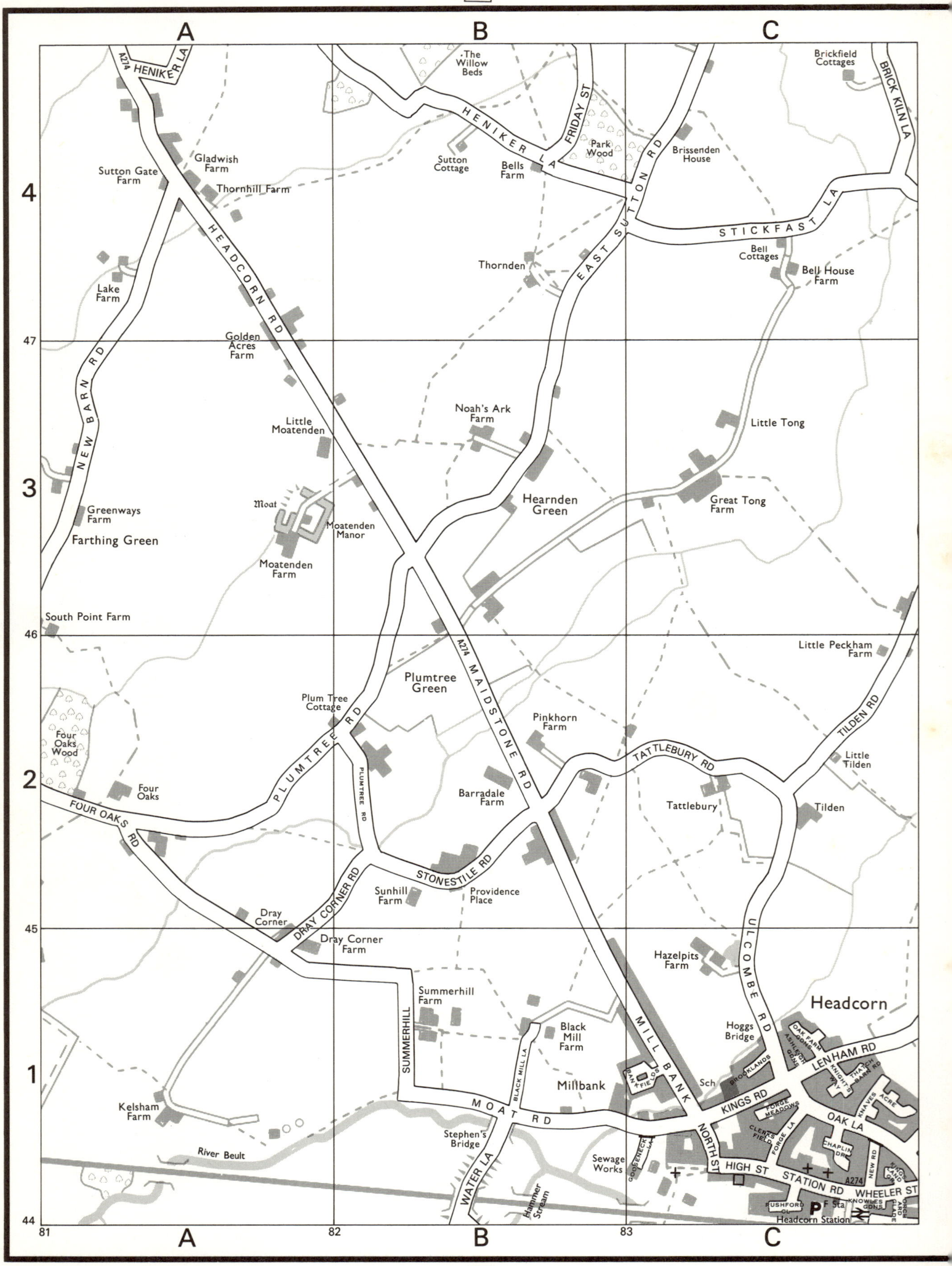
A
B
C
4
3
2
1
47
46
45
44
81
82
83
A274 HENIKER LA
The Willow Beds
HENIKER LA
FRIDAY ST
Park Wood
Brissenden House
Brickfield Cottages
BRICK KILN LA
Sutton Gate Farm
Gladwish Farm
Thornhill Farm
Sutton Cottage
Bells Farm
EAST SUTTON RD
STICKFAST LA
Bell Cottages
Bell House Farm
Thornden
Lake Farm
HEADCORN RD
Golden Acres Farm
NEW BARN RD
Little Moatenden
Noah's Ark Farm
Little Tong
Moat
Moatenden Manor
Moatenden Farm
Hearnden Green
Great Tong Farm
Greenways Farm
Farthing Green
South Point Farm
Little Peckham Farm
A274 MAIDSTONE RD
Plumtree Green
Plum Tree Cottage
Pinkhorn Farm
TILDEN RD
Four Oaks Wood
Four Oaks
PLUMTREE RD
TATTLEBURY RD
Little Tilden
Barradale Farm
Tattlebury
Tilden
FOUR OAKS RD
STONESTILE RD
Sunhill Farm
Providence Place
Dray Corner
DRAY CORNER RD
Dray Corner Farm
ULCOMBE RD
Hazelpits Farm
Headcorn
Summerhill Farm
SUMMERHILL
Black Mill Farm
BLACK MILL LA
MILL BANK
Hoggs Bridge
OAK FARM GDNS
ASHLEIGH GDNS
LENHAM RD
BROOKLANDS
KNIGHT'S WAY
THATCH BARN RD
Millbank
BANKFIELDS
Sch
KINGS RD
FORGE MEADOWS
KNAVES ACRE
OAK LA
Kelsham Farm
MOAT RD
NORTH ST
CLERKS FIELD
FORGE LA
CHAPLIN DR
NEW RD
Stephen's Bridge
River Beult
Sewage Works
GOOSENECK LA
HIGH ST
STATION RD
A274
WHEELER ST
WATER LA
Hammer Stream
RUSHFORD CL
P
F Sta
KNOWLES GDNS
ORCHARD GLADE
Headcorn Station

161

127

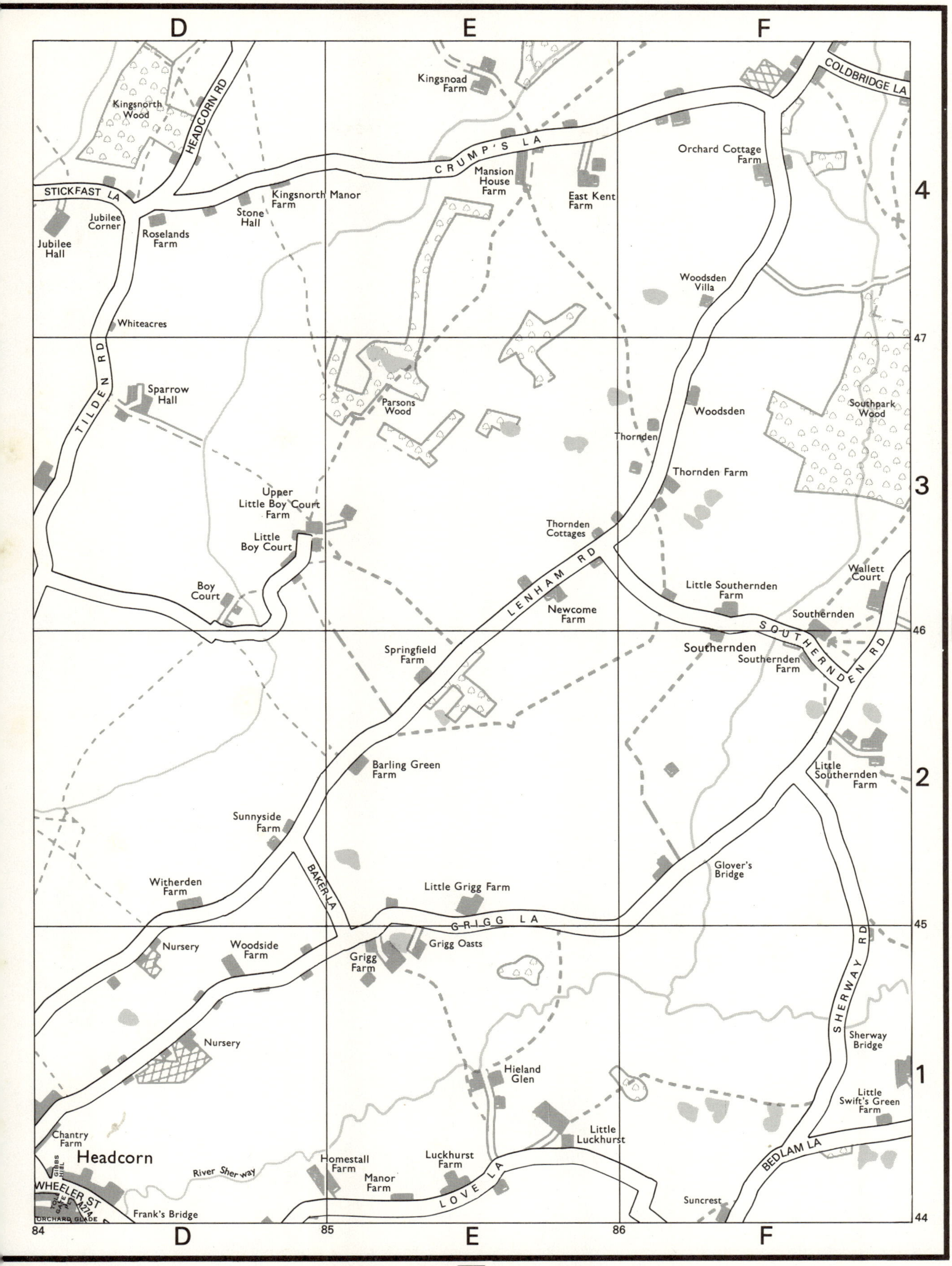
D
E
F
Kingsnoad Farm
COLDBRIDGE LA
Kingsnorth Wood
HEADCORN RD
CRUMP'S LA
Orchard Cottage Farm
Mansion House Farm
STICKFAST LA
Kingsnorth Manor Farm
East Kent Farm
4
Jubilee Corner
Stone Hall
Jubilee Hall
Roselands Farm
Woodsden Villa
Whiteacres
47
TILDEN RD
Sparrow Hall
Parsons Wood
Woodsden
Southpark Wood
Thornden
Thornden Farm
3
Upper Little Boy Court Farm
Little Boy Court
Thornden Cottages
LENHAM RD
Wallett Court
Boy Court
Little Southernden Farm
Newcome Farm
Southernden
46
Springfield Farm
Southernden
SOUTHERNDEN RD
Southernden Farm
Barling Green Farm
Little Southernden Farm
2
Sunnyside Farm
BAKER LA
Glover's Bridge
Witherden Farm
Little Grigg Farm
GRIGG LA
45
Nursery
Woodside Farm
Grigg Oasts
Grigg Farm
SHERWAY RD
Nursery
Sherway Bridge
Hieland Glen
1
Little Swift's Green Farm
Chantry Farm
Little Luckhurst
Headcorn
BEDLAM LA
Homestall Farm
Luckhurst Farm
River Sherway
WHEELER ST
Manor Farm
LOVE LA
Suncrest
Frank's Bridge
ORCHARD GLADE
A274
44
84
85
86
D
E
F

146

162

128

145

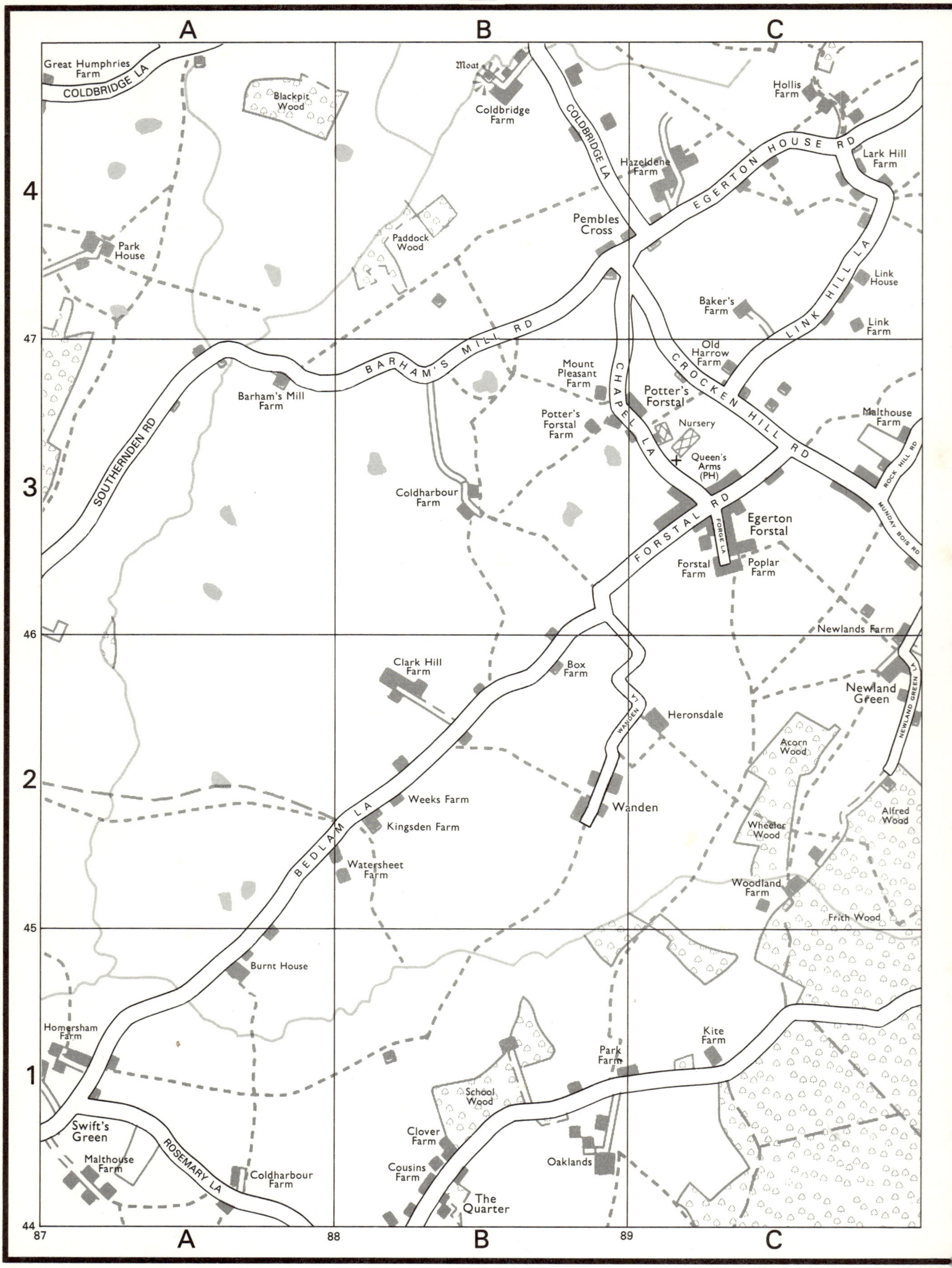
A
B
C
4
3
2
1
47
46
45
44
87
88
89
Great Humphries Farm
COLDBRIDGE LA
Blackpit Wood
Moat
Coldbridge Farm
Hollis Farm
Lark Hill Farm
EGERTON HOUSE RD
Hazeldene Farm
Park House
Paddock Wood
Pembles Cross
Baker's Farm
Link House
Link Farm
LINK HILL LA
BARHAM'S MILL RD
Barham's Mill Farm
Mount Pleasant Farm
Potter's Forstal
Old Harrow Farm
CROCKEN HILL RD
CHAPEL LA
Potter's Forstal Farm
Nursery
Queen's Arms (PH)
Malthouse Farm
SOUTHERNDEN RD
Coldharbour Farm
FORSTAL RD
FORGE LA
Egerton Forstal
Forstal Farm
Poplar Farm
ROCK HILL RD
MUNDAY BOIS RD
Newlands Farm
Clark Hill Farm
Box Farm
Newland Green
NEWLAND GREEN LA
WANDEN LA
Heronsdale
Acorn Wood
Wanden
Weeks Farm
Kingsden Farm
BEDLAM LA
Watersheet Farm
Wheeler Wood
Alfred Wood
Woodland Farm
Frith Wood
Burnt House
Homersham Farm
Kite Farm
Park Farm
School Wood
Swift's Green
Malthouse Farm
ROSEMARY LA
Coldharbour Farm
Clover Farm
Cousins Farm
Oaklands
The Quarter

163

129

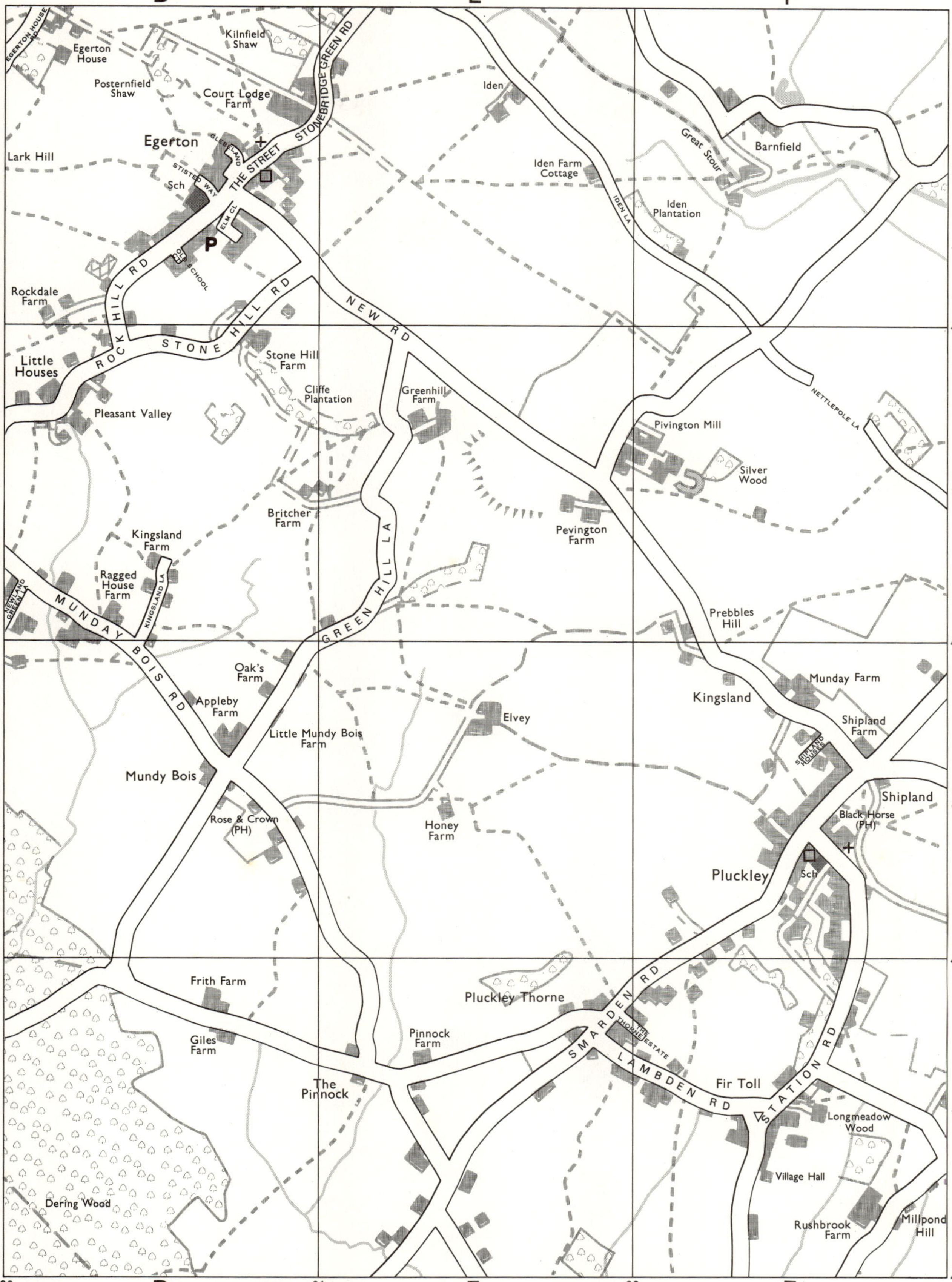

not continued, see key diagram

not continued, see key diagram

131

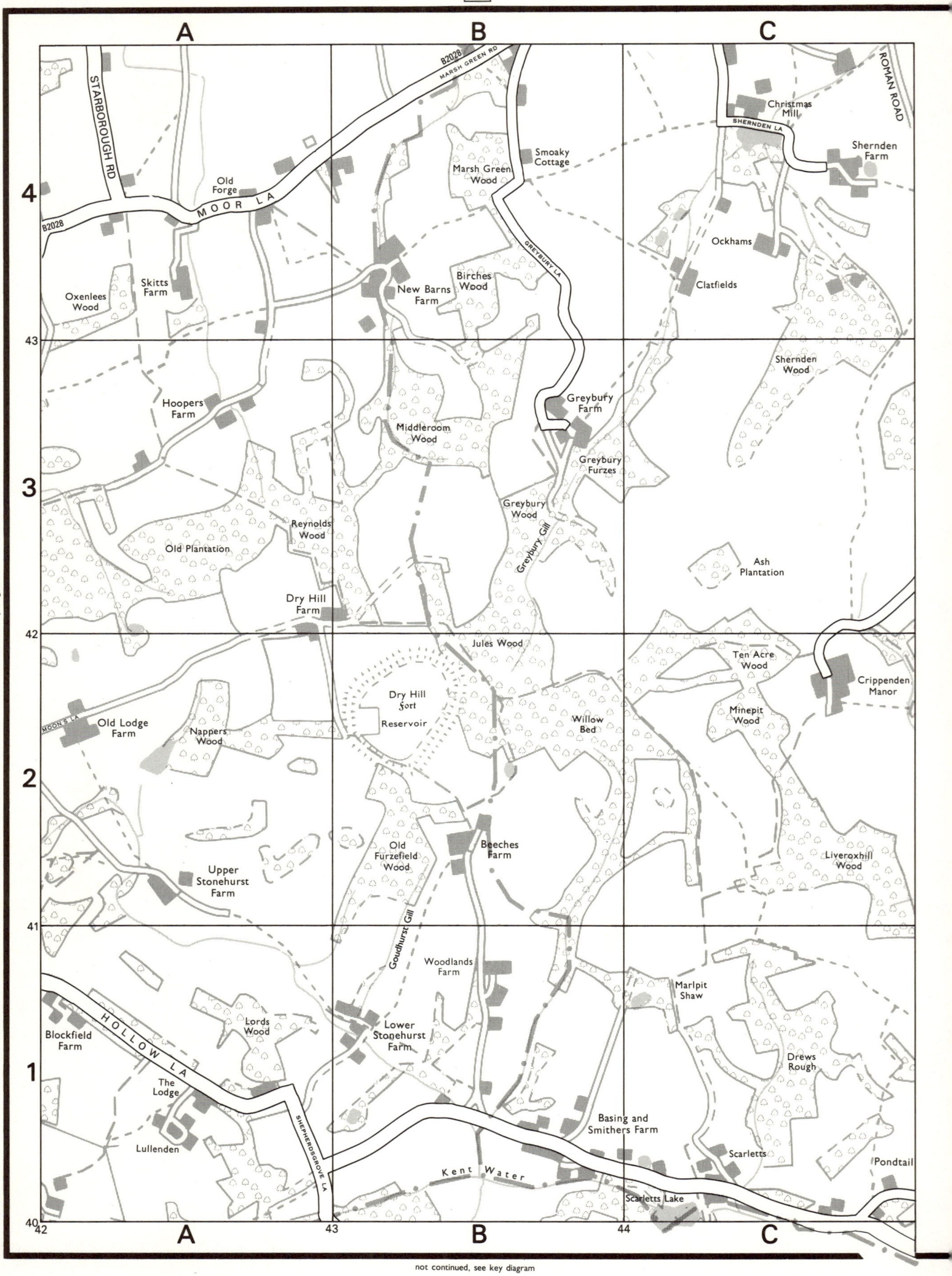

not continued, see key diagram

not continued, see key diagram

132

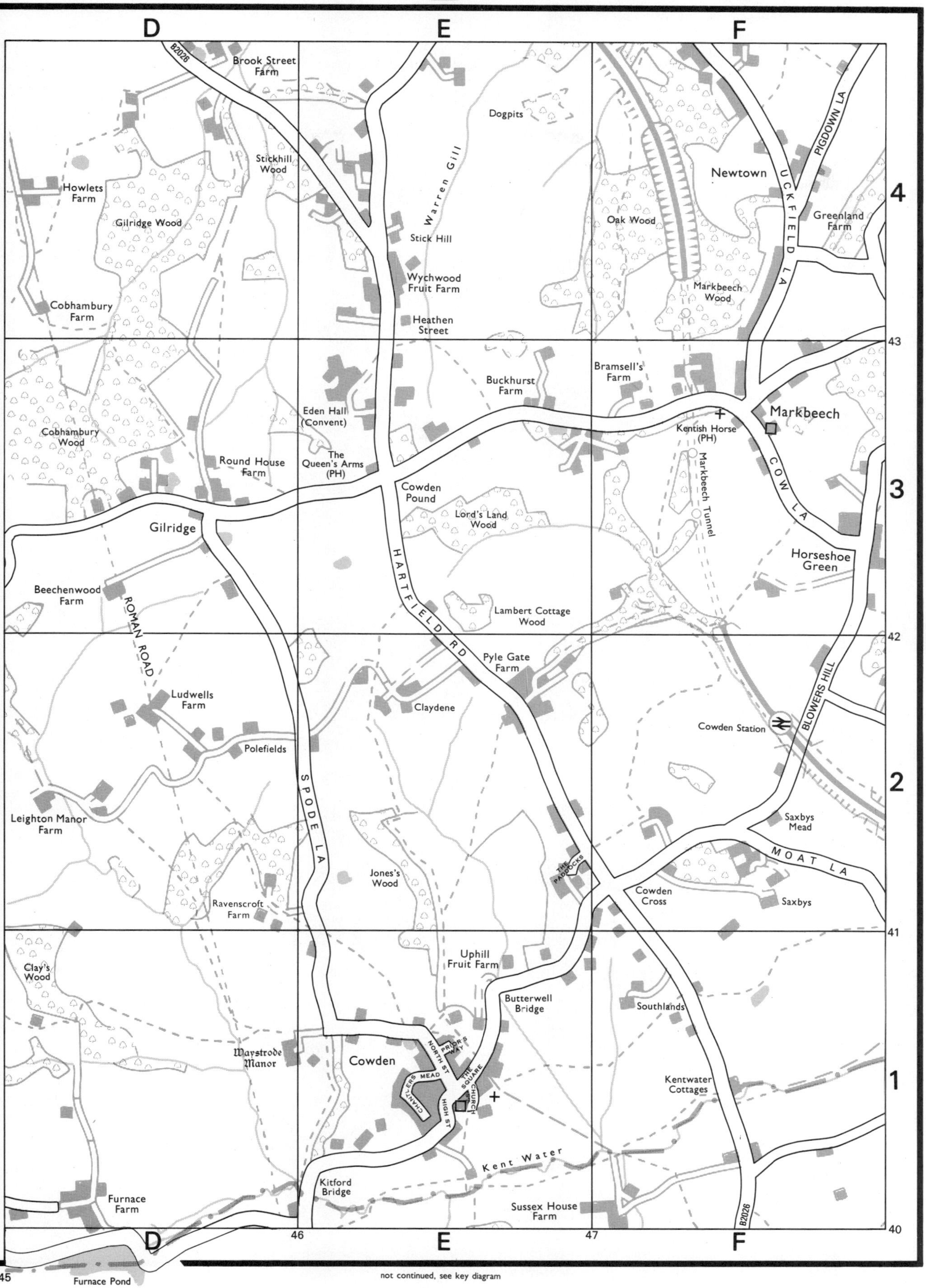

150

not continued, see key diagram

133

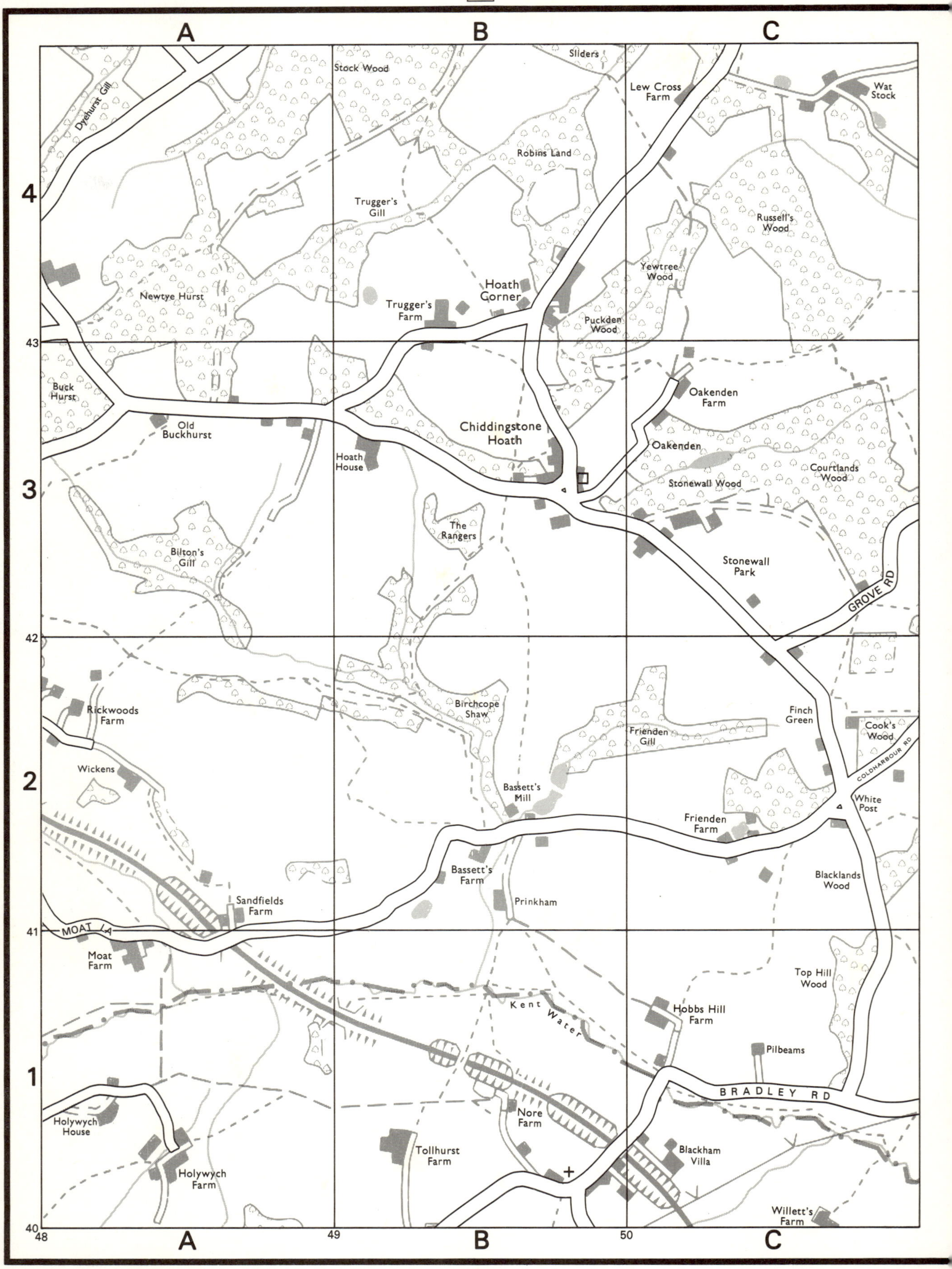
A
B
C
Dyehurst Gill
Stock Wood
Sliders
Lew Cross Farm
Wat Stock
Robins Land
Trugger's Gill
Russell's Wood
Yewtree Wood
Hoath Corner
Newtye Hurst
Trugger's Farm
Puckden Wood
Buck Hurst
Oakenden Farm
Old Buckhurst
Chiddingstone Hoath
Oakenden
Hoath House
Courtlands Wood
Stonewall Wood
The Rangers
Bilton's Gill
Stonewall Park
GROVE RD
Rickwoods Farm
Birchcope Shaw
Finch Green
Cook's Wood
Friendem Gill
COLDHARBOUR RD
Wickens
Bassett's Mill
White Post
Frienden Farm
Bassett's Farm
Blacklands Wood
Sandfields Farm
Prinkham
MOAT LA
Moat Farm
Top Hill Wood
Kent Water
Hobbs Hill Farm
Pilbeams
BRADLEY RD
Holywych House
Nore Farm
Tollhurst Farm
Blackham Villa
Holywych Farm
Willett's Farm
4
3
2
1
43
42
41
40
48
49
50

149

164

134

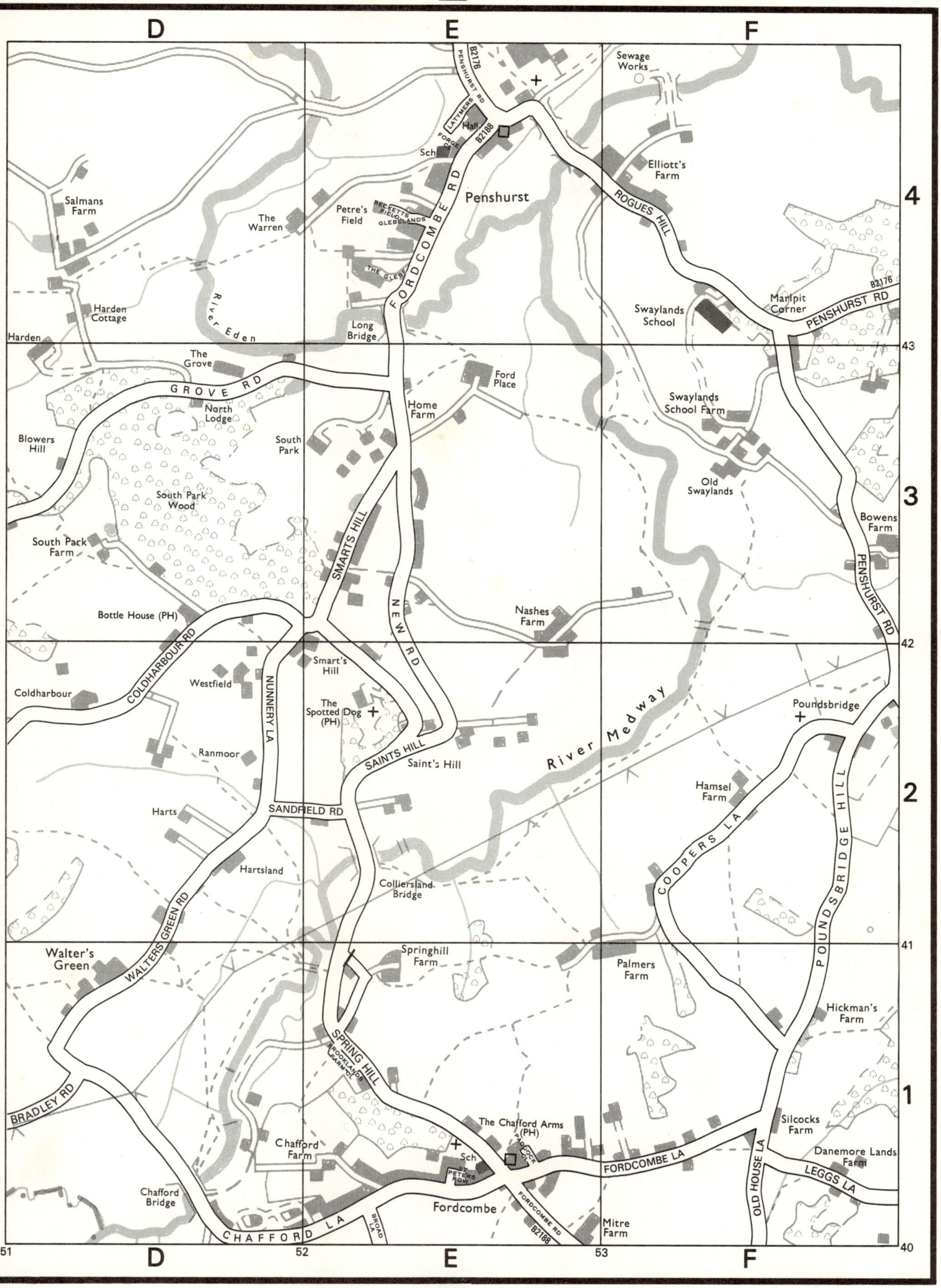
D
E
F
B2176
PENSHURST RD
LATYMERS
Hall
FORGE
B2188
Sch
Sewage Works
Salmans Farm
The Warren
Petre's Field
BECKETTS FIELD
GLEBELANDS
THE GLEBE
FORDCOMBE RD
Penshurst
Elliott's Farm
ROGUES HILL
4
River Eden
Harden Cottage
Harden
Long Bridge
Swaylands School
Marlpit Corner
B2176
PENSHURST RD
43
The Grove
GROVE RD
North Lodge
Ford Place
Home Farm
Swaylands School Farm
Blowers Hill
South Park
South Park Wood
Old Swaylands
3
Bowens Farm
South Park Farm
SMARTS HILL
NEW RD
PENSHURST RD
Bottle House (PH)
Nashes Farm
42
COLDHARBOUR RD
Coldharbour
Westfield
NUNNERY LA
Smart's Hill
The Spotted Dog (PH)
River Medway
Poundsbridge
Ranmoor
SAINTS HILL
Saint's Hill
Hamsel Farm
2
Harts
SANDFIELD RD
COOPERS LA
POUNDSBRIDGE HILL
Hartsland
Colliersland Bridge
WALTERS GREEN RD
41
Walter's Green
Springhill Farm
Palmers Farm
Hickman's Farm
SPRING HILL
BROOKLANDS FARM CL
BRADLEY RD
1
The Chafford Arms (PH)
PADDOCK
Silcocks Farm
Chafford Farm
Sch
ST PETERS ROW
FORDCOMBE LA
Danemore Lands Farm
OLD HOUSE LA
LEGGS LA
Chafford Bridge
Fordcombe
FORDCOMBE RD
B2188
Mitre Farm
CHAFFORD LA
BROAD LA
51
52
53
40
D
E
F

152

165

135

151

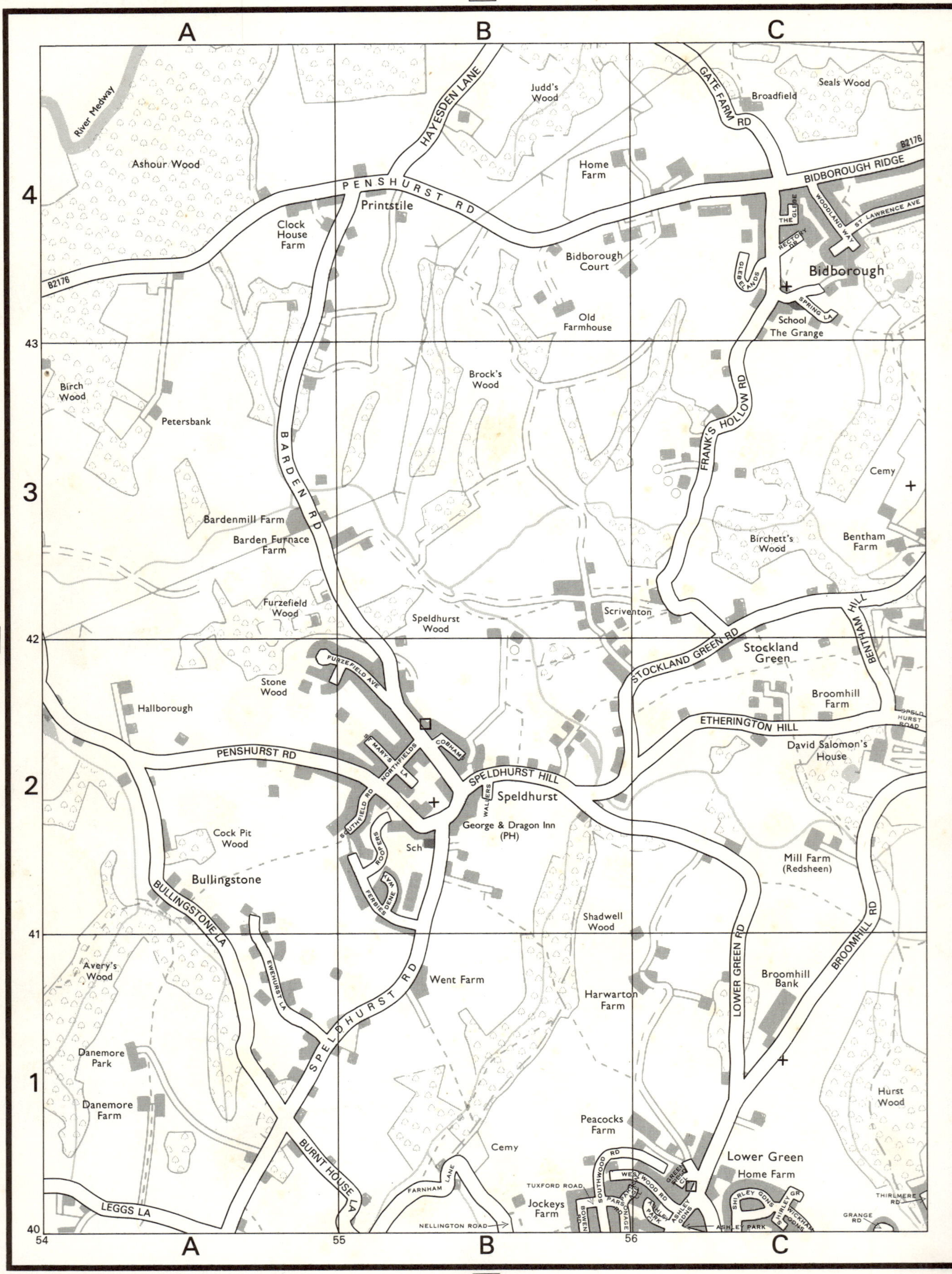
A
B
C
4
3
2
1
43
42
41
40
54
55
56
River Medway
Ashour Wood
HAYESDEN LANE
Judd's Wood
GATE FARM RD
Broadfield
Seals Wood
B2176
BIDBOROUGH RIDGE
Home Farm
PENSHURST RD
Printstile
Clock House Farm
THE GLEBE
WOODLAND WAY
ST LAWRENCE AVE
RECTORY DR
GLEBELANDS
Bidborough Court
Bidborough
SPRING LA
School
The Grange
Old Farmhouse
Brock's Wood
Birch Wood
Petersbank
BARDEN RD
FRANK'S HOLLOW RD
Cemy
Bardenmill Farm
Barden Furnace Farm
Birchett's Wood
Bentham Farm
Furzefield Wood
Speldhurst Wood
Scriventon
BENTHAM HILL
STOCKLAND GREEN RD
Stockland Green
FURZEFIELD AVE
Stone Wood
Hallborough
Broomhill Farm
ETHERINGTON HILL
SPELDHURST ROAD
David Salomon's House
ST MARY'S LA
NORTHFIELDS
COBHAM
SPELDHURST HILL
WALTERS
Speldhurst
SOUTHFIELD RD
George & Dragon Inn (PH)
Cock Pit Wood
ROOPERS
Sch
Mill Farm (Redsheen)
Bullingstone
FERBIES
DENE WAY
BULLINGSTONE LA
Shadwell Wood
Avery's Wood
EWEHURST LA
SPELDHURST RD
Went Farm
LOWER GREEN RD
BROOMHILL RD
Broomhill Bank
Harwarton Farm
Danemore Park
Hurst Wood
Danemore Farm
Peacocks Farm
BURNT HOUSE LA
Cemy
Lower Green
Home Farm
FARNHAM LANE
SOUTHWOOD RD
WESTWOOD RD
TUXFORD ROAD
Jockeys Farm
BOWEN RD
PARSONAGE
ASHLEY GDNS
ASHLEY PARK
SHIRLEY GDNS
SHIRLEY GR
THIRLMERE RD
GRANGE RD
LEGGS LA
NELLINGTON ROAD

166

136

D
E
F
4
3
2
1
43
42
41
40
57
58
59
Waghorn's Wood
Nightingale Farmhouse
Bidborough Corner
BIDBOROUGH RIDGE
B2176
A26
THE CRESCENT
DARNLEY DR
HARLAND WAY
Birch Wood
VAUXHALL LA
Moatenden
Honnington Farm
Forest Farm
Gorse Wood
Minepit Wood
Appletree Wood
Old Forge Farm
BIRCHWOOD AVE
Dr Barnardo's Home
Conneyburrow Wood
High Wood
LONDON RD
CHURCH RD
School
Coll
Southborough Common
Modest Corner
VICTORIA RD
CONSTITUTIONAL HILL RD
HOLDEN RD
PENNINGTON RD
VICARAGE RD
VALLEY VIEW
PENNINGTON PL
THE RIDGEWAY
Brokes Mill Farm
Forge Farm
Barnett's Farm
Brokes Wood
SOUTHBOROUGH
Offices
Chalybeate Spring
The Park
KIBBLES LA
PROSPECT RD
SPRINGFIELD RD
BROOMHILL PARK RD
HOLDEN PARK RD
Schs
Library
Fire Sta
Amb Sta
YEW TREE RD
BRIAN CRES
HILL CREST
BROKES WAY
BLACKTHORNE AVE
Schools
CHESTNUT AVE
High Brooms
High Brooms Industrial Estate
Works
SPELDHURST RD
BROOMHILL RD
Caen Farm
Schools
TA Centre
Smockham Farm
Caenwood Farm
REYNOLDS LA
ST JOHN'S RD
WILMAN RD
NEWLANDS RD
SILVERDALE RD
UPPER GROSVENOR RD
HIGH BROOMS RD
NORTH FARM RD
High Brooms Station
St John's
ALL SAINTS RD
QUEEN'S RD
Sherwood
SANDHURST RD
QUARRY RD
Ferndale
CULVERDEN DOWN
CULVERDEN PARK
CONISTON AVE
BISHOP'S DOWN PARK ROAD
BYNG RD
Sch
Coll

154

167

137

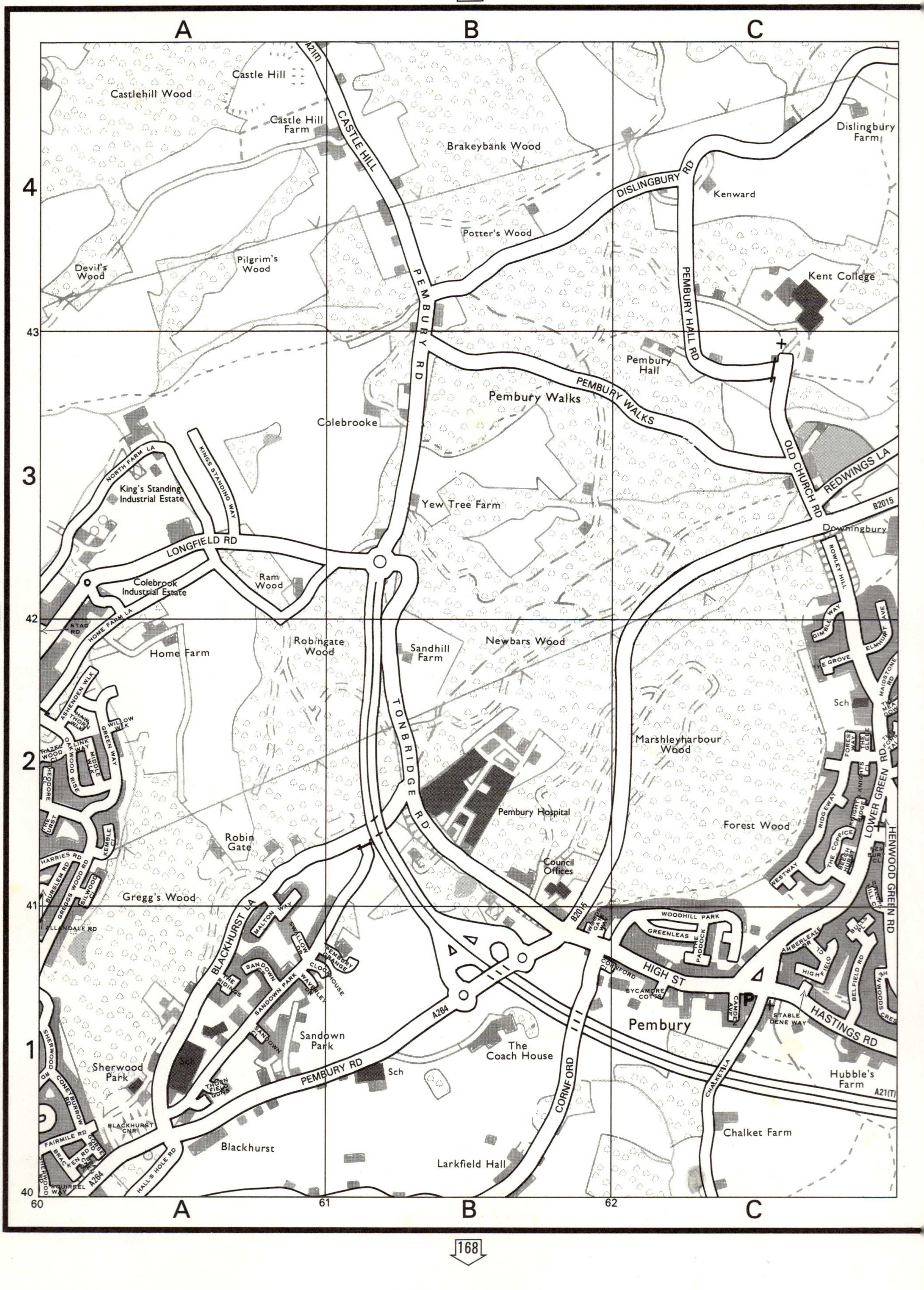
A
B
C
4
3
2
1
43
42
41
40
60
61
62
Castle Hill
Castlehill Wood
Castle Hill Farm
CASTLE HILL
A21(T)
Brakeybank Wood
Dislingbury Farm
DISLINGBURY RD
Kenward
Potter's Wood
Devil's Wood
Pilgrim's Wood
PEMBURY RD
PEMBURY HALL RD
Kent College
Pembury Hall
Pembury Walks
PEMBURY WALKS
Colebrooke
OLD CHURCH RD
REDWINGS LA
B2015
NORTH FARM LA
KINGS STANDING WAY
King's Standing Industrial Estate
Yew Tree Farm
Downingbury
ROWLEY HILL
LONGFIELD RD
Ram Wood
Colebrook Industrial Estate
HOME FARM LA
STAG RD
Home Farm
Robingate Wood
Sandhill Farm
Newbars Wood
GIMBLE WAY
ELMHURST AVE
THE GROVE
MAIDSTONE RD
Sch
ASHENDEN WLK
WILLOW WLK
GREEN WAY
OAKWOOD RISE
MIDDLE WLK
TONBRIDGE RD
Marshleyharbour Wood
FOREST WAY
LOWER GREEN RD
RIDGEWAY
KNIGHTS RIDGE
Pembury Hospital
Robin Gate
Forest Wood
HENWOOD GREEN RD
HARRIES RD
BURSLEM RD
GREGGS WOOD RD
KEMBLE CL
SILWOOD CL
Gregg's Wood
ALLANDALE RD
Council Offices
WESTWAY
THE COPPICE
BLACKHURST LA
MALTON WAY
SWALLOW DR
PEMBURY GRANGE
B2015
WOODHILL PARK
GREENLEAS
THE PADDOCK
AMBERLEAZE DR
HIGH FIELD CL
BELFIELD RD
HENWOOD CRES
THE RIDINGS
SANDOWN PARK
CLOCKHOUSE
WAVERLEY DR
CORNFORD
HIGH ST
SYCAMORE COTTS
CAMDEN AVE
P
STABLE DENE WAY
HASTINGS RD
Pembury
A264
SANDOWN CL
Sandown Park
The Coach House
Sherwood Park
SHERWOOD RD
CONEYBURROW RD
Sch
THORNFIELD GDNS
PEMBURY RD
Sch
CORNFORD
CHALKET LA
Hubble's Farm
A21(T)
BLACKHURST CNR
FAIRMILE RD
BRACKEN RD
Blackhurst
Chalket Farm
Larkfield Hall
SQUIRREL WAY
A264
HALL'S HOLE RD

153

168

138

D
E
F
DISLINGBURY RD
Reeds Farm
Spring Farm
ALDERS RD
Amhurst Bank
Crittenden Farm
Colt's Hill
AMHURST BANK RD
Alder Stream
Tudeley Brook
4
Badsell Park Farm
CRITTENDEN RD
Amhurst Hill Farm
Lord's Wood
Hawkwell Farm
Crittenden
REDWINGS LA
MAIDSTONE RD
43
Spring Grove Farm
Little Hawkwell Farm
CINDERHILL WOOD
3
Cinderhill Wood
Foxhole Farm
CHESTNUT LA
Pippins
Foxhole
Albans Farm
Brenchley Wood
The Star Inn (PH)
STONE COURT LA
Stone Court Farm
FOXHOLE LA
42
The Wheelwrights Arms (PH)
B2160
STONE COURT LA
SNIPE CL
HERONS WAY
THE MEADOW
MIDDLEFIELD
THE GILL
THE FORSTAL
Tutty's Farm
BATCHELORS
PETERSFIELD
Court Farm
OAKFIELD RD
Snipe Wood
2
BEAGLES WOOD RD
Three Towns Farm
BRAMBLE REED LA
MAIDSTONE ROAD
Friars
Lodge Farm
WOODLANDS
Romford
ROMFORD RD
Romford Manor
Hayes View Farm
41
HESKETT PARK
Wellgrove Farm
Henwood Green
WOODSIDE RD
WOODSIDE
HENWOODS CRES
Matfield Grange
KINGS TOLL RD
HENWOOD GREEN ROAD
HENWOODS MOUNT
CANTERBURY RD
SANDHURST
1
King's Toll Farm
SOPHURST LA
HASTINGS RD
Beckett's Grove Farm
A21(T)
Kingsmead
CRYALS ROAD
Kipping's Cross Farm
Kingsmead Farm
B2160
Kipping's Cross
A21(T)
40
63
64
65
D
E
F

156

169

139

155

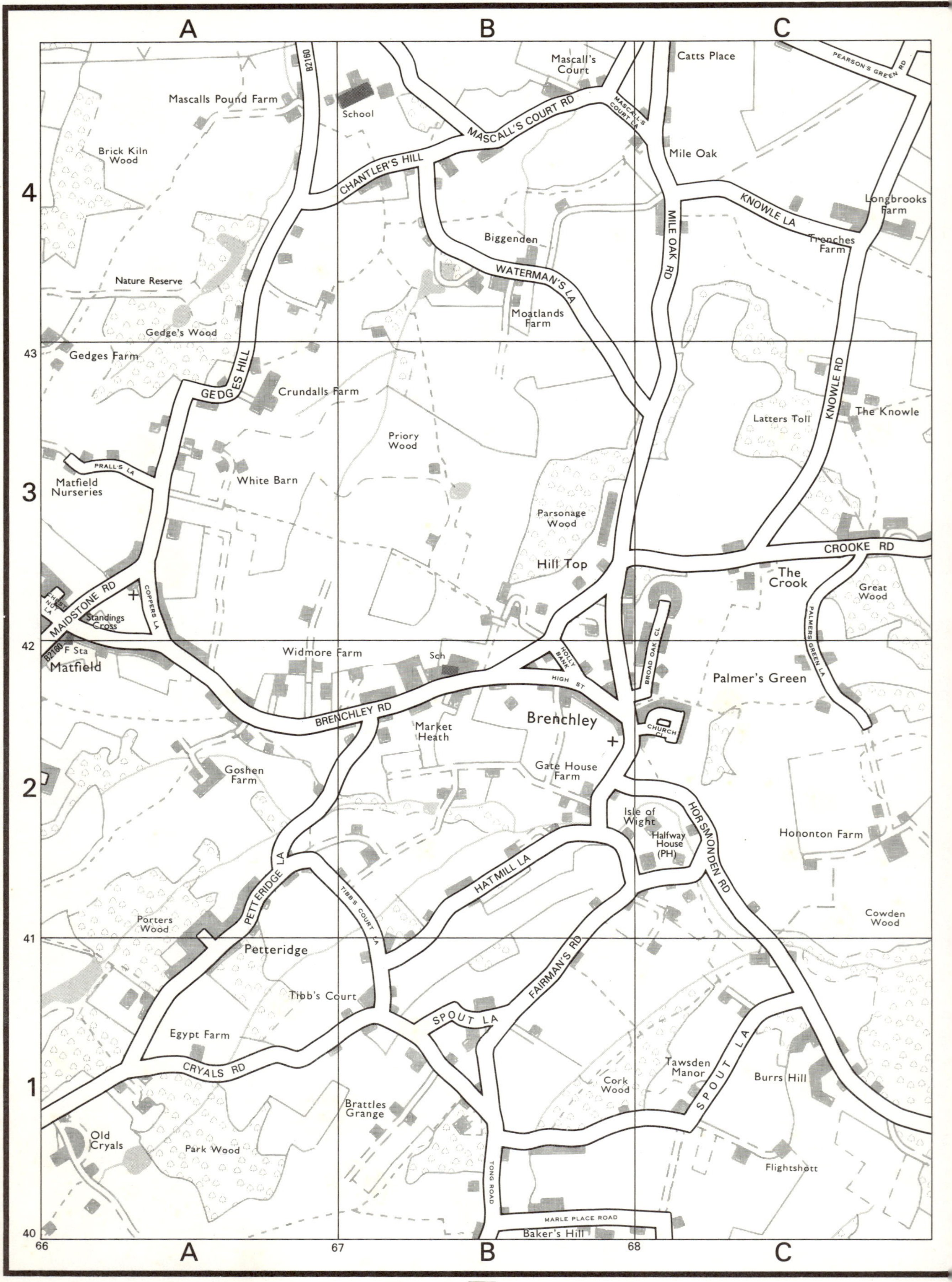
A
B
C
4
3
2
1
43
42
41
40
66
67
68
Mascall's Court
Catts Place
Mascalls Pound Farm
School
B2160
PEARSON'S GREEN RD
MASCALL'S COURT RD
MASCALL'S COURT LA
Brick Kiln Wood
CHANTLER'S HILL
Mile Oak
KNOWLE LA
Longbrooks Farm
Trenches Farm
Biggenden
MILE OAK RD
WATERMAN'S LA
Nature Reserve
Moatlands Farm
Gedge's Wood
Gedges Farm
GEDGES HILL
Crundalls Farm
KNOWLE RD
Latters Toll
The Knowle
Priory Wood
PRALL'S LA
Matfield Nurseries
White Barn
Parsonage Wood
CROOKE RD
Hill Top
The Crook
Great Wood
MAIDSTONE RD
CHESTNUT LA
COPPERS LA
Standings Cross
PALMERS GREEN LA
BROAD OAK CL
HOLLY BANK
F Sta
Matfield
Widmore Farm
Sch
HIGH ST
Palmer's Green
BRENCHLEY RD
Brenchley
CHURCH CL
Market Heath
Goshen Farm
Gate House Farm
Isle of Wight
HORSMONDEN RD
Hononton Farm
Halfway House (PH)
PETTERIDGE LA
HATMILL LA
TIBB'S COURT LA
Porters Wood
Cowden Wood
Petteridge
FAIRMAN'S RD
Tibb's Court
SPOUT LA
Egypt Farm
Tawsden Manor
Burrs Hill
CRYALS RD
Cork Wood
Brattles Grange
Old Cryals
Park Wood
TONG ROAD
Flightshott
MARLE PLACE ROAD
Baker's Hill

170

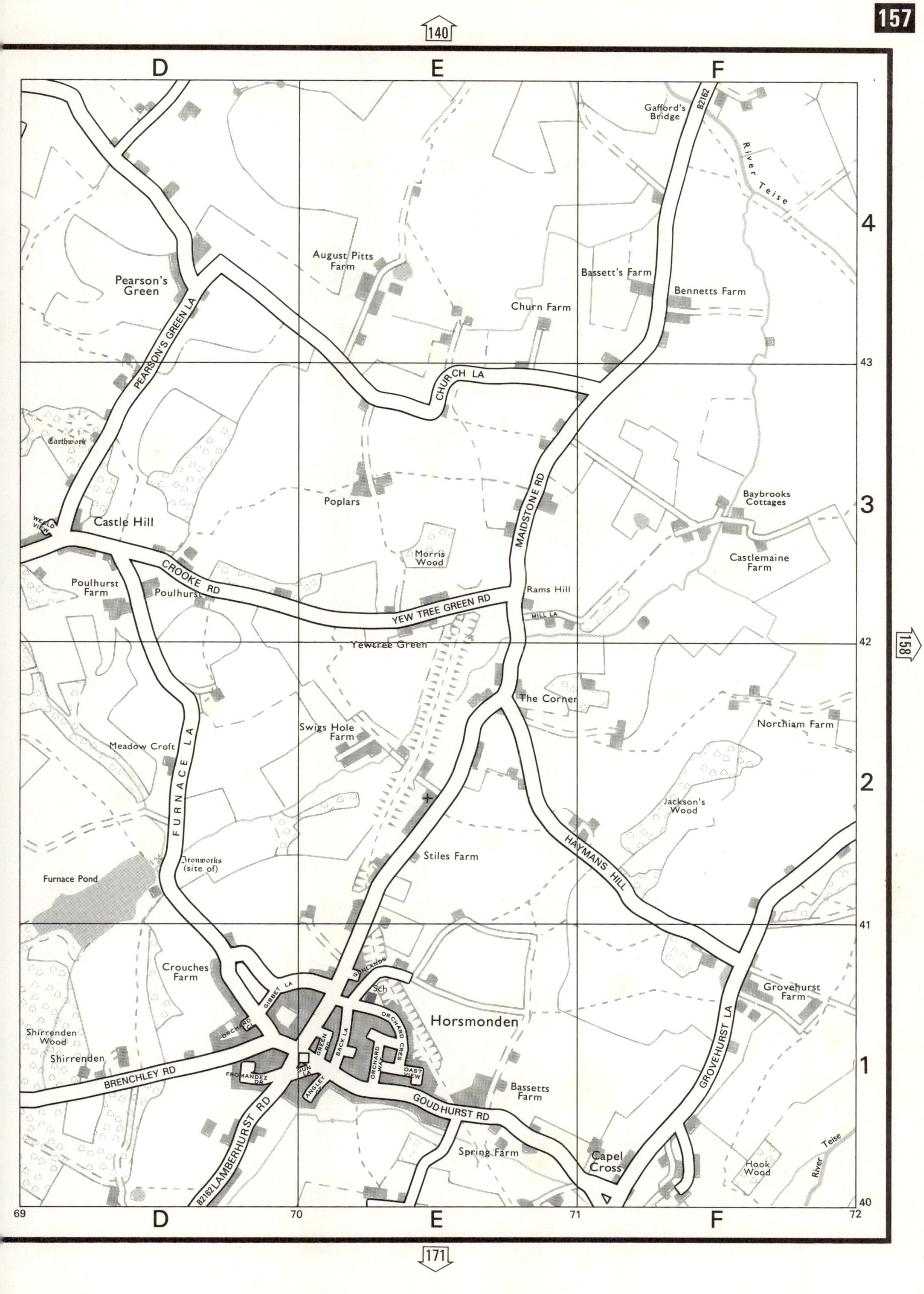
140
D
E
F
Gafford's Bridge
B2162
River Teise
4
Pearson's Green
August Pitts Farm
Bassett's Farm
Bennetts Farm
Churn Farm
PEARSON'S GREEN LA
CHURCH LA
43
Earthwork
Poplars
MAIDSTONE RD
Baybrooks Cottages
3
Castle Hill
WEALD VIEW
Morris Wood
Castlemaine Farm
Poulhurst Farm
Poulhurst
CROOKE RD
YEW TREE GREEN RD
Rams Hill
MILL LA
Yewtree Green
42
158
The Corner
Swigs Hole Farm
Northiam Farm
Meadow Croft
FURNACE LA
2
Jackson's Wood
HAYMANS HILL
Stiles Farm
Ironworks (site of)
Furnace Pond
41
Crouches Farm
GIBBET LA
GONLANDS
Sch
Grovehurst Farm
Horsmonden
Shirrenden Wood
ORCHARD CL
GREEN RD
BACK LA
ORCHARD CRES
ORCHARD WAY
GROVEHURST LA
Shirrenden
BRENCHLEY RD
FROMANDEZ DR
GUN LA
OAST VIEW
1
ANGLEY CT
Bassetts Farm
GOUDHURST RD
B2162 LAMBERHURST RD
Spring Farm
Capel Cross
Hook Wood
River Teise
40
69
70
71
72
171

141

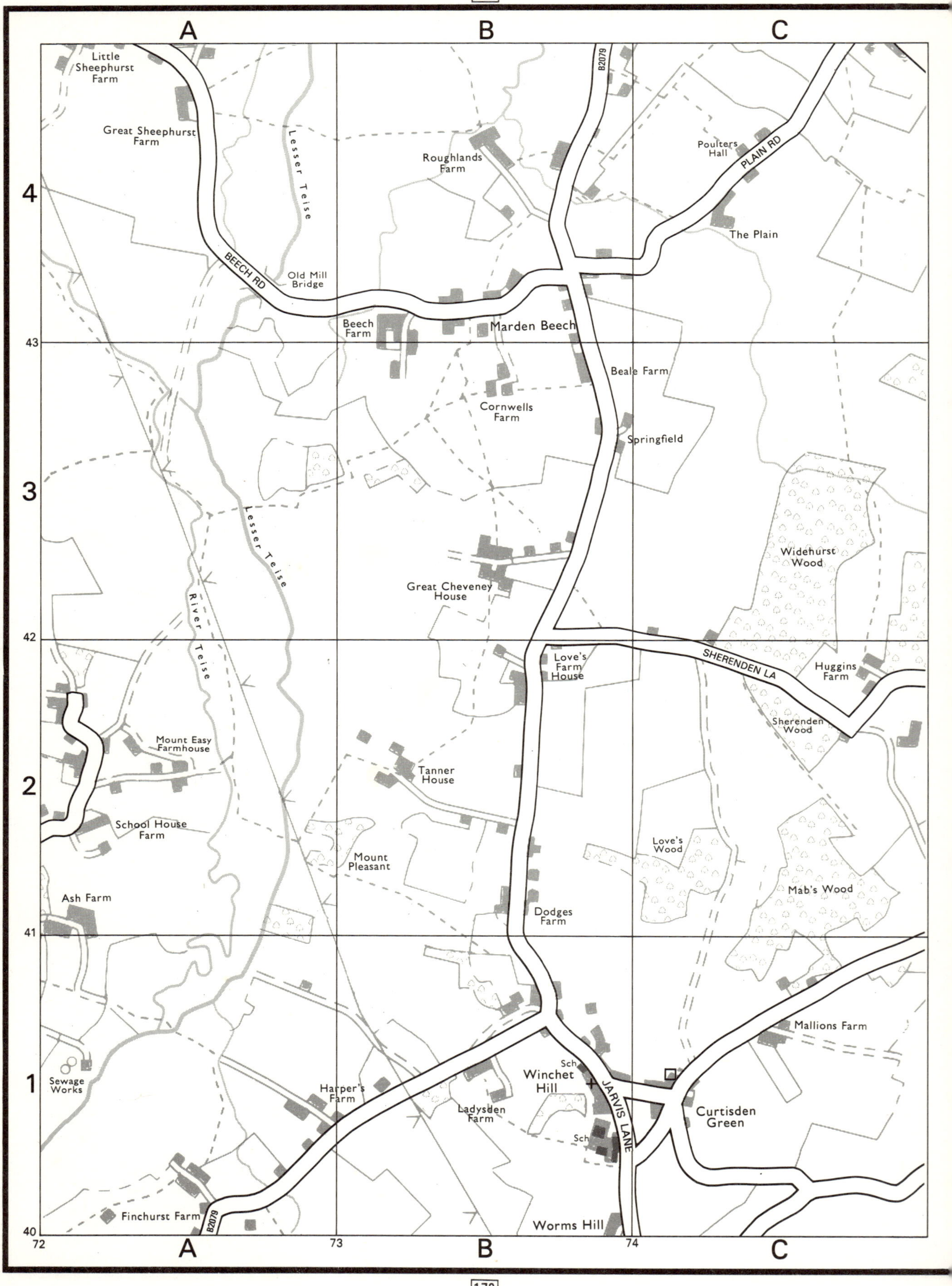

A
B
C
4
3
2
1
43
42
41
40
72
73
74
Little Sheephurst Farm
Great Sheephurst Farm
Lesser Teise
Roughlands Farm
B2079
Poulters Hall
PLAIN RD
The Plain
BEECH RD
Old Mill Bridge
Beech Farm
Marden Beech
Beale Farm
Cornwells Farm
Springfield
Widehurst Wood
Great Cheveney House
River Teise
Love's Farm House
SHERENDEN LA
Huggins Farm
Sherenden Wood
Mount Easy Farmhouse
Tanner House
School House Farm
Mount Pleasant
Love's Wood
Mab's Wood
Ash Farm
Dodges Farm
Mallions Farm
Sewage Works
Harper's Farm
Sch
Winchet Hill
JARVIS LANE
Ladysden Farm
Curtisden Green
Finchurst Farm
Worms Hill

157

172

142

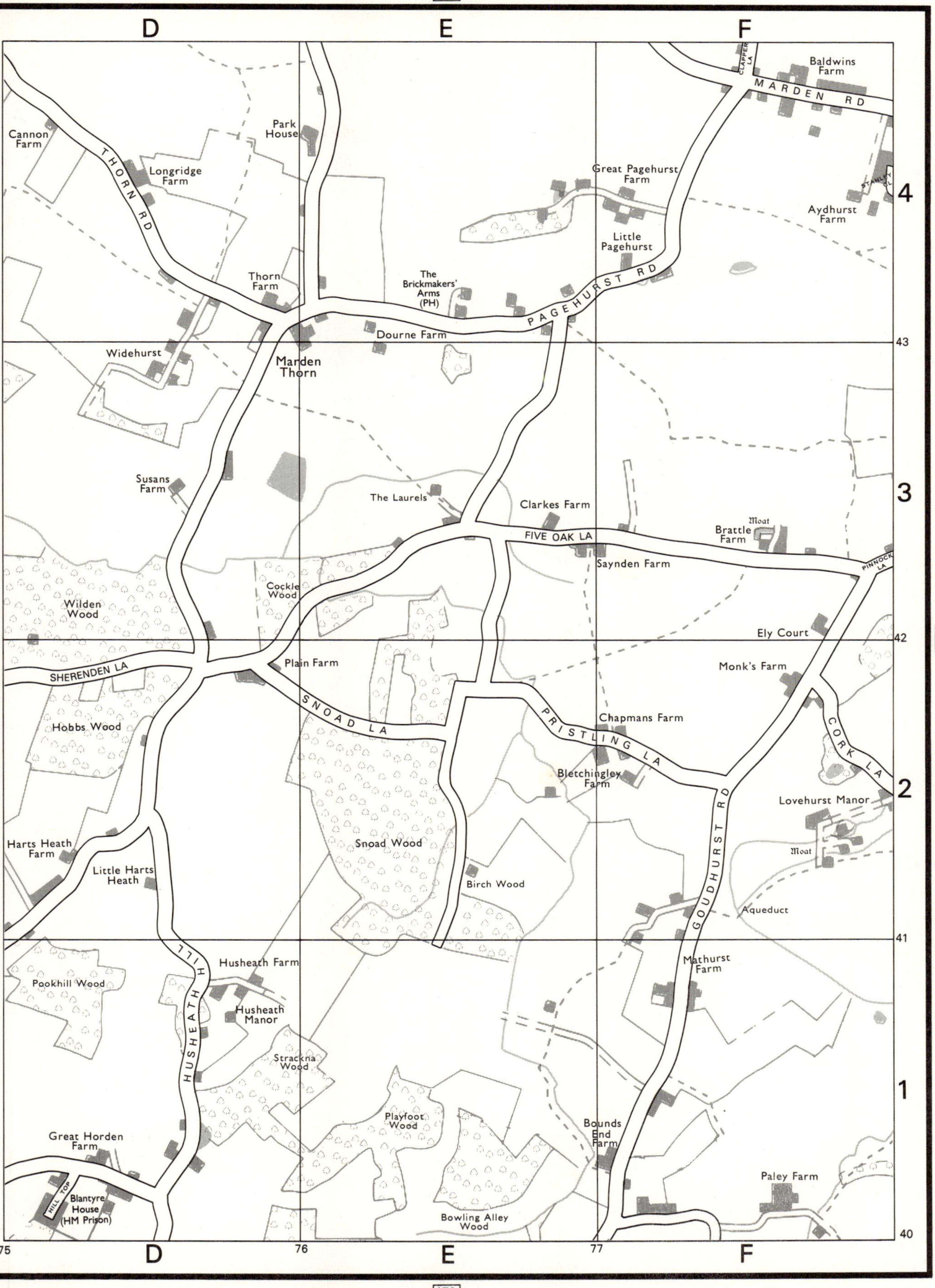
D
E
F
Cannon Farm
Park House
Longridge Farm
THORN RD
Great Pagehurst Farm
Baldwins Farm
MARDEN RD
CLAPPER LA
STANLEY CL
Aydhurst Farm
Little Pagehurst
The Brickmakers' Arms (PH)
Thorn Farm
PAGEHURST RD
Dourne Farm
Widehurst
Marden Thorn
Susans Farm
The Laurels
Clarkes Farm
FIVE OAK LA
Moat
Brattle Farm
Saynden Farm
PINNOCK LA
Cockle Wood
Wilden Wood
Ely Court
SHERENDEN LA
Plain Farm
Monk's Farm
SNOAD LA
Hobbs Wood
Chapmans Farm
PRISTLING LA
CORK LA
Bletchingley Farm
Lovehurst Manor
Moat
GOUDHURST RD
Snoad Wood
Harts Heath Farm
Little Harts Heath
Birch Wood
Aqueduct
HUSHEATH HILL
Husheath Farm
Mathurst Farm
Pookhill Wood
Husheath Manor
Strackna Wood
Playfoot Wood
Bounds End Farm
Great Horden Farm
Paley Farm
HILL TOP
Blantyre House (HM Prison)
Bowling Alley Wood
4
3
2
1
43
42
41
40
75
76
77
D
E
F

160

173

143

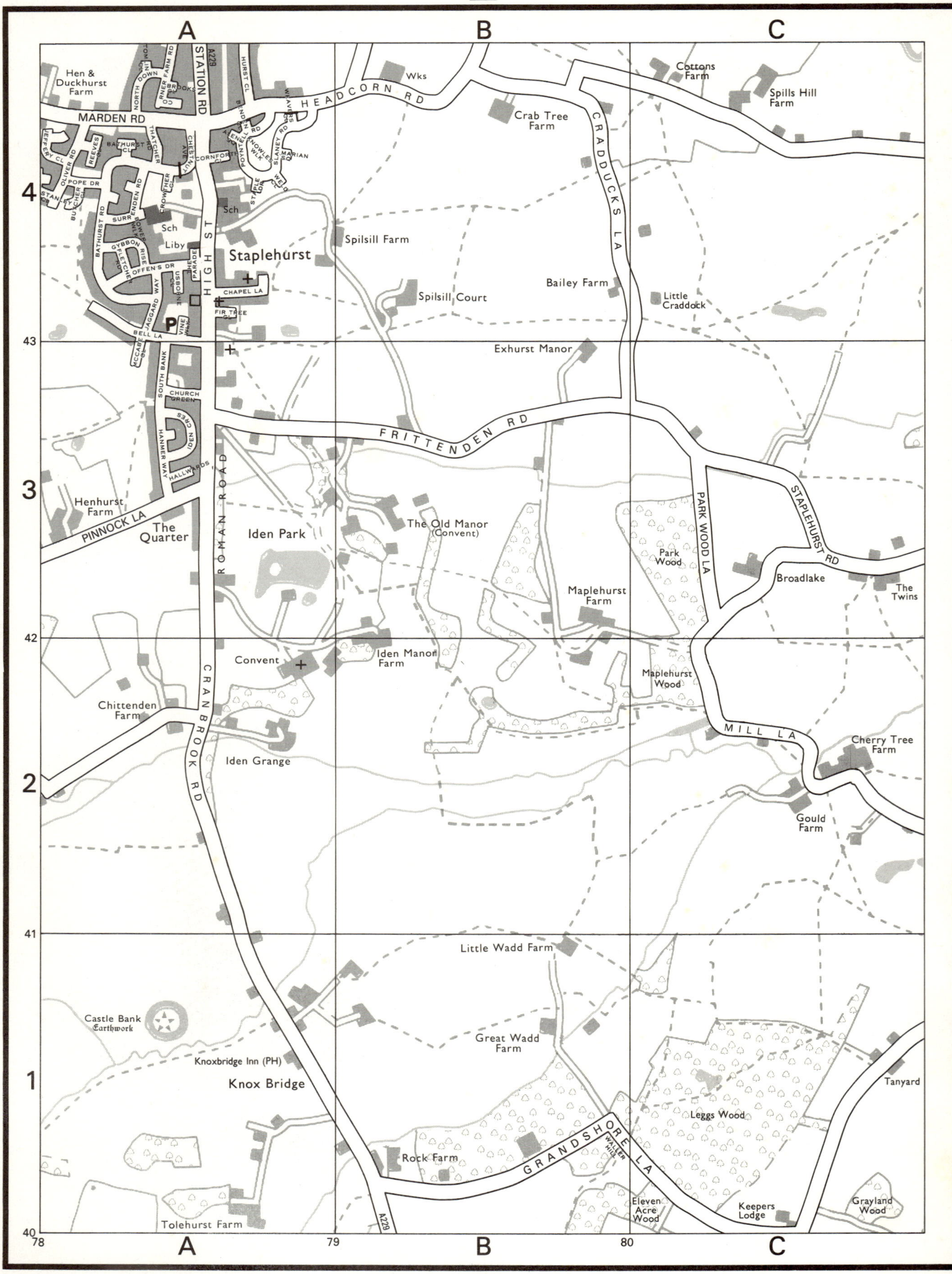
A
B
C
Hen & Duckhurst Farm
MARDEN RD
STATION RD
A229
NORTH DOWN
BROOKS
HURST CL
HEADCORN RD
Wks
Cottons Farm
Spills Hill Farm
Crab Tree Farm
CRADDUCKS LA
JEFFERY CL
OLIVER RD
REEVES
BATHURST CL
THATCHER
CHESTNUT AVE
CORNFORTH
POYNTELL RD
KNOWLES WLK
SLANEY RD
MARIAN
POPE DR
STANLEY CL
BUTCHER CL
CROWTHER
SURRENDEN RD
BATHURST RD
Sch
Liby
GYBBON RISE
FLETCHER
OFFEN'S DR
USBORNE CL
THE PARADE
HIGH ST
Staplehurst
CHAPEL LA
FIR TREE CL
JAGGARD WAY
BELL LA
VINE WALK
P
Spilsill Farm
Spilsill Court
Bailey Farm
Little Craddock
Exhurst Manor
MCCABE CL
SOUTH BANK
CHURCH GREEN
IDEN CRES
HAMMER WAY
HALLWARDS
FRITTENDEN RD
ROMAN ROAD
Henhurst Farm
PINNOCK LA
The Quarter
Iden Park
The Old Manor (Convent)
Park Wood
PARK WOOD LA
STAPLEHURST RD
Broadlake
The Twins
Maplehurst Farm
Convent
Iden Manor Farm
Maplehurst Wood
Chittenden Farm
CRANBROOK RD
Iden Grange
MILL LA
Cherry Tree Farm
Gould Farm
Little Wadd Farm
Castle Bank Earthwork
Great Wadd Farm
Knoxbridge Inn (PH)
Knox Bridge
Tanyard
Leggs Wood
GRANDSHORE LA
WALLER HILL
Rock Farm
Eleven Acre Wood
Keepers Lodge
Grayland Wood
Tolehurst Farm
A229
43
42
41
40
4
3
2
1
78
79
80

159

174

144

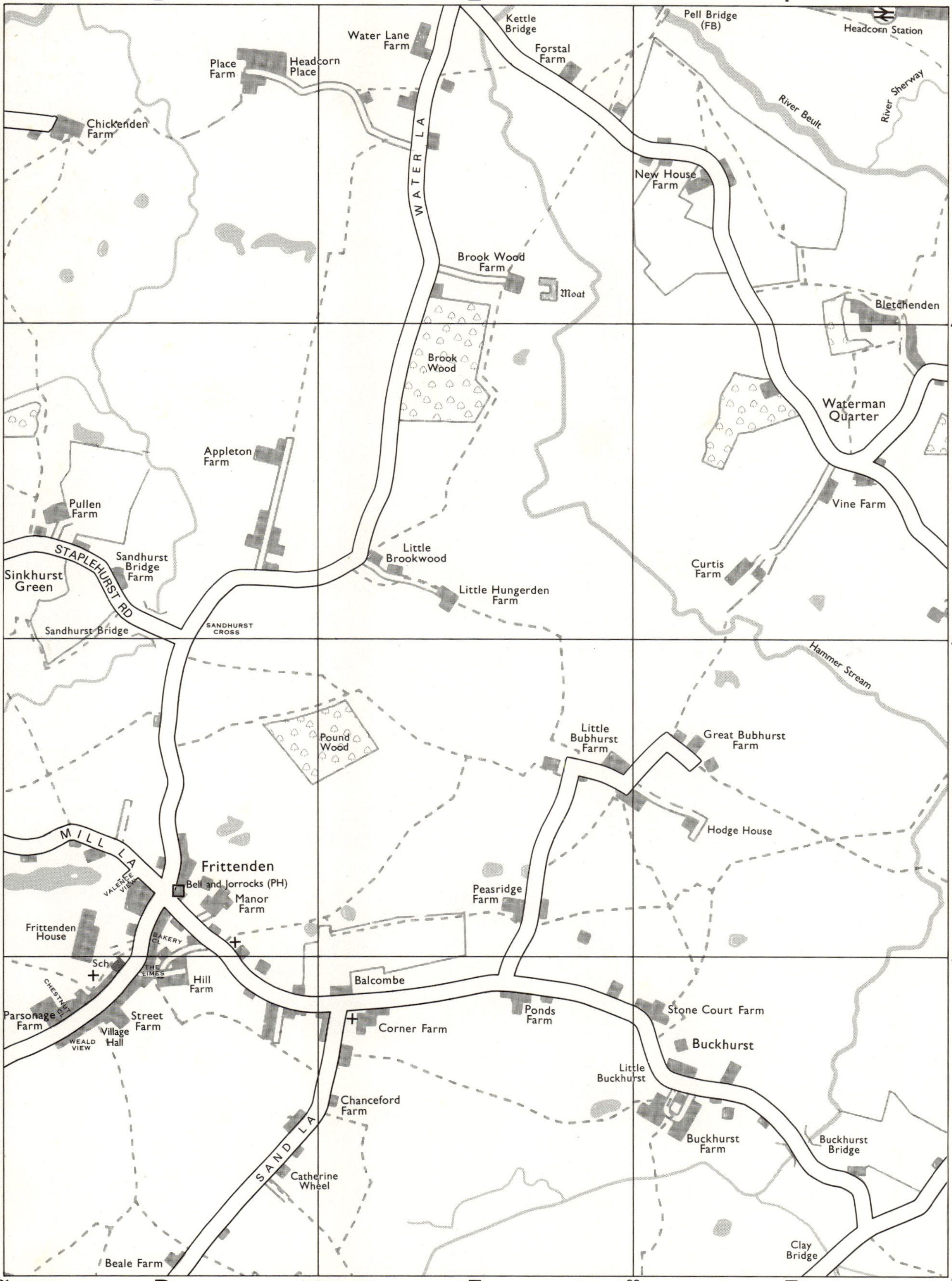
D
E
F
Water Lane Farm
Kettle Bridge
Forstal Farm
Pell Bridge (FB)
Headcorn Station
Place Farm
Headcorn Place
Chickenden Farm
River Beult
River Sherway
WATER LA
New House Farm
Brook Wood Farm
Moat
Bletchenden
Brook Wood
Waterman Quarter
Appleton Farm
Pullen Farm
Vine Farm
Little Brookwood
Curtis Farm
Sinkhurst Green
STAPLEHURST RD
Sandhurst Bridge Farm
Little Hungerden Farm
Sandhurst Bridge
SANDHURST CROSS
Hammer Stream
Pound Wood
Little Bubhurst Farm
Great Bubhurst Farm
MILL LA
Hodge House
Frittenden
Bell and Jorrocks (PH)
VALENCE VIEW
Manor Farm
Peasridge Farm
Frittenden House
BAKERY CL
Sch
THE LIMES
CHESTNUT CL
Hill Farm
Balcombe
Parsonage Farm
Street Farm
Village Hall
WEALD VIEW
Corner Farm
Ponds Farm
Stone Court Farm
Buckhurst
Little Buckhurst
Chanceford Farm
Buckhurst Farm
Buckhurst Bridge
SAND LA
Catherine Wheel
Clay Bridge
Beale Farm
4
3
2
1
43
42
41
40
81
82
83

162

175

145

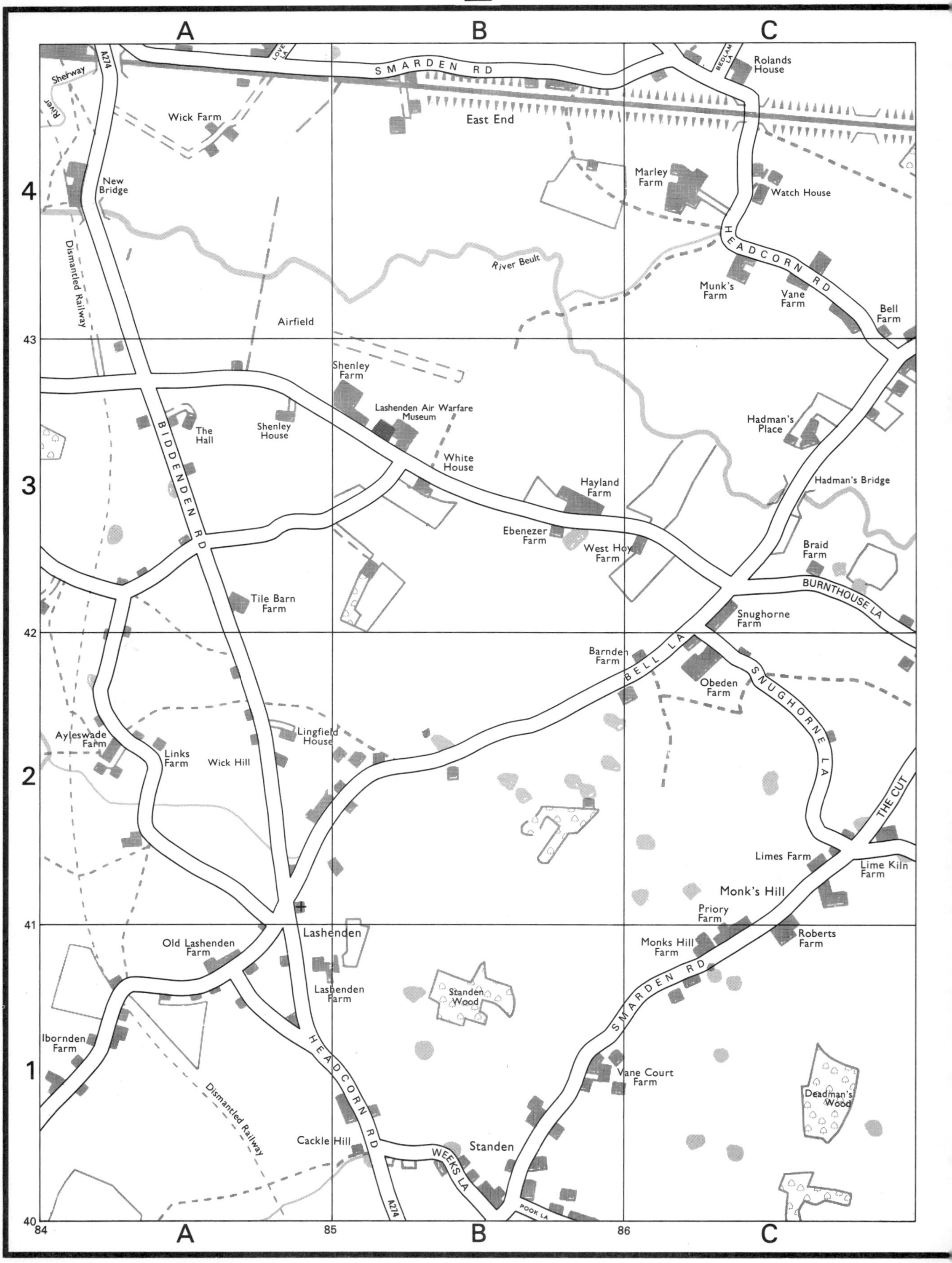
A
B
C
4
3
2
1
43
42
41
40
84
85
86
SMARDEN RD
LOVE LA
BEDLAM LA
Rolands House
A274
Sherway
River
Wick Farm
East End
New Bridge
Marley Farm
Watch House
Dismantled Railway
River Beult
HEADCORN RD
Munk's Farm
Vane Farm
Bell Farm
Airfield
Shenley Farm
Lashenden Air Warfare Museum
The Hall
Shenley House
BIDDENDEN RD
White House
Hadman's Place
Hadman's Bridge
Hayland Farm
Ebenezer Farm
West Hoy Farm
Braid Farm
BURNTHOUSE LA
Tile Barn Farm
Snughorne Farm
Barnden Farm
BELL LA
SNUGHORNE LA
Obeden Farm
Ayleswade Farm
Links Farm
Wick Hill
Lingfield House
THE CUT
Limes Farm
Lime Kiln Farm
Monk's Hill
Priory Farm
Lashenden
Old Lashenden Farm
Monks Hill Farm
Roberts Farm
Lashenden Farm
Standen Wood
SMARDEN RD
Ibornden Farm
Vane Court Farm
Deadman's Wood
Cackle Hill
Standen
WEEKS LA
POOK LA

161

176

146

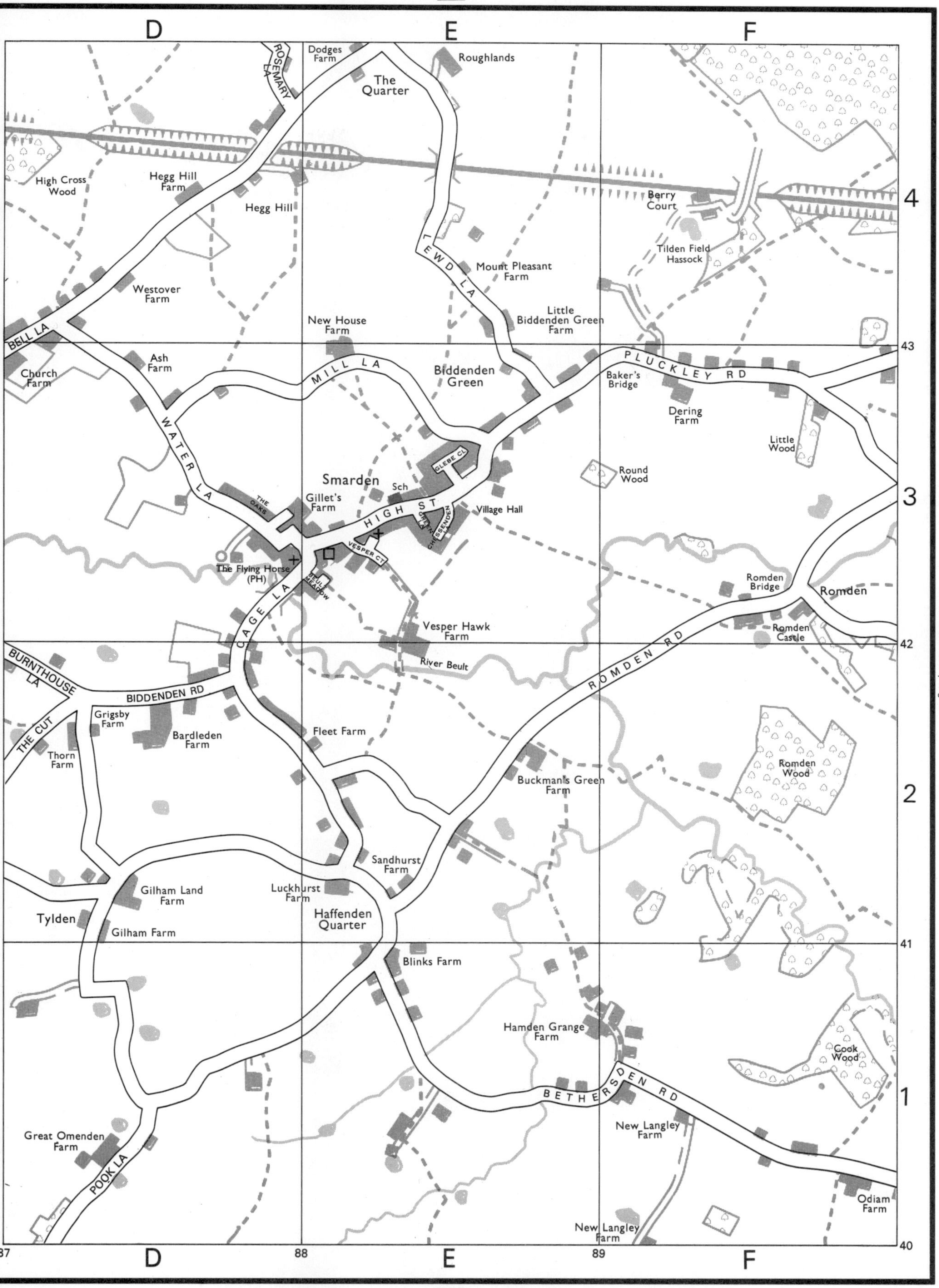
D
E
F
ROSEMARY LA
Dodges Farm
The Quarter
Roughlands
High Cross Wood
Hegg Hill Farm
Hegg Hill
Berry Court
4
Tilden Field Hassock
LEWD LA
Mount Pleasant Farm
Westover Farm
New House Farm
Little Biddenden Green Farm
BELL LA
43
Church Farm
Ash Farm
MILL LA
Biddenden Green
PLUCKLEY RD
Baker's Bridge
Dering Farm
Little Wood
WATER LA
GLEBE CL
Round Wood
Smarden
Sch
3
Gillet's Farm
THE OAKS
HIGH ST
Village Hall
CHESSENDEN
VESPER CT
The Flying Horse (PH)
BEULT MEADOW
Romden Bridge
Romden
CAGE LA
Vesper Hawk Farm
Romden Castle
42
BURNTHOUSE LA
River Beult
ROMDEN RD
BIDDENDEN RD
Grigsby Farm
THE CUT
Bardleden Farm
Fleet Farm
Thorn Farm
Romden Wood
Buckman's Green Farm
2
Sandhurst Farm
Gilham Land Farm
Luckhurst Farm
Tylden
Haffenden Quarter
Gilham Farm
41
Blinks Farm
Hamden Grange Farm
Cook Wood
BETHERSDEN RD
1
New Langley Farm
Great Omenden Farm
POOK LA
Odiam Farm
New Langley Farm
87
88
89
40
not continued, see key diagram

177

150

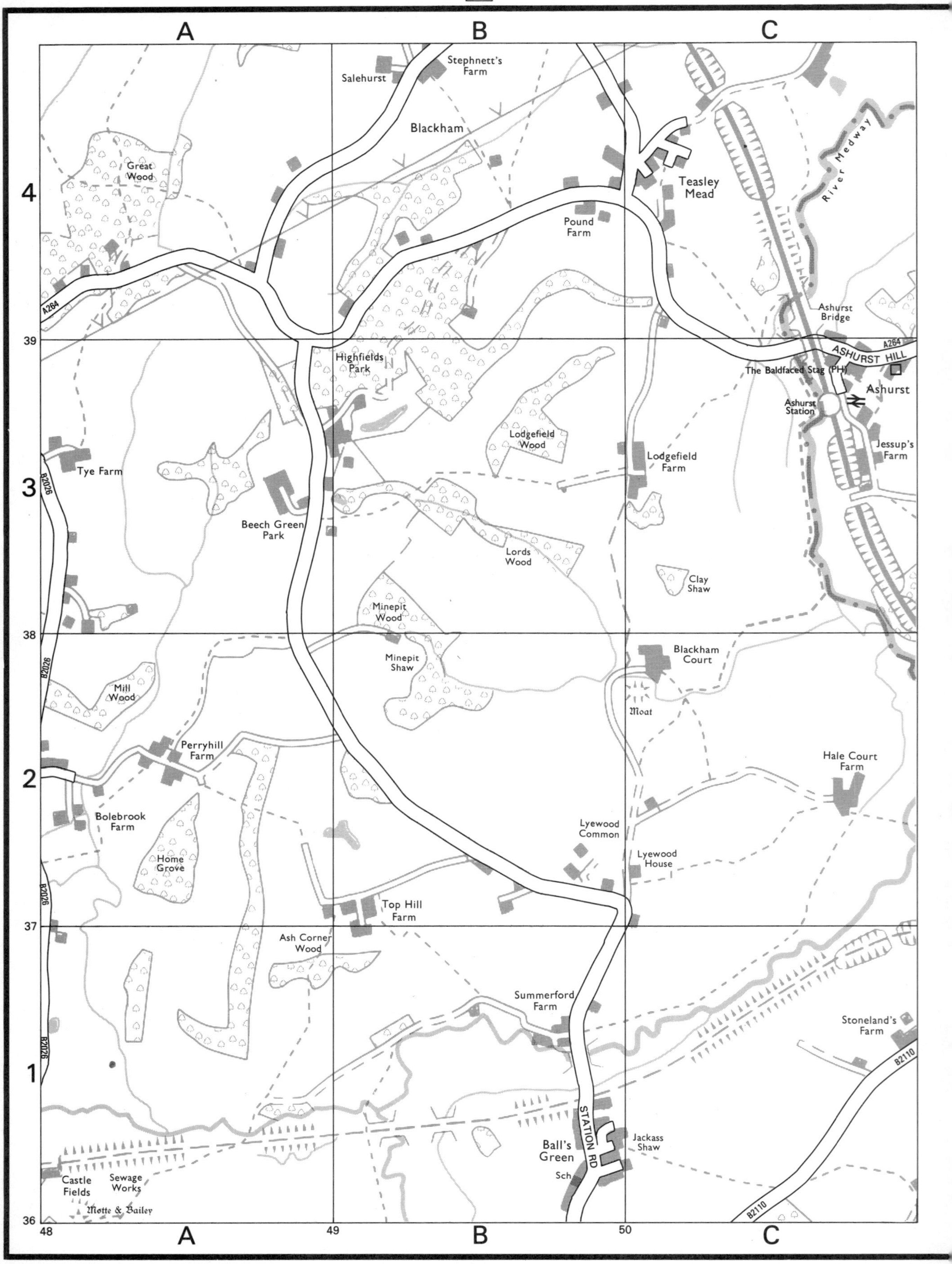

not continued, see key diagram

not continued, see key diagram

151

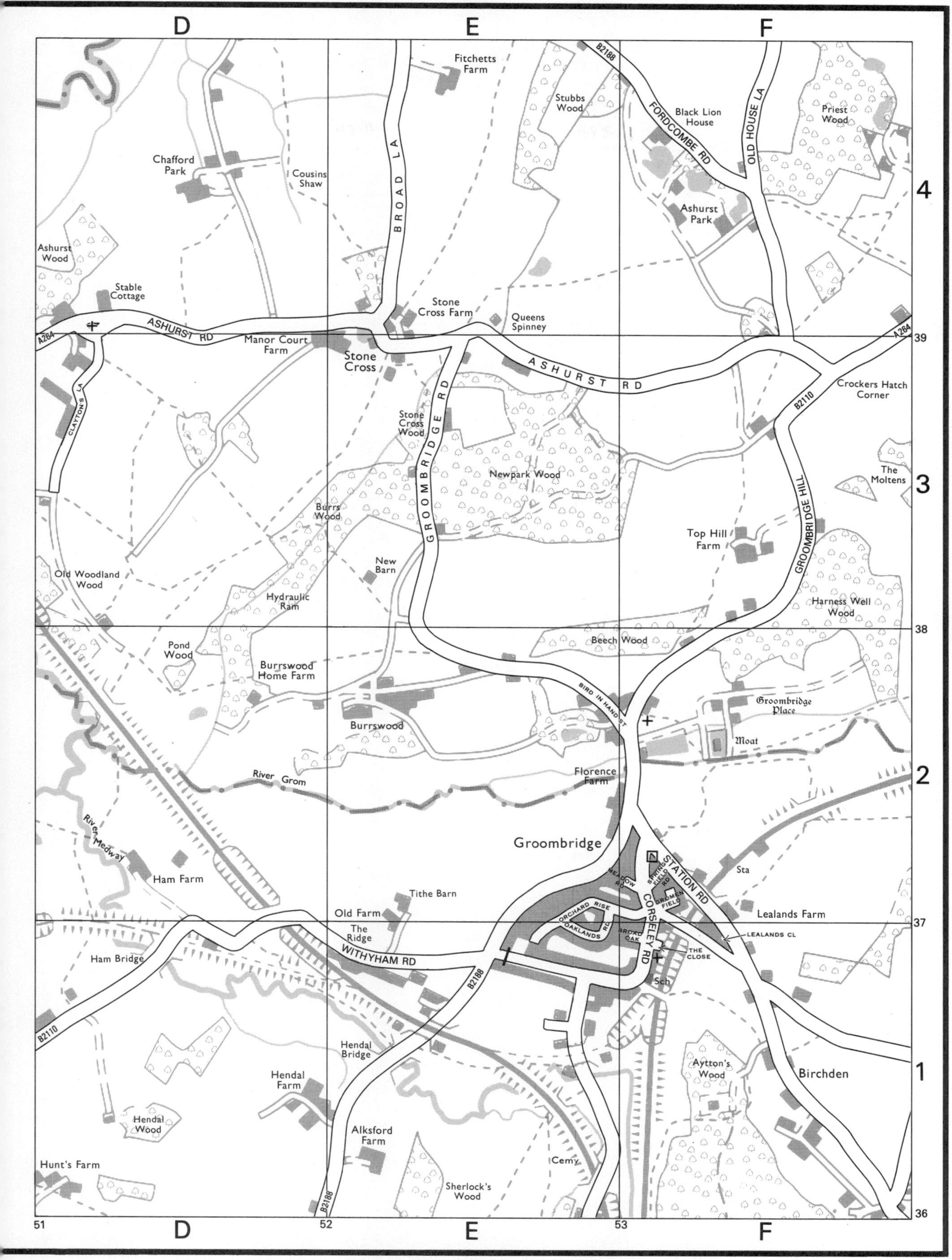

D
E
F
Fitchetts Farm
B2188
Stubbs Wood
FORDCOMBE RD
Black Lion House
OLD HOUSE LA
Priest Wood
Chafford Park
Cousins Shaw
BROAD LA
Ashurst Park
4
Ashurst Wood
Stable Cottage
Stone Cross Farm
Queens Spinney
A264
ASHURST RD
Manor Court Farm
Stone Cross
A264
39
ASHURST RD
Crockers Hatch Corner
B2110
CLAYTON'S LA
Stone Cross Wood
GROOMBRIDGE RD
Newpark Wood
The Moltens
3
Burrs Wood
GROOMBRIDGE HILL
Top Hill Farm
New Barn
Old Woodland Wood
Hydraulic Ram
Harness Well Wood
38
Pond Wood
Beech Wood
Burrswood Home Farm
BIRD IN HAND ST
Groombridge Place
Burrswood
Moat
River Grom
Florence Farm
2
River Medway
Groombridge
MEADOW RD
SPRING FIELD RD
STATION RD
Sta
Ham Farm
Tithe Barn
CROMEN FIELD
CORSELEY RD
Old Farm
ORCHARD RISE
Lealands Farm
37
The Ridge
OAKLANDS RD
BROAD OAK
LEALANDS CL
Ham Bridge
WITHYHAM RD
THE CLOSE
B2188
Sch
B2110
Hendal Bridge
Aytton's Wood
Birchden
1
Hendal Farm
Hendal Wood
Alksford Farm
Hunt's Farm
Cemy
Sherlock's Wood
B2188
36
51
52
53
D
E
F

166

152

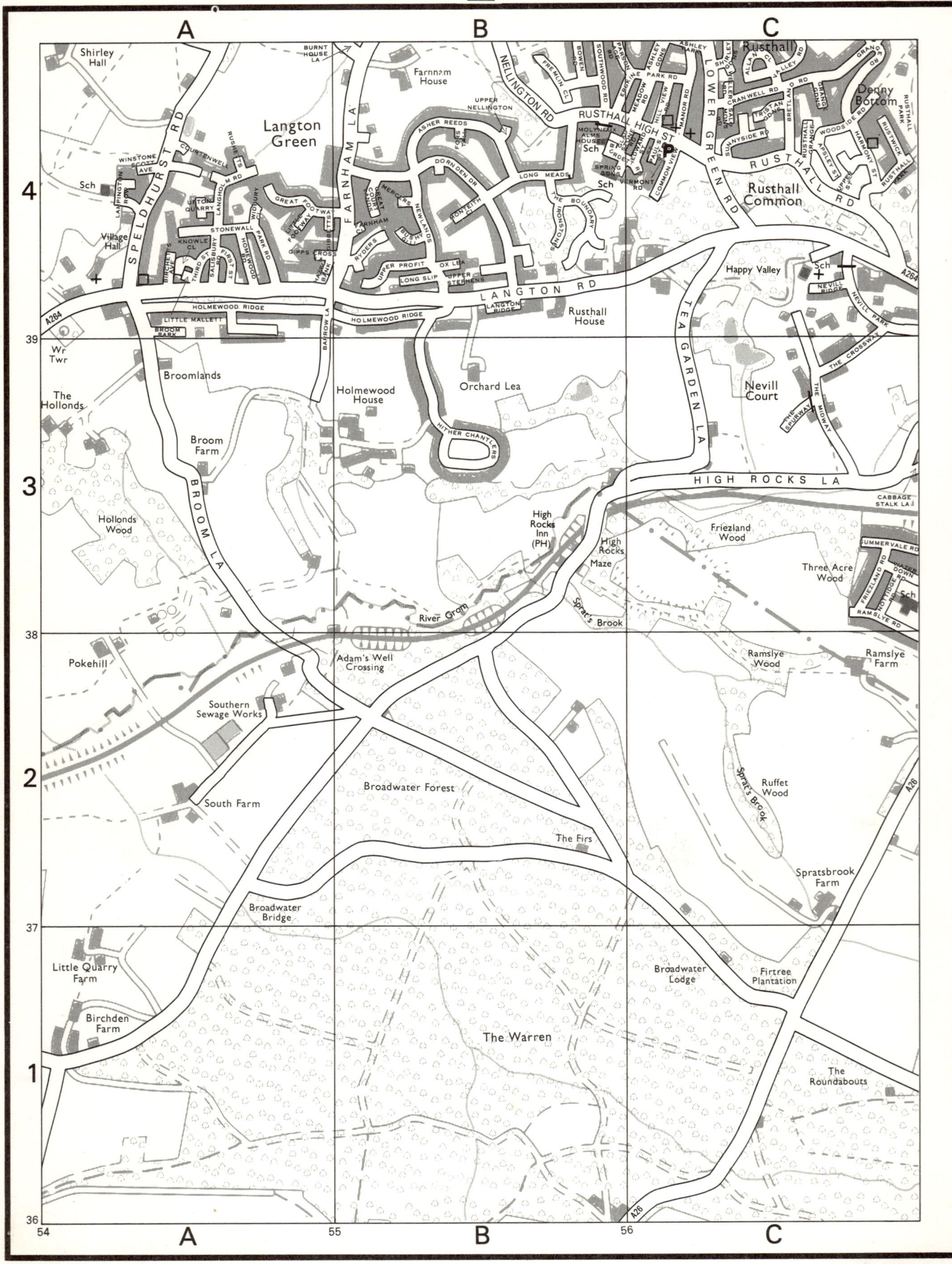
A
B
C
4
3
2
1
39
38
37
36
54
55
56
Shirley Hall
Langton Green
Farnham House
Upper Nellington
Nellington Rd
Rusthall
Rusthall High St
Denny Bottom
Rusthall Common
Rusthall Rd
Lower Green Rd
Burnt House La
Speldhurst Rd
Farnham La
Langton Rd
Holmewood Ridge
Little Mallett
Broom Park
Barrow La
Langton Ridge
Rusthall House
Happy Valley
Nevill Ridge
Nevill Park
The Crossway
The Midway
The Spurway
Nevill Court
Tea Garden La
Wr Twr
Broomlands
The Hollonds
Holmewood House
Orchard Lea
Hither Chantlers
Broom Farm
Broom La
High Rocks La
Cabbage Stalk La
Hollonds Wood
High Rocks Inn (PH)
High Rocks Maze
Friezland Wood
Three Acre Wood
Summervale Rd
Ramslye Rd
River Grom
Sprat's Brook
Adam's Well Crossing
Pokehill
Ramslye Wood
Ramslye Farm
Southern Sewage Works
South Farm
Broadwater Forest
Ruffet Wood
The Firs
Spratsbrook Farm
Broadwater Bridge
Little Quarry Farm
Broadwater Lodge
Firtree Plantation
Birchden Farm
The Warren
The Roundabouts
Village Hall
Sch
A264
A26

165

153

D
E
F
ROYAL TUNBRIDGE WELLS
Kent & Sussex Hospital (General)
Mount Ephraim
Golf Course
Bishop's Down
Hotel
LANGTON RD
BISHOP'S DOWN
MAJOR YORK'S RD
HUNGERSHALL PARK
Tunbridge Wells Common
Hungershall Park
CABBAGE STALK LA
MOUNT EPHRAIM
LONDON RD
MOUNT PLEASANT RD
CHURCH RD
CRESCENT RD
CALVERLEY RD
Calverley Park
Tunbridge Wells Station
GROVE HILL RD
HIGH ST
PROSPECT RD
PEMBURY RD
SANDROCK RD
LANSDOWNE RD
CAMDEN RD
Chilston House
Sch
BAYHALL RD
Camden Park
HALL'S HOLE RD
Madeira Park
Banner Farm
WARWICK PARK
MONTACUTE RD
FRANT RD
FOREST RD
Hawkenbury
HAWKENBURY RD
ERIDGE RD
BROADWATER DOWN
Broadwater Down
BIRLING RD
BENHALL MILL RD
BAYHAM RD
Windmill Farm
Golf Course
Strawberry Hill Farm
Town Court
Stone Farm
Quarry Farm
Hargate Forest
Pinewood Farm
Brickhouse Farm
Sprat's Brook
Tangier Farm
Tangier Lodge Farm
Brook Farm
Kennels
Bohemia
Chase Farm
Chase Wood
Whitehill Wood
Ely Grange
A26
A264
A267
B2023
B2169
4
3
2
1
39
38
37
36
57
58
59
D
E
F

168

154

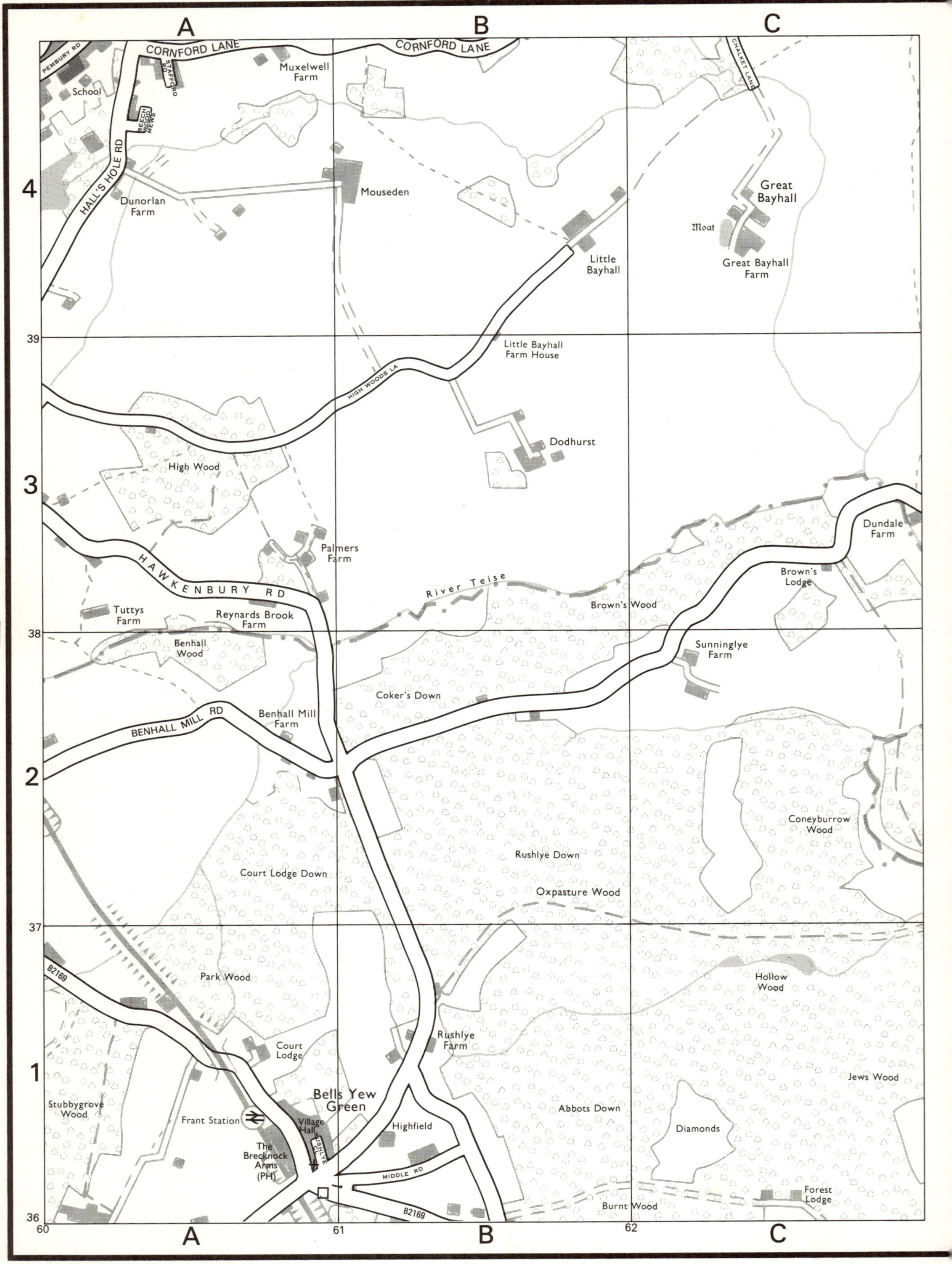

A
B
C
PEMBURY RD
CORNFORD LANE
CORNFORD LANE
STAFFORD RD
CHALKET LANE
School
Muxelwell Farm
BEECH WOOD MEWS
HALL'S HOLE RD
4
Dunorlan Farm
Mouseden
Great Bayhall
Moat
Little Bayhall
Great Bayhall Farm
39
Little Bayhall Farm House
HIGH WOODS LA
Dodhurst
High Wood
3
Palmers Farm
Dundale Farm
HAWKENBURY RD
River Teise
Brown's Lodge
Tuttys Farm
Reynards Brook Farm
Brown's Wood
38
Benhall Wood
Sunninglye Farm
Coker's Down
BENHALL MILL RD
Benhall Mill Farm
2
Coneyburrow Wood
Rushlye Down
Court Lodge Down
Oxpasture Wood
37
B2169
Park Wood
Hollow Wood
Court Lodge
Rushlye Farm
1
Jews Wood
Bells Yew Green
Stubbygrove Wood
Frant Station
Abbots Down
Village Hall
Highfield
Diamonds
The Brecknock Arms (PH)
MIDDLE RD
B2169
Forest Lodge
Burnt Wood
36
60
61
62
A
B
C

167

155

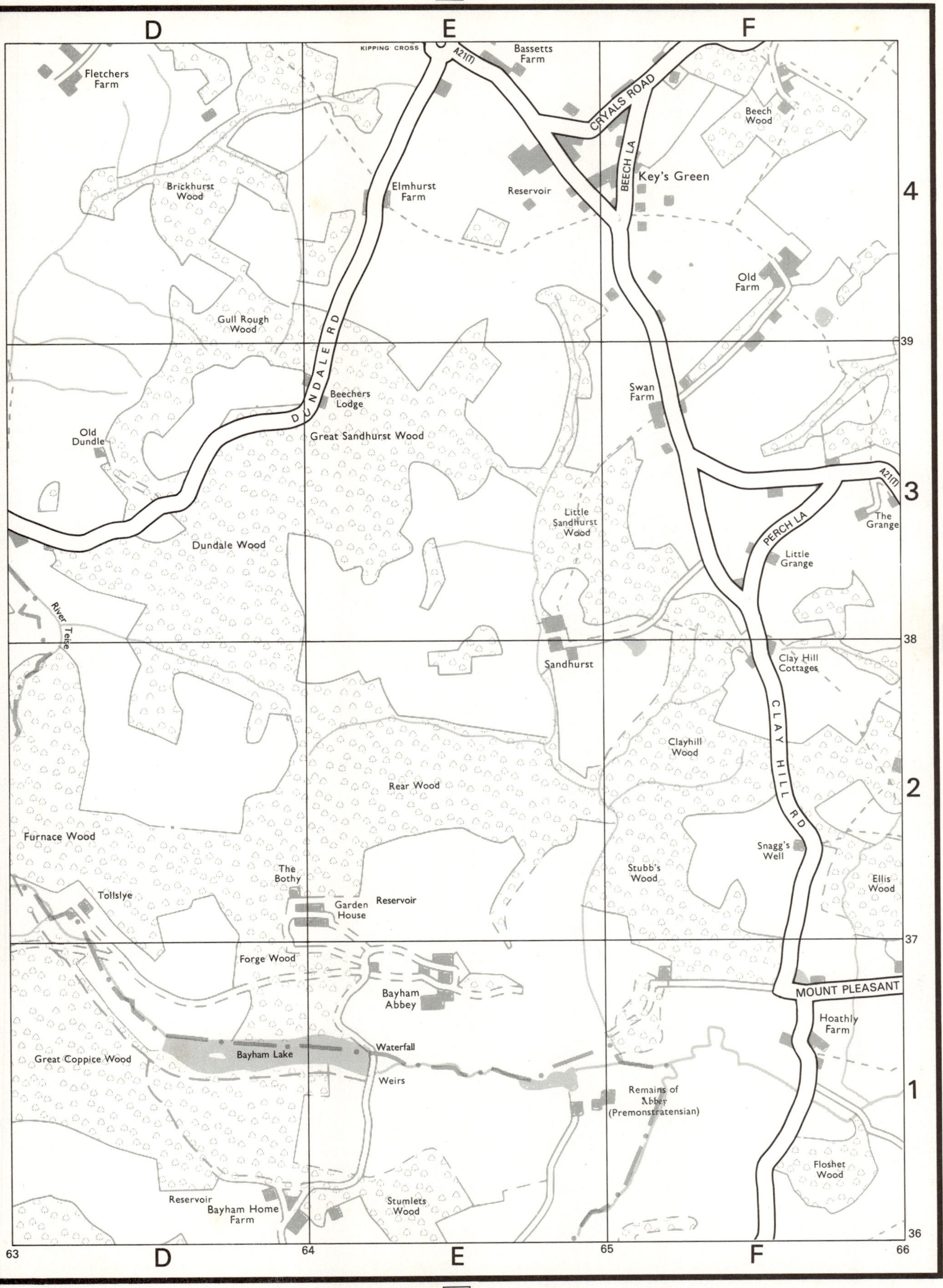
D
E
F
KIPPING CROSS
A21(T)
Bassetts Farm
Fletchers Farm
CRYALS ROAD
Beech Wood
BEECH LA
Key's Green
Brickhurst Wood
Elmhurst Farm
Reservoir
4
Old Farm
Gull Rough Wood
DUNDALE RD
39
Beechers Lodge
Swan Farm
Old Dundle
Great Sandhurst Wood
A21(T)
3
The Grange
Little Sandhurst Wood
PERCH LA
Dundale Wood
Little Grange
River Teise
38
Clay Hill Cottages
Sandhurst
CLAY HILL RD
Clayhill Wood
Rear Wood
2
Furnace Wood
Snagg's Well
The Bothy
Stubb's Wood
Ellis Wood
Tollslye
Garden House
Reservoir
37
Forge Wood
MOUNT PLEASANT
Bayham Abbey
Hoathly Farm
Bayham Lake
Waterfall
Great Coppice Wood
Weirs
1
Remains of Abbey (Premonstratensian)
Floshet Wood
Reservoir
Bayham Home Farm
Stumlets Wood
36
63
64
65
66
D
E
F

170

178

156

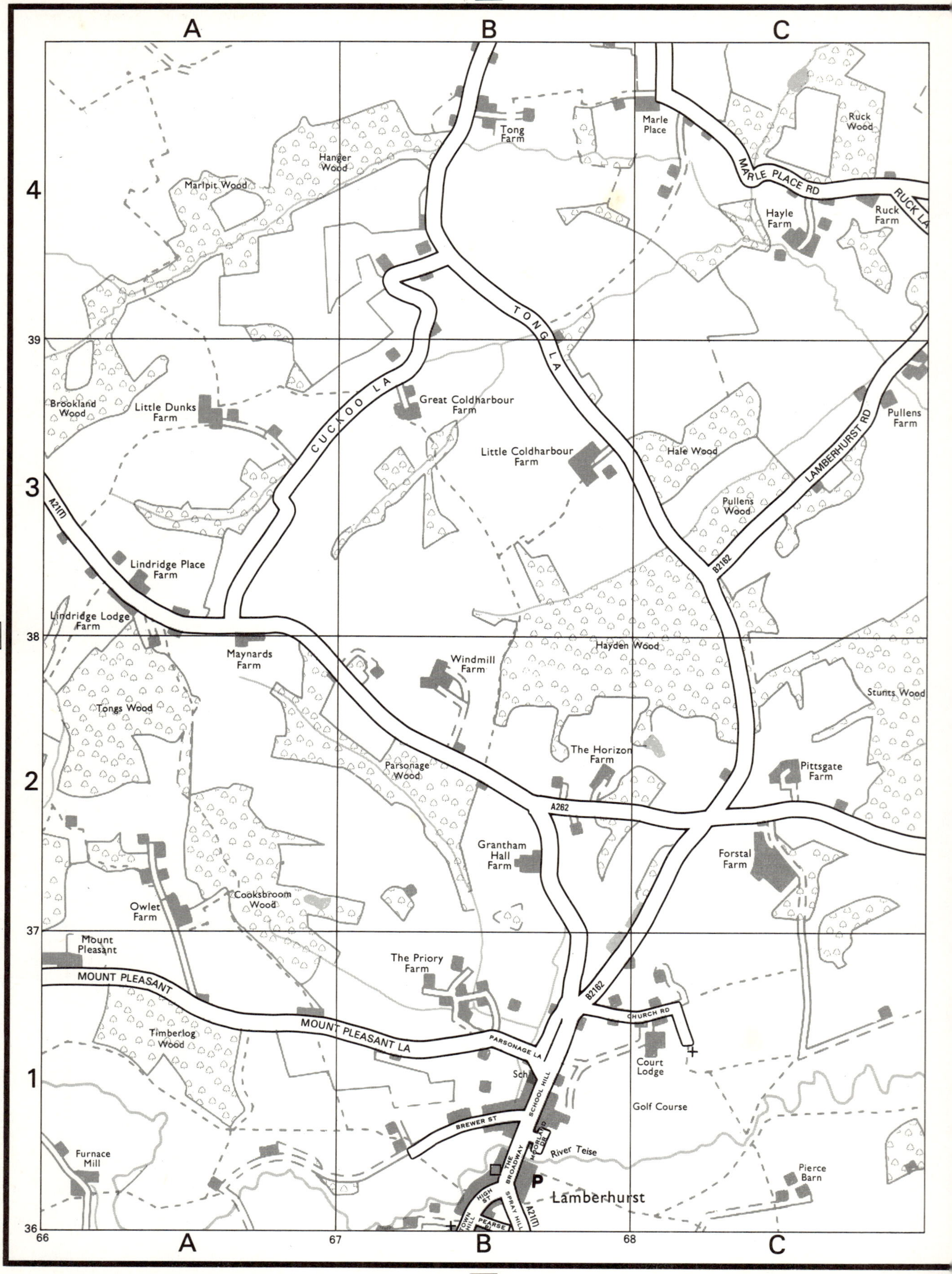
A
B
C
4
3
2
1
39
38
37
36
66
67
68
Tong Farm
Marle Place
Ruck Wood
Hanger Wood
Marlpit Wood
MARLE PLACE RD
RUCK LA
Hayle Farm
Ruck Farm
TONG LA
CUCKOO LA
Great Coldharbour Farm
Brookland Wood
Little Dunks Farm
Pullens Farm
Little Coldharbour Farm
Hale Wood
LAMBERHURST RD
Pullens Wood
A21(T)
B2162
Lindridge Place Farm
Lindridge Lodge Farm
Maynards Farm
Windmill Farm
Hayden Wood
Stunts Wood
Tongs Wood
The Horizon Farm
Parsonage Wood
Pittsgate Farm
A262
Grantham Hall Farm
Forstal Farm
Cooksbroom Wood
Owlet Farm
Mount Pleasant
The Priory Farm
MOUNT PLEASANT
MOUNT PLEASANT LA
PARSONAGE LA
CHURCH RD
Timberlog Wood
Court Lodge
Sch
SCHOOL HILL
Golf Course
BREWER ST
MOORLAND DR
River Teise
Furnace Mill
THE BROADWAY
P
Lamberhurst
Pierce Barn
HIGH ST
SPRAY HILL
TOWN HILL
PEARSE PL

169

179

157

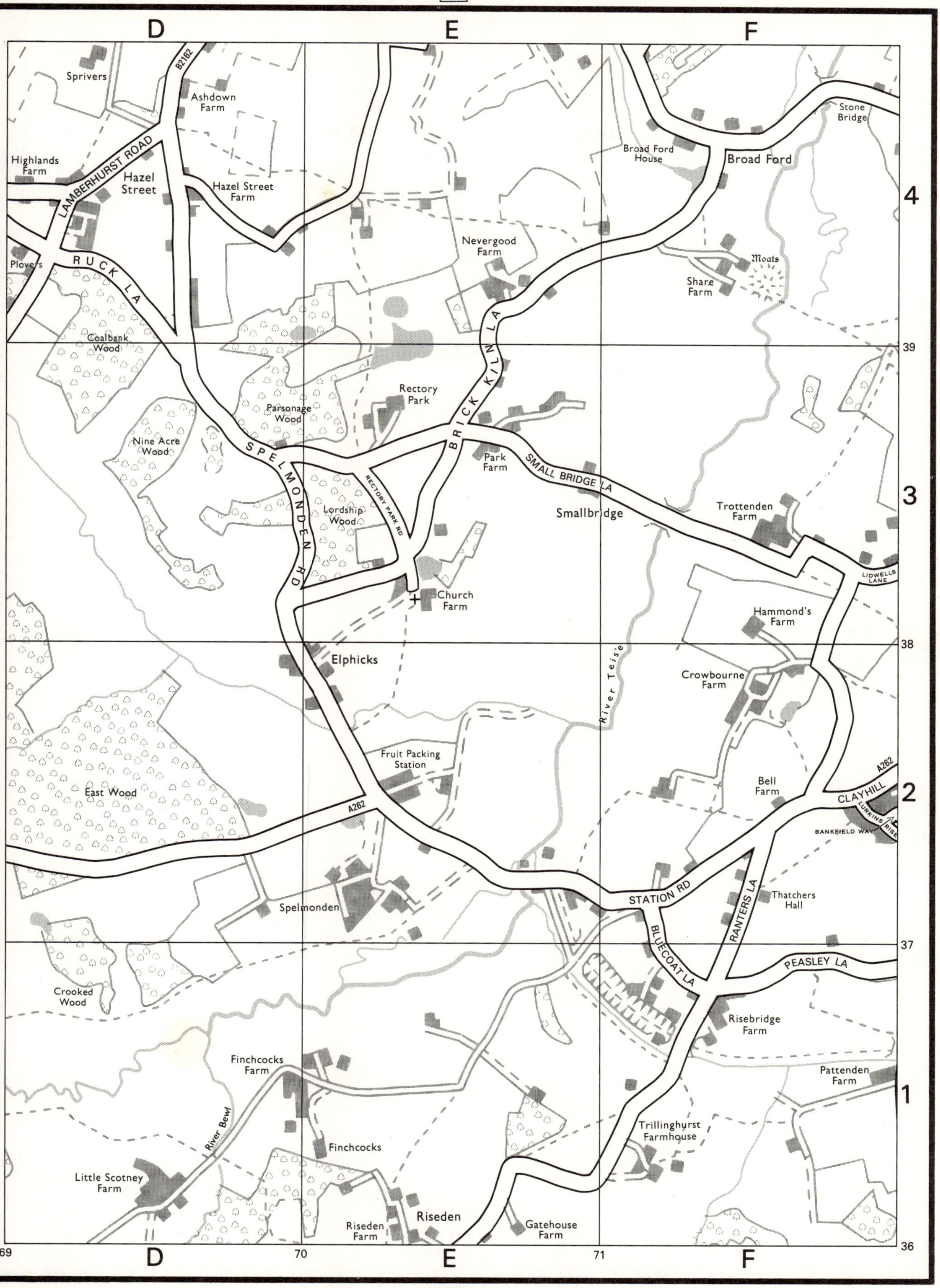
D
E
F
Sprivers
B2162
Ashdown Farm
Highlands Farm
LAMBERHURST ROAD
Hazel Street
Hazel Street Farm
Plovers
RUCK LA
Coalbank Wood
Nine Acre Wood
Parsonage Wood
SPELMONDEN RD
Lordship Wood
RECTORY PARK RD
Rectory Park
Nevergood Farm
BRICK KILN LA
Park Farm
SMALL BRIDGE LA
Smallbridge
Church Farm
Broad Ford House
Broad Ford
Stone Bridge
Moats
Share Farm
Trottenden Farm
LIDWELLS LANE
Hammond's Farm
Crowbourne Farm
River Teise
Elphicks
Fruit Packing Station
East Wood
A262
Bell Farm
A262
CLAYHILL
LURKINS RISE
BANKFIELD WAY
STATION RD
Spelmonden
RANTERS LA
Thatchers Hall
BLUECOAT LA
PEASLEY LA
Crooked Wood
Risebridge Farm
Finchcocks Farm
Pattenden Farm
River Bewl
Finchcocks
Trillinghurst Farmhouse
Little Scotney Farm
Riseden
Riseden Farm
Gatehouse Farm
4
3
2
1
39
38
37
36
69
70
71
D
E
F

172

180

158

171

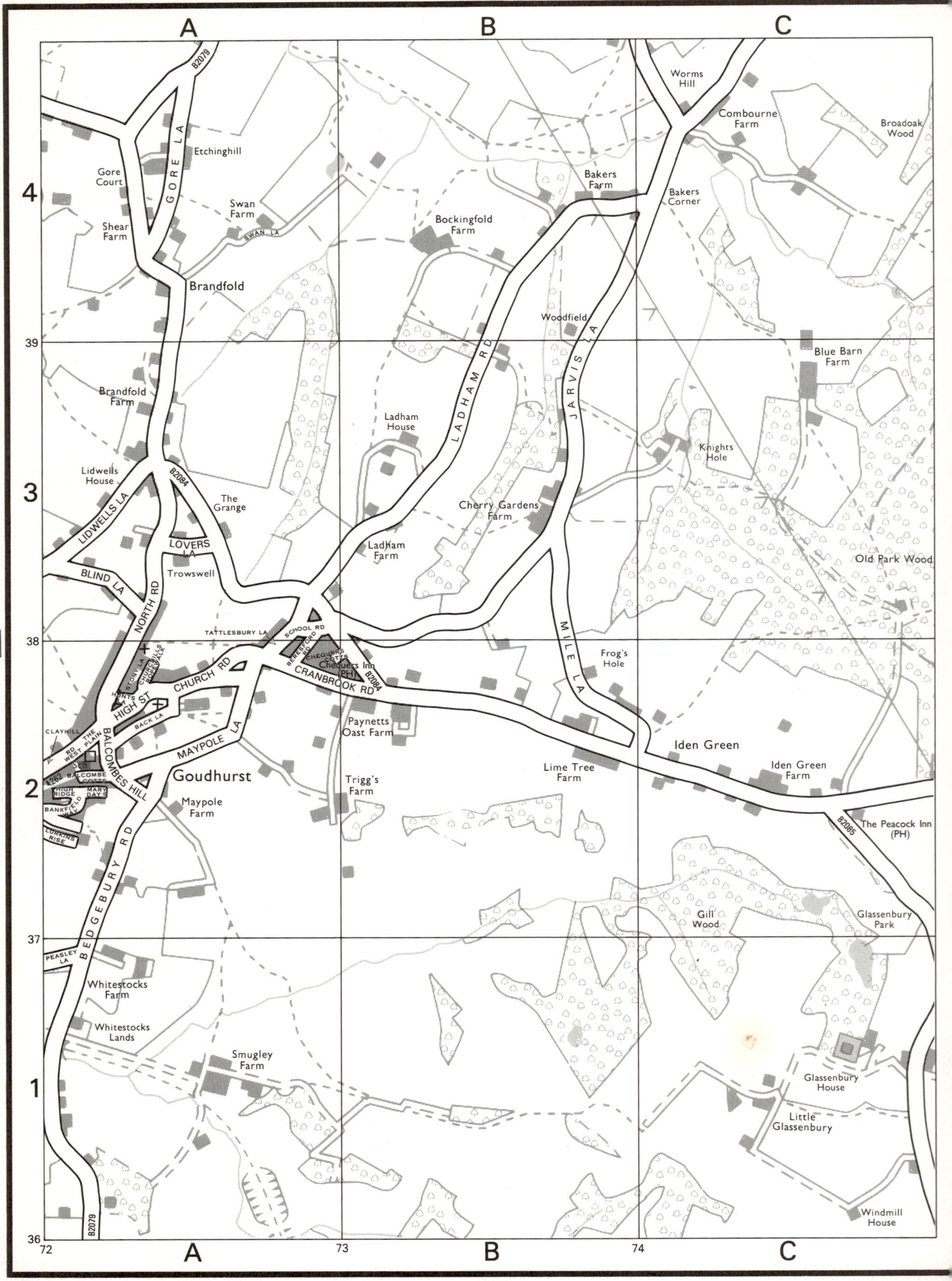
A
B
C
4
3
2
1
39
38
37
36
72
73
74
B2079
GORE LA
Etchinghill
Gore Court
Shear Farm
Swan Farm
SWAN LA
Brandfold
Worms Hill
Combourne Farm
Broadoak Wood
Bakers Farm
Bakers Corner
Bockingfold Farm
Woodfield
Blue Barn Farm
Brandfold Farm
LADHAM RD
JARVIS LA
Ladham House
Knights Hole
Lidwells House
B2084
The Grange
Cherry Gardens Farm
LIDWELLS LA
LOVERS LA
Ladham Farm
Old Park Wood
BLIND LA
Trowswell
NORTH RD
MILE LA
TATTLESBURY LA
SCHOOL RD
BERESFORD RD
CHEQUERS COTTS
Chequers Inn (PH)
Frog's Hole
STONY LA
CHURCH RD
CRANBROOK RD
HUNTS
HIGH ST
BACK LA
Paynetts Oast Farm
CLAYHILL
RD
WEST PLAIN
THE
BALCOMBES HILL
MAYPOLE LA
Sch
BALCOMBE COTTS
Iden Green
Lime Tree Farm
Iden Green Farm
A262
HIGH RIDGE
MARY DAY
Goudhurst
Trigg's Farm
BANKFIELD WAY
Maypole Farm
B2085
The Peacock Inn (PH)
LUCKINS RISE
BEDGEBURY RD
Gill Wood
Glassenbury Park
PEASLEY LA
Whitestocks Farm
Whitestocks Lands
Smugley Farm
Glassenbury House
Little Glassenbury
Windmill House

181

159

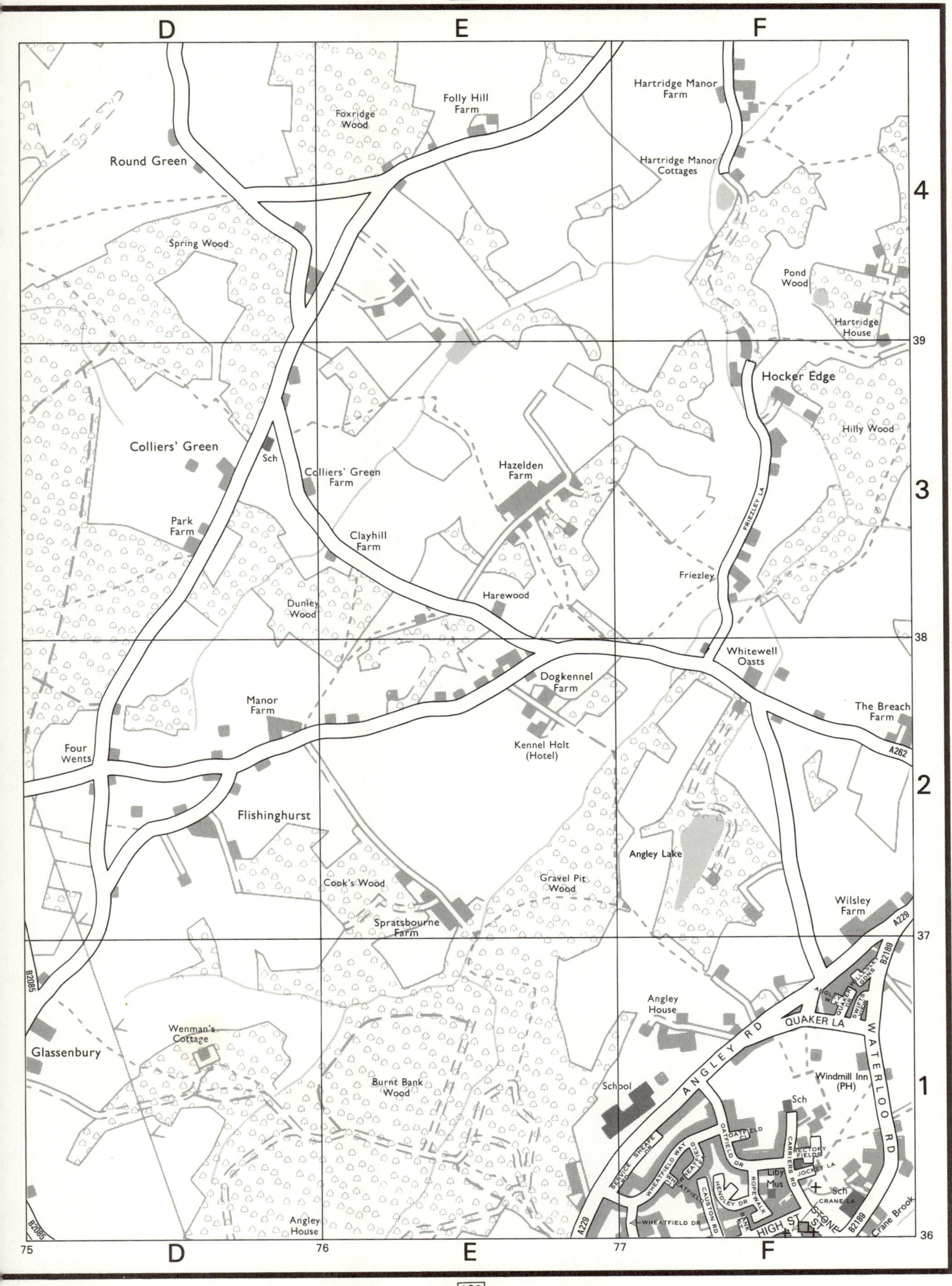
D
E
F
Foxridge Wood
Folly Hill Farm
Hartridge Manor Farm
Round Green
Hartridge Manor Cottages
4
Spring Wood
Pond Wood
Hartridge House
39
Hocker Edge
Hilly Wood
Colliers' Green
Sch
Colliers' Green Farm
Hazelden Farm
3
FRIEZLEY LA
Park Farm
Clayhill Farm
Friezley
Harewood
Dunley Wood
38
Whitewell Oasts
Manor Farm
Dogkennel Farm
The Breach Farm
Kennel Holt (Hotel)
Four Wents
A262
2
Flishinghurst
Angley Lake
Cook's Wood
Gravel Pit Wood
Wilsley Farm
Spratsbourne Farm
A229
37
B2085
B2189
Angley House
QUAKER LA
ANGLEY RD
WATERLOO RD
Wenman's Cottage
Glassenbury
Windmill Inn (PH)
1
School
Burnt Bank Wood
Sch
OATFIELD DR
RECTORY FIELDS
JOCKEY LA
CARRIERS RD
ROPEWALK
HENDLEY DR
CAUSTON RD
WHEATFIELD WAY
Liby
Mus
Sch
CRANE LA
STONE ST
HIGH ST
B2189
Crane Brook
A229
WHEATFIELD DR
Angley House
B2085
36
75
76
77
D
E
F

174

182

160

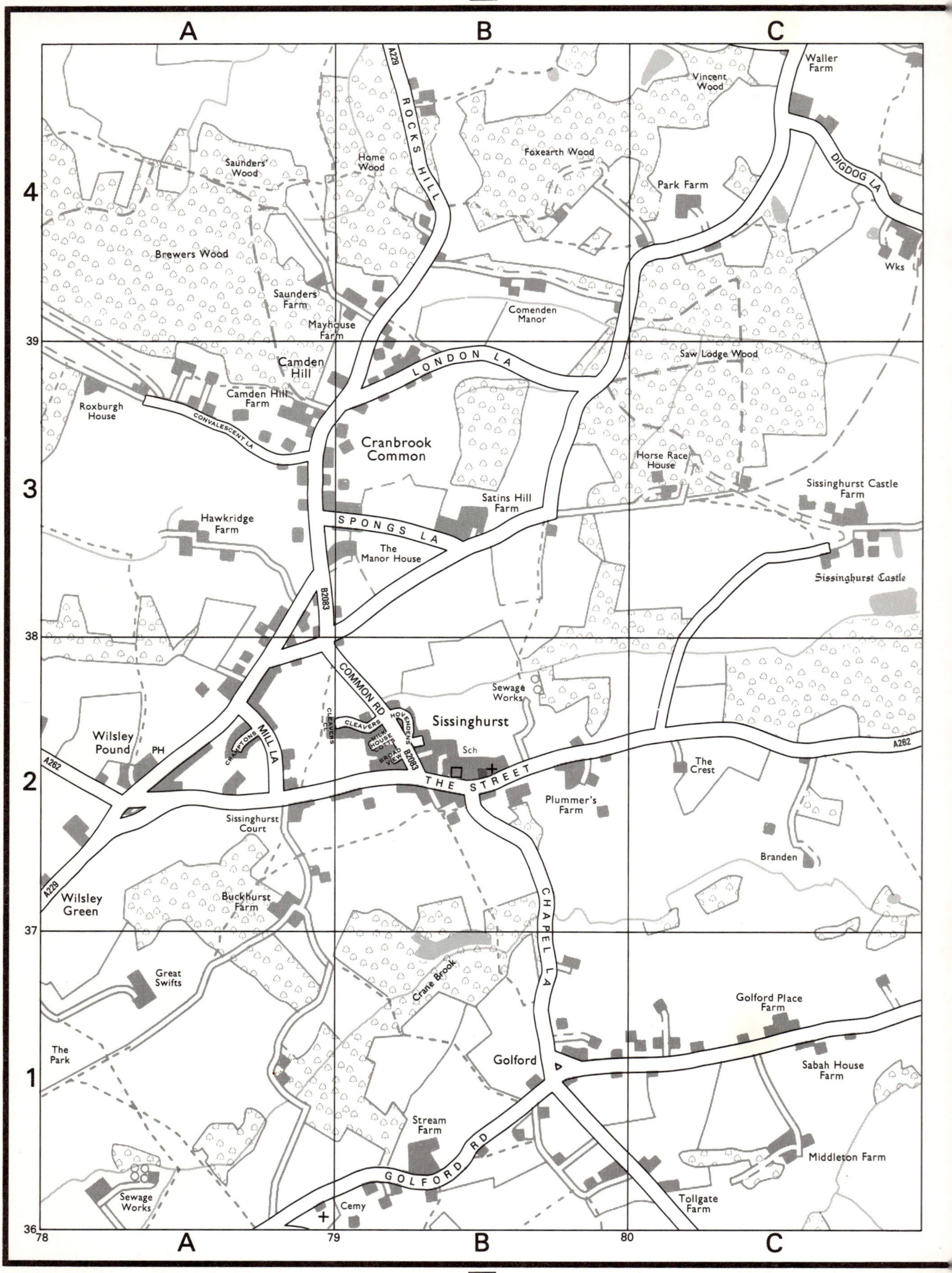
A
B
C
4
3
2
1
39
38
37
36
78
79
80
Waller Farm
Vincent Wood
ROCKS HILL
A229
Home Wood
Foxearth Wood
Saunders' Wood
DIGDOG LA
Park Farm
Brewers Wood
Wks
Saunders Farm
Mayhouse Farm
Comenden Manor
Saw Lodge Wood
LONDON LA
Camden Hill
Roxburgh House
Camden Hill Farm
CONVALESCENT LA
Cranbrook Common
Horse Race House
Sissinghurst Castle Farm
Satins Hill Farm
Hawkridge Farm
SPONGS LA
The Manor House
Sissinghurst Castle
B2083
COMMON RD
Sewage Works
Sissinghurst
HOVENDENS
CLEAVERS
CLEAVERS CL
MILL HOUSE COTTS
BROAD VIEW
CRAMPTONS
MILL LA
Wilsley Pound
PH
Sch
A262
THE STREET
The Crest
Plummer's Farm
Sissinghurst Court
Branden
CHAPEL LA
Wilsley Green
Buckhurst Farm
Great Swifts
Crane Brook
Golford Place Farm
The Park
Golford
Sabah House Farm
Stream Farm
GOLFORD RD
Middleton Farm
Sewage Works
Cemy
Tollgate Farm

173

183

161

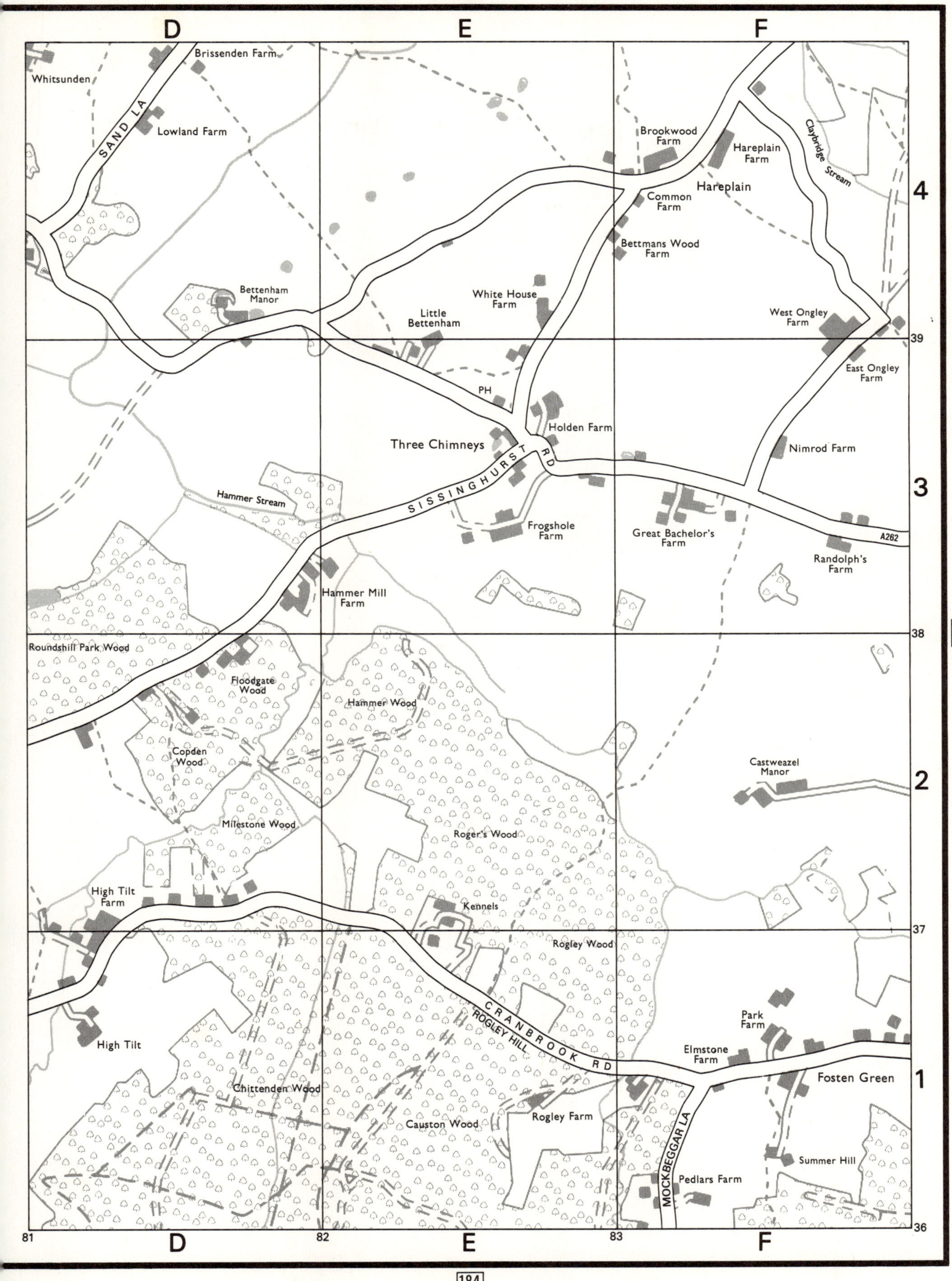
D
E
F
Whitsunden
Brissenden Farm
SAND LA
Lowland Farm
Brookwood Farm
Hareplain Farm
Claybridge Stream
Hareplain
Common Farm
Bettmans Wood Farm
White House Farm
Bettenham Manor
Little Bettenham
West Ongley Farm
East Ongley Farm
PH
Holden Farm
Three Chimneys
Nimrod Farm
SISSINGHURST RD
Hammer Stream
Frogshole Farm
Great Bachelor's Farm
A262
Randolph's Farm
Hammer Mill Farm
Roundshill Park Wood
Floodgate Wood
Hammer Wood
Copden Wood
Castweazel Manor
Milestone Wood
Roger's Wood
High Tilt Farm
Kennels
Rogley Wood
CRANBROOK RD
ROGLEY HILL
Park Farm
Elmstone Farm
High Tilt
Fosten Green
Chittenden Wood
Causton Wood
Rogley Farm
MOCKBEGGAR LA
Summer Hill
Pedlars Farm
4
3
2
1
39
38
37
36
81
82
83

176

184

162

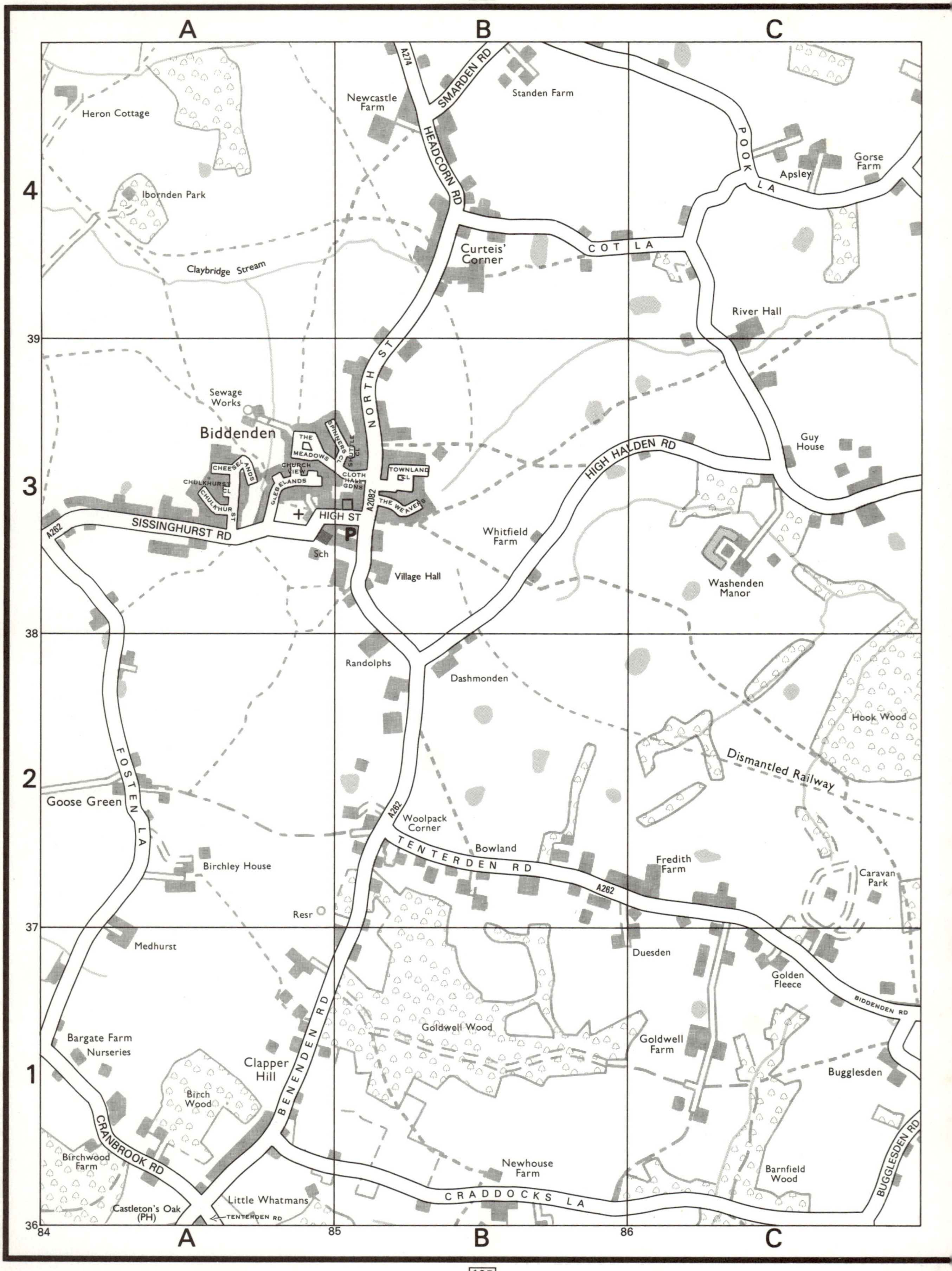
A
B
C
4
3
2
1
39
38
37
36
84
85
86
Heron Cottage
Newcastle Farm
SMARDEN RD
A274
Standen Farm
HEADCORN RD
POOK LA
Apsley
Gorse Farm
Ibornden Park
COT LA
Curteis' Corner
Claybridge Stream
River Hall
NORTH ST
Sewage Works
Biddenden
THE MEADOWS
SPINNERS CL
LITTLE FIELD
CHEESELANDS
CHURCH VIEW
CLOTH HALL GDNS
TOWNLAND CL
CHULKHURST CL
CHULKHURST
GLEBELANDS
HIGH ST
A2082
THE WEAVERS
SISSINGHURST RD
A262
HIGH HALDEN RD
Guy House
P
Sch
Village Hall
Whitfield Farm
Washenden Manor
Randolphs
Dashmonden
Hook Wood
FOSTEN LA
Dismantled Railway
Goose Green
Woolpack Corner
Bowland
TENTERDEN RD
Birchley House
Fredith Farm
Caravan Park
Resr
Medhurst
Duesden
Golden Fleece
BIDDENDEN RD
Goldwell Wood
Bargate Farm
Nurseries
Clapper Hill
BENENDEN RD
Goldwell Farm
Bugglesden
Birch Wood
CRANBROOK RD
Birchwood Farm
Newhouse Farm
Barnfield Wood
BUGGLESDEN RD
CRADDOCKS LA
Little Whatmans
Castleton's Oak (PH)
TENTERDEN RD

175

185

163

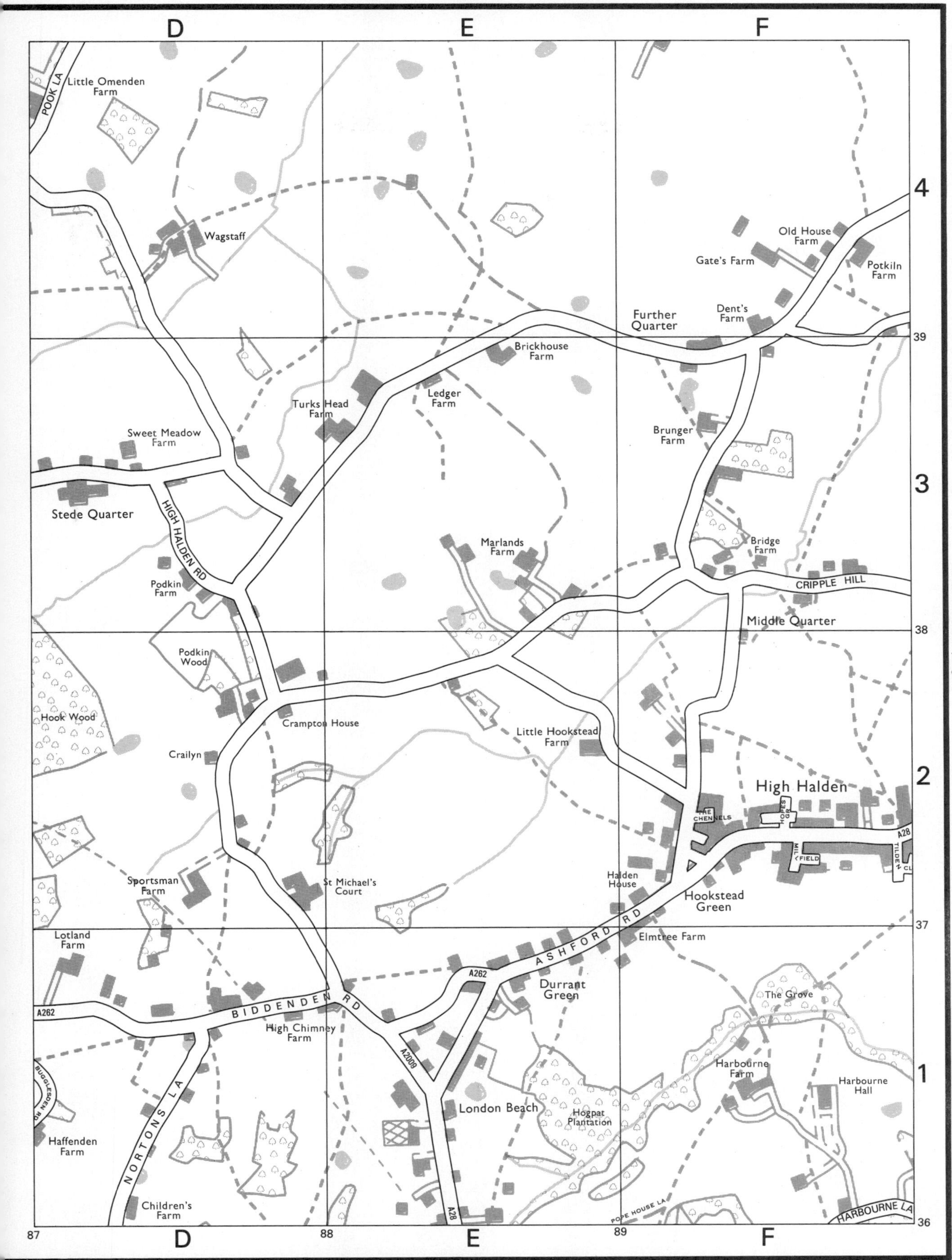
D
E
F
4
3
2
1
39
38
37
36
87
88
89
Little Omenden Farm
POOK LA
Wagstaff
Further Quarter
Dent's Farm
Gate's Farm
Old House Farm
Potkiln Farm
Brickhouse Farm
Ledger Farm
Turks Head Farm
Sweet Meadow Farm
Stede Quarter
HIGH HALDEN RD
Brunger Farm
Marlands Farm
Bridge Farm
CRIPPLE HILL
Middle Quarter
Podkin Farm
Podkin Wood
Hook Wood
Crampton House
Crailyn
Little Hookstead Farm
High Halden
THE CHENNELS
HOPES
MILLFIELD
TILDEN CL
A28
Sportsman Farm
St Michael's Court
Halden House
Hookstead Green
Lotland Farm
ASHFORD RD
Elmtree Farm
A262
Durrant Green
The Grove
BIDDENDEN RD
High Chimney Farm
A2009
BUGGLESDEN RD
NORTONS LA
Haffenden Farm
London Beach
Hogpat Plantation
Harbourne Farm
Harbourne Hall
Children's Farm
POPE HOUSE LA
HARBOURNE LA
not continued, see key diagram

186

169

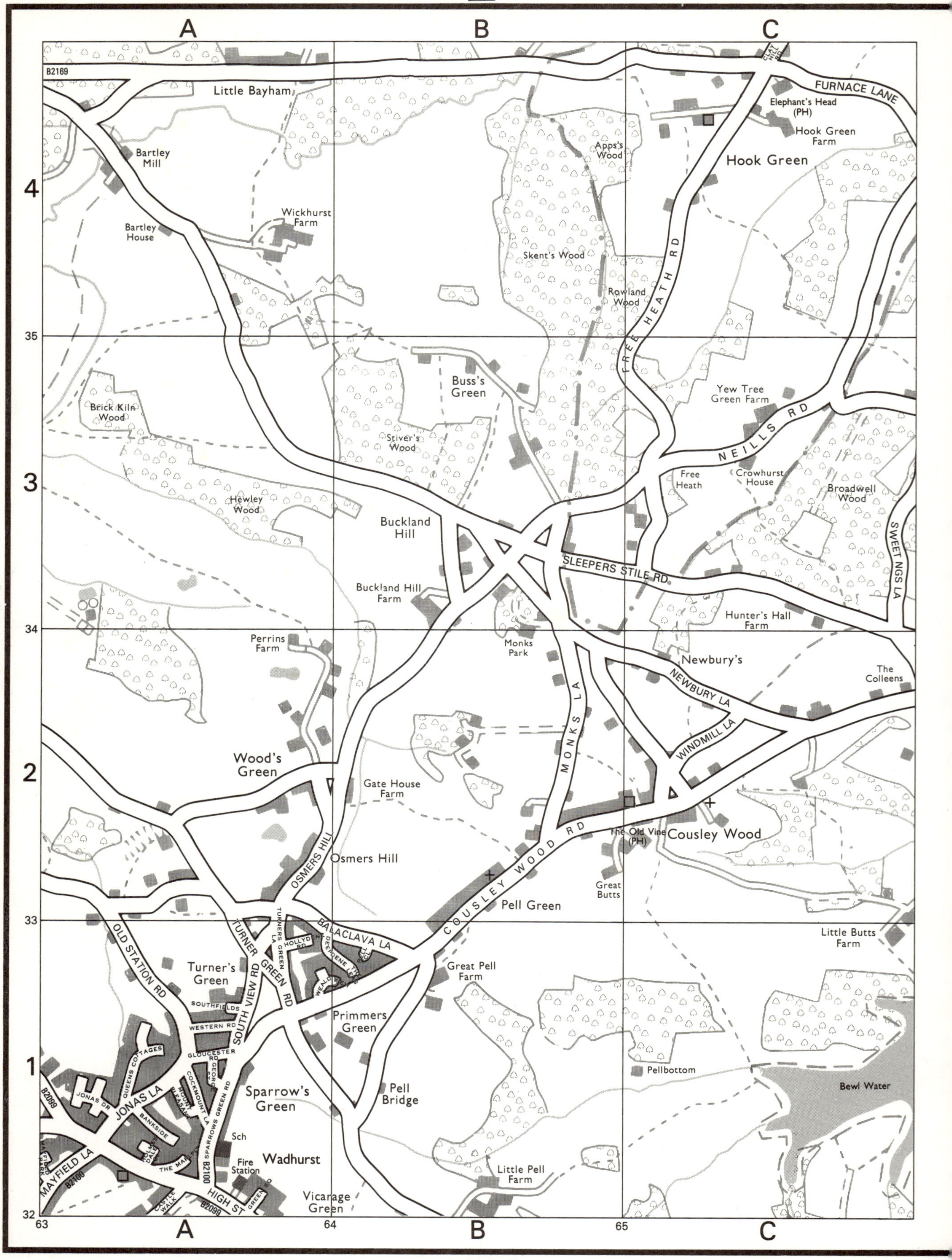

not continued, see key diagram

not continued, see key diagram

170

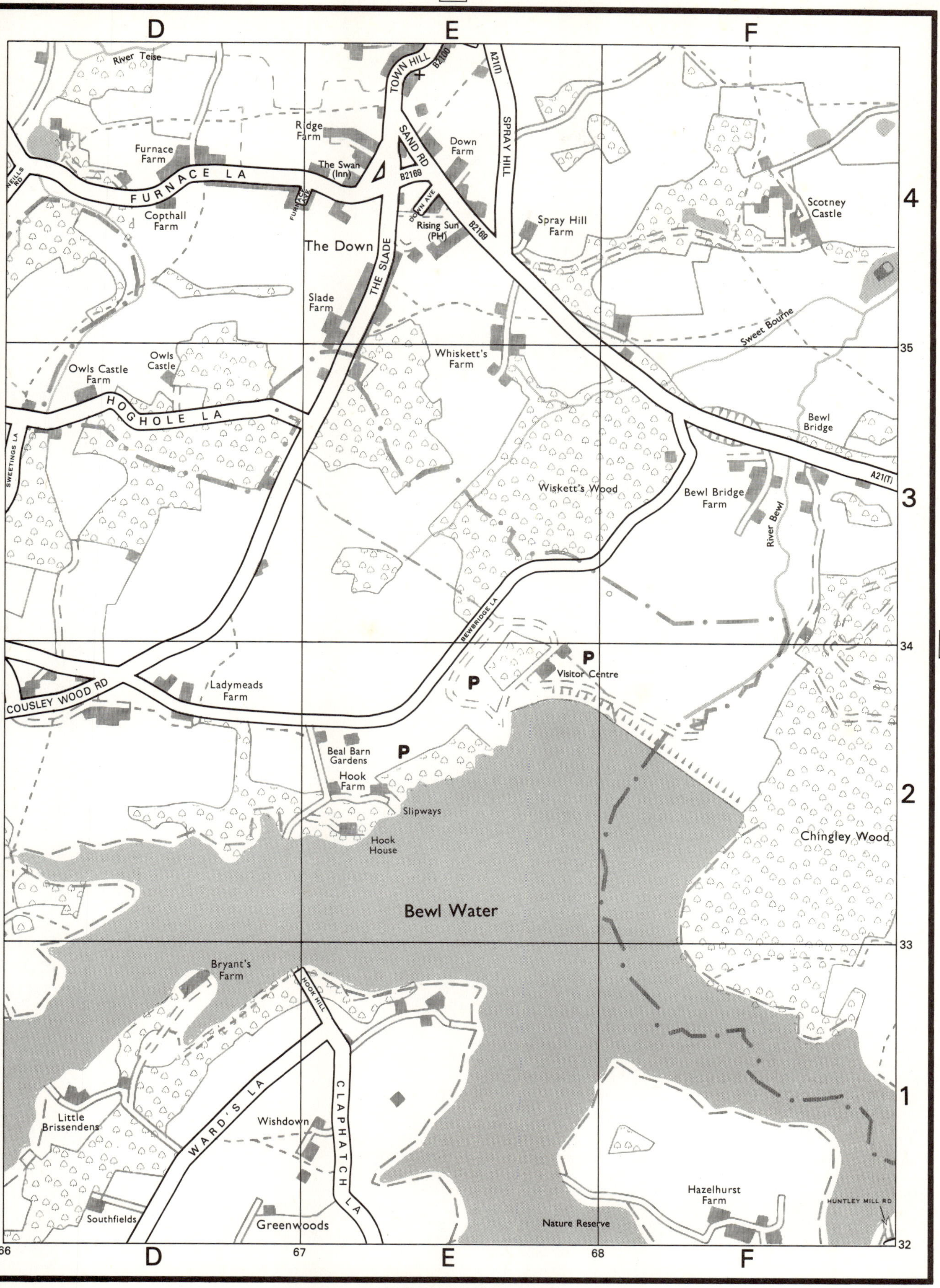

D
E
F
River Teise
TOWN HILL
B2100
A21(T)
SPRAY HILL
Ridge Farm
SAND RD
Down Farm
Furnace Farm
The Swan (Inn)
B2169
FURNACE LA
Copthall Farm
DOWN AVE
Rising Sun (PH)
B2169
Spray Hill Farm
Scotney Castle
The Down
THE SLADE
Slade Farm
Sweet Bourne
Owls Castle
Owls Castle Farm
Whiskett's Farm
HOGHOLE LA
SWEETINGS LA
Bewl Bridge
A21(T)
Wiskett's Wood
Bewl Bridge Farm
River Bewl
BEWBRIDGE LA
P
Visitor Centre
P
COUSLEY WOOD RD
Ladymeads Farm
Beal Barn Gardens
P
Hook Farm
Slipways
Hook House
Chingley Wood
Bewl Water
Bryant's Farm
HOOK HILL
Little Brissendens
WARD'S LA
Wishdown
CLAPHATCH LA
Hazelhurst Farm
HUNTLEY MILL RD
Southfields
Greenwoods
Nature Reserve
4
3
2
1
35
34
33
32
66
67
68
D
E
F

180

171

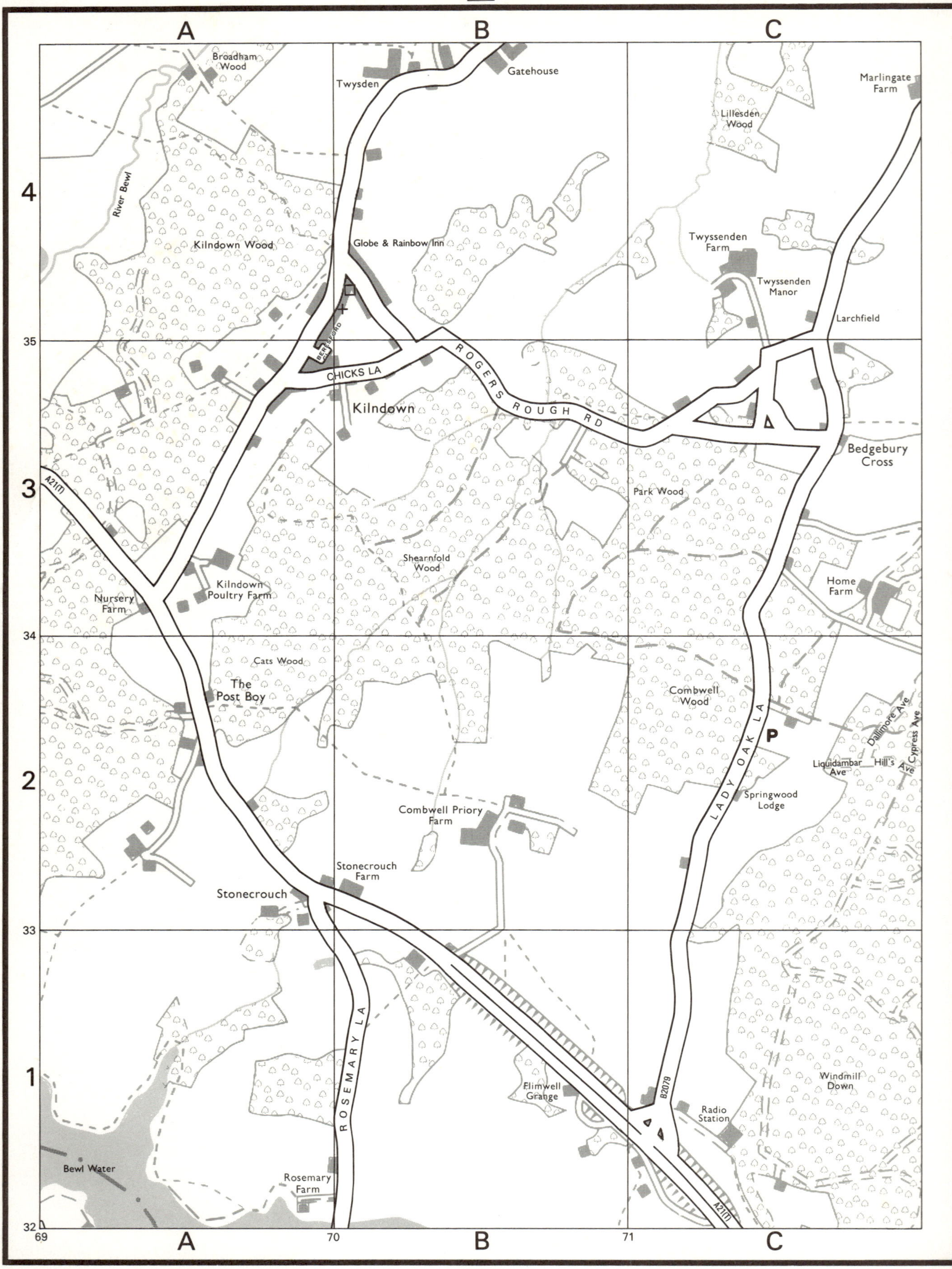
A
B
C
4
35
3
34
2
33
1
32
69
70
71
Broadham Wood
Twysden
Gatehouse
Marlingate Farm
Lillesden Wood
River Bewl
Kilndown Wood
Globe & Rainbow Inn
Twyssenden Farm
Twyssenden Manor
Larchfield
BERESFORD
CHICKS LA
ROGERS ROUGH RD
Kilndown
Bedgebury Cross
A21(T)
Park Wood
Shearnfold Wood
Kilndown Poultry Farm
Nursery Farm
Home Farm
Cats Wood
The Post Boy
Combwell Wood
LADY OAK LA
P
Dallimore Ave
Cypress Ave
Liquidambar Ave
Hill's Ave
Springwood Lodge
Combwell Priory Farm
Stonecrouch Farm
Stonecrouch
ROSEMARY LA
Flimwell Grange
B2079
Radio Station
Windmill Down
Bewl Water
Rosemary Farm
A21(T)

179

187

172

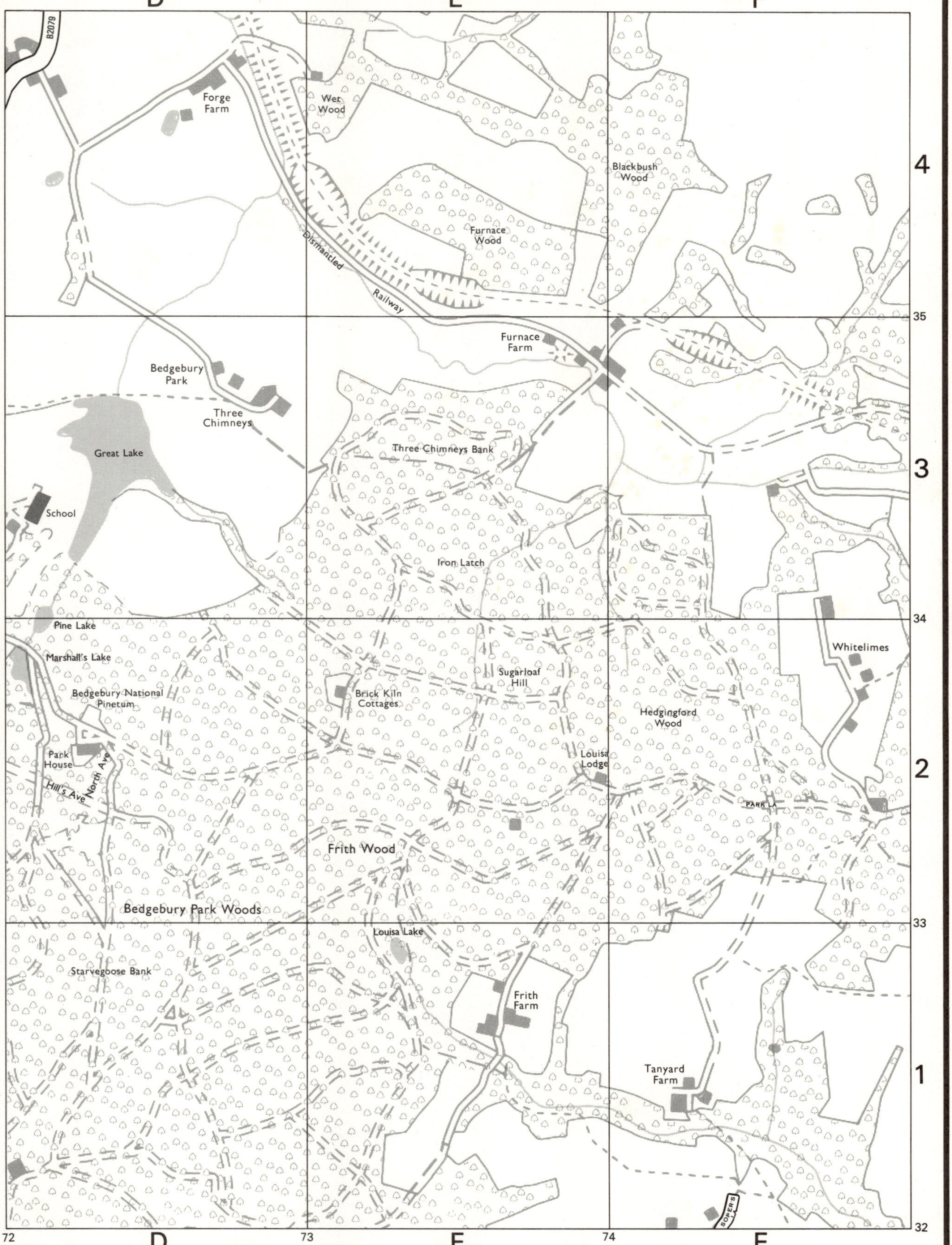
D
E
F
B2079
Forge Farm
Wet Wood
Blackbush Wood
Furnace Wood
Dismantled Railway
4
35
Furnace Farm
Bedgebury Park
Three Chimneys
Great Lake
Three Chimneys Bank
3
School
Iron Latch
34
Pine Lake
Marshall's Lake
Bedgebury National Pinetum
Brick Kiln Cottages
Sugarloaf Hill
Whitelimes
Hedgingford Wood
Park House
North Ave
Hill's Ave
Louisa Lodge
2
PARK LA
Frith Wood
Bedgebury Park Woods
33
Louisa Lake
Starvegoose Bank
Frith Farm
Tanyard Farm
1
SOPER'S
72
73
74
32
D
E
F

182

188

173

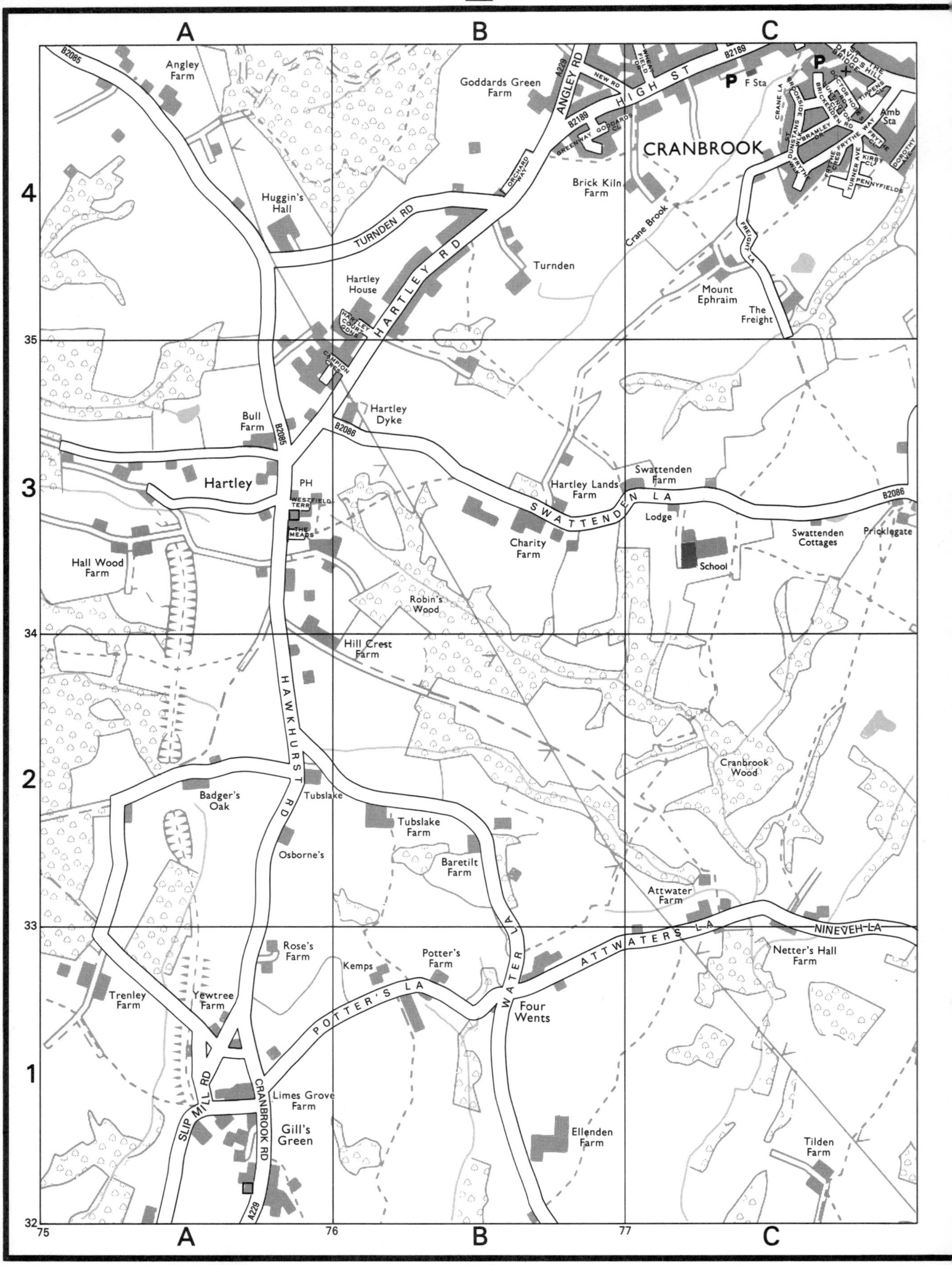
A
B
C
4
3
2
1
35
34
33
32
75
76
77
Angley Farm
Goddards Green Farm
CRANBROOK
HIGH ST
B2189
ANGLEY RD
A229
NEW RD
GOODARDS CL
GREENWAY
ORCHARD WAY
F Sta
Amb Sta
Brick Kiln Farm
Crane Brook
Huggin's Hall
TURNDEN RD
Turnden
HARTLEY RD
Hartley House
Mount Ephraim
The Freight
FREIGHT LA
PENNYFIELDS
TURNER AVE
KIRBY CL
DOROTHY AVE
CRANE LA
BRICKENDEN RD
BRAMLEY DR
FRYTHE WAY
FRYTHE CRES
FRYTHE WALK
ST DUNSTANS WALK
BROOKSIDE
DOCTOR HOPES RD
TIPPENS CL
ST DAVID'S BRIDGE
THE HILL
HARTLEY COURT GDNS
CAMPION CRES
Bull Farm
B2085
Hartley Dyke
B2086
Hartley
PH
WESTFIELD TERR
THE MEADS
Hartley Lands Farm
Swattenden Farm
SWATTENDEN LA
Lodge
Charity Farm
School
Swattenden Cottages
Pricklegate
Hall Wood Farm
Robin's Wood
Hill Crest Farm
HAWKHURST RD
Cranbrook Wood
Badger's Oak
Tubslake
Tubslake Farm
Osborne's
Baretilt Farm
Attwater Farm
ATTWATERS LA
NINEVEH LA
Netter's Hall Farm
Rose's Farm
Kemps
Potter's Farm
WATER LA
POTTER'S LA
Four Wents
Trenley Farm
Yewtree Farm
SLIP MILL RD
CRANBROOK RD
Limes Grove Farm
Gill's Green
A229
Ellenden Farm
Tilden Farm

181

189

174

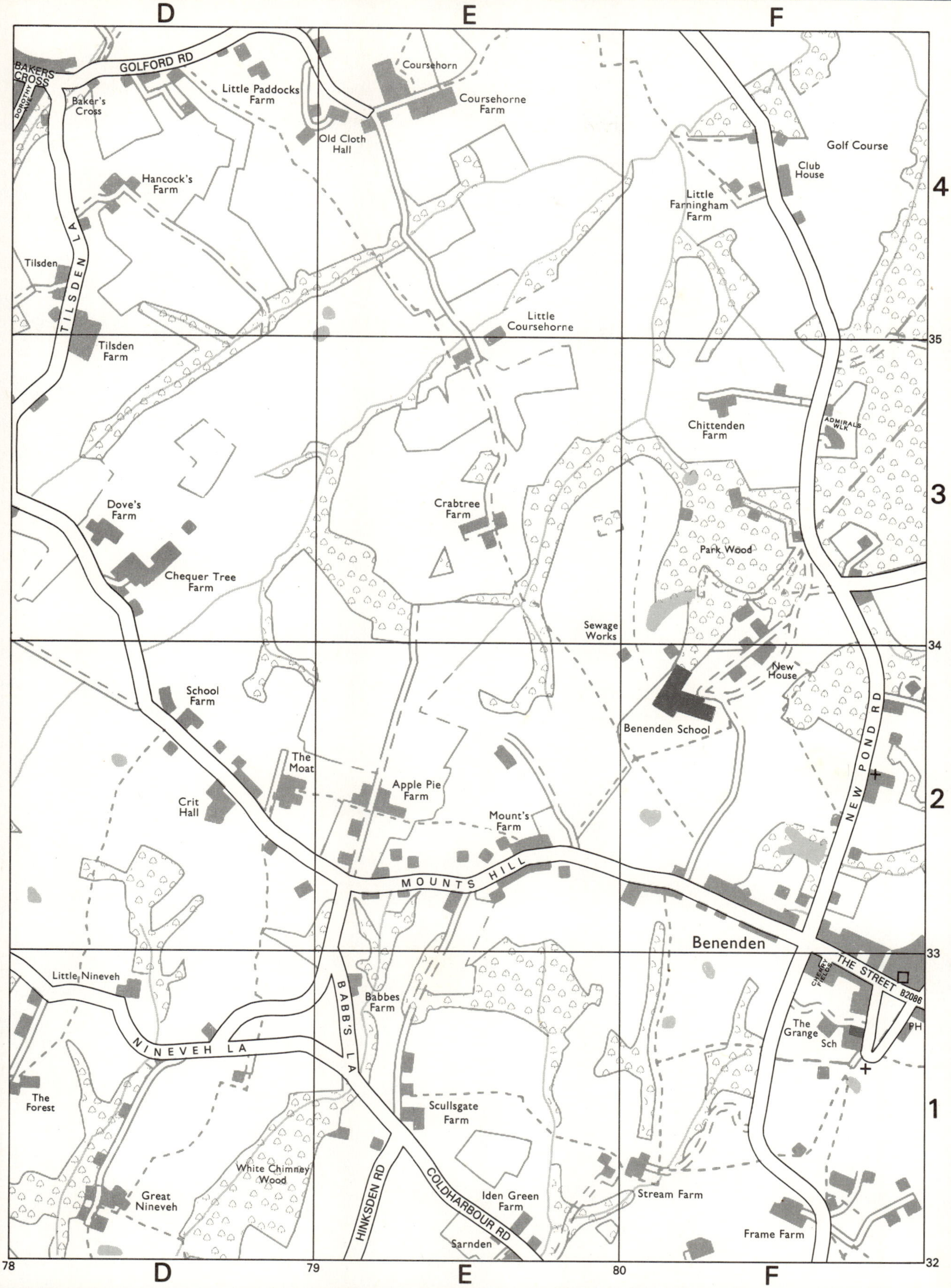
D
E
F
BAKERS CROSS
GOLFORD RD
Baker's Cross
Little Paddocks Farm
Coursehorn
Coursehorne Farm
Old Cloth Hall
Golf Course
Club House
Hancock's Farm
Little Farningham Farm
4
Tilsden
TILSDEN LA
Little Coursehorne
35
Tilsden Farm
Chittenden Farm
ADMIRALS WLK
Crabtree Farm
3
Dove's Farm
Park Wood
Chequer Tree Farm
Sewage Works
34
New House
School Farm
Benenden School
NEW POND RD
The Moat
Apple Pie Farm
Crit Hall
2
Mount's Farm
MOUNTS HILL
Benenden
33
Little Nineveh
BABB'S LA
Babbes Farm
THE STREET
B2086
CHERRY FIELDS
The Grange
Sch
PH
NINEVEH LA
The Forest
Scullsgate Farm
1
White Chimney Wood
Great Nineveh
HINKSDEN RD
COLDHARBOUR RD
Iden Green Farm
Stream Farm
Frame Farm
Sarnden
78
79
80
32

184

190

175

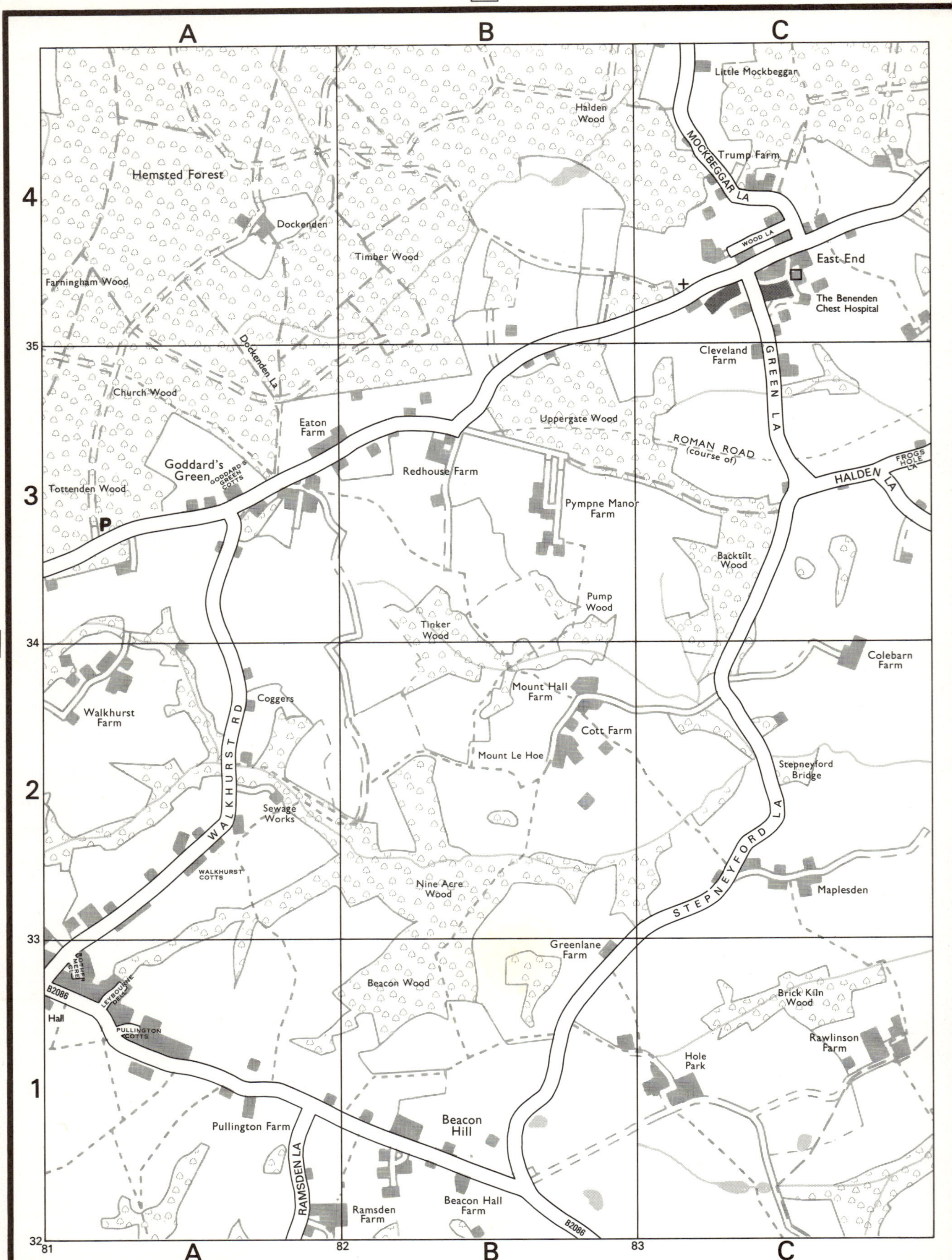
A
B
C
4
3
2
1
35
34
33
32
81
82
83
Hemsted Forest
Dockenden
Farningham Wood
Dockenden La
Church Wood
Tottenden Wood
Goddard's Green
GODDARD'S GREEN COTTS
Eaton Farm
Timber Wood
Halden Wood
Little Mockbeggar
MOCKBEGGAR LA
Trump Farm
WOOD LA
East End
The Benenden Chest Hospital
Cleveland Farm
GREEN LA
Uppergate Wood
ROMAN ROAD (course of)
FROGS HOLE LA
HALDEN LA
Redhouse Farm
Pympne Manor Farm
Backtilt Wood
Pump Wood
Tinker Wood
Colebarn Farm
Walkhurst Farm
Coggers
Mount Hall Farm
Cott Farm
Mount Le Hoe
Stepneyford Bridge
WALKHURST RD
Sewage Works
WALKHURST COTTS
STEPNEYFORD LA
Nine Acre Wood
Maplesden
Greenlane Farm
Beacon Wood
Brick Kiln Wood
B2086
LEYBOURNE DELL
Hall
PULLINGTON COTTS
Rawlinson Farm
Hole Park
Pullington Farm
Beacon Hill
RAMSDEN LA
Ramsden Farm
Beacon Hall Farm
B2086

183

191

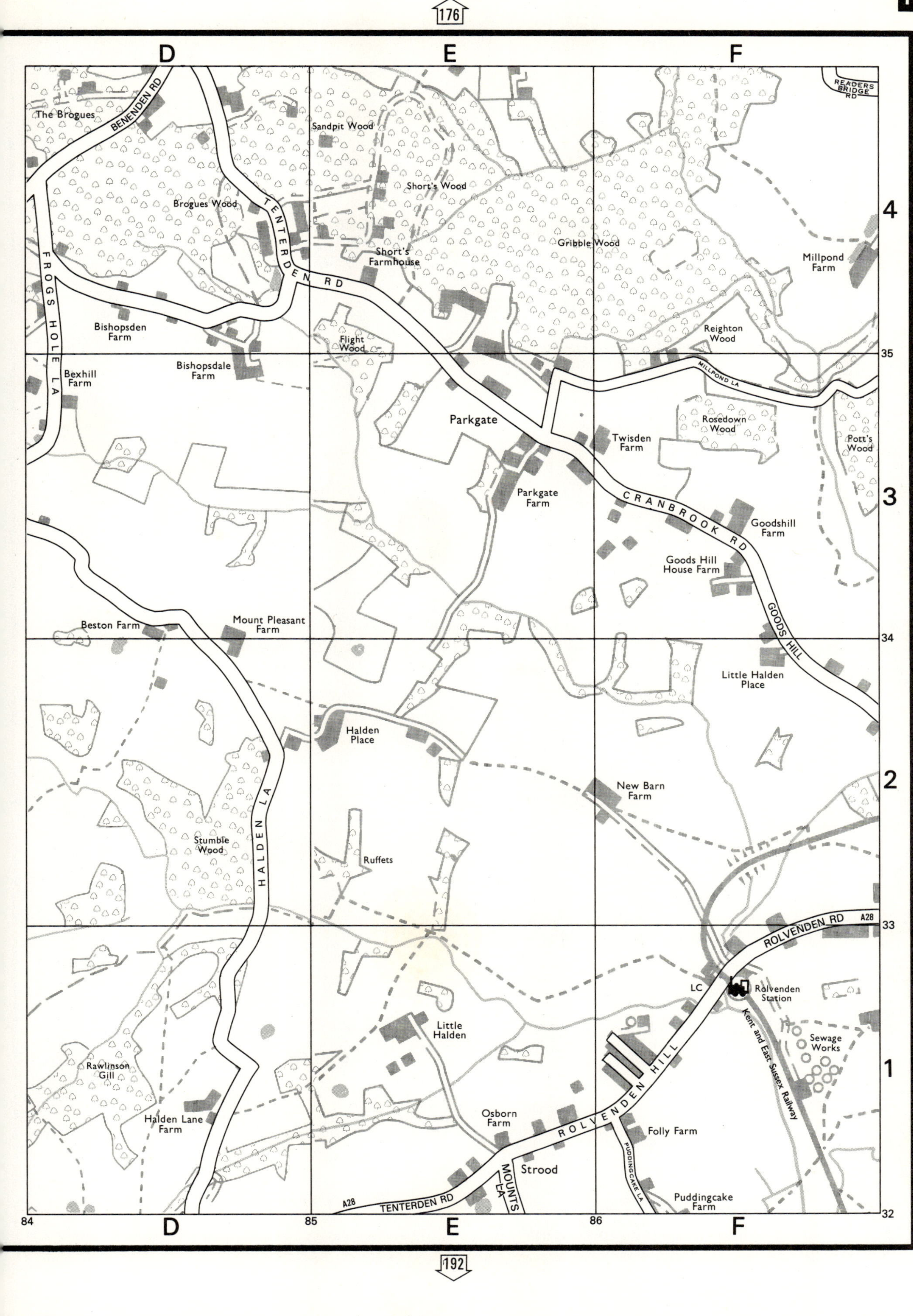
176
D
E
F
READERS BRIDGE RD
The Brogues
BENENDEN RD
Sandpit Wood
Short's Wood
Brogues Wood
TENTERDEN RD
FROGS HOLE LA
Short's Farmhouse
Gribble Wood
Millpond Farm
4
Bishopsden Farm
Flight Wood
Reighton Wood
35
Bexhill Farm
Bishopsdale Farm
MILLPOND LA
Parkgate
Rosedown Wood
Twisden Farm
Pott's Wood
Parkgate Farm
CRANBROOK RD
3
Goodshill Farm
Goods Hill House Farm
GOODS HILL
Beston Farm
Mount Pleasant Farm
34
186
Little Halden Place
Halden Place
New Barn Farm
2
Stumble Wood
HALDEN LA
Ruffets
ROLVENDEN RD
A28
33
LC
Rolvenden Station
Little Halden
Sewage Works
Kent and East Sussex Railway
1
Rawlinson Gill
ROLVENDEN HILL
Osborn Farm
Folly Farm
Halden Lane Farm
Strood
MOUNTS LA
PUDDINGCAKE LA
A28
TENTERDEN RD
Puddingcake Farm
84
85
86
32
D
E
F
192

177

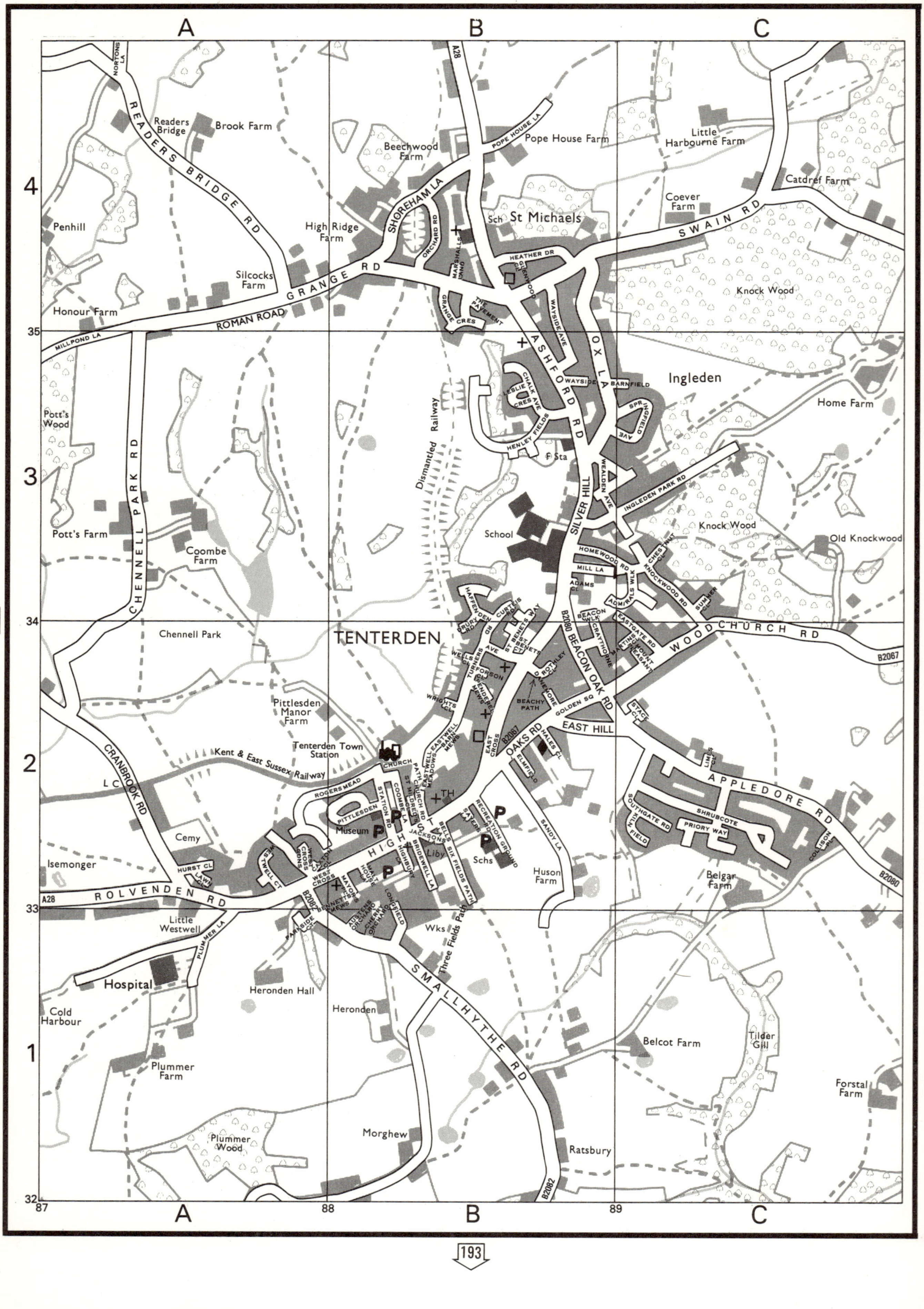
A
B
C
4
3
2
1
35
34
33
32
87
88
89
Readers Bridge
Brook Farm
READERS BRIDGE RD
NORTONS LA
Beechwood Farm
Pope House Farm
POPE HOUSE LA
Little Harbourne Farm
Catdref Farm
Coever Farm
Penhill
High Ridge Farm
SHOREHAM LA
ORCHARD RD
Sch
St Michaels
SWAIN RD
HEATHER DR
Silcocks Farm
GRANGE RD
Knock Wood
Honour Farm
ROMAN ROAD
GRANGE CRES
THE PAVEMENT
WAYSIDE AVE
MILLPOND LA
ASHFORD RD
OX LA
WAYSIDE
BARNFIELD
Ingleden
Home Farm
Pott's Wood
CHALK AVE
LESLIE CRES
HENLEY FIELDS
Dismantled Railway
SPRINGFIELD AVE
F Sta
SILVER HILL
WEALDEN AVE
INGLEDEN PARK RD
CHENNELL PARK RD
School
Knock Wood
Old Knockwood
Pott's Farm
Coombe Farm
HOMEWOOD RD
MILL LA
CHESTNUT CL
KNOCKWOOD RD
ADAMS CL
ADMIRALS WLK
SUMMER CL
HAFFENDEN RD
CURTEIS RD
BEACON WLK
EASTGATE RD
Chennell Park
TENTERDEN
B2080 BEACON OAK RD
WOODCHURCH RD
B2067
ST BENETS WAY
CRAYTHORNE
MOUNT PLEASANT
DROTFLEY CL
BEACHY PATH
GOLDEN SQ
STACE CL
Pittlesden Manor Farm
EAST HILL
Tenterden Town Station
Kent & East Sussex Railway
LIMES CL
CRANBROOK RD
OAKS RD
HALES CL
ELMFIELD
APPLEDORE RD
CHURCH
B2067
EAST CROSS
ROGERS MEAD
PITTLESDEN
STATION RD
COOMBE LA
TH
SOUTHGATE RD
SHRUBCOTE
PRIORY WAY
KILN FIELD
COLLISON PL
Museum
RECREATION GROUND
SANDY LA
Cemy
HIGH ST
JACKSONS
BELLS LA
SIX FIELDS PATH
BRIDEWELL LA
Liby
Schs
Isemonger
HURST CL
LAWN CL
WESTWELL CT
WEST CROSS
HIGHBURY LA
Huson Farm
Belgar Farm
B2080
A28
ROLVENDEN RD
B2082
MAYORS PL
LONGFIELD
Three Fields Path
Little Westwell
PLUMMER LA
Wks
PARKSIDE CT
Hospital
Heronden Hall
Heronden
SMALLHYTHE RD
Cold Harbour
Belcot Farm
Tilder Gill
Plummer Farm
Forstal Farm
Plummer Wood
Morghew
Ratsbury
B2082
A28

185

193

180

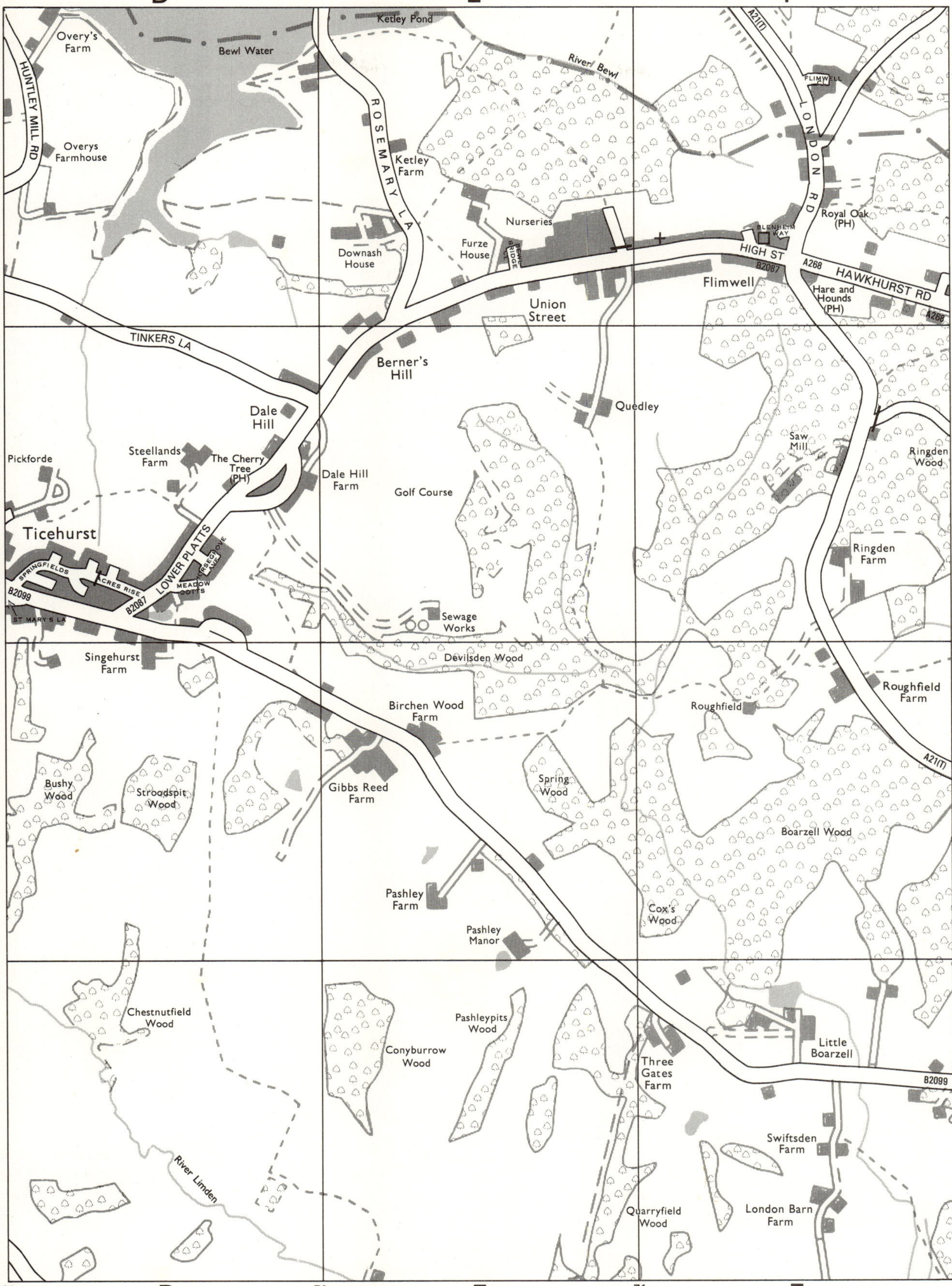

188

not continued, see key diagram

181

187

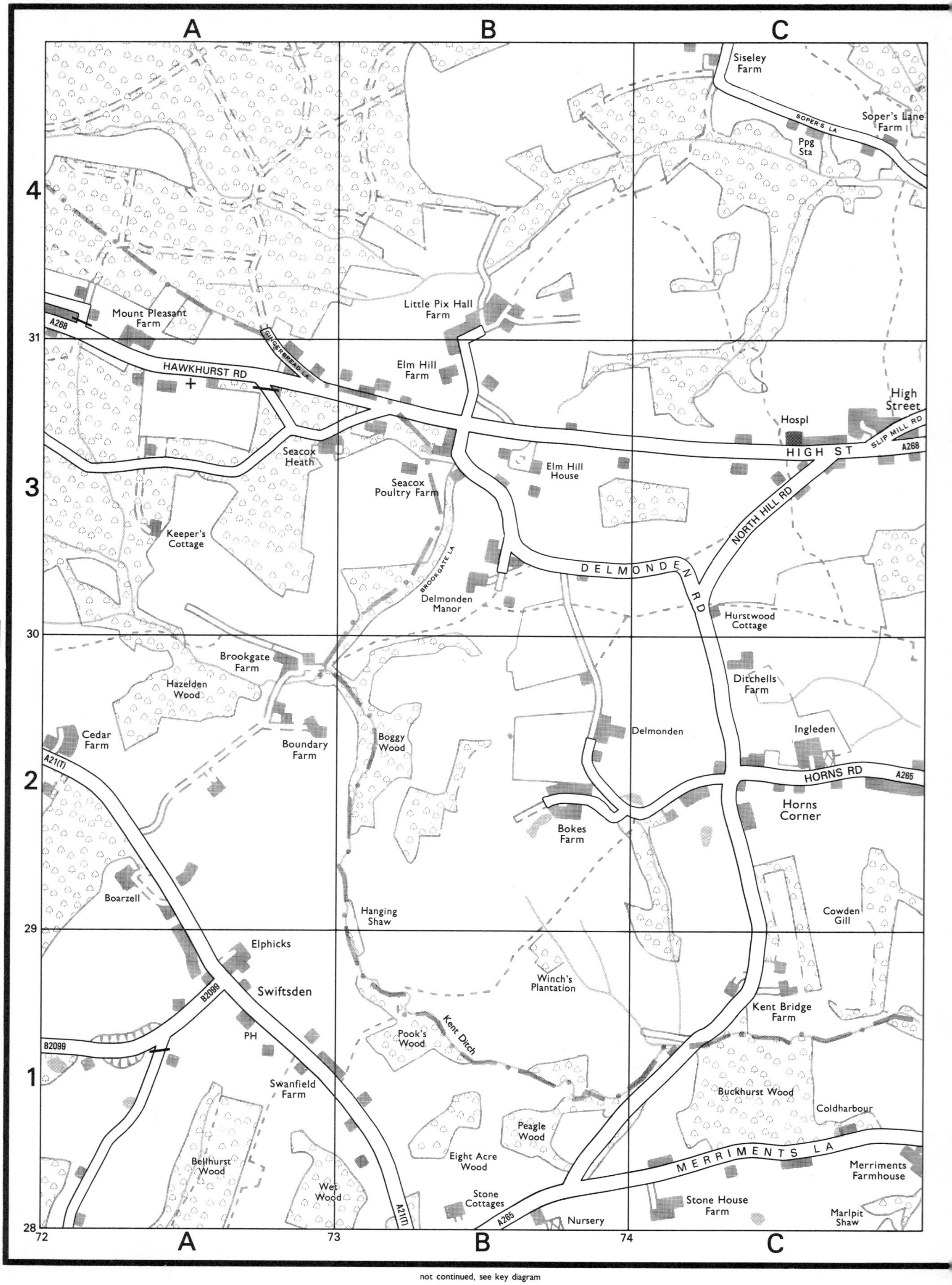

not continued, see key diagram

182

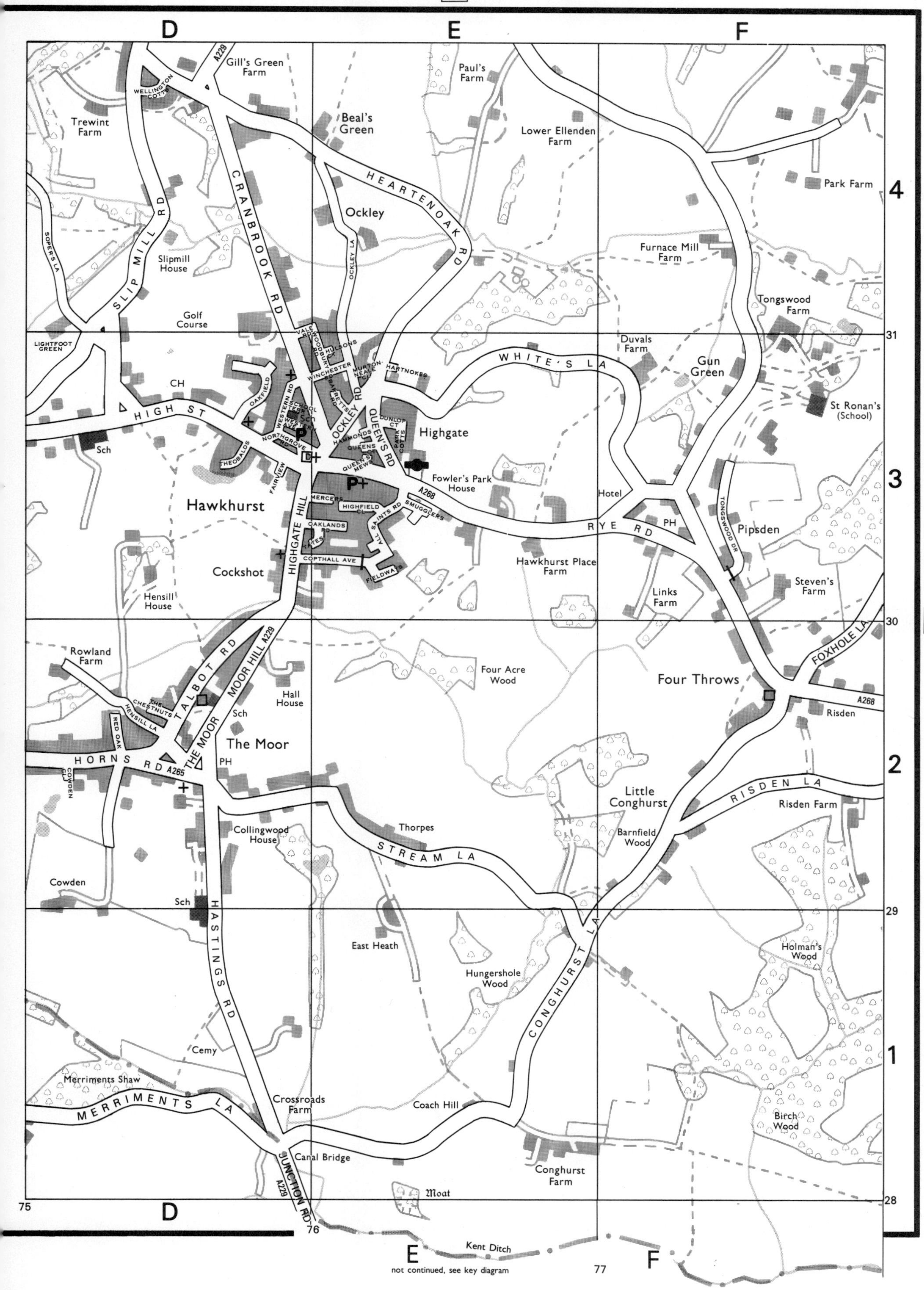

190

not continued, see key diagram

183

189

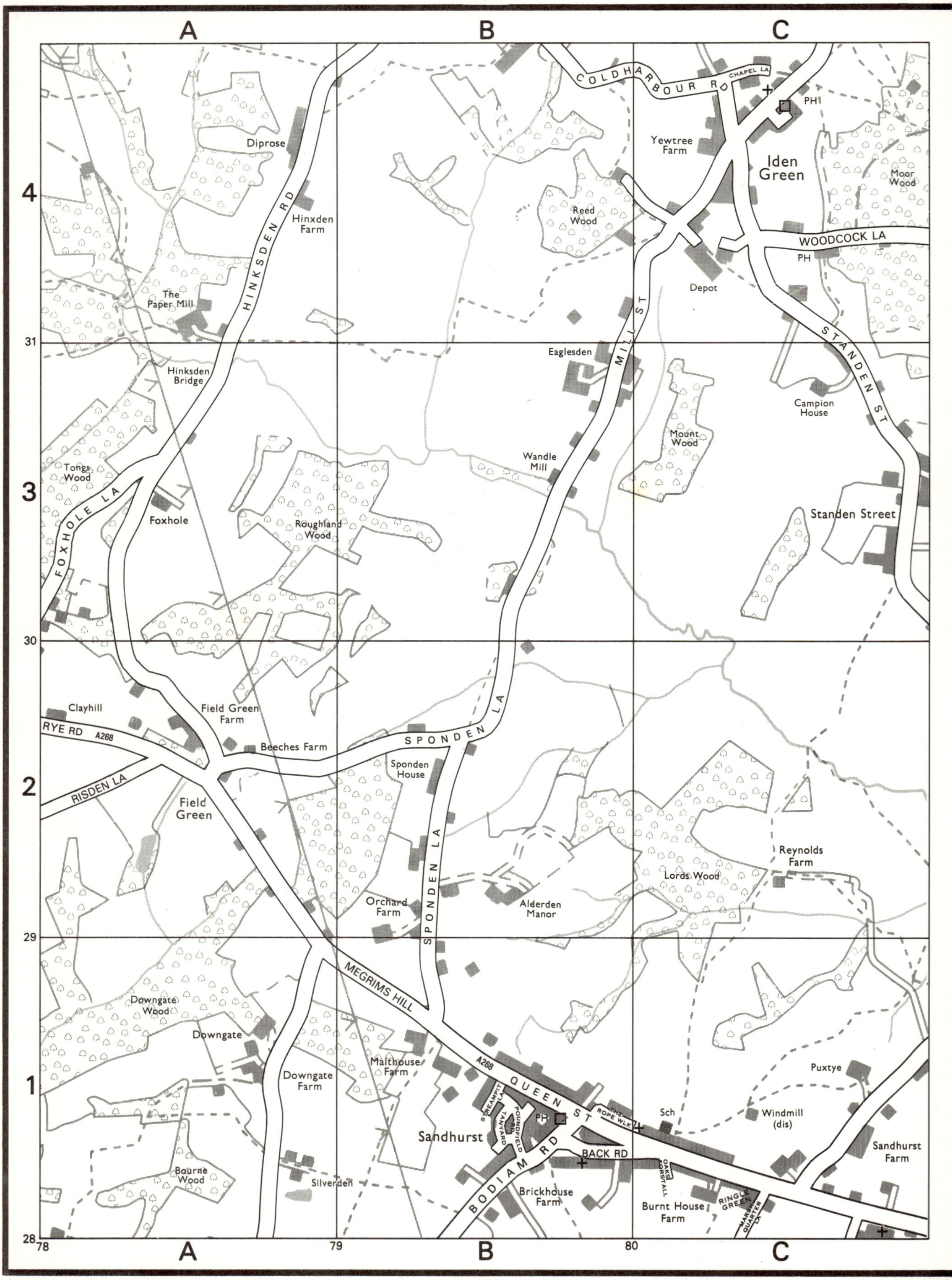
A
B
C
4
3
2
1
31
30
29
28
78
79
80
COLDHARBOUR RD
CHAPEL LA
PH
Yewtree Farm
Iden Green
Moor Wood
Diprose
Hinxden Farm
HINKSDEN RD
Reed Wood
WOODCOCK LA
PH
Depot
The Paper Mill
MILL ST
STANDEN ST
Eaglesden
Hinksden Bridge
Campion House
Mount Wood
Wandle Mill
Tongs Wood
FOXHOLE LA
Foxhole
Roughland Wood
Standen Street
Clayhill
Field Green Farm
RYE RD
A268
Beeches Farm
SPONDEN LA
Sponden House
RISDEN LA
Field Green
Reynolds Farm
Lords Wood
Orchard Farm
Alderden Manor
SPONDEN LA
MEGRIMS HILL
Downgate Wood
Downgate
Malthouse Farm
A268
QUEEN ST
Puxtye
Downgate Farm
STREAMPIT LA
TANYARD
POUNDFIELD RD
PH
THE ROPE WLK
Sch
Windmill (dis)
Sandhurst
BACK RD
OAKS FORSTALL
BODIAM RD
Sandhurst Farm
Bourne Wood
Silverden
Brickhouse Farm
Burnt House Farm
RINGLE GREEN
MARSH QUARTER LA

184

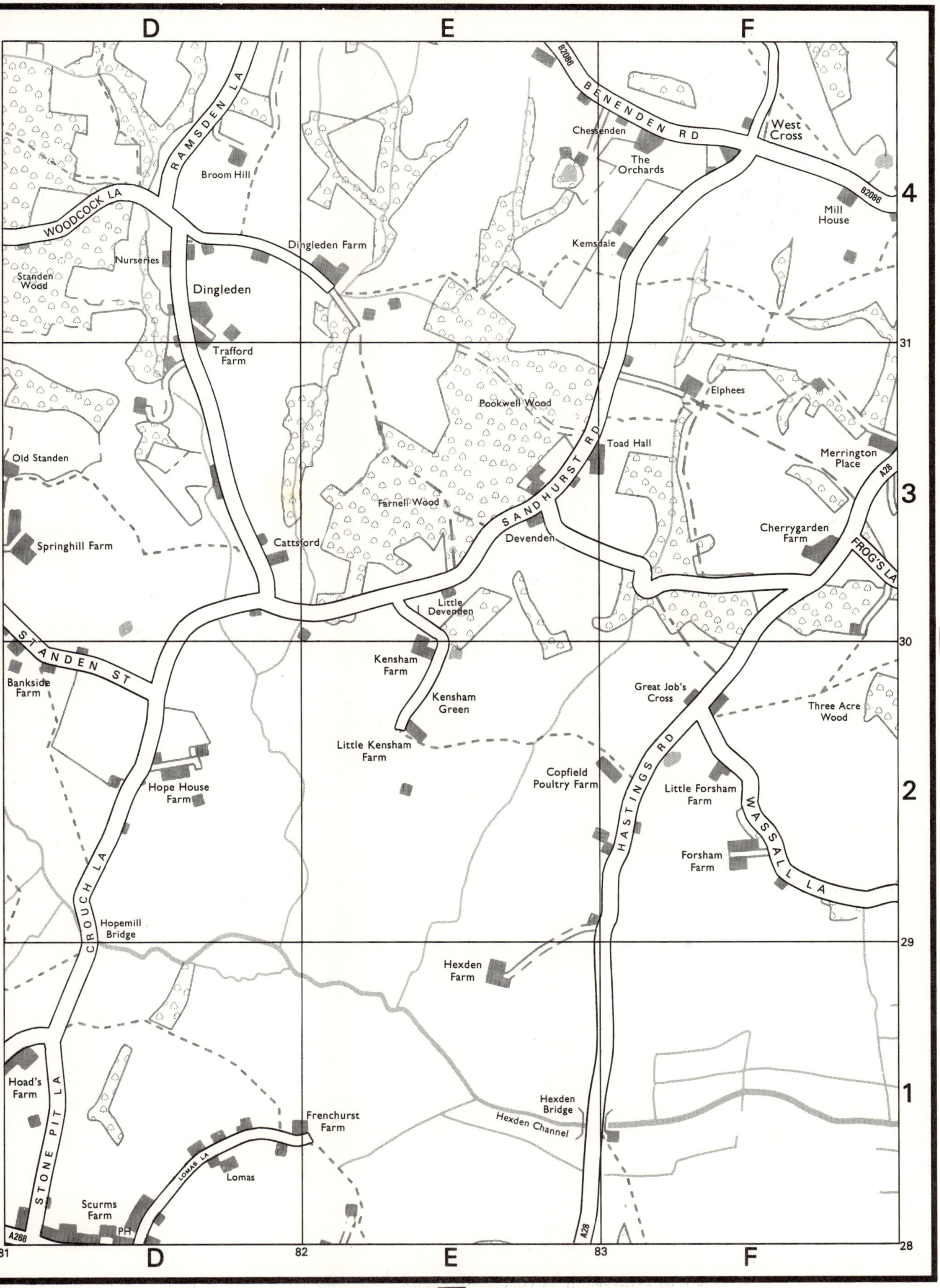
D
E
F
BENENDEN RD
B2086
West Cross
Chessenden
The Orchards
RAMSDEN LA
Broom Hill
WOODCOCK LA
Mill House
4
Kemsdale
Nurseries
Dingleden Farm
Standen Wood
Dingleden
Trafford Farm
31
Elphees
Pookwell Wood
Old Standen
Toad Hall
Merrington Place
A28
3
Farnell Wood
SANDHURST RD
Cherrygarden Farm
Springhill Farm
Cattsford
Devenden
FROG'S LA
Little Devenden
STANDEN ST
30
Kensham Farm
Bankside Farm
Great Job's Cross
Kensham Green
Three Acre Wood
Little Kensham Farm
Copfield Poultry Farm
HASTINGS RD
Hope House Farm
Little Forsham Farm
2
WASSALL LA
Forsham Farm
CROUCH LA
Hopemill Bridge
29
Hexden Farm
Hoad's Farm
STONE PIT LA
Hexden Bridge
Hexden Channel
1
Frenchurst Farm
LOMAS LA
Lomas
Scurms Farm
PH
A268
A28
81
82
83
28

192

195

185

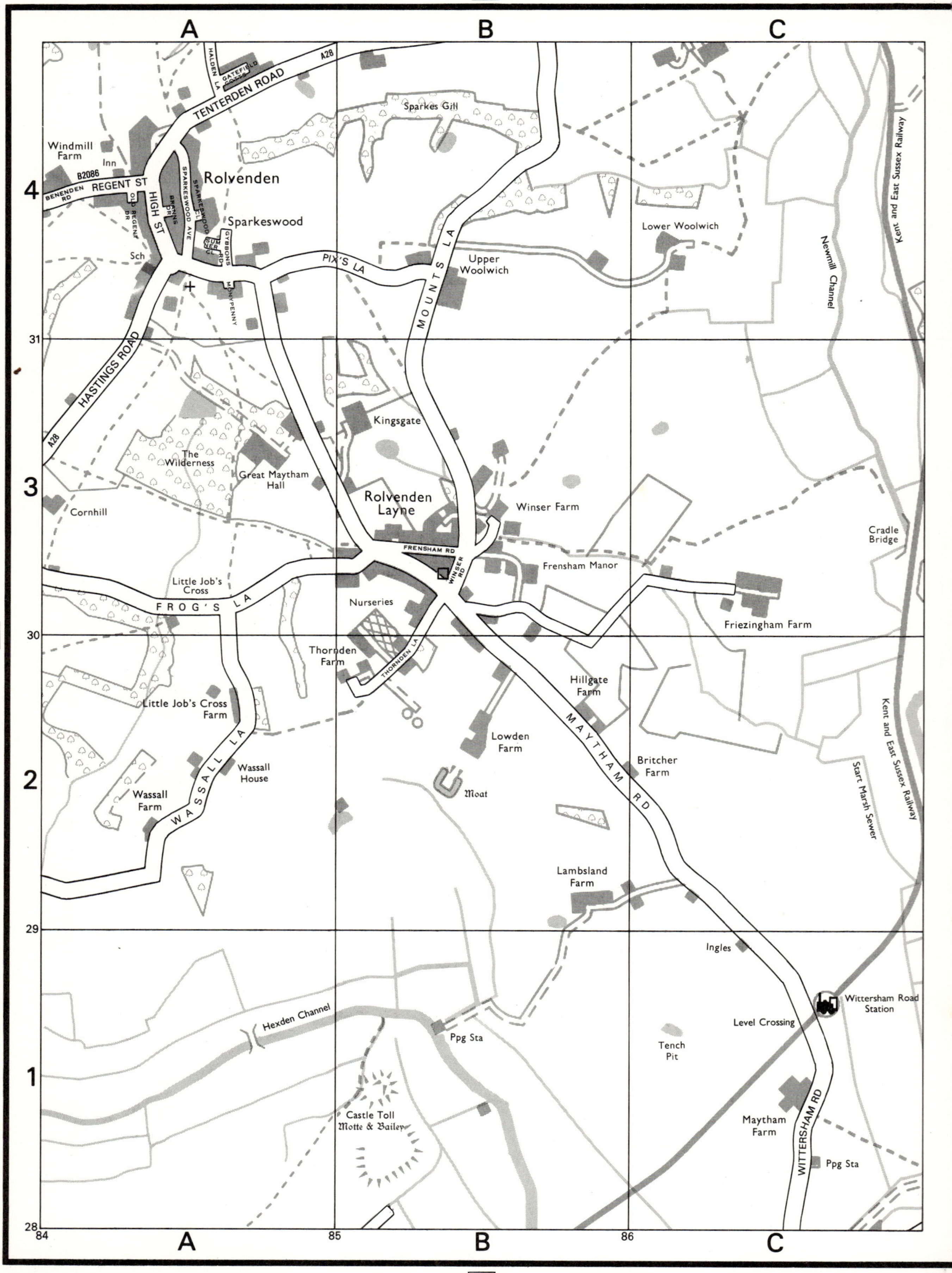
A
B
C
4
3
2
1
31
30
29
28
84
85
86
A28
TENTERDEN ROAD
HALDEN LA
GATEFIELD COTTS
Sparkes Gill
Windmill Farm
Inn
B2086
REGENT ST
BENENDEN RD
Rolvenden
OLD REGENT DR
HIGH ST
SPARKESWOOD AVE
SPARKESWOOD CL
Sparkeswood
GYBBONS RD
Sch
PIX'S LA
MONYPENNY
Upper Woolwich
MOUNTS LA
Lower Woolwich
Newmill Channel
Kent and East Sussex Railway
HASTINGS ROAD
A28
Kingsgate
The Wilderness
Great Maytham Hall
Cornhill
Rolvenden Layne
Winser Farm
FRENSHAM RD
WINSER RD
Frensham Manor
Cradle Bridge
Little Job's Cross
FROG'S LA
Nurseries
Friezingham Farm
Thornden Farm
THORNDEN LA
Hillgate Farm
Little Job's Cross Farm
Lowden Farm
MAYTHAM RD
Britcher Farm
Kent and East Sussex Railway
Start Marsh Sewer
Wassall House
Moat
Wassall Farm
WASSALL LA
Lambsland Farm
Ingles
Wittersham Road Station
Level Crossing
Hexden Channel
Ppg Sta
Tench Pit
Castle Toll
Motte & Bailey
Maytham Farm
WITTERSHAM RD
Ppg Sta

191

196

186

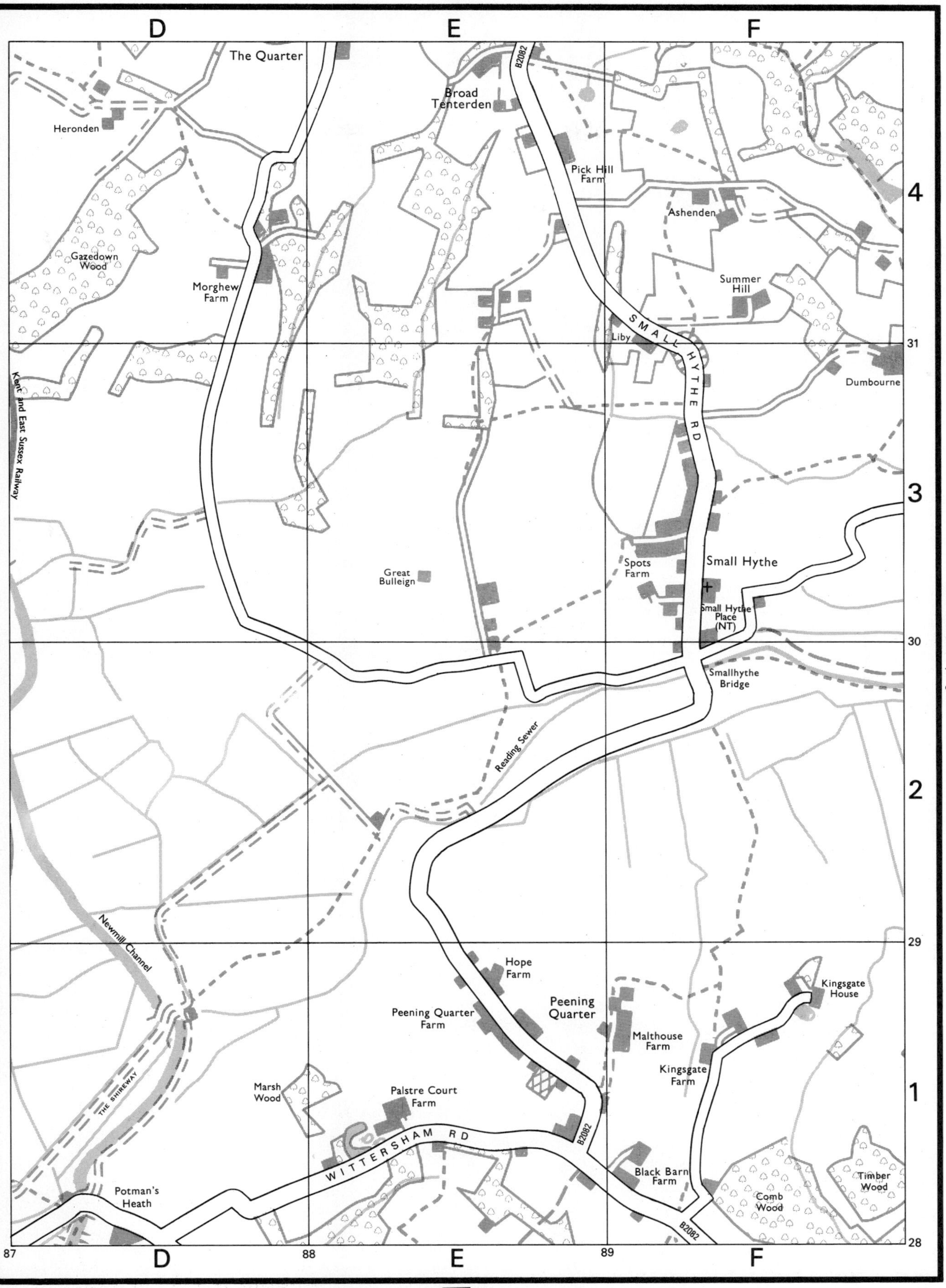

not continued, see key diagram

197

190

not continued, see key diagram

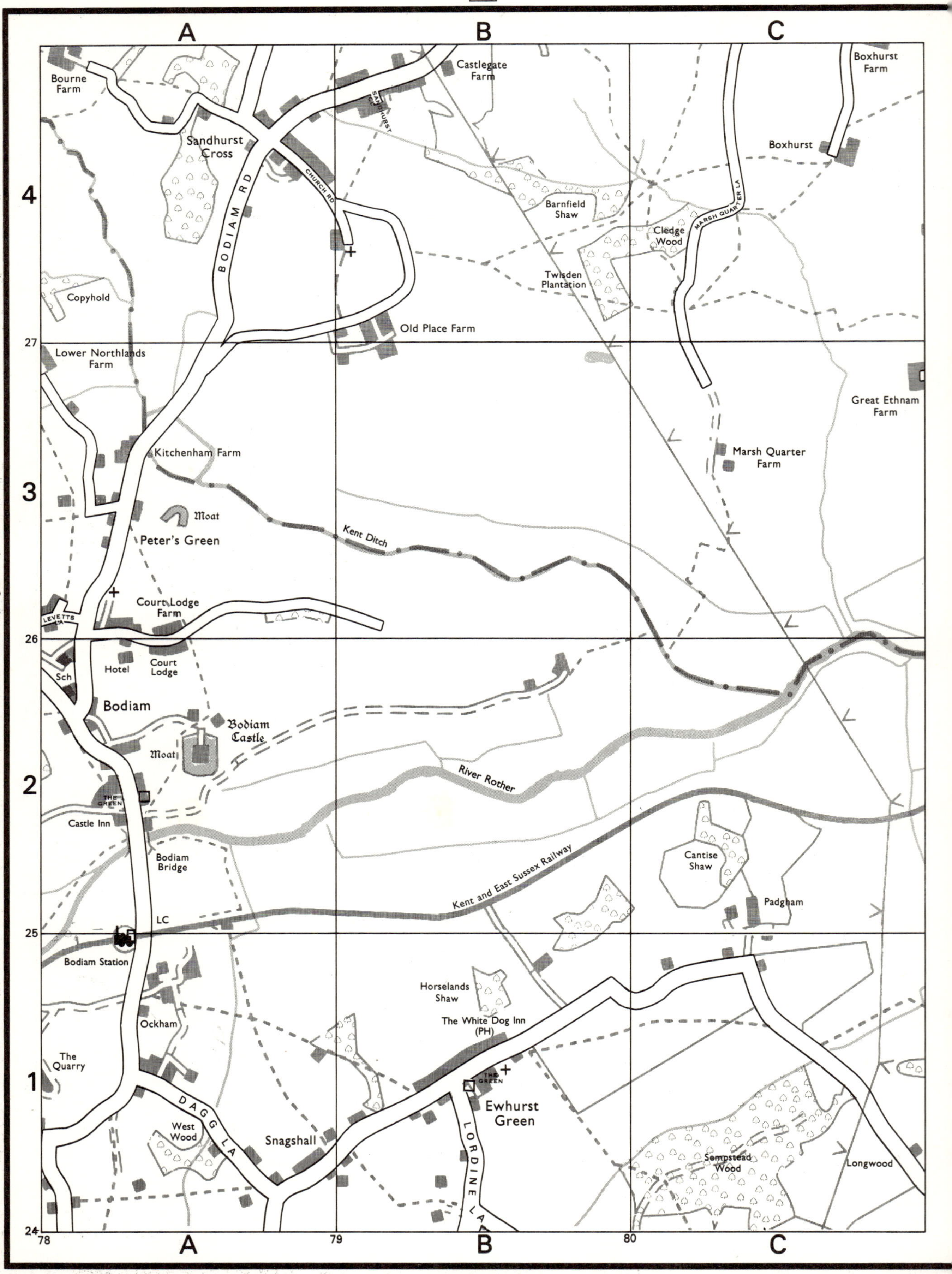

not continued, see key diagram

191

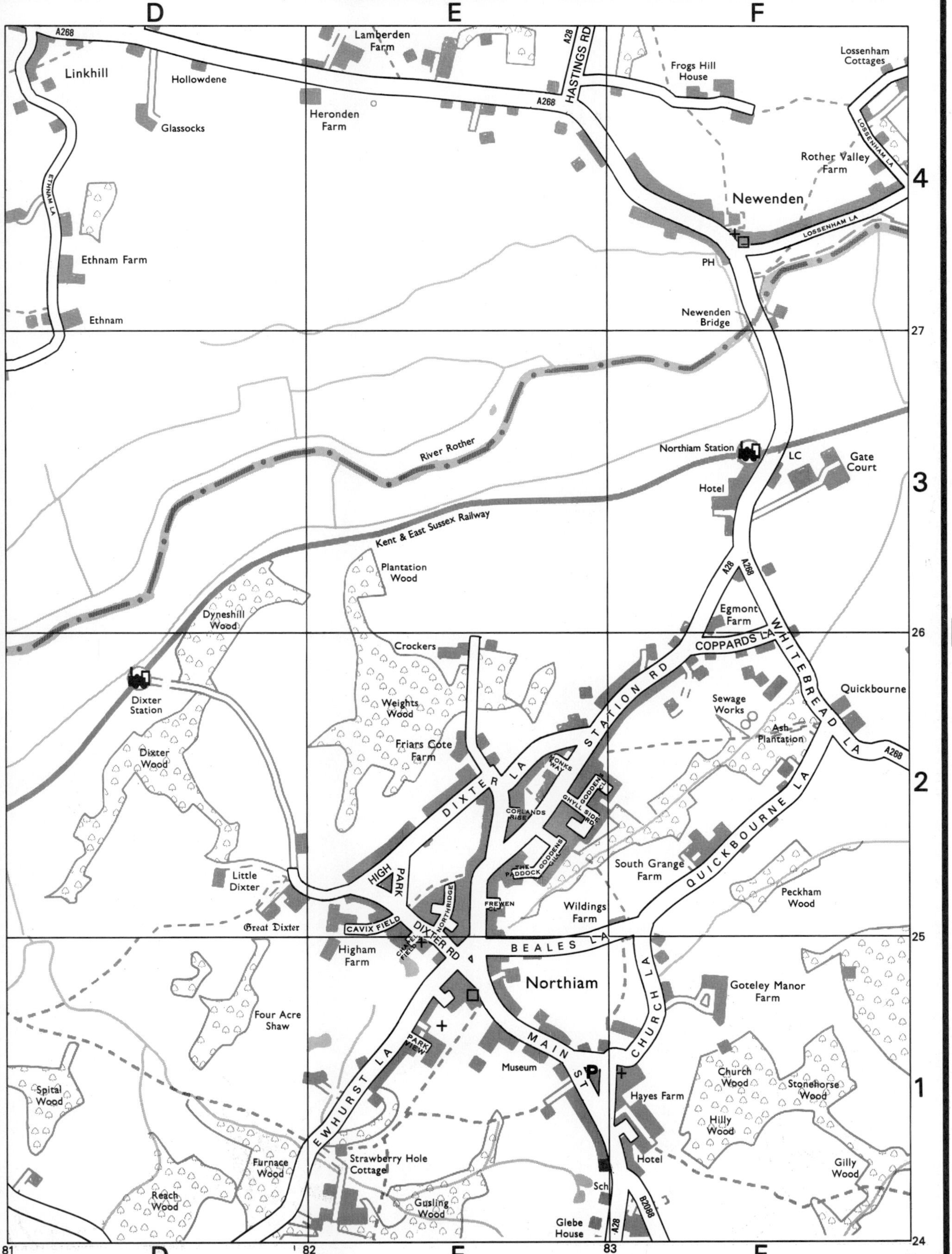

196

not continued, see key diagram

192

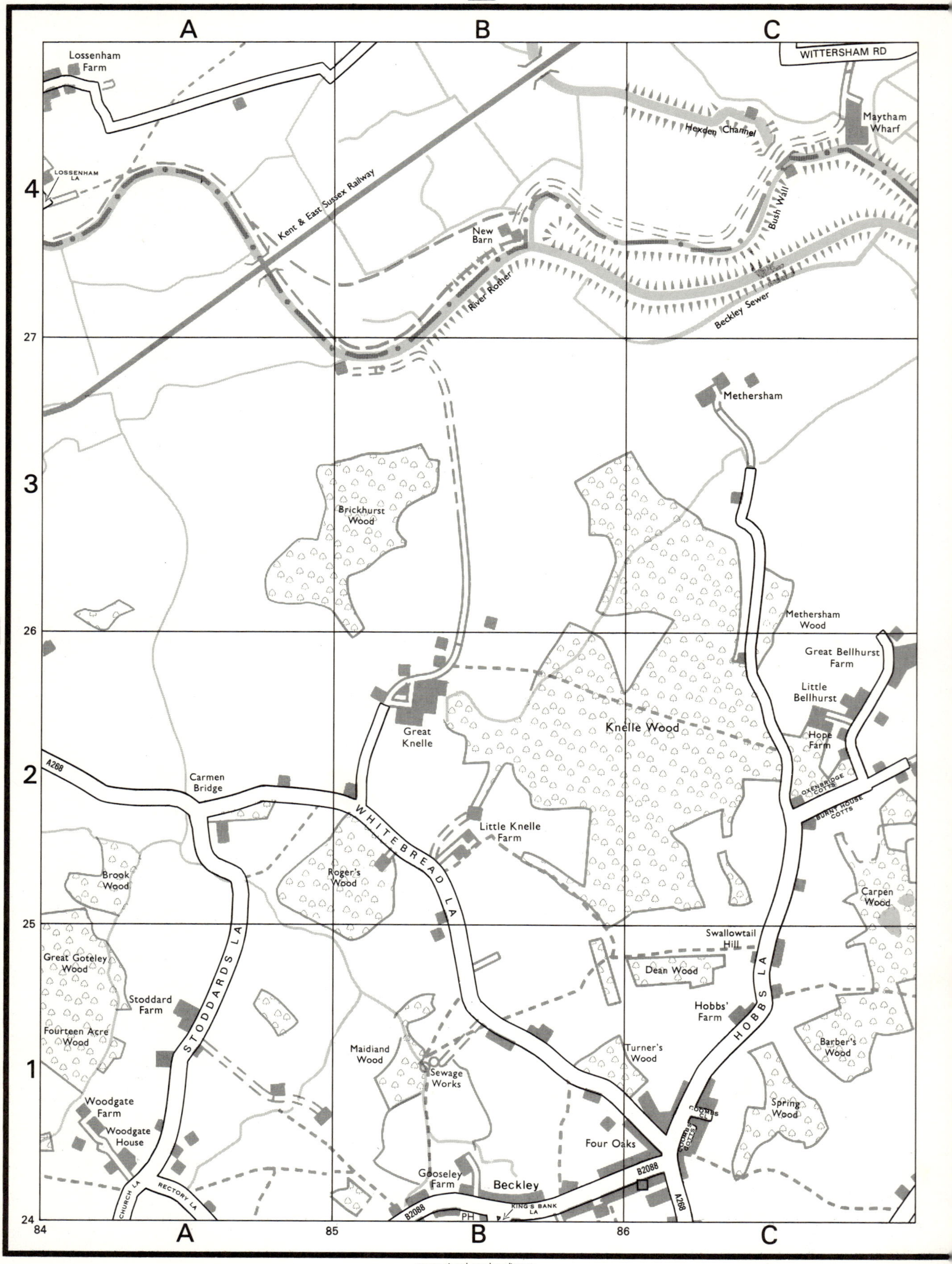

A
B
C
WITTERSHAM RD
Lossenham Farm
LOSSENHAM LA
Kent & East Sussex Railway
Hexden Channel
Maytham Wharf
Bush Wall
New Barn
River Rother
Beckley Sewer
4
27
Methersham
3
Brickhurst Wood
Methersham Wood
26
Great Bellhurst Farm
Little Bellhurst
Great Knelle
Knelle Wood
Hope Farm
2
A268
Carmen Bridge
WHITEBREAD LA
OXENBRIDGE COTTS
BURNT HOUSE COTTS
Little Knelle Farm
Brook Wood
Roger's Wood
Carpen Wood
25
Great Goteley Wood
Swallowtail Hill
Dean Wood
STODDARDS LA
Stoddard Farm
HOBBS LA
Hobbs' Farm
Fourteen Acre Wood
Maidland Wood
Turner's Wood
Barber's Wood
1
Sewage Works
Woodgate Farm
COOMBS CL
Spring Wood
Woodgate House
COOMBS COTTS
Four Oaks
Gooseley Farm
B2088
Beckley
CHURCH LA
RECTORY LA
B2088
PH
KING'S BANK LA
A268
24
84
85
86

195

193

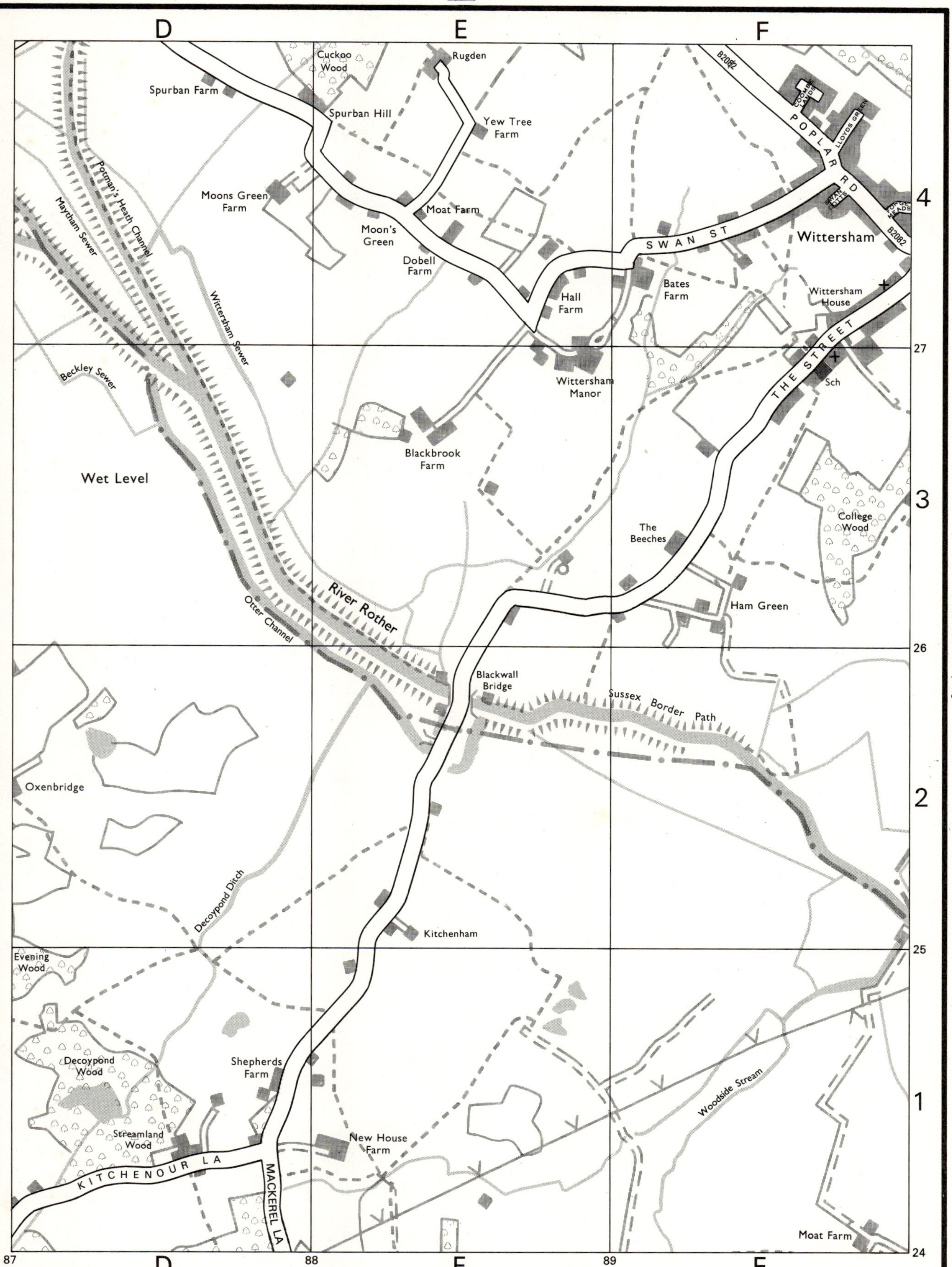

not continued, see key diagram

not continued, see key diagram

USER'S NOTES

EXPLANATION OF THE STREET INDEX REFERENCE SYSTEM

Street names are listed alphabetically and show the locality, the map page number and a reference to the square in which the name falls on the map page.

Example:	Redgate Dr. Brom...*48* B2
Redgate Dr.	This is the full street name, which may have been abbreviated on the map.
Brom	This is the abbreviation for the town, village or locality in which the street falls.
48	This is the page number of the map on which the street name appears.
B2	The letter and figure indicate the square on the map in which the centre of the street falls. The square can be found at the junction of the vertical column carrying the appropriate letter and the horizontal row carrying the appropriate figure.

ABBREVIATIONS USED IN THE INDEX

Road Names

Approach	App
Avenue	Ave
Broadway	Bwy
Causeway	Cswy
Common	Comm
Corner	Cnr
Cottages	Cotts
Court	Ct
Crescent	Cres
Drive	Dr
Drove	Dro
East	E
Gardens	Gdns
Grove	Gr
Heights	Hts
Lane	La
North	N
Orchard	Orch
Parade	Par
Passage	Pas
Place	Pl
Pleasant	Plea
Precinct	Prec
Promenade	Prom
Road	Rd
South	S
Square	Sq
Street, Saint	St
Terrace	Terr
Walk	Wlk
West	W
Yard	Yd

Towns, Villages and Rural Localities

Allhallows	All	13	F2
Ashurst	Asht	164	C3
Aylesford	Ayld	88	B4
Bean	Bean	22	B1
Beckley	Beckl	196	B1
Bells Yew Green	Bel G	168	B1
Belvedere	Belv	4	A3
Benenden	Ben	183	F2
Bexley	Bex	19	E3
Bexleyheath	Bexh	19	D4
Biddenden	Bidd	176	A3
Biggin Hill	Bigg	78	A3
Bidborough	Bid	152	C4
Birling	Birl	71	E1
Blackham	Bla	164	B4
Bodiam	Bod	194	A2
Borden	Bor	77	F3
Borough Green	Bor G	84	B2
Boughton Malherbe	Bou Mal	128	B2
Boughton Monchelsea	Bou Mon	124	B4
Boxley	Box	89	F3
Brasted	Bras	96	C4
Bredgar	Bredg	77	F1
Bredhurst	Bredh	75	E3
Brenchley	Brenc	156	B2
Bromley	Brom	33	F3
Broomfield (Maidstone)	Broom (M)	108	C1
Burham	Burh	73	D2
Charing	Char	130	C2
Charing Heath	Char He	130	A2
Chart Sutton	Chart S	125	E3
Chatham	Chath	60	B3
Chevening	Chev	80	A2
Chiddingstone	Chid	133	F2
Chiddingstone Causeway	Chid C	134	A3
Chislehurst	Chis	34	C3
Church Street	Ch St	26	C3
Cliffe	Cli	10	C1
Cliffe Woods	Cli W	27	E2
Cobham	Cob	42	A1
Cooling	Coo	28	A4
Cowden	Cow	149	E1
Coxheath	Cox	123	F4
Cranbrook	Cran	182	C4
Crockenhill	Croc	51	F4
Crockham Hill	Croc H	113	F3
Crayford	Cray	20	B3
Cuxton	Cux	58	C3
Darenth	Dare	38	C4
Dartford	Dart	20	B2
Ditton	Dit	87	F3
Doddington	Dod	94	C2
Downe	Dow	63	D2
Dunton Green	Dunt	81	D2
East Farleigh	E Far	105	E2
East Peckham	E Pec	121	D1
Eastling	Elng	112	C4
Edenbridge	Ede	131	F3
Egerton	Ege	147	D4
Egerton Forstal	Ege F	146	C3
Erith	Eri	5	D3
Ewhurst Green	Ewh G	194	B1
Eynsford	Eyn	53	D2
Eythorne Street	Eyh	108	C3
Farningham	Farn	53	E3
Fawkham Green	Faw	54	B2
Five Oak Green	Five O G	138	B2
Four Elms	Four E	114	B1
Frinstead	Frins	93	F2
Frittenden	Frit	161	D2
Gillingham	Gil	46	A1
Golden Green	Gol G	120	A1
Goudhurst	Gou	172	A2
Grain	Grain	15	E1
Gravesend	Grave	24	C3
Grays	Grays	8	A4
Greenhithe	Gree	22	B3
Greenwich	Grch	1	A3
Groombridge	Gro	165	E2
Hadlow	Had	120	A2
Halling	Hall	58	B1
Halstead	Hals	65	E2
Harrietsham	Harr	109	F1
Hartley (Sevenoaks)	Hart (S)	55	E4
Hartley (Tunbridge Wells)	Hart (T)	182	A3
Hawkhurst	Hawkt	189	D3
Hawley	Haw	38	A4
Hayes	Hay	48	B3
Headcorn	Head	144	C1
Hever	Hev	132	C1
Hextable	Hex	37	E3
High Halden	H Hald	177	F2
High Halstow	H Hals	29	D4
Higham	Higham	43	F4
Hildenborough	Hild	118	A1
Hollingbourne	Holli	109	D4
Hoo St Werburgh	Hoo S W	28	C1
Horsmonden	Hors	157	E1
Horton Kirby	Hort	38	C1
Hunton	Hunt	122	C2
Ightham	Ight	83	F1
Isle of Grain	I o G	15	D1
Istead Rise	Ist	41	D3
Kemsing	Kemsg	82	A3
Keston	Kes	48	C1
Kilndown	Kiln	180	B3
Knockholt	Kno	79	E3
Knockholt Pound	Kno P	80	A4
Lamberhurst	Lam	170	B1
Langley Heath	Lan H	126	A4
Leeds	Lee	108	B2
Leigh	Lei	135	D3
Lenham	Len	110	C1
Limpsfield	Lim	78	A1
Limpsfield Chart	Lim C	95	D2
Linton	Lint	124	A3
Longfield	Lon	40	A1
Loose	Loose	106	A1
Lower Stoke	Low St	13	F1
Maidstone	Maid	106	C3
Marden	Mard	141	F1
Markbeech	Mark	149	F3
Matfield	Mat	156	A2
Meopham	Meo	56	B2
Mereworth	Merew	102	C2
Milstead	Mils	94	A3
Nettlestead	Net	103	F1
Newenden	Newe	195	F4
Newington (Gillingham)	New (G)	62	C1
Newnham	Newn	112	B4
North Ash	N Ash	55	D2
Northiam	Norm	195	E1
Offham	Off	85	F2
Orpington	Orp	49	F1
Otford	Otf	81	E4
Otham	Oth	107	E2
Paddock Wood	Padd W	139	E2
Pembury	Pem	154	C1
Penshurst	Pen	151	E4
Platt's Heath	Pla H	128	A3
Plaxtol	Plax	101	D2
Pluckley	Plu	147	F2
Pratt's Bottom	Pra	64	C3
Purfleet	Pur	6	B2
Rainham (Kent)	Rai (K)	62	B2
Rochester	Roc	44	B1
Rodmersham	Rod	94	C4
Rolvenden	Rol	192	A4
Roseacre	Rose	107	E4
St Mary's Hoo	St M H	12	C1
Sandhurst	Sand	190	B1
Seal	Seal	82	B1
Sevenoaks	Sev	98	C3
Sevenoaks Weald	Sev W	116	B4
Shipbourne	Ship	100	C1
Shoreham	Shorm	66	A2
Shorne	Shor	43	D4
Sidcup	Sid	35	F4
Sissinghurst	Siss	174	B2
Smarden	Sma	163	E3
Snodland	Snod	72	B2
Southborough	Soub	153	E3
South Darenth	S Dar	38	C2
Southfleet	Souf	40	B3
South Green	S Grn	77	E1
South Ockendon	S Ock	6	C4
South Stifford	S Stiff	7	F3
Speldhurst	Spel	152	B2
Stalisfield Green	Stal	112	C1
Stansted	Stans	69	D3
Staplehurst	Stapt	160	A4
Stockbury	Sto	77	D2
Stone	Stone	22	A3
Sundridge	Sund	97	D4
Sutton-at-Hone	Sutt H	38	B3
Sutton Valence	Sutt V	126	A2
Swanley	Swan	37	E1
Swanscombe	Swans	22	C3
Tenterden	Ten	186	B2
Teston	Tes	104	B2
Thurnham	Thu	90	C2
Ticehurst	Tic	187	D3
Tilbury	Tilb	24	C4
Tonbridge	Ton	136	A2
Trottiscliffe	Trot	70	B1
Tudeley	Tud	137	F2
Tunbridge Wells, Royal	T W	167	D4
Ulcombe	Ulc	127	D2
Upchurch	Upc	62	C3
Wadhurst	Wad	178	A1
Walderslade	Wald	74	C4
Wateringbury	Waty	104	A2
Welling	Well	18	B4
Westerham	Whm	95	F2
West Farleigh	W Far	104	C1
West Kingsdown	W Kin	68	A4
West Malling	W Mall	86	B2
West Peckham	W Pec	102	B1
West Thurrock	W Thu	7	E3
West Wickham	W Wick	48	A3
Wilmington	Wilm	37	F4
Wittersham	Witt	197	F4
Woolwich	Woolw	2	C2
Wormshill	Worm	93	E2
Wouldham	Wou	58	C1
Wrotham	Wro	84	B4
Wrotham Heath	Wro H	85	D2
Yadling	Yal	122	A3

Abbey Cres. Belv 4 B3
Abbey Gr. SE2 3 F3
Abbey Rd. Belv 4 A4
Abbey Rd. Bexh 19 D4
Abbey Rd. Grave 25 D2
Abbey Rd. Gree 22 C3
Abbey Rd. Rai (K) 61 E3
Abbey Rd. Roc 44 A2
Abbey Terr. SE2 3 F3
Abbey Wood Rd. SE2 3 F3
Abbeyhill Rd. Sid 18 C1
Abbots Cl. Orp 49 F3
Abbots Field. Grave 41 F3
Abbots Field. Maid 105 E3
Abbotsbury Rd. Brom 48 A2
Abbotswood Cl. Belv 4 A4
Abbott Rd. Bor G 84 A2
Abbotts Cl. Chath 59 E4
Abbotts Cl. Swan 37 E1
Abbott's Wlk. Bexh 3 F2
Aberford Gdns. SE18 2 A1
Abergeldie Rd. SE12 16 B3
Abernethy Rd. SE13 16 A4
Abery St. SE18 3 D3
Abingdon Rd. Maid 105 D3
Abingdon Way. Orp 50 B1
Abinger Cl. Brom 34 A1
Abinger Dr. Wald 74 C3
Acacia Cl. Orp 49 F4
Acacia Rd. Dart 20 C2
Acacia Rd. Gree 22 A3
Acacia Wlk. Swan 36 C2
Acadamy Dr. Chath 61 D3
Academy Pl. SE18 2 A1
Academy Rd. SE18 2 A2
Acer Ave. T W 167 F2
Achilles Rd. Wald 74 C3
Acorn Cl. Chis 34 C4
Acorn Gr. Dit 87 F2
Acorn Pl. Maid 107 D1
Acorn Rd. Gil 61 D4
Acre Cl. Chath 60 A3
Acres Rise. Tic 187 D3
Adam Cl. Cox 123 F4
Adams Cl. Ten 186 B3
Adams Sq. Bexh 19 D4
Adcot Wlk. Orp 50 A1
Adderley Gdns. SE9 34 B4
Addington La. Trot 85 E4
Addington Rd. W Wick 48 A2
Addison Cl. Dit 87 D3
Addison Cl. Orp 49 F4
Addison Gdns. Grays 8 C3
Addison Rd. Brom 48 C4
Addlestead La. E Pec 120 C1
Addlestead Rd. E Pec 121 D1
Adelaide Rd. Chis 34 B4
Adelaide Rd. Gil 60 C4
Adelaide The. Higham 26 C1
Adisham Dr. Maid 88 B2
Admaston Rd. SE18 2 C2
Admers Wood. Meo 70 B2
Admiral Moore Dr. Dit 88 A3
Admiral Seymour Rd. SE9 17 D4
Admirals Wlk. Ben 183 F3
Admiral's Wlk. Chath 45 D2
Admirals Wlk. Ten 186 C3
Admirals Wlk. Wald 74 B4
Admiralty Rd. Roc 45 D3
Admiralty Terr. Gil 45 E2
Admiralty Terr. Roc 45 D3
Afghan Rd. Chath 60 A4
Agaton Path. SE9 17 F1
Agaton Rd. SE9 17 F1
Ainsdale Cl. Orp 49 F3
Aintree Cl. Grave 24 B1
Aintree Rd. Wald 74 C4
Airedale Cl. Dart 21 F2
Airey Neave Ct. Grays 8 B4
Aislibie Rd. SE12 16 A4
Ajax Rd. Chath 59 F2
Akehurst La. Sev 98 C3
Alabama St. SE18 3 D2
Alamein Ave. Chath 60 A2
Alamein Gdns. Dart 21 F2
Alamein Rd. Swans 2 C3
Alan Cl. Dart 20 C4
Alanbrooke. Grave 24 C2
Alanthus Cl. SE12 16 A3
Alban Cres. Farn 53 E3
Albany Cl. Bex 18 C2
Albany Cl. Ton 136 C2
Albany Hill. T W 153 F1
Albany Rd. Belv 4 A2
Albany Rd. Bex 18 C2
Albany Rd. Chath 60 B3
Albany Rd. Chath 59 F4
Alany Rd. Chis 34 B4
Albany Rd. Gil 60 C4
Albany St. Maid 89 E1
Albany Terr. Chath 60 A4
Albatross Ave. Roc 43 F1
Albatross St. SE18 3 D2
Albemarle Cl. Grays 8 B4
Albermarle Rd. Wald 74 C3
Albert Cl. Grays 8 C4
Albert Pl. Roc 44 B2
Albert Rd. Belv 4 A3
Albert Rd. Bex 19 E2
Albert Rd. Brom 49 D4
Albert Rd. Chath 60 B4
Albert Rd. Chath 59 F4
Albert Rd. Dart 20 C1
Albert Rd. E16 2 B4
Albert Rd. Gil 60 C4
Albert Rd. Orp 50 B1
Albert Rd. Orp 50 B4
Albert Rd. SE9 17 D1
Albert Rd. Swans 23 D3
Albert Rd.Ton 136 B3
Albert St. Maid 89 D1
Albert St. T W 167 E4
Albert Wlk. E16 2 B4
Alberta Rd. Eri 4 C1
Albion Par. Grave 24 C3
Albion Pl. Maid 106 B4
Albion Pl. Roc 45 E4
Albion Rd. Bexh 19 E4
Albion Rd. Grave 24 C2
Albion Rd. Mard 141 F1
Albion Rd. T W 153 F1
Albion Rd. Wald 74 B3
Albion Terr. Grave 24 C3
Albion Way. Ede 131 F4
Albury Ave. Bexh 4 A1
Albury Cl. Wald 74 C3
Albyfield. Brom 34 A1
Aldeburgh St. SE10 1 B3
Alder Cl. Soub 153 F3
Alder Rd. Sid 18 A1
Alder Way. Swan 36 C2
Aldermary Rd. Brom 33 E2
Alderney Rd. Eri 5 E2
Alders Meadow. Ton 136 A3
Alders Rd. Five O G 155 E4
Alders Rd. Tud 138 A1
Alders The. Merew 102 C2
Aldersgrove Ave. SE9 16 C1
Aldershot Rd. Chath 60 B2
Alderwood Rd. SE9 17 F3
Aldington La. Thu 90 C2
Aldington Rd. Rose 107 D4
Aldington Rd. SE18 1 C4
Aldon Cl. Maid 89 F1
Aldwick Cl. SE9 17 F1
Alen Sq. Stapt 160 A4
Alers Rd. Bexh 18 C3
Alexander Cl. Brom 48 B3
Alexander Cl. Sid 18 A3
Alexander Ct. SE3 1 B1
Alexander Rd. Bexh 3 F1
Alexander Rd. Chis 34 B4
Alexander Rd. Gree 22 C3
Alexandra Ave. Gil 61 D4
Alexandra Cl. Swan 37 D2
Alexandra Cres. Brom 33 D3
Alexandra Rd. Chath 60 B3
Alexandra Rd. Eri 5 D2
Alexandra Rd. Grave 25 D2
Alexandra Rd. Ton 136 B2
Alexandra St. Maid 89 D2
Alfan La. Sid 36 C4
Alford Rd. Eri 4 C3
Alfred Cl. Chath 60 B3
Alfred Pl. Grave 24 A2
Alfred Rd. Belv 4 A3
Alfred Rd. Grave 24 B1
Alfred Rd. Sutt H 38 A4
Alfred St. Grays 8 C2
Alkerden La. Gree 22 C3
Alkerden La. Swans 22 C3
Alkham Rd. Maid 89 F1
All Saints Cl. Swans 23 D3
All Saints Dr. SE3 1 A1
All Saints Rd. All 13 F2
All Saints' Rd. Grave 24 A2
All Saints Rd. Hawkt 189 E3
All Saints Rd. T W 153 E1
All Saints Rise. T W 153 E1
Allan Cl. T W 166 C4
Allandale Pl. Orp 50 C2
Allandale Rd. T W 153 F2
Allard Cl. Orp 50 C3
Allen Cl. Wald 60 C1
Allen St. Maid 89 E1
Allenby Cres. Grays 8 C3
Allenby Rd. Bigg 78 A3
Allendale Cl. Dart 21 F2
Allens La. Plax 101 E2
Allenswood Rd. SE9 2 A1
Allhallows-on-Sea Estate. All 14 A3
Alliance Rd. SE18 3 E2
Alliance Way. Padd W 139 D1
Allington Cl. Grave 25 D2
Allington Dr. Roc 44 A2
Allington Dr. Ton 119 E1
Allington Gdns. Waty 104 A2
Allington Rd. Orp 50 A3
Allington Rd. Padd W 139 D2
Allington Rd. Rai (K) 61 E4
Allington Way. Maid 88 B1
Allison Ave. Chath 61 D3
Alma Pl. Roc 44 B2
Alma Rd. Ayld 73 D1
Alma Rd. Orp 50 C2
Alma Rd. Sid 18 B1
Alma Rd. Swans 23 D3
Alma Rd. W Mal 86 B2
Almon Pl. Chath 44 C1
Almond Cl. Brom 49 E3
Almond Dr. Swan 36 C2
Almond Gr. Rai (K) 75 E4
Almond Rd. Dart 21 F2
Almond Way. Brom 49 E3
Almonds The. Rose 107 E4
Alnwick Rd. SE12 16 B2
Alpine Copse. Brom 34 B2
Alsike Rd. Belv 4 A4
Altash Way. SE9 17 E1
Alton Cl. Bex 19 D2
Alverstone Gdns. SE9 17 F2
Alwold Cres. SE12 16 B3
Amanda Cl. Wald 74 A4
Amber La. Chart S 125 E3
Amberleaze Dr. Pem 154 C1
Amberley Ct. Sid 35 F4
Amberley Rd. SE2 3 F2
Amblecote Cl. SE12 16 B1
Amblecote Rd. SE12 16 B1
Ambleside Rd. Bexh 4 B1
Ambley Rd. Rai (K) 61 E3
Ambrook Rd. Belv 4 B4
Ambrose Cl. Orp 50 A2
Ambrose Hill. Chath 60 C3
Ames Ave. Rose 107 E4
Ames Rd. Swans 23 D3
Amesbury Rd. Brom 33 F1
Amethyst Ave. Wald 60 A1
Amherst Bank Rd. Tud 138 A1
Amherst Cl. Maid 105 F4
Amherst Cl. Orp 35 E1
Amherst Dr. Orp 35 E1
Amherst Hill. Chath 45 E1
Amherst Hill. Sev 98 A4
Amherst Rd. Chath 59 F4
Amherst Rd. Sev 81 E1
Amherst Rd. T W 153 E1
Amherst Redoubt. Gil 45 E1
Amhurst Bank Rd. Pem 155 D4
Ampleforth Rd. SE2 3 F4
Amsbury Rd. Cox 123 E3
Ancaster St. SE18 3 D2
Anchor and Hope La. SE7 1 C3
Anchor Bvd. Dart 21 F4
Anchor Rd. Chath 59 F3
Anchorage Clo. Low St 30 C4
Ancona Rd. SE18 2 C3
Anderson Way. Belv 4 B4
Andover Rd. Orp 50 A3
Andover Wlk. Maid 107 D1
Andrew Cl. Dart 19 F3
Andrew Rd. Soub 153 F2
Andrews Cl. Orp 35 F1
Andrews Cl. T W 153 F1
Andwell Cl. SE2 3 E4
Anerley Cl. Maid 88 C2
Angel La. Ton 136 B3
Angel Wlk. Ton 136 B3
Angerstein La. SE3 1 A1
Angle Rd. Grays 7 F2
Anglesea Ave. SE18 2 B3
Anglesea Centre. Grave 24 B3
Anglesea Pl. Grave 24 B3
Anglesea Rd. Orp 50 C4
Anglesea Rd. SE18 2 B3
Anglesey Ave. Maid 106 B2
Anglesey Cl. Chath 60 B2
Angley Ct. Hors 157 E1
Angley Rd. Cran 173 F1
Angley Wlk. Cran 173 F1
Ankerdine Cres. SE18 2 B1
Ann St. SE18 2 C3
Annandale Rd. Sid 18 A2
Anne of Cleves Rd. Dart 20 C3
Annesley Rd. SE3 1 B1
Annie Rd. Snod 72 A1
Ansell Ave. Chath 60 B3
Anson Cl. Chath 60 C1
Anstridge Path. SE9 17 F3
Anstridge Rd. SE9 17 F3
Antelope Rd. SE18 2 A4
Anthony Cl. Dunt 81 D2
Anthony Rd. Well 3 E1
Anthonys La. Hex 37 E2
Anthonys Way. Roc 44 C3
Aperfield Rd. Bigg 78 A3
Aperfield Rd. Eri 5 D2
Apollo Ave. Brom 33 E2
Apollo Way. SE18 2 C4
Apple Cl. Snod 72 B1
Apple Tree Cl. Maid 105 D3
Apple Tree La.T W 153 F2
Appleby Cl. Chath 59 F2
Appledore Ave. Bexh 4 C1
Appledore Cl. Brom 48 B4
Appledore Cres. Sid 18 A1
Appledore Rd. Rai (K) 61 E4
Appledore Rd. Ten 186 C2
Appleshaw Cl. Grave 41 E4
Appleton Rd. SE9 17 D4
Appletons. Had 120 A2
Appold St. Eri 5 D2
Approach The. Orp 50 A2
April Cl. Orp 50 A1
Apsledene. Grave 41 F3
Apsley St. T W 166 C4
Aragon Cl. Brom 49 D3
Arbroath Rd. SE9 17 D4
Arbrook Cl. Orp 35 E1
Arbuthnot La. Bex 19 D3
Arcadia Rd. Ist 41 D2
Arcadian Ave. Bex 19 D3
Arcadian Cl. Bex 19 D3
Arcadian Rd. Bex 19 D3
Archer Rd. Orp 50 B4
Archer Rd. Wald 60 B1
Archer Way. Swan 37 E2
Archery Cl. Cli W 27 E2
Archery Rd. SE9 17 D3
Arcus Rd. Brom 33 D3
Arden St. Gil 45 F1
Ardenlee Dr. Maid 89 E1
Ardgowan Rd. SE6 16 A2
Arethusa Rd. Chath 59 F2
Argent St. Grays 8 B2
Argyle Cl. Chath 60 A2
Argyle Rd. Sev 98 B3
Argyle Rd. Soub 153 E3
Argyll Rd. Grays 8 B3
Ariel Cl. Grave 42 A4
Arlington Cl. Sid 18 A2
Armoury Dr. Grave 24 C2
Armstrong Cl. Hals 80 B4
Armstrong Rd. Maid 106 B3
Armytage Cl. Hoo S W 46 A4
Arndale Centre The. Dart 21 D3
Arne Cl. Ton 119 D1
Arne Gr. Orp 50 A2
Arne Wlk. SE3 16 A4
Arnhem Dr. Chath 60 A2
Arnold Ave. Meo 56 B2
Arnold Rd. Grave 24 C1
Arnolds La. Sutt H 38 B3
Arnside Rd. Bexh 4 B1
Arran Cl. Eri 4 C2
Arran Green. Roc 43 F2
Arran Rd. Maid 106 B1
Arsenal Rd. SE9 17 D4
Artemis Cl. Grave 25 D2
Arterial Road North Stifford. Grays 7 F4
Arterial Road Purfleet. Pur 6 C3
Arterial Road West Thurrock. Grays 7 E4
Arthur Gr. SE18 2 C3
Arthur Rd. Chath 59 F4
Arthur Rd. Rai (K) 62 A2
Arthur Ruxley Estate. Sid 35 F3
Arthur St. Eri 5 D2
Arthur St. Grave 24 B2
Arthur St. Grays 8 C2
Arthur St W. Grave 24 B2
Artillery Pl. SE18 2 B3
Artillery Row. Grave 24 C2
Artington Cl. Orp 49 F1
Arundel Cl. Bex 19 D3
Arundel Cl. Wald 74 C3
Arundel Dr. Orp 50 B1
Arundel Rd. T W 167 E3
Arundel St. Maid 89 E2
Ascot Cl. Bor G 84 B2
Ascot Cl. Wald 74 C3
Ascot Rd. Grave 24 B1
Ascot Rd. Orp 35 D1
Ash Cl. Chath 60 C3
Ash Cl. Dit 88 A3
Ash Cl. Orp 49 F4
Ash Cl. Sid 18 B1
Ash Cl. Swan 36 C2
Ash Cres. Higham 43 F4
Ash Gr. Maid 88 C1
Ash Keys. Meo 70 B2
Ash Platt Rd. Sev 82 A1
Ash Rd. Dart 20 C2
Ash Rd. Grave 41 F4
Ash Rd. Hart (S) 55 D3
Ash Rd. N Ash 54 C1
Ash Rd. Orp 64 A4
Ash Rd. Roc 44 A1
Ash Rd. Sutt H 38 A4
Ash Rd. Whm 96 A3
Ash Row. Brom 49 E4
Ash Tree Cl. W Kin 21 F1
Ash Tree Dr. W Kin 21 F1
Ash Tree La. Chath 60 C3
Ashbee Cl. Snod 72 B2
Ashbourne Ave. Bexh 4 A2
Ashbourne Rise. Orp 50 A1
Ashburnham Rd. Belv 4 C3
Ashburnham Rd. Maid 89 E2
Ashburnham Rd. Ton 136 C4
Ashby Cl. Hall 72 B4
Ashcombe Dr. Ede 131 E4
Ashcroft Ave. Sid 18 B3
Ashcroft Cres. Sid 18 B3
Ashcroft Rd. Padd W 139 E1
Ashdale Rd. SE12 16 B2
Ashden Wlk. Ton 118 C2
Ashdown Cl. Maid 105 F4
Ashdown Cl. T W 167 D4
Ashdown Rd. Len 111 D4
Ashen Dr. Dart 20 B3
Ashen Grove Rd. W Kin 67 E3
Ashenden Cl. Roc 44 C3
Ashenden Wlk. T W 154 A2
Asher Reeds. Spel 166 B4
Ashes La. Had 119 E2
Ashfield La. Chis 34 C3
Ashford Dr. Broom (m) 126 C4
Ashford Rd. Broom (m) 109 E1
Ashford Rd. Char 130 C2
Ashford Rd. H Hald 177 E1
Ashford Rd. Harr 110 B1
Ashford Rd. Lee 108 B3
Ashford Rd. Len 129 E4
Ashford Rd. Maid 106 C4
Ashford Rd. Rose 107 E4
Ashford Rd. Ten 186 B3
Ashgrove Rd. Sev 98 B2
Ashlar Pl. SE18 2 B3
Ashleigh Cl. Meo 70 B3
Ashleigh Gdns. Head 144 C1
Ashley Cl. Sev 98 B4
Ashley Gdns. Orp 50 A1
Ashley Gdns. T W 152 C1
Ashley Park. T W 152 C1
Ashley Park Cl. T W 152 C1
Ashley Rd. Rai (K) 61 F3
Ashley Rd. Sev 98 B4
Ashley Rd. Ton 136 A4
Ashmead Cl. Wald 74 C4
Ashmore Gr. Well 18 A4
Ashridge Cres. SE18 2 C2
Ashurst Cl. Dart 20 A4
Ashurst Hill. Asht 164 C3
Ashurst Rd. Maid 89 F1
Ashurst Rd. Spel 65 D4
Ashwater Rd. SE12 16 B2
Ashwood Cl. Cli W 27 F2
Askern Cl. Bexh 18 C4
Askew Farm La. Grays 8 A3
Aspdin Rd. Grave 24 A1
Aspen Cl. Orp 50 B1
Aspen Cl. Swan 36 C2
Aspen Copse. Brom 34 A2
Aspen Green. Belv 4 A4
Aspen Way. Soub 153 F3
Aspen Way. Wald 74 A4
Aspian Dr. Cox 123 F4
Asquith Rd. Rai (K) 61 F1
Association Wlk. Chath 59 F2
Aster Rd. Hoo S W 46 A4
Astley St. Maid 106 B4
Aston Cl. Sid 18 B1
Aston Cl. Wald 74 B3
Astor Rd. W Kin 68 A4
Astra Dr. Grave 42 A4
Athelstan Green. Lee 108 C3
Athelstan Rd. Chath 60 A3
Athol Rd. Eri 4 C3
Atkinson Cl. Orp 50 B1
Atlas Gdns. SE7 1 C3
Attlee Ct. Grays 8 B4
Attlee Dr. Dart 21 E3
Attwaters La. Hawkt 182 B1
Atwater Ct. Len 110 C1
Auckland Rd. T W 153 F1
Auden Rd. Dit 87 E4
Audley Ave. Chath 61 D3
Audley Ave. Ton 136 A3
Audley Rise. Ton 136 A3
Augustine Rd. Grave 24 C2
Augustine Rd. Orp 35 F1
Austen Cl. Gree 22 C3
Austen Gdns. Dart 21 D4
Austen Way. Dit 87 D4
Austens Orchard. Ten 186 B2
Austin Ave. Brom 49 D4
Austin Cl. Chath 61 D3
Austin Rd. Grave 24 A2
Austin Rd. Orp 50 B4
Austral Cl. Sid 18 A1
Autumn Glade. Bredh 74 C2
Avalon Cl. Orp 50 C2
Avalon Rd. Orp 50 C2
Avard Gdns. Orp 49 F1
Avebury Ave. Ton 136 B3
Avebury Rd. Orp 49 F2
Aveling Cl. Hoo S W 28 C1
Avenue Rd. Belv 4 C3
Avenue Rd. Bexh 19 D4
Avenue Rd. Eri 4 C2
Avenue Rd. Lim 78 A2
Avenue Rd. Sev 98 C4
Avenue The. Bex 18 C2
Avenue The. Bor G 84 B2
Avenue The. Brom 48 C2
Avenue The. Brom 33 F1
Avenue The. Dit 88 A3
Avenue The. Grave 24 B2
Avenue The. Grays 22 B4
Avenue The. Orp 50 A2
Avenue The. Orp 35 E3
Avenue The. Ton 136 B3
Avenue The. Whm 95 E4
Avenue The. W Wick 48 A3
Averenches Rd. Thu 90 A1
Avery Cl. All 14 A3
Avery Cl. Maid 106 A3
Avery Hill Rd. SE9 17 F2
Avery La. Lan H 107 F1
Avery La. Lee 108 A1
Avery Way. All 13 F2
Aviemore Gdns. Rose 107 D4
Avington Cl. Maid 106 A3
Avocet Mews. SE28 2 C4
Avocet Wlk. Wald 74 C3
Avon C. Grave 24 C1
Avon Cl. Ton 118 C1
Avon St. T W 153 F1
Avondale Rd. Brom 33 D3
Avondale Rd. Gil 45 F1
Avondale Rd. SE9 17 D1
Avondale Rd. Well 3 F1
Awliscombe Rd. Well 3 D1
Axminster Cres. Well 3 F1
Axtaine Rd. Orp 50 C3
Axtane. Souf 40 A3
Axtane Cl. Sutt H 38 C2
Aycliffe Cl. Brom 34 A1
Ayelands. N Ash 55 D2
Ayelands La. N Ash 55 D2
Aylesbury Rd. Brom 33 E1
Aylesford Cres. Rai (K) 61 E4
Aylesham Rd. Orp 50 A3
Aynscombe Angle. Orp 50 B3
Azalea Dr. Swan 37 D1

Babbacombe Rd. Brom 33 E2
Babb's La. Ben 183 E1
Babylon La. Chart S 143 F3
Babylon La. Sutt V 143 F3
Back La. Bex 19 E2
Back La. Bou Mon 125 D3
Back La. Gou 172 A2
Back La. Grays 7 E4
Back La. Hors 157 E1
Back La. Ight 100 C4
Back La. Seal 99 E3
Back La. Sev 97 F3
Back La. Ship 118 C4
Back La. Sund 97 F3
Back Rd. Sand 190 B1
Back Rd. Sid 35 E4
Back St. Lee 108 A1
Backfields. Chath 59 E4
Baden Powell Rd. Sev 81 D1
Baden Rd. Gil 45 F2
Bader Cres. Chath 60 B2
Bader Wlk. Grave 24 A1
Badger Rd. Bredh 74 C3
Badger Rd. Wald 74 C3
Badgers Copse. Orp 50 A2
Badgers Croft. SE9 17 E1
Badgers Rd. Shorm 65 E3
Badlow Cl. Eri 5 D2

Badsell Rd. Five O G 138 C2
Badsell Rd. Padd W 139 D1
Bailey Dr. Rai (K) 61 E3
Baizdon Rd. SE3 1 A1
Baker Hill Cl. Grave 41 D4
Baker La. Head 145 E2
Baker La. Sutt V 126 A2
Baker Rd. SE18 2 A1
Baker St. Burh 73 D3
Baker St. Chath 59 F4
Bakers Ave. W Kin 68 A4
Bakers Cross. Cran 183 D4
Baker's Wlk. Chath 44 C1
Bakery Cl. Frit 161 D2
Balaclava La. Wad 178 B1
Balcaskie Rd. SE9 17 D3
Balchen Rd. SE3 1 C1
Balcombes Hill. Gou 172 A2
Balder Rise. SE12 16 B1
Bldwyn's Park. Bex 19 F1
Baldwyn's Rd. Bex 19 F2
Balfour Rd. Brom 48 C4
Balfour Rd. Chath 60 A3
Balfour Rd. Grays 8 C3
Balgowan St. SE18 3 D3
Ballamore Rd. Brom 16 B1
Ballard Business Park. Roc 44 A1
Ballard Cl. Mard 141 F1
Ballard Way. Padd W 139 E2
Ballens Rd. Wald 74 C4
Balliol Rd. Well 3 E1
Balmer Cl. Rai (K) 61 F2
Balmoral Gdns. Bex 19 D2
Balmoral Rd. Gil 45 F1
Balmoral Rd. Sutt H 38 B3
Baltic Rd. Ton 136 B2
Baltimore Pl. Well 3 D1
Banbury Villas. Souf 40 A3
Banchory Rd. SE3 1 B2
Banckside. Hart (S) 40 A1
Bancroft Gdns. Orp 50 A3
Bancroft Rd. Wro 84 A4
Bangor Rd. Roc 43 F1
Bank Ct. Dart 21 D3
Bank La. Hild 117 E4
Bank La. Seal 117 E4
Bank St. Chath 60 B4
Bank St. Cran 173 F1
Bank St. Grave 24 B3
Bank St. Maid 106 A4
Bank St. Sev 98 C3
Bank St. Ton 136 C3
Bankfield Way. Gou 172 A2
Bankfields. Head 144 C1
Bankfoot. Grays 8 B3
Bankfoot Rd. Brom 33 D4
Banks La. Bexh 19 D4
Banks Rd. Roc 44 C2
Bankside. Chath 60 B2
Bankside. Grave 23 F3
Bankside. Wad 178 A1
Bankside Cl. Sid 36 C4
Bankwell Rd. SE13 16 A4
Banky Fields Cl. Rai (K) 62 B3
Banky Meadow. Maid 105 D4
Banner Farm Rd. T W 167 E3
Banning St. Roc 44 B2
Bannister Gdns. Orp 35 F1
Bannister Rd. Maid 89 E2
Bannockburn Rd. SE18 3 D3
Banwell Rd. Bex 18 C3
Bapchild Pl. Orp 35 F1
Barberry Ave. Wald 60 A1
Barchester Way. Ton 119 D1
Barclay Ave. Ton 119 E1
Barclay Way. Grays 7 D3
Bardell Terr. Chath 44 C1
Barden Park Rd. Ton 136 B3
Barden Rd. Bid 152 A3
Barden Rd. Ton 136 B3
Barden St. SE18 3 D2
Bardsley Cl. E Pec 121 E2
Barfield. Sutt H 38 B2
Barfield Rd. Brom 34 B1
Barfreston Cl. Maid 106 A3
Bargate Cl. SE8 3 D3
Barge House Rd. E16 2 B4
Bargrove Rd. Maid 89 F1
Barham Cl. Brom 49 D3
Barham Cl. Chis 34 B4
Barham Cl. Maid 107 D1
Barham Rd. Chis 34 B4
Barham Rd. Dart 21 E2
Barham's Mill Rd. Ege 146 B3
Baring Cl. SE12 16 B1
Baring Rd. SE12 16 B1
Bark Hart Rd. Orp 50 B3
Barker Rd. Maid 106 A4
Barkis Cl. Chath 59 F2
Barley Corn. Birl 87 D3
Barleycorn Dr. Rai (K) 62 A1
Barleyfields. Thu 106 C4
Barleymow Cl. Chath 60 C2
Barling Cl. Burh 73 F3
Barlow Cl. Rai (K) 62 A1
Barming Rd. Tes 104 A3
Barn End Dr. Dart 20 C1
Barn End La. Dart 37 F4
Barn Hill. Hunt 123 D3
Barn Meadow. Hall 72 A4
Barnaby Terr. Chath 59 F3
Barnard Cl. Chis 34 C2
Barnard Cl. SE18 2 B4
Barncroft Dr. Rai (K) 75 D4
Barned Ct. Maid 105 D3
Barnehurst Ave. Bexh 4 C1
Barnehurst Ave. Eri 4 C1
Barnehurst Cl. Eri 4 C1
Barnehurst Rd. Bexh 4 C1
Barnes Cray Rd. Dart 20 B4
Barnes La. Lint 123 F2
Barnesdale Cres. Orp 50 B4
Barnet Dr. Brom 49 D2
Barnet Wood Rd. Brom 48 C2
Barnett Cl. Eri 5 D1
Barnetts Rd. Lei 135 E3
Barnetts Way. Soub 153 F2
Barney Cl. SE7 1 C3
Barnfield. Chath 60 B2
Barnfield. T W 167 D2
Barnfield. Ten 186 C3
Barnfield Cl. Lon 40 C1
Barnfield Cl. Swan 51 F3
Barnfield Cres. Kemsg 82 A3
Barnfield Gdns. SE18 2 B2
Barnfield Rd. Belv 4 A2
Barnfield Rd. Orp 35 F1
Barnfield Rd. SE18 2 B2
Barnfield Rd. Sev 98 A4
Barnhill Ave. Brom 48 A4
Barnhurst Rd. Maid 89 E2
Barnsole Rd. Gil 61 D4
Barnwood Cl. Chath 59 E2
Baron Cl. Gil 46 A2
Baron Cl. Thu 90 A1
Barr Rd. Grave 25 D1
Barrack Rd. Gil 45 E2
Barrack Row. Grave 24 B3
Barrel Arch Cl. Mard 141 F1
Barretts Rd. Dunt 81 D2
Barretts Rd. Hawkt 189 E3
Barrie Dr. Dit 87 D4
Barrier Rd. Chath 45 D1
Barrington Cl. Wald 60 A1
Barrington Rd. Bexh 3 F1
Barrington Villas. SE18 2 B1
Barrow La. Spel 166 A3
Barry Ave. Bexh 4 A2
Barry Cl. Orp 50 A2
Barth Rd. SE18 3 D3
Bartholdmew Way. Swan 37 D1
Bartlett Cl. Wald 74 C3
Bartlett Rd. Grave 24 B2
Bartlett Rd. Whm 95 F3
Barton C. Bexh 19 D3
Barton Rd. Maid 106 B3
Barton Rd. Roc 44 B2
Barton Rd. Sid 36 A3
Barton Rd. Sutt H 38 B2
Bashford Barn La. Bredg 93 E4
Basi Cl. Roc 44 C3
Basildon Rd. SE2 3 E3
Basilon Rd. Bexh 4 A1
Basing Cl. Maid 106 B4
Basing Dr. Bex 19 D3
Basinghall St. T W 167 E4
Basket Gdns. SE9 17 D3
Basmere Cl. Maid 89 F1
Bassant Rd. SE18 3 D2
Bassetts Cl. Orp 49 E1
Bassetts Way. Orp 49 E1
Basted La. Bor G 101 E4
Bastion Rd. SE2 3 E3
Baston Rd. Brom 48 B2
Batchelor St. Chath 60 B4
Batchelors. Pem 155 D2
Batchwood Green. Orp 35 E1
Bates Cl. Dit 87 E4
Bates Hill. Ight 83 F1
Bateson St. SE18 3 D3
Bath Hard. Chath 44 C1
Bath d. Dart 20 B2
Bath St. Grave 24 B3
Baths Rd. Brom 33 F1
Bathurst Cl. Stapt 160 A4
Bathurst Rd. Stapt 160 A4
Bathway. SE18 2 B3
Battersby Rd. SE6 16 A1
Battle La. Mard 142 B2
Battle Rd. Belv 4 C3
Battle Rd. Eri 4 C3
Battle St. Cob 42 A1
Battlefields Rd. Wro 84 B4
Battlesmere Rd. Cli W 27 E2
Batt's Rd. Cob 57 E4
Baudwin Rd. SE6 16 A1
Baugh Rd. Sid 35 F4
Bay Cl. Hoo S W 46 A4
Bay Manor La. Grays 7 D2
Bay Tree Cl. Brom 33 F2
Bayfield Rd. SE9 16 C4
Bayhall Rd. T W 167 F4
Bayham Rd. Sev 98 C4
Bayham Rd. T W 167 E2
Bayley Wlk. SE2 4 A3
Bayley's Hill. Sev W 116 A4
Bayly Rd. Dart 21 E3
Bayswater Dr. Rai (K) 76 A4
Bawell. Dit 87 D3
Bazes Shaw. N Ash 55 D2
Beacham Cl. SE7 1 C2
Beachy Path. Ten 186 B2
Beacon Cl. Rai (K) 61 F2
Beacon Dr. Dart 22 C1
Beacon Hill. Chath 60 C3
Beacon Hill. Pur 6 B3
Beacon Hill La. Hoo S W 45 D4
Beacon Oak Rd. Ten 186 B2
Beacon Rd. Chath 60 C3
Beacon Rd. Eri 5 E2
Beacon Rd. Len 110 C1
Beacon Rise. Sev 98 B3
Beacon Wlk. Ten 186 B3
Beaconfields. Sev 98 B3
Beacons The. Cox 123 F3
Beaconsfield Ave. Gil 46 A1
Beaconsfield Cl. SE3 1 B2
Beaconsfield Rd. Bex 20 A1
Beaconsfield Rd. Brom 33 F1
Beaconsfield Rd. Chath 60 A4
Beaconsfield Rd. Maid 106 A3
Beaconsfield Rd. SE3 1 B2
Beaconsfield Rd. SE9 34 A4
Beadon Rd. Brom 48 B4
Beagles Cl. Orp 50 C2
Beagles Wood Rd. Pem 155 D2
Beal Cl. Well 3 E1
Beales La. Norm 195 E1
Beamish Rd. Orp 50 C3
Beams The. Maid 107 D3
Bean La. Dart 22 B1
Bean Rd. Bexh 18 C4
Bean Rd. Gree 22 B2
Beanshaw. SE9 34 B4
Bearsted Cl. Rai (K) 61 E4
Bearsted Rd. Thu 90 A1
Beatrice Gdns. Grave 24 A1
Beatty Ave. Gil 61 D4
Beatty Rd. Chath 59 F2
Beaufighter Rd. Merew 103 D4
Beaufort Rd. Roc 44 A2
Beaufort Wlk. Maid 125 D4
Beaulieu Rd. Ton 136 B4
Beaulieu Rise. Chath 59 F3
Beaulieu Wlk. Maid 88 C2
Beaumanor Gdns. SE9 34 B4
Beaumont Dr. Grave 24 A2
Beaumont Rd. Maid 105 E3
Beaumont Rd. Orp 49 F4
Beauworth Park. Maid 107 D2
Beaverbank Rd. SE9 17 F2
Beaverwood Rd. Chis 35 D3
Bebbington Rd. SE18 3 D3
Beblets Cl. Orp 50 A1
Beckenham Dr. Maid 88 C2
Beckenham Gr. Brom 33 D2
Beckenham La. Brom 33 D2
Beckett Cl. Belv 4 A4
Becketts Cl. Orp 50 A2
Becketts Field. Pen 151 E4
Beckley Cl. Grave 25 E1
Beckman Cl. Hals 80 C4
Becks Rd. Sid 18 B1
Becksbourne Cl. Maid 89 E2
Becton Pl. Eri 4 C1
Bedale Wlk. Dart 21 E2
Beddington Green. Orp 35 D2
Beddington Rd. Orp 35 D2
Beddow Way. Ayld 88 B3
Bedens Rd. Sid 36 A4
Bedford Ave. Rai (K) 61 F3
Bedford Pl. Maid 106 A4
Bedford Rd. Dart 21 E2
Bedford Rd. Grave 24 A1
Bedford Rd. Grays 8 B3
Bedford Rd. Orp 50 B3
Bedford Rd. Sid 18 A1
Bedford Rd. Soub 153 E3
Bedford Terr. T W 167 E3
Bedgebury Cl. Maid 89 F1
Bedgebury Rd. Gou 172 A2
Bedgebury Rd. SE9 16 C4
Bedivere Rd. Brom 16 B1
Bedlam La. Ege 146 B2
Bedlam La. Sma 146 B2
Bedonwell Rd. Bexh 4 A2
Bedonwell Rd. SE2 4 B2
Bedson Wlk. Rai (K) 62 B3
Bedwell Rd. Belv 4 B3
Bedwin Cl. Chath 59 F2
Beech Ave. Sid 18 B2
Beech Ave. Swan 37 D1
Beech Copse. Brom 34 A2
Beech Dell. Kes 49 D1
Beech Dr. Maid 88 C1
Beech Gr. Higham 43 F4
Beech Gr. S Ock 6 C4
Beech Hurst. Pem 154 C2
Beech La. Mat 169 F4
Beech Mast. Meo 70 B2
Beech Rd. Dart 20 C2
Beech Rd. Dit 87 D2
Beech Rd. Hoo S W 46 A4
Beech Rd. Mard 158 A4
Beech Rd. Merew 102 C3
Beech Rd. Orp 64 B4
Beech Rd. Roc 44 A1
Beech Rd. Sev 98 B3
Beech St. T W 153 E1
Beech Wlk. Dart 20 B4
Beecham Rd. Ton 119 D1
Beechcroft. Chis 34 B3
Beechcroft Ave. Bexh 4 C1
Beechcroft Cl. Orp 49 F1
Beechcroft Rd. Orp 49 F1
Beechen Bank Rd. Wald 74 B3
Beechenlea La. Hex 37 E1
Beechenlea La. Swan 37 E1
Beeches Ct. Brom 33 E3
Beeches The. Cob 41 F1
Beeches The. Dit 88 A3
Beeches The. Wald 74 B4
Beechfield Rd. Brom 33 F2
Beechfield Rd. Eri 5 D2
Beechhill Rd. SE9 17 E3
Beechin Wood La. Bor G 84 C1
Beeching Rd. Wald 74 B4
Beechings Green. Rai (K) 61 F4
Beechings Way. Rai (K) 61 F4
Beechlands Cl. Hart (S) 55 E4
Beechmont Cl. Brom 33 D4
Beechmont Rd. Sev 98 B1
Beechmont Rise. Ton 118 B1
Beechmore Dr. Wald 74 B3
Beechway. Bex 18 C3
Beechwood Ave. Chath 60 C3
Beechwood Ave. Orp 64 A4
Beechwood Cres. Bexh 19 D4
Beechwood Dr. Kes 48 C1
Beechwood Dr. Meo 70 B3
Beechwood Gdns. Meo 70 B3
Beechwood Mews. T W 168 A4
Beechwood Rd. Maid 105 D4
Beechwood Rise. Chis 34 B4
Beechy Lees Rd. Kemsg 82 B4
Beeken Dene. Orp 49 F1
Beesfield La. Farn 53 E3
Begbie Rd. SE3 1 C1
Beggars La. Whm 96 A4
Begonia Ave. Rai (K) 61 F3
Beke Rd. Rai (K) 75 F4
Belcroft Cl. Brom 33 D3
Beldam Haw. Hals 65 E2
Belfield Rd. Pem 154 C1
Belford Gr. SE18 2 B3
Belgrave Cl. Orp 35 F1
Belgrave Rd. T W 167 E4
Belgrave St. Ayld 73 D1
Belgravia Gdns. Brom 33 D3
Belgrove. T W 167 E3
Bell Cl. Gree 22 A3
Bell Cres. Burh 73 D2
Bell Gdns. Orp 50 C4
Bell La. Bredh 74 B2
Bell La. Burh 73 D2
Bell La. Dit 87 E3
Bell La. Rose 90 B1
Bell La. Sma 162 C2
Bell La. Stapt 160 A4
Bell Rd. Maid 107 D1
Bell Water Gate. SE18 2 B4
Bell Way. Broom (m) 127 D3
Belle Vue Rd. Dow 63 E3
Bellefield Rd. Orp 50 B4
Bellegrove Cl. Well 3 D1
Bellegrove Rd. Well 3 D1
Bellevue Rd. exh 19 D3
Bellgrove Ct. Wald 74 B2
Bellman Ave. Grave 25 D2
Bellmeadow. Maid 107 D1
Bellows La. Bor G 84 A2
Bellring Cl. Belv 4 B2
Bells Farm Rd. E Pec 120 C2
Bell's La. Hoo S W 29 D1
Bells La. Ten 186 B2
Belmont Ave. Well 18 A4
Belmont La. Chis 34 C4
Belmont Park. SE13 16 A4
Belmont Park Cl. SE13 16 A4
Belmont Rd. Chis 34 B4
Belmont Rd. Eri 4 B1
Belmont Rd. Gil 60 C4
Belmont Rd. Grays 8 A2
Belmont Rd. Maid 105 D3
Belmont Rd. Sev 98 C4
Belson Rd. SE18 2 A3
Beltana Dr. Grave 42 A4
Belton Rd. Sid 35 E4
Beltring Rd. E Pec 139 E4
Beltring Rd. T W 153 E1
Beltwood Rd. Belv 4 C3
Belvedere Cl. Grave 24 C2
Belvedere Rd. Bexh 4 A1
Belvedere Rd. Bigg 78 A3
Belvior Cl. SE9 17 D1
Benares Rd. SE18 3 D3
Benden Cl. Stapt 160 A4
Bendmore Ave. SE2 3 E3
Bendon Way. Rai (K) 61 F2
BenedictCl. Belv 4 A4
Benedict Cl. Orp 50 A2
Benenden Green. Brom 48 B4
Benenden Rd. Bidd 176 A1
Benenden Rd. Roc 44 C3
Benenden Rd. Rol 191 F4
Benhall Mill Rd. Bel G 168 A2
Benhall Mill Rd. T W 167 F2
Bennett Cl. Well 3 E1
Bennett Park. SE3 16 A4
Bennett Way. Dart 38 C4
Bennetts Ave. W Kin 68 C2
Bennetts Copse. Chis 34 A3
Bennetts Mews. Ten 186 B2
Benover Rd. Yal 122 A2
Benson Rd. Grays 8 C2
Bensted Cl. Hunt 122 C2
Bentfield Gdns. SE9 16 C1
Bentham Hill. Soub 152 C3
Bentley Cl. Dit 88 A3
Bentley Cl. Lon 40 C2
Bentley Cl. Wald 74 C3
Bentley St. Grave 24 C3
Bentley St Indl Est. Grave 24 C3
Bentley's Meadow. Seal 82 A2
Bentlif Cl. Maid 88 C1
Berber Rd. Roc 44 B2
Bercta Rd. SE9 17 F1
Berengrave La. Rai (K) 62 A3
Berens Rd. Orp 50 C4
Berens Way. Chis 35 D1
Beresford Ave. Chath 60 A3
Beresford Cl. Kiln 180 A3
Beresford Dr. Brom 34 A1
Beresford Hill. Bou Mon 124 B4
Beresford Rd. Ayld 73 F2
Beresford Rd. Gil 60 C4
Beresford Rd. Gou 172 A3
Beresford Rd. Grave 4 A2
Beresford Sq. SE18 2 B3
Beresford St. SE18 2 B4
Berger Cl. Orp 50 A4
Berkeley Ave. Bexh 3 F1
Berkeley Cl. Chath 59 F2
Berkeley Cres. Dart 21 D2
Berkeley Rd. T W 167 E3
Berkely Cl. Orp 50 A3
Berkhampstead Rd. Belv 4 B3
Berkley Cres. Grave 24 C3
Berkley Rd. Grave 24 B3
Berkshire Cl. Chath 60 C2
Bernard St. Grave 24 B3
Berry Rd. Hoo S W 46 A4
Berryfields. Brom 34 A2
Berryhill. SE9 17 E4
Berryhill Gdns. SE9 17 E4
Berrylands. Hart (S) 55 E4
Berrylands. Orp 50 C2
Berry's Green Rd. igg 78 B3
Berry's Hill. Dow 78 C4
Bersham La. Grays 8 A3
Berwick Cres. Sid 18 A3
Berwick Rd. Well 3 E1
Berwick Way. Sev 81 E2
Berwyn Gr. Maid 106 B1
Bessels Green Rd. Sev 97 F4
Bessels Meadow. Sev 97 F4
Bessels Way. Sev 97 F4
Best St. Chath 60 A4
Betenson Ave. Sev 81 D1
Bethel Rd. Sev 98 C4
Bethel Rd. Well 18 C4
Bethersden Rd. Sma 163 E1
Betjeman Cl. Dit 87 D4
Betsham Rd. Eri 5 D2
Betsham Rd. Grave 40 A4
Betsham Rd. Maid 107 D1
Betsham Rd. Swans 23 D2
Betterton Dr. Sid 19 D1
Bettescombe Rd. Rai (K) 62 A2
Beulah Rd. T W 167 F4
Beult Meadow. Sma 163 E3
Beult Rd. Dart 20 B4
Bevan Pl. Swan 37 D1
Bevan Rd. SE2 3 E3
Bevans Cl. Gree 22 C3
Bevercote Wlk. Belv 4 A2
Beverley Ave. Sid 18 A2
Beverley Cl. Rai (K) 62 A2
Beverley Cres. Ton 136 A2
Beverley Rd. Bexh 4 C1
Beverley Rd. Brom 49 D2
Beverley Rd. Maid 105 D3
Bevis Cl. Dart 21 F2
Bewl Bridge Cl. Tic 187 E4
Bewlbridge La. Wad 179 E3
Bewley La. Plax 100 C3
Bexley Cl. Dart 20 A3
Bexley High St. Bex 19 E2
Bexley La. Dart 20 A3
Bexley La. Sid 18 C1
Bexley Rd. Eri 4 C2
Bexley Rd. SE9 17 F3
Bexon La. Bredg 93 F4
Bickley Cres. Brom 34 A1
Bickley Park Rd. Brom 34 A1
Bickley Rd. Brom 34 A2
Bickley Rd. Ton 136 B2
Bicknor La. Bredg 92 C4
Bicknor La. S Grn 92 C4
Bicknor Rd. Maid 107 D1
Bicknor Rd. Orp 50 A3
Bidborough Cl. Brom 48 A4
Bidborough Ridge. Bid 152 C4
Biddenden Cl. Rose 107 D4
Biddenden Rd. H Hald 177 D1
Biddenden Rd. Head 162 A3
Biddenden Rd. Sma 163 D2
Biddenden Way. Ist 41 D3
Biddenden Way. SE9 34 B4
Bideford Rd. Brom 16 A1
Bideford Rd. SE2 3 E2
Big Alley. Ede 131 E1
Bilberry Cl. Thu 90 A1
Bill Hamling Cl. SE9 17 D1
Bill Street Rd. Roc 44 C3
Billet Hill. N Ash 54 C1
Billings Hill Shaw. Hart (S) 55 D4
Bilsby Gr. SE9 33 F4
Bilsington Cl. Wald 60 B1
Bilton Rd. Eri 5 E2
Binbury La. Sto 76 B1
Bines The. Padd W 139 E1
Bingham Rd. Roc 44 C3
Bingley Cl. Snod 72 A2
Bingley Rd. Chath 60 A4
Binland Gr. Wald 59 F1
Binnacle Rd. Chath 59 F2
Binney Rd. All 13 F2
Binsey Wlk. SE2 3 F4
Birbetts Rd. SE9 17 D1
Birch Cl. Eyn 52 C2
Birch Cl. Lon 40 C2
Birch Cl. Mat 155 F3
Birch Cl. Sev 98 B4
Birch Cl. Ton 136 A4
Birch Cl. T W 153 F2
Birch Cres. Dit 87 F2
Birch Dr. Bredh 74 C3
Birch Gr. Rai (K) 61 E1
Birch Gr. SE12 16 A2
Birch Gr. Well 18 B4
Birch Mead. Orp 49 E2
Birch Pl. Gree 22 A3
Birch Rd. Hoo S W 46 A4
Birch Rd. Padd W 139 E1
Birch Row. Brom 49 E3
Birch Tee Ave. W Wick 48 A1
Birch Tree Way. Maid 106 B4
Birch Way. T W 153 F2
Birch Wlk. Eri 4 C2
Birchbeck Rd. Sid 18 B1
Birches The. Orp 49 E1
Birches The. SE7 1 B2
Birches The. Swan 37 D2
Birches The. Ton 136 B2

Broadway. Rai (K) 61 E4
Broadway. Swan 51 F4
Broadway The. Lam 170 B1
Broadwood Rd. Hoo S W 45 E4
Brockenhurst Ave. Maid 106 C3
Brockenhurst Cl. Rai (K) 61 F2
Brockway. Bor G 84 B2
Brockwell Cl. Orp 50 A4
Brodrick Gr. SE2 3 E3
Brogden Cres. Lee 108 A2
Brokes Way. Soub 153 E2
Brome Rd. SE9 17 D4
Bromhedge. SE9 17 D1
Bromley Ave. Brom 33 D3
Bromley Cl. Wald 74 B4
Bromley Comm. Brom 48 C4
Bromley Cres. Brom 33 D1
Bromley Ct.Brom 33 D3
Bromley Gdns. Brom 33 D1
Bromley Hill. Brom 33 D3
Bromley La. Chis 34 C3
Bromley Rd. Brom 33 D2
Bromley Rd. Chis 34 C3
Brompton Dr. Eri 5 E2
Brompton Farm Rd. Roc 44 B3
Brompton Hill. Chath 45 D1
Brompton La. Roc 44 B2
Brompton Rd. Gil 45 E1
Bronholm Rd. SE2 3 E4
Bronington Cl. Wald 60 B1
Bronte Cl. Dit 87 D4
Bronte Gr. Dart 21 D4
Bronte View. Grave 24 C2
Brook. Chath 60 B4
Brook Farm Dr. Dow 64 C3
Brook Hill Cl. SE18 2 B3
Brook La. Bex 18 C3
Brook La. Bexh 18 C3
Brook La. Brom 33 E3
Brook La. Plax 101 E2
Brook La. SE3 1 B1
Brook La. Snod 72 B1
Brook Rd. Dit 87 D4
Brook Rd. Grave 24 A2
Brook Rd. Swan 36 C2
Brook Rd. Tw 153 F2
Brook St. Eri 4 B2
Brook St. Snod 72 B2
Brook St. Ton 136 B2
Brook Vale. Eri 4 B1
Brookbank. Maid 89 E2
Brookdale Rd. Bex 19 D3
Brookdene Rd. SE18 3 D3
Brooke Dr. Grave 25 E2
Brooke Rd. Grays 8 B3
Brookend Rd. Sid 18 A2
Brookfield. Four E 114 B1
Brookfield. Kemsg 82 A3
Brookfield Ave. Dit 87 E4
Brookfields. Had 120 A3
Brookgate La. Hawkt 188 B3
Brookhill Rd. SE18 2 B3
Brookhurst Gdns. Soub 153 D4
Brooklands. Head 144 C1
Brooklands. T W 153 F2
Brooklands Ave. SE9 17 F1
Brooklands Farm Cl. Pen 151 E1
Brooklands Park. SE3 16 B4
Brooklands Rd. Dit 87 E4
Brooklyn Paddock. Gil 45 F1
Brooklyn Rd. Brom 48 C4
Brookmead. Ton 136 A4
Brookmead Ave. Brom 49 D4
Brookmead Cl. Orp 50 B4
Brookmead Rd. Cli W 27 F2
Brookmead Way. Orp 50 B4
Brooks Cl. Stapt 160 A4
Brooks Pl. Maid 106 B4
Brooks Way. Orp 35 F2
Brookside. Cran 182 C4
Brookside. Hoo S W 29 D1
Brookside. Orp 50 A3
Brookside Rd. Ist 41 D3
Brookway. SE3 16 B4
Broom Ave. Orp 35 E2
Broom Cl. Brom 49 D4
Broom Hill Rd. Roc 44 A2
Broom La. Spel 166 A3
Broom Mead. Bexh 19 E3
Broom Park. Spel 166 A4
Broomcroft Rd.Rai (K) 62 A3
Broomfield Rd. Bexh 19 E3
Broomfield Rd. Sev 81 D1
Broomfield Rd. Swans 23 D3
Broomhill Park Rd. Soub 153 D2
Broomhill Rd. Dart 20 B3
Broomhill Rd. Orp 50 B3
Broomhil Rd. T W 152 C2
Broomhill Rise. Bexh 19 E3
Broomhills. Grave 40 A4
Broomlands La. Lim 95 D2
Broomshaw Rd. Maid 105 D4
Broomwood Rd. Orp 35 E2
Broughton Rd. Orp 49 F2
Broughton Rd. Otf 81 E4
Brown Rd. Grave 25 D2
Brown St. Rai (K) 62 A3
Browndens Rd. Hall 72 A4
Brownelow Copse. Wald 74 B3
Brownhill Cl. Wald 74 B4
Browning Cl. Dit 87 D4
Browning Cl. Well 3 D1
Browning Rd. Dart 21 D4
Brownings. Ede 131 F4
Brownspring Dr. SE9 17 F1
Broxbourne Rd. Orp 50 A3
Bruce Cl. Well 3 E1
Bruce Gr. Orp 50 B3
Brucks The. Waty 104 A2
Brummel Cl. Bexh 19 F4
Brunel Cl. Tilb 24 B4
Brungers Wlk. Ton 118 B1
Brunswick Cl. Bexh 18 C4
Brunswick Rd. Bexh 19 D4
Brunswick St. Maid 106 B4
Brunswick St E. Maid 106 B4
Brunswick Terr. T W 167 E3
Brunswick Wlk. Grave 24 C3
Bruton Cl. Chis 34 A3
Bryant Cl. Net 103 F1
Bryant Rd. Roc 44 B2
Bryant St. Chath 60 B4
Bubblestone Rd. Otf 81 E4
Buckden Cl. SE12 16 A3
Buckham Thorns Rd. Whm 95 F3
Buckhurst Ave. Sev 98 C3
Buckhurst La. Sev 98 C3
Buckhurst Rd. Bigg 78 B2
Buckingham Ave. Well 18 A4
Buckingham Cl. Orp 50 A3
Buckingham Dr. Chis 34 B4
Buckingham Rd. Gil 45 F1
Buckingham Rd. Grave 23 F2
Buckingham Rd. T W 167 E3
Buckingham Row. Maid 107 D2
Buckland Cl. Wald 74 B3
Buckland Hill. Maid 89 D1
Buckland La. Maid 88 C1
Buckland Rd. Cli W 27 E2
Buckland Rd. Cob 57 E2
Buckland Rd. Maid 106 A4
Buckland Rd. Orp 50 A1
Bucklers Cl. T W 167 F4
Buckley Cl. Dart 5 D1
Bucks Cross Rd. Grave 24 A1
Bucks Cross Rd. Orp 51 D1
Buckwheat Ct. Belv 3 F4
Budgin's Hill. Dow 64 C2
Budleigh Cres. Well 3 F2
Bugglesden Rd. Ten 177 D1
Bugsby's Way. SE7 1 B3
Bull Alley. Well 18 B4
Bull Fields. Snod 72 B2
Bull Hill. Len 129 E3
Bull La. Ayld 73 D1
Bull La. Chath 44 C1
Bull La. Chis 34 C3
Bull La. Higham 26 C2
Bull La. New(G) 77 D4
Bull La. Sto 77 D4
Bull La. Wro 84 B4
Bull Orch. Maid 105 D3
Bull Rd. Birl 71 F1
Bull Yd. Grave 24 B3
Bullace La. Dart 21 D3
Bullbanks Rd. Belv 4 C3
Bulldog Rd. Wald 74 B3
Bullen La. E Pec 121 D2
Buller Rd. Chath 60 A3
Bullers Cl. Sid 36 A4
Bullers Wood Dr. Chis 34 A3
Bullfinch Cl. add W 139 E1
Bullfinch Cl. Sev 80 C1
Bullfinch Corner. Sev 81 D1
Bullfinch Dene. Sev 80 C1
Bullfinch La. Sev 81 D1
Bullingstone La. Spel 152 A1
Bullion Cl. Padd W 139 D1
Bulls Head Yd. Dart 21 D3
Bulls Pl. Pem 154 C1
Bulrush Cl. Wald 74 A4
Bumbles Cl. Chath 59 F2
Bunce Court Rd. Len 112 B2
Bunker's Hill. Belv 4 B3
Bunker's Hill. N Ash 69 F4
Bunkers Hill. Sid 19 D1
Bunters Hill Rd. Cli W 44 B4
Bunton St. SE18 2 B4
Burberry La. Lee 108 B1
Burch Rd. Grave 24 A3
Burcharbro Rd. SE2 3 F2
Burdett Ave. Shor 43 D4
Burdett Cl. Sid 36 A4
Burdett Rd. T W 166 B4
Burfield Dr. Orp 50 C4
Burford Rd. Brom 34 A1
Burgate Cl. Dart 20 A4
Burgess Hall Dr. Lee 108 A1
Burgess Rd. Roc 44 B2
Burghclere Dr. Maid 105 E3
Burghfield Rd. Ist 41 D3
Burham Rd. Chath 59 D2
Burial Ground La. Maid 106 A3
Burleigh Ave. Sid 18 A3
Burleigh Cl. Roc 44 A2
Burleigh Rd. Char 130 C2
Burliegh Dr. Maid 89 D3
Burlings La. Kno P 79 D3
Burlington Cl. Orp 49 E2
Burlington Gdns. Rai (K) 76 A4
Burma Way. Chath 60 A1
Burmarsh Cl. Wald 60 B1
Burnaby Rd. Grave 24 A3
Burnell Ave. Well 3 E1
Burnett Rd. Eri 5 F2
Burnham Cres. Dart 20 C4
Burnham Rd. Dart 20 C4
Burnham Rd. Sid 19 D1
Burnham Wlk. Rai (K) 76 A4
Burns Ave. Sid 18 B3
Burns Cl. Eri 5 D1
Burns Cl. Well 3 D1
Burns Cres. Ton 136 B2
Burn's Rd. Gil 45 F2
Burns Rd. Maid 105 F3
Burnt Ash Hill. SE12 16 B2
Burnt Ash La. Brom 33 E4
Burnt Ash Rd. SE12 16 A3
Burnt House Cl. Roc 44 C3
Burnt House Cotts. Beckl 196 C2
Burnt House La. Dart 21 D1
Burnt House La. Spel 152 B1
Burnt House La. Sutt H 38 A4
Burnt Oak La. Sid 18 B2
Burnt Oak Terr. Gil 45 F1
Burntash Rd. Dit 88 A2
Burnthouse La. Sma 162 C3
Burntwood Gr. Sev 98 B2
Burntwood Rd. Sev 98 B2
Burr Cl. Bexh 19 D4
Burrage Gr. SE18 2 C3
Burrage Pl. SE18 2 B3
Burrage Rd. SE18 2 C3
Burrows La. Low St 30 C4
Bursdon Cl. Sid 18 A1
Burslem Rd. T W 154 A2
Burston Rd. Cox 123 E3
Burwash Rd. SE18 2 C3
Burwood Ave. Brom 48 B2
Busbridge Rd. Loose 106 A1
Busbridge Rd. Snod 72 A2
Bush Rd. Cux 58 B3
Bush Rd. E Pec 121 D2
Bush Row. Ayld 88 B4
Bushell Way. Chis 34 B4
Bushey Ave. Orp 49 F3
Bushfield Wlk. Swans 23 D3
Bushmeadow Rd. Rai (K) 62 A3
Bushmoor Cres. SE18 2 B2
Bushy Gill. Spel 166 B4
Bushy Gr. Broom (m) 126 C3
Busty La. Ight 83 F1
Butcher Cl. Stapt 160 A4
Butcher Wlk. Swans 23 D2
Butchers Hill. Shor 43 D4
Butcher's La. Merew 102 C3
Butler's Pl. N Ash 55 D2
Butt Green La. Lint 124 B2
Butt Haw Cl. Hoo S W 29 D1
Butterfly La. E9 17 E3
Buttermere Cl. Gil 46 B1
Buttermere Rd. Orp 35 F1
Buttmarsh Cl. SE18 2 B3
Button Dr. Low St 13 F1
Button La. Rose 107 E3
Button St. Farn 37 F1
Button St. Swan 37 F1
Butts Rd. Brom 33 D4
Butts The. Otf 81 E3
Buttway La. Cli 10 B1
Buxton Cl. Maid 106 B2
Buxton Cl. Wald 74 C3
Buxton Rd. Eri 4 C2
Bycliffe Terr. Grave 24 A2
Byland Cl. SE2 3 E4
Byng Rd. T W 153 D1
Bynon Ave. Bexh 19 D4
Byrneside. Ton 136 A4
Byron Rd. Dart 21 E4
Byron Rd. Gil 60 C4
Byron Rd. Maid 89 E2

Cabbage Stalk La. T W 167 D3
Cacket's La. Kno P 79 D4
Cade La. Sev 98 C2
Cadlocks Hill. Hals 65 D3
Cadnam Cl. Roc 44 A2
Cadogan Ave. Dart 21 F2
Cadogan Gdns. T W 167 E4
Cadwallon Rd. SE9 17 F1
Caerleon Cl. Sid 35 F4
Caernarvon Dr. Maid 106 A3
Cage Green Rd. Ton 118 C1
Cage La. Sma 163 D3
Cairndale Cl. Brom 33 D3
Cairns Cl. Dart 20 C3
Caistor Rd. Ton 136 B3
Caithness Gdns. Sid 18 A3
Calcott Wlk. SE9 33 F4
Calder Rd. Maid 89 D2
Calderwood St. SE18 2 B3
Caldew Ave. Rai (K) 61 F3
Caldy Rd. Belv 4 B4
Calehill Cl. Maid 89 F1
Caley Rd. T W 153 F2
Calfstock La. Hort 38 A1
Caling Croft. N Ash 55 D3
Caliph Cl. Grave 25 D1
Callaghan Cl. SE13 16 A4
Callams Cl. Rai (K) 61 F1
Callis Way. Rai (K) 61 F1
Calmont Rd. Brom 33 D3
Calverley Park. T W 167 E4
Calverley Park Cres. T W 167 E4
Calverley Park Gdns. T W 167 F4
Calverley Rd. T W 167 E4
Calverley St. T W 167 E4
Calvert Cl. Belv 4 B3
Calvert Cl. Sid 36 A3
Calvin Cl. Orp 35 F1
Calydon Rd. SE7 1 B3
Cambert Way. SE3 16 B4
Camberwell La. Sund 115 D4
Camborne Rd. Sid 18 C1
Camborne Rd. Well 3 D1
Cambray Rd. Orp 50 A3
Cambria Ave. Chath 59 D3
Cambria Cl. Sid 17 F2
Cambria Cres. Grave 42 A4
Cambrian Gr. Grave 24 B2
Cambrian Rd. T W 153 F2
Cambridge Ave. Well 18 A4
Cambridge Barracks Rd. 2 A3
Cambridge Cres. Maid 106 C2
Cambridge Dr. SE12 16 B3
Cambridge Gdns. T W 167 E3
Cambridge Green. SE9 17 E2
Cambridge Rd. Brom 33 E3
Cambridge Rd. Rai (K) 67 F1
Cambridge Rd. Roc 44 B2
Cambridge Rd. Sid 35 D4
Cambridge Row. SE18 2 B3
Cambridge St. T W 167 F4
Cambridge Terr. Chath 60 A4
Camdale Rd. SE18 3 D2
Camden Ave. Pem 154 C1
Camden Cl. Chis 34 C3
Camden Cl. Wald 60 B1
Camden Cnr. Chis 34 B2
Camden Gr. Chis 34 B3
Camden Hill. T W 167 E4
Camden Park. T W 167 F3
Camden Park Rd. Chis 34 3
Camden Rd. Bex 19 D2
Camden Rd. Gil 45 F2
Camden Rd. Sev 81 E1
Camden Rd. T W 167 E4
Camden Row. SE3 1 A1
Camden St. Maid 89 E1
Camden Way. Chis 34 B3
Camellia Cl. Rai (K) 61 F2
Camelot Cl. SE18 2 C4
Camer Park Rd. Meo 56 C3
Camer St. Meo 56 C4
Cameron Cl. Bex 20 A1
Cameron Cl. Chath 60 B2
Cameron Rd. Brom 33 E1
Camlan Rd. Brom 33 D4
Camp Hill. Chid 134 A3
Camp Hill. Lei 134 A3
Camp Way. Maid 106 C1
Campbell Cl. SE18 2 B1
Campbell Rd. Grave 24 A2
Campbell Rd. Maid 106 B4
Campbell Rd. T W 153 E1
Campfield Rd. SE9 16 C2
Campion Cl. Grave 41 D4
Campion Cl. Wald 74 A4
Campion Cres. Cran 182 B3
Campleshon Rd. Rai (K) 61 F1
Camrose Ave. Eri 4 B2
Camrose St. SE2 3 E3
Canada Farm Rd. Faw 54 B4
Canada Farm Rd. Hort 39 E1
Canadian Ave. Gil 61 D4
Canal Basin. Grave 24 C3
Canal Rd. Grave 24 C3
Canal Rd. Higham 26 C2
Canal Rd. Roc 44 C2
Canberra Rd. Bexh 3 F2
Canberra Rd. SE7 1 C2
Canbury Path. Orp 35 E1
Canning St. Maid 89 E1
Cannon La. Ton 136 C3
Cannon Pl. SE7 2 A3
Cannon Rd. Bexh 4 A1
Cannon Wlk. Grave 24 C2
Canon Cl. Chath 59 E3
Canon La. Waty 103 F3
Canon Rd. Brom 33 F1
Canons Wlk. Bras 96 B1
Canterbury Ave. Sid 18 C1
Canterbury Cl. Dart 21 E2
Canterbury Cres. Ton 118 C1
Canterbury La. Upc 62 C3
Canterbury Rd. Grave 24 C1
Canterbury Rd. Pem 155 D1
Canterbury St. Gil 60 C4
Cantwell Rd. SE18 2 B2
Capel Cl. Brom 49 D3
Capel Cl. Rai (K) 75 F4
Capel Pl. Dart 37 F4
Capelands. N Ash 55 E2
Capell Cl. Cox 123 F4
Capstan Ct. Dart 21 F4
Capstone Rd. Brom 33 D4
Capstone Rd. Chath 60 C3
Capstone Rd. Wald 61 D1
Captain's Cl. Sutt V 126 A1
Cardens Rd. Cli W 27 E2
Cardiff St. SE18 3 D2
Cardinal Cl. Chis 35 D2
Cardinal Cl. Ton 136 C2
Cardwell Rd. SE18 2 B3
Carey Ct. Bexh 19 E3
Caring La. Lee 108 A3
Caring Rd. Lee 107 F3
Carisbrooke Ave. Bex 18 C2
Carisbrooke Dr. Maid 88 C1
Carisbrooke Rd. Brom 33 F1
Carisbrooke Rd. Roc 44 A3
Carleton Pl. Hort 38 C1
Caleton Rd. Dart 21 E2
Carlisle Cl. Roc 45 F1
Carlisle Rd. Dart 21 E3
Carlton Ave. Gil 61 D4
Carlton Ave. Gree 22 A3
Carlton Cres. Chath 60 C2
Carlton Cres. T W 167 F4
Carlton Gdns. Maid 106 B2
Carlton Par. Orp 50 B3
Carlton Rd. Eri 4 C2
Carlton Rd. Sid 35 D4
Carlton Rd. T W 167 F4
Carlton Rd. Well 18 B4
Carluke Cl. SE7 1 C3
Carlyle Ave. Brom 33 F1
Carmelite Way. Hart (S) 55 D4
Carnation Cl. Dit 87 E3
Carnation Cres. Dit 87 D3
Carnation Rd. Roc 44 A1
Carnation St. SE 3 E3
Carnbrook Rd. SE3 16 C4
Carnecke Gdns. SE9 17 D3
Caroline Cres. Maid 88 C2
Carolyn Dr. Orp 50 B2
Carpeaux Cl. Chath 60 B4
Carpenters La. Had 119 F3
Carpenters La. Mard 142 C2
Carpenters La. Stapt 142 C2
Carriageway The. Bras 96 C4
Carrick Dr. Sev 98 B4
Carriers Rd. Cran 173 F1
Carrill Way. Belv 3 F4
Carrington Rd. Dart 21 E3
Carroll Gdns. Dit 87 D4
Carronade Pl. SE18 2 C4
Carsington Gdns. Dart 20 C1
Carston Cl. SE12 16 A3
Carter's Hill. Seal 99 E1
Carters Hill Cl. SE9 16 C2
Carters Hill La. Meo 70 A3
Carters Row. Grave 24 A2
Cartmel Rd. Bexh 4 B1
Carton Cl. Chath 59 F3
Carton Rd. Higham 43 E4
Carville Ave. Soub 153 D3
Carvoran Way. Rai (K) 61 F1
Cassilda Rd. SE2 3 E3
Casstine Cl. Hex 37 D3
Casterbridge Rd. SE3 16 B4
Castile Rd. SE18 2 B3
Castillon Rd. SE6 16 A1
Castle Ave. Chath 59 F4
Castle Dene. Maid 89 D2
Castle Dr. Kemsg 82 A3
Castle Farm Rd. Shorm 66 B3
Castle Hill. Chath 44 C1
Castle Hill. Faw 54 C4
Castle Hill. Hart (S) 55 D4
Castle Hill. Thu 90 C3
Castle Hill. Tud 137 D1
Castle La. Grave 25 E1
Castle Rd. Chath 60 B3
Castle Rd. Grays 8 A2
Castle Rd. Maid 88 C2
Castle Rd. Swan 66 B4
Castle Rd. Swans 23 D3
Castle Rd. T W 167 E4
Castle St. Gree 22 B3
Castle St. Roc 45 D3
Castle St. Soub 153 D3
Castle St. Swans 23 D3
Castle St. T W 167 E3
Castle St. Ton 136 C3
Castle St. Wou 72 C4
Castle View Rd. Roc 44 B2
Castle Walk. Wad 178 A1
Castle Way. Birl 87 D4
Castlecombe Rd. SE9 34 A4
Castlefields. Ist 41 D2
Castleford Ave. SE9 17 E2
Castlemaine Ave. Gil 46 A1
Castleton Ave. Bexh 4 C1
Castleton Rd. SE9 33 F4
Castlewood Dr. SE9 2 A1
Catcart Dr. Orp 50 A3
Catherine Pl. T W 167 E4
Catherine St. Chat 59 F4
Catkin Cl. Wald 74 A3
Catlyn Cl. Dit 87 E2
Catterick Rd. Wald 74 C3
Cattistock Rd. SE9 34 A4
Causton Rd. Cran 173 F1
Cave Hill. Maid 106 A3
Cavell Cres. Dart 21 E4
Cavendish Ave. Eri 4 C2
Cavendish Ave. Gil 46 A1
Cavendish Ave. Sev 81 E1
Cavendish Ave. Sid 18 B2
Cavendish Ave. Well 18 A4
Cavendish Cl. Ton 118 C2
Cavendish Dr. T W 167 E3
Cavendish Rd. Chath 59 F4
Cavendish Way. Rose 107 E4
Caveside Cl. Chis 34 B2
Cavix Field. Norm 195 E2
Caxton Cl. Hart (S) 40 A1
Caxton Cl. Ten 186 A2
Caxton La. Had 120 A2
Caxton La. Lim C 113 D4
Caygill Cl. Brom 33 D1
Cayser Dr. Broom (M) 127 D3
Cazeneuve St. Chath 44 C1
Cecil Ave. Rai (K) 61 E3
Cecil Ave. Roc 44 B2
Cecil Rd. Chath 59 F4
Cecil Rd. Grave 24 A2
Cecil Way. Brom 48 B3
Cedar Ave. Grave 41 F4
Cedar Ave. Sid 18 B2
Cedar Cl. Brom 49 D2
Cedar Cl. Dit 87 F2
Cedar Cl. Meo 56 B4
Cedar Cl. Swan 36 C2
Cedar Copse. Brom 34 A2
Cedar Cres. Brom 49 D2
Cedar Cres. Ton 118 C2
Cedar Ct. T W 153 E1
Cedar Dr. Ede 131 E3
Cedar Dr. Maid 105 D3
Cedar Dr. Sutt H 38 B2
Cedar Gdns. Sto 77 D2
Cedar Gr. Bex 18 C3
Cedar Gr. Rai (K) 61 E1
Cedar Mount. SE9 16 C2
Cedar Pl. SE7 1 C3
Cedar Rd. Brom 33 F2
Cedar Rd. Dart 20 C2
Cedar Rd. Eri 5 E1
Cedar Rd. Hoo S W 46 A4
Cedar Rd. Roc 44 A1
Cedar Ridge. T W 153 F1
Cedar Terrace Rd. Sev 98 C4
Cedarhurst Dr. SE9 16 C3

Cedric Rd. SE9 17 F1
Celestine Cl. Wald 74 B3
Celtic Ave. Brom 33 D1
Cemetery La. Had 120 B3
Cemetery La. SE7 2 A2
Cemetery Rd. Hall 72 B4
Cemetery Rd. Snod 72 A3
Central Ave. Gil 45 E2
Central Ave. Grave 24 B1
Central Ave. Grays 7 D3
Central Ave. S Ock 6 C4
Central Ave. Well 3 E1
Central Par. Chath 59 F3
Central Park Gdns. Chath 60 A3
Central Rd. Dart 21 D3
Central Rd. Dit 87 E4
Central Rd. Roc 44 B2
Central Terr. Hoo S W 28 A1
Centre Common Rd. Chis 34 C3
Centre Rd. N Ash 55 D2
Centurian Way. Belv 4 B4
Centurian Way. Pur 6 A3
Century Rd. Rai (K) 62 A3
Ceres Rd. SE18 3 D3
Cerne Rd. Grave 25 D1
Cervia Way. Grave 25 D1
Chada Ave. Gil 61 D4
Chadd Dr. Brom 34 A1
Chadwell Rd. Grays 8 C3
Chadwick Cl. Grave 24 A1
Chaffinch Cl. Chath 60 B2
Chaffinch Way. Padd W 139 E1
Chafford La. Pen 151 D1
Chalcombe Rd. SE2 3 E4
Chalcrft Rd. SE13 16 A3
Chalet Cl. Sid 36 C4
Chalfont Dr. Rai (K) 61 F1
Chalice Way. Gree 22 A3
Chalk Ave. Ten 186 B3
Chalk Pit Ave. Orp 35 F1
Chalk Pit Hill. Chath 60 B4
Chalk Rd. Grave 25 E1
Chalk Rd. Higham 26 C1
Chalkenden Ave. Rai (K) 61 E3
Chalket La. Pem 154 C1
Chalkways. Kemsg 82 B4
Chalky Bank. Grave 41 E4
Chalky Bank Rd. Rai (K) 62 A3
Chalky Rd. Sto 76 C1
Challenge Cl. Grave 42 A4
Challenger Cl. Padd W 139 D1
Challock Wlk. Maid 89 F1
Chamberlain Ave. Maid 105 F3
Chamberlain Cl. SE18 2 C4
Chamberlain Rd. Chath 60 B3
Chancel Cl. W Kin 68 A4
Chancellor Way. Sev 81 E1
Chancelot Rd. SE2 3 E3
Chancery La. Maid 106 B4
Chancery Rd. Cli 10 B1
Chanctonbury Cl. SE9 17 E1
Chandler's Hill. Meo 56 C1
Chandler's Rd. Meo 56 C1
Chandos Rd. T W 153 F1
Chantler's Hill. Paddw 156 B4
Chantlers Mead. Cow 149 E1
Chantrey Cl. Sid 36 A4
Chantry Ave. Hart (S) 55 D4
Chantry La. Brom 48 C4
Chantry Pl. Mard 141 F1
Chantry Rd. Mard 141 F1
Chapel Cl. Birl 71 D1
Chapel Cl. Dart 20 A3
Chapel Cl. Grays 7 E2
Chapel Ct. Swans 23 D3
Chapel Farm Rd. SE9 17 D1
Chapel Field. Norm 195 E2
Chapel Hill. Dart 20 A3
Chapel La. Ben 190 C4
Chapel La. Bredh 75 E3
Chapel La. Cran 174 B2
Chapel La. Ege 146 B3
Chapel La. Hall 71 F4
Chapel La. Stapt 160 A4
Chapel La. Thu 90 B1
Chapel Pl. T W 167 E3
Chapel Rd. Bexh 19 E4
Chapel Rd. I o G 15 E1
Chapel Rd. Snod 72 B2
Chapel Rd. Sutt V 126 A2
Chapel Row. Ight 83 F1
Chapel St. Birl 71 D1
Chapel St. Dit 87 E1
Chapel Way. Brom 33 E2
Chapel Wood. N Ash 55 D2
Chapel Wood Rd. N Ash 55 D2
Chaplin Dr. Head 144 C1
Chapman Ave. Maid 107 D2
Chapman Rd. Belv 4 B3
Chapman Way. Dit 87 D2
Chapman Way. Soub 153 F2
Chapman's Hill. Meo 70 A4
Chapmans La. Orp 36 A2
Chapmans La. Orp 36 B2
Chapmans Rd. Sund 97 D4
Chapter Rd. Roc 44 A2
Charing Cl. Orp 50 A1
Charing Heath Rd. Char 130 B1
Charing Heath Rd. Char 130 B2
Charing Hill. Char 130 C2
Charing Rd. Rai (K) 61 E4
Charlbury Cl. Maid 105 F4
Charldane Rd. SE9 17 E1
Charles Cl. Sid 35 E4
Charles Cl. Snod 72 B2
Charles Dickens Ave. Higham 43 F3
Charles Dr. Cux 58 B4
Charles Grinling Wlk. SE18 2 B3
Charles Rd. Shorm 65 E3
Charles St. Chath 60 A4
Charles St. Grays 8 C2
Charles St. Gree 22 A3
Charles St. Maid 106 A4
Charles St. Roc 44 B2
Charles St. Soub 153 E2
Charlesfield. SE9 16 C1
Charlesford Ave. Broom (m) 126 C4
Charlieville Rd. Eri 4 C2
Charlotte Cl. Wald 60 B1
Charlotte Dr. Rai (K) 61 F3
Charlotte Pl. Grays 7 E2
Charlton Church La. SE7 1 C3
Charlton Dene. SE7 1 C2
Charlton La. E Far 105 D1
Charlton La. SE7 1 C3
Charlton La. Sutt V 126 C2
Charlton La. W Far 104 C2
Charlton Park La. SE7 1 C2
Charlton Park Rd. SE7 1 C2
Charlton Rd. SE3 1 B2
Charlton Rd. SE7 1 C2
Charlton St. Grays 7 F2
Charlton St. Maid 105 F3
Charlton Terr. Ton 136 C3
Charlton Way. SE3 1 A2
Charlton's Way. T W 167 D3
Charminster Rd. SE9 33 F4
Charmouth Rd. Well 3 F1
Charmwood La. Dow 64 B3
Charne The. Otf 81 E3
Charnock. Swan 37 D1
Chart Cl. Brom 33 D2
Chart Hill Rd. Chart S 125 E2
Chart La. Bras 96 B2
Chart Pl. Rai (K) 75 F4
Chart Rd. Chart S 125 F2
Chart Rd. Sutt V 125 F2
Chart View. Kemsg 82 B3
Charter Dr. Bex 19 D2
Charter St. Chath 60 A3
Charter St. Gil 45 F2
Charterhouse Dr. Sev 98 B4
Charterhouse Rd. Orp 50 B2
Charton Cl. Belv 4 A2
Chartway. Sev 98 C4
Chartway St. Broom (M) 126 B3
Chartway St. Sutt V 126 B3
Chartwell Cl. Roc 44 B3
Chartwell Cl. SE9 17 F1
Chartwell Dr. Orp 49 F1
Chase Sq. Grave 24 B3
Chase The. Bexh 19 E4
Chase The. Brom 33 E1
Chase The. Chath 59 F3
Chase The. Dow 64 B3
Chase The. Grays 7 F2
Chase The. Kemsg 82 B4
Chase The. Rai (K) 61 E3
Chase The. T W 167 F3
Chase The. Ton 118 C1
Chastilian Rd. Dart 20 B2
Chatham Ave. Brom 48 B3
Chatham Gr. Chath 60 A3
Chatham Hill. Chath 60 B4
Chatham Hill Rd. Sev 81 F1
Chatham Rd. Ayld 73 F1
Chatham Rd. Burh 73 F2
Chatham Rd. Maid 73 F1
Chatham Rd. Orp 49 F1
Chatsworth Ave. Brom 33 E4
Catsworth Ave. Sid 18 B2
Chatsworth Cl. Wick 48 A2
Chatsworth Dr. Roc 44 B3
Chatsworth Rd. Dart 20 C4
Chatsworth Rd. Gil 45 F1
Chattenden Ct. Maid 89 E2
Chattenden La. Hoo S W 45 D4
Chatterton Rd. Brom 48 C4
Chaucer Gdns. Ton 136 A2
Chaucer Industrial Park. Kemsg 82 C2
Chaucer Rd. Gil 60 C4
Chaucer Rd. Grave 23 F1
Chaucer Rd. Sid 18 C2
Chaucer Rd. Well 3 D1
Chaucer Way. Dart 21 D4
Chaucer Way. Dit 87 E4
Chaundrye Cl. SE9 17 D3
Chave Rd. Dart 21 D1
Cheeselands. Bidd 176 A3
Chegwell Dr. Wald 74 B4
Chegworth Rd. Harr 109 D1
Chelmar Rd. Chath 60 B4
Chelmsford Rd. Roc 43 F1
Chelsfield Hill. Orp 64 C3
Chelsfield La. Orp 50 C2
Chelsfield La. Shorm 65 E3
Chelsfield Rd. Orp 50 C4
Chelsworth Dr. SE18 2 C2
Cheltenham Rd. Orp 50 B2
Cheney Cl. Rai (K) 61 F1
Chenies Cl. T W 167 E2
Chenies The. Dart 37 D4
Chenies The. Orp 50 A4
Chennell Park Rd. Ten 186 A3
Chennels The. H Hald 177 F2
Chequers Cl. Ist 41 D2
Chequers Cl. Orp 35 D1
Chequers Hill Cotts. Chid 133 E3
Cherbourg Cres. Chath 60 A2
Cheriton Ave. Brom 48 B4
Cheriton Dr. SE18 2 C2
Cheriton Rd. Rai (K) 61 F2
Cheriton Way. Maid 88 C2
Cherries The. Maid 105 E3
Cherry Amber Cl. Rai (K) 62 A2
Cherry Ave. Swan 36 C1
Cherry Cl. Len 110 C1
Cherry Gr. Ton 119 D1
Cherry Orch. Dit 87 F2
Cherry Orch. SE7 1 C2
Cherry Orchard. Ten 186 B1
Cherry Orchard Cl. Orp 50 C4
Cherry Orchard Rd. Brom 49 D2
Cherry Orchard The. Had 120 A3
Cherry Orchard Way. Maid 105 E4
Cherry Rd. Hoo S W 46 A4
Cherry Tree Cl. Grays 8 C2
Cherry Tree Gr. W Kin 67 F3
Cherry Tree Rd. Char 130 A2
Cherry Tree Rd. Rai (K) 62 A2
Cherry Tree Rd. T W 167 D3
Cherry Tree Wlk. W Wick 48 A1
Cherry Trees. Hart (S) 55 D4
Cherry Wlk. Brom 48 B3
Cherrycot Hill. Orp 49 F1
Cherrycot Rise. Orp 49 F1
Cherrydown Rd. Sid 18 C1
Cherryfields. Ben 183 F1
Cherrywood Dr. Grave 24 A1
Chervilles. Maid 105 E3
Cherwell Cl. Ton 136 B4
Chesfield Cl. Had 120 A3
Chesham Ave. Orp 49 E4
Chesham Dr. Rai (K) 62 A1
Cheshire Rd. Maid 107 D2
Cheshunt Rd. Belv 4 B3
Chessenden La. Sma 163 E3
Chessington Ave. Bexh 4 A2
Chester Ave. T W 167 F3
Chester Cl. Roc 43 F1
Chester Rd. Gil 60 C3
Chester Rd. Sid 18 A3
Chesterfield Cl. Orp 36 A1
Chesterfield Dr. Sev 80 C1
Chesterton Rd. Dit 87 D4
Chestfield Cl. Rai (K) 62 A3
Chestnut Ave. Grays 8 B4
Chestnut Ave. Lim 78 A1
Chestnut Ave. Soub 153 E2
Chestnut Ave. Stapt 160 A4
Chestnut Ave. W Wick 48 A1
Chestnut Ave. Wald 74 A4
Chestnut Ave. Whm 78 A1
Chestnut Cl. Ede 131 E3
Chestnut Cl. Frit 161 D1
Chestnut Cl. Grave 24 A3
Chestnut Cl. Meo 56 B4
Chestnut Cl. Orp 50 B1
Chestnut Cl. Soub 153 E2
Chestnut Cl. Ten 186 C3
Chestnut Cl. Ulc 127 D1
Chestnut Dr. Bexh 19 D4
Chestnut Dr. Broom (M) 126 C3
Chestnut Dr. Cox 123 E4
Chestnut La. Mat 155 F3
Chestnut La. Meo 70 B2
Chestnut La. Sev 98 B4
Chestnut Rd. Dart 20 C2
Chestnut Rd. Roc 44 A1
Chestnut Rise. SE18 3 D3
Chestnut Wlk. Dit 87 E3
Chestnut Wlk. Sev 99 D2
Chestnut Wlk Ton 136 A3
Chestnuts The. Hawkt 189 D2
Chestnuts The. Wro H 85 F4
Cheswick Cl. Dart 20 A4
Chesworth Cl. Eri 5 D1
Chetney Cl. Roc 43 F2
Cheveney Wlk. Brom 33 E1
Chevening Cl. Wald 60 B1
Chevening La. Kno P 80 A4
Chevening Rd. Chev 80 B1
Chevening Rd. Sund 97 D4
Chevenings The. Sid 18 C1
Cheviot Cl. Bexh 5 D1
Cheviot Cl. Ton 136 C4
Cheviot Gdns. Oth 107 E3
Cheyne Cl. Brom 49 D2
Cheyne Wlk. Meo 56 B2
Chicago Ave. Gil 46 A1
Chichester Cl. Rai (K) 62 B2
Chichester Cl. SE3 1 C1
Chichester Dr. Sev 98 A3
Chichester Rd. Gree 22 A3
Chichester Rd. Ton 136 B2
Chichester Rise. Grave 41 F4
Chickfield Gdns. Chath 60 C3
Chicks La. Kiln 180 B3
Chiddingstone Ave. Bexh 4 A2
Chiddingstone Cl. Maid 107 D1
Chidley Cross Rd. E Pec 121 D1
Chieftan Cl. Rai (K) 61 E3
Chieftan Dr. Pur 6 B3
Chieveley Dr. T W 167 F3
Chieveley Rd. Bexh 19 E4
Chiffinch Gdns. Grave 24 A1
Childs Cres. Swans 22 C3
Childs Way. Wro 84 A4
Childsbridge La. Kemsg 82 A2
Childsbridge La. Seal 82 A2
Childsbridge Way. Seal 82 A2
Childscroft Rd. Rai (K) 62 A3
Chilham Cl. Chath 60 A4
Chilham Rd. Maid 88 C2
Chilham Rd. Rai (K) 61 E4
Chilham Rd. SE9 34 A4
Chilham Way. Brom 48 B3
Chillington Cl. Hall 72 A4
Chillington St. Maid 89 D1
Chillwack Rd. Hoo S W 28 A1
Chilston Cl. T W 153 E1
Chilston Rd. Len 110 C1
Chilston Rd. T W 153 E1
Chiltern Cl. Bexh 5 D1
Chiltern Gdns. Brom 33 D1
Chiltern Rd. Grave 24 A1
Chiltern Way. Ton 136 C4
Chiltern Wlk. T W 167 F4
Chilton Ct. Rai (K) 62 A3
Chilton Dr. Higham 43 E4
Chiltonian Ind Est. SE12 16 A3
Chinbrook Cres. SE12 16 B1
Chinbrook Rd. SE12 16 B1
Chingley Cl. Brom 33 D3
Chippendale Cl. Wald 74 A3
Chipperfield Rd. Orp 35 E2
Chipstead Cl. Dit 88 C1
Chipstead La. Sev 80 C1
Chipstead Park. Sev 80 C1
Chipstead Park Cl. Sev 80 C1
Chipstead Rd. Eri 5 D2
Chipstead Rd. Rai (K) 75 F4
Chipstead Sq. Sev 80 C1
Chislehurst Cl. Maid 107 D1
Chislehurst High St. Chis 34 B3
Chislehurst Rd. Brom 34 A2
Chislehurst Rd. Chis 34 A2
Chislehurst Rd. Orp 50 A4
Chislehurst Rd. Sid 35 E4
Chislet Wlk. Rai (K) 75 F4
Chiswell Sq. SE3 1 B1
Chorleywood Cres. Orp 35 E2
Christ Church Ave. Eri 5 D2
Christ Church Ave. T W 167 E3
Christ Church Cres. Grave 24 C2
Christ Church Rd. Grave 24 C2
Christchurch Rd. Dart 20 C3
Christchurch Rd. Sid 18 A1
Christen Way. Maid 125 D4
Christian Fields Ave. Grave 41 F4
Christie Cl. Wald 60 B1
Christie Dr. Dit 87 D4
Christies Ave. Shorm 65 E3
Christmas La. H Hals 29 D4
Christmas St. Gil 46 A2
Christopher Cl. Sid 18 A3
Chulkhurst. Bidd 176 A3
Chulkhurst Cl. Bidd 176 A3
Church Ave. Sid 35 E4
Church Cl. Brenc 156 C2
Church Cl. Cli 10 B1
Church Cl. Merew 102 C2
Church Cotts. Swan 51 F3
Church Cres. Harr 110 A1
Church Dr. W Wick 48 A2
Church Farm Cl. Swan 51 F4
Church Field. Dart 20 C1
Church Field. Sev 81 D1
Church Field. Snod 72 B2
Church Fields. W Mal 86 B2
Church Green. Mard 141 F1
Church Green. Roc 44 C2
Church Green. Stapt 160 A3
Church Hill. Bou Mon 124 C2
Church Hill. Char 129 F2
Church Hill. Chath 60 C3
Church Hill. Dart 20 A4
Church Hill. Dart 20 C1
Church Hill. Dow 78 C4
Church Hill. Gree 22 A3
Church Hill. Lei 135 D3
Church Hill. Orp 50 B3
Church Hill. Plax 101 D2
Church Hill. SE18 2 A4
Church Hill. Sto 77 D2
Church Hill Wood. Orp 50 A4
Church La. Beckl 196 A1
Church La. Brom 49 D3
Church La. Chath 45 D2
Church La. Chis 34 C2
Church La. E Pec 121 D2
Church La. Grave 25 F1
Church La. Had 120 A2
Church La. Harr 110 A1
Church La. Hors 157 E3
Church La. Kemsg 82 B3
Church La. Norm 195 F1
Church La. Pur 6 B3
Church La. Rose 107 F4
Church La. Sto 77 D2
Church La. Sutt V 126 B2
Church La. Ton 136 C3
Church La. Trot 70 B1
Church La. Tud 138 A1
Church La. W Far 104 C2
Church Manor Way. SE2 3 D3
Church Manorway. Eri 4 C4
Church Mews. Rai (K) 62 A2
Church Path. Gil 46 A1
Church Path. Gil 45 E1
Church Path. Grays 8 A2
Church Path. Gree 22 A3
Church Path. Roc 44 B2
Church Path. Ten 186 B2
Church Rd. Bexh 19 D4
Church Rd. Bigg 78 A3
Church Rd. Bou Mal 128 A2
Church Rd. Bras 96 B4
Church Rd. Brom 33 D1
Church Rd. Brom 33 E2
Church Rd. Char 130 C3
Church Rd. Chart S 125 F2
Church Rd. Cob 41 F2
Church Rd. Eri 4 C3
Church Rd. Gou 172 A2
Church Rd. Grave 41 F3
Church Rd. Gree 22 A3
Church Rd. Hals 65 D2
Church Rd. Harr 110 A1
Church Rd. Hart (S) 55 E3
Church Rd. Hex 37 F2
Church Rd. Hild 117 F1
Church Rd. Ist 41 F2
Church Rd. Lam 170 C1
Church Rd. Maid 106 A3
Church Rd. N Ash 55 E3
Church Rd. Off 86 A3
Church Rd. Orp 64 C4
Church Rd. Orp 49 F1
Church Rd. Oth 107 D2
Church Rd. Padd W 139 E1
Church Rd. Pem 154 C2
Church Rd. S Grn 92 A3
Church Rd. Sand 194 A4
Church Rd. Seal 82 A1
Church Rd. Seal 100 A4
Church Rd. Sev W 116 B4
Church Rd. Sid 35 E4
Church Rd. Soub 153 D3
Church Rd. Sund 97 D3
Church Rd. Sutt H 38 B3
Church Rd. Swan 51 F3
Church Rd. Swans 23 D3
Church Rd. T W 167 E4
Church Rd. Ten 186 B2
Church Rd. W Kin 68 A4
Church Rd. W Mal 86 A4
Church Rd. W Pec 102 B1
Church Rd. Well 3 E1
Church Row. Chis 34 C2
Church Sq. Len 110 C1
Church St. Bou Mon 124 B4
Church St. Burh 73 D3
Church St. Chath 60 B4
Church St. Chath 59 F4
Church St. Cli 10 B1
Church St. Cow 149 E1
Church St. E16 2 B4
Church St. Ede 131 F3
Church St. Gil 46 A1
Church St. Grave 24 B3
Church St. Grays 8 C2
Church St. Higham 26 C2
Church St. Hoo S W 46 A4
Church St. Loose 106 A1
Church St. Maid 106 A3
Church St. Maid 106 B4
Church St. Seal 82 B2
Church St. Shorm 66 B2
Church St. Souf 40 B4
Church St. Tes 104 B2
Church St. Ton 136 C3
Church Terr. Chath 60 C3
Church Terr. SE13 16 A4
Church View. Bidd 176 A3
Church View. S Ock 6 C4
Church View. Swan 36 C1
Church Wlk. Ayld 88 B4
Church Wlk. Dart 20 C1
Church Wlk. Dit 87 E2
Church Wlk. Eyn 53 D2
Church Wlk. Grave 24 C2
Churchbury Rd. SE9 16 C2
Churchdown. Brom 33 D4
Churchfield. Ede 131 F3
Churchfield. Wro H 85 F4
Churchfield Rd. Well 18 B4
Churchfields Terr. Chath 59 E4
hurchill Ave. Chath 60 B2
Churchill Rd. Grave 24 A2
Churchill Rd. Grays 8 C2
Churchill Rd. Hort 38 C1
Churchills Ropewalk. Gou 172 A2
Churchside. Meo 70 B2
Chute Cl. Rai (K) 75 F4
Chyngton Cl. Sid 18 A1
Cimba Wood. Grave 42 A4
Cinder Hill La. Lei 134 C3
Cinderford Way. Brom 33 D4
Cinderhill Wood. Mat 155 F3
Cinnabar Cl. Wald 74 B3
Circuit Rd. SE28 3 D4
Circular Way. SE18 2 B2
Cirrus Cres. Grave 42 A4
City Way. Chath 59 F3
Clacket La. Lim 95 D3
Clandon Rd. Wald 74 C3
Clanricarde Gdns. T W 167 E4
Clanricarde Rd. T W 167 E4
Claphatch La. Wad 179 E1
Clapper La. Stapt 142 C1
Clara Pl. SE18 2 B3
Clare Ave. Ton 136 A3
Clare Cnr. SE9 17 E2
Clare La. Dit 87 D2
Clare Way. Bexh 4 A1
Clare Way. Sev 98 C2
Claremont Cl. Grays 8 C4
Claremont Cl. Orp 49 E1
Claremont Cres. Dart 20 A4
Claremont Gdns. T W 167 E3
Claremont Rd. Brom 34 A1
Claremont Rd. Hex 37 D3
Claremont Rd. Maid 89 E1
Claremont Rd. T W 167 E3
Claremont St. E16 2 B4
Claremont Way. Chath 60 A4
Clrence Ave. Brom 34 A1
Clarence Ave. Chath 59 F4
Clarence Cres. Sid 18 B1
Clarence Ct. Thu 107 D4
Clarence Pl. Grave 24 B2
Clarence Rd. Bexh 19 D4
Clarence Rd. Bigg 78 A3
Clarence Rd. Brom 34 A1
Clarence Rd. Chath 60 B3
Clarence Rd. Grays 8 B3
Clarence Rd. SE9 17 D1
Clarence Rd. Sid 18 B1
Clarence Rd. T W 167 E4
Clarence Row. Grave 24 B2
Clarence Row. T W 167 E4
Clarendon Cl. Orp 35 E1
Clarendon Cl. Rose 107 E4
Clarendon Gdns. Dart 21 F2

Clarendon Gdns. T W 167 E3
Clarendon Gr. Orp 35 E1
Clarendon Green. Orp 35 E1
Clarendon Path. Orp 35 E1
Clarendon Pl. Maid 106 B4
Clarendon Rd. Grave 24 C3
Clarendon Rd. Sev 98 B3
Clarendon Way. Chis 35 D1
Clarendon Way. Orp 35 E1
Clarendon Way. T W 167 E3
Clareville Rd. Orp 49 F2
Clark Cl. Eri 5 E1
Clark Mews. Dit 88 A3
Clarkbourne Dr. Grays 8 C2
Clarke's Green Rd. Shorm 67 E1
Clarks La. Hals 65 D2
Clarks La. Lim 95 D4
Claston Cl. Dart 20 A4
Clavadal Rd. Padd W 139 E2
Clavadel Rd. Padd W 139 E2
Clavell Cl. Rai (K) 76 A4
Clay Hill Rd. Lam 169 F2
Clay Wood Cl. Orp 50 A3
Claybridge Rd. SE12 33 F4
Clayfarm Rd. SE9 17 F1
Claygate. Maid 106 C3
Claygate La. Ship 119 D4
Claygate Rd. Yal 140 B4
Clayhill. Gou 171 F2
Clayhill Cres. SE9 33 F4
Clayton Croft Rd. Dart 20 B1
Clayton's La. Asht 165 D3
Claywood La. Dart 22 C1
Clayworth Cl. Sid 18 B3
Cleanthus Cl. SE18 2 B1
Cleanthus Rd. SE18 2 B1
Clearmount Dr. Char 130 C2
Clearway. Wro H 85 E3
Cleave Ave. Orp 64 A4
Cleave Rd. Gil 61 D4
Cleavers. Cran 174 B2
Cleavers Cl. Cran 174 B2
Cleavesland. Yal 122 A1
Cleeve Ave. T W 167 F3
Clematis Ave. Rai (K) 61 E1
Clement Ct. Maid 88 C1
Clement St. Sutt H 38 A3
Clenches Farm La. Sev 98 B3
Clenches Farm Rd. Sev 98 B3
Clendon Way. SE18 2 C3
Clerks Field. Head 144 C1
Clermont Cl. Rai (K) 75 E4
Cleve Rd. Sid 18 C1
Cleveland. T W 153 F1
Cleveland Rd. Gil 45 F1
Cleveland Rd. Well 3 D1
Clevely Cl. SE7 1 C3
Cleves Rd. Kemsg 82 A3
Clewson Rise. Maid 89 E2
Cliff Hill. Bou Mon 124 C4
Cliff Hill Rd. Bou Mon 124 C4
Cliffe Rd. Roc 44 B3
Clifford Ave. Chis 34 A3
Clifton Cl. Maid 89 E1
Clifton Cl. Orp 49 F1
Clifton Cl. Roc 44 A2
Clifton Gr. Grave 24 B2
Clifton Marine Par. Grave 24 B3
Clifton Pl. T W 167 E3
Clifton Rd. Gil 45 F2
Clifton Rd. Grave 24 B3
Clifton Rd. Sid 35 D4
Clifton Rd. T W 153 F2
Clifton Rd. Well 18 C4
Clinch St. H Hals 29 E4
Clinton Ave. Roc 44 A2
Clinton Ave. Well 18 B4
Clinton Cl. Cox 123 E4
Clinton La. Chid 133 D3
Clinton La. Four E 132 C4
Clipper Cres. Grave 42 A4
Clive Ave. Dart 20 A3
Clive Rd. Belv 4 B3
Clive Rd. Chath 59 F4
Clive Rd. Grave 24 B3
Clock House La. Sev 98 B4
Clockhouse. T W 154 A1
Clockhouse La. Grays 8 A4
Cloisterham Rd. Chath 59 F2
Cloisters Ave. Brom 49 D4
Cloonmore Ave. Orp 50 A1
Close The. Bex 19 E2
Close The. Birl 71 E1
Close The. Bor G 84 B2
Close The. Chath 59 F4
Close The. Dart 20 C1
Close The. Grays 8 C4
Close The. Gro 165 F1
Close The. Lon 40 B2
Close The Orp 50 A4
Close The. Sev 98 A4
Close The. Sid 35 E4
Close The. Wro H 85 F3
Close The. Ight 83 F1
Cloth Hall Gdns. Bidd 176 B3
Cloudesley Rd. Bexh 4 A1
Cloudesley Rd. Eri 5 D1
Clovelly Rd. Bexh 4 A2
Clovelly Way. Orp 50 A4
Clover Ct. Grays 8 C2
Clover Rd. Hoo S W 46 A4
Clover St. Chath 60 A4
Clover Wlk. Ede 131 F4
Cloverdale Gdns. Sid 18 A3
Clovers The. Grave 41 D4
Club Gardens Rd. Brom 48 B3
Clyde Rd. Ton 118 C1
Clydon Cl. Eri 5 D2
Coach and Horses Pas. T W 167 E3
Coach Drive The. Meo 70 A2
Coach Rd. Char 129 D1
Coach Rd. Ege 129 D1
Coach Rd. Grave 24 A3
Coach Rd. Ight 100 B3
Coalpit La. Len 94 B1
Coastguard Cotts. I o G 15 E1
Coates Hill Rd. Brom 34 B2
Cob Cl. Ight 83 F1
Cob Dr. Shor 43 D4
Cobb Cl. Roc 43 F2
Cobbett Cl. Dit 87 D2
Cobbett Rd. SE9 17 D4
Cobbett's Ride. T W 167 D3
Cobblestones. Rai (K) 61 D1
Cobbs Cl. Padd W 139 D1
Cobbs Cl. Waty 104 A2
Cobden Rd. Chath 60 B3
Cobden Rd. Orp 49 F1
Cobden Rd. Sev 98 C4
Cobdown Cl. Dit 87 F3
Cobdown Gr. Rai (K) 62 B3
Cobfield. Chart S 125 E3
Cobham. Grays 8 B4
Cobham Cl. Brom 49 D3
Cobham Cl. Maid 106 A4
Cobham Cl. Roc 44 A2
Cobham St. Grave 24 B2
Cobhambury Rd. Cob 57 E4
Cobhams. Spel 152 B2
Cobland Rd. SE12 33 F4
Cobsdene. Grave 41 F3
Cobtree Cl. Chath 60 C2
Cobtree Rd. Cox 123 F4
Cockerhurst Rd. Shorm 66 A3
Cockmannings La. Orp 50 C3
Cockmannings Rd. Orp 50 C3
Cockmount La. Wad 178 A1
Cocksett Ave. Orp 64 A4
Codrington Cres. Grave 41 F4
Codrington Gdns. Grave 41 F4
Cogate Rd. Padd W 139 D1
Colchester Cl. Chath 60 B2
Cold Arbor Rd. Sev 97 F4
Cold Blow Cres. Bex 19 F2
Cold Harbour Rd. Len 112 B1
Coldblow La. Thu 91 E3
Coldbridge La. Bou Mal 128 B1
Coldbridge La. Ege 146 B4
Coldharbour La. Ayld 88 B3
Coldharbour La. Hild 118 A2
Coldharbour La. S Grn 91 E3
Coldharbour Rd. Ben 190 C4
Coldharbour Rd. Grave 24 A1
Coldharbour Rd. Pen 151 D2
Coldred Rd. Maid 125 D4
Coldrum La. Trot 70 C1
Colebrook Industrial Estate. T W 154 A3
Colebrook Rd. Soub 153 F2
Colebrooke Rise. Brom 33 D2
Colegate Dr. Rose 107 F4
Coleman Rd. Belv 4 B3
Colemans Heath. SE9 17 E1
Colepits Wood Rd. SE9 17 F3
Coleraine Rd. SE3 1 A2
Coleridge Cl. Dit 87 D4
Coleridge Rd. Dart 21 E4
Coleridge Way. Orp 50 B4
Coles La. Bras 96 C4
Coleshall Cl. Maid 107 D1
Colets Orchard. Otf 81 E4
Colewood Dr. Higham 43 E2
Colin Blythe Rd. Ton 119 D1
Colin Chapman Way. W Kin 54 A1
Colin Cl. Dart 21 E3
Colin Cl. W Wick 48 A2
College Ave. Gil 60 B4
College Ave. Grays 8 C3
College Ae. Maid 106 A4
College Ave. Ton 136 B2
College Dr. T W 167 F4
College Rd. Brom 33 E2
College Rd. Chath 45 E2
College Rd. Dit 87 E4
College Rd. Grave 23 E3
College Rd. Grays 8 C3
College Rd. Hex 37 D3
College Rd. Maid 106 A4
College Slip. Brom 33 E2
College View. SE9 16 C2
College Yd. Chath 44 C1
Coller Cres. Dart 39 D4
Collet Wlk. Rai (K) 75 F4
Collett Rd. Kemsg 82 A3
Colliers Wood. Kes 48 C1
Collindale Ave. Eri 4 B2
Collindale Ave. Sid 18 B2
Collings Wlk. Rai (K) 75 F4
Collington Cl. Grave 24 A2
Collington Terr. Maid 125 D4
Collingwood Rd. Ayld 73 F2
Collins Sq. SE3 1 A1
Collins St. SE3 1 A1
Collis St. Roc 44 B2
Collison Pl. Ten 186 C2
Colne Rd. Ton 118 B1
Colney Rd. Dart 21 D3
Colonel's Way. Soub 153 E3
Coltness Cres. SE2 3 E3
Coltsfoot Ct. Grays 8 C2
Coltstead. N Ash 55 D2
Columbine Cl. Dit 87 D3
Columbine Cl. Roc 44 A2
Columbine Rd. Dit 87 D2
Columbine Rd. Roc 44 A2
Colview Ct. SE9 16 C2
Colyer Cl. SE9 17 E1
Colyer Rd. Grave 23 F1
Colyers Cl. Eri 4 C1
Colyers La. Eri 4 C1
Colyers Wlk. Eri 5 D1
Colyton Cl. Well 3 F1
Combe Ave. SE3 1 A2
Combedale Rd. SE10 1 B3
Combeside. SE18 3 D2
Combwell Cres. SE2 3 E4
Comet Cl. Pur 6 B3
Comfrey Ct. Grays 8 C2
Command Rd. Maid 89 D2
Commercial Pl. Grave 24 C3
Commercial Rd. Padd W 139 D1
Commercial Rd. Roc 44 B2
Commercial Rd. Ton 136 C2
Commercial Rd. T W 153 E1
Commissioner's Rd. Roc 44 C2
Commodore Rd. Maid 89 F1
Common La. Cli 10 C1
Common La. Dart 20 B1
Common Rd. Burh 73 E3
Common Rd. Cli W 44 B4
Common Rd. Cran 174 B2
Common Rd. Had 120 A3
Common Rd. Ight 100 B4
Common View. T W 166 C4
Common Wall. Cli 10 C1
Commonside. Kes 48 C1
Commonwealth Way. SE2 3 F3
Commority Rd. Meo 70 B2
Comp La. Bor G 84 C1
Comp La. Off 85 E2
Compasses Rd. Lei 134 B3
Compton Cl. Wald 74 C3
Compton Pl. Eri 5 D2
Concord Ave. Wald 60 A1
Concord Cl. Padd W 139 D2
Concord Cl. T W 167 F4
Condover Cres. SE18 2 B2
Conduit Rd. SE18 2 B3
Coney Hill Rd. W Wick 48 A2
Coneyburrow Rd. T W 154 A1
Conference Rd. SE2 3 F3
Conghurst La. Hawkt 189 E1
Congleton Gr. SE18 2 C3
Congo Rd. SE18 2 C3
Congress Rd. SE2 3 F3
Congreve Rd. SE9 17 D4
Conifer Ave. Hart (S) 55 D4
Conifer Cl. Orp 49 F1
Conifer Dr. Bredh 74 C3
Conifer Dr. Meo 70 A3
Conifer Way. Swan 36 C2
Coniston Ave. T W 153 D1
Coniston Ave. Well 18 A4
Coniston Cl. Bexh 4 C1
Coniston Cl. Dart 20 B2
Coniston Cl. Eri 5 D2
Coniston Cl. Gil 46 B1
Coniston Rd. Bexh 4 C1
Coniston Rd. Brom 33 D3
Connaught Ave. Grays 8 B4
Connaught Cl. Maid 125 D4
Connaught Rd. Chath 60 C3
Connaught Rd. Gil 45 F1
Connaught Rd. SE18 2 B3
Connaught Way. T W 153 D1
Conquest Industrial Estate. Roc 44 B1
Conrad Cl. Grays 8 B4
Conrad Cl. Rai (K) 75 F4
Conrad Gdns. Grays 8 B4
Consort Cl. Maid 89 E1
Constable Rd. Grave 24 A1
Constable Rd. Ton 119 D1
Constance Cres. Brom 48 A3
Constitution Hill. Chath 60 B4
Constitution Hill. Grave 24 C2
Constitution Hill. Snod 72 A2
Constitution Rd. Chath 60 C3
Constitution Rise. SE18 2 B1
Constitutional Hill Rd. Soub 153 D3
Contessa Cl. Orp 50 A1
Convalescent La. Cran 174 A3
Conway Cl. Roc 44 A3
Conway Gdns. Grays 8 B2
Conway Rd. Maid 88 C1
Conway Rd. SE18 3 D3
Conyerd Rd. Bor G 84 A1
Conyers Wlk. Rai (K) 75 F4
Cooden Cl. Brom 33 E3
Cooden Cl. Rai (K) 62 B3
Cook Cl. Wald 60 C1
Cookham Dene Cl. Chis 34 C2
Cookham Hill. Chath 59 E3
Cookham Rd. Orp 36 B2
Cookham Wood Rd. Chath 59 E2
Cookhill Rd. SE2 3 E4
Cooling Cl. Maid 89 F1
Cooling Rd. Cli 27 F4
Cooling Rd. H Hals 28 C4
Cooling Rd. Roc 44 B3
Coomb Field. Ede 131 F2
Coombe Ave. Sev 81 E2
Coombe Cl. Wald 74 B4
Coombe La. Ten 186 B2
Coombe Lands. Witt 197 F4
Coombe Lea. Brom 34 A1
Coombe Lodge. SE7 1 C2
Coombe Rd. Grave 24 C1
Coombe Rd. Hoo S W 29 D1
Coombe Rd. Maid 106 A3
Coombe Rd. Otf 81 F4
Coombfield Dr. Dart 39 D4
Coombs Cl. Beckl 196 C1
Coombs Cotts. Beckl 196 C1
Cooper Cl. Gree 22 A3
Cooper Rd. Snod 72 A1
Cooper Rd. Wald 74 B4
Coopers Cl. Dart 38 C2
Coopers La. Pen 151 F2
Coopers La. SE12 16 B1
Coopers Rd. Grave 24 A2
Coote Rd. Bexh 4 A1
Copenhagen Rd. Gil 60 C4
Coplands Rise. Norm 195 E2
Copley Dene. Brom 33 F2
Coppards La. Norm 195 F2
Coppelia Rd. SE3 16 A4
Copper Beech Cl. Grave 24 C2
Copper La. Mard 142 A1
Copper Tree Ct. Maid 106 B1
Copper Tree Wlk. Wald 74 C3
Copperfield Cl. Grave 25 E2
Copperfield Cres. Higham 43 F3
Copperfield Dr. Lan H 126 A4
Copperfield Rd. Chath 59 F3
Copperfield Way. Chis 34 C3
Copperfields. Kemsg 82 A3
Copperfields Cl. Kemsg 82 A3
Copperfields Orch. Kemsg 82 A3
Copperfields Way. Kemsg 82 A3
Coppergate. Rai (K) 61 D1
Copperhouse La. Rai (K) 46 B1
Copperhouse Rd. Roc 43 F2
Coppers La. Mat 156 A3
Coppice Ct. Rai (K) 75 E4
Coppice Rd. Wald 74 C3
Coppice The. Dit 88 A3
Coppice The. Meo 70 B2
Coppice The. Pem 154 C2
Coppice The. Seal 99 F3
Coppice View. Thu 90 A1
Coppings Rd. Lei 134 C4
Copse Bank. Seal 82 A2
Copse Rd. Ton 136 A4
Copse Side. Hart (S) 40 A1
Copse The. Hoo S W 46 A4
Copsehill. Dit 87 D3
Copsewood Way. Rose 107 E4
Copt Hall Rd. Ight 100 B4
Copt Hall Rd. Meo 41 E1
Coptefield Dr. Belv 3 F4
Copthall Ave. Hawkt 189 E3
Copthorne Ave. Brom 49 D2
Coralline Wlk. SE2 3 F4
Corbylands Rd. Sid 18 A2
Cordelia Cres. Chath 59 E3
Cordwell Rd. SE13 16 A3
Corelli Rd. SE3 2 A1
Corinthian Manorway. Eri 4 C3
Corinthian Rd. Eri 4 C3
Cork La. Stapt 159 F2
Cork St. Ayld 73 D1
Corkwell St. Chath 6 A4
Cormorant Cl. Roc 43 F2
Corn Mill Dr. Orp 50 B3
Cornel Gdns. Swan 36 C2
Cornelia Pl. Eri 5 D2
Cornell Cl. Sid 36 A3
Corner Farm Rd. Stapt 160 A4
Corner Green. SE3 1 B1
Cornfield Way. Ton 118 C1
Cornflower Cl. Thu 107 D4
Cornford. T W 154 B1
Cornford Cl. Brom 48 B4
Cornford Cl. Pem 154 B1
Cornforth Cl. Stapt 160 A4
Cornwall Ave. Well 18 A4
Cornwall Cl. Maid 107 D2
Cornwall Cres. Wou 72 C4
Cornwall Dr. Sid 35 F3
Cornwall Gate. Pur 6 B3
Cornwall Rd. Chath 59 F4
Cornwall Rd. Gil 45 F1
Cornwallis Ave. Chath 60 A3
Cornwallis Ave. Gil 61 E4
Cornwallis Ave. Lint 124 A2
Cornwallis Ave. SE9 17 F1
Cornwallis Ave. Ton 137 D4
Cornwallis Rd. Maid 105 F4
Cornwallis Wlk. SE9 17 D4
Cornwell Ave. Grave 24 C1
Corona Rd. SE12 16 B2
Coronation Cl. Bex 18 C3
Coronation Cotts. Low St 30 B4
Coronation Rd. Chath 60 C3
Coronation Rd. I o G 15 E1
Corporation Rd. Gil 45 F2
Corporation St. Chath 44 C1
Corral Cl. Chath 60 C3
Corrance Green. Maid 106 B2
Correnden Rd. Ton 136 B4
Corseley Rd. Gro 165 F2
Cossack St. Chath 59 F4
Cossington Rd. Wald 74 B3
Costells Meadow. Whm 95 F3
Cot La. Bidd 176 B4
Cotleigh Ave. Bex 18 C1
Cotman Way. E Pec 121 D1
Cotmandene Cres. Orp 35 E2
Cotman's Ash La. Kemsg 82 C4
Cotman's Ash La. Shorm 67 E1
Coton Rd. Well 18 B4
Cotswold Cl. Bexh 5 D1
Cotswold Gdns. Oth 107 E3
Cotswold Rd. Grave 24 A1
Cotswold Rise. Orp 50 A4
Cottage Ave. Brom 49 D3
Cottage Field Cl. Bex 18 C2
Cottage Rd. Chath 45 D1
Cottall Ave. Chath 60 A3
Cottenham Cl. Dit 87 D1
Cotton La. Dart 21 F3
Coulman St. Gil 45 F1
Coulters Cl. Maid 89 F1
Coulton Ave. Grave 24 A2
Council Ave. Grave 23 F3
County Gate. SE9 17 F1
County Gr. W Mal 86 B2
County Rd. Maid 89 E1
Coupland Pl. SE18 2 C3
Course The. SE9 17 E1
Court Ave. Belv 4 A3
Court Broomes. Sutt V 126 C2
Court Cres. Swan 37 D1
Court Dr. Maid 105 F4
Court Farm Rd. SE9 17 D1
Court La. Had 120 B2
Court La. Sto 75 F1
Court Lane Pl. Had 120 A2
Court Lodge. Shor 43 D3
Court Lodge Rd. Gil 46 A1
Court Meadow. Wro 84 A4
Court Rd. Burh 73 D2
Court Rd. Dart 39 D4
Court Rd. SE9 17 D2
Court Rd. T W 167 D4
Court Rd (Orpington by-pass). Orp 50 B3
Court St. Brom 33 E2
Court Yd. SE9 17 D3
Courtenay Rd. Maid 106 A3
Courteney Rd. Rai (K) 61 E2
Courtenwell. Spel 166 A4
Courtfield Ave. Wald 74 B4
Courthope. Padd W 139 E1
Courtlands. Tes 104 B2
Courtlands. Ton 136 B4
Courtlands Ave. Brom 48 A3
Courtlands Ave. SE12 16 B3
Courtlands Cl. Tes 104 B2
Courtleet Dr. Eri 4 B1
Courtwood Dr. Sev 98 B4
Cousley Wood Rd. Wad 178 B2
Couthurst Rd. SE3 1 B2
Coutts Ave. Shor 43 D4
Coventry Cl. Roc 43 F1
Coventry Rd. Ton 118 C1
Coverdale Ave. Maid 106 C1
Coverdale Cl. Chath 60 B2
Covert The. Meo 70 A2
Covert The. Orp 50 A4
Covert The. Wald 74 B3
Covey Hall Rd. Snod 72 B3
Cow La. Hev 149 F3
Cowbeck Cl. Rai (K) 61 F1
Cowden Cl. Hawkt 189 D2
Cowden Rd. Maid 89 F1
Cowden Rd. Orp 50 A3
Cowdrey Cl. Chath 59 E3
Cowdrey Cl. Maid 105 E3
Cowdrey Ct. Dart 20 B2
Cowper Cl. Brom 33 F1
Cowper Cl. Well 18 B3
Cowper Rd. Belv 4 B3
Cowper Rd. Brom 33 F1
Cowper Rd. Gil 60 C4
Cowstead La. Rai (K) 62 A4
Cowstead Rd. New(a) 76 C4
Cox St. Sto 76 A2
Coxmount Rd. SE7 1 C3
Cox's Cl. Snod 72 A2
Coxwell Rd. SE18 2 C3
Cozenton Cl. Rai (K) 62 A3
Crabb Croft Cl. Orp 49 F1
Crabtree Manorway. Belv 4 C4
Crabtree Rd. Rai (K) 61 F2
Craddock Way. Rai (K) 61 F1
Craddocks La. Bidd 176 B1
Cradducks La. Stapt 160 B4
Cradles Rd. Sto 76 C3
Cradley Rd. SE9 17 F2
Cragie Wlk. Rai (K) 76 A4
Craigerne Rd. SE3 1 B2
Craigholm. SE18 2 B1
Craigton Rd. SE9 17 D4
Cramptons. Cran 174 A2
Crampton's Rd. Sev 81 E2
Cranborne Ave. Maid 106 B2
Cranbrook Cl. Brom 48 B4
Cranbrook Cl. Maid 107 D2
Cranbrook Cl. Rai (K) 61 F4
Cranbrook Rd. Bexh 4 A1
Cranbrook Rd. Bidd 175 E1
Cranbrook Rd. Gou 172 A2
Cranbrook Rd. Hawkt 182 A1
Cranbrook Rd. Stapt 160 A2
Cranbrook Rd. Ten 186 A2
Crandalls. Lei 135 D3
Crane La. Cran 173 F1
Crane Rd. Chath 45 E2
Cranford Cl. Rai (K) 61 F3
Cranford Rd. Dart 21 D2
Cranford Rd. Ton 119 E1
Cranleigh Cl. Bex 19 E3
Cranleigh Cl. Orp 50 B2
Cranleigh Dr. Swan 37 D1
Cranleigh Gdns. Chath 59 F4
Cranleigh Gdns. Maid 88 C2
Cranmer Ct. Maid 106 B2
Cranmer Rd. Sev 98 A4
Cranmore Rd. Brom 16 A1
Cranmore Rd. Chis 34 A4
Cranwell Rd. T W 166 C4
Crathie Rd. SE12 16 B3
Craven Rd. Orp 50 C2
Crawfords. Hex 37 D3
Crawshay Cl. Sev 98 B4
Cray Ave. Orp 50 B4
Cray Cl. Dart 20 B4
Cray Rd. Belv 4 B2
Cray Rd. Sid 35 F3
Cray Rd. Swan 51 F4
Cray Valley Rd. Orp 35 E1
Craybrooke Rd. Sid 35 E4
Crayburne. Grave 40 A4
Craybury End. SE9 17 F1
Craydene Rd. Eri 5 D1
Crayford Cl. Maid 89 F1

Crayford High St. Dart ... 20 A3
Crayford Rd. Dart ... 20 A3
Crayford Way. Dart ... 20 A4
Craylands. Orp ... 35 F1
Craylands La. Swans ... 22 C3
Craylands Sq. Swans ... 22 C3
Craythorne. Ten ... 186 B2
Credenhall Dr. Brom ... 49 D3
Credo Way. Grays ... 7 E2
Creek The. Grave ... 23 E3
Cremorne Rd. Grave ... 24 A2
Crendon Park. Soub ... 153 E3
Crescent Ave. Grays ... 8 C2
Crescent Dr. Orp ... 49 F4
Crescent Gdns. Swan ... 36 C2
Crescent Gr. S Ock ... 6 C4
Crescent Rd. Brom ... 33 E3
Crescent Rd. Dunt ... 81 D2
Crescent Rd. Eri ... 5 D2
Crescent Rd. S Ock ... 6 C4
Crescent Rd. SE18 ... 2 B3
Crescent Rd. Sid ... 18 A1
Crescent Rd. T W ... 167 E4
Crescent The. Bex ... 18 C2
Crescent The. Bor G ... 84 B2
Crescent The. Dit ... 88 A2
Crescent The. Grave ... 24 A1
Crescent The. Gree ... 22 C3
Crescent The. Lon ... 40 A1
Crescent The. Maid ... 89 D2
Crescent The. Sev ... 81 F1
Crescent The. Sid ... 35 D4
Crescent The. Soub ... 153 D4
Crescent The. Ton ... 136 B3
Crescent The. W Wick ... 48 A4
Crescent Way. Orp ... 50 A1
Crescent Way. Wald ... 59 F1
Crescent Wlk. S Ock ... 6 C4
Cressey Ct. Chath ... 60 A4
Cresswell Park. SE3 ... 16 A4
Crest Cl. Shorm ... 65 E2
Crest Industrial Estate. Mard ... 141 F1
Crest Rd. Brom ... 48 A3
Crest Rd. Chath ... 59 F3
Crest View Dr. Orp ... 49 F4
Cresthill Ave. Grays ... 8 C3
Crestway. Chath ... 60 C2
Crete Hall Rd. Grave ... 24 A3
Creton St. SE18 ... 2 B4
Creve Coeur Cl. Thu ... 90 B1
Cricket Ground Rd. Chis ... 34 B2
Cricketers Cl. Eri ... 5 D3
Cricketers Cl. Harr ... 109 F1
Cricketers Dr. Meo ... 56 B2
Cripple Hill. H Hald ... 177 F3
Cripple St. Maid ... 106 B2
Crismill La. Lee ... 108 A4
Crismill La. Thu ... 108 A4
Crispe Cl. Rai (K) ... 75 F4
Crispin Rd. Roc ... 44 A2
Crittenden Rd. Paddw ... 155 F4
Crocken Hill Rd. Ege ... 146 C3
Crockenhall Way. Ist ... 41 D3
Crockenhill La. Eyn ... 52 C3
Crockenhill La. Swan ... 52 C3
Crockenhill Rd. Orp ... 51 D4
Crockenhill Rd. Swan ... 51 D4
Crockham Way. SE9 ... 34 B4
Croft Cl. Belv ... 4 A3
Croft Cl. Chis ... 34 A4
Croft Cl. Ton ... 119 D1
Croft Cl. Wald ... 74 C3
Croft Ct. Ede ... 131 F3
Croft Gdns. Len ... 110 C1
Croft La. Ede ... 131 F3
Croft Rd. Brom ... 33 E3
Croft Rd. Whm ... 95 F3
Croft The. Birl ... 87 D3
Croft The. Swan ... 36 C1
Croft Way. Sev ... 98 A3
Croft Way. Sid ... 18 A1
Crofton Ave. Bex ... 18 C2
Crofton Ave. Orp ... 49 F2
Crofton La. Orp ... 49 F3
Crofton Rd. Orp ... 49 F2
Croftside. Meo ... 70 B2
Crombie Rd. Sid ... 17 F2
Cromer Pl (off Andover Rd). Orp ... 50 A3
Cromer Rd. Roc ... 44 B2
Cromer St. Ton ... 136 B3
Cromford Cl. Orp ... 50 A2
Cromlix Cl. Chis ... 34 B2
Cromwell Ave. Brom ... 33 E1
Cromwell Cl. Brom ... 33 E1
Cromwell Rd. Grays ... 8 B3
Cromwell Rd. Maid ... 89 E1
Cromwell Rd. T W ... 167 F4
Cromwell Terr. Chath ... 60 B4
Cronin Cl. Dit ... 87 D4
Crook Log. Bexh ... 18 C4
Crooke Rd. Brenc ... 156 C3
Crooked La. Grave ... 24 B3
Crookston Rd. SE9 ... 17 E4
Crosley Rd. Gil ... 60 C4
Cross Dr. Broom (M) ... 126 B3
Cross Keys. Rose ... 107 F4
Cross Keys Cl. Sev ... 98 B2
Cross La. Bex ... 19 D2
Cross Lane E. Grave ... 24 B1
Cross Lane W. Grave ... 24 B1
Cross Rd. Brom ... 49 D2
Cross Rd. Dart ... 20 C3
Cross Rd. Grave ... 24 A3
Cross Rd. Orp ... 50 B4
Cross Rd. Sid ... 35 E4
Cross Rd. Sutt H ... 38 A4
Cross St. Chath ... 60 B4
Cross St. Eri ... 5 D2
Cross St. Gil ... 45 F1
Cross St. Grave ... 24 B3
Cross St. Maid ... 89 E1
Cross St. Roc ... 44 B2
Cross Way. Chath ... 59 F4
Crossbrook Rd. SE3 ... 17 D4
Crossmead. SE9 ... 17 D2
Crossway. Orp ... 34 C1
Crossway. Wald ... 60 A1
Crossway The. SE9 ... 16 C1
Crossway The. T W ... 166 C3
Crossways Bvd. Dart ... 21 F4
Crouch Croft. SE9 ... 17 E1
Crouch House Rd. Ede ... 131 E3
Crouch La. Bor G ... 84 B1
Crouch La. Sand ... 191 D2
Crow Dr. Hals ... 80 C4
Crow Hill Rd. Bor G ... 84 B2
Crow La. Chath ... 44 C1
Crowhurst La. Plax ... 101 D4
Crowhurst La. W Kin ... 68 B4
Crowhurst Rd. Bor G ... 84 A1
Crowhurst Way. Orp ... 50 C4
Crown Acres. E Pec ... 121 E1
Crown Cl. Orp ... 50 B1
Crown Ct. SE12 ... 16 B3
Crown Green. Shor ... 43 D4
Crown La. Brom ... 49 D4
Crown La. Chis ... 34 C2
Crown La. Shor ... 43 D4
Crown Lane Spur. Brom ... 48 C4
Crown Rd. Ede ... 131 F4
Crown Rd. Grays ... 8 B2
Crown Rd. Orp ... 50 B1
Crown Rd. Shorm ... 66 A3
Crown St. Gil ... 45 F1
Crown Woods Way. SE9 ... 17 F3
Crownfields. Sev ... 98 B3
Crowstone Rd. Grays ... 8 C4
Crowther Cl. Stapt ... 160 A4
Croxley Cl. Orp ... 35 E2
Croxley Green. Orp ... 35 E2
Croyde Cl. Sid ... 17 F2
Croydon Cl. Wald ... 74 C4
Croydon Rd. Brom ... 48 C2
Croydon Rd. Whm ... 95 E3
Croydon Rd. W Wick ... 48 A2
Cruden Rd. Grave ... 25 D1
Crump's La. Ulc ... 145 E4
Crumpsall St. SE2 ... 3 F3
Crundale Rd. Rai (K) ... 61 F4
Crundwell Rd. Soub ... 153 D3
Crusader Cl. Pur ... 6 A3
Crusader Cl. Rai (K) ... 61 E2
Crusoe Rd. Eri ... 4 C3
Crutches La. Higham ... 43 E3
Cruthchley Rd. SE6 ... 16 A1
Cryals Rd. Mat ... 156 A1
Cuckoo La. Brenc ... 170 A3
Cuckoo La. Grays ... 8 A4
Cuckoo La. Ton ... 119 E2
Cuckoowood Ave. Maid ... 89 D3
Cudham Cl. Maid ... 89 F1
Cudham La. Dow ... 64 A4
Cudham La N. Dow ... 63 F2
Cudham La S. Bigg ... 79 D3
Cudham Park Rd. Dow ... 64 A3
Cudham Rd. Dow ... 63 E2
Cudham Rd. Lim ... 78 A2
Cuff Cres. SE9 ... 16 C3
Culcroft. Hart (S) ... 40 A1
Culford Rd. Grays ... 8 C4
Culpepper Cl. Holli ... 109 D3
Culpepper Rd. Cox ... 123 E4
Culpepper Rd. Rai (K) ... 75 F4
Culverden Ave. T W ... 153 E1
Culverden Down. T W ... 153 D1
Culverden Park. T W ... 153 D1
Culverden Park Rd. T W ... 153 E1
Culverden Sq. T W ... 153 E1
Culverden St. T W ... 167 E4
Culverstone Cl. Brom ... 48 A4
Culvey Cl. Hart (S) ... 55 D4
Cumberland Ave. Grave ... 24 C2
Cumberland Ave. Maid ... 106 C2
Cumberland Ave. Well ... 18 A4
Cumberland Ct. Ton ... 136 B4
Cumberland Dr. Bexh ... 4 A2
Cumberland Dr. Dart ... 21 D2
Cumberland Gdns. T W ... 167 E3
Cumberland Rd. Brom ... 33 D1
Cumberland Rd. Gil ... 45 E2
Cumberland Wlk. T W ... 167 E3
Cumberland Yd. T W ... 167 E3
Cumbrian Ave. Bexh ... 5 D1
Cunningham Cres. Chath ... 60 B2
Cunningham Rd. T W ... 153 E2
Cupola Cl. Brom ... 33 E4
Curlew Cres. Roc ... 43 F1
Curlews The. Grave ... 24 C1
Curling La. Grays ... 8 A3
Curran Ave. Sid ... 18 A3
Currie Rd. T W ... 153 E1
Curteis Rd. Ten ... 186 B3
Curtismill Cl. Orp ... 35 E1
Curtismill Way. Orp ... 35 E1
Curzon Cl. Orp ... 49 F1
Curzon Rd. Chath ... 60 A4
Curzon Rd. Maid ... 89 E1
Cut The. Chath ... 45 D1
Cut The. Chath ... 45 E2
Cut The. Sma ... 163 D2
Cutmore St. Grave ... 24 B2
Cutter Ridge Rd. Cob ... 57 E3
Cutty Sark Ct. Gree ... 22 B3
Cuxton Cl. Bexh ... 19 D3
Cuxton Industrial Estate. Cux ... 58 C3
Cuxton Rd. Maid ... 107 D1
Cuxton Rd. Roc ... 44 A1
Cyclamen Rd. Swan ... 36 C1
Cygnet Cl. Dit ... 87 E3
Cygnet Gdns. Grave ... 24 A1
Cygnet Rd. Wald ... 74 C3
Cygnet View. Grays ... 7 D3
Cypress Ave. Hoo S W ... 46 A4
Cypress Gr. T W ... 167 F2
Cypress Rd. Roc ... 44 C3
Cyril Rd. Bexh ... 4 A1
Cyril Rd. Orp ... 50 B3

Dacre Gdns. SE13 ... 16 A4
Dacre Park. SE13 ... 16 A4
Dacre Pl. SE13 ... 16 A4
Daerwood Cl. Brom ... 49 D3
Daffodil Rd. Roc ... 44 A2
Dagg La. Ewh G ... 194 A1
Dagmar Rd. Chath ... 60 B3
Dagonet Gdns. Brom ... 16 B1
Dagonet Rd. Brom ... 16 B1
Dahlia Dr. Swan ... 37 D2
Dahlia Rd. SE2 ... 3 E3
Dainton Cl. Brom ... 33 E2
Dairsie Rd. SE9 ... 17 E4
Dairy Cl. Sutt H ... 38 B3
Dairy La. Mard ... 141 D4
Dairy La. SE18 ... 2 A3
Dairy La. Whm ... 113 E3
Dalberg Way. Belv ... 3 F4
Dale Cl. Dart ... 20 A3
Dale Cl. SE3 ... 16 B4
Dale Ct. Maid ... 89 D1
Dale End. Dart ... 20 A3
Dale Rd. Chath ... 59 F4
Dale Rd. Dart ... 20 A3
Dale Rd. Souf ... 40 B4
Dale Rd. Swan ... 36 C1
Dale St. Chath ... 60 A3
Dale St. T W ... 167 E4
Dale The. Kes ... 48 C1
Dale View. Eri ... 5 D1
Dale Wlk. Dart ... 21 F2
Dale Wood Rd. Orp ... 50 A3
Daleside. Orp ... 50 B1
Daleside Cl. Orp ... 64 B4
Dallin Rd. Bexh ... 18 C4
Dallin Rd. SE18 ... 2 B2
Dallinger Rd. SE12 ... 16 A3
Dalmeny Rd. Bexh ... 4 B1
Dalton Cl. Dart ... 20 A4
Dalton Cl. Orp ... 50 A2
Dalton St. Gil ... 45 F1
Daltons Rd. Swan ... 51 F2
Damien Cl. Chath ... 60 B3
Damigos Rd. Grave ... 25 D2
Damon Cl. Sid ... 18 B1
Damson Dr. Hoo S W ... 46 A4
Dando Cres. SE3 ... 16 B4
Dandridge Cl. SE10 ... 1 A3
Dane Cl. Bex ... 19 E2
Dane Cl. New(G) ... 62 C1
Dane Cl. Orp ... 49 F1
Dane Cl. Wald ... 74 C3
Dane Ct. Cox ... 123 F3
Dane La. New(G) ... 62 C1
Dane Rd. Otf ... 81 D3
Danehill Wlk. Sid ... 18 B1
Danemore. Ten ... 186 B2
Danes Cl. Grave ... 23 F1
Danes Hill. Gil ... 46 B1
Danescombe. SE12 ... 16 B1
Danns La. Merew ... 103 E3
Dansington Rd. Well ... 18 B4
Danson Cres. Well ... 18 B4
Danson La. Well ... 18 B4
Danson Mead. Well ... 18 C4
Danson Rd. Bex ... 18 C3
Danson Rd. Bexh ... 18 C4
Danson Underpass. Sid ... 18 C3
Danson Way. Rai (K) ... 61 F3
Danvers Rd. Ton ... 136 B3
Darby Gdns. Higham ... 43 E4
Darent Cl. Chev ... 80 C1
Darent Mead. Sutt H ... 38 B2
Darenth Ave. Ton ... 118 C1
Darenth Dr. Grave ... 25 E2
Darenth Gdns. Whm ... 95 F3
Darenth Hill. Dart ... 38 C4
Darenth La. Dunt ... 81 D1
Darenth Rd. Dart ... 38 B4
Darenth Rd. Dart ... 21 E1
Darenth Rd. Well ... 3 E1
Darenth Rise. Wald ... 74 B4
Darenth Way. Shorm ... 66 B2
Drenth Wood Rd. Dart ... 22 A1
Dargate Cl. Maid ... 88 C2
Dargets Rd. Wald ... 74 B4
Darland Ave. Chath ... 61 D3
Darman La. Yal ... 139 F4
Darnets Field. Otf ... 81 D3
Darnley Cl. Roc ... 43 F1
Darnley Dr. Soub ... 153 D4
Darnley Rd. Grave ... 24 B2
Darnley Rd. Grays ... 8 B2
Darnley Rd. Roc ... 44 A1
Darnley St. Grave ... 24 B2
Darns Hill. Swan ... 51 F3
Darrick Wod Rd. Orp ... 49 F2
Dart Cl. Roc ... 44 A1
Dartford Rd. Bex ... 19 F2
Dartford Rd. Dart ... 20 B3
Dartford Rd. Farn ... 53 E4
Dartford Rd. Hort ... 38 B1
Dartford Rd. Sev ... 98 C4
Dartmouth Rd. Brom ... 48 B3
Darwin Cl. Orp ... 49 F1
Darwin Dr. Ton ... 118 C1
Darwin Rd. Well ... 18 A4
Dashmonden Cl. Roc ... 44 C3
Dashwood Cl. Bexh ... 19 E3
Dashwood Rd. Grave ... 24 B1
Davenport Ave. Gil ... 46 A2
Davenport Rd. Sid ... 19 D1
David Coffer Ct. Belv ... 4 B3
Davis Ave. Grave ... 24 A2
Davy's Pl. Grave ... 42 A3
Dawes St. Gil ... 45 F1
Dawson Ave. Orp ... 35 E2
Dawson Cl. SE18 ... 2 C3
Dawson Dr. Hex ... 37 D3
Days La. Sid ... 18 A2
Dayton Dr. Eri ... 5 F2
De Lapre Cl. Orp ... 50 C3
De Luci Rd. Eri ... 4 C3
De Lucy St. SE2 ... 3 E3
De Mere Cl. Rai (K) ... 61 F1
Deacon Cl. Roc ... 44 A2
Deacon Estate The. Ayld ... 88 B3
Deacon Trading Centre. Roc ... 44 B2
Deacons Leas. Orp ... 49 F1
Deakin Leas. Ton ... 136 B2
Dean La Meo ... 56 C1
Dean Rd. Cob ... 57 D2
Dean Rd. Meo ... 57 D2
Dean Rd. Roc ... 44 A2
Dean St. E Far ... 105 F2
Dean St. Maid ... 105 F2
Deanery Rd. Whm ... 113 F3
Deans Hill Rd. Bredg ... 77 F1
Deanwood Cl. Rai (K) ... 61 F1
Deanwood Dr. Rai (K) ... 75 F4
Debrabant Cl. Eri ... 4 C2
Decoy Hill Rd. H Hals ... 12 A1
Deepdale Ave. Brom ... 33 D1
Deepdene. Wad ... 178 A1
Deepdene Ct. Brom ... 33 D1
Deepdene Rd. Well ... 18 B4
Deerhurst Cl. Lon ... 40 C1
Deerhurst Gdns. Maid ... 106 A4
Deerleap La. Kno P ... 65 D1
Defiance Wlk. SE18 ... 2 A4
Defiant Cl. Chath ... 60 B1
Defoe Cl. Eri ... 20 A4
Degema Rd. Chis ... 34 B4
Delacourt Rd. SE3 ... 1 B2
Delafield Rd. Grays ... 8 C3
Delafield Rd. SE7 ... 1 C3
Delagarde Rd. Whm ... 95 F3
Delamere Gdns. Snod ... 72 B2
Delamere Rd. Snod ... 72 B2
Delce Rd. Chath ... 59 F4
Delius Dr. Ton ... 119 D1
Dell Dr. T W ... 167 F4
Dell Industrial Estate The. W Kin ... 21 F1
Dell Rd. Grays ... 8 B3
Dell The. Bex ... 20 A2
Dell The. SE2 ... 3 E3
Delme Cres. SE3 ... 1 B1
Delmonden Rd. Hawkt ... 188 C3
Delvan Cl. SE18 ... 2 B2
Delves Ave. T W ... 167 F3
Den La. Yal ... 140 C4
Denbeigh Dr. Ton ... 118 C1
Denberry Dr. Sid ... 18 B1
Denbigh Ave. Rai (K) ... 61 F3
Denbigh Cl. Chis ... 34 A3
Denbigh Rd. T W ... 153 F2
Denbridge Rd. Brom ... 34 A2
Dene Ave. Sid ... 18 B2
Dene Cl. Bex ... 37 D4
Dene Cl. Brom ... 48 A3
Dene Dr. Lon ... 40 B2
Dene Dr. Orp ... 50 B2
Dene Holm Rd. Grave ... 24 A1
Dene Lodge Cl. Bor G ... 84 A2
Dene Rd. Dart ... 21 D2
Dene The. Sev ... 98 B3
Dene Way. Spel ... 152 B2
Dene Wlk. Lon ... 40 A1
Denecroft Gdns. Grays ... 8 C4
Denesway. Meo ... 56 B4
Denham Cl. Well ... 18 C4
Denham St. SE10 ... 1 B3
Deniston Ave. Bex ... 19 D2
Denmark Rd. Brom ... 33 E2
Dennettsland Rd. Whm ... 113 F3
Dennis Rd. Grave ... 24 B1
Denstead Wlk. Maid ... 107 D1
Denton Cl. Maid ... 107 D2
Denton Court Rd. Grave ... 25 D2
Denton Green. Rai (K) ... 61 E4
Denton Rd. Bex ... 20 A2
Denton Rd. Dart ... 20 A2
Denton Rd. Well ... 3 F2
Denton St. Grave ... 25 D2
Denver Cl. Orp ... 50 A4
Denver Rd. Dart ... 20 B2
Derby Cl. Hild ... 118 A1
Derby Rd. Chath ... 61 D3
Derby Rd. Grays ... 8 B3
Derby Rd. Maid ... 106 C2
Derby Road Bridge. Grays ... 8 B2
Deringwood Dr. Oth ... 107 D3
Dernier Rd. Ton ... 136 C4
Derrick Gdns. SE7 ... 1 C3
Derry Downs. Orp ... 50 C4
Derwent Cl. Dart ... 20 B2
Derwent Cres. Bexh ... 4 B1
Derwent Dr. Orp ... 49 F3
Derwent Dr. T W ... 153 D1
Derwent Rd. Ton ... 118 C1
Derwent Way. Rai (K) ... 61 F2
Detling Cl. Rai (K) ... 61 F3
Detling Hill. Sto ... 90 B3
Detling Rd. Brom ... 33 E4
Detling Rd.Eri ... 4 C2
Detling Rd. Grave ... 23 F2
Devenish Rd. SE2 ... 3 E4
Devon Cl. Chath ... 60 C2
Devon Cl. Rai (K) ... 62 A3
Devon Rd. Dart ... 38 C2
Devon Rd. Maid ... 106 C2
Devon Rd. Sutt H ... 38 C2
Devonshire Ave. Dart ... 20 B3
Devonshire Cl. T W ... 167 D2
Devonshire Rd. Bexh ... 19 D4
Devonshire Rd. Gil ... 45 F2
Devonshire Rd. Grave ... 24 B1
Devonshire Rd. Orp ... 50 B3
Devonshire Rd. SE9 ... 17 D1
Devonshire Sq. Brom ... 33 E1
Dewlands Ave. Dart ... 21 E2
Dexter Cl. Grays ... 8 B4
Dhekelia Cl. Maid ... 89 E2
Dial Cl. Gil ... 46 A1
Dial Rd. Gil ... 46 A1
Diameter Rd. Orp ... 49 F4
Dianthus Cl. SE2 ... 3 E3
Dibden La. Sev ... 98 C3
Dickens Ave. Dart ... 21 E4
Dickens Cl. Hart (S) ... 55 D4
Dickens Cl. Lan H ... 126 A4
Dickens Ct. Roc ... 44 C2
Dickens Dr. Chis ... 34 C3
Dickens Dr. Dit ... 87 D3
Dickens Rd. Chath ... 59 F3
Dickens Rd. Grave ... 25 D2
Dickens Rd. Maid ... 89 D2
Dickley La. Harr ... 110 B1
Dickson Rd. SE9 ... 17 D4
Digdog La. Frit ... 174 C4
Dignals Cl. Rai (K) ... 62 A3
Dilhorne Cl. SE12 ... 16 B1
Dillon Way. T W ... 153 F1
Dillywood La. Cli W ... 44 A3
Dimmock Cl. Padd W ... 139 E2
Dinsdale Rd. SE3 ... 1 A2
Dippers Cl. Kemsg ... 82 A3
Dislingbury Rd. Pem ... 154 C4
Dislingbury Rd. Tud ... 138 A1
Disraeli Cl. Maid ... 107 D1
Dittisham Rd. SE9 ... 34 A4
Ditton Court Cl. Dit ... 87 E3
Ditton Pl. Dit ... 87 E3
Ditton Rd. Bexh ... 19 D3
Dixon Cl. Maid ... 106 A3
Dixter La. Norm ... 195 E2
Dixter Rd. Norm ... 195 E1
Dixwell Cl. Rai (K) ... 61 F1
Dobell Rd. SE9 ... 17 D3
Dobson Rd. Grave ... 42 A4
Dock Head Rd. Chath ... 45 E2
Dock Head Rd. Gil ... 45 E2
Dock Rd. Chath ... 45 D1
Dock Rd. Grays ... 8 C2
Dock Rd. Tilb ... 24 B4
Doctor Hope's Rd. Cran ... 182 C4
Dodd Rd. Ton ... 119 D1
Doddington Ct. Maid ... 89 D1
Doddington Rd. Rai (K) ... 61 F4
Doggetts Row. I o G ... 15 E1
Dogwood Cl. Bredh ... 74 C3
Dogwood Cl. Grave ... 41 D4
Dolphin Dr. Rai (K) ... 62 A1
Dolphin Yd The. Grave ... 24 B3
Dombey Cl. Chath ... 59 F4
Dombey Cl. Higham ... 43 E4
Domonic Dr. SE9 ... 17 E1
Donaldson Rd. SE18 ... 2 B1
Donet Cl. Rai (K) ... 61 F1
Dongola Rd. Roc ... 44 B2
Donkey Field. Lei ... 135 D3
Donkey La. Farn ... 53 E2
Donnington Rd. Dunt ... 80 C2
Doon Brae. Soub ... 153 E3
Dorado Gdns. Orp ... 50 C2
Doran Gr. SE18 ... 2 C2
Dorchester Ave. Bex ... 18 C2
Dorchester Cl. Cli W ... 27 E2
Dorchester Cl. Dart ... 21 D2
Dorchester Cl. Orp ... 35 E3
Dorchester Rd. Grave ... 24 C1
Dorcis Ave. Bexh ... 4 A1
Doria Dr. Grave ... 25 D1
Doric Ave. Soub ... 153 D3
Doric Cl. Soub ... 153 D3
Doris Ave. Eri ... 4 C1
Dorking Rd. T W ... 153 F1
Dormers Dr. Meo ... 56 B3
Dornberg Cl. SE3 ... 1 B2
Dornberg Rd. SE3 ... 1 B2
Dornden Dr. Spel ... 166 B4
Dornden Gdns. Wald ... 74 B3
Dorney Rise. Orp ... 35 D1
Dorothy Ave. Cran ... 183 D4
Dorothy Evans Cl. Bexh ... 19 E4
Dorrit Way. Chath ... 59 F3
Dorrit Way. Chis ... 34 C3
Dorset Ave. Well ... 18 A4
Dorset Cres. Grave ... 42 A4
Dorset Rd. SE9 ... 17 D1
Dorset Rd. T W ... 167 F3
Dorset Sq. Rai (K) ... 61 F3
Dorset St. Sev ... 98 C3
Dorset Way. Maid ... 106 C2
Dorville Rd. SE12 ... 16 B3
Dot Hill Rd. SE18 ... 2 C2
Dotterel Cl. Wald ... 74 C3
Doug Siddons Ct. Grays ... 8 C2
Douglas Rd. Len ... 110 C1
Douglas Rd. Maid ... 106 A4
Douglas Rd. Ton ... 136 B2
Douglas Rd. Well ... 3 E1
Dove Cl. Chath ... 60 B1
Dove Rd. Ton ... 118 C1
Dovedale Cl. Well ... 3 E1
Dovedale Rd. Dart ... 21 F2
Doveney Cl. Orp ... 35 F1

Dover Rd. Grave 23 F2
Dover Rd. SE18 2 B1
Dover Rd. Well 2 C1
Dover Rd E. Grave 24 A2
Dover St. Maid 105 F3
Doves Cl. Brom 49 D2
Dowanhill Rd. SE6 16 A2
Dowding Wlk. Grave 24 A1
Dower House Cres. Soub 153 D4
Dowgate Cl. Ton 136 C2
Dowlerville Rd. Orp 64 A4
Dowling Cl. Snod 72 A2
Down Ave. Lam 179 E4
Down Court Rd. Dod 94 C3
Down Court Rd. Mils 94 C3
Downbank Ave. Bexh 4 C1
Downderry Rd. Brom 33 D4
Downderry Way. Dit 87 E3
Downe Ave. Dow 63 F2
Downe Cl. Well 3 F2
Downe Rd. Dow 63 D3
Downe Rd. Dow 63 F1
Downend. SE18 2 B2
Downham Way. Brom 33 E4
Downleys Cl. SE9 17 D1
Downman Rd. SE9 17 D4
Downs Ave. Chis 34 A4
Downs Ave. Dart 21 E2
Downs Cl. Char 130 C2
Downs Cl. Maid 89 E2
Downs Hill. Ist 40 C3
Downs Rd. Ist 40 C4
Downs Rd. Maid 89 E2
Downs Rd. Yal 122 B3
Downs The. Burh 73 F3
Downs Valley. Hart (S) 40 A1
Downs View. Burh 73 D3
Downs View Cl. Dow 64 C3
Downs View Rd. Maid 89 E2
Downs Way. Char 130 C2
Downs Wood. Meo 70 A2
Downside. Roc 44 B2
Downsview. Chath 60 C2
Downsview Cl. Swan 37 D1
Downsview Rd. Sev 98 A3
Downsway. Orp 50 A1
Doyle Cl. Eri 5 D1
Drage Rd. E Pec 121 D1
Drake's Ave. Roc 44 A2
Draper Cl. Belv 4 A3
Draper St. Soub 153 D3
Drawell Cl. SE18 3 D3
Dray Corner Rd. Head 144 A2
Drays Field. Worm 93 E2
Drayton Ave. Orp 49 E3
Drayton Rd. Ton 136 C2
Dreadnoght St. SE10 1 A4
Drewery Dr. Rai (K) 61 F1
Driffield Gdns. Ton 136 A2
Drift The. Brom 48 C2
Drive The. Bex 18 C2
Drive The. Chis 35 D1
Drive The. Chis 35 D2
Drive The. Eri 4 B2
Drive The. Grave 42 A4
Drive The. Lon 40 B1
Drive The. Orp 50 A2
Drive The. Sev 98 B4
Drive The. Sid 35 E4
Drive The. T W 167 E3
Drive The. Ton 136 B2
Drove Way The. Ist 41 D3
Drudgeon Way. Dart 22 C1
Drummond Cl. Eri 5 D1
Drury Rd. Ten 186 B3
Dry Bank Ct. Ton 136 C4
Dry Bank Rd. Ton 136 C4
Dry Hill Park Cres. Ton 136 C4
Dry Hill Park Rd. Ton 136 B4
Dry Hill Rd. Ton 136 B4
Dryden Rd. Well 3 D1
Dryden Way. Orp 50 B3
Dryhill. Sund 97 E4
Dryhill Rd. Belv 4 A2
Dryland Ave. Orp 50 A1
Dryland Rd. Bor G 84 A1
Dryland Rd. Snod 72 A2
Duchess Cl. Roc 44 A2
Duchess Of Kent Dr. Wald 74 B4
Duchess' Wlk. Sev 98 C3
Ducketts Rd. Dart 20 A3
Duddington Cl. SE9 33 F4
Dudley Rd. Grave 24 A2
Dudley Rd. T W 167 E4
Dudsbury Rd. Dart 20 B3
Dudsbury Rd. Sid 35 F3
Duke Humphrey Rd. SE3 1 A1
Dukes Ave. Grays 8 B4
Dukes Meadow Dr. Rai (K) 61 D1
Dukes Orch. Bex 19 F2
Dukes Rd. T W 153 F1
Dukes Way. W Wick 48 A2
Dully Rd. Rod 94 C4
Dulverton Rd. SE9 17 F1
Dumbreck Rd. SE9 17 E4
Dunblane Rd. SE9 2 A1
Duncan Rd. Gil 45 F1
Duncroft. SE18 3 D2
Dundale Rd. Lam 169 E3
Dunera Dr. Maid 89 D2
Dunkerry Rd. SE9 17 D1
Dunkin Rd. Dart 21 E4
Dunkirk Cl. Grave 41 F4
Dunkirk Dr. Chath 60 A1
Dunk's Green Rd. Ship 101 E1
Dunlop Ct. Hawkt 189 E3
Dunn Street Rd. Bredh 75 D2
Dunning's La. Chath 59 F4
Dunstall Welling Estate. Well 3 E1
Dunstan Gr. T W 153 E1
Dunstan Rd. T W 153 E1
Dunvegan Rd. SE9 17 D4
Dunwich Rd. Bexh 4 A1
Dupree Rd. SE7 1 B3
Durant Rd. Hex 37 E3
Durham Ave. Brom 33 D1
Durham Cl. Maid 107 D3
Durham Hill. Brom 33 D4
Durham Rd. Brom 33 D1
Durham Rd. Rai (K) 61 F2
Durham Rd. Sid 35 E4
Durham Rise. SE18 2 C3
Durley Gdns. Orp 50 B1
Durling Ct. Rai (K) 62 B3
Durndale La. Grave 41 D4
Durrant Way. Orp 49 F1
Durrant Way. Swans 23 D2
Dursley Cl. SE3 1 C1
Dursley Gdns. SE3 1 C1
Dursley Rd. SE3 1 C1
Duval Dr. Chath 60 A2
Dux Hill. Plax 101 D2
Dux La. Plax 101 D3
Dyke Dr. Orp 50 C3
Dykes Way. Brom 33 D1
Dykewood Cl. Bex 20 A1
Dylan Rd. Belv 4 B4
Dyneley Rd. SE12 16 C1
Dynes Rd. Kemsg 82 A3
Dynevor Rd. T W 153 F2

Eagle Cl. Dit 87 E3
Eaglesfield Rd. SE18 2 B1
Eaglestone Cl. Bor G 84 B2
ealden Way. Dit 88 A2
Ealdham Sq. SE9 16 C4
Ealing Cl. Wald 74 C4
Eardemont Cl. Dart 20 A4
Eardley Rd. Belv 4 B3
Eardley Rd. Sev 98 B4
Earl Cl. Wald 74 B4
Earl Rd. Grave 24 A1
Earl Rise. SE18 2 C3
Earl St. Maid 106 A4
Earl's Rd. T W 167 D4
Earlshall Rd. SE9 17 E4
East Cliff Rd. T W 153 E1
East Crescent Rd. Grave 24 C3
East Cross. Ten 186 B2
East Dr. Orp 50 B4
East End Rd. Gil 45 F2
East Hall Hill. Bou Mon 125 D2
East Hall Rd. Orp 51 D3
East Hill. Dart 38 C2
East Hill. Dart 21 D2
East Hill. Ten 186 B2
East Hill Dr. Dart 21 D2
East Hill Rd. Shorm 67 E2
East Hill Rd. W Kin 67 E2
East Holme. Eri 4 C1
East Kent Ave. Grave 23 F3
East Milton Rd. Grave 24 C2
East Park Rd. Ayld 88 B3
East Rd. Chath 45 E2
East Rd. Well 3 E1
East Rochester Way. Bex 19 D3
East Rochester Way. Sid 18 B3
East Row. Chath 44 C1
East St. Bexh 19 E4
East St. Birl 86 A4
East St. Brom 33 E2
East St. Chath 60 B4
East St. Gil 45 F1
East St. Grays 8 A2
East St. Grays 8 C2
East St. Harr 110 B1
East St. Hunt 123 D2
East St. Off 85 F4
East St. Snod 72 B2
East St. Ton 136 C3
East Sutton Rd. Head 144 B4
East Sutton Rd. Sutt V 126 B2
East Sutton Rd. Sutt V 126 C1
East Terr. Grave 24 C3
East Thurrock Rd. Grays 8 C2
East Woodside. Bex 19 D2
Eastbrook Rd. SE3 1 B1
Eastbury Rd. Orp 49 F4
Eastcombe Ave. SE7 1 B2
Eastcote. Orp 50 A3
Eastcote Rd. Well 2 C1
Eastcourt Green. Rai (K) 61 E4
Eastcourt La. Rai (K) 61 E4
Easterfields. Dit 87 F1
Eastern Ave. Grays 7 D3
Eastern Ave. S Ock 6 C4
Eastern Rd. Gil 46 A1
Eastern Rd. Grays 8 C3
Eastern Way. Belv 4 B4
Eastern Way. Grays 8 B3
Eastern Way. SE28 3 E4
Eastfield Gdns. Ton 119 D1
Eastgate. Chath 44 C1
Eastgate Ct. Chath 44 C1
Eastgate Rd. Ten 186 C2
Eastgate Terr. Chath 44 C1
Eastlands Cl. T W 167 D2
Eastlands Rd. T W 167 D3
Eastleigh Rd. Bexh 19 F4
Eastling Cl. Rai (K) 61 F4
Eastmead Cl. Brom 34 A2
Eastmoor Pl. SE7 1 C4
Eastmoor St. SE7 1 C3
Eastnor Rd. SE9 17 F2
Eastry Ave. Brom 48 A4
Eastry Cl. Maid 88 C2
Eastry Rd. Eri 4 B2
Eastview Ave. SE18 3 D2
Eastway. Brom 48 B3
Eastwell Barn Mews. Ten 186 B2
Eastwell Cl. Maid 89 F1
Eastwell Cl. Padd W 139 D2
Eastwell Meadows. Ten 186 B2
Eaton Ct. Chis 34 C3
Eaton Rd. Sid 18 C1
Ebbsfleet Industrial Estate. Grave 23 E3
Ebbsfleet Wlk. Grave 23 E3
Ebdon Way. SE3 16 B4
Ebony Wlk. Maid 105 E4
Ebury Cl. Brom 49 D2
Eccles Row. Ayld 73 D1
Eccleston Cl. Orp 49 F3
Eccleston Rd. Maid 106 A3
Echo Cl. Maid 107 D1
Ector Rd. SE6 16 A1
Eddington Cl. Maid 106 B1
Eden Ave. Chath 60 B2
Eden Cl. Sid 36 C4
Eden Rd. H Hals 29 D4
Eden Rd. Sid 36 C4
Eden Rd. T W 167 E3
Eden Wlk. T W 167 E3
Edenbridge Cl. Orp 35 F1
Edenbridge Trading Centre. Ede 131 F2
Edendale Rd. Bexh 4 C1
Edgar Cl. Swan 37 D1
Edgar Rd. Kemsg 82 A3
Edge Hill. SE18 2 B2
Edgeborough Way. Brom 33 F2
Edgebury . Chis 34 B4
Edgebury Wlk. Chis 17 F1
Edgefield Cl. Dart 21 E2
Edgehill Gdns. Ist 41 D2
Edgehill Rd. Chis 34 C4
Edgewood Dr. Orp 50 B1
Edgeworth Rd. SE9 16 C4
Edgington Way. Orp 35 F3
Edinburgh Rd. Chath 60 C3
Edinburgh Rd. Gil 45 F1
Edinburgh Rd. I o G 15 E1
Edinburgh Sq. Maid 106 C2
Edington Rd. SE2 3 E4
Edisbury Wlk. Rai (K) 61 F1
Edison Gr. SE18 3 D2
Edison Rd. Brom 33 E2
Edison Rd. Well 3 D1
Edith Rd. Orp 50 B1
Ediva Rd. Meo 56 B4
Edmund Cl. Meo 56 B4
Edmund Rd. Orp 50 C4
Edmund Rd. Well 18 B4
Edmunds Ave. Orp 35 F1
Edna Rd. Maid 89 D2
Edward Rd. Bigg 78 A3
Edward Rd. Brom 33 F3
Edward Rd. Chis 34 B4
Edward St. Chath 60 B4
Edward St. Roc 44 B2
Edward St. Soub 153 D2
Edward St. T W 166 C4
Edward Wlk. Dit 87 D2
Edwards Cl. Rai (K) 61 F1
Edwards Gdns. Swan 36 C1
Edwards Rd. Belv 4 B3
Ewin Cl. Bexh 4 A2
Edwin Rd. Dart 20 C1
Edwin Rd. Rai (K) 61 F2
Edwin St. Grave 24 B2
Effingham Rd. SE12 16 A3
Egdean Wlk. Sev 98 C4
Egerton Ave. Hex 37 D2
Egerton Cl. Dart 20 B2
Egerton House Rd. Ege 129 D1
Egerton Rd. Maid 89 D2
Eggpie La. Hild 117 D2
Eggpie La. Lei 117 D2
Eglantine La. Farn 53 E4
Eglington Rd. SE18 2 B2
Eglinton Hill. SE18 2 B2
Eglinton Rd. Swans 23 D3
Egremont Rd. Rose 107 D3
Eight Dock East Rd. Gil 45 E3
Elaine Ave. Roc 44 A2
Elantine La. Hort 53 E4
Elder Cl. Broom (M) 126 C3
Elder Cl. Hoo S W 46 A4
Elderslie Rd. SE9 17 E3
Eldon St. Chath 60 B4
Eldon Way. Padd W 139 D2
Eldred Rd. Orp 50 C2
Elford Cl. SE3 16 C4
Elgal Cl. Orp 49 E1
Elgar Cl. Ton 119 D1
Elgin Gdns. Roc 43 F1
Elham Cl. Brom 33 F3
Elham Cl. Rai (K) 61 E4
Elibank Rd. SE9 17 E4
Eliot Cotts. SE3 1 A1
Eliot Pl. SE3 1 A1
Eliot Rd. Dart 21 E3
Elizabeth Cl. Maid 106 B4
Elizabeth Ct. Grave 24 B3
Elizabeth Ct. Rai (K) 61 F3
Elizabeth Rd. Grays 8 A4
Elizabeth St. Gree 22 A3
Elizabeth Terr. SE9 17 D3
Elizabeth Way. Orp 50 C4
Ellen Cl. Brom 33 F1
Ellenborough Rd. Sid 36 A4
Ellenswood Cl. Oth 107 E3
Ellingham Leas. Maid 106 C2
Elliott Rd. Brom 33 F1
Elliott St. Grave 24 C2
Elliotts La. Bras 96 C4
Ellis Cl. SE9 17 F1
Elliscombe Rd. SE7 1 C2
Ellison Rd. Sid 17 F2
Ellison Way. Rai (K) 62 B3
Elm Ave. Chath 60 A3
Elm Ave. Hoo S W 45 E4
Elm Cl. Dart 20 C2
Elm Cl. Ege 147 D4
Elm Cl. Higham 43 F4
Elm Cres. Dit 87 D2
Elm Dr. Swan 36 C2
Elm Gr. Eri 4 C2
Elm Gr. Maid 106 B4
Elm Gr. Orp 50 A3
Elm Gr. Ton 136 A4
Elm La. Ton 136 C4
Elm Rd. Dart 20 C2
Elm Rd. Eri 5 E1
Elm Rd. Gil 46 A1
Elm Rd. Grave 24 C1
Elm Rd. Grays 8 C2
Elm Rd. Gree 22 A3
Elm Rd. Hoo S W 46 A4
Elm Rd. Orp 64 B4
Elm Rd. Sid 35 E4
Elm Rd. Soub 153 D3
Elm Rd. Whm 96 A3
Elm Terr. Grays 7 E2
Elm Terr. SE9 17 E3
Elm Tree Drive. Chath 59 E3
Elm Wlk. Brom 49 D2
Elm Wlk. Dit 88 A3
Elmbourne Dr. Belv 4 B3
Elmbrook Gdns. SE9 17 D4
Elmcroft Ave. Sid 18 B3
Elmcroft Rd. Orp 50 B3
Elmdene Rd. SE18 2 B3
Elmfield. Rai (K) 61 E4
Elmfield. Ten 186 B2
Elmfield Cl. Grave 24 B2
Elmfield Cl. Sev W 116 B3
Elmfield Park. Brom 33 E1
Elmfield Rd. Brom 33 E1
Elmhurst. Belv 4 A2
Elmhurst Ave. Pem 154 C2
Elmhurst Gdns. Chath 60 A4
Elmhurst Rd. SE9 17 D1
Elmington Cl. Bex 19 E3
Elmlee Cl. Chis 34 A3
Elmley St. SE18 2 C3
Elmscott Rd. Brom 33 D4
Elmshurst Gdns. Ton 118 C2
Elmstead Ave. Chis 34 A4
Elmstead Cl. Sev 81 D1
Elmstead Glade. Chis 34 A3
Elmstead La. Chis 34 A4
Elmstead Rd. Eri 5 D1
Elmsted Cres. Well 3 F2
Elmstone Cl. Maid 105 E3
Elmstone Hole Rd. Len 127 F3
Elmstone La. Maid 105 E3
Elmstone Rd. Rai (K) 61 F2
Elmstone Terr. Orp 35 F1
Elmtree Cotts. Kno P 80 A4
Elmwood Dr. Bex 19 D2
Elmwood Rd. Hoo S W 28 A1
Elphick's Pl. T W 167 E2
Elrick Cl. Eri 5 D2
Elsa Rd. Well 3 F1
Elstow Cl. SE9 17 D3
Elstow Cl. SE9 17 E3
Elstree Gdns. Belv 4 A3
Elstree Hill. Brom 33 D3
Eltham Green Rd. SE9 16 C4
Eltham High St. SE9 17 E3
Eltham Hill. SE9 16 C3
Eltham Palace Rd. SE9 16 C3
Eltham Park Gdns. SE9 17 E4
Eltham Rd. SE12 16 B3
Eltham Rd. SE9 16 B3
Elvington Cl. Maid 88 C1
Elvington Green. Brom 48 A4
Elwill Way. Ist 41 D2
Elwyn Gdns. SE12 16 B2
Ely Cl. Eri 5 D1
Ely Cl. Rai (K) 62 A3
Elysian Ave. Orp 50 A4
Embassy Ct. Sid 18 B1
Embassy Ct. Well 18 B4
Ember Cl. Orp 49 F3
Emerald Cl. Chath 59 F2
Emes Rd. Eri 4 C2
Emily Rd. Wald 60 B1
Emmet La. Yal 122 A1
Empress Dr. Chis 34 B3
Empress Rd. Grave 25 D2
Emsworth Gr. Maid 89 F1
Engineer Cl. SE18 2 B2
Englefield Cl. Orp 35 D1
Englefield Cres. Cli W 27 E2
Englefield Cres. Orp 35 E1
Englefield Path. Orp 35 E1
Ennerdale Rd. Bexh 4 B1
Ennis Rd. SE18 2 C2
Ensfield Rd. Lei 135 D2
Enslin Rd. SE9 17 E2
Enterprise Cl. Roc 44 C2
Enterprise Way. Ede 131 F4
Epaul La. Chath 44 C1
Epsom Cl. Bexh 19 E4
Epsom Cl. Maid 107 D1
Epsom Cl. W Mal 86 B2
Erica Ct. Swan 37 D1
Eridge Rd. T W 167 D3
Erin Cl. Brom 33 D3
Erindale. SE18 2 C2
Erindale Terr. SE18 2 C2
Erith Cl. Maid 89 E2
Erith Ct. Pur 6 B3
Erith High St. Eri 5 D3
Erith Rd. Belv 4 B3
Erith Rd. Bexh 19 E4
Erith Rd. Eri 4 B1
Ermington Rd. SE9 17 F1
Ernest Dr. Maid 88 B1
Ernest Rd. Chath 60 B4
Erskine Park Rd. T W 166 C4
Erskine Rd. Meo 70 B2
Erwood Rd. SE7 2 A3
Escott Gdns. SE9 34 A4
Escreet Gr. SE18 2 B3
Eshcol Rd. Hoo S W 29 F1
Esher Cl. Bex 19 D2
Eskdale Cl. Dart 21 F2
Eskdale Rd. Bexh 4 B1
Esplanade. Chath 44 B1
Esplanade. Roc 44 B1
Essenden Rd. Belv 4 B3
Essex Cl. T W 167 D2
Essex Rd. Dart 20 C3
Essex Rd. Grave 24 B2
Essex Rd. Grays 7 E2
Essex Rd. Hall 58 B1
Essex Rd. Lon 39 F2
Essex Rd. Maid 107 D1
Estelle Cl. Chath 59 F2
Estridge Way. Ton 119 D1
Etfield Gr. Sid 35 E4
Ethelbert Cl. Brom 33 E1
Ethelbert Rd. Brom 33 E1
Ethelbert Rd. Chath 59 F4
Ethelbert Rd. Eri 4 C2
Ethelbert Rd. Orp 35 F1
Ethelbert Rd. Sutt H 38 A4
Etherington Hill. Spel 152 C2
Ethnam La. Sand 195 D4
Ethronvi Rd. Bexh 19 D4
Eton Cl. Wald 74 A4
Eton Gr. SE13 16 A4
Eton Rd. Orp 50 B1
Euclid Way. Grays 7 D3
Europe Rd. SE18 2 A4
Eustace Pl. SE18 2 A3
Eva Rd. Gil 60 C4
Evans Cl. Gree 22 B3
Evans Rd. SE6 16 A1
Evelyn Rd. Maid 106 A4
Evelyn Rd. Otf 81 F4
Evenden Rd. Meo 56 B3
Everard Ave. Brom 48 B3
Everest Cl. Grave 24 A1
Everest Dr. Hoo S W 46 A4
Everest La. Roc 44 B3
Everest Pl. Swan 36 C1
Everest Rd. SE9 17 D3
Everett Wlk. Belv 4 A3
Everglades The. Rai (K) 61 D1
Evergreen Cl. Birl 87 D3
Evergreen Cl. Higham 43 E4
Evergreen Cl. Rai (K) 61 E1
Eversley Ave. Bexh 5 D1
Eversley Cl. Maid 88 C1
Eversley Cross. Bexh 5 D1
Eversley Rd. SE7 1 B2
Evesham Rd. Grave 24 C1
Evry Rd. Sid 35 F3
Ewart Rd. Chath 60 A3
Ewehurst La. Spel 152 A1
Ewell Ave. W Mal 86 B2
Ewell La. E Far 105 D1
Ewell La. W Far 104 C1
Ewhurst La. Norm 195 E1
Exedown Rd. Wro 83 F4
Exeter Cl. Ton 136 C4
Exeter Rd. Grave 24 C1
Exeter Rd. Well 3 D1
Exeter Wlk. Chath 59 F2
Exford Gdns. SE12 16 B2
Exford Rd. SE12 16 B2
Exmouth Rd. Brom 33 E1
Exmouth Rd. Gil 45 F2
Exmouth Rd. Grays 8 B2
Exmouth Rd. Well 3 F2
Exton Cl. Wald 74 C3
Eyhorne St. Holli 108 C3
Eynsford Cl. Orp 49 F3
Eynsford Cres. Bex 18 C2
Eynsford Rd. Eyn 53 D3
Eynsford Rd. Farn 53 D3
Eynsford Rd. Gree 22 C3
Eynsford Rd. Maid 88 C2
Eynsford Rd. Swan 52 A3
Eynsham Dr. SE2 3 E4
Eynswood Dr. Sid 35 F4

Fackenden La. Shorm 66 B2
Factory Rd. E16 2 A4
Factory Rd. Grave 23 F3
Faesten Way. Dart 20 A1
Fair Acres. Brom 48 B4
Fairbank Ave. Orp 49 E2
Fairbourne La. Harr 109 F1
Fairby La. Hart (S) 55 D4
Fairby Rd. SE12 16 B3
Fairfax Cl. Rai (K) 61 F1
Fairfax Gdns. SE3 1 C1
Fairfax Rd. Grays 8 B3
Fairfield Ave. T W 153 F1
Fairfield Cl. Sid 18 A3
Fairfield Cres. Ton 136 C2
Fairfield Gr. SE7 1 C3
Fairfield Rd. Bexh 4 A1
Fairfield Rd. Bor G 84 A2
Fairfield Rd. Brom 33 E3
Fairfield Rd. Orp 50 A3
Fairfield Way. Hild 118 A1
Fairford Ave. Bexh 4 C1
Fairlands Ct. SE9 17 E3
Fairlawn. SE7 1 C2
Fairlawn Ave. Bexh 3 F1
Fairlawn Cl. Tes 104 B2

Fairlawn Ct. SE7 1 C2
Fairlead Rd. Chath 59 F3
Fairlight Cl. Soub 153 E3
Fairlight Cross. Lon 40 C1
Fairmans La. Brenc 156 B1
Fairmead. Brom 34 A1
Fairmead Cl. Brom 34 A1
Fairmead Rd. Ede 113 F1
Fairmeadow. Maid 106 A4
Fairmile Rd. T W 154 A1
Fairoak Cl. Orp 49 E3
Fairoak Dr. SE9 17 F3
Fairseat La. Stans 69 E3
Fairseat La. Stans 69 F1
Fairthorn Rd. SE10 1 B3
Fairtrough Rd. Dow 64 B2
Fairview. Eri 5 D2
Fairview. Faw 54 B2
Fairview. Hawkt 189 D3
Fairview Ave. Rai (K) 61 E1
Fairview Cl. Ton 136 B2
Fairview Dr. Higham 43 E4
Fairview Dr. Orp 50 A1
Fairview Gdns. Meo 56 B4
Fairview Rd. Ist 41 D3
Fairwater Ave. Well 18 B4
Fairway. Bexh 19 D3
Fairway. Orp 49 F4
Fairway Cl. Chath 59 F3
Fairway Dr. Dart 21 E2
Fairway The. Brom 49 D4
Fairway The. Chath 59 F3
Fairway The. Grave 24 B1
Fairways The. Soub 153 E2
Falcon Ave. Brom 34 A1
Falcon Cl. Dart 21 D3
Falcon Green. Dit 87 D3
Falcon Mews. Grave 24 A
Falconwood Ave. Well 3 D1
Falconwood Par. Well 18 A4
Falkland Pl. Wald 74 A3
Fallowfield. Chath 60 B2
Falmouth Cl. SE12 16 A3
Falmouth Pl. Five O G 138 C2
Fanconi Rd. Wald 74 B4
Fancy Row. Thur 90 C1
Fane Way. Rai (K) 75 F4
Fanns Rise. Pur 6 B3
Fant La. Maid 105 E3
Faraday Ave. Sid 18 B1
Faraday Rd. Maid 89 E2
Faraday Rd. Well 18 B4
Faraday Ride. Ton 118 C2
Faraday Way. Orp 35 E1
Faraday Way. SE18 1 C4
Fareham Wlk. Maid 107 D1
Faringdon Ave. Brom 49 E3
Farjeon Rd. SE3 1 C1
Farleigh Ave. Brom 48 B3
Farleigh Hill. Maid 106 A3
Farleigh La. Maid 105 E3
Farley Cl. Wald 74 C3
Farley La. Whm 95 E2
Farley Rd. Grave 25 D2
Farleycroft. Whm 95 F3
Farlow Cl. Grave 24 A1
Farm Ave. Swan 36 C1
Farm Cl. W Wick 48 A2
Farm Hill Ave. Roc 44 A3
Farm Holt. N Ash 55 D3
Farm La. Ton 136 B4
Farm Pl. Dart 20 B4
Farm Rd. Sev 81 F2
Farm Rd. Wald 74 A4
Farm Vale. Bex 19 E3
Farmcombe Cl. T W 167 E3
Farmcombe La. T W 167 E3
Farmcombe Rd. T W 167 F3
Farmcote Rd. SE12 16 B2
Farmcroft. Grave 24 B1
Farmdale Ave. Chath 59 D3
Farmdale Rd. SE10 1 B3
Farmer Cl. Lee 108 B1
Farmfield Rd. Brom 33 D4
Farmland Wlk. Chis 34 B4
Farmstead Dr. Ede 131 F4
Farnaby Dr. Sev 98 B3
Farnaby Rd. Brom 33 D2
Farnaby Rd. SE9 16 C4
Farnborough Cl. Maid 105 F3
Farnborough Comm. Brom 49 D2
Farnborough Comm. Orp 49 E1
Farnborough Ct. Orp 49 F1
Farnborough Hill. Orp 49 F1
Farne Cl. Maid 106 B1
Farnham Cl. Rai (K) 62 B3
Farnham Cl. Spel 166 B4
Farnham La. Spel 166 B4
Farnham Rd. Well 3 F1
Farningham Cl. Maid 89 F1
Farningham Hill Rd. Farn 52 C4
Farnol Rd. Dart 21 E4
Faro Cl. Brom 34 B2
Farraday Cl. Chath 59 F2
Farrant Cl. Orp 64 B4
Farrier Cl. Thu 90 A1
Farriers Cl. Grave 25 D2
Farrington Ave. Orp 35 E1
Farrington Pl. Chis 34 C3
Fartherwell Ave. W Mal 86 B2
Fartherwell Rd. W Mal 86 B2
Farthing Cl. Dart 21 D4
Farthing Cnr. Rai (K) 76 A4
Farthing St. Dow 63 D3
Farthing Wall. Cli 10 B2
Farthingfield. Wro 84 B4
Farwell Rd. Sid 35 F4
Farwig La. Brom 33 E2
Fashoda Rd. Brom 33 F1
Fauchon's Cl. Rose 107 D4
Fauchon's La. Rose 107 D4
Faversham Rd. Len 111 E3
Fawkham Ave. Lon 40 C1
Fawkham Green Rd. Faw 54 B2
Fawkham Rd. Faw 39 F1
Fawkham Rd. Lon 39 F1
Fawkham Rd. W Kin 68 B4
Fawley Cl. Maid 89 D2
Faygate Cres. Bexh 19 E3
Fearon St. SE10 1 B3
Featherby Rd. Rai (K) 61 E4
Federation Rd. SE2 3 F3
Felderland Cl. Maid 107 D1
Felderland Dr. Maid 107 D1
Felderland Rd. Maid 107 D1
Feldspar Cl. Wald 74 A3
Felhampton Rd. SE9 17 E1
Felixstowe Rd. SE2 3 E4
Fell Mead. E Pec 121 D1
Fellowes Way. Hild 118 A1
Fellows Cl. Rai (K) 61 E1
Felltram Way. SE7 1 B3
Felspar Cl. SE18 3 D3
Felstead Rd. Orp 50 B2
Felton Cl. Orp 49 E4
Felton Lea. Sid 35 D4
Fen Gr. Sid 18 A3
Fen Pond Rd. Ight 83 F2
Fen Pond Rd. Wro 83 F2
Fendyke Rd. Belv 3 F4
Fenn Cl. Brom 33 E3
Fennell St. SE18 2 B2
Fens Way. Hex 37 E3
Fenton Cl. Chis 34 A4
Fenwick Cl. SE18 2 B2
Ferbies. Spel 152 B2
Ferguson Ave. Grave 41 F4
Fern Down. Meo 70 B2
Fernbank Cl. Wald 74 A3
Fernbrook Ave. Sid 18 A3
Fernbrook Rd. SE13 16 A3
Ferndale. Brom 33 F2
Ferndale. T W 153 F1
Ferndale Cl. T W 167 F4
Ferndale Rd. Gil 46 A1
Ferndale Rd. Grave 24 B1
Ferndale Way. Orp 49 F1
Ferndell Ave. Bex 19 F1
Ferndene. Lon 40 C1
Ferndown Ave. Orp 49 F3
Ferndown Cl. Rai (K) 61 E1
Ferndown Rd. SE9 16 C2
Fernheath Way. Sid 36 C4
Fernhill Rd. Maid 105 E3
Fernhill St. E16 2 A4
Fernholt. Ton 118 C2
Fernhurst Cres. Soub 153 E3
Fernleigh Rise. Dit 87 E3
Ferns The. Dit 87 E3
Ferns The. T W 167 F4
Fernside La. Sev 98 C1
Fernwood Cl. Brom 33 F2
Ferranti Cl. SE18 1 C4
Ferry La. Wou 72 C4
Ferry Pl. SE18 2 B4
Ferry Rd. Hall 72 B4
Ferry Rd. Tilb 24 B4
Ferry Rd. Tilb 24 B4
Festival Ave. Lon 40 C1
Festival Cl. Bex 18 C2
Festival Cl. Eri 5 D2
Ffinch Cl. Dit 87 F2
Field Cl. Brom 33 F2
Field Cl. Wald 60 A1
Field Dr. Ede 131 F4
Field Mill Rd. Char 129 E1
Fielding Dr. Dit 87 E4
Fields La. Waty 104 A2
Fieldside Cl. Orp 49 F1
Fieldway. Orp 49 F4
Fieldways. Hawkt 189 E3
Fieldworks Rd. Gil 45 E2
Fifth Ave. Grays 7 E2
Filborough Way. Grave 25 E1
Filmer La. Sev 82 A1
Filston La. Dunt 80 C4
Filston La. Shorm 66 A1
Filston Rd. Eri 4 C3
Finchale Rd. SE2 3 E4
Finchley Cl. Dart 21 E3
Finchley Rd. Grays 8 B2
Finglesham Ct. Maid 106 C2
Fintonagh Dr. Maid 89 E2
Finucane Dr. Orp 50 C3
Finwell Rd. Rai (K) 62 B3
Fir Dene. Orp 49 E2
Fir Tree Cl. Hild 118 A1
Fir Tree Cl. Orp 50 A1
Fir Tree Cl. Stapt 160 A4
Fir Tree Gr. Bredh 74 C3
Fir Tree Gr. Bredh 75 E3
Fir Tree Rd. T W 167 D4
Fircroft Way. Ede 131 F4
Firecrest Cl. Lon 40 B1
Firethorn Cl. Gil 46 A1
Firmin Rd. Dart 20 C3
Firmingers Rd. Shorm 51 F1
Firs Cl. Dit 88 A3
Firs La. Lee 108 A3
Firs The. Bex 19 F2
First Ave. Bexh 3 F2
First Ave. Chath 60 C3
First Ave. Gil 61 D4
First Ave. Grave 24 A2
First Ave. Grays 7 E2
First St. Spel 166 A4
Fisher Rd. Chath 60 B2
Fisher St. Maid 89 E1
Fishermen's Hill. Grave 23 E3
Fishers Cl. Stapt 143 D1
Fishers Rd. Stapt 143 D1
Fisher's Way. Belv 4 C4
Fishponds Rd. Kes 48 C1
Fitzwilliam Rd. Thu 90 A1
Five Bells La. Chath 59 F4
Five Elms Rd. Brom 48 C2
Five Oak Green Rd. Five O G 138 A2
Five Oak Green Rd. Ton 136 C2
Five Oak Green Rd. Tud 137 E2
Five Oak La. Stapt 159 E3
Five Ways. T W 167 E4
Five Wents. Swan 37 E2
Fiveash Rd. Grave 24 A2
Flack Gdns. Hoo S W 29 D1
Flamingo Cl. Chath 60 B2
Flamsteed Rd. SE7 2 A3
Flaxman Dr. Maid 88 C1
Flaxton Rd. SE18 3 D2
Fleet Ave. Dart 21 F2
Fleet Dale Par. Dart 21 F2
Fleet Rd. Chath 59 F3
Fleet Rd. Dart 21 F2
Fleet Rd. Grave 23 E4
Fleming Way. Had 119 D2
Fletcher Rd. Stapt 160 A4
Fletchers Cl. Brom 33 E1
Fletching Rd. SE7 1 C2
Flimwell Cl. Brom 33 D4
Flimwell Cl. Kiln 187 F4
Flint Green. Wald 74 C4
Flint St. Grays 7 E2
Flintmill Cres. SE3 2 A1
Flora St. Belv 4 A3
Florence Cl. Grays 8 A2
Florence Rd. Brom 33 E2
Florence Rd. Maid 106 A4
Florence Rd. SE2 3 F3
Florence St. Roc 44 B2
Florida Ct. Brom 33 D1
Flowerfield. Otf 81 D3
Flowerhill Way. Ist 41 D3
Floyd Rd. SE7 1 C3
Fludyer St. SE13 16 A4
Flyers Way The. Whm 95 F3
Foalhurst Cl. Ton 137 D4
Foley St. Maid 89 E1
Fontwell Cl. Maid 107 D1
Fontwell Dr. Brom 49 E4
Foord Rd. Len 110 C1
Foord St. Chath 59 F4
Footbury Hill Rd. Orp 50 B3
Foots Cray High St. Sid 35 F3
Foots Cray La. Sid 18 C2
Footscray Rd. SE9 17 E2
Force Green La. Whm 95 F4
Ford La. Trot 85 D4
Ford La. Wro H 85 D4
Ford Rd. Grave 23 E3
Fordcombe Cl. Maid 107 D2
Fordcombe La. Pen 151 F1
Fordcombe Rd. Pen 151 E4
Fordcombe Rd. Spel 165 F4
Fordcroft Rd. Orp 50 B4
Forde Ave. Brom 33 F1
Fordwich Cl. Maid 88 B2
Fordwich Cl. Orp 50 A3
Fordwich Green. Rai (K) 61 F4
Foreland St. SE18 2 C3
Foremans Barn Rd. Hunt 123 D4
Forest Dr. Kes 49 D1
Forest Dr. Wald 74 A3
Forest Gr. Ton 118 C1
Forest Hill. Maid 106 A3
Forest Rd. Eri 5 E1
Forest Rd. Padd W 139 E1
Forest R. T W 167 F3
Forest Ridge. Kes 49 D1
Forest Way. Orp 50 B4
Forest Way. Pem 154 C2
Forest Way. Sid 17 F2
Forest Way. T W 167 F3
Forestdale Rd. Wald 74 B2
Foresters Cl. Wald 74 A3
Foresters Cres. Bexh 19 E4
Forge Cl. Brom 48 B3
Forge Cl. Pen 151 E4
Forge Croft. Ede 131 F3
Forge La. Box 89 F4
Forge La. Bredh 75 E3
Fore La. Chart S 125 D1
Forge La. E Far 105 E2
Forge La. Ege 146 C3
Forge La. Gil 46 A2
Forge La. Grave 25 D1
Forge La. H Hals 29 D4
Forge La. Head 144 C1
Forge La. Higham 43 F4
Forge La. Hort 38 C1
Forge La. Lee 108 A2
Forge La. Shor 43 D4
Forge La. W Kin 68 B3
Forge La. W Pec 102 B1
Forge La. Ya 140 B4
Forge Meadow. Harr 109 F1
Forge Meadows. Head 144 C1
Forge Meads. Witt 197 F4
Forge Rd. Soub 153 E3
Forge Sq. Lei 135 D3
Forge View. Seal 99 E1
Forge Way. Shorm 66 A2
Formby Rd. Hall 58 B2
Forsham La. Sutt V 143 F4
Forson Cl. Ten 186 B2
Forstal Cl. Brom 33 E1
Forstal La. Cox 123 F4
Forstal Rd. Ayld 88 C3
Forstal Rd. Ege 146 C3
Forstal Rd. Maid 89 D3
Forstal The. Pem 155 D2
Forstall. Spel 166 B4
Forstall The. Lei 135 E3
Forsters. Lan H 126 A4
Fort Pitt Hill. Chath 60 A4
Fort Pitt St. Chath 60 A4
Fort Rd. Hals 80 C4
Fort Rd. Tilo 24 B4
Fort St. Chath 59 F4
Fortune Wlk. SE18 2 C4
Fossdene Rd. SE7 1 B3
Fosse Bank Cl. Ton 136 B2
Fosse Rd. Ton 136 B3
Fossington Rd. Belv 3 F3
Fosten La. Bidd 176 A2
Foster St. Maid 106 B4
Fosters Cl. Chis 34 A4
Fostington Way. Wald 74 A3
Foulds Cl. Rai (K) 61 E1
Fountain Ct. Eyn 53 D2
Fountain La. Maid 105 E3
Fountain Rd. Roc 44 A3
Fountain Wlk. Grave 24 A3
Four Elmes Rd. Ede 132 A4
Four Elms Hill. Hoo S W 45 D4
Four Elms Rd. Four E 114 B1
Four Oaks Rd. Head 144 A2
Fourth Ave. Gil 61 D4
Fourth Ave. Grays 7 E2
Fourwents Rd. Hoo S W 28 C2
Fowey Cl. Wald 60 C1
Fowler Cl. Rai (K) 75 F4
Fowler Cl. Sid 36 A4
Fox Cl. Orp 50 B1
Fox House Rd. Belv 4 B3
Fox La. Kes 48 C1
Fox St. Gil 45 F1
Foxburrow Cl. Rai (K) 61 F1
Foxbury. N Ash 55 D2
Foxbury Ave. Chis 34 C3
Foxbury Cl. Brom 33 E3
Foxbury Cl. Orp 50 B1
Foxbury Dr. Orp 64 B4
Foxbury Rd. Brom 33 E3
Foxbush. Hild 117 F1
Foxcroft Rd. SE18 2 B1
Foxden Dr. Oth 107 D3
Foxearth Cl. Bigg 78 A3
Foxendown La. Meo 56 B3
Foxes Dale. SE3 16 B4
Foxfield Rd. Orp 49 F2
Foxglove Cl. Ede 131 F4
Foxglove Cres. Wald 74 A4
Foxglove Row. Hall 58 B1
Foxhole La. Hawkt 190 A3
Foxhole La. Mat 155 F3
Foxhole Rd. SE9 17 D3
Foxhome Cl. Chis 34 B3
Foxton Rd. Grays 7 F2
Foxwood Rd. Dart 22 B1
Foxwood Rd. SE3 16 A4
Foxwood Way. Lon 40 C2
Foyle Rd. SE3 1 A2
Framley Rd. Ton 119 D1
Framlingham Cres. SE9 34 A4
Frances St. SE18 2 A3
Francis Ave. Bexh 4 B1
Francis Dr. Wald 74 B3
Francis La. Maid 107 D1
Francis Rd. Dart 20 C3
Francis Rd. Hild 117 F1
Francis Rd. Orp 35 F1
Frank Woolley Rd. Ton 119 D1
Frankfield Rise. T W 167 E3
Franklin Dr. Thu 106 C4
Franklin Pas. SE9 17 D4
Franklin Rd. Bexh 4 A1
Franklin Rd. Gil 45 F1
Franklin Rd. Grave 41 F4
Franks Ct. Rai (K) 61 E3
Frank's Hollow Rd. Bid 152 C3
Franks La. Hort 53 E4
Franks Wood Ave. Orp 49 F4
Frant Field. Ede 131 F3
Frant Rd. T W 167 E3
Fraser Cl. Bex 19 F2
Fraser Rd. Eri 4 C3
Frederick Andrews Ct. Grays 8 C2
Frederick Pl. SE18 2 B3
Frederick Rd. Gil 60 C4
Free Heath Rd. Lam 178 C4
Freehold. E Pec 121 D1
Freehold The. Had 119 F3
Freelands Gr. Brom 33 E2
Freelands Rd. Brom 33 E2
Freelands Rd. Snod 72 A2
Freeman Gdns. Chath 60 A3
Freeman Rd. Grave 25 D1
Freeman Way. Maid 107 D2
Freesia Cl. Orp 50 A1
Freight La. Cran 182 C4
Fremantle Rd. Belv 4 B3
Fremlin Cl. T W 166 B4
Fremlins Rd. Rose 107 F4
Frensham Rd. Rol 192 B3
Frensham Rd. SE9 17 F1
Frensham Wlk. Wald 74 A3
Freshwater Rd. Chath 60 B2
Freta Rd. Bexh 19 D3
Frewen Cl. Norm 195 E2
Friar Rd. Orp 50 B4
Friars Ave. Wald 74 A3
Friars Mews. SE9 17 E3
Friars Way. T W 153 F1
Friars Wlk. SE2 3 F3
Friary Pl. Roc 44 B2
Friday Rd. Eri 4 C3
Fridy St. Sutt V 126 B1
Friezland Rd. T W 166 C3
Friezley La. Cran 173 F3
Frimley Ct. Sid 35 F4
Frindsbury Hill. Roc 44 C3
Frindsbury Rd. Roc 44 C2
Frinstead Cl. Orp 35 F1
Frinstead Rd. Eri 4 C2
Frinstead Wlk. Maid 88 C2
Frinsted Cl. Rai (K) 61 F4
Frinton Rd. Sid 19 D1
Frithwood Cl. Oth 107 D3
Frittenden Rd. Roc 44 C3
Frittenden Rd. Stapt 160 B3
Frobisher St. SE10 1 A2
Frobisher Way. Grave 42 A4
Frog La. T W 167 E3
Frog La. W Mal 86 C2
Froghole La. Whm 113 F4
Frogmore Wlk. Len 110 C1
Frognal Ave. Sid 35 E3
Frognal Cnr. Sid 35 D3
Frognal Pl. Sid 35 E4
Frogs Hole La. Ben 185 D4
Frog's La. Rol 192 A3
Froissart Rd. SE9 17 D3
Fromandez Dr. Hors 157 D1
Frome Ct. Ton 118 B1
Froyle Cl. Maid 88 C1
Fry Cl. I o G 15 E1
Frythe Cl. Cran 182 C4
Frythe Cres. Cran 182 C4
Frythe Way. Cran 182 C4
Frythe Wlk. Cran 182 C4
Fuchsia St. SE2 3 E3
Fuggles Cl. Padd W 139 D1
Fulbert Dr. Thu 90 A1
Fuller Cl. Orp 50 A1
Fullers Cl. Rose 107 E4
Fullers Hill. Whm 95 F3
Fulmar Rd. Roc 43 F1
Fulthorp Rd. SE3 1 B1
Fulwich Rd. Dart 21 D3
Furfield Cl. Maid 107 D1
Furnace Ave. Lam 179 E4
Furnace La. Brenc 157 D2
Furnace La. Lam 179 D4
Furner Cl. Dart 20 A4
Furrell's Rd. Chath 44 C1
Further Green Rd. SE6 16 A2
Furze Bank. Four E 114 B1
Furzefield Ave. Spel 152 B2
Furzefield Cl. Chis 34 B3
Furzefield Rd. SE3 1 B2
Fyfe Way. Brom 33 E2

Gable Cl. Dart 20 B3
Gables The. Lon 40 C2
Gabriel Gdns. Grave 42 A4
Gabriel's Hill. Maid 106 B4
Gabrielspring Rd. Farn 53 F2
Gabrielspring Rd. Hort 54 A2
Gads Hill. Gil 46 A1
Gainsborough Ave. Dart 20 C3
Gainsborough Cl. Rai (K) 61 F1
Gainsborough Dr. Grave 23 F1
Gainsborough Gdns. Ton 119 D1
Gainsborough Sq. Bexh 18 C4
Gaitskell Rd. SE9 17 F2
Galahad Ave. Roc 44 A1
Galahad Rd. Brom 33 E4
Galena Cl. Wald 74 B3
Gallants La. E Far 105 D1
Galleon Bvd. Dart 21 F4
Galleon Cl. Chath 59 F2
Galley Hill Rd. Swans 23 D3
Galley Hill Trading Estate. Swans 23 D3
Gallions Rd. SE7 1 B3
Gallon Cl. SE7 1 C3
Gallops The. Meo 70 A2
Gallosson Rd. SE18 3 D3
Gallus Sq. SE3 16 B4
Galsworthy Cres. SE3 1 C1
Gandy's La. Bou Mon 124 C3
Gapp Cl. W Kin 68 A4
Garden Ave. Bexh 19 E4
Garden Cl. Bras 114 C4
Garden Cl. Maid 107 D2
Garden Cl. SE12 16 B1
Garden Cotts. Lei 135 E3
Garden La. Brom 33 E3
Garden Pl. Dart 20 C1
Garden Rd. Brom 33 E3
Garden Rd. Sev 81 F1
Garden Rd. T W 167 E4
Garden Rd. Ton 136 C3
Garden Row. Grave 24 A1
Garden St. Gil 45 E1
Garden St. T W 167 E4
Gardenia Cl. Roc 44 B3
Gardiner Cl. Orp 35 F2
Gardiner St. Gil 45 F1
Gareth Gr. Brom 33 E4
Garfield Rd. Gil 45 F1
Garibaldi St. SE18 3 D3
Garland Rd. SE18 2 C2
Garlands. Hild 117 F2
Garlinge Rd. Soub 153 E3
Garnett Cl. SE9 17 D4
Garrard Cl. Bexh 19 E4
Garrard Cl. Chis 34 B4
Garrick Rd. SE18 2 C4
Garrick St. Grave 24 B3
Garrington Cl. Maid 89 F1
Garrison Cl. SE18 2 B2
Garth Rd. Sev 98 C2
Garvock Dr. Sev 98 B3
Gas House Rd. Chath 44 C1
Gascoyne Dr. Dart 20 A4
Gasson Rd. Swans 23 D3

Gassons Rd. Snod 72 A2
Gatcombe Cl. Wald 60 B1
Gate Farm Rd. Bid 152 C4
Gatefield Cotts. Rol 192 A4
Gates Green Rd. Kes 48 B1
Gates Green Rd. W Wick 48 B1
Gatland La. Maid 105 E3
Gatling Rd. SE2 3 E3
Gaton Rd. SE2 3 F4
Gatwick Rd. Grave 24 B1
Gault Cl. Rose 107 E3
Gavestone Cres. SE12 16 B2
Gavestone Rd. SE12 16 B2
Gayhurst Cl. Rai (K) 61 F1
Gaza Trading Estate. Lei 116 C2
Gazelle Glade. Grave 42 A4
Gedges Hill. Mat 156 A3
General Gordons Pl. SE18 2 B3
Genesta Glade. Grave 42 B4
Genesta Rd. SE18 2 C2
Geneva Ave. Rai (K) 61 E3
Gentian Cl. Thu 90 A1
Gentian Cl. Wald 74 A4
George La. Brom 48 B3
George La. Chath 44 C1
George La. Lee 108 B2
George St. Grays 8 B2
George St. Hunt 123 E2
George St. Maid 106 B4
George St. Stapt 143 D1
George St. T W 167 F4
George St. Ton 136 B2
George St. Wad 178 A1
Georges Cl. Orp 35 F1
Georgian Cl. Brom 48 B3
Georgian Dr. Cox 123 F4
Georgian Way. Rai (K) 75 F4
Geraint Rd. Brom 33 E4
Gerald Ave. Chath 60 A3
Gerald Rd. Grave 25 D2
Gerda Rd. SE9 17 F1
Gerdview Dr. Dart 37 F4
Gerrard Ave. Chath 60 A2
Gertrude Rd. Belv 4 B3
Ghyll Side Rd. Norm 195 E2
Gibbet La. Hors 157 D1
Gibbetts. Spel 166 A4
Gibbs Hill. Head 145 D1
Gibbs Hill. Net 103 F1
Gibraltar Ave. Gil 45 E2
Gibraltar Hill. Chath 60 A4
Gibraltar La. Maid 89 D2
Gibson Cl. Grave 24 A1
Giddyhorn La. Maid 88 C1
Gideon Cl. Belv 4 B3
Giggs Hill. Orp 35 E2
Gighill Rd. Dit 87 D4
Gilbert Cl. Rai (K) 61 E1
Gilbert Cl. Swans 22 C3
Gilbert Rd. Belv 4 B4
Gilbert Rd. Brom 33 E3
Gilbourne Rd. SE18 3 D2
Gildenhill Rd. Hex 37 F3
Gildersome St. SE18 2 B2
Gill Ave. Roc 44 C3
Gill Cres. Grave 24 A1
Gill The. Pem 155 D2
Gillets La. Dit 87 E1
Gillies Rd. W Kin 54 A1
Gillingham Green. Gil 46 A1
Gillingham Rd. Gil 45 F1
Gillmans Rd. Orp 50 B3
Gill's Rd. Dart 39 E2
Gilroy Way. Orp 50 B3
Gilton Rd. SE6 16 A1
Gimble Way. Pem 154 C2
Gingerbread La. Tic 188 A3
Gipps Cross La. Spel 166 A4
Gipsy La. Grays 8 C2
Gipsy Rd. Well 3 F1
Glade The. Brom 33 F2
Glade The. SE7 1 C2
Glade The. Sev 98 B4
Glade The. Wald 74 B3
Glades The. Grave 41 F3
Gladeswood Rd. Belv 4 B3
Gladstone Rd. Chath 60 A3
Gladstone Rd. Dart 21 D3
Gladstone Rd. Maid 89 E1
Gladstone Rd. Orp 49 F1
Gladstone Rd. T W 166 B4
Gladstone Rd. Ton 136 B3
Gladwell Rd. Brom 33 E3
Gladwyn Cl. Rai (K) 75 F4
Glamford Rd. Roc 43 F1
Glamis Cl. Wald 60 B1
Glanville Rd. Brom 33 E1
Glanville Rd. Gil 45 F1
Glanville Rd. Roc 44 B2
Glasbrook Rd. SE9 16 C2
Glass Yd. SE18 2 B4
Glassmill La. Brom 33 D2
Gleaming Wood Dr. Bredh 74 C2
Gleaners Cl. Thu 107 D4
Gleanings Mews. Chath 44 C1
Glebe Cl. Sma 163 E3
Glebe Ct. SE3 16 A4
Glebe Gdns. Len 111 D1
Glebe House Dr. Brom 48 B3
Glebe La. Maid 105 E3
Glebe La. Sev 98 B3
Glebe Meadow. Waty 104 A2
Glebe Pl. Hort 38 C1
Glebe Rd. Brom 33 E2
Glebe Rd. Gil 61 D4
Glebe Rd. Grave 24 A2
Glebe Rd. Sev W 116 C4
Glebe The. Bid 152 C4
Glebe The. Char 130 C2
Glebe The. Chis 34 C2
Glebe The. Cux 58 C3
Glebe The. Pem 154 C2
Glebe The. Pen 151 E4
Glebe The. SE3 16 A4
Glebe Way. Eri 5 D2
Glebefield The. Sev 98 A4
Glebeland. Ege 147 D4
Glebelands. Bid 152 C4
Glebelands. Bidd 176 A3
Glebelands. Dart 20 A4
Glebelands. Pen 151 E4
Gleeson Dr. Orp 50 A1
Glen The. Brom 33 D2
Glen The. Orp 49 E2
Glen View. Grave 24 C2
Glen View Rd. Brom 33 F2
Glenalvon Way. SE18 2 A3
Glenbarr Cl. SE9 17 E4
Glenbow Rd. Brom 33 D4
Glencoe Rd. Chath 60 B3
Glendale. Swan 52 A4
Glendale Cl. SE9 17 E4
Glendale Rd. Eri 4 C3
Glendale Rd. Grave 24 A1
Glendower Cres. Orp 50 B4
Glendown Rd. S2 3 E3
Gleneagles Cl. Orp 49 F3
Gleneagles Dr. Maid 106 B3
Gleneagles Green. Orp 49 F3
Glenesk Rd. SE9 17 E4
Glengall Rd. Bexh 19 D4
Glenhead Cl. SE9 17 E4
Glenhouse Rd. SE9 17 E3
Glenhurst Ave. Bex 19 D2
Glenister St. E16 2 B4
Glenlea Rd. SE9 17 E4
Glenluce Rd. SE3 1 B2
Glenlyon Rd. SE9 17 E3
Glenmore Park. T W 167 D2
Glenmore Rd. Well 3 D2
Glenmount Path. SE18 2 C3
Glenrosa Gdns. Grave 42 B4
Glenshiel Rd. SE9 17 E3
Glenton Rd. SE13 16 A4
Glentrammon Ave. Orp 64 A4
Glentrammon Cl. Orp 50 A1
Glentrammon Gdns. Orp 64 A4
Glentrammon Rd. Orp 64 A4
Glenure Rd. SE9 17 E3
Glenview. SE2 3 F2
Glenwood Cl. Chath 60 C3
Glenwood Cl. Maid 88 C1
Glenwood Cl. Rai (K) 61 E2
Glenwood Cl. Ten 186 B4
Glimpsing Green. Belv 4 A4
Glistening Glade. Rai (K) 62 A1
Gload Rd. Orp 50 C2
Globe La. Chath 45 D1
Gloucester Ave. Grays 8 C4
Gloucester Ave. Sid 18 A1
Gloucester Ave. Well 18 A4
Gloucester Cl. Rai (K) 62 B2
Gloucester Rd. Belv 4 A3
Gloucester Rd. Dart 20 B2
Gloucester Rd. Grave 41 F4
Gloucester Rd. Maid 106 C2
Gloucester Rd. Wad 178 A1
Gloxinia Rd. Souf 40 B3
Glyn Dr. Sid 35 E4
Glynde Rd. Bexh 19 D4
Glyndebourne Park. Orp 49 E2
Glyndon Rd. SE18 2 C3
Glynne Cl. Rai (K) 61 F1
Goad Ave. Wald 74 B4
Goddards Cl. Cran 182 B4
Goddard's Green Cotts. Ben 184 A3
Godden Rd. Snod 72 A2
Goddens Cl. Norm 195 E2
Goddens Gill. Norm 195 E2
Goddings Dr. Chath 59 E4
Goddington Chase. Orp 50 B1
Goddington La. Harr 109 E1
Goddington La. Orp 50 B2
Goddington Rd. Roc 44 B2
Godfrey Cl. Roc 44 A3
Godfrey Evans Cl. Ton 119 D1
Godfrey Hill. SE18 2 A3
Godfrey Rd. SE18 2 A3
Godstow Rd. SE2 3 F4
Godwin Rd. Brom 33 F1
Goffers Rd. SE3 1 A1
Gold St. Cob 57 D4
Golden Sq. Ten 186 B2
Golden Wood Cl. Bredh 74 C2
Goldfinch Cl. Dit 87 E3
Goldfinch Cl. Orp 50 B1
Goldfinch Cl. Padd W 139 E1
Goldfinch Rd. SE28 2 C4
Golding Cl. Dit 87 F3
Golding Gdns. E Pec 121 E1
Golding Rd. Sev 81 F1
Golding St. T W 167 E4
Goldings. Padd W 139 D1
Goldings The. Rai (K) 61 F2
Goldsel Rd. Swan 37 D1
Goldsmid Rd. Ton 136 C2
Goldsmid St. SE18 3 D3
Goldsmith's Bottom. Sev 98 A2
Goldstone Wlk. Wald 74 B3
Goldthorne Cl. Maid 106 C4
Golf Links Ave. Grave 41 E4
Golf Rd. Brom 34 B1
Golford Rd. Cran 174 B1
Gollogly Terr. SE7 1 C3
Goodall Cl. Rai (K) 62 A1
Goodbury Rd. Shorm 57 E1
Goodhart Way. W Wick 48 A4
Goodley Stock. Whm 95 E2
Goodmead Rd. Orp 50 B3
Goods Hill. Ten 185 F3
Goods Station Rd. T W 167 E4
Goodwin Dr. Maid 89 E2
Goodwin Dr. Sid 18 C1
Goodwin Rd. Cli W 27 E2
Goodwins The. T W 167 D3
Goodwood Cl. H Hals 29 D4
Goodwood Cres. Grave 41 F3
Goodworth Rd. Wro 84 A4
Goosander Way. SE18 2 C4
Goose Cl. Chath 60 B2
Goose Green Cl. Orp 35 E2
Gooseneck La. Head 144 C1
Gordon Pl. Grave 24 C3
Gordon Rd. Belv 4 C3
Gordon Rd. Chath 60 B3
Gordon Rd. Dart 20 C2
Gordon Rd. Gil 46 A1
Gordon Rd. Gil 45 E2
Gordon Rd. Grave 24 A2
Gordon Rd. Hoo S W 28 C1
Gordon Rd. Roc 44 B2
Gordon Rd. Sev 98 B3
Gordon Rd. Sid 18 A3
Gordon Rd. Soub 153 F2
Gordon Terr. Chath 59 F4
Gore Court. Maid 107 D1
Gore Green Rd. Higham 27 D2
Gore La. Gou 172 A4
Gore Rd. Dart 21 F1
Gorham Cl. Snod 72 A2
Gorham Dr. Oth 107 E3
Gorham Dr. Ton 137 D2
Gorman Rd. SE18 2 A3
Gorringe Ave. Hort 38 C2
Gorse Ave. Wald 74 A4
Gorse Cres. Dit 87 F2
Gorse Hill. Farn 53 F2
Gorse Rd. Orp 51 E2
Gorse Rd. Roc 44 A2
Gorse Rd. T W 154 A1
Gorse Way. Hart (S) 55 E4
Gorse Wood Rd. Hart (S) 40 B1
Gorst St. Gil 45 F1
Goss Hill. Hex 37 F3
Gossage Rd. SE18 2 C3
Gosshill Rd. Chis 34 B2
Gossington Cl. Chis 34 B4
Gothic Cl. Dart 20 C1
Goudhurst Cl. Maid 106 A4
Goudhurst Rd. Brom 33 D4
Goudhurst Rd. Hors 157 D1
Goudhurst Rd. Mard 141 E1
Goudhurst Rd. Rai (K) 61 E4
Goudhurst Rd. Stapt 159 F2
Gouge Ave. Grave 24 A2
Gould Rd. Wald 74 B4
Gourock Rd. SE9 17 E3
Gover Hill. Plax 102 A1
Grace Ave. Bexh 4 A1
Grace Ave. Maid 88 C1
Grace Cl. SE9 16 C1
Gracious La. Sev W 98 B1
Grafton Ave. Chath 60 A2
Graham Rd. Bexh 19 D4
Grain Rd. I o G 31 E4
Grain Rd. Low St 31 E4
Grain Rd. Rai (K) 75 F4
Graineyfield. New(G) 77 D4
Grainger Wlk. Ton 119 D1
Grampian Cl. Orp 50 A4
Grampian Cl. T W 153 F1
Grampian Way. Oth 107 E3
Granada St. Maid 106 B4
Granary. Padd W 139 E1
Granary Cl. Rai (K) 62 A3
Granary Cl. Thu 90 A1
Granby Rd. Grave 23 F3
Granby Rd. SE9 17 D4
Grand Depot Rd. SE18 2 B3
Grandshore La. Frit 160 B1
Grange Cl. Birl 86 C3
Grange Cl. Ede 131 F3
Grange Cl. Sid 18 B1
Grange Cl. Whm 95 F3
Grange Cres. Ten 186 B4
Grange Dr. Chis 34 A3
Grange Dr. Dow 64 C3
Grange Gdns. T W 166 C4
Grange Hill. Chath 60 B4
Grange Hill. Plax 101 D2
Grange La. Box 89 E3
Grange La. Hart (S) 55 E3
Grange La. Maid 89 D3
Grange Rd. Bor G 84 C2
Grange Rd. Gil 46 B1
Grange Rd. Grave 24 B2
Grange Rd. Grays 8 B2
Grange Rd. Orp 49 F2
Grange Rd. Rai (K) 46 B1
Grange Rd. Roc 44 B2
Grange Rd. Sev 98 B2
Grange Rd. T W 166 C4
Grange Rd. Ten 186 B4
Grange The. Dart 38 C2
Grange The. Dit 87 E2
Grange The. W Kin 21 F1
Grange Way. Chath 59 F4
Grange Way. Eri 5 E2
Grange Way. Hart (S) 55 D4
Grangehill Pl. SE9 17 D4
Grangehill Rd. SE9 17 D4
Grangeways Cl. Grave 41 D4
Grangewood. Bex 19 D2
Granite St. SE18 3 D3
Grant Cl. Rai (K) 61 E3
Granton Rd. Sid 35 F3
Granville Rd. Gil 46 A1
Granville Rd. Grave 24 A2
Granville Rd. Maid 89 E1
Granville Rd. Sev 98 B4
Granville Rd. Sid 35 E4
Granville Rd. T W 153 F1
Granville Rd. Well 18 C4
Granville Rd. Whm 95 F3
Grapple Rd. Maid 89 D2
Grasdene Rd. SE18 3 E2
Grasmere Ave. Orp 49 E2
Grasmere Gdns. Orp 49 E2
Grasmere Gr. Roc 44 C3
Grasmere Rd. Bexh 4 C1
Grasmere Rd. Brom 33 D3
Grasmere Rd. Orp 49 E2
Grassington Rd. Sid 35 E4
Grasslands. Lan H 126 A4
Grassmere. Dit 87 D3
Grassy Glade. Rai (K) 61 E1
Grassy La. Sev 98 B2
Gravel Hill. Stal 112 C2
Gravel Hill Cl. Bex 19 E3
Gravel Hill Cl. Bexh 19 E3
Gravel Pit La. SE9 17 F3
Gravel Pit Way. Orp 50 B3
Gravel Rd. Brom 49 D2
Gravel Wlk. Chath 44 C1
Gravelly Bottom Rd. Broom (m) 126 B3
Gravelly Bottom Rd. Lan H 126 B3
Gravelly Bottom Rd. Leeds 126 B3
Gravelly Ways. Yal 121 F1
Gravelwood Cl. Chis 17 F1
Graveney Cl. Cli W 27 F2
Graveney Rd. Maid 107 D2
Graves Estate. Well 3 E1
Gravesend Rd. Higham 44 A2
Gravesend Rd. Meo 70 A2
Gravesend Rd. Roc 44 A2
Gravesend Rd. Shor 43 E4
Gravesend Rd. Stans 69 F1
Grayland Cl. Brom 33 F2
Grayne Ave. I o G 15 E1
Grays End Cl. Grays 8 B4
Grays Farm Rd. Orp 35 E2
Grays Rd. Bigg 78 C1
Grays Town Centre. Grays 8 B2
Grazeley Cl. Bexh 19 F3
Great Bounds Dr. Soub 153 D4
Great Brooms Rd. Soub 153 F2
Great Courtlands. Spel 166 B4
Great Cross Ave. SE10 1 A2
Great Elms. Had 120 A3
Great Elms Rd. Brom 33 F1
Great Footway. Spel 166 A4
Great Hall Arc. T W 167 E4
Great Harry Dr. SE9 17 E1
Great Lines. Gil 45 E1
Great Queen St. Dart 21 D3
Great South Ave. Chath 60 B3
Great Thrift. Orp 34 C1
Greatness La. Sev 81 F1
Greatness Rd. Sev 81 F1
Greatwood. Chis 34 B3
Grebe Cl. Low St 30 C4
Grebe Ct. Dit 87 D3
Grecian Rd. T W 167 E3
Grecian St. Maid 89 E1
Green Bank Cl. Rai (K) 61 E1
Green Cl. Brom 33 D1
Green Cl. Chath 59 F3
Green Court Rd. Swan 51 F4
Green Farm Cl. Orp 50 A1
Green Farm La. Shor 26 A1
Green Gdns. Orp 49 F1
Green Hill. Dow 63 D2
Green Hill. Oth 107 E3
Green Hill. SE18 2 A3
Green Hill La. Ege 147 E3
Green Hill La. Len 127 F3
Green La. Ben 184 C3
Green La. Bou Mon 124 C4
Green La. Bras 114 C2
Green La. Chart S 143 E4
Green La. Cli 10 B1
Green La. I o G 15 E1
Green La. Lan H 126 A4
Green La. Len 128 A3
Green La. Meo 56 B3
Green La. SE9 17 E1
Green La. Shor 42 C3
Green La. Sma 163 E3
Green La. Sto 77 D3
Green La. Trot 70 B1
Green La. Yal 141 D2
Green La The. Lei 135 D3
Green Lands. Cob 56 C4
Green Manor Way. Grave 23 D4
Green Pl. Dart 20 A3
Green Rd. Hors 157 E1
Green Rd. Stal 112 C1
Green Sq. Wad 178 A1
Green St. Gil 45 F1
Green Street Green RD. Dart 39 E3
Green Street Green RD. Grave 39 E3
Green The. Bexh 4 B1
Green The. Bod 194 A2
Green The. Brom 16 B1
Green The. Brom 48 B3
Green The. Ewh G 194 B1
Green The. Lei 135 E3
Green The. Orp 49 E1
Green The. Orp 35 E3
Green The. Sev 81 F1
Green The. Sid 35 E4
Green The. Well 18 A4
Green The. Whm 95 F3
Green Vale. Bexh 18 C3
Green View Ave. Lei 135 E3
Green Way. Brom 49 D4
Green Way. Hart (S) 55 D4
Green Way. Maid 105 E4
Green Way. SE9 16 C3
Green Way. T W 154 A2
Green Wlk. Dart 20 A4
Greenacre Cl. Swan 37 D1
Greenacres. SE9 17 E3
Greenacres Cl. Orp 49 F1
Greenbank. Chath 60 B2
Greenbanks. Dart 21 D1
Greenbay Rd. SE7 1 C2
Greenborough Cl. Maid 107 D1
Greencourt Rd. Orp 50 A4
Greendale Wlk. Grave 24 A1
Greenfield. Ede 131 F3
Greenfield Cl. Ayld 73 E1
Greenfield Cl. T W 152 C1
Greenfield Gdns. Orp 49 F3
Greenfield Rd. Gil 45 F1
Greenfield Rd. Sid 36 C4
Greenfields. Maid 107 D2
Greenfields Cl. Roc 44 C4
Greenfinches. Lon 40 B1
Greenfinches. Rai (K) 61 D1
Greenfrith Dr. Ton 118 B1
Greenhill Rd. Grave 24 A1
Greenhill Rd. Otf 66 C1
Greenhill Terr. SE18 2 A3
Greenhithe. Maid 106 B4
Greenhithe Cl. Sid 18 A2
Greenholm Rd. SE9 17 E3
Greening St. SE2 3 F3
Greenlands. Bor G 84 C2
Greenlands Rd. Kemsg 82 B2
Greenlaw St. SE18 2 B4
Greenleas. Pem 154 C1
Green's End. SE18 2 B3
Greensand Rd. Rose 107 E3
Greenside. Bex 19 D2
Greenside. Maid 106 B4
Greenside. Swan 36 C2
Greentrees Ave. Ton 119 D1
Greenvale Gdns. Rai (K) 61 E3
Greenvale Rd. SE9 17 E4
Greenview Cres. Ton 136 A4
Greenview Wlk. Gil 61 E4
Greenway. Chis 34 B4
Greenway. Cran 182 B4
Greenway. Wald 59 F1
Greenway Court Rd. Holli 109 E3
Greenway Court Rd. Lee 109 E3
Greenway La. Harr 109 E2
Greenway The. Orp 50 B4
Greenways. Lon 40 C1
Greenways. Thu 90 A1
Greenways The. Padd W 139 D1
Greenwich Cl. Maid 105 F4
Greenwich Cl. Wald 74 B4
Greenwood Cl. Orp 50 A4
Greenwood Cl. Sid 18 B1
Greenwood Rd. Sid 36 C4
Greenwood Way. Sev 98 A3
Greggs Wood Rd. T W 154 A2
Gregor Mews. SE3 1 B2
Gregory Cl. Rai (K) 76 A4
Gregory Cres. SE9 16 C2
Grenada Rd. SE7 1 C2
Grenville Cl. Meo 56 B2
Gresham Ave. Hart (S) 55 D4
Gresham Cl. Bex 19 D3
Gresham Rd. Cox 123 F4
Gresswell Cl. Sid 18 B1
Grey Wethers. Ayld 89 D4
Greybury La. Ede 148 B4
Greyhound Way. Dart 20 A3
Greys Park Cl. Kes 48 C1
Greystone Pk. Sund 97 D3
Greystones Cl. Kemsg 82 A3
Greystones Rd. Rose 107 E3
Grieves Rd. Grave 24 A1
Griffin Manor Way. SE28 2 C4
Griffin Manor Way. SE28 3 D4
Griffin Rd. SE18 2 C3
Griffin Wlk. Gree 22 A3
Griffins The. Grays 8 B4
Grigg La. Head 145 E2
Griggs Way. Bor G 84 B2
Gromenfield. Gro 165 F2
Groombridge Cl. Well 18 B3
Groombridge Hill. Spel 165 F3
Groombridge Rd. Spel 165 E3
Groombridge Sq. Maid 107 D1
Grosmont Rd. SE18 3 D3
Grosvenor Ave. Chath 60 A4
Grosvenor Bridge. T W 153 E1
Grosvenor Cres. Dart 20 C3
Grosvenor Pk. T W 167 E4
Grosvenor Rd. Belv 4 B2
Grosvenor Rd. Bexh 19 D3
Grosvenor Rd. Orp 50 A4
Grosvenor Rd. Rai (K) 61 E3
Grosvenor Rd. T W 167 E4
Grosvenor Wlk. T W 167 E4
Grote's Bldgs. SE3 1 A1
Grote's Pl. SE3 1 A1
Grove Ave. T W 167 E3
Grove Cl. Brom 48 B2
Grove Green La. Thu 90 A1
Grove Green Rd. Thu 90 A1
Grove Hill Gdns. T W 167 E4
Grove Hill Rd. T W 167 E4
Grove La. Hunt 122 C2
Grove Market Pl. SE9 17 D3
Grove Park Rd. SE9 16 C1
Grove Rd. Belv 4 A2
Grove Rd. Bexh 19 F4
Grove Rd. Chath 60 B3
Grove Rd. Gil 46 B1
Grove Rd. Grave 23 E3

Grove Rd. Grays 8 C2
Grove Rd. Hall 58 A1
Grove Rd. Maid 106 C2
Grove Rd. Pen 151 D3
Grove Rd. Roc 44 B2
Grove Rd. Seal 82 B1
Grove Rd. Sev 81 F1
Grove The. Bexh 18 C4
Grove The. Bigg 78 A3
Grove The. Grave 24 B2
Grove The. Pem 154 C2
Grove The. Rose 107 E4
Grove The. Sid 36 A4
Grove The. Swan 37 D1
Grove The. Swans 23 D3
Grove The. W Kin 21 F1
Grove Vale. Chis 34 B3
Grovebury Cl. Eri 4 C2
Grovebury Rd. SE2 3 E4
Grovehill Ct. Brom 33 D3
Grovehurst La. Hors 157 F1
Grovelands R. Orp 35 E3
Grovelands Way. Grays 8 A3
Grover St. T W 167 E4
Groves The. Snod 72 A2
Grovewood Dr. Thu 90 A1
Grovewood Dr. Thu 107 D4
Guardian Ct. Rai (K) 61 F3
Guestwick. Ton 119 D1
Guibal Rd. SE12 16 B2
Guild Rd. Eri 5 D2
Guild Rd. SE7 1 C3
Guildables La. Whm 113 D2
Guildford Gdns. Roc 43 F1
Guildford Rd. T W 167 E4
Gullands. Lan H 126 A4
Gulliver Rd. Sid 18 A1
Gumley Rd. Grays 7 F2
Gumping Rd. Orp 49 F2
Gun La. Hors 157 E1
Gun La. Roc 44 B2
Gundulph Rd. Brom 33 F1
Gundulph Rd. Chath 60 A4
Gundulph Sq. Chath 44 C1
Gunfleet Cl. Grave 25 D2
Gunlands. Hors 157 E1
Gunn Rd. Swans 23 D3
Gunner La. SE18 2 B3
Gunning St. SE18 3 D3
Gunnis' Cl. Rai (K) 75 F4
Gurdon Rd. SE7 1 B3
Guston Rd. Maid 89 F1
Gwillim Cl. Sid 18 B3
Gwydyr Rd. Brom 33 D1
Gwynn Rd. Grave 23 F1
Gybbon Rise. Stapt 160 A4
Gybbons Rd. Rol 192 A4

Hackney Rd. Maid 105 F3
Hadden Rd. SE28 3 D4
Haddon Gr. Sid 18 B2
Haddon Rd. Orp 50 C4
Hadleigh Ct. Rai (K) 75 E4
Hadley Cl. Meo 56 B2
Hadley Ct. T W 153 D1
Hadley Rd. Belv 4 A3
Hadlow Park. Had 120 A3
Hadlow Rd. Maid 89 F1
Hadlow Rd. Sid 35 E4
Hadlow Rd. Ton 136 C4
Hadlow Rd. Well 3 F2
Hadlow Stair Rd. Ton 137 D4
Hadlow Way. Ist 41 D3
Haffenden Cl. Mard 141 F1
Haffenden Meadow. Char 130 C2
Haffenden Rd. Ten 186 B3
Hafton Rd. SE6 16 A2
Ha-Ha Rd. SE18 2 A2
Haig Ave. Chath 60 B3
Haig Ave. Chath 59 F3
Haig Ave. Gil 61 D4
Haig Rd. Bigg 78 A3
Haig Villas. Hoo S W 28 B1
Hailey Rd. Belv 4 B4
Haileybury Rd. Orp 50 B1
Hailstone Cl. Had 120 A2
Haimo Rd. SE9 16 C3
Hainault St. SE9 17 E2
Halcot Ave. Bexh 19 E3
Halden Cl. Maid 107 D1
Halden La. Ben 185 D2
Halden La. Rol 185 D2
Hale Cl. Orp 49 F1
Hale Ct. E Pec 121 E2
Hale La. Otf 81 D3
Hale Oak Rd. Chil 134 A4
Hale Oak Rd. Sev W 116 B2
Hale Rd. Cli W 27 F2
Hale St. E Pec 121 E2
Hales Cl. Ten 186 B2
Haley Cl. Cux 58 C3
Haleys Pl. Burh 73 E2
Half Moon La. Hild 117 F1
Halfpene La. Cob 42 B1
Halfway Ct. Pur 6 B3
Halfway St. Sid 18 A2
Halifax Cl. Chath 60 B1
Hall Ave. S Ock 6 C4
Hall Cres. S Ock 6 C4
Hall Hill. Seal 99 F4
Hall Place Cres. Bex 19 F3
Hall Rd. Dart 21 D4
Hall Rd. Dit 88 A3
Hall Rd. Grave 23 F1
Hall Rd. S Ock 6 C4
Hall Rd. Wald 74 C4
Hall Rd. Wou 72 C4
Hall Terr. S Ock 6 C4
Hall The. SE3 16 B4
Hall View. SE9 16 C1
Hallam Cl. Chis 34 A4
Hallfield Dr. Belv 4 A4
Hallford Way. Dart 20 C3
Hall's Hole Rd. T W 167 F4
Hall's Hole Rd. T W 168 A4
Hallsfield Rd. Wald 73 F3
Hallwards. Stapt 160 A3
Hallwood Cl. Rai (K) 61 F1
Halons Rd. SE9 17 E2
Halsbrook Rd. SE3 16 C4
Halstead La. Kno P 65 D1
Halstead Rd. Eri 5 D1
Halstead Wlk. Maid 88 C2
Halstow Cl. Maid 106 B1
Halstow Rd. SE10 1 B3
Halt Robin La. Belv 4 B3
Halt Robin Rd. Belv 4 B3
Ham La. Len 110 C1
Ham La. Wald 75 D4
Ham River Hill. Cli W 27 E1
Ham Shades Cl. Sid 18 B1
Ham Wall. Cli 10 B2
Hamble Rd. Ton 118 B1
Hambledon Ct. Maid 105 E4
Hambledown Rd. Sid 17 F2
Hambro Ave. Brom 48 B3
Hamelin Rd. Chath 61 D2
Hamerton Rd. Grave 23 E3
Hamilton Rd. Bexh 4 A1
Hamilton Rd. Gil 45 F2
Hamilton Rd. Sid 35 E4
Hamlea Cl. SE12 16 B3
Hamlet Cl. SE13 16 A4
Hamlin Rd. Sev 81 D1
Hammelton Rd. Brom 33 E2
Hammonds. Hawkt 189 E3
Hamond Hill. Chath 60 A4
Hampden Rd. Grays 8 B3
Hampshire Cl. Chath 60 C2
Hampshire Dr. Maid 106 C2
Hampson Way. Rose 107 E4
Hampstead La. Net 121 F3
Hampstead La. Yal 121 F3
Hampton Cl. Wald 60 B1
Hampton Cres. Grave 25 D1
Hampton Rd. Maid 89 F1
Hamptons Rd. Ship 101 E1
Hamptons Rd. W Pec 119 F4
Hamwick Green. Wald 74 C3
Hanbury Cl. Waty 104 A2
Hanbury Wlk. Bex 20 A1
Handel Wlk. Ton 119 D1
Handen Rd. SE12 16 A3
Hang Grove Hill. Dow 63 E1
Hanmer Way. Stapt 160 A3
Hanover Dr. Chis 34 B4
Hanover Dr. Rai (K) 75 F4
Hanover Rd. Cox 123 F4
Hanover Rd. T W 167 E4
Hanover Way. Bexh 18 C4
Hansol Rd. Bexh 19 D3
Hanway. Rai (K) 61 E3
Harbex Cl. Bex 19 E2
Harbledown Pl. Orp 35 F1
Harborough Ave. Sid 18 A2
Harbour The. Sutt V 126 A1
Harbourland Cl. Maid 89 E2
Harbourne La. H Hald 177 F1
Harcourt Ave. Sid 18 C2
Harcourt Gdns. Rai (K) 76 A4
Harcourt Rd. Bexh 19 D4
Harden Ct. SE18 2 A3
Harden Rd. Grave 24 A1
Hardens Manorway. SE7 1 C4
Hardie Cl. Dit 87 D3
Harding Rd. Bexh 4 A1
Hardinge Ave. Soub 153 D4
Hardinge Cl. Rai (K) 75 F4
Hardman Rd. SE7 1 B3
Hardres Terr. Orp 50 C3
Hards Town. Chath 60 B4
Hardwick Rd. Hild 118 A1
Hardy Ave. Grave 24 A1
Hardy Cl. Wald 60 B1
Hardy Gr. Dart 21 E4
Hardy Rd. SE3 1 A2
Hardy St. Maid 89 E1
Hare and Billet Rd. SE3 1 A1
Hare St. Chath 60 B4
Hare St. SE18 2 B4
Harebell Cl. Thu 90 A1
Harebell Cl. Wald 74 A4
Haredale Cl. Chath 59 F2
Harefield Rd. Sid 18 C1
Harescroft. T W 167 D2
Hargood Rd. SE3 1 C1
Harland Ave. SE9 18 A1
Harland Rd. SE12 16 B2
Harland Way. Soub 153 D4
Harlands Gr. Orp 49 E1
Harley Gdns. Orp 50 A1
Harleyford. Brom 33 F2
Harlington Rd. Bexh 19 D4
Harman Ave. Grave 41 E4
Harman Dr. Sid 18 A3
Harmer Rd. Swans 23 D3
Harmer St. Grave 24 C3
Harmony St. T W 166 C4
Harness Rd. SE28 3 E4
Harnetts Cl. Swan 51 F3
Harold Ave. Belv 4 A3
Harold Ave. Gil 61 D4
Harold Gibbons Ct. SE7 1 C2
Harold Rd. Cux 58 C4
Harold Rd. Sutt H 38 A4
Harp Farm Rd. Bredh 74 C1
Harple La. Sto 90 A3
Harptree Dr. Wald 60 A1
Harraden Rd. SE3 1 C1
Harrap Chase. Grays 8 A3
Harrier Mews. SE28 2 C4
Harries Rd. T W 153 F2
Harrington Way. SE18 1 C4
Harris Cl. Grave 24 A1
Harris Rd. Bexh 4 A1
Harrison Dr. H Hals 29 D4
Harrison Rd. Bor G 84 A2
Harrison Way. Sev 81 E1
Harrow Cl. Ede 131 F4
Harrow Ct. Sto 76 C2
Harrow Gdns. Orp 50 B1
Harrow Manor Way. SE2 3 F4
Harrow Rd. Kno P 80 A4
Harrow Rd. Rai (K) 61 D1
Harrowby Gdns. Grave 24 A1
Hart Dyke Cres. Swan 36 C1
Hart Dyke Rd. Orp 50 C3
Hart Dyke Rd. Swan 36 C1
Hart Hill. Char 130 B3
Hart Shaw. Lon 40 B2
Hart St. Maid 106 A4
Hartfield Cl. Ton 119 D1
Hartfield Cres. W Wick 48 B2
Hartfield Pl. Grave 23 F2
Hartfield Rd. Cow 149 E3
Hartfield Rd. Ede 132 A1
Hartfield Rd. W Wick 48 B1
Hartford Rd. Bex 19 E3
Harting Rd. SE9 17 D1
Hartington St. Chath 60 B4
Hartlake Rd. Had 138 A4
Hartlake Rd. Tud 137 F3
Hartley Bottom Rd. Lon 55 F3
Hartley Bottom Rd. N Ash 55 F3
Hartley Cl. Brom 34 A2
Hartley Cl. Maid 107 D1
Hartley Court Gdns. Cran 182 B4
Hartley Hill. N Ash 55 E3
Hartley Rd. Cran 182 B4
Hartley Rd. Lon 40 A2
Hartley Rd. Well 3 F2
Hartley Rd. Whm 96 A3
Hartnokes. Hawkt 189 E3
Hartnup St. Maid 105 F3
Harton Cl. Brom 33 F2
Hartpiece Cl. Rai (K) 62 A3
Hartshill Rd. Grave 24 A1
Hartsland Rd. Sev 98 C4
Hartslock Dr. SE2 3 F4
Hartsmead Rd. SE9 17 D1
Hartville Rd. SE18 3 D3
Harty Ave. Rai (K) 75 E4
Harvel Ave. Roc 44 A2
Harvel Cres. SE2 3 F3
Harvel La. Meo 70 B3
Harvel Rd. Meo 70 B2
Harvel St. Meo 70 C4
Harvest Bank Rd. W Wick 48 A2
Harvest Rd. Ton 118 C1
Harvest Ridge. Birl 86 C3
Harvest Way. Swan 36 C2
Harvest Way. Swan 51 F3
Harvester Way. Thu 106 C4
Harvesters Cl. Rai (K) 62 A2
Harvey. Grays 8 B4
Harvey Gdns. SE7 1 C3
Harvey Rd. Rai (K) 62 A2
Harvill Rd. Sid 36 A4
Harwood Ave. Brom 33 E2
Harwood Rd. Rai (K) 62 B3
Haslemere Estate. Maid 107 D1
Haslemere Rd. Bexh 4 A1
Hasletts Cl. T W 153 E1
Hassendean Rd. SE3 1 B2
Hassock Way. Kes 49 D1
Hassop Wlk. SE9 34 A4
Haste Hill Cl. Bou Mon 124 B4
Haste Hill Rd. Bou Mon 124 B4
Hasted Cl. Gree 22 C3
Hasted Rd. SE7 1 C3
Hasteds. Lee 108 C3
Hastings Rd. Brom 49 D2
Hastings Rd. Hawkt 189 D1
Hastings Rd. Maid 106 B4
Hastings Rd. Newe 191 F2
Hastings Rd. Pem 155 D1
Hastings Rd. Rol 191 F2
Hatch Rd. Len 110 C1
Hatches La. E Pec 120 C1
Hatcliffe Cl. SE3 16 A4
Hatfield Rd. Roc 44 B2
Hatham Green La. Stans 68 C3
Hathaway Cl. Brom 49 D3
Hathaway Rd. Grays 8 B3
Hatherall Rd. Maid 89 E1
Hatherley Cres. Sid 18 B1
Hatherley Rd. Sid 18 B1
Hathern Gdns. SE9 34 B4
Hatmill La. Brenc 156 B2
Hattersfield Cl. Belv 4 A3
Hatton Cl. Grave 24 A1
Hatton Cl. SE18 2 C2
Hatton Ct. Chis 34 A3
Hatton Rd. Wald 74 C4
Havant Wlk. Maid 107 D1
Havelock Rd. Belv 4 A3
Havelock Rd. Brom 33 F1
Havelock Rd. Dart 20 B3
Havelock Rd. Grave 24 A2
Havelock Rd. Ton 136 B3
Haven Cl. Chath 59 F3
Haven Cl. Ist 41 D2
Haven Cl. Sid 35 F3
Haven Cl. Swan 37 D2
Haven Hill. N Ash 69 E4
Haven Pl. Grays 8 C4
Havengore Ave. Grave 25 D2
Haverthwaite Rd. Orp 49 F2
Havisham Cl. Chath 59 F3
Havisham Rd. Grave 25 E1
Havock La. Maid 106 A4
Hawbeck Rd. Rai (K) 75 F4
Hawden Cl. Ton 136 A4
Hawden La. Ton 136 A4
Hawden Rd. Ton 136 B3
Hawes Rd. Brom 33 E2
Hawfield Bank. Orp 50 C2
Hawkenbury Cl. T W 167 F3
Hawkenbury Rd. Head 143 F1
Hawkenbury Rd. T W 168 A3
Hawkes Cl. Grays 8 B2
Hawkhurst Rd. Cran 182 A2
Hawkhurst Rd. Hawkt 182 A2
Hawkhurst Rd. Rai (K) 61 E4
Hawkhurst Rd. Tic 188 A3
Hawkinge Wlk. Orp 35 E1
Hawkins Ave. Grave 41 F4
Hawkins Cl. Chath 45 E1
Hawkshead Cl. Brom 33 D3
Hawkwood Cl. Chath 59 F4
Hawkwood La. Chis 34 C2
Hawley Rd. Dart 21 D1
Hawley Rd. Sutt H 38 B4
Hawser Rd. Chath 59 F3
Hawstead La. Orp 51 D1
Hawthorn Cl. Ede 131 F3
Hawthorn Cl. Orp 49 F4
Hawthorn Dr. W Wick 48 A1
Hawthorn La. Sev 81 D1
Hawthorn Rd. Bexh 19 D4
Hawthorn Rd. Dart 20 C2
Hawthorn Rd. Roc 44 A1
Hawthorn Walk. T W 154 A2
Hawthorn Wlk. Ton 118 C2
Hawthorndene Cl. Brom 48 B2
Hawthorndene Rd. Brom 48 A2
Hawthorne Ave. Rai (K) 61 F3
Hawthorne Cl. Brom 34 A1
Hawthorne Rd. Brom 34 A1
Hawthorns. Hart (S) 40 A1
Hawthorns. Wald 74 A3
Hawthorns The. Dit 88 A3
Haxted Rd. Brom 33 E2
Haxted Rd. Ede 131 D2
Haydens Cl. Orp 50 C3
Hayes Cl. Brom 48 B2
Hayes Cl. Higham 43 F4
Hayes Gdn. Brom 48 B3
Hayes Hill. Brom 48 A3
Hayes Hill Rd. Brom 48 A3
Hayes La. Brom 33 D1
Hayes La. Orp 50 B4
Hayes La. S Grn 77 D1
Hayes Mead Rd. Brom 48 A3
Hayes Rd. Brom 33 E1
Hayes Rd. Gree 22 A2
Hayes St. Brom 48 B3
Hayes Way. Beck 33 D1
Hayes Wood Ave. Brom 48 B3
Hayesden La. Bid 135 E1
Hayesford Park Dr. Brom 48 A4
Hayfield. Birl 87 D3
Hayfield Rd. Orp 50 B4
Hayle Mill Rd. Maid 106 A2
Hayle Rd. Maid 106 B4
Hayman Wlk. Ayld 73 D1
Haymans Hill. Hors 157 F2
Haymen St. Chath 60 A4
Haynes Cl. SE3 16 A4
Haynes Rd. Grave 24 B1
Hay's Mead. Cob 57 D4
Haywain Cl. Padd W 139 E1
Hayward Ave. Roc 44 B2
Hayward Cl. Dart 19 F3
Haywood Rd. Brom 33 F1
Haywood Rise. Orp 50 A1
Hazel Ave. Hoo S W 46 A4
Hazel Ave. Maid 88 C1
Hazel Bank. Spel 166 A4
Hazel Cotts. Hals 65 E1
Hazel Dr. Eri 5 E1
Hazel End. Swan 52 A4
Hazel Gr. Chath 60 B2
Hazel Gr. Orp 49 E2
Hazel Rd. Dart 20 C1
Hazel Rd. Eri 5 E1
Hazel Shaw. Ton 118 C2
Hazel Wlk. Brom 49 E4
Hazelbank Rd. SE6 16 A1
Hazelden Cl. W Kin 68 B3
Hazeldene Rd. Well 3 F1
Hazelmere Rd. Orp 34 C1
Hazelmere Way. Brom 48 B4
Hazels The. Rai (K) 61 E1
Hazelwood Cl. T W 154 A2
Hazelwood Rd. Dow 63 F2
Hazlemere Dr. Gil 46 B1
Hazlitt Dr. Maid 88 C1
Headcorn Rd. Bidd 162 B1
Headcorn Rd. Brom 33 E4
Headcorn Rd. Len 128 B3
Headcorn Rd. Rai (K) 61 E4
Headcorn Rd. Sma 162 C4
Headcorn Rd. Stapt 160 B4
Headcorn Rd. Sutt V 144 A4
Headcorn Rd. Ulc 127 D1
Headingley Rd. Maid 88 B1
Healy Dr. Orp 50 A1
Hearns Cl. Orp 35 F1
Hearns Rd. Orp 35 F1
Hearns Rise. Orp 35 F1
Heartenoak Rd. Hawkt 189 E4
Heath Ave. Bexh 3 F2
Heath Cl. Orp 50 C4
Heath Gr. Maid 105 E3
Heath La. Dart 20 B2
Heath La. SE3 16 A4
Heath Rd. Bex 19 F2
Heath Rd. Bou Mon 124 B3
Heath Rd. Cox 123 E4
Heath Rd. Dart 20 A3
Heath Rd. E Far 105 D1
Heath Rd. Lan H 126 A4
Heath Rd. Lint 124 B3
Heath Rd. Maid 105 D3
Heath Rise. Brom 48 B4
Heath Side. Orp 49 F3
Heath St. Dart 20 C2
Heath The. Dit 87 D1
Heath View Gdns. Grays 8 C4
Heath View Rd. Grays 8 C4
Heath Villas. SE18 3 D3
Heath Way. Eri 4 C1
Heathclose Ave. Dart 20 B2
Heathclose Rd. Dart 20 B2
Heathdene Dr. Belv 4 B3
Heathend Rd. Bex 20 A2
Heather Cl. Wald 74 A4
Heather Dr. Dart 20 B2
Heather Dr. Maid 106 B3
Heaher Dr. Ten 186 B4
Heather Rd. SE12 16 B2
Heather Wlk. Ton 118 B2
Heatherbank. Chis 34 B2
Heatherbank. SE9 2 A1
Heatherside Rd. Sid 18 C1
Heatherwood Cl. Broom (m) 127 D3
Heathfield. Chis 34 C3
Heathfield. Lan H 126 A4
Heathfield Ave. Maid 89 F2
Heathfield Cl. Chath 60 B2
Heathfield Cl. Kes 48 C1
Heathfield Cl. Maid 89 E2
Heathfield La. Chis 34 C3
Heathfield Rd. Bexh 19 D4
Heathfield Rd. Brom 33 D3
Heathfield Rd. Kes 48 C1
Heathfield Rd. Maid 89 F2
Heathfield Rd. Sev 81 D1
Heathfield Terr. SE18 3 D2
Heathfield Terr. Swan 36 C2
Heathlands Rise. Dart 20 B3
Heathlee Rd. SE3 16 A4
Heathley End. Chis 34 C3
Heathorn St. Maid 89 E1
Heathside Ave. Bexh 4 A1
Heathside Ave. Cox 123 F4
Heathview Ave. Dart 20 A3
Heathview Cres. Dart 20 B2
Heathview Dr. SE2 3 F2
Heathway. SE3 1 B2
Heathwood Gdns. SE7 2 A3
Heathwood Gdns. Swan 36 C2
Heathwood Wlk. Bex 20 A2
Heaverham Rd. Kemsg 82 C3
Heavitree Cl. SE18 2 C3
Heavitree Rd. SE18 2 C3
Hector St. SE18 3 D3
Hectorage Rd. Ton 136 C2
Hedge Place Rd. Gree 22 B3
Hedges The. Maid 89 E2
Hedgley St. SE12 16 A3
Hedley Ave. Grays 7 F2
Hedley St. Maid 89 E1
Heights The. SE7 1 C3
Helder Gr. SE12 16 A2
Helen Cl. Dart 20 B2
Helen St. SE18 2 B3
Helleborine. Grays 8 A3
Hempstead Rd. Rai (K) 75 D4
Hempstead Valley Dr. Rai (K) 75 E4
Hemsted Rd. Eri 5 D2
Henbane Cl. Thu 90 A1
Henderson Dr. Dart 21 E4
Hendley Dr. Cran 173 F1
Henfield Cl. Bex 19 E3
Hengist Rd. Eri 4 C2
Hengist Rd. SE12 16 B2
Hengist Way. Brom 33 D1
Hengrove Ct. Bex 19 D2
Henham Gdns. E Pec 121 E1
Henhurst Rd. Cob 42 A2
Heniker La. Sutt V 144 B4
Henley Cl. Chath 60 B1
Henley Cl. Rai (K) 61 F2
Henley Cl. T W 153 F1
Henley Deane. Grave 41 D4
Henley Fields. Ten 186 B3
Henley Fields. Thu 90 A1
Henley Rd. E16 2 A4
Henley St. Cob 57 D4
Henry Cooper Way. SE9 16 C1
Henry St. Brom 33 E2
Henry St. Chath 60 B4
Henry St. Grays 8 C2
Henry St. Rai (K) 62 B3
Hensill La. Hawkt 189 D2
Henson Cl. Orp 49 E2
Henville Rd. Brom 33 E2
Henwick Rd. SE9 17 D4
Henwood Green Rd. Pem 154 C2
Henwoods Cres. Pem 154 C1
Henwoods Mount. Pem 155 D1
Hepburn Gdns. Brom 48 A3
Hepplewhite Mews. Wald 74 A3
Herald Wlk. Dart 21 D3
Herbert Pl. SE18 2 B2
Herbert Rd. Bexh 4 A1
Herbert Rd. Brom 49 D4
Herbert Rd. Chath 60 B4
Herbert Rd. Hex 37 E3
Herbert Rd. Rai (K) 62 A2
Herbert Rd. SE18 2 B2
Herbert Rd. Swans 23 D3
Herdsdown. Hoo S W 28 C1

Hereford Cl. Rai (K) 61 F3
Hereford Rd. Maid 106 C2
Heritage Dr. Chath 61 D3
Heritage Hill. Kes 48 C1
Heritage Rd. Chath 60 B1
Herman Terr. Chath 60 B4
Hermitage La. Bou Mon 125 D1
Hermitage La. Dit 88 A1
Hermitage La. Maid 105 E4
Hermitage La. Sto 90 B4
Hermitage Rd. Higham 44 A4
Hern The. Bor G 84 C1
Herne Rd. Rai (K) 61 F3
Hero Wlk. Chath 59 F2
Heron Cl. Ede 131 F4
Heron Cres. Sid 35 D4
Heron Ct. Brom 33 F1
Heron Hill. Belv 4 A3
Heron Hill La. Meo 70 B4
Heron Rd. Dit 87 D3
Heron Way. Chath 60 B2
Heron Way. Grays 7 E3
Heron Way. Low St 30 C4
Heronden Rd. Maid 125 D4
Herongate Rd. Hex 37 D3
Herons Way. Pem 155 D2
Herringham Rd. SE7 1 C4
Hertford Wlk. Belv 4 B3
Herts Cres. Loose 124 A4
Hervey Rd. SE3 1 B1
Hesketh Ave. Dart 21 E2
Heskett Park. Pem 155 D1
Hever Ave. W Kin 68 A4
Hever Cl. Maid 107 D1
Hever Court Rd. Grave 41 F3
Hever Croft. Roc 44 A1
Hever Croft. SE9 34 B4
Hever Gdns. Brom 34 B2
Hever Gdns. Maid 106 A4
Hever Rd. Ede 132 B2
Hever Rd. Hev 132 B2
Hever Rd. W Kin 68 A4
Hever Road Cotts. Hev 133 D3
Hever Wood Rd. W Kin 68 A4
Heverham Rd. SE18 3 D3
Heversham Rd. Bexh 4 B1
Hewett Pl. Swan 36 C1
Hewitts Rd. Orp 65 D4
Hexal Rd. SE6 16 A1
Hextable Cl. Maid 88 C2
Hibernia Dr. Grave 25 D1
Hickin Cl. SE7 1 C3
Hickory Dell. Rai (K) 61 E1
Higgins' La. Chath 45 D1
High Banks. Loose 106 A1
High Beeches. Orp 64 B4
High Beeches. Sid 36 A4
High Beeches. T W 153 F1
High Brooms Rd. Soub 153 F2
High Cross Rd. Ight 100 B3
High Dewar Rd. Rai (K) 62 B2
High Elms. Rai (K) 62 A3
High Elms Rd. Dow 63 E3
High Firs. Swan 37 D1
High Gr. Brom 33 F2
High Gr. SE18 2 C1
High Halden Rd. Bidd 177 D3
High Hilden Cl. Ton 136 B4
High House La. Had 119 F3
High Mead. W Wick 48 A2
High Park. Norm 195 E2
High Point. SE9 17 E1
High Rd. Dart 20 C1
High Ridge. Gou 172 A2
High Rocks La. T W 166 C3
High St. Ayld 88 A4
High St. Bidd 176 B3
High St. Bor G 84 A2
High St. Bras 96 C4
High St. Brenc 156 B2
High St. Brom 33 E2
High St. Char 130 C2
High St. Chath 60 B4
High St. Cow 149 E1
High St. Cran 182 C4
High St. Dart 22 B1
High St. Dart 21 D3
High St. Dit 87 E1
High St. Dow 63 E2
High St. Ede 131 F3
High St. Eyn 53 D2
High St. Farn 53 D3
High St. Gil 45 E1
High St. Gil 45 F1
High St. Gou 172 A2
High St. Grave 24 B3
High St. Grave 23 F3
High St. Grays 8 B2
High St. Grays 22 B4
High St. Had 120 A2
High St. Hall 72 B4
High St. Hawkt 189 D3
High St. Head 144 C1
High St. I o G 15 E1
High St. Kemsg 82 B3
High St. Lam 170 B1
High St. Lei 135 D3
High St. Len 110 C1
High St. Maid 106 A4
High St. Mard 141 F1
High St. Orp 64 A4
High St. Orp 50 B3
High St. Orp 50 C4
High St. Orp 49 F1
High St. Orp 35 F1
High St. Otf 81 E4
High St. Pem 154 C1
High St. Pur 6 B3
High St. Rai (K) 62 A2
High St. Roc 44 B2
High St. Roc 45 D3
High St. Rol 192 A4
High St. Seal 82 A1
High St. Sev 80 C1
High St. Sev 98 C3
High St. Shorm 66 A2
High St. Sid 35 E4
High St. Sma 163 E3
High St. Snod 72 B2
High St. Stapt 160 A4
High St. Sutt V 126 A2
High St. Swan 37 D1
High St. Swans 23 D3
High St. T W 167 E3
High St. Ten 186 B2
High St. Tic 187 F4
High St. Ton 136 C3
High St. W Mal 86 B2
High St. Wad 178 A1
High St. Whm 95 F2
High St. Wou 58 C1
High St. Wro 84 B4
High St. Yal 122 A3
High Tor Cl. Brom 33 E3
High View. Higham 43 F4
High View Ave. Grays 8 C3
High Woods La. T W 168 B3
Higham Cl. Maid 106 A3
Higham Gdns. Ton 119 D1
Higham La. Had 119 D2
Higham Rd. Cli 27 E4
Higham Rd. Roc 44 C4
Higham School Rd. Ton 119 D1
Highbanks Cl. SE2 3 E2
Highberry. Dit 87 D3
Highbrook Rd. SE3 16 C4
Highbury La. Ten 186 B2
Highcombe. SE7 1 B2
Highcombe Cl. SE9 17 D2
Highcroft Green. Maid 125 D4
Highcross Rd. Grave 39 F3
Highfield Ave. Eri 4 B2
Highfield Ave. Orp 50 A1
Highfield Cl. Hawkt 189 E3
Highfield Cl. Pem 154 C1
Highfield Dr. Brom 33 D1
Highfield Gdns. Grays 8 C4
Highfield Rd. Bexh 19 D3
Highfield Rd. Brom 34 A1
Highfield Rd. Chis 35 D1
Highfield Rd. Dart 20 C2
Highfield Rd. Rai (K) 61 F2
Highfield Rd. Soub 153 F2
Highfield Rd N. Dart 20 C3
Highfield Rd S. Dart 20 C2
Highfields Rd. Ede 131 F4
Highfields Rd. Kemsg 82 B4
Highgate Hill. Hawkt 189 D3
Highgrove. T W 167 E2
Highgrove Rd. Wald 60 B1
Highland Rd. Bexh 19 E4
Highland Rd. Brom 33 D2
Highland Rd. Maid 107 D2
Highland Rd. Shorm 65 E3
Highlands Cl. Roc 43 F1
Highlands Hill. Hex 37 E2
Highlands Park. Sev 82 A1
Highlands Rd. Orp 50 C3
Highmead. SE18 3 D2
Highmore Rd. SE3 1 A2
Highridge. Chath 61 D3
Highstead Cres. Eri 5 D2
Highview. Meo 70 B3
Highview Cl. Maid 106 B2
Highview Dr. Wald 59 F1
Highview Rd. Sid 35 E4
Highway The. Orp 50 C1
Highwood Cl. Orp 49 F2
Highwood Dr. Orp 49 F2
Highwoods Cl. Higham 43 E4
Hilary Cl. Eri 4 C1
Hilbert Cl. T W 153 F1
Hilbert Rd. T W 153 F1
Hilborough Way. Orp 49 F1
Hilda May Ave. Swan 37 D2
Hilda Rd. Chath 60 B4
Hilda Vale Cl. Orp 49 E1
Hilda Vale Rd. Orp 49 E1
Hilden Ave. Ton 136 A4
Hilden Dr. Eri 5 E2
Hilden Lea Pl. Brom 33 D2
Hilden Park Rd. Ton 136 A4
Hildenborough Cres. Maid 88 B2
Hildenborough Gdns. Brom 33 D3
Hildenborough Rd. Lei 135 E3
Hildenborough Rd. Seal 117 F4
Hildenborough Rd. Ship 118 B4
Hilders Cl. Ede 131 E4
Hilders La. Ede 131 E4
Hill Brow. Brom 33 F2
Hill Brow. Dart 20 A3
Hill Brow. Rose 98 C4
Hill Chase. Wald 74 A4
Hill Cl. Chis 34 B4
Hill Cl. Ist 41 D3
Hill Cres. Bex 19 F2
Hill Crest. Sev 81 E1
Hill Crest. Sid 18 B2
Hill Crest. Soub 153 E2
Hill Ct. Hoo S W 45 D4
Hill End. Orp 50 A2
Hill End. SE18 2 B1
Hill Farm Cl. H Hals 29 D4
Hill Green Rd. Sto 76 C2
Hill Rd. Chath 59 E3
Hill Rd. Dart 21 D1
Hill Rd. Wou 59 D1
Hill Rise. Dart 39 D4
Hill The. Cran 182 C4
Hill The. Grave 23 F3
Hill Top. Hunt 122 C4
Hill View. Bor G 84 B2
Hill View Cl. Bor G 84 B2
Hill View Dr. Well 3 D1
Hill View Rd. Hild 118 A1
Hill View Rd. Lon 40 B1
Hill View Rd. Orp 50 A2
Hill View Rd. T W 166 C4
Hill View Way. Wald 60 A1
Hillary Ave. Grave 24 A1
Hillary Rd. Maid 89 E2
Hillborough Ave. Sev 81 F1
Hillborough Gr. Wald 74 B4
Hillbrow Cl. Sid 36 C4
Hillbrow Rd. Brom 33 D3
Hillcrest. Four E 114 B1
Hillcrest Ave. Grays 7 E2
Hillcrest Dr. Cux 58 C3
Hillcrest Dr. Gree 22 B3
Hillcrest Dr. T W 153 F2
Hillcrest Rd. Brom 33 E4
Hillcrest Rd. Chath 60 A3
Hillcrest Rd. Dart 20 A2
Hillcrest Rd. Ede 131 F4
Hillcrest Rd. Orp 50 B2
Hillden Shaw. Maid 106 B2
Hilldown Rd. Brom 48 A3
Hilldrop Rd. Brom 33 E3
Hillfield Rd. Dunt 81 D2
Hillgarth. Soub 153 E2
Hillhouse Rd. Dart 21 F2
Hillingdon Ave. Sev 81 F1
Hillingdon Rd. Bexh 19 F4
Hillingdon Rd. Grave 24 B1
Hillingdon Rise. Sev 81 F1
Hillreach. SE18 2 A3
Hills La. W Kin 67 E2
Hills Terr. Chath 60 A4
Hillshaw Cres. Roc 44 A1
Hillside. Chath 59 E3
Hillside. Dart 39 D4
Hillside. Eri 4 C3
Hillside. Farn 53 D3
Hillside. Grays 8 C3
Hillside. Ton 136 B2
Hillside Ave. Grave 24 C1
Hillside Ave. Roc 44 B2
Hillside Ct. Waty 104 A2
Hillside Dr. Grave 24 C1
Hillside La. Brom 48 A2
Hillside Rd. Brom 33 D1
Hilside Rd. Chath 60 B4
Hillside Rd. Dart 20 B3
Hillside Rd. Kemsg 82 A3
Hillside Rd. Lim 78 A2
Hillside Rd. Sev 98 C4
Hillside Rd. Stal 112 C1
Hillside The. Orp 64 B3
Hilltop. Ton 136 B2
Hilltop Gdns. Dart 21 D3
Hilltop Gdns. Orp 50 A2
Hilltop Rd. Grays 7 E2
Hilltop Rd. Roc 44 C3
Hillview Cres. Orp 50 A3
Hillview Rd. Chis 34 B4
Hillydeal Rd. Otf 81 F4
Hillyfield Cl. Roc 44 A3
Hilton Rd. Cli W 27 E2
Hind Cres. Eri 4 C2
Hinksden Rd. Ben 190 A4
Hinksey Path. SE2 3 F4
Hinstock Rd. SE18 2 C1
Hinton Cl. SE9 17 D2
Hinton Cres. Rai (K) 61 E1
Hitchen Hatch La. Sev 98 B4
Hither Chantlers. Spel 166 B3
Hither Field. Char 130 B2
Hither Green La SE12 16 A2
Hive La. Grave 23 E3
Hive The. Grave 23 E3
Hoath Cl. Rai (K) 61 E2
Hoath La. Rai (K) 61 E2
Hoath Way. Rai (K) 61 E2
Hobbs La. Beckl 196 C1
Hoblands End. Chis 35 D3
Hockenden La. Swan 36 B2
Hockers Cl. Thu 90 B2
Hockers La. Thu 90 B2
Hoddesdon Rd. Belv 4 B3
Hodgson Cres. Snod 72 B3
Hodsoll Ct. Orp 50 C4
Hodsoll St. N Ash 69 F3
Hodson Cres. Orp 50 C4
Hog La. Grave 23 F1
Hogbarn La. Harr 110 B3
Hogg La. Grays 8 B3
Hoghole La. Lam 179 D3
Hognore La. Stans 69 F1
Hogtrough Hill. Bras 79 D1
Holbeach Gdns. Sid 18 A3
Holborn La. Chath 45 D1
Holborough Rd. Snod 72 B3
Holbrook La. Chis 34 C3
Holbrook Way. Brom 49 D4
Holburne Cl. SE3 1 C1
Holburne Gdns. SE3 1 C1
Holburne Rd. SE3 1 C1
Holcombe Rd. Chath 60 A3
Holcombe Rd. Chath 59 F4
Holcote Cl. Belv 4 A4
Holden Chr. Soub 153 D3
Holden Park Rd. Soub 153 D2
Holden Rd. Soub 153 D3
Holder Cl. Wald 60 C1
Holding St. Rai (K) 62 A3
Hole La. Ede 113 E1
Holford St. Ton 136 B3
Holgate St. SE7 1 C4
Holland Cl. Brom 48 A2
Holland Rd. Maid 89 E1
Holland Rd. Wald 74 A4
Holland Way. Brom 48 A2
Hollands Cl. Shor 43 D4
Hollies Ave. Sid 18 A2
Hollies The. Grave 41 F3
Hollies The. Sid 18 B2
Holligrave Rd. Brom 33 E2
Hollin Cl. T W 167 D4
Hollingbourne Ave. Bexh 4 A1
Hollingbourne Hill. Holli 109 D4
Hollingbourne Rd. Rai (K) 61 F4
Hollingworth Rd. Maid 107 D1
Hollingworth Rd. Orp 49 E3
Hollingworth Way. Whm 95 F3
Hollis Pl. Grays 8 B3
Hollow La. Ede 148 A1
Hollow La. New(G) 62 C1
Hollow La. Snod 72 A1
Hollowfield Ave. Grays 8 C3
Holly Bank. Brenc 156 B2
Holly Bush La. Sev 98 C4
Holly Cl. Chath 60 C2
Holly Cl. Gil 46 A1
Holly Farm Rd. Lan H 107 F1
Holly Hill Rd. Belv 4 B3
Holly Hill Rd. Eri 4 B3
Holly Rd. Dart 20 C2
Holly Rd. Orp 64 B4
Holly Rd. Roc 44 A1
Holly Rd. Roc 44 C3
Holly Tree Cl. Broom (m) 127 D3
Hollybrake Cl. Chis 34 C3
Hollybush La. Orp 65 E4
Hollybush Rd. Grave 24 C1
Hollydale Dr. Brom 49 D2
Hollydene Rd. Wad 178 A1
Hollyshaw Cl. T W 167 F3
Hollytree Ave. Swan 37 D2
Hollytree Dr. Higham 43 E4
Hollywood La. Roc 44 C3
Hollywood La. W Kin 68 A2
Holm Mill La. Harr 109 E1
Holm Wlk. SE3 1 B1
Holmbury Park. Brom 34 A3
Holmcroft Way. Brom 49 D4
Holmdale Rd. Chis 34 C4
Holmdene Ct. Brom 34 A1
Holme Lacey Rd. SE12 16 A3
Holmes Dale Cl. Wad 178 A1
Holmesdale Cl. Loose 124 A4
Holmesdale Hill. Dart 38 C2
Holmesdale Rd. Bexh 3 F1
Holmesdale Rd. Dart 38 C2
Holmesdale Rd. Sev 98 C4
Holmewood Rd. T W 153 F2
Holmewood Ridge. Spel 166 A4
Holmhurst Rd. Belv 4 B3
Holmleigh Ave. Dart 20 C3
Holmoaks. Maid 89 F1
Holmoaks. Rai (K) 62 A3
Holmsdale Gr. Bexh 20 A4
Holmside. Gil 61 D4
Holstein Way. Belv 4 A4
Holt Wood Ave. Dit 88 A2
Holtwood Cl. Rai (K) 61 F1
Holtye Cres. Maid 106 B3
Holwood Park Ave. Kes 49 D1
Holwood Rd. Brom 33 E2
Holyoake Terr. Sev 98 B4
Holywell Cl. SE3 1 B2
Home Farm La. T W 154 A2
Home Gdns. Dart 21 D3
Home Hill. Hex 37 D3
Home Lea. Orp 50 A1
Home Mead Cl. Gave 24 B2
Home Orch. Dart 21 D3
Homedean Rd. Sev 97 F4
Homefield Cl. Swan 37 D1
Homefield Rd. Brom 33 F2
Homefield Rd. Sev 81 D1
Homefield Rise. Orp 50 B3
Homemead Rd. Brom 49 D4
Homer Cl. Bexh 4 C1
Homesdale Rd. Brom 33 F1
Homesdale Rd. Orp 50 A3
Homestead Rd. Ede 113 E1
Homestead Rd. Orp 64 B4
Homestead The. Dart 20 C3
Homewards Rd. All 13 E2
Homewood Cres. Chis 35 D3
Homewood Rd. Spel 166 A4
Homewood Rd. Ten 186 B3
Hone St. Roc 44 B2
Honey Bee Glade. Rai (K) 62 A1
Honey Cl. Rai (K) 61 E1
Honey La. Oth 107 E1
Honeybourne Way. Orp 49 F3
Honeycrock Hill. Sto 77 D2
Honeyden Rd. Sid 36 A3
Honeypot Cl. Roc 44 B2
Honeypot La. Kemsg 82 C2
Honeypot La. N Ash 69 F3
Honeysuckle Cl. Wald 74 A4
Honiton Rd. Well 3 D1
Honywood Rd. Len 110 C1
Hoo Common. Hoo S W 45 E4
Hoo Rd. Roc 44 C4
Hood Ave. Orp 50 B4
Hook Cl. Wald 60 A1
Hook Farm Rd. Brom 48 C4
Hook Green La. Dart 20 B1
Hook Green Rd. Grave 40 A3
Hook Green Rd. Souf 40 A3
Hook Hill. Had 179 E1
Hook La. Char 130 B2
Hook La. Harr 109 F1
Hook La. Well 18 A4
Hook Rd. Snod 72 A2
Hook St. Len 129 D2
Hookfields. Grave 24 A1
Hookwood Rd. Dow 64 C2
Hooper's Pl. Chath 59 F4
Hooper's Rd. Chath 59 F4
Hoopers Yd. Sev 98 C3
Hop Pocket La. Padd W 139 E2
Hope Ave. Had 120 A3
Hope Cl. SE12 16 B1
Hope Park. Brom 33 D3
Hope Rd. Swans 23 D3
Hope St. Chath 60 B4
Hope St. Maid 89 D1
Hopedale Rd. SE7 1 B2
Hopes Gr. H Hald 177 F2
Hopewell Dr. Chath 60 C2
Hopewell Dr. Grave 42 A4
Hopgarden Cl. Ede 131 F4
Hopgarden La. Sev 98 B2
Hopgarden Rd. Ton 118 C1
Hopwood Gdns. T W 153 E1
Horley Cl. Bexh 19 E3
Horley Rd. SE9 34 A4
Horn La. SE10 1 B3
Horn Yd. Grave 24 B3
Hornbeam Ave. Wald 74 B3
Hornbeam Cl. Dit 87 E3
Hornbeam Cl. Padd W 139 D1
Hornbeam La. Bexh 4 C1
Hornbeam Way. Brom 49 E4
Hornbeams. Meo 70 B2
Horncastle Cl. SE12 16 B2
Horncastle Rd. SE12 16 B2
Hornfair Rd. SE7 1 C2
Hornfield Cotts. Meo 70 C4
Horning Cl. SE9 34 A4
Hornpark La. SE12 16 B3
Horns La. Merew 102 C3
Horns Lodge La. Ton 118 C2
Horn's Oak Rd. Meo 56 B1
Horns Rd. Hawkt 189 D2
Horsa Rd. Eri 4 C2
Horsa Rd. SE12 16 C2
Horsecroft Cl. Orp 50 B3
Horsegrove Ave. Tic 187 D3
Horsell Rd. Orp 35 E2
Horseshoe Cl. Rai (K) 61 D1
Horseshoes La. Lan H 125 F4
Horsewash La. Chath 44 C1
Horsfeld Gdns. SE9 17 D3
Horsfeld Rd. SE9 16 C3
Horsham Hill. Rai (K) 62 C4
Horsham La. Rai (K) 62 C4
Horsham Rd. Bexh 19 D3
Horsley Rd. Brom 33 E2
Horsley Rd. Chath 59 E4
Horsmonden Cl. Orp 50 A3
Horsmonden Rd. Brenc 156 C2
Horsted Ave. Chath 60 A3
Horsted Way. Chath 59 F2
Horton Downs. Oth 107 D3
Horton Rd. Dart 38 C1
Horton Rd. Hort 38 C1
Horton Way. Farn 53 D3
Hortons Way. Whm 95 F3
Horwood Cl. Chath 59 E2
Hoselands View. Hart (S) 40 A1
Hoser Ave. SE12 16 B1
Hosey Common La. Whm 114 B4
Hosy Common Rd. Whm 113 F4
Hosey Hill. Whm 96 A2
Hospital La. Chath 60 A4
Hospital Rd. Lee 109 D2
Hospital Rd. Sev 81 F1
Hothfield Rd. Rai (K) 62 A3
Hottsfield. Hart (S) 40 A1
Houghton Ave. Rai (K) 75 E4
Houselands Rd. Ton 136 B3
Hovendens. Cran 174 B2
How Green La. Four E 132 C3
How Green La. Hev 132 C3
Howard Ave. Bex 18 C2
Howard Ave. Chath 59 F4
Howard Dr. Maid 88 B1
Howard Rd. Brom 33 E3
Howard Rd. Dit 87 D2
Howarth Rd. SE2 3 E3
Howbury La. Eri 5 E1
Howbury Wlk. Rai (K) 75 F4
Howells Cl. W Kin 68 A4
Howick Cl. Dit 88 A2
Howland Rd. Mard 142 A1
Hubbards Hill. Len 111 E1
Hubbard's Hill. Sev W 116 B4
Hubbard's La. Loose 124 B4
Hubble Dr. Maid 107 D2
Huckleberry Cl. Wald 74 B4
Hudson Cl. Rai (K) 61 F3
Hudson Pl. SE18 2 C3
Hudson Rd. Bexh 4 A1
Huggens's College. Grave 23 3
Hughes Dr. Roc 44 C3
Hulsewood Cl. Dart 20 B1
Hulsons Ct. Hawkt 189 E3
Humber Cres. Roc 44 A2
Humber Rd. SE3 1 A2
Humboldt Ct. T W 153 F1
Hume Ave. Tilb 24 B4
Hungershall Park. T W 167 D3
Hunsdon Dr. Sev 98 B4
Hunstanton Cl. Rai (K) 76 A4
Hunt Rd. Grave 24 A1
Hunt Rd. Ton 119 D1
Hunt St. W Far 104 B1
Hunter's Gr. Orp 49 F1
Hunters Way. Chath 61 D3
Hunters Way. T W 167 D3

Hunters Way W. Chath 61 D3
Huntersfield Cl. Wald 74 C3
Huntingdon Wlk. Maid 107 D2
Huntingfield Rd. Meo 56 B3
Huntington Cl. Cran 182 C4
Huntington Rd. Cox 123 E4
Huntley Ave. Grave 23 F3
Huntley Mill Rd. Kiln 187 D4
Hunton Hill. Hunt 123 D3
Hunts Cl. SE3 1 B1
Hunts Farm Cl. Bor G 84 B2
Hunts La. Gou 172 A2
Hunts Mead Cl. Chis 34 A3
Huntsman La. Maid 106 B4
Huntsman La. Wro H 85 D3
Huntsmans Cl. Chath 60 A3
Hurlfield. Dart 20 C1
Hurlingham Rd. Bexh 4 A2
Hurren Cl. SE3 16 A4
Hurricane Rd. Merew 103 D4
Hurst Cl. Brom 48 A3
Hurst Cl. Stapt 160 A4
Hurst Cl. Ten 186 A2
Hurst Cl. Wald 60 A1
Hurst Farm Rd. Sev W 116 B4
Hurst Hill. Wald 74 A3
Hurst La. Char 130 A1
Hurst La. SE2 3 F3
Hurst La. Sev W 116 B3
Hurst Pl. Rai (K) 62 A2
Hurst Pl. SE2 3 F3
Hurst Rd. Bex 19 D2
Hurst Rd. Eri 4 C2
Hurst Rd. Sid 18 B1
Hurst Springs. Bex 19 D2
Hurst The. Plax 101 F3
Hurst The. T W 154 A2
Hurst Way. Maid 105 D3
Hurst Way. Sev 98 C2
Hurst Wood Rd. Len 112 A2
Hurstdene Ave. Brom 48 A3
Hurstfield. Brom 48 B4
Hurstings The. Maid 105 F3
Hurstwood. Wald 74 A4
Hurstwood Ave. Bex 19 D2
Hurstwood Ave. Bexh 5 D1
Hurstwood Ave. Eri 5 D1
Hurstwood Dr. Brom 34 A1
Hurstwood La. T W 167 D4
Hurstwood Rd. Bredh 75 E2
Husheath Hill. Gou 159 D1
Husseywell Cres. Brom 48 B3
Hutsford Cl. Rai (K) 61 F1
Huxley Rd. Well 18 A4
Hyacinth Rd. Roc 44 A1
Hybrid Cl. Chath 59 F3
Hyde Rd. Bexh 4 A1
Hyde Rd. Maid 88 C1
Hylton St. SE18 3 D3
Hyperion Dr. Roc 44 A3
Hythe Ave. Bexh 4 A2
Hythe Cl. Orp 35 F1
Hythe Cl. Soub 153 E3
Hythe St. Dart 21 D3

Ickleton Rd. SE9 34 A4
Ide Hill Rd. Sund 115 D3
Iden Cl. Brom 33 D1
Iden Cres. Stapt 160 A3
Iden La. Ege 147 E4
Iden Rd. Roc 44 C3
Idenwood Cl. Rai (K) 61 F1
Idleigh Court Rd. N Ash 55 F2
Ifield Cl. Maid 107 D2
Ifield Rd. Meo 56 A1
Ifield Way. Grave 41 F3
Ightham by-pass. Ight 83 F2
Ightham Rd. Eri 4 B2
Ightham Rd. Ship 100 C1
Ilfracombe Rd. Brom 16 A1
Illustrious Cl. Wald 60 B1
Impala Gdns. T W 153 E1
Imperial Dr. Grave 42 A4
Imperial Rd. Gil 60 C4
Imperial Way. Chis 17 F1
Impton La. Wald 74 B3
Inca Dr. SE9 17 E2
Independents Rd. SE3 16 A4
Indus Rd. SE7 1 C2
Ingle Rd. Chath 60 A3
Ingleby Way. Chis 34 B4
Ingleden Park Rd. Ten 186 C3
Ingledew Rd. SE18 2 C3
Ingleside Gr. SE3 1 A2
Ingleton Ave. Well 18 B3
Inglewood. Chis 34 C3
Inglewood Copse. Brom 34 A2
Inglewood Rd. Bexh 19 F4
Ingoldsby Rd. Grave 25 D2
Ingram Rd. Dart 21 D2
Ingram Rd. Gil 46 A1
Ingram Rd. Grays 8 C3
Ingres Terr. Grave 40 A4
Ingress Gdns. Gree 22 C3
Inigo Jones Rd. SE7 2 A2
Institute Rd. Chath 60 B4
Instone Rd. Dart 20 C2
Inverary Pl. SE18 2 C2
Inverine Rd. SE7 1 B3
Invermore Pl. SE18 2 C3
Invicta Cl. Chis 34 B4
Invicta Rd. Dart 21 E3
Invicta Rd. SE3 1 B2
Iona Cl. Bredh 74 C3
Iona Rd. Maid 106 B2
Irene Rd. Orp 50 A3
Ireton Pl. Grays 8 B3
Iris Ave. Bex 19 D3
Iris Cl. Wald 74 B2
Iris Cres. Bexh 4 A2
Iron Mill La. Dart 20 A4
Iron Mill Pl. Dart 20 A4
Ironside Cl. Chath 60 B2
Ironstones. T W 166 B4
Irvine Rd. Higham 43 E4
Irvine Way. Orp 50 A3
Irving Way. Swan 36 C2
Irving Wlk. Swans 23 D2
Irwin Ave. SE18 3 D2
Isabella Dr. Orp 49 F1
Isla Rd. SE18 2 C2
Islehurst Cl. Chis 34 B2
Ismays Rd. Ight 100 B4
Istead Rise. Ist 41 D3
Itchingwood Common Rd. Lim C 113 D3
Ivedon Rd. Well 3 F1
Ivens Way. Harr 109 F1
Iverhurst Cl. Bexh 18 C3
Iversgate Cl. Rai (K) 62 A3
Ives Rd. Ton 136 A3
Ivor Gr. SE9 17 E2
Ivorydown. Brom 33 E4
Ivy Bower Cl. Gree 22 B3
Ivy Cl. Broom (M) 126 C3
Ivy Cl. Dart 21 E2
Ivy Cl. Grave 24 C1
Ivy House La. Dunt 80 C3
Ivy La. Kno P 80 A4
Ivy Mews. Broom (M) 127 D3
Ivy St. Rai (K) 62 A2
Izane Rd. Bexh 19 D4

Jackass La. Kes 48 B1
Jacklin Cl. Wald 74 A3
Jackson Ave. Chath 60 A2
Jackson Rd. Brom 49 D3
Jackson St. SE18 2 B2
Jacksons La. Ten 186 B2
Jacob's La. Hoo S W 29 E1
Jaffray Rd. Brom 33 F1
Jaggard Way. Stapt 160 A4
Jagger Cl. Dart 21 F2
Jago Cl. SE18 2 C2
Jail La. Bigg 78 A4
James Rd. Cux 58 C3
James Rd. Dart 20 B3
James St. Chath 60 A4
James St. Chath 59 F4
James St. Gil 45 F1
James St. Maid 89 E1
Jarrett Ave. Roc 44 C3
Jarvis La. Gou 172 B3
Jasmine Cl. Dit 87 D2
Jasmine Cl. Orp 49 E2
Jasmine Cl. Wald 74 A4
Jasmine Rd. Dit 87 D2
Jason Wlk. SE9 34 B4
Jasper Ave. Chath 59 F3
Javelin Rd. Merew 103 D4
Jefferson Dr. Rai (K) 61 F3
Jefferson Wlk. SE18 2 B2
Jeffery Cl. Stapt 160 A4
Jeffery St. Gil 45 F1
Jeffrey St. Maid 89 E1
Jeken Rd. SE9 16 C4
Jellicoe Ave. Grave 24 C1
Jellicoe Ave W. Grave 24 C1
Jenkins' Dale. Chath 60 A4
Jenkins Dr. Maid 107 D1
Jenner Rd. Chath 59 F4
Jenner Way. Ayld 73 D1
Jennifer Rd. Brom 16 A1
Jenningtree Rd. Eri 5 E2
Jenningtree Way. Belv 4 C4
Jenton Ave. Bexh 4 A1
Jerome Rd. Dit 87 D4
Jersey Dr. Orp 49 F4
Jersey Rd. Roc 44 B2
Jeskyns Rd. Cob 42 A1
Jesmond Rd. Grays 8 C4
Jessamine Pl. Dart 21 F2
Jessamine Terr. Swan 36 C2
Jessup Cl. SE18 2 C3
Jevington Way. SE12 16 B2
Jewell Gr. Mard 141 F1
Jeyes Rd. Gil 60 C4
Jezreels Rd. Gil 60 C4
Jim Bradley Cl. SE18 2 B3
Jiniwin Rd. Chath 59 F2
Joan Cres. SE9 16 C2
Jockey La. Cran 173 F1
Jodrell Way. Grays 7 D3
John Newton Ct. Well 18 B4
John St. Chath 59 F4
John St. Grays 8 C2
John St. Maid 89 E2
John St. T W 153 E1
John Wilson St. SE18 2 B3
John Woolley Cl. SE13 16 A4
Johns Cl. Hart (S) 55 D4
John's Rd. Meo 56 A4
Johnson Cl. Grave 23 F1
Johnson Rd. Brom 48 C4
Johnsons Ave. Shorm 65 E3
Johnsons Way. Gree 22 C3
Joiners Ct. Chath 60 B3
Jonas Dr. Wad 178 A1
Jonas La. Wad 178 A1
Jordan Cl. Maid 107 D1
Joslin Rd. Pur 6 C3
Joy Rd. Grave 24 C2
Joyce Green La. Dart 21 D4
Joyce Green Wlk. Dart 21 D4
Joyden's Wood Rd. Bex 20 A1
Joyden's Wood Rd. Sid 36 C4
Jubilee Cl. Gree 22 C3
Jubilee Cres. Grave 25 D1
Jubilee Cres. Ight 83 F1
Jubilee Rd. Grays 7 E2
Jubilee Rd. Orp 65 E4
Jubilee Rise. Seal 82 A1
Jubilee Terr. Gil 45 F1
Jubilee Way. Sid 18 B1
Judd Rd. Ton 136 B2
Judeth Gdns. Grave 42 A4
Judkins Cl. Wald 60 C1
Juglands Rd. Orp 50 B3
Julian Rd. Orp 64 B4
Julians Cl. Sev 98 B2
Julians Way. Sev 98 B2
Juliet Way. Pur 6 A4
Junction Rd. Dart 20 C3
Junction Rd. Gil 60 C4
Junction Rd. Hawkt 189 D1
Juniper Cl. Bigg 78 A3
Juniper Cl. Wald 74 B4
Juniper Wlk. Swan 36 C2
Jury St. Grave 24 B3
Jutland Cl. All 13 F2

Kale Rd. Belv 4 A4
Karen Ct. Brom 33 D2
Kashgar Rd. SE18 3 D3
Kashmir Rd. SE7 1 C2
Katherine Gdns. SE9 16 C4
Katherine Rd. Ede 131 F2
Kay St. Well 3 E1
Keary Rd. Swans 23 D2
Keats Rd. Belv 4 C4
Keats Rd. Dit 87 D4
Keats Rd. Well 3 D1
Kechill Gdns. Brom 48 B3
Kedleston Dr. Orp 50 A4
Keeble Cl. SE18 2 B2
Keedonwood Rd. Brom 33 D4
Keel Gdns. Soub 153 D2
Keeling Rd. SE9 16 C3
Keemor Cl. SE18 2 B2
Keep The. SE3 1 B1
Keightley Dr. SE9 17 F2
Keith Ave. Sutt H 38 B3
Kelbrook Rd. SE3 17 D4
Kelby Path. SE9 17 E1
Kelchers La. Had 120 A1
Kellaway Rd. SE3 1 C1
Kellaway Rd. Wald 74 B3
Kellerton Rd. SE13 16 A3
Kellner Rd. SE28 3 D4
Kelsall Cl. SE3 1 B1
Kelsey Rd. Orp 35 E2
Kelso Dr. Grave 42 A4
Kelvin Cl. Ton 118 C2
Kelvin Par. Orp 50 A3
Kelvin Rd. Well 18 B4
Kemble Cl. T W 154 A2
Kemble Dr. Brom 49 D2
Kemnal Rd. Chis 34 C4
Kemnal Warren. Chis 34 C3
Kemp Cl. Wald 74 A4
Kempley Ct. Grays 8 C2
Kempt St. SE18 2 B2
Kempton Cl. Eri 4 C2
Kempton Cl. Wald 74 C3
Kemsing Cl. Bex 19 D2
Kemsing Cl. Brom 48 A2
Kemsing Rd. SE10 1 B3
Kemsing Rd. Wro 83 E3
Kemsley Cl. Grave 41 D4
Kemsley Cl. Gree 22 B3
Kemsley Street Rd. Bredh 75 F3
Kendal Cl. Ton 136 C4
Kendal Dr. Ton 136 C3
Kendal Park. T W 153 D1
Kendal Way. Rai (K) 61 F2
Kendale Rd. Brom 33 D4
Kenia Wlk. Grave 25 D1
Kenilworth Dr. Rai (K) 61 F2
Kenilworth Gdns. Rai (K) 61 F2
Kenilworth Gdns. SE18 2 B1
Kenilworth Rd. Orp 49 F4
Kenley Cl. Bex 19 E2
Kenley Cl. Chis 35 D1
Kenmere Rd. Well 3 F1
Kennard Cl. Chath 59 D3
Kennedy Cl. Orp 49 F3
Kennedy Gdns. Sev 81 F1
Kennel Barn Rd. S Grn 92 B4
Kennelling Rd. Stal 112 C1
Kennet Rd. Dart 20 B4
Kennet Rd. Ton 118 C1
Kennington Cl. Maid 107 D2
Kennington Cl. Rai (K) 61 E4
Kensington St. T W 167 E4
Kent Ave. Maid 106 C2
Kent Ave. Well 18 A3
Kent Cl. Chath 59 F2
Kent Cl. Orp 64 A4
Kent Cl. Padd W 139 E1
Kent Hatch Rd. Limc 113 E4
Kent Hatch Rd. Whm 113 E4
Kent Kraft Industrial Estate. Grave 23 D3
Kent Rd. Dart 21 D3
Kent Rd. Grave 24 B2
Kent Rd. Grays 8 C3
Kent Rd. Hall 58 B1
Kent Rd. Lon 39 F2
Kent Rd. Orp 50 B4
Kent Rd. Snod 72 B1
Kent Rd. T W 153 E1
Kent St. Merew 103 D3
Kent Terr. Upc 62 C3
Kent View. S Ock 6 C4
Kentish Rd. Belv 4 B3
Kentish Way. Brom 33 E2
Kentmere Rd. SE18 3 D3
Kenward Ct. Had 120 A2
Kenward Rd. Maid 88 C1
Kenward Rd. SE9 16 C3
Kenward Rd. Yal 122 A4
Kenwood Ave. Lon 40 C1
Kenwood Ave. Wald 74 B4
Kenya Rd. SE7 1 C2
Kenyon Wlk. Rai (K) 75 E4
Kerry Ave. Pur 6 A4
Kersey Gdns. SE9 34 A4
Kestlake Rd. Bex 18 C3
Keston Ave. Kes 48 C1
Keston Cl. Well 3 F2
Keston Ct. Rai (K) 61 E3
Keston Gdns. Kes 48 C1
Keston Mark. Brom 49 D2
Keston Park Cl. Kes 49 D2
Kestrel Cl. Ede 131 F4
Kestrel Rd. Wald 74 C3
Keswick Cl. Ton 136 C3
Keswick Rd. Bexh 4 B1
Keswick Rd. Orp 50 B3
Keswick Rd. W Wick 48 A2
Ketridge La. Waty 103 F3
Kettle La. E Far 105 D1
Kettlewell Ct. Swan 37 D2
Kevington Cl. Orp 35 D1
Kevington Dr. Chis 35 D1
Kewlands. Maid 89 F1
Keyes Ave. Chath 60 A3
Keyes Gdns. Ton 136 A2
Keyes Rd. Dart 21 D4
Keynsham Gdns. SE9 17 D3
Keynsham Rd. SE9 17 D3
Keyworth Cl. Padd W 139 D1
Khartoum Rd. Chath 45 D1
Khyber Rd. Gil 45 E2
Kibbles La. Soub 153 D2
Kidbrooke Gdns. SE3 1 B1
Kidbrooke Gr. SE3 1 B1
Kidbrooke La. SE9 17 D4
Kidbrooke Park Cl. SE3 1 B1
Kidbrooke Park Rd. SE3 16 B4
Kidbrooke Way. SE3 1 B1
Kidd Pl. SE7 2 A3
Killewarren Way. Orp 50 C4
Killick Rd. Hoo S W 28 C1
Kiln Barn Rd. Dit 87 F2
Kiln Field. Ten 186 C2
Kiln La. Lei 135 D3
Kiln Way. Grays 8 A3
Kiln Way. Padd W 139 E1
Kilndown. Grave 41 F3
Kilndown Cl. Maid 88 C2
Kilnfields. Orp 65 E4
Kimberley Dr. Sid 18 C1
Kimberley Rd. Gil 60 C4
Kimbolton Cl. SE12 16 A3
Kimmeridge Gdns. SE9 34 A4
Kimmeridge Rd. SE9 34 A4
Kincraig Dr. Sev 98 B4
King Arthur's Dr. Roc 44 B3
King Edward Ave. Dart 20 C3
King Edward Rd. Chath 60 A3
King Edward Rd. Chath 44 C1
King Edward Rd. Gil 46 A1
King Edward Rd. Gree 22 B3
King Edward Rd. Maid 106 A3
King George Rd. Wald 74 A4
King George V Hill. T W 153 F1
King Harolds Way. Bexh 4 A2
King Hill. W Mal 103 D4
King John's Wlk. SE9 17 D2
King St. Chath 60 B4
King St. Chath 44 C1
King St. Gil 45 F1
King St. Grave 24 B3
King St. Maid 106 B4
King St. W Mal 86 C2
King William Rd. Gil 45 F2
Kingfisher Cl. Orp 35 F1
Kingfisher Dr. Chath 60 C2
Kingfisher Rd. Dit 87 E3
Kings Acre. Oth 107 E3
Kings Ave. Brom 33 D3
King's Ave. Chath 59 F4
King's Bank La. Beckl 196 B1
King's Bastion. Gil 45 E1
Kings Cl. Dart 20 A4
King's Cotts. Net 103 F1
Kings Dr. Grave 24 C1
King's Highway. SE18 3 D2
Kings La. Yal 140 C2
King's Orch. SE9 17 D3
King's Orchard. Chath 44 C1
King's Rd. Chath 60 C3
Kings Rd. Head 144 C1
Kings Rd. Orp 50 A1
King's Rd. Ton 136 C2
Kings Standing Way. T W 154 A3
Kings Toll Rd. Mat 155 E1
Kings Wlk. Grays 8 B2
Kingsand Rd. SE12 16 B1
Kingsbridge Gdns. Dart 20 C3
Kingsdale Rd. SE18 3 D2
Kingsdown Cl. Grave 25 D2
Kingsdown Cl. Maid 106 A4
Kingsdown Cl. Rai (K) 75 E4
Kingsdown Rd. Rod 94 C4
Kingsdown Way. Brom 48 B3
Kingsgate Cl. Bexh 4 A1
Kingsgate Cl. Maid 105 F4
Kingsgate Cl. Orp 35 F1
Kingsground. SE9 17 D3
Kingshill Dr. Hoo S W 28 C1
Kingsholm Gdns. SE9 17 D4
Kingshurst Rd. SE12 16 B2
Kingsingfield Cl. W Kin 68 A4
Kingsingfield Rd. W Kin 68 A3
Kingsland Gr. Head 144 C1
Kingsland La. Ege 147 D3
Kingsley Ave. Dart 21 E3
Kingsley Rd. Maid 106 B4
Kingsley Rd. Orp 64 A4
Kingsley Wood Dr. SE9 17 D1
Kingsman Par. SE18 2 A4
Kingsman St. SE18 2 A3
Kingsmead Cl. Sid 18 B1
Kingsnorth Rd. Hoo S W 29 E1
Kingsnorth Rd. Ri (K) 61 F4
Kingston Cres. Wald 74 B4
Kingston Ct. Grave 23 E3
Kingston Dr. Maid 106 B2
Kingsway. Chath 61 D3
Kingsway. Orp 49 F4
Kingsway. W Wick 48 A2
Kingswood Ave. Belv 4 A3
Kingswood Ave. Brom 33 D1
Kingswood Ave. Chath 60 A3
Kingswood Ave. Swan 37 D1
Kingswood Cl. Dart 20 C3
Kingswood Cl. Orp 49 F3
Kingswood Cl. T W 167 F4
Kingswood Pl. SE13 16 A4
Kingswood Rd. Ayld 73 F2
Kingswood Rd. Brom 33 D1
Kingswood Rd. Dunt 81 D2
Kingswood Rd. Gil 45 F1
Kingswood Rd. T W 167 F4
Kinlet Rd. SE18 2 C1
Kinnaird Ave. Brom 33 D3
Kinnaird Cl. Brom 33 D3
Kinnings Row. Ton 136 C3
Kinross Cl. Chath 60 B2
Kinveachy Gdns. SE7 2 A3
Kipling Dr. Dit 87 D4
Kipling Rd. Bexh 4 A1
Kipling Rd. Dart 21 E3
Kipping's Cross. Mat 155 E1
Kippington Cl. Sev 98 A4
Kippington Dr. SE9 16 C2
Kippingtn Rd. Sev 98 B3
Kirby Cl. Cran 182 C4
Kirby Rd. Dart 21 F2
Kirby Rd. Hoo S W 28 A1
Kirk La. SE18 2 C2
Kirkdale. Maid 106 A1
Kirkdale Cl. Wald 74 C3
Kirkdale Rd. Maid 106 A1
Kirkdale Rd. T W 167 E4
Kirkham St. SE18 3 D2
Kirkland Cl. SE9 18 A3
Kirkside Rd. SE3 1 B2
Kirkstone Way. Brom 33 D3
Kit Hill Ave. Wald 74 A4
Kitchener Ave. Chath 60 B3
Kitchener Ave. Grave 24 C1
Kitchener Rd. Hoo S W 45 D4
Kitchener Rd. Roc 44 B2
Kitchenour La. Beckl 197 D1
Knatts La. W Kin 68 A2
Knatts Valley Rd. W Kin 67 F3
Knave Wood Rd. Kemsg 82 A3
Knaves Acre. Head 144 C1
Knavesacre Ct. Rai (K) 61 F1
Knee Hill. SE2 3 F3
Knee Hill Cres. SE2 3 F3
Knight Ave. Gil 45 F2
Knight Rd. Roc 44 B1
Knight Rd. Ton 119 D1
Knighton Rd. Otf 81 D3
Knightrider St. Maid 106 B4
Knights Cl. Hoo S W 29 D1
Knights Cl. Pem 154 C2
Knights Croft. N Ash 55 D2
Knights Manor Way. Dart 21 E3
Knights Rd. E16 1 B4
Knights Rd. Hoo S W 28 C1
Knights Ridge. Orp 50 B1
Knight's Ridge. Pem 154 C2
Knight's Way. Head 144 C1
Knightsbridge Cl. T W 153 D1
Knock Mill Lane. W Kin 68 B1
Knockhall Chase. Gree 22 C3
Knockhall Rd. Gree 22 C3
Knockholt Rd. Hals 65 D1
Knockholt Rd. SE9 16 C3
Knockwood Rd. Ten 186 C3
Knole Cl. Sev W 116 B3
Knole La. Sev 98 C3
Knole Rd. Dart 20 B2
Knole Rd. Sev 98 C4
Knole Rd. Wald 74 C4
Knole The. Ist 41 D3
Knole The. SE9 34 B4
Knole Way. Sev 98 C3
Knoll Rd. Bex 19 E3
Knoll Rd. Sid 35 E4
Knoll Rise. Orp 50 A3
Knoll The. Brom 48 B3
Knotts Pl. Sev 98 B4
Knowle Ave. Bexh 4 A2
Knowle Cl. Spel 166 A4
Knowle La. Padd W 156 C4
Knowle Rd. Brenc 156 C3
Knowle Rd. Brom 49 D2
Knowle Rd. Maid 89 E1
Knowle Rd. Wou 72 C4
Knowles Gdns. Head 144 C1
Knowles Wlk. Stapt 160 A4
Knowlton Gdns. Maid 105 E3
Knowlton Green. Brom 48 A4
Knowsley Way. Hild 117 F1
Kydbrook Cl. Orp 49 F3
Kyetop Wlk. Rai (K) 61 F1
Kynaston Rd. Brom 33 E4
Kynaston Rd. Orp 50 B3

La Providence. Chath 44 C1
La Tourne Gdns. Orp 49 F2

Labour-in-Vain Rd. Stans 69 D1
Laburnam Gr. Grave 23 F2
Laburnum Ave. Dart 20 C2
Laburnum Ave. Swan 36 C1
Laburnum Dr. Dit 87 E3
Laburnum Rd. Roc 44 A1
Laburnum Way. Brom 49 E3
Lacey Cl. Lan H 126 A4
Laceys La. Lint 123 F2
Ladbrooke Cres. Sid 18 C1
Ladds La. Snod 72 B3
Ladds Way. Swan 36 C1
Ladham Rd. Gou 172 B3
Lady Amherst's Dr. Sund 115 F4
Lady Oak La. Kiln 180 C2
Lady Vane Cl. Ship 100 C1
Ladyclose Ave. Cli W 27 E2
Ladycroft Gdns. Orp 49 F1
Ladycroft Way. Orp 49 F1
Ladyfields. Grave 24 A1
Ladyfields. Wald 74 C3
Lady's Gift Rd. Soub 153 D2
Ladysmith Rd. SE9 17 E3
Ladywood Ave. Orp 50 A4
Ladywood Rd. Cux 58 B3
Ladywood Rd. Dart 39 D4
Lagoon Rd. Orp 50 C4
Laird Ave. Grays 8 C4
Lake Ave. Brom 33 E3
Lake Dr. Higham 26 C1
Lake Rd. Dit 88 A2
Lake Rd. T W 167 D4
Lake Rise. Grays 7 E3
Lake View Rd. Sev 98 B4
Lakedale Rd. SE18 3 D3
Lakelands. Harr 110 A1
Lakelands. Maid 106 B2
Laker Rd. Chath 59 F1
Laker Rd. Wou 59 F1
Lakes Rd. Kes 48 C1
Lakeside. Snod 72 A1
Lakeside Cl. Sid 18 C3
Lakeside Dr. Brom 49 D2
Lakeswood Rd. Orp 49 F4
Lakeview Cl. Snod 72 B1
Lakeview Rd. Well 18 B4
Lakewood Dr. Rai (K) 61 F1
Lambarde Ave. SE9 34 B4
Lambarde Cl. Hall 72 B4
Lambarde Rd. Sev 81 E1
Lambardes. N Ash 55 D2
Lambden Rd. Plu 147 F1
Lamberhurst Cl. Orp 50 C3
Lamberhurst Green. Rai (K) 61 E4
Lamberhurst Rd. Hors 170 C3
Lamberhurst Rd. Maid 88 B2
Lamberts Rd. T W 153 F2
Lambert's Yd. Ton 136 B3
Lambes Ct. Rai (K) 61 F1
Lambeth Cl. Wald 74 B4
Lambourn Way. T W 167 F3
Lambourn Way. Wald 74 C3
Lambourne Pl. Rai (K) 62 B3
Lambourne Pl. SE3 1 B1
Lambourne Rd. Rose 107 D3
Lambscroft Ave. SE9 16 C1
Lambsfrith Gr. Rai (K) 75 E4
Lamerock Rd. Brom 33 D4
Lamorbey Cl. Sid 18 A2
Lamorna Ave. Grave 24 C1
Lamorna Cl. Orp 50 B3
Lampington Row. Spel 166 A4
Lamplighters Cl. Rai (K) 61 E1
Lampmead Rd. SE12 16 A4
Lamport Cl. SE18 2 A3
Lancashire Rd. Maid 107 D2
Lancaster Cl. Brom 33 D1
Lancaster Ct. Rai (K) 61 F2
Lancelot Ave. Roc 44 A2
Lancelot Cl. Roc 44 A1
Lancelot Rd. Well 18 B4
Lances Cl. Meo 56 B3
Lancet La. Maid 106 B1
Lancey Cl. SE7 1 C3
Lancing Rd. Orp 50 B2
Land Way. Higham 26 C1
Lander Rd. Grays 8 C3
Landor Ct. Rai (K) 75 E4
Landsdowne Ave. Bexh 3 F2
Landseer Ave. Grave 24 A1
Landseer Cl. Ton 119 D1
Landstead Rd. SE18 2 C2
Landway. Seal 82 A2
Landway The. Bor G 84 A2
Landway The. Kemsg 82 B3
Landway The. Orp 35 F1
Landway The. Rose 107 E4
Lane Ave. Gree 22 C3
Lane End. Bexh 19 E4
Lane The. SE3 16 B4
Lanes Ave. Grave 24 B1
Laneside. Chis 34 C4
Langafel Cl. Lon 40 A1
Langbrook Rd. SE3 1 C1
Langdale Ave. Orp 49 E2
Langdale Cl. Rai (K) 61 F3
Langdale Cres. Bexh 4 B1
Langdale Rise. Maid 88 C1
Langdale Wlk. Grave 24 A1
Langdon Rd. Brom 33 E1
Langdon Rd. Chath 59 F4
Langdon Shaw. Sid 35 D4
Langford Pl. Sid 18 B1
Langham Gr. Maid 105 F4
Langholm Rd. Spel 166 A4
Langlands Dr. Dart 39 D4
Langley Gdns. Brom 33 F2
Langley Gdns. Orp 49 E4
Langley Rd. Well 3 F2
Langley Way. W Wick 48 A3
Langmore Ct. Bexh 18 C4
Langthorne Cres. Grays 8 C3
Langton Cl. Maid 89 F1
Langton Rd. Spel 166 B4
Langton Rd. T W 166 C4
Langton Ridge. T W 166 B4
Langton Way. SE3 1 B1
Langworth Cl. Dart 20 C1
Lankester Parker Rd. Chath 59 F1
Lannoy Rd. SE9 17 F2
Lanridge Rd. Belv 3 F4
Lansbury Cres. Dart 21 E3
Lansdown Rd. Grave 24 A2
Lansdown Rd. Sid 18 B1
Lansdowne Ave. Maid 106 C1
Lansdowne Ave. Orp 49 E3
Lansdowne La. SE7 1 C3
Lansdowne Mews. SE7 1 C3
Lansdowne Rd. Brom 33 E3
Lansdowne Rd. Chath 60 A3
Lansdowne Rd. T W 167 E4
Lansdowne Rd. Ton 136 B3
Lansdowne Sq. Grave 24 A3
Lansdowne Sq. T W 167 E4
Lapis Cl. Grave 25 E2
Lapwing Rd. I o G 15 E1
Lapwings. Lon 40 B1
Lapwings The. Grave 24 C1
Lapworth Cl. Orp 50 C2
Larch Cl. Dit 87 E3
Larch Cres. Hoo S W 46 A4
Larch Cres. Ton 118 C1
Larch Dene. Orp 49 E2
Larch Gr. Padd W 139 D1
Larch Rd. Dart 20 C2
Larch Way. Brom 49 E3
Larch Wlk. Swan 36 C2
Larch Wood Cl. Bredh 74 C3
Larchcroft. Wald 74 B4
Larches The. Higham 43 F4
Larchwood Rd. SE9 17 E1
Larkfield. Five O G 138 B2
Larkfield Ave. Gil 61 D4
Larkfield Cl. Brom 48 B2
Larkfield Cl. Dit 87 E3
Larkfield Rd. Dit 87 E3
Larkfield Rd. Sev 97 F4
Larkfield Rd. Sid 18 A1
Larkfield Trading Estate. Snod 72 B1
Larkfields. Grave 24 A1
Larkin Cl. Roc 44 B3
Larks Field. Hart (S) 40 A1
Larkspur Cl. Dit 87 E3
Larkspur Cl. Orp 50 C2
Larkspur Rd. Dit 87 D3
Larkspur Rd. Wald 74 A4
Larkwell La. Hart (S) 40 A1
Larner Rd. Eri 5 D2
Lassa Rd. SE9 17 D3
Lassel St. SE10 1 A3
Latham Rd. Bexh 19 E3
Latona Dr. Grave 42 A4
Latymers. Pen 151 E4
Launcelot Rd. Brom 33 E4
Launder Way. Maid 106 A3
Laura Dr. Hex 37 E3
Laura Pl. Chath 59 D3
Laurel Ave. Grave 24 C1
Laurel Bank. Soub 153 E2
Laurel Cl. Dart 20 C2
Laurel Cl. Sid 18 B1
Laurel Gr. Broom (m) 126 C3
Laurel Rd. Gil 45 F2
Laurel Rd. T W 153 F2
Laurel Way. T W 153 F2
Laurel Wlk. Rai (K) 62 A1
Laurels The. Dart 20 C1
Laurels The. Lon 40 C1
Lavenda Cl. Rai (K) 75 E4
Lavender Cl. Dit 87 D2
Lavender Cl. Wald 74 A4
Lavender Hill. Swan 36 C1
Lavender Hill. Ton 136 C2
Lavender Rd. Dit 87 D2
Lavender Wlk. Dit 87 D2
Lavenders Rd. W Mal 86 C1
Lavernock Rd. Bexh 4 B1
Laverstoke Rd. Maid 88 C2
Lavidge Rd. SE9 17 D1
Lavinia Rd. Dart 21 D3
Lawford Gdns. Dart 20 C3
Lawn Cl. Brom 33 E3
Lawn Cl. Chath 60 B3
Lawn Cl. Swan 36 C2
Lawn Cl. Ten 186 A2
Lawn Park. Sev 98 B2
Lawn Rd. Grave 23 F3
Lawn Rd. Ton 136 B2
Lawn Terr. SE3 16 A4
Lawns Cres. Grays 8 C2
Lawns The. SE3 16 A4
Lawns The. Sid 35 E4
Lawnside. SE3 16 A4
Lawrence Cl. Maid 106 B2
Lawrence Dr. Cob 42 B1
Lawrence Hill Gdns. Dart 20 C3
Lawrence Hill Rd. Dart 20 C3
Lawrence Rd. Ton 119 D1
Lawrence Rd. W Wick 48 B1
Lawrence St. Gil 45 F1
Lawson Rd. Dart 20 C4
Laxey Rd. Orp 64 A4
Laxey The. Maid 106 A3
Laxton Cl. Rose 107 D4
Laxton Dr. Chart S 125 E3
Laxton Gdns. Padd W 139 D2
Layfield Rd. Gil 46 A2
Layhams Rd. W Wick 48 A1
Laymarsh Cl. Belv 4 A4
Layzell Wlk. SE9 16 C2
Le May Ave. SE12 16 B1
Le Temple Rd. Padd W 139 E2
Lea Rd. Sev 98 C2
Lea Vale. Bexh 19 F4
Leafy Glade. Rai (K) 61 E1
Leafy Gr. Kes 48 C1
Leafy Oak Rd. SE12 16 C1
Leahurst Rd. SE13 16 A3
Lealands Ave. Lei 135 E3
Lealands Cl. Gro 165 F1
Leamington Ave. Brom 33 F4
Leamington Ave. Orp 50 A1
Leamington Cl. Brom 33 F4
Lender Dr. Grave 42 A4
Leander Rd. Chath 59 F2
Leas Dale. SE9 17 E1
Leas Green. Chis 35 D3
Leas The. Wad 178 B1
Leather Bottle Green. Belv 4 A4
Lebrun Sq. SE3 16 B4
Leckwith Ave. Bexh 4 A2
Leconfield Cl. Ton 136 A2
Leda Rd. SE18 2 A4
Lee Church St. SE13 16 A4
Lee Green. Orp 50 B4
Lee Green. SE12 16 A3
Lee Green Rd. Cli W 44 C4
Lee Green Rd. Cli W 27 E1
Lee High Rd. SE12 16 A4
Lee Park. SE3 16 A4
Lee Rd. Chath 60 C3
Lee Rd. SE3 16 A4
Lee Rd. Snod 72 B2
Lee Terr. SE3 16 A4
Leechcroft Ave. Sid 18 A3
Leechcroft Ave. Swan 37 D1
Leeds Rd. Lan H 126 A4
Leeds Rd. Sutt V 126 A4
Leeds Sq. Rai (K) 61 E4
Leegate. SE12 16 A3
Lees Rd. Yal 122 A2
Leesness Ave. Bexh 3 F2
Leesons Hill. Orp 35 E1
Leesons Way. Orp 35 D2
Leet Cl. Gil 46 A1
Leeward Rd. Chath 59 F3
Leewood Pl. Swan 36 C1
Legatt Rd. SE9 16 C3
Legge La. Birl 71 F1
Leggs La. Spel 152 A1
Leghorn Rd. SE18 2 C3
Leicester Rd. Maid 106 C2
Leigh Ave. Maid 106 B1
Leigh Pl. Well 3 E1
Leigh Rd. Grave 24 B1
Leigh Rd. Hild 135 F4
Leighton Cl. Soub 153 E2
Leitch Row. Gil 45 E2
Leith Hill. Orp 35 E2
Leith Hill Green. Orp 35 E2
Leith Park Rd. Grave 24 B2
Lemmon Rd. SE10 1 A2
Lemonwell Dr. SE9 17 F3
Lendon Rd. Bor G 84 A1
Leneda Dr. T W 167 D2
Leney Rd. Waty 104 A2
Lenfield Ave. Maid 106 B4
Lenham Heath Rd. Len 129 E2
Lenham Rd. Bexh 4 A2
Lenham Rd. Bou Mal 145 E3
Lenham Rd. Broom (m) 127 E3
Lenham Rd. Head 145 E3
Lenham Rd. Len 128 A3
Lenham Rd. SE12 16 A4
Lenham Rd. Ulc 127 E3
Lenham Way. Rai (K) 61 E4
Lenmore Ave. Grays 8 C4
Lennard Ave. W Wick 48 A2
Lennard Cl. W Wick 48 A2
Lennard Rd. Brom 49 D3
Lennard Rd. Dunt 81 D2
Lennox Ave. Grave 24 B3
Lennox Rd. Grave 24 A2
Lennox Road E. Grave 24 B2
Lennox Row. Gil 45 E2
Lenor Cl. Bexh 19 D4
Lensbury Way. SE2 3 F4
Lenside Dr. Rose 107 E3
Lenthall Ave. Grays 8 B4
Lentmead Rd. Brom 16 A1
Lenton St. SE18 2 C3
Leonard Ave. Otf 81 E4
Leonard Ave. Swans 23 D2
Leonard Cl. Maid 88 B1
Leonard Rd. Chath 60 B3
Leopold Rd. Chath 60 B4
Lesley Cl. Bex 19 E2
Lesley Cl. Ist 41 D2
Lesle Cl. Swan 36 C1
Leslie Cres. Ten 186 B3
Leslie Pl. Maid 89 D1
Leslie Rd. Gil 45 F2
Leslie Smith Sq. SE18 2 B2
Lesney Park. Eri 4 C2
Lesney Park Rd. Eri 4 C2
Lessness Park. Belv 4 B3
Lessness Rd. Belv 4 B3
Lested La. Chart S 125 E3
Lester Rd. Chath 60 B4
Letchworth Ave. Chath 60 A3
Letchworth Cl. Brom 48 B4
Letchworth Dr. Brom 48 B4
Letter Box La. Sev 98 C1
Leverholme Gdns. SE9 34 B4
Levett Cl. I o G 15 E1
Levetts La. Bod 194 A3
Lewd La. Sma 163 E4
Lewes Rd. Brom 33 F2
Lewin Rd. Bexh 19 D4
Lewis Ave. Rai (K) 61 E3
Lewis Court Dr. Bou Mon 124 C4
Lewis Rd. Ist 41 D2
Lewis Rd. Sid 18 C1
Lewis Rd. Swans 23 D3
Lewis Rd. Well 18 C4
Leybank. Ton 136 A4
Leybourne Cl. Brom 48 B4
Leybourne Cl. Wald 74 B3
Leybourne Dell. Ben 184 A1
Leybourne Rd. Roc 44 A2
Leybourne Way. Dit 87 E4
Leybridge Ct. SE12 16 B3
Leycroft Gdns. Eri 5 E1
Leydenhatch La. Swan 36 C2
Leyhill Cl. Swan 37 D1
Leyland Rd. SE12 16 B3
Leysdown Ave. Bexh 19 F4
Leysdown Rd. SE9 17 D1
Leyton Ave. Chath 61 D3
Leyton Cross Rd. Dart 20 A1
Leywood Rd. Meo 70 C3
Lezayre Rd. Orp 64 A4
Lichfield Cl. Rai (K) 61 F3
Lichlade Cl. Orp 50 A1
Liddon Rd. Brom 33 F1
Lidsing Rd. Box 89 F4
Lidsing Rd. Bredh 75 D2
Lidwells La. Gou 172 A3
Liffler Rd. SE18 3 D3
Lightfoot Green. Hawkt 189 D4
Lila Pl. Swan 37 D1
Lilac Cres. Roc 44 A1
Lilac Gdns. Swan 36 C1
Lilac Green. Dit 87 E2
Lilac Pl. Meo 56 B3
Lilac Rd. Roc 44 A1
Lilburne Gdns. SE9 17 D3
Lilburne Rd. SE9 17 D3
Lilk Hill. Rose 107 E4
Lillieburn. Birl 86 C3
Lime Ave. Grave 23 F2
Lime Cl. Mard 141 F1
Lime Cres. Dit 87 E2
Lime Ct. Rai (K) 75 F4
Lime Gr. Orp 49 E2
Lime Gr. Sid 18 A3
Lime Hill Rd. T W 167 E4
Lime Pit La. Dunt 80 C3
Lime Rd. Swan 36 C1
Lime Row. Belv 4 A4
Lime Tree C. Ton 136 C3
Lime Tree Wlk. Sev 98 B3
Lime Tree Wlk. W Wick 48 A1
Limes Cl. Ten 186 C2
Limes The. Brom 49 D2
Limes The. Ede 131 F3
Limes The. Frit 161 D1
Limes The. Orp 49 E1
Limes The. Pur 6 B3
Limestone Wlk. Belv 3 F4
Limetree Cl. Chath 60 B2
Limewood Rd. Eri 4 C2
Linchmere Rd. SE12 16 A2
Lincoln Cl. Eri 5 D1
Lincoln Cl. Roc 43 F1
Lincoln Green Rd. Orp 50 A4
Lincoln Rd. Eri 5 D1
Lincoln Rd. Gil 45 F2
Lincoln Rd. Maid 106 C2
Lincoln Rd. Sid 35 E4
Lincombe Rd. Brom 16 A1
Linden Ave. Dart 20 C2
Linden Chase. Sev 81 E1
Linden Cl. Orp 50 B1
Linden Cl. Padd W 139 E1
Linden Cl. Pur 6 C2
Linden Gdns. T W 167 D3
Linden Park Rd. T W 167 E3
Linden Rd. Cox 123 F4
Linden Rd. Gil 46 A1
Linden Sq. Sev 81 D1
Lindenfield. Chis 34 B2
Lindens The. Dit 88 A3
Lindisfarne Cl. Grave 25 D1
Lindridge La. Stapt 142 C1
Lindsey Cl. Brom 34 A1
Lineacre Cl. Rai (K) 61 F1
Ling Rd. Eri 4 C2
Lingey Cl. Sid 18 A1
Lingfield Ave. Dart 21 E2
Lingfield Cres. SE9 17 F4
Lingfield Rd. Bor G 84 B2
Lingfield Rd. Ede 131 D1
Lingfield Rd. Grave 24 B1
Lingley Dr. Roc 44 C3
Lingwood. Bexh 4 B1
Link Hill La. Ege 146 C4
Link Way. Brom 49 D3
Link Way. T W 154 A2
Linkfield. Brom 48 B4
Links The. Chath 60 B2
Linkway. Dit 87 F3
Linnet Ave. Padd W 139 E1
Linslade Rd. Orp 64 B4
Linsted Ct. SE9 18 A3
Linton Cl. Well 3 E1
Linton Dann Cl. Hoo S W 28 C1
Linton Gore. Cox 123 F4
Linton Hill. Lint 124 A2
Linton Rd. Loose 106 A1
Lintorn Simmonds Rd. Hoo S W 28 A1
Linwood Ave. Roc 44 A2
Lion Rd. Bexh 19 D4
Lionel Gdns. SE9 16 C3
Lionel Rd. SE9 16 C3
Lionel Rd. Ton 136 B2
Lions Cl. SE9 16 C1
Liphook Way. Maid 88 C2
Lipscombe Rd. T W 153 F1
Liptraps La. T W 153 F2
Lipwell Hill. Coo 28 B4
Liskeard Cl. Chis 34 C3
Liskeard Gdns. SE3 1 B1
Lisle Cl. Grave 25 E1
Lisle Pl. Grays 8 B4
Lismore Cl. Maid 106 B2
Lister Cl. Dit 87 D2
Listmas Rd. Chath 60 B4
Little Alley. Ede 131 E1
Little Birches. Sid 18 A1
Little Boundes Cl. Soub 153 D4
Little Browns La. Ede 131 D4
Little Buckland Ave. Maid 88 C1
Little Ct. W Wick 48 A2
Little Footway. Spel 166 A4
Little Heath. SE7 2 A3
Little Heath Rd. Bexh 4 A2
Little John Ave. Wald 74 A3
Little Julians Hill. Sev 98 B2
Little Mallett. Spel 166 A4
Little Market Row. Birl 87 D3
Little Mount Sion. T W 167 E3
Little Orchard. Cox 123 F4
Little Oxley. Dit 87 D3
Little Queen St. Dart 21 D2
Little Redlands. Brom 34 A2
Little Thrift. Orp 34 C1
Little Wood. Sev 81 F1
Littlebourne Ave. Rai (K) 61 E4
Littlebourne Rd. Maid 89 F1
Littlebrook Manor Way. Dart 21 E3
Littlecombe. SE7 1 B2
Littlecourt Rd. Sev 98 B4
Littlecroft. Ist 41 D3
Littlecroft. SE9 17 E4
Littledale. SE2 3 E2
Littlejohn Rd. Orp 50 B4
Littlemede. SE9 17 D1
Littlemore Rd. SE2 3 E4
Livesey St. Tes 104 B3
Livingstone Circus. Gil 45 F1
Livingstone Gdns. Grave 41 F4
Livingstone Rd. Gil 46 A1
Livingstone Rd. Grave 41 F4
Livingstone Wlk. Maid 107 D1
Lizban St. SE3 1 B2
Llanover Rd. SE18 2 B2
Lloyds Green. Witt 197 F4
Lloyd's Pl. SE3 1 A1
Loampits Cl. Ton 136 C4
Lobby Rd. SE28 3 D4
Lobelia Cl. Gil 46 A1
Locarno Ave. Rai (K) 61 E3
Lochaber Rd. SE13 16 A4
Lochat Rd. Hoo S W 28 A1
Lochmere Cl. Eri 4 B2
Lock Chase. SE3 16 A4
Lock La. Maid 88 C3
Lock St. Gil 45 F1
Lockesley Dr. Orp 50 B4
Lockington Cl. Ton 136 A2
Lockington Gr. Chath 44 C1
Lock's Yd. Sev 98 C3
Locksley Cl. Wald 74 A3
Lockyer Rd. Pur 6 C2
Lockyers Hill. Meo 57 D1
Loddington La. Lint 124 B2
Lodge Ave. Dart 20 C3
Lodge Cl. Orp 50 B3
Lodge Cl. Waty 103 F2
Lodge Cres. Orp 50 B3
Lodge Gdns. Ulc 127 D1
Lodge Hill. Well 3 F2
Lodge Hill La. Hoo S W 28 A1
Lodge La. Bex 18 C3
Lodge La. Cob 42 B1
Lodge La. Grays 8 B4
Lodge La. Whm 95 F2
Lodge Oak La. Ton 136 C2
Lodge Rd. Brom 33 F3
Lodge Rd. Stapt 143 D1
Lodge Rd. Ton 136 B3
Logs Hill. Chis 34 A2
Logs Hill Cl. Chis 34 A2
Lomas La. Sand 191 D1
Lombard St. Hort 38 C1
Lombard Wall. SE7 1 B3
Lombardy Cl. Rai (K) 61 E1
Lombardy Dr. Maid 89 F1
London La. Brom 33 D3
London La. Cran 174 B3
London Rd. Brom 33 D2
London Rd. Dart 19 F3
London Rd. Dart 21 F3
London Rd. Dit 88 B2
London Rd. Dit 87 E3
London Rd. Dunt 81 D2
London Rd. Farn 53 D4
London Rd. Grave 24 A3
London Rd. Grays 8 A2
London Rd. Gree 22 B3
London Rd. Hals 65 D3
London Rd. Hild 117 E3
London Rd. Maid 88 B2
London Rd. Pur 6 B4
London Rd. Rai (K) 61 F3
London Rd. Roc 44 B2
London Rd. S Ock 6 B4
London Rd. Sev 81 D1
London Rd. Shorn 65 F1
London Rd. Soub 153 D3
London Rd. Stans 68 B2
London Rd. Swan 36 C2
London Rd. Swans 23 D3
London Rd. T W 167 E4

London Rd. Tic 187 F4
London Rd. Ton 136 B4
London Rd. Upc 62 C2
London Rd. W Kin 68 B2
London Rd. W Mal 86 B3
London Rd. Whm 95 F3
London Rd. Wro 84 B4
London Rd. Wro H 85 E3
London Rd E. Dit 88 A2
London Road Purfleet. Pur 6 B3
London Road West Thurrock. Grays 7 E2
Lone Barn Rd. Len 111 E3
Lonewood Way. Had 120 A3
Long Acre. Orp 50 C2
Long Barn Rd. Sev W 116 B3
Long Catlis Rd. Rai (K) 75 F4
Long Ct. Pur 6 B3
Long La. Bexh 4 A1
Long La. Bou Mon 124 C1
Long La. Grays 8 B4
Long Mead Way. Ton 136 B4
Long Meads. T W 166 B4
Long Mill La. Bor G 84 C1
Long Mill La. Plax 101 E3
Long Pond Rd. SE3 1 A1
Long Rede La. Maid 105 D4
Long Slip. Spel 166 B4
Long Wlk. Lim C 113 E4
Long Wlk. SE18 2 B2
Longbury Dr. Orp 35 E2
Longcroft. SE9 17 E1
Longdon Wood. Kes 49 D1
Longfellow Rd. Gil 60 C4
Longfield. Brom 33 D2
Longfield. Ten 186 B2
Longfield Ave. H Hals 29 D4
Longfield Ave. Ist 40 C2
Longfield Ave. Lon 40 C2
Longfield Pl. Maid 106 C2
Longfield Rd. Meo 56 A4
Longfield Rd. T W 154 A3
Longford Cl. Rai (K) 62 B2
Longham Copse. Oth 107 D3
Longhill Ave. Chath 60 B4
Longhurst Dr. Wald 74 A3
Longhurst Rd. SE13 16 A3
Longlands Park Cres. Sid 18 A1
Longlands Rd. Sid 18 A1
Longleigh La. SE2 3 F2
Longley Rd. Chath 59 F4
Longley Rd. Rai (K) 62 A3
Longmarsh View. Sutt H 38 B2
Longmead. Chis 34 B2
Longmead Dr. Sid 18 C1
Longmeadow Rd. Sid 18 A2
Longparish Cl. Maid 107 D1
Longreach Rd. Eri 5 E2
Longshaw Rd. Maid 107 D1
Longview Way. T W 153 F2
Longwlk. Ist 41 D2
Lonsdale Cl. SE9 16 C1
Lonsdale Cres. Dart 21 F2
Lonsdale Dr. Rai (K) 62 A2
Lonsdale Gdns. T W 167 E4
Lonsdale Rd. Bexh 4 A1
Loop Rd. Chis 34 C3
Loose Rd. Maid 106 B2
Lord Roberts Terr. SE18 2 B3
Lord Romney's Hill. Rose 107 D4
Lord St. Grave 24 B2
Lord Warwick St. SE18 2 A4
Lordine La. Ewh G 194 B1
Lords Wood Cl. Wald 74 B3
Lords Wood La. Wald 74 B3
Lordswood Cl. Dart 39 D4
Lorton Cl. Grave 25 D1
Lossenham La. Newe 195 F4
Lotus Rd. Bigg 78 A3
Louisville Ave. Gil 60 C4
Louvain Rd. Gree 22 A2
Love La. Bex 19 E3
Love La. Brom 33 E2
Love La. Chath 44 C1
Love La. Grave 24 C2
Love La. Head 145 E1
Love La. S Ock 6 C4
Love La. SE18 2 B3
Love La. Waty 103 F2
Lovel Ave. Well 3 E1
Lovelace Ave. Brom 49 E4
Lovelace Cl. Rai (K) 75 F4
Lovelace Cl. W Kin 68 A2
Lovelace Green. SE9 17 D4
Lovers La. Gou 172 A3
Lover's La. Gree 22 C4
Lovers' Wlk. SE10 1 A2
Lovers' Wlk. Ton 136 C4
Lovibonds Ave. Orp 49 F2
Low Cl. Gree 22 B3
Lower Bell La. Dit 87 E3
Lower Boxley Rd. Maid 89 D1
Lower Camden. Chis 34 A2
Lower Croft. Swan 37 D1
Lower East Rd. Gil 45 E2
Lower Fant Rd. Maid 106 A3
Lower Farm Rd. Bou Mon 124 C1
Lower Gravel Rd. Brom 49 D3
Lower Green. Lei 135 D3
Lower Green Rd. Pem 154 C2
Lower Green Rd. Spel 152 C1
Lower Green Rd. T W 166 C4
Lower Hartlip Rd. New(G) 76 C4
Lower Haysden La. Ton 135 F3
Lower Higham Rd. Grave 25 E2
Lower Park Rd. Belv 4 B3
Lower Rainham Rd. Gil 46 B1
Lower Rainham Rd. Rai (K) 62 B4
Lower Range Rd. Grave 25 D2
Lower Rd. Belv 4 C4
Lower Rd. E Far 105 E2
Lower Rd. Grave 23 E4
Lower Rd. Hex 37 E3
Lower Rd. Maid 106 B4
Lower Rd. Orp 50 B4
Lower Rd. Shor 26 A1
Lower Rd. Sutt V 126 A2
Lower Rd. Tilb 24 B4
Lower Rd. W Far 104 C2
Lower Rochester Rd. Cli W 44 B4
Lower Rochester Rd. Higham 44 B4
Lower St. Hild 117 D1
Lower St. Lee 108 B2
Lower Station Rd. Dart 20 A3
Lower Stone St. Maid 106 B4
Lower Tovil. Maid 106 A3
Lower Twydall La. Rai (K) 61 F4
Lower Warren Rd. Ayld 74 A1
Lower Woodlands Rd. Gil 46 B1
Lowfield St. Dart 21 D2
Lownds Ave. Brom 33 E2
Loxwood Cl. Orp 50 C2
Lubbock Cl. Maid 107 D1
Lubbock Rd. Chis 34 A3
Lubbock Wlk. Rai (K) 61 F1
Lucas Rd. Grays 8 B4
Lucas Rd. Snod 72 A2
Lucerne Rd. Orp 50 A3
Lucerne St. Maid 89 E1
Lucilina Dr. Ede 131 F2
Lucknow Rd. Padd W 139 E2
Lucknow St. SE18 3 D2
Lucks Hill. Dit 87 D2
Lucks La. Chart S 125 D1
Lucks La. Padd W 139 F2
Luck's Way. Mard 141 E1
Lucorn Cl. SE12 16 A3
Luddenham Cl. Maid 89 F1
Luddesdon Rd. Eri 4 B2
Luddesdown Rd. Cob 57 E3
Ludlow Cl. Brom 33 E1
Ludlow Pl. Grays 8 B4
Luffield Rd. SE2 3 E4
Luffman Rd. SE12 16 B1
Lughorse La. Hunt 122 C3
Lughorse La. Yal 122 C3
Lullingstone Ave. Swan 37 D1
Lullingstone Cl. Orp 35 E3
Lullingstone Cres. Orp 35 E3
Lullingstone La. Eyn 52 C2
Lullingstone La. Swan 52 C2
Lullingstone Rd. Belv 4 A2
Lullingstone Rd. Maid 88 C2
Lullington Garth. Brom 33 D3
Lulworth Rd. SE9 17 D1
Lulworth Rd. Well 3 D1
Lumley Cl. Belv 4 B3
Lumsden Terr. Chath 60 A4
Lunedale Rd. Dart 21 F2
Lunsford La. Dit 87 D4
Lunsford La. Snod 72 A1
Lupton Cl. SE12 33 E4
Lurkins Rise. Gou 171 F2
Lushington Rd. Maid 89 D2
Lusted Rd. Dunt 81 D2
Luton High St. Chath 60 C3
Luton Rd. Chath 60 B3
Luton Rd. Sid 18 C1
Luxfield Rd. SE9 17 D2
Luxon Rd. Meo 71 D4
Luxted Rd. Dow 63 E1
Lyall Way. Rai (K) 76 A4
Lych Gate Rd. Orp 50 B3
Lydd Cl. Sid 18 A1
Lydd Rd. Bexh 4 A2
Lydd Rd. Wald 60 B1
Lydden Ct. SE9 18 A3
Lydens La. Ede 132 A1
Lydia Rd. Eri 5 D2
Lydstep Rd. Chis 34 B4
Lyford St. SE18 2 A3
Lyle Cl. Roc 44 B2
Lyle Park. Sev 98 B4
Lyme Farm Rd. SE12 16 B4
Lyme Rd. Well 3 E1
Lyminge Cl. Rai (K) 61 F3
Lyminge Cl. Sid 35 D4
Lymington Ct. Maid 125 D4
Lyndale Cl. SE3 1 A2
Lynden Way. Swan 36 C1
Lyndhurst Ave. Rai (K) 61 F2
Lyndhurst Cl. Bexh 19 E4
Lyndhurst Dr. Sev 98 A4
Lyndhurst Rd. Bexh 19 E4
Lyndhurst Rd. Maid 106 C2
Lyndhurst Way. Ist 41 D2
Lyndon Ave. Sid 18 A3
Lyndon Rd. Belv 4 B3
Lynette Ave. Roc 44 B3
Lyngs Cl. Yal 122 A2
Lynmead Cl. Ede 131 E4
Lynmere Rd. Well 3 E1
Lynmouth Rise. Orp 35 E1
Lynne Cl. Orp 64 A4
Lynors Ave. Roc 44 B3
Lynstead Cl. Bexh 19 E3
Lynstead Cl. Brom 33 F2
Lynsted Gdns. SE9 16 C4
Lynsted Rd. Rai (K) 61 E4
Lynton Ave. Orp 35 E1
Lynton Dr. Wald 74 B4
Lynton Rd. Grave 24 B2
Lynton Road S. Grave 24 B2
Lynwood Gr. Orp 50 A3
Lyons Cres. Ton 136 C3
Lyoth Rd. Orp 49 F2
Lysander Rd. Merew 103 D4
Lysander Way. Orp 49 F2
Lytchet Rd. Brom 33 E3
Lyveden Rd. SE3 1 B2
Mabel Rd. Hex 37 E3
Mabledon Rd. Ton 136 B2
Macaul Cl. Dit 87 E4
Macbean St. SE18 2 B4
Macdonald Rd. Gil 45 F1
Mace La. Dow 63 F1
Mackenders Cl. Ayld 73 E1
Mackenders La. Ayld 73 E1
Mackenzie Way. Grave 41 F3
Macklands Way. Rai (K) 62 B3
Macleod Cl. Grays 8 C3
Macmillan Gdns. Dart 21 E4
Macoma Rd. SE18 2 C2
Macoma Terr. SE18 2 C2
Mada Rd. Orp 49 E2
Madan Rd. Whm 96 A3
Madden Ave. Wald 60 A1
Madden Cl. Swans 23 D3
Maddocks Cl. Sid 36 A4
Madeira Ave. Brom 33 D3
Madeira Park. T W 167 E3
Madginford Cl. Rose 107 E3
Madginford Rd. Rose 107 E3
Madison Cres. Bexh 3 F2
Madison Gdns. Bexh 3 F2
Madison Gdns. Brom 33 D1
Madison Way. Sev 98 A4
Mafeking Rd. Wald 74 A4
Magdalen Cl. Rai (K) 75 E4
Magdelan Gr. Orp 50 B1
Magnolia Ave. Rai (K) 61 E1
Magnolia Cl. Ton 136 C2
Magnolia Dr. Bigg 78 A4
Magpie Bottom. Shorm 67 D1
Magpie Cl. Dit 87 E3
Magpie Green. Ede 131 F4
Magpie Hall Cl. Brom 49 D4
Magpie Hall La. Brom 49 D4
Magpie Hall Rd. Chath 60 B3
Magpie La. New(G) 76 A3
Maida Rd. Belv 4 B4
Maida Rd. Chath 60 B3
Maida Vale Rd. Dart 20 B3
Maiden Erlegh Ave. Bex 19 D2
Maiden La. Dart 20 B4
Maidstone Rd. Bor G 84 B2
Maidstone Rd. Burh 73 F3
Maidstone Rd. Char 130 B3
Maidstone Rd. Chath 60 A3
Maidstone Rd. Chath 59 F3
Maidstone Rd. E Pec 139 E3
Maidstone Rd. Five O G 138 C1
Maidstone Rd. Grays 8 B2
Maidstone Rd. Had 120 A3
Maidstone Rd. Head 144 B2
Maidstone Rd. Len 110 C1
Maidstone Rd. Maid 157 E3
Maidstone Rd. Mard 142 A3
Maidstone Rd. Mat 156 A3
Maidstone Rd. Net 121 F3
Maidstone Rd. New(G) 77 F3
Maidstone Rd. Padd W 139 E3
Maidstone Rd. Rai (K) 61 F1
Maidstone Rd. Seal 82 C1
Maidstone Rd. Sev 81 D1
Maidstone Rd. Sid 36 A3
Maidstone Rd. Stapt 143 D2
Maidstone Rd. Sutt V 126 A3
Maidstone Rd. Wald 59 F1
Maidstone Rd. Wro H 85 D2
Maidstone Rd. Yal 139 E3
Mailyns The. Rai (K) 61 F2
Main Gate Rd. Chath 45 D2
Main Rd. Bigg 78 A3
Main Rd. Ede 113 E2
Main Rd. Farn 53 E3
Main Rd. Grave 39 F2
Main Rd. Hex 37 D2
Main Rd. Hoo S W 45 E4
Main Rd. Kno P 79 E3
Min Rd. Lon 40 B1
Main Rd. Orp 35 F2
Main Rd. Sid 35 D4
Main Rd. Sund 97 D4
Main Rd. Sutt H 38 B3
Main Rd. Swan 51 F4
Main Rd. Whm 113 E2
Main St. Norm 195 E1
Mainridge Rd. Chis 34 B4
Majendie Rd. SE18 2 C3
Major York's Rd. T W 167 D3
Malan Cl. Bigg 78 A3
Malden Dr. Maid 89 D2
Mall The. Brom 33 E1
Mallard Cl. Dart 21 D3
Mallard Way. Ede 131 F4
Mallard Way. Low St 30 C4
Mallard Wlk. Dit 87 D3
Mallard Wlk. Sid 35 F3
Malling Rd. Merew 103 D3
Malling Rd. Snod 72 A1
Malling Rd. Tes 104 B3
Malling Terr. Maid 105 F4
Malling Way. Brom 48 A3
Mallingdene Cl. Cli W 27 E2
Mallings Dr. Rose 107 F4
Mallings La. Rose 107 F4
Mallow Cl. Grave 41 D4
Mallow Ct. Grays 8 C2
Mallow Way. Wald 74 A4
Malmaynes Hall Rd. Low St 30 A4
Malt House La. Ten 186 B2
Malt Mews. Chath 44 C1
Malta Ave. Chath 60 B2
Maltby Cl. Orp 50 B3
Malthouse Cl. Len 110 C1
Malthouse Hill. Loose 124 A4
Malthouse La. Shor 43 D4
Malthouse Rd. Stans 69 D3
Maltings Cl. Had 120 A2
Maltings Mews. Sid 18 B1
Maltings The. Bou Mon 124 B4
Maltings The. Orp 50 A3
Maltings The. Rai (K) 62 B2
Maltings The. Thu 90 A1
Malton St. SE18 3 D2
Malton Way. T W 154 A1
Malvern Ave. Bexh 4 A2
Malvern Rd. Gil 61 D4
Malvern Rd. Orp 50 B1
Malvina Ave. Grave 24 C1
Malyons Rd. Hex 37 D3
Mamignot Cl. Thu 90 B1
Manchester Cl. Chath 60 C1
Mandeville Cl. SE3 1 B2
Mangold Way. Belv 4 A4
Mangravet Ave. Maid 106 C2
Manister Rd. SE2 3 E4
Mann Sq. Ton 136 C2
Manning Rd. Orp 50 C4
Manor Cl. Dart 20 A4
Manor Cl. Dart 20 B1
Manor Cl. Grave 25 E1
Manor Cl. Rose 107 E4
Manor Cl. T W 167 D4
Manor Dr. Hart (S) 55 E4
Manor Field. Shor 43 D4
Manor Forstal. N Ash 55 D2
Manor Gr. Ton 136 C4
Manor House Dr. Maid 105 F4
Manor House Gdns. Ede 131 F3
Manor La. Chath 59 D3
Manor La. Faw 54 C3
Manor La. Hart (S) 55 E4
Manor La. SE12 16 A3
Manor Lane Terr. SE13 16 A3
Manor Park. Chis 34 C2
Manor Park. SE13 16 A3
Manor Park. T W 167 D4
Manor Park Rd. Chis 34 C2
Manor Pl. Chis 34 C2
Manor Rd. Bex 19 E2
Manor Rd. Chath 60 A4
Manor Rd. Cob 56 C4
Manor Rd. Dart 20 A4
Manor Rd. Ede 131 E3
Manor Rd. Eri 5 E2
Manor Rd. Grave 24 B3
Manor Rd. Grays 8 C2
Manor Rd. Grays 7 F2
Manor Rd. Lim 78 A2
Manor Rd. Lon 55 F4
Manor Rd. Mils 94 A3
Manor Rd. Sand 96 C4
Manor Rd. Sid 18 B1
Manor Rd. Soub 153 D3
Manor Rd. Swans 23 D2
Manor Rd. T W 166 C4
Manor Rise. Rose 107 E4
Manor St. Gil 45 E1
Manor Way. Bex 19 E2
Manor Way. Bexh 19 F4
Manor Way. Brom 49 D4
Manor Way. Grave 23 E4
Manor Way. Grays 8 B2
Manor Way. Grays 8 C2
Manor Way. Orp 34 C1
Manor Way. SE3 16 B4
Manor Way. Swans 23 D4
Manorbrook. SE3 16 B4
Manorside Cl. SE2 3 F3
Manse Par. Swan 37 E1
Manse Way. Swan 37 E1
Mansel Dr. Chath 59 E3
Mansergh Cl. SE18 2 A2
Mansfield Cl. Orp 50 C3
Mansfield Rd. Hex 37 D3
Mansion Row. Gil 45 E1
Manthorpe Rd. SE18 2 C3
Manton Rd. SE2 3 E3
Maple Ave. Gil 46 A1
Maple Ave. Maid 88 C1
Maple Cl. Dit 87 E3
Maple Cl. Orp 49 F4
Maple Cl. Swan 37 D2
Maple Cl. T W 167 E3
Maple Cres. Sid 18 B3
Maple Dene. Chis 34 C4
Maple Rd. Dart 20 C2
Maple Rd. Grave 41 F4
Maple Rd. Grays 8 C2
Maple Rd. Hoo S W 46 A4
Maple Rd. Roc 44 A1
Maplescombe La. Farn 53 E1
Maplesden Cl. Maid 105 D4
Mapleton Cl. Brom 48 B4
Mapleton Rd. Whm 114 A3
Maplins Cl. Rai (K) 62 A3
Maran Way. Belv 3 F4
Marathon Paddock. Gil 60 C4
Marbrook Ct. SE12 16 C1
Marcellina Way. Orp 50 A2
Marcet Rd. Dart 20 C3
Marconi Rd. Grave 23 F1
Marcus Rd. Dart 20 B2
Mardale Cl. Rai (K) 62 B3
Marden Ave. Brom 48 B4
Marden Cres. Bex 19 F3
Marden Rd. Roc 44 C3
Marden Rd. Stapt 159 F4
Marechal Neil Ave. Sid 17 F1
Margaret Gardner Dr. SE9 17 D1
Margaret Rd. Bex 18 C3
Margate Cl. Gil 46 A1
Margetts La. Burh 72 C3
Margetts La. Burh 72 C3
Margetts Pl. Roc 45 E4
Marian Sq. Stapt 160 A4
Marina Cl. Brom 33 E1
Marina Dr. Dart 21 E2
Marina Dr. Grave 24 A3
Marina Dr. Well 3 D1
Marine Dr. Hoo S W 46 A4
Marine Dr. SE18 2 A3
Marion Cl. Wald 74 B3
Marion Cres. Maid 106 B2
Marion Cres. Orp 50 B4
Mark Cl. Bexh 4 A1
Mark Cl. Kes 49 D1
Mark La. Grave 25 D3
Mark Way. Swan 52 B4
Market Alley. Grave 24 B3
Market Bldgs. Maid 106 A4
Market Hill. SE18 2 B4
Market Meadow. Orp 35 F1
Market Pl. Bexh 19 E4
Market Pl. Char 130 C2
Market Pl. Chath 60 B4
Market Pl. SE18 2 B3
Market Pl. T W 167 E3
Market Rd. T W 167 E4
Market Sq. Brom 33 E2
Market Sq. Whm 95 F3
Market St. Dart 21 D2
Market St. Maid 106 A4
Market St. SE18 2 B3
Market St. Stapt 143 D1
Market St. T W 167 E3
Market Way. Whm 95 F3
Marlborough Cl. Grays 8 C4
Marlborough Cl. Orp 50 A4
Marlborough Cl. T W 167 D4
Marlborough Cres. Sev 98 A4
Marlborough La. SE7 1 C2
Marlborough Park Ave. Sid 18 B2
Marlborough Rd. Bexh 18 C4
Marlborough Rd. Brom 33 F1
Marlborough Rd. Dart 20 C3
Marlborough Rd. Gil 45 E1
Marle Place Rd. Brenc 170 C4
Marley Ave. Bexh 3 F2
Marley Rd. Harr 110 A1
Marley Rd. Hoo S W 28 C1
Marley Way. Chath 59 F3
Marlhurst. Ede 131 E4
Marling Way. Grave 42 A4
Marlings Cl. Chis 35 D1
Marlings Park Ave. Chis 35 D1
Marlow Ave. Pur 6 B3
Marlow Copse. Wald 74 A3
Marlowe Cl. Chis 34 C3
Marlowe Gdns. SE9 17 E3
Marlowe Rd. Dit 87 E4
Marlowes The. Bexh 19 F4
Marlpit Cl. Ede 131 F4
Marlpit The. Wad 178 A1
Marmadon Rd. SE18 3 D3
Marne Ave. Well 18 B4
Marriot Rd. Dart 21 E2
Marsden Way. Orp 50 A1
Marsh Cres. H Hals 29 D4
Marsh Green Rd. Ede 131 F1
Marsh La. Cli 10 B1
Marsh Quarter La. Sand 194 C4
Marsh Rd. Hall 58 B1
Marsh St. Dart 21 E4
Marsh St. Roc 44 B2
Marsh Way. Dit 87 E4
Marshall Gdns. Had 120 A3
Marshall Rd. Rai (K) 61 F2
Marshalls Gr. SE18 2 A3
Marshalls Land. Ten 186 B4
Marsham Cl. Chis 34 B4
Marsham Cres. Chart S 125 E3
Marsham St. Maid 106 B4
Marshbrook Cl. SE3 16 C4
Marshgate Path. SE18 2 C4
Marshland View. Low St 13 F1
Marston Cl. Wald 74 A4
Marston Dr. Maid 89 F1
Marston Rd. Maid 89 E1
Marston Wlk. Wald 74 A4
Martens Ave. Bexh 19 F4
Martens Cl. Bexh 19 F4
Martin Bowes Rd. SE9 17 D4
Martin Dene. Bexh 19 D3
Martin Dr. Dart 21 E3
Martin Hardie Way. Ton 119 D1
Martin Rd. Dart 20 C1
Martin Rd. Roc 44 B2
Martin Rise. Bexh 19 D3
Martin Sq. Dit 87 E3
Martindale Ave. Orp 50 B1
Martins Cl. Higham 26 C1
Martins Cl. Orp 35 F1
Martins Cl. Ten 186 C2
Martins La. E Pec 121 D3
Martin's Rd. Brom 33 D2
Martin's Shaw. Sev 80 C1
Martins Slip. Brom 33 D2
Marvels Cl. SE12 16 B1
Marvels La. SE12 16 C1
Marwell. Whm 95 F3
Marwood Cl. Well 18 B4
Mary Burrows Gdns. Kemsg 82 B3
Mary Day's. Gou 172 A2
Marybank. SE18 2 A3
Maryfield Cl. Bex 20 A1
Maryland Ct. Rai (K) 62 A1
Maryland Dr. Maid 105 D3
Maryland Rd. T W 167 F3
Maryon Gr. SE7 2 A3
Maryon Rd. SE7 2 A3
Mascall's Court La. Padd W 156 B4
Mascall's Court Rd. Padd W 156 B4

Mascalls Ct. SE7 1 C2
Mascalls Park. Padd W 139 D1
Mascalls Rd. SE7 1 C2
Masefield Cl. Eri 5 D1
Masefield Dr. Cli W 27 E2
Masefield Rd. Dart 21 E3
Masefield Rd. Dit 87 D4
Masefield Rd. Grave 23 F1
Masefield View. Orp 49 F2
Masefield Way. Ton 136 A2
Mason Cl. Bexh 19 E4
Mason's Hill. Brom 33 E1
Masons Hill. SE18 2 B3
Master Gunners' Pl. SE18 2 A1
Masters La. Birl 71 E1
Masthead Cl. Dart 21 F4
Matchless Dr. SE18 2 B2
Matfield Cl. Brom 48 B4
Matfield Cl. Maid 89 F1
Matfield Cres. Maid 89 F1
Matfield Rd. Belv 4 B2
Matilda Cl. Rai (K) 61 E3
Matthews La. W Pec 120 A4
Mattinson Pl. Worm 93 D2
Matts Hill Rd. Rai (K) 76 A4
Maude Rd. Hex 37 E3
Maudslay Rd. SE9 17 D4
Maunders Cl. Chath 60 C2
Mavelstone Cl. Brom 34 A2
Mavelstone Rd. Brom 34 A2
Maxey Rd. SE18 2 C3
Maxim Rd. Dart 20 A3
Maxim Rd. Eri 4 C3
Maximfeldt Rd. Eri 5 D3
Maxton Cl. Thu 90 A1
Maxwell Dr. Maid 88 B1
Maxwell Gdns. Orp 50 A2
Maxwell Rd. Gil 45 E1
Maxwell Rd. Well 18 B4
May Ave. Grave 24 A2
May Ave. Orp 50 B4
May Avenue Estate. Grave 24 A2
May Rd. Chath 59 F4
May Rd. Gil 60 C4
May Rd. Sutt H 38 A4
May St. Cux 58 B3
May St. Snod 72 B2
May St. Well 3 E1
May Terr. Gil 45 E2
Maybury Ave. Dart 21 F2
Maybury Cl. Orp 49 E4
Maycroft Ave. Grays 8 C3
Maycroft Gdns. Grays 8 C3
Mayday Gdns. SE3 2 A1
Mayerne Rd. SE9 16 C3
Mayes Cl. Swan 37 E1
Mayeswood Rd. SE12 33 F4
Mayfair. Roc 44 C2
Mayfair Ave. Bexh 3 F1
Mayfair Ave. Maid 106 B2
Mayfair Rd. Dart 20 C3
Mayfield. Bexh 19 D4
Mayfield. SE3 1 B1
Mayfield Ave. Orp 50 A3
Mayfield Cl. Rai (K) 62 A3
Mayfield Cl. Wald 74 B3
Mayfield La. Wad 178 A1
Mayfield Park. Wad 178 A1
Mayfield Rd. Belv 4 C3
Mayfield Rd. Brom 49 D4
Mayfield Rd. Grave 24 A2
Mayfield Rd. T W 167 D4
Mayfields. Grays 8 C4
Mayford Rd. Wald 74 C3
Mayhill Rd. SE7 1 B2
Maylands Dr. Sid 18 C1
Maynard Cl. Eri 5 D2
Maynard Pl. Chath 60 C3
Maynards. Mard 141 F1
Mayor's Pl. Ten 186 B2
Mayplace Ave. Dart 20 B4
Mayplace Cl. Bexh 19 E4
Mayplace La. SE18 2 B2
Mayplce Rd E. Bexh 19 F4
Mayplace Rd W. Bexh 19 E4
Maypole Cres. Eri 5 F2
Maypole La. Gou 172 A2
Maypole Rd. Grave 25 D2
Maypole Rd. Orp 65 D4
May's Hill Rd. Brom 33 D1
Maytham Rd. Rol 192 B2
Mayweed Ave. Wald 74 A4
Maze Hill. SE3 1 A2
Mc Kenzie Rd. Wald 74 B3
McAlpine Cres. Loose 124 A4
McCabe Cl. Stapl 160 A3
McCall Cres. SE7 2 A3
McDermott Rd. Bor G 84 A2
McKenzie Cl. Dit 88 A2
McLeod Rd. SE2 3 E3
Mead Cl. Grays 8 B4
Mead Cl. Swan 52 B4
Mead Cres. Dart 20 C2
Mead Green. Wald 74 C4
Mead Rd. Chis 34 C3
Mead Rd. Dart 20 C2
Mead Rd. Ede 131 F2
Mead Rd. Grave 24 B1
Mead The. Birl 87 D3
Mead Wall. Cli 10 A2
Mead Way. Brom 48 A4
Meades Cl. Mard 141 E1
Meadfield Rd. Meo 56 B2
Meadow Bank. Lei 135 D3
Meadow Bank. W Mal 86 C2
Meadow Bank Cl. W Kin 21 F1
Meadow Cl. Chis 34 B4
Meadow Cl. Hall 72 A4
Meadow Cl. Sev 98 B4
Meadow Cl. Wald 60 A1
Meadow Cres. Hall 72 A4
Meadow Croft. Brom 34 A1
Meadow Hill Rd. T W 167 E4
Meadow La. Ede 131 E4
Meadow La. Meo 70 B3
Meadow Rd. Brom 33 D2
Meadow Rd. Grave 24 B1
Meadow Rd. Grave 23 F2
Meadow Rd. Gro 165 F2
Meadow Rd. Soub 153 D3
Meadow Rd. T W 166 C4
Meadow Rd. T W 167 E4
Meadow Rd. Ton 136 B2
Meadow The. Bidd 176 A3
Meadow The. Chis 34 C3
Meadow The. Pem 155 D2
Meadow View. Sid 18 B2
Meadow Viw Rd. Bou Mon 124 B4
Meadow Way. Dart 21 F2
Meadow Way. Mard 142 A1
Meadow Way. Orp 49 E2
Meadow Wlk. Dart 37 F4
Meadow Wlk. Maid 106 B4
Meadow Wlk. Snod 72 A2
Meadowbank. SE3 16 A4
Meadowbank Rd. Chath 60 B4
Meadowcourt Rd. SE3 16 A4
Meadowdown Cl. Rai (K) 75 E4
Meadowlands. Seal 82 A2
Meadows The. Bidd 176 A3
Meadows The. Hals 65 D1
Meadows The. Orp 64 C4
Meadowside. Dart 21 D2
Meadowside. SE9 16 C4
Meadowview. Orp 35 F1
Meadowview Rd. Bex 19 D3
Meads The. Cran 182 A3
Meadside Wlk. Wald 60 A1
Meadway. Grays 8 C3
Meadway. Hals 65 D1
Meadway. Hild 118 A1
Meadway The. Orp 64 B4
Meadway The. Sev 81 D1
Meath Cl. Orp 50 B4
Medebourne Cl. SE3 16 B4
Medhurst Cres. Grave 25 D1
Medhurst Gdns. Grave 25 D1
Medina Rd. Dit 87 F3
Medina Rd. Grays 8 C3
Medina Rd. Ton 118 C1
Medlar Gr. Rai (K) 75 E4
Medlar Rd. Grays 8 C2
Medlars The. Maid 89 F1
Medlars The. Meo 56 B4
Medway Ave. H Hals 29 D4
Medway Ave. Yal 122 A3
Medway Gdns. Chath 45 D2
Medway Meadows. E Pec 121 E1
Medway Rd. Dart 20 B4
Medway Rd. Gil 45 F2
Medway Rd. Rai (K) 62 A3
Medway Rd. T W 153 E1
Medway St. Chath 45 D1
Medway St. Maid 106 A4
Medway Trading Est. Maid 106 A4
Medway View. Had 120 A1
Medway Wharf Rd. Ton 136 C3
Meerbrook Rd. SE3 16 C4
Meeson's La. Grays 8 A3
Meeting House La. Chath 60 A4
Megby Cl. Rai (K) 61 F1
Megrims Hill. Sand 190 B1
Melanda Cl. Chis 34 A4
Melanie Cl. Bexh 4 A1
Melbourne Cl. Orp 50 A3
Melbourne Rd. Chath 60 B4
Melbury Cl. Chis 34 A3
Meldrum Cl. Orp 50 C4
Melliker La. Meo 56 B4
Melling St. SE18 3 D2
Mells Cres. SE9 34 A4
Melody Cl. Rai (K) 75 F4
Melrose Cl. Maid 106 B2
Melrose Cl. SE12 16 B2
Melrose Cres. Orp 49 F1
Melthorpe Gdns. SE3 2 A1
Melville Rd. Maid 106 B4
Melville Rd. Sid 18 C1
Mendip Rd. Bexh 5 D1
Mendip Walk. T W 153 F1
Meness Path. SE18 2 B2
Mera Dr. Bexh 19 E4
Mercer Dr. Harr 110 A1
Mercer St. T W 153 E1
Mercer Way. Chart S 125 E3
Mercers. Hawkt 189 E3
Mercers. Spel 166 B4
Mercers Cl. Padd W 139 D1
Merchland Rd. SE9 17 F2
Mercury Cl. Chath 59 E4
Mere Cl. Orp 49 E2
Meresborough La. New(G) 62 B1
Meresborough Rd. Rai (K) 62 B1
Mereside. Orp 49 E2
Merewood Cl. Brom 34 B2
Merewood Rd. Bexh 4 C1
Mereworth Cl. Brom 48 A4
Mereworth Cl. Rai (K) 61 E4
Mereworth Dr. SE18 2 C2
Mereworth Rd. Merew 102 C2
Mereworth Rd. T W 153 E1
Mereworth Rd. W Pec 102 C2
Meridan Rd. SE7 1 C2
Meriden Cl. Brom 33 F3
Merifield Rd. SE9 16 C4
Merino Pl. Sid 18 B3
Merivale Gr. Wald 74 B4
Merlewood. Sev 98 B4
Merlewood Dr. Chis 34 A2
Merlin Ave. Dit 87 D3
Merlin Cl. Ton 137 D4
Merlin Gdns. Brom 16 B1
Merlin Rd. Well 18 B4
Mermaid Cl. Chath 60 B1
Mermerus Gdns. Grave 42 A4
Merrals Wood Rd. Roc 44 A1
Merrilees Rd. Sid 18 A2
Merriman Rd. SE3 1 C1
Merriments La. Tic 188 C1
Merrion Cl. T W 153 E2
Merrion Way. T W 153 E2
Merryboys Rd. Cli W 27 E2
Merrydown Way. Chis 34 A2
Merryfield. SE3 1 A1
Mersey Rd. Ton 118 B1
Merton Ave. Hart (S) 40 A1
Merton Cl. Wald 60 C1
Merton Gdns. Orp 49 E4
Merton Rd. Rose 107 D3
Mervyn Ave. SE9 17 F1
Mesne Way. Shorm 66 A2
Messent Rd. SE9 16 C3
Messeter Pl. SE9 17 E3
Meteor Rd. Merew 103 D4
Methuen Rd. Belv 4 B3
Methuen Rd. Bexh 19 D4
Mews The. Roc 44 A2
Mews The. Sev 98 B4
Mews The. Sid 35 E4
Meyer Rd. Eri 4 C2
Micawber Cl. Wald 74 B3
Michael Gdns. Grave 42 A4
Michaels Cl. SE13 16 A4
Michaels La. Faw 54 B2
Micheldever Rd. SE12 16 A3
Mickleham Cl. Orp 35 E2
Mickleham Rd. Orp 35 E2
Middle Field. Pem 155 D2
Middle La. Seal 82 A1
Middle Park Ave. SE9 16 C3
Middle Rd. Bel G 168 B1
Middle St. Gil 45 E1
Middle Walk. T W 154 A2
Middlefields. Rai (K) 62 B2
Middlesex Rd. Maid 106 C2
Middleton Ave. Sid 35 F4
Middleton Cl. Rai (K) 76 A4
Middleton Rd. Sid 35 F3
Middlings Rise. Sev 98 A3
Middlings The. Sev 98 A3
Middlings Wood. Sev 98 B3
Midfield Ave. Bexh 19 F4
Midfield Ave. Hex 37 E3
Midfield Par. Bexh 19 F4
Midfield Way. Orp 35 E2
Midhurst Hill. Bexh 19 E3
Midley Cl. Maid 88 C2
Midsummer Rd. Snod 72 A2
Midway The. T W 166 C3
Miers Court Rd. Rai (K) 62 A1
Mierscourt Cl. Rai (K) 62 B2
Mierscourt Rd. Rai (K) 62 A2
Milborough Cres. SE12 16 A3
Milburn Rd. Gil 45 F2
Mildmay Pl. Shorm 66 A2
Mildred Cl. Dart 21 E3
Mildred Rd. Eri 5 D3
Mile La. Gou 172 B2
Mile Oak Rd. Brenc 156 C4
Mile Oak Rd. Padd W 156 C4
Mile Stone Rd. Dart 21 E3
Milebush La. Mard 142 A3
Miles Pl. Chath 59 F4
Milford Cl. Maid 88 C1
Milford Cl. SE2 4 A2
Military Rd. Chath 45 D1
Milk House Cotts. Cran 174 B2
Milk St. Brom 33 E3
Milking La. Dow 63 D2
Mill Bank. Head 144 C1
Mill Brook Rd. Orp 35 F1
Mill Cl. Len 128 C4
Mill Cl. Roc 44 B3
Mill Cres. Ton 136 C3
Mill Hall Business Estate. Dit 87 F3
Mill Hall Rd. Dit 87 F4
Mill Hill. Ede 131 F2
Mill Hill La. Shor 42 C4
Mill La. Chath 60 C3
Mill La. Cox 123 F4
Mill La. Cran 174 A2
Mill La. Dow 63 E3
Mill La. Eyn 53 D3
Mill La. Frit 160 C2
Mill La. Grays 7 F3
Mill La. Hild 117 F3
Mill La. Hors 157 E3
Mill La. Ight 83 F1
Mill La. Lim C 113 D4
Mill La. Maid 89 D1
Mill La. SE18 2 B3
Mill La. Seal 117 F3
Mill La. Sev 81 F1
Mill La. Shorm 66 A3
Mill La. Sma 163 E3
Mill La. Snod 72 B2
Mill La. Ten 186 B3
Mill La. Ton 136 C3
Mill La. Waty 103 F2
Mill La. Whm 95 F2
Mill La. Yal 122 B2
Mill Lane. Burh 73 F3
Mill Pl. Chis 34 B2
Mill Pl. Dart 20 B4
Mill Pond Rd. Dart 21 D3
Mill Rd. Dunt 81 D1
Mill Rd. Eri 4 C2
Mill Rd. Gil 45 F1
Mill Rd. Grave 24 A2
Mill Rd. Pur 6 B2
Mill Rd. Roc 44 B2
Mill Rd. Sutt H 38 A4
Mill St. Ben 190 C4
Mill St. Dit 87 D2
Mill St. Loose 106 A1
Mill St. Maid 106 A4
Mill St. Snod 72 B2
Mill St. Whm 95 F2
Mill Stone Cl. Sutt H 38 C2
Mill Vale. Brom 33 D2
Mill Wlk. Maid 105 E4
Millbank Way. SE12 16 B3
Millbro. Hex 37 E2
Millbrook. Birl 86 C3
Millbrook Ave. Well 17 F4
Millcroft Rd. Cli 27 E4
Miller Rd. Grave 25 E1
Miller Way. Roc 44 C3
Millers Wharf. Maid 106 A3
Millfield. H Hald 177 F2
Millfield. N Ash 55 D2
Millfield La. N Ash 55 D2
Millfield Rd. W Kin 67 F4
Millfields Cl. Orp 35 E1
Millfordhope Rd. Roc 43 F2
Millhall. Ayld 88 A3
Millhouse La. Wro H 85 F4
Millpond La. Ten 186 A3
Mills Cres. Seal 82 A2
Mills Rd. Dit 88 A2
Mills Terr. Chath 60 B4
Milward Wlk. SE18 2 B2
Millwood Rd. Orp 35 F1
Milne Gdns. SE9 17 D3
Milner Rd. Gil 45 F2
Milroy Ave. Grave 24 A1
Milstead Cl. Maid 89 F1
Milsted Rd. Rai (K) 61 F4
Milton Ave. Cli W 27 E2
Milton Ave. Grave 24 C2
Milton Ave. Shorm 65 E3
Milton Dr. T W 153 F2
Milton Gdns. Ton 136 A2
Milton Hall Rd. Grave 24 C2
Milton Pl. Grave 24 C3
Milton Rd. Belv 4 B3
Milton Rd. Dunt 81 D1
Milton Rd. Gil 60 C4
Milton Rd. Grave 24 C2
Milton Rd. Grays 8 B3
Milton Rd. Swans 23 D3
Milton Rd. Well 3 D1
Milton St. Maid 105 F3
Milton St. Swans 22 C3
Milverton Way. SE9 34 B4
Mimosa Cl. Orp 50 C2
Minard Rd. SE6 16 A2
Mincers Cl. Wald 74 C3
Mineral St. SE18 3 D3
Minerva Cl. Sid 35 D4
Minerva Rd. Roc 44 B2
Ministry Way. SE9 17 D1
Minor Canon Row. Chath 44 C1
Minster Rd. Brom 33 E3
Minster Rd. Rai (K) 61 F4
Mintching Wood La. Mils 94 A3
Minters Orch. Bor G 84 B2
Mirfield St. SE7 1 C4
Miriam Rd. SE18 3 D3
Mirror Path. SE9 16 C1
Miskin Rd. Dart 20 C2
Miskin Rd. Hoo S W 29 D1
Miskin Way. Grave 41 F3
Mitchell Ave. Chath 60 A3
Mitchell Ave. Grave 23 F1
Mitchell Cl. Dart 21 D1
Mitchell Cl. SE2 3 F3
Mitchell Rd. Brom 33 F2
Mitchell Rd. Orp 50 A1
Mitchell Way. Brom 33 E2
Mitchell Wlk. Swans 23 D2
Mitchem Cl. W Kin 68 A4
Mitre Rd. Chath 59 E4
Moat Cl. Orp 64 A4
Moat Farm. T W 167 E2
Moat La. Cow 150 A2
Moat La. Eri 5 E1
Moat Rd. Head 144 B1
Moat The. Char 130 C2
Mockbeggar La. Bidd 184 C4
Model Farm Cl. SE9 17 D1
Moira Rd. SE9 17 D4
Molash Rd. Orp 35 F1
Molescroft. SE9 17 F1
Molescroft Way. Ton 136 A2
Molyneux Almshouses. T W 166 B4
Molyneux Park Rd. T W 167 D4
Monarch Cl. Wald 60 B1
Monarch Rd. Belv 4 B4
Monckton's Ave. Maid 89 D2
Monckton's Dr. Maid 89 D2
Monk St. SE18 2 B3
Monkdown. Oth 107 E3
Monks Cl. SE2 3 F3
Monks La. Lim C 113 D1
Monks La. Wad 178 B2
Monks Orchard. Dart 20 C1
Monks Way. Norm 195 E2
Monks Way. Orp 49 F3
Monks Wlk. Char 130 C2
Monks Wlk. Souf 40 B3
Monkton Rd. Bor G 84 A2
Monkton Rd. Well 3 D1
Monkton's La. Maid 89 D2
Monkwood Cl. Chath 59 E2
Monmouth Cl. Rai (K) 61 F3
Monmouth Cl. Well 18 B4
Mons Way. Brom 49 D4
Monson Rd. T W 167 E4
Montacute Gdns. T W 167 D3
Montacute Rd. T W 167 E3
Montague Rd. Swan 37 D1
Montbelle Rd. SE9 17 E1
Montcalm Cl. Brom 48 B4
Montcalm Rd. SE7 1 C2
Monteith Cl. Spel 166 B4
Monterey Cl. Bex 19 F1
Montfort Rd. Kemsg 82 A3
Montfort Rd. Roc 44 B2
Montfort Rd. Wald 74 A3
Montgomery Ave. Chath 60 B2
Montgomery Cl. Grays 8 C4
Montgomery Cl. Sid 18 A3
Montgomery Rd. Dart 38 C2
Montgomery Rd. Gil 60 C4
Montgomery Rd. T W 153 E2
Montpelier Ave. Bex 18 C2
Montpelier Row. SE3 1 A1
Montpelier Vale. SE3 1 A1
•Montreal Rd. Sev 98 A4
Montreal Rd. Tilb 24 B4
Montrose Ave. Chath 61 D3
Montrose Ave. Sid 18 B2
Montrose Ave. Well 18 A4
Montrose Cl. Well 18 A4
Monypenny. Rol 192 A4
Moon's La. Ede 148 A2
Moor Hill. Hawkt 189 D2
Moor La. Ede 148 A4
Moor Park Cl. Rai (K) 62 B2
Moor Rd The. Sev 81 F2
Moor St. Rai (K) 62 B2
Moor The. Hawkt 189 D2
Moorden La. Lei 134 B3
Moordown. SE18 2 B1
Moore Ave. Grays 8 A3
Moore Rd. Swans 23 D3
Moore St. Roc 44 B2
Moorehead Way. SE3 16 B4
Mooreland Rd. Brom 33 D3
Moorfield Rd. Orp 50 B3
Moorhouse Rd. Lim C 95 E1
Mooring Rd. Chath 59 F3
Moorland Dr. Lam 170 B1
Moorside Rd. Brom 33 D4
Morants Court Rd. Dunt 80 C2
Morden Rd. SE3 1 B1
Morden Road Mews. SE3 1 B1
Morden St. Chath 59 F4
Morden Wharf Rd. SE10 1 A4
Mordred Rd. SE6 16 A1
Moreland Ave. Grays 8 C4
Morella Wlk. Len 110 C1
Morement Rd. Hoo S W 28 C1
Moreton Cl. Swan 37 D2
Morewood Cl. Sev 98 A4
Morgan Dr. Gree 22 A2
Morgan Rd. Brom 33 E3
Morhen Cl. Snod 72 A2
Morland Ave. Dart 20 B3
Morley Cl. Orp 49 E2
Morley Rd. Chis 34 C2
Morley Rd. Ton 136 C3
Morley's Rd. Sev W 116 C3
Mornington Ave. Brom 33 F1
Mornington Ct. Bex 19 F2
Morris Cl. Dit 87 D3
Morris Cl. Orp 50 A2
Morris Gdns. Dart 21 E3
Morry La. Sutt V 126 C2
Morston Gdns. SE9 34 A4
Mortgramit Sq. SE18 2 B4
Mortimer Rd. Eri 4 C2
Mortimer Rd. Orp 50 B3
Mortimers Ave. Cli W 27 E2
Morvale Cl. Belv 4 A3
Moselle Rd. Bigg 78 A3
Mosquito Rd. Merew 103 D4
Mossbank. Wald 74 B4
Mossdown Cl. Belv 4 B3
Mosslea Rd. Brom 48 C4
Mosslea Rd. Orp 49 F2
Mossy Glade. Rai (K) 62 A1
Mostyn Rd. Maid 106 C4
Mosul Way. Brom 49 D4
Mosyer Dr. Orp 50 C2
Mote Ave. Maid 106 B4
Mote Rd. Ight 100 B2
Mote Rd. Maid 106 B4
Mote Rd. Ship 100 B2
Motherwell Way. Grays 7 E3
Motney Hill Rd. Rai (K) 62 B4
Mottingham Gdns. SE9 16 C2
Mottingham La. SE9 16 C2
Mottingham Rd. SE9 17 D1
Mottisfont Rd. SE2 3 E4
Moultain Hill. Swan 37 E1
Mound The. SE9 17 E1
Mount Ave. Yal 122 B3
Mount Cl. Brom 34 A2
Mount Cl. Sev 98 A4
Mount Ct. W Wick 48 A2
Mount Culver Ave. Sid 35 F3
Mount Dr. Bexh 19 D3
Mount Dr. Rose 107 E4
Mount Edgcumbe Rd. T W 167 E4
Mount Ephraim. T W 167 E4
Mount Ephraim Rd. T W 167 E4
Mount Harry Rd. Sev 98 B4
Mount La. New(G) 76 C4
Mount La. Rose 107 E4
Mount Pleasant. Ayld 88 B4
Mount Pleasant. Chath 60 B4
Mount Pleasant. Hild 117 F1
Mount Pleasant. Lam 170 A1

Mount Pleasant. Padd W 139 D2
Mount Pleasant. Ten 186 C2
Mount Pleasant. Wad 178 A1
Mount Pleasant Ave. T W 167 E4
Mount Pleasant Dr. Rose 90 B1
Mount Pleasant La. Lam 170 B1
Mount Pleasant Rd. Dart 21 D3
Mount Pleasant Rd. Sev W 116 B3
Mount Pleasant Rd. T W 167 E4
Mount Pleasant Wlk. Bex 19 F3
Mount Rd. Bexh 19 D3
Mount Rd. Chath 60 A4
Mount Rd. Chath 59 E3
Mount Rd. Dart 20 A3
Mount Sion. T W 167 E3
Mountbatten Ave. Chath 60 B2
Mountbatten Ave. Higham 43 F4
Mountbatten Cl. SE18 3 D2
Mountfield. Bor G 84 B2
Mountfield Cl. Meo 70 A3
Mountfield Gdns. T W 167 E4
Mountfield Park. Ton 136 C2
Mountfield Rd. T W 167 E4
Mountfield Way. Orp 35 F1
Mounthurst Rd. Brom 48 A3
Mountjoy Cl. SE2 3 E4
Mounts Hill. Ben 183 E2
Mounts La. Rol 192 B4
Mounts Pond Rd. SE3 1 A1
Mounts Rd. Gree 22 B3
Mountsfield Cl. Maid 88 C1
Mountview Rd. Orp 50 B3
Moyle Cl. Rai (K) 75 F4
Muggins La. Shor 42 C4
Muir Rd. Maid 106 B3
Mulberry Cl. Meo 56 B4
Mulberry Cl. Rai (K) 75 E4
Mulberry Dr. Pur 6 A3
Mulberry Rd. Grave 41 D4
Mulberry Way. Belv 4 C4
Mullien Ct. Grays 8 C2
Multon Rd. W Kin 68 A4
Munday Bois Rd. Ege 147 D3
Munford Dr. Swans 23 D2
Mungo Park Rd. Grave 41 F4
Mungo Park Way. Orp 50 C4
Murchison Ave. Bex 19 D2
Murrain Dr. Oth 107 E3
Murray Ave. Brom 33 E2
Murray Rd. Orp 35 E1
Murray Rd. Roc 44 C2
Murrays Yd. SE18 2 B3
Murton-Neale Cl. Hawkt 189 E3
Museum St. Maid 106 A4
Musket La. Lee 108 B3
Mussenden La. Hort 54 A3
Mustang Rd. Merew 103 D4
Mycenae Rd. SE3 1 B2
Mynn Cres. Rose 107 E4
Myra St. SE2 3 E3
Myrtle Alley. SE18 2 B4
Myrtle Cl. Eri 5 D1
Myrtle Cres. Wald 60 A1
Myrtle Gr. S Ock 6 C4
Myrtle Pl. Dart 21 F2
Myrtle Rd. Dart 20 C1
Myrtledene Rd. SE2 3 E3

Nadine St. SE7 1 C3
Nags Head La. Chath 59 F4
Nag's Head La. Well 18 B4
Nansen Rd. Grave 41 F4
Napier Rd. Belv 4 A3
Napier Rd. Brom 33 E1
Napier Rd. Gil 60 C4
Napier Rd. Grave 24 A2
Napier Rd. T W 167 F3
Napoleon Wlk. Len 110 C1
Napwood Cl. Rai (K) 61 F1
Nares Rd. Rai (K) 75 F4
Narrow Way. Brom 49 D4
Nash Bank. Ist 41 D2
Nash Cl. Wald 74 C3
Nash Croft. Grave 41 D4
Nash Green. Brom 33 E3
Nash La. Kes 48 B1
Nash St. Ist 41 E2
Nashenden La. Chath 59 D3
Natal Rd. Chath 60 B4
Nathan Way. SE28 3 D4
Neal Rd. W Kin 54 A1
Neale St. Chath 60 A3
Neal's Yd. Eri 4 C2
Neills Rd. Lam 178 C3
Nellington Rd. T W 166 B4
Nelson Ave. Ton 136 B3
Nelson Cl. Bigg 78 A3
Nelson Pl. Sid 35 E4
Nelson Rd. Belv 4 A3
Nelson Rd. Brom 33 F1
Nelson Rd. Dart 20 C3
Nelson Rd. Gil 60 C4
Nelson Rd. Grave 24 A1
Nelson Rd. Sid 35 E4
Nelson Rd. T W 167 F3
Nelson Rd. Wou 58 C1
Nelson Terr. Chath 60 C3
Nepicar La. Stans 84 C4
Nesbit Cl. SE3 1 A1
Nesbit Rd. SE9 16 C4
Ness Rd. Eri 5 F2
Nestor Ct. Tes 104 B2
Netley Cl. Maid 89 F1
Nettlepole La. Lit C 147 F3
Nettlestead La. Waty 103 E1
Nevill Gate. T W 167 E3
Nevill Park. T W 166 C4
Nevill Pl. Snod 72 B2
Nevill Rd. Snod 72 B2
Nevill Ridge. T W 166 C4
Nevill St. T W 167 E3
Nevill Terr. T W 167 D3
Neville Cl. Maid 89 E2
Neville Cl. Sid 35 D4
Neville Rd. Chath 60 A3
New Barn Rd. Lon 40 C3
New Barn Rd. Souf 40 C3
New Barn Rd. Sutt V 144 A3
New Barn Rd. Swan 37 D2
New Barns Rd. Maid 89 E2
New Covenant Pl. Chath 59 F4
New Ct. Dart 21 D3
New Cut. Chath 60 A4
New Cut. E Far 105 F2
New Cut Rd. Thu 90 A1
New England Rd. T W 153 E2
New Farm Ave. Brom 33 E1
New House La. Grave 24 A1
New Hythe La. Dit 87 E4
New Lydenburg St. SE7 1 C4
New Pond Rd. Ben 183 F2
New Pound La. Merew 102 C3
New Rd. Burh 73 D3
New Rd. Chath 60 B4
New Rd. Chath 59 F4
New Rd. Cli 27 E4
New Rd. Cran 182 B4
New Rd. Dart 38 C2
New Rd. Dit 87 E2
New Rd. Dit 87 F3
New Rd. Ege 147 E4
New Rd. Grave 24 B3
New Rd. Grays 8 B2
New Rd. Head 144 C1
New Rd. Hex 37 D3
New Rd. Lan H 107 F1
New Rd. Meo 56 A4
New Rd. Orp 50 B3
New Rd. Padd W 139 E1
New Rd. Pen 151 E3
New Rd. SE2 3 F3
New Rd. Sund 97 D3
New Rd. Swan 37 D1
New Rd. Well 3 E1
New Road Ave. Chath 60 A4
New Road Hill. Dow 63 D3
New St. Chath 60 A4
New St. Whm 95 F2
New Stairs. Chath 45 D1
New Street Hill. Brom 33 F4
New Street Rd. N Ash 55 F1
New Wharf Rd. Ton 136 B3
New Wlk. Wro 84 A4
New Yeaps La. Kno P 79 E4
Newark Yd. Roc 44 B2
Newbarn La. Bigg 78 C4
Newbery Rd. Eri 5 D1
Newbury Ave. Maid 88 C1
Newbury Cl. Cli W 27 E2
Newbury La. Wad 178 C2
Newbury Rd. Brom 33 E1
Newchurch Rd. Maid 106 B3
Newcomen Rd. T W 153 E1
Newenden Cl. Maid 89 F1
Newenden Rd. Roc 44 C3
Newhaven Gdns. SE9 16 C4
Newick Cl. Bex 19 E3
Newing Green. Brom 33 F3
Newington Wlk. Maid 89 F1
Newitt Rd. Hoo S W 29 D1
Newland Green La. Ege 146 C2
Newland Green La. Ege 147 D3
Newlands. Spel 166 B4
Newlands Ct. SE9 17 E3
Newlands La. Meo 70 A3
Newlands Rd. Char 130 A1
Newlands Rd. T W 153 E2
Newlands Rise. T W 153 E1
Newlands Way. T W 153 E2
Newlyn Ct. Maid 106 B4
Newlyn Dr. Stapt 143 D1
Newlyn Rd. Well 3 D1
Newman Rd. Brom 33 E2
Newman's Rd. Grave 24 A1
Newmarket Green. SE9 16 C2
Newnham Cl. Rai (K) 61 F3
Newnham St. Chath 60 B4
Newnhams Cl. Brom 34 A1
Newports. Swan 51 F3
Newstead Ave. Orp 50 A2
Newstead Rd. SE12 16 A2
Newton Abbot Rd. Grave 24 A1
Newton Ave. Had 119 D2
Newton Cl. Maid 106 A4
Newton Cl. Wald 74 C3
Newton Gdns. Padd W 139 D2
Newton Rd. T W 167 E4
Newton Rd. Tilb 24 B4
Newton Rd. Well 18 B4
Nichol La. Brom 33 E3
Nicklaus Dr. Wald 74 A4
Nickleby Cl. Chath 59 F3
Nickleby Rd. Grave 25 E2
Nicolson Rd. Orp 50 C3
Nicolson Way. Sev 81 F1
Nigeria Rd. SE7 1 C2
Nightingale Cl. Dit 87 D3
Nightingale Cl. Grave 41 D4
Nightingale Cl. Rai (K) 62 A1
Nightingale Gr. Dart 21 E4
Nightingale La. Brom 33 F2
Nightingale La. Sund 97 E1
Nightingale Pl. SE18 2 B2
Nightingale Rd. Kemsg 82 A3
Nightingale Rd. Orp 49 F4
Nightingale Vale. SE18 2 B2
Nightingale Way. Swan 37 D1
Nile Path. SE18 2 B2
Nile Rd. Gil 60 C4
Nine Acres Rd. Cux 58 B4
Nine Elms Gr. Grave 24 B2
Nineveh La. Ben 183 D1
Ninhams Wood. Orp 49 E1
Nithdale Rd. SE18 2 B2
Nizels La. Hild 117 D2
Noah's Ark. Kemsg 82 B3
Noble Tree Cross. Hild 117 E1
Noble Tree Rd. Hild 117 E1
Nook The. Yal 122 A3
Norah La. Higham 43 E4
Nordenfeldt Rd. Eri 4 C3
Nore Cl. Chath 61 D3
Norfield Rd. Sid 36 C4
Norfolk Cl. Rai (K) 61 F3
Norfolk Cl. Wald 74 C4
Norfolk Cres. Sid 18 A2
Norfolk Gdns. Bexh 4 A1
Norfolk Pl. Well 3 E1
Norfolk Rd. Grave 24 C2
Norfolk Rd. Maid 106 C2
Norfolk Rd. T W 167 E3
Norfolk Rd. Ton 136 B3
Norlands Cres. Chis 34 B2
Norman Cl. Kemsg 81 F3
Norman Cl. Maid 89 E1
Norman Cl. Orp 49 F2
Norman Cl. Rai (K) 61 E1
Norman Rd. Belv 4 B4
Norman Rd. Dart 21 D2
Norman Rd. Snod 72 B1
Norman Rd. T W 153 E1
Norman Rd. W Mal 86 B2
Norman St. Sund 97 D1
Normandy Way. Eri 5 D1
Normanhurst Ave. Bexh 3 F1
Normanhurst Rd. Bor G 84 B2
Normanhurst Rd. Orp 35 E2
Normans Cl. Grave 24 B2
Normans La. Ede 131 F3
Norreys Rd. Rai (K) 62 A2
Norrington Rd. Maid 106 B1
Norris Way. Dart 20 A4
Norstead Gdns. Soub 153 E2
Norsted La. Dow 64 B2
North Ash Rd. N Ash 55 D2
North Bank Cl. Roc 44 A1
North Basin One Rd. Gil 45 E3
North Basin Two Rd. Gil 45 F3
North Cl. Bexh 18 C4
North Cray Rd. Bex 19 E2
North Cray Rd. Sid 36 A4
North Cres. Cox 123 F4
North Dane Way. Chath 60 C1
North Dane Way. Wald 74 C4
North Down. Stapt 160 A4
North Dr. Orp 50 A1
North End La. Dow 63 E3
North Farm La. T W 154 A3
North Farm Rd. Soub 153 F2
North Folly Rd. Hunt 123 D4
Nrth Glade The. Bex 19 D2
North Hill Rd. Hawkt 188 C3
North Kent Ave. Grave 23 F3
North Lockside Rd. Gil 45 F2
North Meadow. Off 85 F2
North Park. SE9 17 E3
North Pole Rd. Maid 105 D4
North Pole Rd. Tes 104 B3
North Pondside Rd. Chath 45 E2
North Rd. Belv 4 B4
North Rd. Brom 33 E2
North Rd. Cli 10 B1
North Rd. Dart 20 B3
North Rd. Gil 45 E2
North Rd. Gou 172 A3
North Rd. Pur 6 C3
North Rd. SE18 3 D3
North Side Three Rd. Gil 45 F2
North St. Bexh 19 E4
North St. Bidd 176 B3
North St. Brom 33 E2
North St. Cow 149 E1
North St. Dart 20 C2
North St. Grave 24 B2
North St. Head 144 C1
North St. Maid 105 D3
North St. Roc 44 B2
North St. Sutt V 126 A2
North St. T W 167 F4
North Terr. Hoo S W 28 A1
North View. Maid 106 B3
North View Rd. Sev 81 F1
North Way. Maid 89 E2
Northall Rd. Bexh 4 C1
Northbourne. Brom 48 B3
Northbourne Rd. Rai (K) 61 E4
Northbrook Rd. SE13 16 A3
Northcote Rd. Grave 24 A2
Northcote Rd. Roc 44 B2
Northcote Rd. Sid 35 D4
Northcote Rd. Ton 136 B3
Northdown Cl. Maid 89 E2
Northdown Cl. Padd W 139 D1
Northdown Rd. Kemsg 82 A3
Northdown Rd. Lon 40 A2
Northdown Rd. Well 3 F1
Northdown View. Harr 110 A1
Northend Rd. Eri 5 D1
Northern By-Pass. Char 130 C2
Northfield. Hart (S) 40 A1
Northfield Rd. Orp 50 C4
Northfields. Grays 8 C3
Northfields. Maid 105 D3
Northfields. Spel 152 B2
Northfleet Cl. Maid 89 F1
Northgate. Chath 44 C1
Northgrove Rd. Hawkt 189 D3
Northlands Ave. Orp 50 A1
Northleigh Cl. Maid 106 B1
Northolme Cl. Grays 8 C4
Northolme Rise. Orp 50 A2
Northover. Brom 16 A1
Northridge. Norm 195 E2
Northridge Rd. Grave 24 C1
Northside Rd. Brom 33 E2
Northumberland Ave. Rai (K) 62 A3
Northumberland Ave. Well 18 A4
Northumberland Cl. Eri 4 C2
Northumberland Park. Eri 4 C2
Northumberland Rd. Ist 41 D3
Northumberland Rd. Maid 106 C2
Northumberland Way. Eri 4 C1
Northview. Swan 37 D2
Northwood Ave. H Hals 29 D4
Northwood Pl. Belv 4 A4
Northwood Rd. Ton 118 B1
Norton Cres. Ton 118 B2
Norton Gr. Wald 74 A4
Norton Rd. Chart S 125 F3
Norton Rd. Soub 153 E3
Nortons La. Ten 177 D1
Nortons Way. Five O G 138 B2
Norwich Ave. Ton 118 C1
Norwich Cl. Roc 43 F1
Norwich Pl. Bexh 19 E4
Norwood La. Meo 56 B4
Nottidge Rd. T W 166 C3
Nottingham Ave. Maid 106 C2
Nottingham Wlk. Roc 43 F1
Novar Cl. Orp 50 A3
Novar Rd. SE9 17 F2
Nower The. Bigg 79 D2
Nuffield Rd. Hex 37 E3
Nunnery La. Pen 151 D2
Nunnington Cl. SE9 17 D1
Nunns Way. Grays 8 C3
Nursery Ave. Bexh 19 D4
Nursery Ave. Maid 88 B1
Nursery Ave. Rose 107 E4
Nursery Cl. Dart 21 F2
Nursery Cl. Orp 50 B3
Nursery Cl. Sev 81 F1
Nursery Cl. Swan 36 C2
Nursery Cl. Ton 137 D4
Nursery Pl. Sev 97 F4
Nursery Rd. Dit 87 F3
Nursery Rd. Meo 56 B4
Nursery Rd. Padd W 139 D2
Nursery Rd. Rai (K) 61 F2
Nursery Rd. Soub 153 E2
Nursery The. Eri 5 D2
Nursery The. Whm 95 F2
Nurstead Ave. Lon 40 C1
Nurstead La. Lon 40 C1
Nurstead La. Meo 40 C1
Nurstead Rd. Eri 4 B2
Nut Tree Cl. Orp 50 C2
Nutberry Ave. Grays 8 B4
Nutberry Cl. Grays 8 B4
Nutfield Cl. Chath 60 B2
Nutfield Way. Orp 49 E2
Nuthatch. Lon 40 B2
Nuthatch Gdns. SE28 2 C4
Nutley Cl. Hex 37 D2
Nutmead Cl. Bex 19 F2
Nuttall Ct. Orp 35 E1
Nuxley Rd. Belv 4 B3
Nyanza St. SE18 2 C2

Oak Ave. Gil 46 A1
Oak Ave. Sev 98 B2
Oak Cl. Dart 20 A4
Oak Cl. Hoo S W 46 A4
Oak Cottage Cl. SE6 16 A2
Oak Cotts. Four E 114 B1
Oak Dr. Dit 87 E3
Oak Dr. Higham 43 E4
Oak End Cl. Soub 153 E3
Oak Farm Gdns. Head 144 C1
Oak Farm La. N Ash 70 A2
Oak Hill Rd. Sev 98 B3
Oak La. Head 144 C1
Oak La. Sev 98 B2
Oak La. Upc 62 3
Oak Lodge La. Whm 95 F3
Oak Rd. Eri 4 C2
Oak Rd. Eri 5 E1
Oak Rd. Five O G 138 B2
Oak Rd. Grave 24 C1
Oak Rd. Grays 8 C2
Oak Rd. Gree 22 A3
Oak Rd. Hoo S W 46 A4
Oak Rd. Orp 64 B4
Oak Rd. Roc 44 A1
Oak Rd. T W 153 F2
Oak Rd. Whm 95 F3
Oak Tree Ave. Maid 106 C2
Oak Tree Cl. Mard 141 F1
Oak Tree Cl. T W 167 E3
Oak Tree Gdns. Brom 33 E4
Oak View. Ede 131 E3
Oakapple La. Maid 105 E4
Oakbrook Cl. SE12 33 E4
Oakdale La. Whm 113 F3
Oakdale Rd. T W 167 D4
Oakdene Ave. Chis 34 B4
Oakdene Ave. Eri 4 C2
Oakdene Rd. Orp 50 B4
Oakdene Rd. Sev 81 E1
Oakendn Rd. Cob 57 D3
Oakfield. Hawkt 189 D3
Oakfield Court Rd. T W 167 F4
Oakfield La. Dart 20 C1
Oakfield La. Kes 48 C1
Oakfield Park Rd. Dart 20 C1
Oakfield Pl. Dart 20 C1
Oakfield Rd. Ede 113 E1
Oakfield Rd. Orp 50 B3
Oakfield Rd. Pem 155 F2
Oakfields. Sev 98 B3
Oakham Dr. Brom 33 D1
Oakhill Rd. Orp 50 A2
Oakhouse Rd. Bexh 19 E3
Oakhurst Ave. Bexh 4 A2
Oakhurst Cl. Wald 74 A4
Oakhurst Gdns. Bexh 4 A2
Oakland Cl. Wald 74 A4
Oaklands Ave. Sid 18 A2
Oaklands Cl. Bexh 19 D3
Oaklands Cl. Orp 50 A4
Oaklands Cl. W Kin 68 A4
Oaklands Rd. Bexh 19 D4
Oaklands Rd. Brom 33 D3
Oaklands Rd. Dart 21 F2
Oaklands Rd. Grave 41 D4
Oaklands Rd. Gro 165 E1
Oaklands Rd. Hawkt 189 E3
Oaklands Way. Ton 136 A4
Oaklea Rd. Padd W 139 D1
Oakleigh Cl. Wald 74 A3
Oakleigh Gdns. Orp 50 A1
Oakleigh Park Ave. Chis 34 B2
Oakley Dr. Brom 49 D2
Oakley Dr. SE9 17 F2
Oakley Park. Sid 18 C2
Oakley Rd. Brom 49 D2
Oakmead. Meo 56 B2
Oakmead. Ton 118 C1
Oakmead Ave. Brom 48 B4
Oakmere Rd. SE2 3 E2
Oakmont Pl. Orp 49 F3
Oakridge Rd. Brom 33 D4
Oaks Dene. Wald 74 A3
Oaks Forstall. Sand 190 C1
Oaks Rd. Ten 186 B2
Oaks The. Dit 88 A3
Oaks The. SE18 2 C3
Oaks The. Sma 163 D3
Oaks The. Swan 37 D2
Oakum Ct. Chath 60 B3
Oakway Cl. Bex 19 D3
Oakways. SE9 17 E3
Oakwood Ave. Brom 33 E1
Oakwood Cl. Chis 34 A3
Oakwood Cl. Dart 21 E2
Oakwood Ct. Maid 105 F4
Oakwood Dr. Bexh 19 F4
Oakwood Gdns. Orp 49 F2
Oakwood Rd. Maid 105 F4
Oakwood Rd. Orp 49 F2
Oakwood Rise. Lon 40 A1
Oakwood Rise. T W 154 A2
Oarenden Rd. Meo 56 C3
Oast Cl. T W 153 F2
Oast Ct. Yal 122 A3
Oast House Way. Orp 35 E1
Oast View. Hors 157 E1
Oast Way. Hart (S) 55 D4
Oasts The. Rose 107 F4
Oastview. Rai (K) 62 B2
Oatfield Cl. Cran 173 F1
Oatfield Dr. Cran 173 F1
Oatfield Rd. Orp 50 A3
Occupation La. SE18 2 B1
Ockham Dr. Orp 35 E3
Ockley La. Hawkt 189 E4
Ockley Rd. Hawkt 189 E3
Odiham Dr. Maid 88 C2
Offenham Rd. SE9 34 A4
Offen's Dr. Stapt 160 A4
Offham Rd. W Mal 86 B2
Officers' Rd. Gil 45 E2
Ogilby St. SE18 2 A3
Oilver Cl. Grays 7 D2
Okehampton Cres. Well 3 F1
Okemore Gdns. Orp 35 F1
Old Ashford Rd. Len 111 D1
Old Barn Cl. Rai (K) 61 D1
Old Barn Rd. Birl 87 D3
Old Barn Way. Bexh 19 F4
Old Bexley La. Bex 19 F1
Old Bexley La. Dart 20 A2
Old Carriageway The. Sev 80 C1
Old Castle Wlk. Rai (K) 75 F4
Old Chapel Rd. Swan 51 F3
Old Chatham Rd. Ayld 73 F2
Old Chatham Rd. Maid 89 D3
Old Church Rd. Burh 72 C3
Old Church Rd. E Pec 102 C1
Old Church Rd. Pem 154 C3
Old Clem Sq. SE18 2 B2
Old Coach Rd. Stans 69 D1
Old Dover Rd. SE3 1 B2
Old Downs. Hart (S) 55 D4
Old Dr. Maid 106 B1
Old Farm Ave. Sid 18 A1
Old Farm Gdns. Swan 37 D1
Old Farm Rd E. Sid 18 B1
Old Farm Rd W. Sid 18 A1
Old Forge La. S Grn 92 A4
Old Forge Way. Sid 35 E4
Old Garden The. Sev 97 F4
Old Gardens Cl. T W 167 E2
Old Hadlow Rd. Ton 137 D4
Old Harrow La. Bigg 78 C2
Old Hill. Chis 34 B2
Old Hill. Dow 63 F4
Old Hill. Orp 64 A4
Old Homesdale Rd. Brom 33 F1
Old House La. Pen 151 F1
Old House La. Spel 165 F4
Old House Rd. New(G) 77 D4
Old Kent Rd. Padd W 139 E1
Old La. Ight 100 B4
Old Lain. Harr 110 A1

Old London Rd. Kno P 80 A4
Old London Rd. Shorm 65 E2
Old London Rd. Ton 136 C4
Old London Rd. Wro 84 B4
Old Loose Cl. Loose 106 A1
Old Loose Hill. Loose 106 A1
Old Maidstone Rd. Sid 36 A3
Old Manor Dr. Grave 24 C2
Old Manor Way. Bexh 4 C1
Old Mill La. Ayld 88 C4
Old Mill Rd. Lee 108 A2
Old Mill Rd. SE18 2 C2
Old Orchard. Lei 134 B4
Old Orchard La. Birl 86 C3
Old Otford Rd. Otf 81 E3
Old Park Rd. SE2 3 E3
Old Parsonage Ct. W Mal 86 C2
Old Pattens La. Chath 59 F3
Old Perry St. Chis 35 D3
Old Perry St. Grave 24 A1
Old Polhill. Shorm 80 C4
Old Rd. Bexh 19 F4
Old Rd. Chath 60 A4
Old Rd. E Pec 121 E1
Old Rd. SE13 16 A4
Old Rd. Waty 103 F2
Old Regent Dr. Rol 192 A4
Old Road E. Grave 24 C1
Old Road W. Grave 24 B2
Old School Ct. Ege 147 D4
Old School Ct. Hoo S W 45 D4
Old School La. Birl 86 B4
Old Soar Rd. Plax 101 E2
Old Station Rd. Wad 178 A1
Old Terry's Lodge Rd. Wro 83 E4
Old Timber Top Cotts The. Sev 98 C4
Old Tovil Rd. Maid 106 B3
Old Trafford Cl. Maid 88 B1
Old Tranyard. SE18 3 D3
Old Tree La. Bou Mon 124 C4
Old Tye Ave. Bigg 78 A4
Old Watling St. Grave 41 E4
Old Watling St. Higham 43 E2
Old Watling St. Shor 43 E2
Old Wlk The. Otf 81 F3
Old Woolwich Rd. SE10 1 A3
Old Yews The. Lon 40 B1
Oldbury Cl. Ight 83 E1
Oldbury Cl. Orp 35 F1
Oldbury La. Ight 83 E1
Oldfield Cl. Brom 34 A1
Oldfield Cl. Maid 107 D3
Oldfield Cl. Rai (K) 61 F2
Oldfield Grange. Brom 34 A1
Oldfield Rd. Bexh 4 A1
Oldfield Rd. Brom 34 A1
Oleander Cl. Orp 49 F1
Olive Rd. Dart 20 C2
Oliver Cl. Chath 60 B3
Oliver Cres. Farn 53 D3
Oliver Ct. SE18 2 C3
Oliver Rd. Grays 7 D2
Oliver Rd. Stapt 160 A4
Oliver Rd. Swan 36 C1
Olivers Mill. N Ash 55 D2
Olivine Cl. Wald 74 B2
Olliffe Cl. Wald 74 A3
Olron Cres. Bexh 19 D3
Olven Rd. SE18 2 C2
Olyffe Ave. Well 3 E1
O'Neill Path. SE18 2 B2
Onslow Cres. Chis 34 B2
Onslow Dr. Sid 18 C1
Onslow Rd. Chath 59 F4
Opal Green. Wald 74 B3
Openshaw Rd. SE2 3 E3
Orache Dr. Thu 90 A1
Orange Court La. Dow 63 E3
Orange Terr. Chath 44 C1
Orangery La. SE9 17 D3
Orbit Cl. Wald 74 B2
Orchard Ave. Belv 4 A2
Orchard Ave. Dart 20 B2
Orchard Ave. Dit 88 A3
Orchard Ave. Grave 41 E4
Orchard Ave. Roc 44 A3
Orchard Cl. Bexh 4 A1
Orchard Cl. Cox 123 F4
Orchard Cl. Ede 131 E3
Orchard Cl. Hors 157 D1
Orchard Cl. Lan H 126 A4
Orchard Cl. Lon 40 B2
Orchard Cl. Sev 81 F2
Orchard Cl. T W 153 F1
Orchard Cres. Hors 157 E1
Orchard Dr. Ede 131 E3
Orchard Dr. Grays 8 B4
Orchard Dr. Meo 56 A4
Orchard Dr. SE3 1 A1
Orchard Dr. Thu 107 D4
Orchard Dr. Ton 119 D1
Orchard Glade. Head 144 C1
Orchard Gr. Dit 87 E3
Orchard Gr. Orp 50 A3
Orchard Green. Orp 50 A2
Orchard Hill. Dart 20 A3
Orchard Industrial Estate. Maid 125 D4
Orchard Lea. Hild 118 A1
Orchard Pl. Maid 106 A4
Orchard Rd. Belv 4 B3
Orchard Rd. Brom 33 F2
Orchard Rd. Dow 64 C3
Orchard Rd. E Pec 121 E1
Orchard Rd. Grave 23 F1
Orchard Rd. Orp 50 C2
Orchard Rd. Otf 81 D4
Orchard Rd. SE18 2 C3
Orchard Rd. Sev 81 D1
Orchard Rd. Sid 35 D4
Orchard Rd. Swans 23 D3
Orchard Rd. Ten 186 B4
Orchard Rd. Well 18 B4
Orchard Rise. Gro 165 E2
Orchard Rise E Sid 18 A3
Orchard Rise W. Sid 18 A3
Orchard St. Dart 21 D3
Orchard St. Maid 106 B4
Orchard St. Rai (K) 62 A2
Orchard The. Swan 36 C2
Orchard Way. Cran 182 B4
Orchard Way. Dart 20 C1
Orchard Way. Hors 157 E1
Orchard Way. Kemsg 82 B3
Orchard Way. Snod 72 A2
Orchid Cl. Roc 43 F1
Orchis Gr. Grays 8 A3
Ordnance Cres. SE10 1 A4
Ordnance Rd. Grave 24 C3
Ordnance Rd. SE18 2 B2
Ordnance St. Chath 60 A4
Ordnance Terr. Chath 60 A4
Oregon Sq. Orp 49 F3
Oriole Way. Dit 87 D3
Orion Rd. Chath 59 F2
Orissa Rd. SE18 3 D3
Orlestone Gdns. Orp 51 D1
Orlick Rd. Grave 25 E2
Ormisto Rd. SE10 1 B3
Ormonde Ave. Orp 49 F2
Ormsby Green. Rai (K) 76 A4
Orpines The. Waty 104 A2
Orpington By-Pass Rd. Shorm 65 E3
Orpington Rd. Chis 35 D1
Orsett Rd. Grays 8 B3
Orwell Cl. Dit 87 D4
Osberton Rd. SE12 16 B3
Osborn Terr. SE3 16 A4
Osborne Rd. Belv 4 A2
Osborne Rd. Gil 45 F1
Osgood Ave. Orp 50 A1
Osgood Gdns. Orp 50 A1
Osmers Hill. Wad 178 A2
Osney Way. Grave 25 D1
Osprey Ave. Chath 61 D3
Osprey Wlk. Dit 87 D3
Ospringe Ct. SE9 17 F3
Osterberg Rd. Dart 21 D4
Ostlers Ct. Snod 72 B2
Otford Cl. Bex 19 E3
Otford Cl. Brom 34 B1
Otford La. Hals 65 E1
Otford Rd. Otf 81 E2
Otford Rd. Sev 81 E2
Otham La. Oth 107 F3
Otham St. Oth 107 E2
Otlinge Cl. Orp 35 F1
Otterbourne Pl. Maid 107 D3
Otterden Cl. Orp 50 A1
Otterden Road. Elng 112 C4
Otterham Quay La. Upc 62 B3
Otteridge Rd. Rose 107 E4
Otway St. Chath 60 B4
Otway St. Gil 45 F1
Otway Terr. Chath 60 B4
Oval Gdns. Grays 8 C4
Oval The. Lon 40 C1
Oval The. Sid 18 B2
Ovenden Rd. Sund 80 A1
Over Minnis. N Ash 55 D2
Overcliff Rd. Grays 8 C3
Overcliffe. Grave 24 B2
Overcourt Cl. Sid 18 B3
Overdale. Sev W 116 B3
Overmead. Sid 17 F2
Overmead. Swan 52 A4
Overton Rd. SE2 3 F4
Overy Liberty. Dart 21 D2
Overy St. Dart 21 D3
Owen Cl. Dit 87 D2
Owenite St. SE2 3 E3
Owens Way. Gil 46 B1
Ox La. Ten 186 B3
Ox Lea. Spel 166 B4
Oxenbridge Cotts. Beckl 196 C2
Oxenden Wood Rd. Orp 64 C4
Oxenhill Rd. Kemsg 82 A3
Oxfield. Ede 131 F4
Oxford Cl. Grave 25 D1
Oxford Rd. Gil 60 C4
Oxford Rd. Maid 106 C2
Oxford Rd. Sid 35 E4
Oxford St. Snod 72 B2
Oxhawth Cres. Brom 49 E4
Oxleas Cl. Well 2 C1
Oxley Shaw La. Dit 87 D3

Packham Rd. Grave 24 A1
Packhorse Rd. Sev 97 F4
Packmores Rd. SE9 17 F3
Paddlesworth Rd. Snod 71 F3
Paddock Cl. Bor G 84 C1
Paddock Cl. Dart 38 C2
Paddock Cl. Orp 49 E1
Paddock Cl. Pen 151 E1
Paddock Green. Orp 49 E1
Paddock Rd. Bexh 19 D4
Paddock The. Chath 60 A4
Paddock The. Had 120 A3
Paddock The. Meo 70 A2
Paddock The. Norm 195 E2
Paddock The. Pem 154 C1
Paddock The. Whm 95 F3
Paddock Way. Chis 35 C3
Paddocks Cl. Orp 50 C2
Paddocks The. Cow 149 E2
Padsole La. Maid 106 B4
Page Cl. Dart 22 C1
Page Cres. Eri 5 D2
Page Heath La. Brom 33 F1
Page Heath Villas. Brom 33 F1
Pagehurst Rd. Stapt 159 E4
Paget Gdns. Chis 34 B2
Paget Rise. SE18 2 B2
Paget Row. Gil 45 F1
Paget St. Gil 45 F1
Paget Terr. SE18 2 B2
Pagette Way. Grays 8 B3
Pagitt St. Chath 60 A4
Paiges Farm Cl. Sev W 116 C3
Paine Ct. SE3 1 A2
Painters Ash La. Grave 23 F1
Palace Ave. Maid 106 B4
Palace Gr. Brom 33 E2
Palace Rd. Brom 33 E2
Palace Rd. Whm 78 B1
Palace View. Brom 33 E1
Palace View. SE12 16 B1
Palewell Cl. Orp 35 E2
Pallant Way. Orp 49 E2
Pallet Way. SE18 2 A1
Palm Ave. Sid 35 F3
Palmar Cres. Bexh 4 B1
Palmar Rd. Bexh 4 B1
Palmar Rd. Maid 88 C1
Palmarsh Cl. Orp 35 F1
Palmeira Rd. Bexh 18 C4
Palmer Ave. Grave 41 F4
Palmer's Ave. Grays 8 C3
Palmers Dr. Grays 8 C3
Palmers Green La. Brenc 156 C3
Palmers Orchard. Shorm 66 A2
Palmerston Cres. SE18 2 C2
Palmerston Gdns. Grays 7 F3
Palmerston Rd. Chath 60 A3
Palmerston Rd. Grays 7 F3
Palmerston Rd. Orp 49 F1
Panfield Rd. SE2 3 E4
Pankhurst Rd. Hoo S W 28 C1
Pannell Rd. I o G 15 E1
Panter's. Hex 37 D3
Pantiles The. Bexh 4 A2
Pantiles The. Brom 34 A1
Pantiles The. T W 167 E3
Panton Cl. Wald 74 C4
Papillons Wlk. SE3 1 B1
Papion Gr. Wald 74 A3
Parade The. Stapt 160 A4
Paradise Pl. SE18 2 A3
Paragon Pl. SE3 1 A1
Paragon The. SE3 1 B1
Parham Rd. Chath 60 A3
Parish Gate Dr. SE9 18 A3
Park App. Well 18 B4
Park Ave. Brom 33 D3
Park Ave. Ede 131 E3
Park Ave. Gil 60 C4
Park Ave. Grave 24 A2
Park Ave. Grave 24 C2
Park Ave. Grays 7 E2
Park Ave. Hild 118 A1
Park Ave. Lint 124 A3
Park Ave. Maid 89 E1
Park Ave. Orp 50 B2
Park Ave. Orp 49 E2
Park Corner Rd. Grave 23 E1
Park Cotts. Hawkt 189 E3
Park Cres. Chath 60 A2
Park Cres. Eri 4 C2
Park Crescent Rd. Eri 4 C2
Park Dr. Lon 40 A1
Park Dr. SE7 2 A2
Park End. Brom 33 D2
Park Farm Rd. Birl 71 D1
Park Farm Rd. Brom 33 F2
Park Gdns. Eri 4 C3
Park Gr. Bexh 19 F4
Park Gr. Brom 33 E2
Park Hill. Brom 34 A1
Park Hill. Meo 41 D1
Park Hill Rd. Brom 33 D2
Park Hill Rd. Kemsg 82 B4
Park House Gdns. Soub 153 E3
Park La. Bou Mon 124 C3
Park La. Hawkt 181 F2
Park La. Hex 37 F2
Park La. Kemsg 82 B3
Park La. Maid 89 D2
Park La. Seal 99 E4
Park La. Sev 98 C4
Park Mead. Sid 18 B3
Park Pl. Grave 24 C2
Park Pl. Sev 97 F4
Park Rd. Birl 86 C4
Park Rd. Brom 33 E2
Park Rd. Chis 34 B3
Park Rd. Dart 21 E2
Park Rd. Grave 24 B2
Park Rd. Grays 8 B3
Park Rd. Orp 50 C4
Park Rd. Soub 153 E3
Park Rd. Swan 37 D1
Park Rd. Swans 23 D3
Park Rd. T W 153 E1
Park Rd. W Pec 101 F1
Park Rd. Waty 103 D1
Park Rd. Wro H 85 F4
Park Road Industrial Estate. Swan 37 D1
Park St. T W 167 F4
Park Terr. Gree 22 B3
Park The. Sid 35 E4
Park View. N Ash 69 F3
Park View. Norm 195 E1
Park View Cl. Ede 131 E3
Park View Gdns. Grays 8 B3
Park View Rd. SE9 17 E1
Park Vew Rd. Well 18 C4
Park Villas. Had 120 A3
Park Vista. SE10 1 A2
Park Way. Cox 123 F4
Park Way. Dart 20 A1
Park Way. Maid 106 B3
Park Wood Green. Rai (K) 61 F1
Park Wood La. Frit 160 C3
Park Wood Trading Estate. Maid 107 D1
Park Wood Trading Estate. Maid 125 D4
Parkcroft Rd. SE12 16 A2
Parkdale Rd. SE18 3 D3
Parker Cl. Rai (K) 62 A1
Parker Rd. Grays 8 A3
Parkfield. Hart (S) 40 A1
Parkfield. Seal 99 D4
Parkfield. Sev 99 D4
Parkfield Rd. Rai (K) 62 A3
Parkfield Way. Brom 49 D4
Parkfields. Roc 43 F2
Parkgate. SE3 16 A4
Parkgate Rd. Shorm 51 F1
Parkhill Rd. Bex 19 D2
Parkhill Rd. Sid 18 A1
Parkhurst Gdns. Bex 19 E2
Parkhurst Rd. Bex 19 E2
Parkland Cl. Sev 98 C1
Parkside. Cli W 27 E2
Parkside. Grays 8 C4
Parkside. Hals 65 D1
Parkside. Rai (K) 61 E1
Parkside. SE3 1 A2
Parkside. Sid 18 B1
Parkside Ave. Bexh 5 D1
Parkside Ave. Brom 34 A1
Parkside Cross. Bexh 5 D1
Parkside Ct. Ten 186 A2
Parkside Rd. Belv 4 C3
Parkway. Belv 4 A4
Parkway. Ton 118 C1
Parkwood Cl. T W 153 F1
Parkwood Rd. Bex 19 D2
Parkwood Rd. Lim 78 A1
Paroma Rd. Belv 4 B4
Parr Ave. Gil 45 F1
Parrock Ave. Grave 24 C2
Parrock Rd. Grave 24 C2
Parrock St. Grave 24 B2
Parrock The. Grave 24 C2
Parry Pl. SE18 2 B3
Parsonage Cl. T W 152 B1
Parsonage La. Lam 170 B1
Parsonage La. Roc 44 C2
Parsonage La. Sid 36 B4
Parsonage La. Sutt H 38 B3
Parsonage Manorway. Belv 4 B2
Parsonage Rd. T W 152 B1
Parsons La. Dart 20 B1
Parsons La. Stans 69 D3
Partridge Ave. Dit 87 D4
Partridge Dr. Orp 49 F2
Partridge Green. SE9 17 E1
Partridge Rd. Sid 35 D4
Pasley Rd. Gil 45 E2
Pasley Rd E. Gil 45 E2
Pasley Rd N. Gil 45 E2
Pasley Rd W. Gil 45 E2
Passey Pl. SE9 17 D3
Paston Cres. SE12 16 B2
Pasture Rd. SE6 16 A2
Patch The. Sev 81 D1
Patricia Ct. SE2 3 E2
Patrixbourne Ave. Rai (K) 61 F3
Pattenden Gdns. E Pec 121 E2
Pattenden La. Mard 141 F2
Pattens Gdns. Chath 59 F3
Pattens La. Chath 60 A3
Pattens Pl. Chath 59 F3
Patterdale Cl. Brom 33 D3
Patterdale Rd. Dart 21 F2
Pattison Wlk. SE18 2 C3
Paulinus Cl. Orp 35 F1
Pavement The. Ten 186 B4
Paviion La. Merew 103 E2
Pavilion The. Ton 136 B3
Pavings The. Lee 108 C3
Paxton Rd. Brom 33 E3
Payden St. Len 111 F2
Paynell Ct. SE3 16 A4
Paynes Cotts. Dunt 80 C3
Payne's La. Maid 106 B2
Peach Croft. Grave 41 D4
Peachum Rd. SE3 1 A2
Peacock St. Grave 24 C2
Peakes Pl. SE18 2 B3
Pear Tree Ave. Dit 87 F3
Pear Tree Cl. Eri 4 C1
Pear Tree Cl. Swan 36 C2
Pear Tree La. Maid 106 B1
Pear Tree La. Rai (K) 61 D2
Peareswood Rd. Eri 5 D1
Pearman Cl. Rai (K) 62 B3
Pearse Pl. Lam 170 B1
Pearson's Green La. Padd 157 D4
Peartree La. Shor 43 E3
Pease Hill. N Ash 69 D4
Peasley La. Gou 171 F1
Peatfield Cl. Sid 18 A1
Peckham Cl. Roc 44 C2
Pedham Place Estate. Farn 52 B4
Peel Rd. Orp 49 F1
Peel St. Maid 89 E1
Peel St Hedges. Maid 89 E2
Peens La. Bou Mon 124 C2
Pegasus Ct. Grave 24 C1
Peggoty Cl. Higham 43 E4
Pegley Gdns. SE12 16 B1
Pegwell St. SE18 3 D2
Pelham Rd. Bexh 19 E4
Pelham Rd. Grave 24 B2
Pelham Rd S. Grave 24 A2
Pelham Terr. Grave 24 A2
Pelican Cl. Roc 43 F1
Pelinore Rd. SE6 16 A1
Pell Cl. Wad 178 B1
Pellipar Gdns. SE18 2 A3
Pells La. W Kin 68 B2
Pemberton Gdns. Swan 37 D1
Pemberton Sq. Roc 44 C2
Pemble Cl. Five O G 138 B2
Pembroke Gdns. Rai (K) 76 A4
Pembroke Mews. Sev 98 B3
Pembroke Pl. Sutt H 38 B2
Pembroke Rd. Brom 33 F2
Pembroke Rd. Cox 123 F4
Pembroke Rd. Eri 4 C3
Pembroke Rd. Gil 45 E2
Pembroke Rd. Sev 98 B3
Pembroke Rd. Ton 136 B3
Pembroke Rise. Chath 45 E2
Pembury Cl. Brom 48 A3
Pembury Cl. Pem 154 C2
Pembury Cres. Sid 19 D1
Pembury Gdns. Maid 105 F4
Pembury Gr. Ton 136 C2
Pembury Grange. T W 154 B1
Pembury Hall Rd. Pem 154 C4
Pembury Rd. Bexh 4 A2
Pembury Rd. Pem 154 B3
Pembury Rd. Ton 136 C2
Pembury Rd. Tud 137 D1
Pembury Rd. T W 154 A1
Pembury Walks. Pem 154 C3
Pembury Way. Rai (K) 62 A3
Pen Way. Ton 119 D1
Penda Rd. Eri 4 B2
Pendennis Rd. Orp 50 C2
Pendennis Rd. Sev 98 B4
Penderel Mews. Ten 186 B2
Pendragon Rd. Brom 16 B1
Pendrell St. SE18 2 C2
Peneden. N Ash 55 D2
Penenden Heath Rd. Maid 89 F2
Penenden St. Maid 89 E1
Penfield La. Rod 94 B4
Penfold Cl. Chath 60 B2
Penfold Cl. Maid 107 D1
Penfold Hill. Lee 108 B2
Penfold La. Bex 18 C2
Penfold Way. Maid 106 A1
Penfolds Cl. Ton 118 C1
Penford Gdns. SE9 16 C4
Pengarth Rd. Bex 18 C3
Penguin Cl. Roc 43 F1
Penhall Rd. SE7 1 C3
Penhill Rd. Bex 18 C2
Penhurst Wlk. Brom 48 A4
Penlee Cl. Ede 131 F3
Penmon Rd. SE2 3 E4
Penn Gdns. Chis 34 B2
Penn La. Bex 19 D3
Pennant Rd. Chath 59 F2
Penney Cl. Dart 20 C2
Pennine Walk. T W 153 F1
Pennine Way. Bexh 5 D1
Pennine Way. Grave 24 A1
Pennine Way. Oth 107 E3
Pennington Pl. Soub 153 E3
Pennington Rd. Soub 153 E3
Pennyfields. Cran 182 C4
Penpool La. Well 18 B4
Penshurst Ave. Sid 18 B3
Penshurst Cl. Rai (K) 62 A3
Penshurst Cl. W Kin 68 A4
Penshurst Green. Brom 48 A4
Penshurst Rd. Bexh 4 A1
Penshurst Rd. Bid 152 B4
Penshurst Rd. Lei 134 B2
Penshurst Rd. Pen 151 F3
Penshurst Rd. Spel 152 A2
Penstocks The. Maid 105 F3
Pepingstraw Cl. Off 85 F2
Pepper Alley. Maid 89 D2
Pepper Hill. Grave 23 F1
Pepperhill La. Grave 23 F1
Pepys Cl. Dart 21 E4
Pepys Cl. Grave 23 F1
Pepys Rise. Orp 50 A3
Pepy's Way. Roc 44 A2
Perch La. Lam 169 F3
Percival Rd. Orp 49 F2
Percy Rd. Bexh 4 A1
Percy St. Grays 8 C2
Perimeter Rd. Dit 87 F4
Periton Rd. SE9 16 C4
Perks Cl. SE3 1 A1
Perpins Rd. SE9 18 A3
Perran Cl. Hart (S) 40 A1
Perry Gr. Dart 21 E4
Perry Hall Cl. Orp 50 B3
Perry Hall Rd. Orp 50 B3
Perry St. Chath 60 A4
Perry St. Chis 35 D3
Perry St. Dart 20 A4
Perry St. Grave 24 A2
Perry St. Maid 89 D1
Perryfield St. Maid 89 D1
Perrys La. Kno P 64 C1
Persand Rd. SE6 16 A1
Pescot Ave. Lon 40 B1
Pested Bars Rd. Maid 106 C1
Peter St. Grave 24 B2
Peterborough Gdns. Roc 43 F1
Peters Cl. Well 3 D1
Petersfield. Pem 155 D2
Petersfield Dr. Meo 70 A3
Petersham Dr. Orp 35 E1
Petersham Gdns. Orp 35 D2
Peterstone Rd. SE2 3 E4
Petham Gr. Rai (K) 61 F3

Pett La. Char 130 C2
Pett St. SE18 2 A3
Petten Cl. Orp 50 C3
Petten Gr. Orp 50 C3
Petteridge La. Brenc 156 A2
Petteridge La. Mat 156 A2
Pettman Cres. SE28 2 C4
Petts Wood Rd. Orp 49 F4
Petworth Rd. Bexh 19 E3
Peverel Cl. Thu 90 B1
Pheasant La. Maid 106 B2
Pheasant Rd. Chath 60 C3
Phelps Cl. W Kin 68 A4
Philipot Path. SE9 17 E3
Philippa Gdns. SE9 16 C3
Phillip Ave. Swan 36 C1
Phillips Cl. Dart 20 B3
Phillips Ct. Rai (K) 61 E3
Phillips Way. Brom 33 E2
Philpots La. Hild 117 D1
Phineas Pett Rd. SE9 17 D4
Phoenix Cl. Wick 48 A2
Phoenix Dr. Brom 48 C2
Phoenix Dr. Waty 104 A2
Phoenix Pl. Dart 20 C2
Phoenix Rd. Wald 74 B3
Picardy Manorway. Belv 4 B4
Picardy Rd. Belv 4 B3
Picardy St. Belv 4 B4
Pickering St. Maid 106 B1
Pickford Cl. Bexh 4 A1
Pickford La. Bexh 4 A1
Pickford Rd. Bexh 19 D4
Pickhurst Green. Brom 48 A3
Pickhurst La. W Wick 48 A4
Pickhurst Mead. Brom 48 A3
Pickhurst Park. Brom 48 A4
Pickhurst Rise. W Wick 48 A3
Pickles Way. Cli 10 B1
Pickmoss La. Otf 81 E4
Pickwick Cres. Chath 59 F4
Pickwick Ct. SE9 17 D2
Pickwick Gdns. Grave 23 F1
Pickwick Way. Chis 34 C3
Piedmont Rd. SE18 2 C3
Pier Approach Rd. Gil 45 F2
Pier Rd. E16 2 B4
Pier Rd. Eri 5 D2
Pier Rd. Gil 46 A2
Pier Rd. Grave 24 A3
Pier Rd. Grays 22 B4
Pier Rd Industrial Estate. Gil 45 F2
Pier Way. SE18 2 C4
Pierce Mill Rd. E Pec 120 C1
Pierce Mill Rd. Had 120 C1
Pigdown La. Hev 149 F4
Piggs Cnr. Grays 8 C4
Pigsdean Rd. Cob 57 E3
Pike Cl. Brom 33 E4
Pikefish La. Yal 140 A3
Pikey La. Dit 87 D1
Pilgrim' Rd. Swans 23 D4
Pilgrims La. Grays 7 F4
Pilgrims La. Lim 95 D4
Pilgrims Way. Ayld 73 E1
Pilgrims Way. Box 89 F4
Pilgrims Way. Char 130 C2
Pilgrims Way. Cux 58 C4
Pilgrim's Way. Dunt 81 D4
Pilgrims Way. Hall 58 A2
Pilgrims Way. Harr 110 B2
Pilgrims Way. Holli 91 E1
Pilgrims Way. Kemsg 82 B3
Pilgrims Way. Len 110 B2
Pilgrims Way. Stans 84 C4
Pilgrims Way. Sto 90 A3
Pilgrims Way. Thu 90 C3
Pilgrims Way. Trot 70 B2
Pilgrims Way. Wou 59 D1
Pilgrims Way. Wro 84 A4
Pilgrim's Way Cotts. Kemsg 82 B3
Pilgrims Way . Otf 81 F4
Pilgrims Way W. Dunt 80 C3
Pilgrims Way W. Otf 81 D4
Pilkington Rd. Orp 49 F2
Pillar Box Rd. Seal 83 D1
Pillmans Cl. Sid 35 F3
Pilot Rd. Chath 59 F2
Pimpernel Way. Wald 74 A4
Pinchbeck Rd. Orp 64 A4
Pincott Rd. Bexh 19 E4
Pincroft Wood. Lon 40 C1
Pine Ave. Grave 24 C2
Pine Cl. Dit 87 E3
Pine Cl. Swan 37 D1
Pine Glade. Kes 49 D1
Pine Gr. Ede 131 E3
Pine Gr. Maid 89 E1
Pine Gr. Rai (K) 61 E1
Pine Lodge. Maid 105 F4
Pine Rd. Roc 44 A1
Pine Ridge. Ton 118 B1
Pine Rise. Meo 56 B4
Pine Tree La. Ight 100 B3
Pine View. Bor G 84 C2
Pinecroft. SE2 3 E2
Pinehurst. Sev 82 A1
Pinehurst Wlk. Orp 50 A3
Pineneedle La. Sev 98 B4
Pines Rd. Brom 34 A2
Pinesfield La. Trot 70 B1
Pinewood Ave. Sev 81 F1
Pinewood Ave. Sid 18 A2
Pinewood Cl. Orp 49 F3
Pinewood Cl. Padd W 139 D1
Pinewood Dr. Bredh 74 C2
Pinewood Dr. Orp 50 A1
Pinewood Gdns. Soub 153 E3
Pinewood Rd. Brom 33 E1
Pinewood Rd. SE2 3 F2
Pinewood Rd. T W 153 F1
Pink Alley. T W 167 E3
Pinkham. E Pec 121 E1
Pinks Hill. Swan 52 A4
Pinnacle Hill. Bexh 19 E4
Pinnell Rd. SE9 16 C4
Pinnock La. Stapt 160 A3
Pinnock's Ave. Grave 24 B2
Pintail Cl. I o G 15 E1
Pinto Way. SE3 16 B4
Pipers Green Rd. Bras 96 B2
Pipers La. Bras 96 B3
Pippin Cl. Cox 123 E3
Pippin Croft. Rai (K) 61 E1
Pippin Rd. E Pec 121 D1
Pippins The. Meo 56 B4
Pip's View. Coo 11 D1
Pirbright Cl. Wald 74 C3
Pirrip Cl. Grave 25 D1
Pit La. Ede 131 F4
Pitfield. Hart (S) 40 A1
Pitfield Dr. Meo 56 A2
Pitfold Cl. SE12 16 B3
Pitfold Rd. SE12 16 B3
Pitsmead Ave. Brom 48 B3
Pitt Rd. Broom (M) 126 B3
Pitt Rd. Lan H 126 B3
Pitt Rd. Maid 105 E3
Pitt Rd. Orp 49 F1
Pittlesden. Ten 186 B2
Pixfield Ct. Brom 33 D2
Pixot Hill. Brenc 156 B3
Pix's La. Rol 192 B4
Pizien Well Rd. Wty 103 E2
Place Farm Ave. Orp 49 F3
Place La. New(G) 62 C1
Plain Rd. Mard 158 C4
Plain The. Gou 172 A2
Plains Ave. Maid 106 C3
Plaistow Gr. Brom 33 E3
Plaistow La. Brom 33 F2
Plaistow Sq. Maid 89 F1
Plane Ave. Grave 23 F2
Plane Wlk. Ton 118 C2
Plantation Dr. Orp 50 C3
Plantation La. Rose 107 E4
Plantation Rd. Eri 5 E1
Plantation Rd. Gil 46 B1
Plantation Rd. Hex 37 E3
Plantation The. SE3 1 B1
Plat The. Ede 131 F3
Platt Comm. Bor G 84 C2
Platt House La. Stans 69 F1
Platt Industrial Estate. Bor G 84 B2
Platt The. Sutt V 126 A2
Platters The. Rai (K) 61 F2
Plaxtol Cl. Brom 33 F2
Plaxtol La. Plax 100 C2
Plaxtol Rd. Eri 4 B2
Pleasance Rd. Orp 35 E1
Pleasant View. Eri 5 D3
Pleasant View. Orp 49 F1
Pleasure House Rd. Sutt V 126 B2
Plomley Cl. Rai (K) 75 F4
Plough Hill. Bor G 101 D4
Plough Wents Rd. Chart S 125 E3
Plough Wlk. Ede 131 F4
Ploughmans Way. Rai (K) 62 A1
Pover Cl. Ede 131 F4
Plover Cl. Wald 74 C3
Plover Rd. Dit 87 D3
Plowenders Cl. Wro H 85 F3
Pluckley Cl. Rai (K) 61 F4
Pluckley Rd. Char 130 B1
Pluckley Rd. Sma 163 F3
Plug La. Meo 56 C1
Plum La. SE18 2 C2
Plum Tree Rd. Sto 76 B2
Plummer La. Ten 186 A1
Plumpton Wlk. Maid 107 D1
Plumstead Common Rd. SE18 2 C2
Plumstead High St. SE18 3 D3
Plumstead Rd. SE18 2 C3
Plumtree Gr. Rai (K) 75 E4
Plumtree Rd. Head 144 B2
Plumtrees. Maid 105 E3
Plymouth Dr. Sev 98 C4
Plymouth Park. Sev 98 C4
Plymouth Rd. Brom 33 E2
Plympton Cl. Belv 4 A4
Plymstock Rd. Well 3 F2
Poachers Cl. Wald 60 C1
Podkin Wood. Wald 74 A2
Pole Cat Alley. Brom 48 A2
Polebrook Rd. SE3 16 C4
Polesden Rd. T W 167 F3
Polhill. Dunt 80 C4
Polhill Dr. Wald 74 A3
Police Station Rd. W Mal 86 C2
Pollard Wlk. Sid 35 F3
Pollyhaugh. Eyn 53 D2
Polperro Cl. Orp 50 A4
Polthorne Gr. SE18 2 C3
Polytechnic St. SE18 2 3
Pond Cl. SE3 1 A1
Pond Farm Rd. S Grn 91 F3
Pond La. Seal 100 A3
Pond Rd. SE3 1 A1
Pondfield La. Shor 43 D3
Pondfield Rd. Brom 48 A3
Pondfield Rd. Orp 49 E2
Pontefract Rd. Brom 33 D4
Pontoise Cl. Sev 81 D1
Pook La. Bidd 177 D4
Poona Rd. T W 167 E3
Pootings Rd. Four E 114 A1
Pootings Rd. Whm 114 A1
Pope Dr. Stapt 160 A4
Pope House La. H Hald 186 B4
Pope Rd. Brom 48 C4
Pope St. Maid 105 F3
Poplar Ave. Grave 41 F4
Poplar Ave. Orp 49 E2
Poplar Cl. Hoo S W 46 A4
Poplar Cl. Roc 44 A1
Poplar Gr. Maid 88 C1
Poplar Mount. Belv 4 B3
Poplar Rd. Roc 44 A1
Poplar Rd. Witt 197 F4
Poplar Wlk. Meo 56 B4
Poplars Cl. Lon 40 C1
Poplicans Rd. Cux 58 B4
Porchester Cl. Hart (S) 40 A1
Porchester Cl. Maid 106 B1
Porchfield Cl. Grave 24 C1
Porcupine Cl. SE9 17 D1
Porrington Cl. Chis 34 B2
Port Ave. Gree 22 B3
Port Cl. Thu 90 B1
Port Cl. Wald 74 B4
Port Hill. Dow 64 B2
Port Victoria Rd. I o G 32 C4
Porters Wlk. Lan H 126 A4
Porthkerry Ave. Well 18 B4
Portland Ave. Grave 24 B1
Portland Ave. Sid 18 B3
Portland Cres. SE9 17 D1
Portland Pl. Snod 72 B2
Portland Rd. Brom 33 F4
Portland Rd. Gil 46 A1
Portland Rd. Grave 24 B2
Portland Rd. Grave 23 F3
Portland Rd. SE9 17 D1
Portland Rd. Wou 72 C4
Portland St. Chath 60 B3
Portman Cl. Bex 20 A2
Portman Cl. Bexh 19 D4
Portman Pk. Ton 136 C4
Portmeadow Wlk. SE2 3 F4
Portsdown Cl. Maid 105 E3
Portsmouth Cl. Roc 43 F1
Portway Gdns. SE18 1 C2
Portway Rd. Cli W 27 E2
Post Barn Rd. Chath 60 A3
Postern La. Ton 136 C3
Postern La. Tud 137 D3
Postley Rd. Maid 106 B3
Postmill Dr. Maid 106 A3
Potash La. Bor G 84 C1
Potter's La. Hawkt 182 B1
Pottery Rd. Bex 19 F1
Pottery Rd. Hoo S W 28 C1
Poulters Wood. Kes 48 C1
Pound Bank Cl. W Kin 21 F1
Pound Cl. Orp 49 F2
Pound Court Dr. Orp 49 F2
Pound La. Kno P 79 F4
Pound La. Sev 98 C4
Pound Park Rd. SE7 1 C3
Pound Pl. SE9 17 E3
Pound Rd. E Pec 121 D1
Poundfield Rd. Sand 190 B1
Poundsbridge Hill. Pen 151 F2
Pounsley Rd. Dunt 81 D1
Pout Rd. Snod 72 A2
Poverest Rd. Orp 50 B4
Povey Ave. Roc 44 C3
Powder Mill Cl. Soub 153 F2
Powder Mill La. Dart 21 D1
Powder Mill La. Lei 135 F3
Powder Mill La. Soub 153 F2
Powell Cl. Ayld 88 B4
Powerscroft Rd. Sid 35 F3
Powis St. SE18 2 B4
Powlett Rd. Roc 44 C3
Powster Rd. Brom 33 E4
Powys Cl. Bexh 3 F2
Poynings Cl. Orp 50 C2
Poyntell Cres. Chis 34 C2
Poyntell Rd. Stapt 160 A4
Pragnell Rd. SE12 16 B1
Prall's La. Mat 156 A3
Pratling St. Ayld 88 C4
Premier Ave. Grays 8 C4
Prendergast Rd. SE3 16 A4
Prentiss Ct. SE7 1 C3
Prescott Ave. Orp 49 E4
Prestbury Sq. SE9 34 A4
Preston Ave. Chath 61 D3
Preston Dr. Bexh 3 F1
Preston Rd. Brom 48 B2
Preston Rd. Grave 24 A2
Preston Rd. Ton 136 B3
Preston Way. Rai (K) 61 F3
Pretoria Rd. Chath 60 A3
Pretoria Rd. Gil 60 C4
Prettymans La. Ede 132 A4
Prickley Wood. Brom 48 A3
Pridmore Rd. Snod 72 A2
Priestfield Rd. Gil 46 A1
Priestfields. Chath 59 E4
Priestlands Park Rd. Sid 18 A1
Priestley Ct. Grays 8 C3
Priestley Dr. Dit 87 D4
Priestley Dr. Had 119 D2
Priest's Wlk. Grave 25 E1
Priestwood Rd. Meo 56 C1
Primrose Ave. Rai (K) 61 E1
Primrose Cl. Chath 60 A2
Primrose Dr. Dit 87 F3
Primrose Rd. Hall 58 A1
Prince Arthur Rd. Gil 45 E2
Prince Charles Ave. Hort 38 C2
Prince Charles Ave. Wald 74 B4
Prince Charles Rd. SE3 1 A1
Prince Consort Dr. Chis 34 C2
Prince Henry Rd. SE7 1 C2
Prince Imperial Rd. Chis 34 B3
Prince Imperial Rd. SE18 2 B1
Prince John Rd. SE9 17 D3
Prince Of Wales Rd. SE3 1 A1
Prince Rupert Rd. SE9 17 D4
Princes Ave. Chath 60 B1
Princes Ave. Dart 21 E2
Princes Ave. Orp 50 A4
Princes Ave. Wald 74 B4
Princes Cl. Sid 18 C1
Prince's Plain. Brom 49 D3
Princes Rd. Dart 20 B3
Princes Rd. Dart 21 D2
Princes Rd. Grave 24 C1
Princes Rd. Hex 37 E3
Princes St. Bexh 19 D4
Prince's St. Chath 59 F4
Princes St. Grave 24 B3
Princes St. Maid 89 E1
Prince's St. T W 167 F4
Princes View. Dart 21 E2
Princes Way. Thu 90 B3
Princes Way. W Wick 48 A2
Princess Mary Ave. Gil 45 E2
Princess Par. Orp 49 E2
Prinys Dr. Rai (K) 75 F4
Priolo Rd. SE7 1 C3
Prior Chase. Grays 8 A3
Prior's Way. Cow 149 E1
Priorsdean Cl. Maid 105 D3
Priorsford Ave. Orp 35 E1
Priory Ave. Orp 49 F4
Priory Cl. Chis 34 A2
Priory Cl. Dart 20 C3
Priory Cl. E Far 105 F2
Priory Ct. Rai (K) 61 E3
Priory Dr. SE2 3 F3
Priory Fields. Eyn 53 D2
Priory Gdns. Dart 20 C3
Priory Gr. Dit 87 F3
Priory Gr. Ton 136 B2
Priory Hill. Dart 20 C3
Priory La. Eyn 53 D3
Priory Park. SE3 16 A4
Priory Pl. Dart 20 C3
Priory Rd. Dart 20 C3
Priory Rd. Maid 106 B4
Priory Rd. Rai (K) 61 E3
Priory Rd. Roc 44 B1
Priory Rd. Ton 136 C2
Priory St. Ton 136 B2
Priory The. SE3 16 A4
Priory Way. Ten 186 C2
Priory Wlk. Ton 136 B2
Pristling La. Stapt 159 E2
Progress Estate The. Maid 125 D4
Proof ButtsRd. SE28 3 D4
Prospect Ave. Roc 44 B2
Prospect Cl. Belv 4 B3
Prospect Gr. Grave 24 C2
Prospect Park. Soub 153 D3
Prospect Pl. Brom 33 E1
Prospect Pl. Dart 21 D3
Prospect Pl. Grave 24 C2
Prospect Pl. Grays 8 B2
Prospect Pl. Maid 106 A4
Prospect Rd. Sev 98 C4
Prospect Rd. Soub 153 D2
Prospect Rd. T W 167 F4
Prospect Row. Chath 60 B4
Prospect Row. Gil 45 E1
Prospect Vale. SE18 2 A3
Provender Way. Thu 90 A1
Providence St. Gree 22 B3
Pudding La. Maid 106 A4
Pudding La. Seal 82 A1
Pudding Rd. Rai (K) 62 A2
Puddingcake La. Rol 185 F1
Puddledock La. Bras 114 B3
Puddledock La. Dart 37 D3
Puddledock La. Hex 37 D3
Puffin Rd. I o G 15 E1
Pullington Cotts. Ben 184 A1
Pump Cl. Birl 86 C3
Pump La. Rai (K) 61 F4
Pump La. Shorn 51 E1
Punch Croft. N Ash 55 D2
Purbeck Rd. Chath 60 A3
Purcell Ave. Ton 119 D1
Purfleet By-Pass. Pur 6 C3
Purfleet Rd. S Ock 6 B4
Purland Rd. SE28 3 E4
Purneys Rd. SE9 16 C4
Purrett Rd. SE18 3 D3
Puttenden Rd. Had 119 D4
Puttenden Rd. Ship 119 D4
Pym Orchard. Bras 96 C4
Pym Pl. Grays 8 B3
Pynham Cl. SE2 3 E4

Quadrant The. Bexh 3 F2
Quadrant The. Pur 6 C3
Quaggy Wlk. SE3 16 B4
Quaker Dr. Cran 173 F1
Quaker La. Cran 173 F1
Quakers Cl. Hart (S) 40 A1
Quaker's Hall La. Sev 81 F1
Quantock Rd. Bexh 5 D1
Quarry Hill. Grays 8 B3
Quarry Hill. Sev 98 C4
Quarry Hill. Ton 136 B1
Quarry Hill Par. Ton 136 B2
Quarry Hill Rd. Bor G 84 A1
Quarry Hill Rd. Ton 136 B2
Quarry Mews. Pur 6 B3
Quarry Rd. Bou Mon 124 C4
Quarry Rd. Maid 106 B3
Quarry Rd. T W 153 E1
Quarry Rise. Ton 136 B2
Quarry Sq. Maid 89 E1
Quarry Way. Grays 7 D2
Quebec Ave. Whm 95 F3
Quebec Sq. Whm 95 F3
Queen Anne Ave. Brom 33 D1
Queen Anne Gate. Bexh 18 C4
Queen Anne Rd. Maid 106 B4
Queen Elizabeth Pl. Tilb 24 B4
Queen Elizabeth Sq. Maid 106 C1
Queen Mother Ct The. Chath 59 E4
Queen St. Bexh 19 D4
Queen St. Chath 60 B4
Queen St. Chath 59 F4
Queen St. Eri 5 D2
Queen St. Grave 24 B3
Queen St. Padd W 139 F2
Queen St. Sand 190 B1
Queen St. Yal 140 A3
Queendown Ave. Rai (K) 61 F1
Queen's Ave. Maid 88 C1
Queen's Ave. Snod 72 B2
Queens Cottages. Wad 178 A1
Queens Ct. Ede 131 F3
Queens Ct. Hawkt 189 E3
Queen's Dr. Sev 81 F2
Queen's Farm Rd. Shor 26 A2
Queens Gate Gdns. Chis 34 C2
Queens Gdns. Dart 21 E2
Queen's Gdns. T W 153 E1
Queen's Mead Rd. Brom 33 D2
Queen's Mews. Hawkt 189 E3
Queens Pas. Chis 34 B3
Queen's Rd. Brom 33 E2
Queens Rd. Chath 60 C3
Queen's Rd. Chis 34 B3
Queen's Rd. Eri 5 D2
Queen's Rd. Gil 60 C4
Queens Rd. Grave 24 C1
Queen's Rd. Hawkt 189 E3
Queen's Rd. Maid 105 F4
Queen's Rd. Snod 72 B2
Queen's Rd. T W 153 E1
Queen's Rd. Well 3 E1
Queenscroft Rd. SE9 16 C3
Queensway. All 13 F3
Queensway. Orp 49 F4
Queensway. Thu 90 B3
Queensway. W Wick 48 A1
Queenswood Rd. Ayld 73 F2
Queenswood Rd. Sid 18 A3
Quentin Pl. SE13 16 A4
Quentin Rd. SE13 16 A4
Quern The. Maid 106 A3
Quernmore Cl. Brom 33 E3
Quernmore Rd. Brom 33 E3
Quested Way. Harr 109 F1
Quickbourne La. Norm 195 F2
Quickrells Ave. Cli 10 B1
Quickthorn Cres. Wald 60 A1
Quiet Nook. Brom 48 C2
Quilter Rd. Orp 50 C3
Quincewood Gdns. Ton 118 B2
Quinion Cl. Wald 74 B2
Quinnell St. Rai (K) 62 A3
Quixote Cres. Roc 44 B3

Rabbits Rd. Dart 39 D2
Racefield Cl. Shor 43 D3
Radfield Way. Sid 17 F2
Radnor Ave. Well 18 B3
Radnor Cl. Chis 35 D3
Raeburn Ave. Dart 20 B3
Raeburn Cl. Ton 119 D1
Raeburn Rd. Sid 18 A3
Rafford Way. Brom 33 E1
Rag Hill. Lim 78 A1
Rag Hill Cl. Lim 78 A1
Rag Hill Rd. Lim 78 A1
Ragge Way. Seal 82 A2
Raggleswood. Chis 34 B2
Raglan Rd. Belv 4 A3
Ragan Rd. Brom 33 F1
Raglan Rd. SE18 2 C3
Ragstone Ct. Dit 87 F2
Ragstone Rd. Rose 107 E3
Railway App. Ton 136 B3
Railway Pl. Belv 4 B4
Railway Pl. Grave 24 B3
Railway St. Chath 60 A4
Railway St. Gil 45 F1
Railway St. Grave 23 E3
Railway Terr. Whm 95 F3
Rainham Cl. Maid 106 B3
Rainham C. SE9 18 A3
Rainham Rd. Chath 60 C3
Rainton Rd. SE7 1 B3
Raleigh Cl. Wald 60 B1
Ramac Way. SE7 1 B3
Ramillies Cl. Wald 60 B1
Ramillies Rd. Sid 18 B3
Rampion Cl. Thu 90 A1
Ramsden Cl. Orp 50 C3
Ramsden La. Ben 191 D4
Ramsden Rd. Eri 4 C2
Ramsden Rd. Orp 50 B3
Ramslye Rd. T W 167 D2
Ramus Wood Ave. Orp 50 A1
Rancliffe Gdns. SE9 17 D4
Randall Cl. Eri 4 C2
Randall Hill Road. Wro 84 A4
Randall Rd. Chath 60 A3
Randall St. Maid 89 D1
Randle's La. Kno P 64 C1
Randolph Cl. Bexh 19 F4
Randolph Cotts. Roc 44 B3
Randolph Rd. Gil 45 F1
Ranelagh Gdns. Grave 24 A2
Range Rd. Grave 25 D2
Rangefield Rd. Brom 33 D4

Rankine Rd. T W 153 F2
Ranleigh Gdns. Bexh 4 A2
Ranmore Path. Orp 35 E1
Ranscombe Cl. Roc 44 A1
Ransom Rd. SE7 1 C3
Ranters La. Gou 171 F2
Ranworth Cl. Eri 5 D1
Raphael Rd. Grave 24 C2
Rapier Cl. Pur 6 B3
Rashleigh Way. Hort 38 C1
Ratcliffe Highway. All 13 E2
Ratcliffe Highway. H Hals 29 E3
Ratcliffe Highway. Hoo S W 28 C1
Ratcliffe Highway. Hoo S W 45 E4
Rathmore Rd. Grave 24 B2
Rathmore Rd. SE7 1 B3
Raven Cl. Dit 87 E3
Ravens Cl. Brom 33 D2
Ravens Dane Cl. Oth 107 E3
Ravens Knowle. Wou 72 C4
Ravens Mews. SE12 16 B3
Ravens Way. SE12 16 B3
Ravensbourne Ave. Brom 33 D2
Ravensbourne Rd. Brom 33 E1
Ravensbourne Rd. Dart 20 B4
Ravensbury Rd. Orp 35 E1
Ravenscar Rd. Brom 33 D4
Ravenscourt Rd. Orp 35 E2
Ravenshill. Chis 34 B2
Ravenswood. Bex 19 D2
Ravenswood Ave. Roc 44 B3
Ravenswood Ave. T W 153 F1
Ravensworth Rd. SE9 34 A4
Ravine Gr. SE18 3 D2
Rawdon Rd. Maid 106 B4
Rawling St. Mils 94 A4
Rawling St. Rod 94 A4
Rawlings Cl. Orp 50 A1
Rayfield Cl. Brom 49 D4
Rayford Ave. SE12 16 A2
Rayford Cl. Dart 20 C3
Rayleas Cl. SE18 2 B1
Raymer Rd. Maid 89 E2
Raymere Gdns. SE18 3 D2
Rayners Ct. Grave 23 E3
Rayners Hill. Len 111 F1
Raynham Villas. Mard 141 E4
Rays Hill. Hort 53 F4
Read Way. Grave 42 A4
Readers Bridge Rd. Ten 186 A4
Readscroft Rd. Rai (K) 75 F4
Recreation Ave. Snod 72 B2
Recreation Cl. Maid 89 E1
Recreation Ground Rd. Ten 186 B2
Recreation Rd. Brom 33 D2
Rectory Cl. Dart 20 A4
Rectory Cl. Sid 35 E4
Rectory Cl. Snod 72 B2
Rectory Cl. Wou 58 C1
Rectory Dr. Bid 152 C4
Rectory Field Cres. SE7 1 C2
Rectory Fields. Cran 173 F1
Rectory Grange. Chath 59 F3
Rectory La. Beckl 196 A1
Rectory La. Bras 96 C4
Rectory La. Harr 110 A1
Rectory La. Ight 83 F1
Rectory La. Lim 95 D4
Rectory La. Maid 105 E3
Rectory La. Sev 98 C3
Rectory La. Sid 35 F4
Rectory La. Sutt V 126 A2
Rectory Lane N. Birl 87 D3
Rectory Lane S. Birl 87 D3
Rectory Meadow. Souf 40 B3
Rectory Park Rd. Hors 171 E3
Rectory Pl. SE18 2 B3
Rectory Rd. Cli 27 E3
Rectory Rd. Grays 8 C3
Rectory Rd. N Ash 55 F1
Rectory Rd. Swans 23 D2
Reculver Wlk. Maid 107 D2
Red Barracks Rd. SE18 2 A3
Red Cedars Rd. Orp 50 A3
Red Hill. Chis 34 B4
Red Hill. Waty 104 A2
Red House Gdns. Waty 103 F2
Red House La. Bexh 19 D4
Red Lion Cl. Orp 50 C4
Red Lion La. SE18 2 B1
Red Lion Pl. SE18 2 B1
Red Lodge Cres. Bex 20 A1
Red Lodge Rd. Bex 19 F1
Red Oak. Hawkt 189 D2
Red Oak Cl. Orp 49 E2
Red St. Souf 40 B3
Redbank. Dit 87 D3
Redbridge Cl. Wald 74 C4
Redcliffe La. Maid 89 E2
Reddy Rd. Eri 5 D2
Rede Court Rd. Roc 44 A2
Rede Wood Rd. Maid 105 D4
Redfern Ave. Gil 46 A1
Redgate Dr. Brom 48 B2
Redhill Rd. N Ash 55 D1
Redhill Wood. N Ash 55 E2
Redlands Rd. Sev 98 A4
Redleaf Cl. Belv 4 B2
Redleaf Cl. T W 153 F1
Redmans La. Shorm 66 A4
Redmans Pl. Sev 98 C3
Redpoll Way. Belv 4 A4
Redpoll Wlk. Padd W 139 E1
Redsell's Cl. Oth 107 E3
Reduers Rd. Chath 60 B3
Redwall La. Lint 123 F1
Redwell La. Ight 100 B4
Redwing Cl. Dit 87 E3
Redwing Path. SE18 2 C4
Redwings La. Pem 155 D4
Redwood Cl. Wald 74 B3
Reed Ave. Orp 50 A2
Reed Cl. SE12 16 B3
Reed St. Cli 10 B1
Reedham Cres. Cli W 27 F2
Reeds La. Ship 101 D1
Reeves Cl. Stapt 160 A4
Reeves Cres. Swan 36 C1
Reform Rd. Chath 60 B3
Regency Cl. Rai (K) 75 F4
Regency Cl. W Kin 68 A4
Regency Way. Bexh 18 C4
Regent Cl. Grays 8 C4
Regent Dr. Maid 106 B2
Regent Rd. Gil 60 C4
Regent Sq. Belv 4 B3
Regent St. Rol 192 A4
Regents Dr. Kes 48 C1
Regent's Pl. SE3 1 B1
Reginald Ave. Cux 58 C4
Reginald Rd. Maid 106 A4
Reidhaven Rd. SE18 3 D3
Reigate Rd. Brom 16 B1
Reinden Gr. Oth 107 D3
Rembrandt Cl. Ton 119 D1
Rembrandt Dr. Grave 24 A1
Rembrandt Rd. SE13 16 A4
Rennets Cl. Sid 18 A3
Rennets Wood Rd. SE9 17 F3
Renown Rd. Wald 74 C3
Renshaw Cl. Belv 4 A2
Renton Dr. Orp 50 C3
Repository Rd. SE18 2 A3
Repton Rd. Orp 50 B1
Repton Way. Wald 74 A4
Resolution Cl. Wald 60 B1
Resolution Wlk. SE18 2 A4
Restell Cl. SE3 1 A2
Restharrow Rd. Thu 107 D4
Restons Cres. SE9 18 A3
Retreat The. Grays 8 B2
Retreat The. Orp 64 B4
Revell Rise. SE18 3 D2
Revenge Rd. Wald 74 C2
Reventlow Rd. SE9 17 2
Reynard Cl. Brom 34 B1
Reynolds Cl. Ton 119 D1
Reynolds Fields. Higham 26 C1
Reynolds La. T W 153 D1
Reynolds Pl. SE3 1 B2
Rhode St. Chath 60 A4
Rhodewood Cl. Oth 107 E3
Rhododendron Ave. Meo 70 B3
Ribblesdale Rd. Dart 21 F2
Ribston Cl. Brom 49 D3
Ribston Gdns. Padd W 139 D2
Richard Cl. SE18 2 A3
Richard St. Chath 60 A4
Richard St. Chath 59 F4
Richard's Cl. Chid 134 A3
Richardson Rd. T W 153 E1
Richborough Cl. Orp 35 F1
Richmer Rd. Eri 5 E2
Richmond Cl. Roc 45 D3
Richmond Cl. Wald 74 B4
Richmond Pl. SE18 2 C3
Richmond Rd. Gil 45 F2
Richmond Rd. Grays 8 C3
Richmond Way. Maid 106 B2
Richmount Gdns. SE3 16 B4
Ricketts Hill Rd. Lim 78 A2
Rickyard Path. SE9 17 D4
Riddlesdale Ave. T W 153 E1
Riddons Rd. SE12 33 F4
Rideout St. SE18 2 A3
Rider Cl. SE9 18 A3
Ridge Ave. Dart 20 A3
Ridge La. Meo 70 B3
Ridge The. Bex 19 D2
Ridge The. Orp 49 F2
Ridge Way. Dart 20 A3
Ridge Way. Ede 131 F4
Ridgebrook Rd. SE3 16 C4
Ridgecroft Cl. Bex 19 F2
Ridgeway. Brom 48 B2
Ridgeway. Dart 39 D4
Ridgeway. Pem 154 C2
Ridgeway Ave. Grave 24 B1
Ridgeway Cres. Orp 50 A2
Ridgeway Cres. Ton 136 C4
Ridgeway Cres Gdns. Orp 50 A2
Ridgeway Dr. Brom 33 E4
Ridgeway E. Sid 18 A3
Ridgeway The. Chath 60 A2
Ridgeway The. Gil 45 F2
Ridgeway The. Shor 43 D3
Ridgeway The. Ton 136 C4
Ridgeway W. Sid 18 A3
Ridgewaye The. Soub 153 E3
Ridgway. Maid 105 E3
Riding La. Hild 117 F2
Riding Pk. Hild 117 F2
Ridings The. Bigg 78 A3
Ridings The. T W 154 A1
Ridlads Gr. Lim C 95 D1
Ridlands La. Lim C 95 D1
Ridlands Rise. Lim C 95 D1
Ridley Rd. Brom 33 D1
Ridley Rd. Chath 59 F4
Ridley Rd. Well 3 E1
Riefield Rd. SE9 17 F4
Riggs Way. Wro 84 A4
Rigshill Rd. Len 112 B1
Rigshill Rd. Stal 112 B1
Ring Cl. Brom 33 E3
Ringden Ave. Padd W 139 D1
Ringer's Rd. Brom 33 E1
Ringle Green. Sand 190 C1
Ringlestone Rd. Holli 110 A4
Ringlestone Rd. Maid 89 D2
Ringmer Way. Brom 49 D4
Rings Hill. Hild 117 E1
Ringshall Rd. Orp 35 E1
Ringwood Ave. Dow 64 C3
Ringwood Cl. Rai (K) 61 F2
Ringwood Rd. Maid 106 C2
Ripley Rd. Belv 4 B3
Ripon Ave. Rai (K) 61 E3
Ripon Cl. Rai (K) 61 F4
Ripon Rd. SE18 2 B2
Rippersley Rd. Well 3 E1
Rippolson Rd. SE18 3 D3
Risden La. Sand 189 F2
Rise The. Bex 18 C2
Rise The. Chath 59 F4
Rise The. Dart 20 A4
Rise The. Grave 42 A4
Rise The. Rai (K) 75 E4
Rise The. Sev 98 C2
Risedale Rd. Bexh 19 F4
Ritch Rd. Snod 72 A2
Ritter St. SE18 2 B2
River Cl. E Far 105 E2
River Dr. Roc 44 A2
River Lawn Rd. Ton 136 B3
River St. Gil 45 E1
River Way. Dit 87 E4
River Way. SE10 1 A4
River Wlk. Ton 136 B3
Riverdale Estate. Ton 136 C2
Riverdale Rd. Bex 19 D3
Riverdale Rd. Eri 4 C3
Riverdale Rd. SE18 3 D3
Riverhead Cl. Maid 88 C1
Riverhill. Sev W 99 D2
Rivers Wlk. Len 110 C1
Riversdale. Grave 24 A1
Riverside. Ede 131 F3
Riverside. Eyn 52 C2
Riverside. SE7 1 C4
Riverside East Rd. Gil 45 F3
Riverside North Rd. Gil 45 E3
Riverside Rd. Sid 19 D1
Riverside Way. Dart 21 D3
Riverside West Rd. Gil 45 E3
Riverview Rd. Gree 22 B3
Riverwood La. Chis 34 C2
Roach St. Roc 44 B2
Robert St. E16 2 B4
Robert St. SE18 2 C3
Roberton Dr. Brom 33 F2
Roberts Orchard Rd. Maid 105 D4
Roberts Rd. Belv 4 B3
Roberts Rd. Rai (K) 62 A2
Roberts Rd. Snod 72 A2
Robin Hill Dr. Chis 34 A3
Robin Hood Green. Orp 50 B4
Robin Hood La. Bexh 19 D3
Robin Hood La. Burh 73 F3
Robin Hood La (Lower). Wald 74 A3
Robin Hood La (Upper). Wald 74 A3
Robin Way. Orp 35 E1
Robina Cl. Bexh 18 C4
Robinia Ave. Grave 23 F2
Robins Ave. Len 110 C1
Robins Cl. Len 128 C4
Robins Ct. SE12 16 C1
Robins Gr. W Wick 48 B2
Robson Dr. Ayld 88 A3
Robson Dr. Hoo S W 28 C1
Robyns Croft. Grave 24 A1
Robyns Way. Ede 131 F2
Robyns Way. Sev 81 D1
Rocfort Rd. Snod 72 B2
Rochdale Rd. SE2 3 E3
Rochdale Rd. T W 153 F1
Rochester Ave. Brom 33 E2
Rochester Ave. Chath 59 F4
Rochester Cl. Sid 18 B3
Rochester Cres. Hoo S W 28 C1
Rochester Dr. Bex 19 E3
Rochester Rd. Ayld 88 B4
Rochester Rd. Burh 73 D3
Rochester Rd. Dart 21 E2
Rochester Rd. Grave 25 E1
Rochester Rd. Hall 58 C3
Rochester Rd. Ton 136 C4
Rochester Rd. Wou 58 C1
Rochester Rd. Wou 73 D3
Rochester Rd. Wou 73 F4
Rochester St. Chath 60 A4
Rochester Way. Bex 20 A2
Rochester Way. Dart 20 A2
Rochester Way. SE9 17 E4
Rock Ave. Gil 60 C4
Rock Hill. Shorm 65 E4
Rock Hill Rd. Ege 147 D3
Rock Rd. Bor G 84 A2
Rock Rd. Maid 89 E2
Rock Villa Rd. T W 167 E4
Rockdale Rd. Sev 98 C3
Rockmount Rd. SE18 3 D3
Rocks Cl. Dit 87 E1
Rocks Hill. Frit 174 B4
Rocks Rd The. Dit 87 E1
Rocky Hill. Maid 106 A4
Rocque La. SE3 16 A4
Rodmell Rd. T W 167 E3
Rodney Ave. Ton 137 D4
Rodney Gdns. W Wick 48 B1
Rodway Rd. Brom 33 E2
Roebourne Way. E16 2 B4
Roebuck Rd. Chath 44 C1
Roedean Cl. Orp 50 B1
Roedean Rd. T W 167 E3
Roehampton Cl. Grave 25 D2
Roehampton Dr. Chis 34 C3
Roffen Rd. Chath 59 F3
Rogers Ct. Swan 37 E1
Rogers Rd. Grays 8 C3
Rogers Rough Rd. Kiln 180 B3
Rogers Wood La. Faw 54 B1
Rogersmead. Ten 186 B2
Rogley Hill. Bidd 175 E1
Rogues Hill. Pen 151 F4
Rokesby Cl. Well 2 C1
Rolinsden Way. Kes 48 C1
Rolleston Ave. Orp 49 E4
Rolleston Cl. Orp 49 E3
Rollo Rd. Hex 37 D3
Rolvenden Ave. Rai (K) 61 F4
Rolvenden Gdns. Brom 33 F3
Rolvenden Hill. Rol 185 E1
Rolvenden Rd. Roc 44 C3
Rolvenden Rd. Ten 186 A2
Roman Heights. Maid 89 F1
Roman Rd. Grave 23 F1
Roman Rd. Snod 72 A2
Roman Villa Rd. Dart 38 C3
Roman Way. Dart 20 A3
Roman Way. Roc 59 D4
Romanhurst Ave. Brom 33 D1
Romanhurst Gdns. Brom 33 D1
Romany Rd. Rai (K) 61 F3
Romany Rise. Orp 49 F3
Romden Rd. Sma 163 F2
Romero Sq. SE3 16 C4
Romford Rd. Pem 155 D2
Romney Cl. Rose 107 E4
Romney Dr. Brom 33 F3
Romney Gdns. Bexh 4 A1
Romney Pl. Maid 106 B4
Romney Rd. Grave 24 A1
Romney Rd. Wald 60 B1
Romney Way. Ton 119 D1
Romsey Cl. Orp 49 F1
Romsey Cl. Roc 44 A2
Ronalds Rd. Brom 33 E2
Ronaldstone Rd. Sid 18 A3
Ronfearn Ave. Orp 50 C4
Ronver Rd. SE12 16 A2
Rookdean. Sev 80 C1
Rookery Cres. Cli 10 B1
Rookery Ct. Grays 7 E2
Rookery Gdns. Orp 50 C4
Rookery Hill. Snod 72 A2
Rookery La. Brom 48 C4
Rookery Rd. Dow 63 E3
Rookery The. Grays 7 E2
Rookery View. Grays 8 C3
Rookesley Rd. Orp 50 C3
Rooks Hill. Seal 99 F2
Rookwood Cl. Grays 8 B3
Roopers. Spel 152 B2
Roosevelt Ave. Chath 60 B2
Rope Wlk. Chah 45 D1
Rope Wlk The. Sand 190 B1
Rope Yard Rails. SE18 2 B4
Ropemakers Ct. Chath 60 B3
Roper Cl. Rai (K) 75 F4
Roper St. SE9 17 E3
Roper's Gate. T W 167 D3
Roper's Green La. Hoo S W 29 E2
Roper's La. Hoo S W 29 E2
Ropewalk. Cran 173 F1
Rose Ave. Grave 25 D2
Rose Dale. Orp 49 E2
Rose St. Chath 59 F4
Rose St. Grave 23 E3
Rose St. Ton 136 C2
Rose Way. SE12 16 B3
Rose Yd. Maid 106 B4
Roseacre La. Rose 107 E4
Roseacre Rd. Well 18 B4
Rosebank Wlk. SE18 2 A3
Roseberry Gdns. Dart 20 C2
Roseberry Gdns. Orp 50 A2
Rosebery Ave. Sid 18 A2
Rosebery Rd. Chath 60 A3
Rosebery Rd. Gil 45 F2
Rosebery Rd. Grays 8 A2
Rosecroft Cl. Orp 50 C4
Rosedale Cl. Dart 21 E2
Rosedale Cl. SE2 3 E4
Rosedale Rd. Grays 8 C3
Rosedene Ct. Dart 20 C2
Rosefield. Sev 98 B4
Rosegarth. Ist 41 D2
Rosehill Wlk. T W 167 E4
Roseholme. Maid 105 F3
Roseleigh Ave. Maid 88 C1
Rosemary Cl. Wald 74 A4
Rosemary La. Kiln 180 B1
Rosemary La. N Ash 69 F4
Rosemary La. Sma 163 D4
Rosemary La. Tic 187 E4
Rosemary Rd. Dit 87 D3
Rosemary Rd. Rose 107 E4
Rosemary Rd. Well 3 D1
Rosemount Cl. Loose 124 A4
Rosemount Dr. Brom 34 A1
Rosenheath Cl. Orp 64 C3
Roseveare Rd. SE12 33 F4
Rosewood. Bex 37 D4
Rosewood Cl. Sid 18 C1
Rosewood Ct. Brom 33 F2
Rosherville Way. Grave 24 A2
Roslin Way. Brom 33 E4
Ross Rd. Dart 20 B3
Ross St. Chath 59 F4
Ross Way. SE9 17 D4
Rossdale. T W 153 F1
Rosse Mews. SE3 1 B1
Rossland Cl. Bexh 19 E3
Rosslyn Cl. W Wick 48 A2
Rother Rd. Ton 118 C1
Rother Vale. Wald 74 C4
Rothermere Cl. Ben 184 A1
Rothley Cl. Ten 186 B2
Rouge La. Grave 24 B2
Roughetts Rd. Birl 86 A4
Roughetts Rd. W Mal 86 A4
Roughway La. Plax 101 F2
Round Ash Way. Hart (S) 55 D4
Round St. Cob 41 F1
Roundhay. Birl 87 D3
Roundhill Rd. T W 167 F3
Roundtable Rd. Brom 16 A1
Roundwell. Rose 107 F4
Roundwood. Chis 34 B2
Rover Rd. Wald 74 B3
Row The. N Ash 55 D2
Rowan Cl. Dit 88 A3
Rowan Cl. Meo 56 B4
Rowan Cres. Dart 20 C2
Rowan Rd. Bexh 19 D4
Rowan Rd. Swan 36 C1
Rowan Shaw. Ton 118 C1
Rowan Tree Rd. T W 167 D3
Rowan Wlk. Brom 49 D2
Rowbrooke Cl. Rai (K) 75 F4
Rowdow. Otf 82 A4
Rowdow La. Shorm 66 C1
Rowfield. Ede 131 F4
Rowhill Rd. Dart 37 E4
Rowhill Rd. Hex 37 E4
Rowland Ave. Chath 61 D3
Rowlatt Cl. Dart 37 F4
Rowley Ave. Sid 18 B2
Rowley Hill. Pem 154 C3
Rowton Rd. SE18 2 C2
Rowzill Rd. Hex 37 D3
Royal Ave. Ton 136 C2
Royal Chase. T W 167 D4
Royal Oak Rd. Bexh 19 D4
Royal Par. Chis 34 C3
Royal Par. SE3 1 A1
Royal Pier Rd. Grave 24 C3
Royal Rd. Sid 18 C1
Royal Rd. Sutt H 38 B4
Royal Sovereign Ave. Gil 45 E2
Royal West Kent Ave. Ton 136 C4
Roydene Rd. SE18 3 D3
Roydon Hall Rd. E Pec 121 D4
Royston Rd. Dart 20 A3
Royston Rd. Rose 107 E4
Roystons Cl. Rai (K) 62 A3
Royton Ave. Len 110 C1
Ruck La. Hors 171 D4
Ruckinge Way. Rai (K) 61 F4
Ruddstreet Cl. SE18 2 B3
Rudge Cl. Wald 74 C3
Rudland Rd. Bexh 19 E4
Ruffets Wood. Grave 41 F3
Rugby Cl. Wald 74 A4
Rumania Wlk. Grave 25 D1
Rumstead La. S Grn 91 F4
Rumstead Rd. S Grn 92 A4
Runciman Cl. Dow 64 C3
Runham La. Len 128 A4
Rural Vale. Grave 24 A2
Ruscombe Cl. Soub 153 D3
Rush Cl. Wald 74 B4
Rush Grove St. SE18 2 A3
Rushbrook Rd. SE9 17 F1
Rushdean Rd. Roc 44 A1
Rushdene. SE2 3 F4
Rushdon Cl. Grays 8 B4
Rushet Rd. Orp 35 E2
Rushetts. Spel 166 A4
Rushetts Rd. W Kin 68 A4
Rushford Cl. Head 144 C1
Rushley Cl. Kes 49 D1
Rushlye Cl. Bel G 168 A1
Rushmead Dr. Maid 106 B2
Rushmore Cl. Brom 34 A1
Rushmore Hill. Dow 64 C2
Rushmore Hill. Kno P 65 D1
Rushymead. Kemsg 82 B3
Ruskin Ave. Well 3 E1
Ruskin Cl. Dit 87 D2
Ruskin Ct. SE9 17 D3
Ruskin Dr. Orp 50 A2
Ruskin Dr. Well 18 B4
Ruskin Gr. Dart 21 E3
Ruskin Gr. Well 3 E1
Ruskin Rd. Belv 4 B3
Ruskin Wlk. Brom 49 D4
Rusland Ave. Orp 49 F2
Russel Rd. Grays 8 B3
Russell Cl. Bexh 19 E4
Russell Cl. Dart 20 B4
Russell Cl. SE7 1 C2
Russell Ct. Brom 33 D3
Russell Ct. Chath 60 B4
Russell Pl. Sutt H 38 B2
Russell Rd. Ayld 73 F2
Russell Rd. Grave 24 C3
Russells Ave. Rai (K) 62 B2
Russet Cl. Roc 44 A2
Russets The. Meo 56 B4
Russett Cl. Orp 50 B1
Russett Rd. E Pec 121 D1
Russett Way. Swan 36 C2
Rusthall Grange. T W 166 C4
Rusthall High St. T W 166 C4
Rusthall Park. T W 166 C4
Rusthall Rd. T W 166 C4
Rustwick. T W 166 C4
Rutherford Way. Ton 118 C2
Rutherglen Rd. SE2 3 E2
Ruthin Rd. SE3 1 B2
Rutland Ave. Sid 18 B2
Rutland Cl. Bex 18 C2
Rutland Cl. Dart 20 C2

Rutland Gate. Belv 4 B3
Rutland Gate. Brom 33 D1
Rutland Pl. Rai (K) 75 F4
Rutland Way. Maid 107 D2
Rutland Way. Orp 50 C4
Ruxley Cl. Sid 36 A3
Ruxley Corner Industrial Estate. Sid 35 F3
Ruxton Cl. Swan 37 D1
Ryan Cl. SE3 16 C4
Ryan Dr. Rose 107 E3
Ryarsh Cres. Orp 50 A1
Ryarsh La. W Mal 86 B3
Ryarsh Rd. Birl 71 E1
Rycaut Cl. Rai (K) 75 F4
Rycroft La. Sev 98 A1
Rycuff Sq. SE3 1 A1
Rydal Cl. T W 153 D1
Rydal Dr. Bexh 4 B1
Rydal Dr. T W 153 D1
Ryde Cl. Chath 60 B2
Ryder Cl. Brom 33 E4
Ryders. Spel 166 B4
Rydons Cl. SE9 17 D4
Rye Cl. Bex 19 E3
Rye Cres. Orp 50 C3
Rye Field. Orp 50 C3
Rye La. Dunt 81 D3
Rye La. Otf 81 D3
Rye Rd. Hawkt 189 E3
Ryecroft Rd. Orp 49 F4
Ryecroft Rd. Otf 81 E4
Ryegrass Cl. Chath 60 C1
Ryelands Cres. SE9 16 C3
Rymers Cl. T W 153 F2
Rysted La. Whm 95 F3

Sackville Ave. Brom 48 B3
Sackville Cl. Sev 81 E1
Sackville Rd. Dart 21 D1
Saddington St. Grave 24 C2
Saddler's Park. Eyn 52 C2
Sadlers Cl. Wald 73 F3
Saffron Way. Wald 60 A1
Sailmakers Ct. Chath 60 B3
St.John's Rd. Gil 60 C4
St Aidan's Way. Grave 25 D1
St Albans Cl. Gil 46 A2
St Alban's Cl. Grave 24 C1
St Alban's Gdns. Grave 24 C1
St Alban's Rd. Dart 21 D3
St Albans Rd. Roc 43 F1
St Alfege Rd. SE7 1 C2
St Andrew's Cl. Maid 105 E3
St Andrews Cl. Padd W 139 E1
St Andrews Ct. Soub 153 E3
St Andrews Dr. Orp 50 B3
St Andrews Mews. SE3 1 B2
St Andrew's Park Rd. Soub 153 E3
St Andrews Rd. Gil 45 F2
St Andrew's Rd. Grave 24 B2
St Andrew's Rd. Maid 105 E4
St Andrews Rd. Padd W 139 E1
St Andrews Rd. Sid 18 C1
St Andrew's Rd. Tilb 24 B4
St Andrews Way. Lim C 95 D1
St Andrew's Wlk. All 13 F2
St Anne Ct. Maid 106 A4
St Anthony's Ct. Orp 49 E2
St Aubyns Cl. Orp 50 A2
St Aubyns Gdns. Orp 50 A2
St Audrey Ave. Bexh 4 B1
St Augustine's Ave. Brom 49 D4
St Augustine's Rd. Belv 4 A3
St Barnabas Cl. Gil 60 C4
St Bartholomew's La. Chath 60 A4
St Bartholomew's Terr. Chath 60 A4
St Benedict Rd. Snod 72 A2
St Benedict's Ave. Grave 25 D1
St Benets Ct. Ten 186 B2
St Benets Way. Ten 186 B2
St Bernards Rd. Ton 118 C1
St Blaise Ave. Brom 33 E2
St Botolph Rd. Grave 23 F1
St Botolph's Ave. Sev 98 B4
St Botolph's Rd. Sev 98 B4
St Brides Cl. Belv 3 F4
St Chad's Dr. Grave 25 D1
St Clement's Ave. Grays 7 E2
St Clements Ct. Pur 6 B3
St Clement's Rd. Grays 7 F2
St Clere Hill Rd. W Kin 68 A2
St Columba's Cl. Grave 25 D1
St David's Bridge. Cran 182 C4
St David's Cres. Grave 41 F4
St David's Rd. All 13 F2
St David's Rd. Hex 37 D3
St David's Rd. T W 153 E1
St Dunstan's Dr. Grave 25 D1
St Dunstans Wlk. Cran 182 C4
St Edith's Rd. Kemsg 82 B3
St Edmunds Cl. Belv 3 F4
St Edmunds Rd. Dart 21 E4
St Edmunds Way. Rai (K) 62 B3
St Faith's La. Rose 107 E4
St Faith's St. Maid 106 A4
St Fidelis' Rd. Eri 4 C3
St Francis Ave. Grave 42 A4
St Francis Cl. Orp 50 A4
St Francis' Rd. Eri 4 C3
St Francis Rd. Meo 70 B4
St George's Ave. Grays 8 C3
St George's Centre. Grave 24 B3
St George's Cres. Grave 41 F4
St Georges Mews. Ton 136 B2
St George's Park. T W 167 D2
St Georges Rd. Brom 34 A1
St George's Rd. Gil 45 F1
St Georges Rd. Orp 49 F4
St George's Rd. Sev 81 E1
St George's Rd. Sid 35 F3
St Georges Rd. Swan 37 D1
St Georges Rd W. Brom 34 A2
St George's Sq. Maid 106 A4
St George's Way. Wro 84 A4
St George's Wlk. All 13 F2
St German's Pl. SE3 1 B1
St Giles Rd. Orp 49 F1
St Gregory's Cres. Grave 25 D1
St Gregory's Ct. Grave 25 D1
St Helens La. E Far 105 D2
St Helens Rd. Belv 3 F4
St Hildas. Plax 101 D2
St Hilda's Way. Grave 25 D1
St James Cl. I o G 15 E1
St James' La. Gree 22 A2
St James' Park. T W 153 F1
St James Pl. Dart 20 C3
St James Rd. I o G 15 E1
St James' Rd. T W 153 F1
St James Way. Sid 36 A4
St James's Ave. Grave 24 B3
St James's Cl. SE18 2 C3
St James's Rd. Grave 24 B3
St James's Rd. Sev 81 E1
St James's St. Grave 24 B3
St John's Cl. Higham 43 F4
St John's Hill. Sev 81 F1
St John's La. Hart (S) 55 D4
St John's Park. SE3 1 B2
St John's Park. T W 153 F2
St John's Rd. Dart 21 F2
St John's Rd. Eri 4 C3
St John's Rd. Grave 24 C2
St John's Rd. Higham 43 F4
St Johns Rd. Hoo S W 28 C1
St John's Rd. Orp 50 A4
St John's Rd. Sev 81 E1
St John's Rd. Sid 35 E4
St John's Rd. T W 153 E1
St John's Rd. Well 18 B4
St John's Terr. SE18 2 C2
St Johns Way. Chath 59 E3
St Josephs Cl. Orp 50 A1
St Justin Cl. Orp 35 F1
St Katherine's La. Snod 72 A2
St Katherines Rd. Belv 3 F4
St Keverne Rd. SE9 34 A4
St Kilda Rd. Orp 50 A3
St Laurence Ave. Maid 88 C2
St Laurence Cl. Orp 35 F1
St Lawrence Ave. Bid 152 C4
St Leonards Ave. Chath 60 A3
St Leonards Cl. Maid 88 C2
St Leonards Cl. Well 18 B4
St Leonards Rise. Orp 50 A1
St Leonard's St. W Mal 86 B2
St Luke's Ave. Maid 89 E1
St Lukes Cl. Swan 36 C2
St Lukes Cotts. Swan 36 C2
St Luke's Rd. Maid 89 E1
St Luke's Rd. T W 153 E1
St Luke's Way. All 13 F2
St Margarets Ave. Sid 17 F1
St Margaret's Banks. Chath 44 C1
St Margarets Cl. Maid 105 E3
St Margarets Cl. Orp 50 B1
St Margaret's Cres. Grave 25 D1
St Margarets Dr. Rai (K) 61 F1
St Margaret's Gr. SE18 2 C3
St Margarets Mews. Chath 44 C1
St Margaret's Pas. SE13 16 A4
St Margaret's Path. SE18 2 C3
St Margaret's Rd. Dart 39 D3
St Margaret's Rd. Grave 24 A2
St Margaret's St. Chath 44 C1
St Margaret's Terr. SE18 2 C3
St Margarets Villas. Yal 140 C2
St Mark's Ave. Grave 24 A2
St Marks Ct. Ayld 73 D1
St Mark's Rd. Brom 33 E1
St Mark's Rd. T W 167 D2
St Martins Cl. Belv 3 F4
St Martin's Cl. Thu 90 B2
St Martin's Dr. Eyn 52 C2
St Martins Meadow. Bras 96 C4
St Martin's Rd. Dart 21 D3
St Mary St. SE18 2 B4
St Mary's Ave. Brom 33 D1
St Mary's Church Rd. Sund 97 D3
St Mary's Cl. Bor G 84 C2
St Mary's Cl. Grave 24 C1
St Mary's Cl. Orp 35 F2
St Mary's Cl. Yal 140 A4
St Mary's Dr. Sev 98 A4
St Mary's Gdns. Gil 45 E2
St Mary's La. Spel 152 B2
St Mary's La. Tic 187 D3
St Mary's Rd. Bex 19 F2
St Mary's Rd. Gil 45 E3
St Mary's Rd. Gil 45 F3
St Mary's Rd. Gree 22 A3
St Mary's Rd. Roc 44 B2
St Mary's Rd. Swan 37 D1
St Mary's Rd. Ton 136 B2
St Marys Rd. Wro 84 B3
St Marys Way. Lon 40 A1
St Mary's Wlk. Burh 73 D3
St Matthews Dr. Brom 34 A1
St Matthews Dr. Chath 59 E3
St Matthew's Way. All 13 F2
St Merryn Cl. SE18 2 C2
St Michaels Cl. Ayld 88 C4
St Michaels Cl. Brom 34 A1
St Michael's Cl. Chath 60 A4
St Michaels Cl. SE2 3 F4
St Michaels Dr. Kemsg 82 B4
St Michael's Rd. Maid 105 F4
St Michael's Rd. T W 153 E2
St Michael's Rd. Well 18 B4
St Mildred's Cl. Ten 186 B2
St Mildreds Rd. SE12 16 A2
St Nicholas Dr. Sev 98 C3
St Nicholas Rd. SE18 3 D3
St Nicolas La. Chis 34 A2
St Patrick's Gdns. Grave 24 C1
St Paul's Cl. Roc 43 F1
St Pauls Cl. SE7 1 C3
St Pauls Cl. Ton 118 C1
St Paul's Cray Rd. Chis 34 C2
St Paul's Rd. Eri 4 C2
St Paul's Sq. Brom 33 E2
St Paul's St. T W 166 C4
St Paul's Wood Hill. Orp 35 D2
St Peter St. Chath 59 F4
St Peter St. Maid 106 A4
St Peter's Bridge. Maid 106 A4
St Peters Cl. Chis 34 C3
St Peters Cl. Dit 87 E3
St Peters Ct. SE3 16 A4
St Peters Pl. Ayld 73 D1
St Peters Rd. Dit 87 E3
St Peters Row. Pen 151 E1
St Peter's St. T W 167 F4
St Philip's Ave. Maid 106 B3
St Quentin Rd. Well 18 A4
St Ronan's Cl. Maid 106 C2
St Stephen's Sq. Maid 106 A3
St Stephen's St. Ton 136 B2
St Thomas Ct. Bex 19 E2
St Thomas' Dr. Orp 49 F3
St Thomas Rd. Belv 4 C4
St Thomas Rd. Grave 24 A1
St Thomas's Ave. Grave 24 B2
St Thomas's Pl. Grays 8 C2
St Vincents La. Wro H 85 E3
St Vincents Rd. Dart 21 E3
St Welcume's Way. Harr 110 A1
St Werburgh Cres. Hoo S W 28 C1
St William's Way. Chath 59 F3
St Winifred's Rd. Bigg 78 A3
Saints Hill. Pen 151 E2
Saladin Dr. Pur 6 B3
Salcote Rd. Grave 42 A4
Salem Pl. Grave 23 F2
Salem St. Maid 106 B4
Salisbury Ave. Rai (K) 61 F2
Salisbury Ave. Swan 37 E1
Salisbury Cl. Ton 118 C1
Salisbury Rd. Ayld 73 F2
Salisbury Rd. Bex 19 E2
Salisbury Rd. Brom 49 D4
Salisbury Rd. Chath 60 B4
Salisbury Rd. Dart 21 F2
Salisbury Rd. Grave 24 A2
Salisbury Rd. Grays 8 C3
Salisbury Rd. Maid 89 E1
Salisbury Rd. Soub 153 F2
Salisbury Rd. Spel 166 A4
Salisbury Rd. Ton 136 C4
Salix Rd. Grays 8 C2
Sallows Shaw. Cob 41 F1
Sally Port. Gil 45 E1
Sally Port Gdns. Gil 45 E1
Salmon Rd. Belv 4 B3
Salomons Rd. T W 166 C4
Salt La. Cli 27 D4
Saltash Rd. Well 3 F1
Saltford Cl. Eri 5 D3
Saltings Rd. Snod 72 B2
Salt's Ave. Loose 124 A4
Salts La. Loose 106 A1
Salts La. Loose 124 B4
Saltwood Cl. Orp 50 C1
Saltwood Rd. Maid 106 A3
Sam Bartram Cl. SE7 1 C3
Samara Cl. Wald 74 B3
Samphire Cl. Thu 107 D4
Sampson Cl. Belv 3 F4
Samuel St. SE18 2 A3
Sanctuary Cl. Dart 20 C3
Sanctuary Rd. Rai (K) 61 E4
Sanctuary The. Bex 18 C3
Sand La. Frit 161 D1
Sand Rd. Lam 179 E4
Sandbach Pl. SE18 2 C3
Sandbanks Hill. Dart 39 E3
Sandbourne Dr. Maid 89 D3
Sandby Green. SE9 17 D4
Sandcliff Rd. Eri 4 C3
Sandersons Ave. Shorm 65 E3
Sanderstead Rd. Orp 50 B4
Sandfield Rd. Pen 151 E2
Sandford Rd. Bexh 19 D4
Sandford Rd. Brom 33 E1
Sandgate Rd. Rai (K) 76 A4
Sandgate Rd. Well 3 F2
Sandhurst Ave. Pem 155 D1
Sandhurst Cl. Rai (K) 61 F4
Sandhurst Cl. Sand 194 B4
Sandhurst Cl. T W 153 F1
Sandhurst Cross. Frit 161 D3
Sandhurst Park. T W 153 F1
Sandhurst Rd. Bexh 18 C3
Sandhurst Rd. Orp 50 B1
Sandhurst Rd. Rol 191 E3
Sandhurst Rd. SE6 16 A2
Sandhurst Rd. Sid 18 B1
Sandhurst Rd. T W 153 F1
Sandiland Cres. Brom 48 A2
Sandilands. Sev 80 C1
Sandling La. Maid 89 E2
Sandling Rd. Maid 89 D1
Sandling Rise. SE9 17 E1
Sandown Cl. T W 154 A1
Sandown Dr. Rai (K) 61 F2
Sandown Gr. T W 154 A1
Sandown Park. T W 154 A1
Sandown Rd. Grave 41 F3
Sandown Rd. W Mal 86 B2
Sandpiper Rd. Wald 74 C3
Sandpiper Way. Orp 35 F1
Sandpipers The. Grave 24 C1
Sandpit Pl. SE7 2 A3
Sandpit Rd. Brom 33 D4
Sandpit Rd. Dart 20 C4
Sandringham Dr. Well 3 D1
Sandringham Rd. Brom 33 E4
Sandringham Rd. Rai (K) 76 A4
Sandrock Rd. T W 167 F4
Sandstone Rd. SE12 16 B1
Sandtoft Rd. SE7 1 B2
Sandway Rd. Len 128 A4
Sandway Rd. Orp 35 F1
Sandy Bank Rd. Grave 24 B2
Sandy Bury. Orp 49 F2
Sandy Dell. Rai (K) 75 E4
Sandy Hill Ave. SE18 2 B3
Sandy Hill Rd. SE18 2 B3
Sandy La. Birl 72 A1
Sandy La. Box 89 F2
Sandy La. Dart 22 C1
Sandy La. Grave 40 A4
Sandy La. Grays 7 E2
Sandy La. Ight 100 B4
Sandy La. Maid 89 F2
Sandy La. Orp 50 B3
Sandy La. Orp 35 F2
Sandy La. Rose 90 B1
Sandy La. Sev 98 C4
Sandy La. Ten 186 B2
Sandy La. W Mal 86 B3
Sandy La. Whm 95 F3
Sandy La. Wro H 85 D3
Sandy Mount. Rose 90 B1
Sandy Ridge. Bor G 84 B2
Sandy Ridge. Chis 34 B3
Sandycroft. SE2 3 E2
Sandycroft Rd. Roc 44 A3
Sapho Park. Grave 42 A4
Saphora Cl. Orp 49 F1
Sappers Wlk. Gil 45 F1
Sara Park. Grave 42 A4
Saracen Cl. Rai (K) 61 E3
Sarsen Hts. Wald 74 A3
Sarsens Cl. Cob 42 A1
Sassoon Cl. Dit 87 E4
Saunders Cl. Grave 24 A1
Saunders Rd. SE18 3 D3
Saunders Rd. T W 167 D3
Saunders St. Chath 60 A4
Saunders St. Gil 45 F1
Savage Rd. Wald 74 B4
Savoy Rd. Dart 20 C3
Sawpit Rd. Mils 94 B3
Sawpit Rd. Rod 94 B3
Sawyers Ct. Chath 60 B3
Saxby Wood. Lei 135 D3
Saxbys Rd. Seal 82 C1
Saxon Cl. Grave 23 F1
Saxon Cl. Roc 44 A3
Saxon Pl. Hort 53 F4
Saxon Rd. Brom 33 D3
Saxon Rd. Sutt H 38 A4
Saxon Wlk. Sid 35 F3
Saxons Dr. Maid 89 E1
Saxton St. Gil 45 F1
Saxville Rd. Orp 35 E2
Sayer Rd. Char 130 C2
Sayers' La. Ten 186 B2
Sayes Court Rd. Orp 35 E1
Scabharbour Rd. Sev W 116 C3
Scads Hill Cl. Orp 50 A4
Scarborough La. Burh 73 D3
Scarlet Rd. SE6 16 A1
Scarlett Cl. Wald 60 C1
Scarsbrook Rd. SE3 16 C4
Schofield Wlk. SE3 1 B2
School Ave. Gil 61 D4
School Cl. Meo 56 B3
School Hill. Lam 170 B1
School La. Dart 22 C1
School La. Had 120 A3
School La. Hex 37 E3
School La. Higham 26 C1
School La. Hort 54 A3
School La. Len 128 A3
School La. Maid 107 D3
School La. Plax 101 D1
School La. Seal 82 A1
School La. Ship 101 D1
School La. Stal 112 C1
School La. Sutt V 126 A2
School La. Trot 70 B1
School La. Well 18 B4
School La. Wou 59 D1
School Rd. Char 130 C2
School Rd. Chis 34 C3
School Rd. Gou 172 A3
School Rd. Grave 24 C1
School Rd. W Pec 119 F4
School Terr. Hawkt 189 D3
Schoolfield Rd. Grays 7 E2
Schooner Ct. Dart 21 F4
Scilla Ct. Grays 8 C2
Scimitar Cl. Rai (K) 61 E3
Scords La. Bras 114 C4
Scotby Ave. Wald 74 B4
Scotsdale Cl. Orp 35 D1
Scotsdale Rd. SE12 16 B3
Scott Ave. Rai (K) 62 B3
Scott Cl. Dit 87 F2
Scott Cres. Eri 5 D1
Scott Rd. Grave 41 F4
Scott Rd. Ton 136 A2
Scott St. Maid 89 D1
Scotteswood Ave. Chath 60 A3
Scott's Ave. Brom 33 D2
Scotts Pas. SE18 2 B3
Scotts Rd. Brom 33 E3
Scott's Terr. Chath 60 A4
Scotts Way. Sev 81 D1
Scotts Way. T W 167 D2
Scragged Oak Rd. S Grn 91 F3
Scragged Oak Rd. Sto 75 F1
Scratchers La. W Kin 54 A1
Scratton Fields. Cob 56 C4
Scrubbs La. Maid 106 A4
Scudders Hill. Faw 54 C4
Seabrook Dr. W Wick 48 A2
Seabrook Rd. Ton 136 B4
Seabrooke Rise. Grays 8 B2
Seacourt Rd. SE2 3 F4
Seagull Rd. Roc 43 F1
Seal Dr. Seal 82 A1
Seal Hollow Rd. Sev 98 C4
Seal Rd. Sev 81 F1
Sealcroft Cotts. Seal 82 A2
Seaton Rd. Dart 20 B2
Seaton Rd. Gil 61 D4
Seaton Rd. Well 3 F2
Seaview. I o G 15 E1
Seaview Rd. Gil 60 C4
Second Ave. Chath 60 C3
Second Ave. Gil 61 D4
Second Ave. Grays 7 E2
Secretan Rd. Chath 59 E3
Sedcombe Cl. Sid 35 F4
Sedge Cres. Wald 74 A4
Sedgebrook Rd. SE3 16 C4
Sedgeway. SE6 16 A2
Sedgewood Cl. Brom 48 A3
Sedley. Souf 40 B3
Sedley Cl. Cli W 27 F2
Sedley Cl. Dit 88 A3
Sedley Cl. Rai (K) 75 F4
Sefton Cl. Orp 35 D1
Sefton Rd. Orp 35 D1
Selah Dr. Swan 36 C2
Selborne Ave. Bex 19 D2
Selborne Rd. Sid 35 E4
Selbourne Cl. Lon 40 C1
Selbourne Rd. Gil 45 F2
Selbourne Wlk. Maid 107 D1
Selby Cl. Chis 34 B3
Selby Rd. Maid 125 D4
Selkirk Dr. Eri 5 D1
Sellinge Green. Rai (K) 61 F4
Selsey Cres. Well 3 F1
Selstead Cl. Rai (K) 61 F3
Selwyn Cres. Well 18 B4
Selwyn Pl. Orp 35 E1
Senacre La. Maid 107 D1
Senacre Sq. Maid 107 D2
Senator Way. SE18 2 C4
Senlac Rd. SE12 16 B2
Sennen Wlk. SE9 17 D1
Sequoia Gdns. Orp 50 A3
Sermon Dr. Swan 36 C1
Serpentine Rd. Sev 98 C4
Service Rd. Cran 173 E1
Serviden Dr. Brom 33 F2
Setford Rd. Wald 60 C1
Settington Ave. Chath 60 C3
Seven Acres. N Ash 55 D2
Seven Acres. Swan 51 F4
Seven Mile La. E Pec 121 D3
Seven Mile La. Merew 102 B3
Seven Mile La. Off 85 D1
Sevenoaks Business Centre. Sev 81 F1
Sevenoaks By-Pass. Sev 98 A1
Sevenoaks By-Pass. Sev W 98 A1
Sevenoaks Cl. Bexh 19 E4
Sevenoaks Rd. Bor G 84 A2
Sevenoaks Rd. Ight 100 B4
Sevenoaks Rd. Orp 64 B3
Sevenoaks Rd. Otf 81 E3
Sevenoaks Way. Orp 35 F2
Severn Cl. Ton 118 C1
Severn Rd. Wald 60 C1
Sevington Park. Maid 106 A1
Sewell Rd. SE2 3 E4
Seymour Dr. Brom 49 D3
Seymour Rd. Chath 60 B4
Seymour Rd. Grave 24 A1
Seymour Rd. Rai (K) 62 C2
Shacklands Rd. Shorm 65 F2
Shackleton Cl. Chath 60 B1
Shades The. Roc 43 E2
Shaftesbury Cl. Dit 87 D3
Shaftesbury Dr. Maid 105 F4
Shaftesbury La. Dart 21 E4
Shaftesbury Rd. T W 153 E1
Shakespeare Rd. Bexh 4 A1
Shakespeare Rd. Dart 21 E4
Shakespeare Rd. Gil 60 C4
Shakespeare Rd. Ton 136 A2
Shalford Cl. Orp 49 F1
Shallons Rd. SE9 34 B4
Shambles The. Sev 98 C3
Shamley Rd. Wald 74 C3
Shamrock Rd. Grave 25 D2
Shandon Cl. T W 167 F4
Shanklin Cl. Chath 60 C2
Sharfleet Dr. Roc 43 E2
Sharland Rd. Grave 24 C1
Sharman Ct. Sid 35 E4
Sharnal La. Snod 72 B2
Sharnbrooke Cl. Well 18 C4
Sharon Cres. Wald 74 A4
Sharp Way. Dart 21 D4
Sharsted Way. Rai (K) 75 E4
Sharsted Way. Rose 90 B1
Shaw Cl. Cli W 27 E2
Shaw Path. Brom 16 A1
Shaw Rd. Brom 16 A1

Shaw The. T W 167 F3
Shawbrooke Rd. SE9 16 C4
Shawfield Park. Brom 33 F2
Shaws Way. Chath 59 F4
Shawstead Rd. Chath 60 C1
Shawstead Rd. Wald 74 C4
Sheafe Dr. Cran 173 F1
Sheal's Cres. Maid 106 B3
Shearers Cl. Thu 107 D4
Shearman Rd. SE3 16 A4
Shearwater. Lon 40 B1
Shearwater Cl. Roc 43 F2
Shearwood Cres. Dart 20 B4
Sheen Rd. Orp 35 D1
Sheepcote La. Swan 36 B1
Sheet Hill. Plax 101 D3
Sheffield Rd. Soub 153 D3
Sheiling The. Seal 82 A2
Shelbury Cl. Sid 18 B1
Shelden Dr. Rai (K) 62 A2
Sheldon Rd. Bexh 4 A1
Sheldon Way. Dit 87 E4
Shell Cl. Brom 49 D4
Shellbank La. Dart 39 E4
Shelldrake Cl. I o G 15 E1
Shelley Cl. Orp 50 A2
Shelley Dr. Well 3 D1
Shelley La. Kno P 79 E4
Shelley Rd. Maid 105 F3
Shelton Cl. Ton 118 C1
Shenden Cl. Sev 98 C2
Shenden Way. Sev 98 C2
Shenley Gr. Box 89 D3
Shenley Rd. Dart 21 E2
Shenstone Cl. Bexh 19 F4
Shepherd St. Grave 23 F2
Shepherds Cl. Orp 50 A2
Shepherds Gate. Rai (K) 61 D1
Shepherds Gate Dr. Thu 90 A1
Shepherds La. Dart 20 B2
Shepherds Way. Lan H 126 A4
Shepherds Way. Low St 30 C4
Shepherds Wlk. T W 167 F4
Shepherdsgrove La. Ede 148 A1
Shepperton Cl. Wald 74 C4
Shepperton Rd. Orp 49 F4
Sheppey Cl. Eri 5 E2
Sheppey Rd. Maid 106 B2
Sheppy Pl. Grave 24 B2
Sherard Rd. SE9 17 D3
Sheraton Ct. Wald 74 A3
Sherborne Cl. T W 167 F3
Sherborne Rd. Orp 50 A4
Sherbourne Cl. W Kin 68 A4
Sherbourne Dr. Maid 105 E3
Sherbrooke Cl. Bexh 19 E4
Sherenden La. Mard 158 C2
Sherenden La. Stapt 159 D2
Sherenden Park. Had 120 B1
Sherenden Rd. Tud 137 F2
Sherfield Rd. Grays 8 B2
Sheridan Cl. Chath 60 C2
Sheridan Cl. Maid 89 D2
Sheridan Cl. Swan 37 D1
Sheridan Cres. Chis 34 B2
Sheridan Ct. Dart 21 E4
Sheridan Rd. Belv 4 B3
Sheridan Rd. Bexh 19 D4
Sheriff Dr. Wald 74 B3
Sherington Rd. SE7 1 B2
Sherlies Ave. Orp 50 A2
Sherman Cl. Rai (K) 61 E3
Sherman Rd. Brom 33 E2
Shermanbury Pl. Eri 5 D2
Shernden La. Ede 131 F1
Shernolds. Maid 106 B2
Sherway Rd. Head 145 F1
Sherwood Ave. Wald 74 B3
Sherwood Cl. Bex 18 C3
Sherwood Park Ave. Sid 18 B3
Sherwood Rd. T W 153 F1
Sherwood Rd. Well 18 A4
Sherwood Way. T W 153 F1
Shieldhall St. SE2 3 F3
Shillingheld Cl. Thu 90 A1
Shingle Barn La. Yal 122 C4
Shinglewell Rd. Eri 4 B2
Ship La. Chath 60 A4
Ship La. S Ock 7 D4
Ship La. Sutt H 38 A2
Shipbourne Rd. Had 118 C3
Shipbourne Rd. Ton 118 C1
Shipbourne Rd. Ton 136 C4
Shipland Houses. Plu 147 F2
Shipley Hills Rd. Meo 56 A3
Shipwrights Ave. Chath 60 B3
Shire Ct. Belv 3 F4
Shire La. Dow 63 E4
Shire La. Orp 64 A4
Shire La. Stal 112 C1
Shirebrook Rd. SE3 16 C4
Shirehall Rd. Dart 37 F4
Shirehall Rd. Sutt H 38 A4
Shirley Ave. Bex 18 C2
Shirley Ave. Wald 59 F1
Shirley Cl. Dart 20 C4
Shirley Cl. Grave 25 E1
Shirley Gdns. T W 152 C1
Shirley Gr. T W 152 C1
Shirley House Dr. SE7 1 C2
Shirley Rd. Sid 18 A1
Shirley Way. Rose 107 E4
Sholden Gdns. Orp 50 C4
Sholden Rd. Roc 44 C3
Shooters Hill. SE18 2 B1
Shooters Hill Rd. SE18 2 A1
Shore The. Grave 24 A3
Shore The. Grave 23 F3
Shoreham Cl. Bex 18 C2
Shoreham La. Hals 65 E2
Shoreham La. Sev 98 A4
Shoreham La. Shorm 65 E4
Shoreham La. Ten 186 B4
Shoreham Pl. Shorm 66 B2
Shoreham Rd. Orp 35 E2
Shoreham Rd. Otf 81 F4
Shoreham Way. Brom 48 B4
Shoreham Wlk. Maid 107 D2
Shorehill La. Kemsg 82 A4
Shorne Cl. Orp 35 F1
Shorne Cl. Sid 18 B3
Shorne Ifield Rd. Shor 42 B3
Shornefield Cl. Brom 34 B1
Shornells Way. SE2 3 F3
Short La. Brenc 156 B1
Short La. Brenc 156 C2
Short La. Gil 46 B1
Short Path. SE18 2 B2
Short St. Chath 60 B4
Shortlands Gdns. Brom 33 D2
Shortlands Green. Maid 107 D1
Shortlands Rd. Brom 33 D2
Shorts Way. Chath 59 E4
Shortway. SE9 17 D4
Shottenden Rd. Gil 45 F2
Shottery Cl. SE9 17 D1
Showfields Rd. T W 167 D3
Shrapnel Cl. SE18 2 A2
Shrapnel Rd. SE9 17 D4
Shrewsbury La. SE18 2 B1
Shroffold Rd. Brom 33 D4
Shropshire Terr. Maid 107 D2
Shrubbery Rd. Dart 38 C2
Shrubbery Rd. Grave 24 C2
Shrubcote. Ten 186 C2
Shrublands Ct. T W 167 F4
Shrubsole Dr. Box 89 D4
Shurlock Ave. Swan 36 C2
Shurlock Dr. Orp 49 F1
Shuttle Cl. Bidd 176 B3
Shuttle Cl. Sid 18 A2
Shuttle Rd. Dart 20 B4
Shuttlemead. Bex 19 D3
Sibley Cl. Bexh 19 D3
Sibthorpe Rd. SE12 16 C2
Sidcup By Pass Rd. Sid 35 E3
Sidcup Hill. Sid 35 E4
Sidcup Hill Gdns. Sid 35 F4
Sidcup Rd. SE9 16 C2
Sidewood Rd. SE9 17 F2
Sidmouth Rd. Orp 35 E1
Sidmouth Rd. Well 3 F2
Sidney Cl. T W 167 D2
Sidney Gdns. Otf 81 F3
Sidney Rd. Chath 59 E3
Sidney Rd. Gil 45 F2
Sidney St. Maid 105 F3
Siebert Rd. SE3 1 B2
Siemens Rd. SE18 1 C4
Silchester Ct. Maid 89 F2
Silecroft Rd. Bexh 4 B1
Silk Cl. SE12 16 B3
Silver Birch Ave. Meo 70 A3
Silver Birch Cl. Bex 37 D4
Silver Cl. Ton 136 B1
Silver Hill. Chath 60 A4
Silver Hill. Chath 59 D3
Silver Hill. Ten 186 B3
Silver Rd. Grave 25 D1
Silver Spring Cl. Eri 4 B2
Silverdale. Hart (S) 40 A1
Silverdale. Maid 105 E3
Silverdale Dr. Rai (K) 62 A2
Silverdale Dr. SE9 17 D1
Silverdale La. T W 153 F1
Silverdale Rd. Bexh 4 B1
Silverdale Rd. Orp 34 C1
Silverdale Rd. Orp 35 E1
Silverdale Rd. T W 153 E1
Silverhurst Dr. Ton 118 C2
Silverlocke Rd. Grays 8 C2
Silverspot Cl. Rai (K) 62 A2
Silverstead La. Bigg 78 C1
Silverweed Rd. Wald 74 A4
Silwood Cl. T W 154 A2
Simmonds La. Oth 107 E1
Simmons Rd. SE18 2 B3
Simnel Rd. SE12 16 B2
Simone Cl. Brom 33 F2
Simpson Rd. Snod 72 B1
Simpson's Rd. Brom 33 E1
Sims Wlk. SE3 16 A4
Sinclair Way. Dart 38 C4
Sindals La. Bedh 75 D3
Singapore Dr. Gil 45 E1
Single St. Dow 78 B4
Single's Cross La. Kno P 64 C1
Singlewell Rd. Grave 24 B1
Singlewell Rd. Grave 41 E4
Sion Wlk. T W 167 E3
Sir David's Park. Soub 153 D2
Sir Evelyn Rd. Chath 59 E3
Sir Thomas Longley Rd. Roc 45 D1
Sirdar Strand. Grave 42 A4
Siskin Gdns. Padd W 139 E1
Siskin Wlk. Dit 87 D3
Sissinghurst Rd. Bidd 175 E3
Sittingbourne Rd. Maid 89 E1
Siward Rd. Brom 33 F1
Six Bells La. Sev 98 C3
Six Fields Path. Ten 186 B2
Skeet Hill La. Orp 51 E2
Skene Cl. Rai (K) 62 B3
Skeynes Rd. Ede 131 E3
Skibbs La. Orp 51 D2
Skinner St. Chath 60 A4
Skinner St. Gil 45 F1
Skinners Cl. Ayld 73 E1
Skinners La. Ede 131 F3
Skinner's Terr. Ton 136 B2
Skinner's Way. Lan H 126 A4
Skye Cl. Maid 106 B2
Slade Cl. Wald 74 B3
Slade Gdns. Eri 5 D1
Slade Green Rd. Eri 5 E2
Slade Rd. Len 111 F2
Slade The. Lam 179 E4
Slade The. SE18 3 D2
Slade The. Ton 136 B3
Sladebrook Rd. SE3 16 C4
Sladedale Rd. SE18 3 D3
Slades Dr. Chis 17 F1
Slaney Rd. Stapt 160 A4
Slaters. Chid 133 D3
Slatin Rd. Roc 44 B2
Sleepers Stile Rd. Lam 178 B3
Slicketts Hill. Chath 60 B4
Slip Mill Rd. Hawkt 189 D4
Slip North Rd. Chath 45 E2
Slip Rd. Chath 45 E2
Slip The. Whm 95 F3
Sloane Gdns. Orp 49 F2
Slough Rd. Rod 94 B4
Small Bridge La. Hors 171 E3
Small Grains. Faw 54 B2
Small Hythe Rd. Ten 193 F3
Small Profits. Yal 122 B4
Smarden Cl. Belv 4 B3
Smarden Gr. SE9 34 A4
Smarden Rd. Bidd 162 C1
Smarden Rd. Head 162 B4
Smarden Rd. Plu 147 E1
Smarden Wlk. Rai (K) 62 B3
Smarts Hill. Pen 151 E3
Smarts Rd. Grave 24 C1
Smith Hill. W Far 104 C1
Smith Rd. Wald 74 B4
Smith St. Roc 44 B2
Smithers Cl. Had 120 A3
Smithers La. E Pec 121 E2
Smithfield Rd. I o G 15 F1
Smithies Rd. SE2 3 E3
Smiths Hill. Yal 122 C4
Smiths La. Whm 113 F3
Smugglers. Hawkt 189 E3
Smythe Cl. Soub 153 D4
Smythe Rd. Sutt H 38 B2
Snag La. Dow 63 F2
Snelling Ave. Grave 24 A1
Snipe Cl. Pem 155 D2
Snoad La. Stapt 159 E2
Snodhurst Ave. Wald 60 A1
Snodland Cl. Dow 63 E3
Snodland Rd. Birl 71 F2
Snoll Hatch Rd. E Pec 121 D1
Snowdon Ave. Maid 89 E1
Snowdon Cl. Chath 60 B2
Snughorne La. Sma 162 C2
Socket La. Brom 48 B4
Sole Street. Cob 56 C4
Solefields Rd. Sev 98 C2
Soleoak Dr. Sev 98 C2
Solomon Rd. Rai (K) 62 B3
Solomons Rd. Chath 60 A4
Somerden Rd. Orp 50 C3
Somerfield Cl. Maid 88 C1
Somerfield La. Maid 106 A4
Somerfield Rd. Maid 105 F4
Somerhill Ave. Sid 18 B2
Somerhill Rd. Ton 136 C2
Somerhill Rd. Well 3 E1
Somerset Ave. Well 18 A4
Somerset Cl. Chath 60 C2
Somerset Rd. Dart 20 B3
Somerset Rd. Maid 106 C2
Somerset Rd. Orp 50 B3
Somerset Rd. T W 153 E1
Somersham Rd. Bexh 4 A1
Somertrees Ave. SE12 16 B1
Somerville Gdns. T W 167 D4
Somerville Rd. Dart 21 D3
Somner Wlk. Maid 125 D4
Soper's La. Hawkt 188 C4
Sophurst La. Mat 155 F1
Sorrel Ct. Grays 8 C2
Sorrel Way. Grave 41 D4
Sorrell Cl. Ede 131 F4
Sorrell Rd. Wald 74 A4
Sounds Lodge. Swan 51 F4
South Ash Rd. Stans 68 C3
South Ave. Rai (K) 61 E3
South Bank. Stapt 160 A3
South Bank. Sutt V 126 A2
South Bank. Whm 95 F3
South Bush La. Rai (K) 62 B2
South Cl. Bexh 18 C4
South Cres. Cox 123 F4
South Dr. Orp 50 A1
South Eastern Rd. Roc 44 C2
South Gate. Pur 6 C3
South Gipsy Rd. Well 18 C4
South Glade The. Bex 19 D2
South Gr. T W 167 E3
South Green La. S Grn 77 D1
South Hill. Chis 34 A3
South Hill Rd. Brom 33 D1
South Hill Rd. Grave 24 C2
South Kent Ave. Grave 23 F3
South La. Sutt V 126 A1
South Park. Sev 98 B3
South Park Cres. SE6 16 A2
South Park Rd. Maid 106 C3
South Pondside Rd. Chath 45 E2
South Rd. Eri 5 D2
South Rd. Gil 45 E2
South Rd. Gil 45 E2
South Rd. Mard 142 A1
South Row. SE3 1 A1
South Side Three Rd. Gil 45 F2
South Side Two Rd. Gil 45 E3
South St. Brom 33 E2
South St. Grave 24 B2
South St. Maid 105 D3
South St. Meo 56 A2
South Street Rd. Sto 76 B2
South View. Brom 33 F2
South View Cl. Bex 19 D3
South View Rd. Dart 20 C1
South View Rd. Grays 7 F2
South View Rd. Soub 153 E2
South View Rd. Wad 178 A1
South Wlk. W Wick 48 A2
Southborough La. Brom 49 D4
Southborough Rd. Brom 34 A1
Southbourne. Brom 48 B3
Southbourne Gdns. SE12 16 B3
Southbourne Gr. Wald 74 B4
Southbrook Rd. SE12 16 A3
Southcroft Ave. Well 18 A4
Southcroft Rd. Orp 50 A2
Southdene. Hals 65 D1
Southend Cl. SE9 17 E3
Southend Cres. SE9 17 E3
Southend Rd. Grays 8 C3
Southern Pl. Swan 36 C1
Southernden Rd. Bou Mal 145 F3
Southey Way. Dit 87 D4
Southfield Rd. Chis 35 E1
Southfield Rd. Spel 152 B2
Southfield Rd. T W 153 E1
Southfield Shaw. Meo 70 B3
Southfields. Chath 59 F4
Southfields. Hex 37 D3
Southfields. Wad 178 A1
Southfields Rd. W Kin 21 F1
Southfields Way. Soub 153 E2
Southfleet Ave. Lon 40 B2
Southfleet Rd. Dart 39 F4
Southfleet Rd. Grave 24 A2
Southfleet Rd. Orp 50 A1
Southfleet Rd. Swans 23 E2
Southgate Rd. Ten 186 C2
Southill Rd. Chath 60 A4
Southill Rd. Chis 34 A3
Southland Rd. SE18 3 D2
Southlands Gr. Brom 34 A1
Southlands Rd. Brom 33 F1
Southlees La. S Grn 92 A4
Southold Rise. SE9 17 D1
Southover. Brom 33 E4
Southport Rd. SE18 2 C3
Southspring. Sid 17 F2
Southvale Rd. SE3 1 A1
Southview Cl. Swan 37 E1
Southwark Pl. Brom 34 A1
Southwark Rd. Roc 43 F1
Southway. Brom 48 B3
Southwell Rd. Roc 43 F1
Southwold Rd. Bex 19 E3
Southwood. Maid 105 D3
Southwood Ave. T W 153 E1
Southwood Cl. Brom 34 A1
Southwood Rd. SE9 17 E1
Southwood Rd. T W 152 B1
Sovereign Bvd. Rai (K) 61 D3
Sovereign Way. Ton 136 C3
Sovereigns Way. Mard 141 F1
Sowerby Cl. SE9 17 D3
Spade La. New(G) 62 C1
Spade La. Upc 62 C1
Sparepenny La. Eyn 53 D3
Sparepenny La. Farn 53 D3
Sparkeswood Ave. Rol 192 A4
Sparkeswood Cl. Rol 192 A4
Sparrow Dr. Orp 49 F3
Sparrows Green Rd. Wad 178 A1
Sparrows La. SE9 17 F2
Spearhead Rd. Maid 89 D2
Spearman St. SE18 2 B2
Speedgate Hill. Faw 54 B2
Speedwell Ave. Wald 74 A4
Speedwell Cl. Ede 131 F4
Speedwell Cl. Thu 90 A1
Speekhill. SE9 17 D1
Spekes Rd. Rai (K) 61 E1
Speldhurst Cl. Brom 48 A4
Speldhurst Ct. Maid 105 F4
Speldhurst Hill. Spel 152 B2
Speldhurst Rd. Soub 153 D2
Speldhurst Rd. Spel 152 A1
Spelmonden Rd. Hors 171 D3
Spencer Cl. Orp 50 A2
Spencer Cl. Wald 60 B1
Spencer Rd. Brom 33 D3
Spencer St. Grave 24 B2
Spencer Way. Maid 107 D2
Spenlow Dr. Wald 74 B2
Spenny La. Yal 140 C2
Speranza St. SE18 3 D3
Speyside. Ton 118 B1
Spielman Rd. Dart 21 D4
Spillway The. Maid 105 F3
Spindle Glade. Maid 89 F1
Spindlewood Cl. Wald 74 B4
Spinel Cl. SE18 3 D3
Spinners Cl. Bidd 176 B3
Spinney Oak. Brom 34 A2
Spinney The. Maid 106 B3
Spinney The. Sid 36 A4
Spinney The. Swan 37 D2
Spinney The. Ton 136 B2
Spinney The. Wald 74 B3
Spinney Way. Dow 63 F2
Spinneys The. Brom 34 A2
Spire Cl. Grave 24 B2
Spires The. Dart 20 C1
Spires The. Maid 105 F4
Spires The. Roc 43 F1
Spital St. Dart 20 C3
Spitfire Cl. Chath 60 B1
Spitfire Rd. Merew 103 D4
Spode La. Cow 149 E2
Sponden La. Sand 190 B2
Spongs La. Cran 174 B3
Sportsfield. Maid 89 E1
Spot La. Oth 107 E3
Spot La. Rose 107 E3
Spout La. Brenc 156 C1
Spout La. Whm 113 F3
Spray Hill. Lam 179 E4
Spray St. SE18 2 B3
Sprig The. Rose 107 E4
Spring Cross. N Ash 55 E2
Spring Gdns. Orp 64 B4
Spring Gdns. T W 166 B4
Spring Gr. Grave 24 B2
Spring Head Rd. Kemsg 82 A3
Spring Hill. Pen 151 E1
Spring La. Bid 152 C4
Spring La. Ight 83 E1
Spring Vale. Bexh 19 E4
Spring Vale. Dart 20 C3
Spring Vale. Gree 22 C3
Spring Vale Cl. Hex 37 D2
Spring Vale N. Dart 20 C3
Spring Vale S. Dart 20 C2
Springbank Rd. SE13 16 A3
Springcroft. Hart (S) 55 E4
Springett Cl. Ayld 73 D1
Springett Way. Cox 123 F4
Springfield Ave. Maid 89 D2
Springfield Ave. Swan 37 D1
Springfield Ave. Ten 186 C3
Springfield Gdns. Brom 34 A1
Springfield Gr. SE7 1 C2
Springfield Rd. Bexh 19 E4
Springfield Rd. Brom 34 A1
Springfield Rd. Dit 87 D4
Springfield Rd. Ede 131 E3
Springfield Rd. Gil 46 A1
Springfield Rd. Grays 8 C4
Springfield Rd. Gro 165 F2
Springfield Rd. Soub 153 D3
Springfield Rd. Well 18 B4
Springfield Wlk. Orp 49 F3
Springfields. Tic 187 D3
Springhead. T W 153 F1
Springhead Enterprise Park. Grave 23 F2
Springhead Rd. Eri 5 D2
Springhead Rd. Grave 23 F2
Springshaw Cl. Sev 97 F4
Springvale. Rai (K) 61 F1
Springwater Cl. SE18 2 B1
Springwell Rd. Ton 136 B2
Springwood Cl. Maid 105 E4
Springwood Rd. Maid 105 E4
Spruce Cl. Dit 87 E3
Sprucedale Cl. Swan 37 D2
Spur Rd. Orp 50 B2
Spurrell Ave. Sid 36 C4
Spurway. Rose 107 E4
Spurway The. T W 166 C3
Square Hill. Maid 106 B4
Square Hill Rd. Maid 106 B4
Square The. Cow 149 E1
Square The. Had 120 A2
Square The. Lei 135 D3
Square The. Len 110 C1
Square The. Sev 81 D1
Square The. Swan 36 C1
Squerryes Mede. Whm 95 F2
Squires Cl. Roc 43 E2
Squires Way. Sid 36 C4
Squires Wood Dr. Chis 34 A3
Squirrel Way. T W 154 A1
Stable Cl. Bex 19 F1
Stable Cl. Wald 60 C1
Stabledene Way. Pem 154 C1
Stables End. Orp 49 F2
Stace Cl. Ten 186 C2
Stacey Cl. Grave 42 A4
Stacey Rd. Ton 136 B4
Staceys St. Maid 89 D1
Stack La. Hart (S) 55 D4
Stack Rd. Hort 39 D1
Stackfield. Ede 131 F4
Stacklands Cl. W Kin 68 A4
Stadium Rd. SE18 2 A2
Stadium Way. Dart 20 A3
Staffa Rd. Maid 106 B2
Stafford Rd. Sid 35 D4
Stafford Rd. Ton 136 B3
Stafford St. Gil 45 F1
Stafford Way. Sev 98 C2
Stag Rd. T W 154 A2
Stag Rd. Wald 60 B1
Stainer Rd. Ton 119 D1
Staines Wlk. Sid 35 F3
Stainmore Cl. Chis 34 C2
Stair Rd. Ton 137 D4
Stairfoot La. Sev 80 C1
Stake La. Hall 58 B1
Staleys Rd. Bor G 84 A2
Stalham Ct. Rai (K) 75 E4
Stalin Ave. Chath 60 B2
Stalisfield Pl. Dow 63 E3
Stalisfield Rd. Stal 112 C2
Stamford Dr. Brom 33 D1
Stampers The. Maid 105 F3
Stan La. W Pec 102 B2
Stanam Rd. Pem 155 D1
Stanbridge Rd. Ede 131 E3
Stanbrook Rd. Grave 24 A2
Stanbrook Rd. SE2 3 E4
Standard Rd. Belv 4 B3

Standard Rd. Bexh 19 D4
Standard Rd. Dow 63 E3
Standen Cl. Rai (K) 76 A4
Standen St. Ben 190 C3
Standen St. T W 153 E1
Stane Way. SE18 2 A2
Stanford Dr. Maid 105 F4
Stanford La. E Pec 120 C3
Stanford Rd. Grays 8 C4
Stanford Way. Cux 58 C3
Stangate Rd. Birl 71 F2
Stangate Rd. Roc 43 F2
Stangrove Rd. Ede 131 F3
Stanham Pl. Dart 20 B4
Stanham Rd. Dart 20 C3
Stanhope Ave. Brom 48 B3
Stanhope Rd. Bexh 4 A1
Stanhope Rd. Maid 89 D2
Stanhope Rd. Roc 44 B2
Stanhope Rd. Sid 35 E4
Stanhope Rd. Swans 23 D3
Stanhope Rd. T W 153 F1
Stanhope Way. Sev 80 C1
Stanley Cl. Gree 22 A3
Stanley Cl. Stapt 159 F4
Stanley Cres. Grave 41 F4
Stanley Rd. Brom 33 F1
Stanley Rd. Gil 45 F1
Stanley Rd. Grave 24 A2
Stanley Rd. Grays 8 B2
Stanley Rd. Mard 141 F1
Stanley Rd. Orp 50 A3
Stanley Rd. Sid 18 B1
Stanley Rd. Swans 23 D3
Stanley Rd. T W 153 E1
Stanley Rd. Wald 60 C1
Stanley Way. Orp 50 B4
Stanmore Rd. Belv 4 C3
Stanstead Cl. Brom 48 A4
Stansted Cl. Maid 88 C2
Stansted Cres. Bex 18 C2
Stansted Hill. Stans 69 E3
Stansted La. W Kin 68 C3
Stanton Cl. Orp 50 C3
Staple Dr. Stapt 160 A4
Stapleford Ct. Sev 98 A4
Staplehurst Rd. Frit 160 C3
Staplehurst Rd. Mard 142 B4
Staplehurst Rd. Rai (K) 61 E4
Staplehurst Rd. SE13 16 A3
Staplers Ct. Maid 89 E2
Stapleton Rd. Bexh 4 A2
Stapleton Rd. Orp 50 A2
Stapley Rd. Belv 4 B3
Star Hill. Chath 44 C1
Star Hill. Dart 20 A3
Star Hill Rd. Chev 80 B3
Star La. Orp 36 A1
Star La. Rai (K) 61 E2
Star Mill La. Chath 60 C3
Starboard Ave. Gree 22 B3
Starborough Rd. Ede 131 D1
Starling Cl. Lon 40 B1
Starts Cl. Orp 49 E2
Starts Hill Ave. Orp 49 E1
Starts Hill Rd. Orp 49 E1
Starvecrow Cl. Ton 118 C2
State Farm Ave. Orp 49 F1
Station App. Bexh 4 A1
Station App. Bexh 4 C1
Station App. Brom 48 B3
Station App. Chis 34 A3
Station App. Chis 34 B2
Station App. Dart 21 D3
Station App. Ede 131 F3
Station App. Grays 8 B2
Station App. Hall 58 B1
Station App. Maid 106 A4
Station App. Orp 50 A2
Station App. Orp 50 B1
Station App. Orp 35 E1
Station App. Padd W 139 E2
Station App. SE3 16 B4
Station App. SE9 17 D2
Station App. Stapt 143 D1
Station App. Swan 37 D1
Station App. Well 3 E1
Station Approach Rd. Tilb 24 B4
Station Cres. SE3 1 B3
Station Hill. Brom 48 B2
Station Hill. Lei 134 B2
Station Rd. Asht 164 B1
Station Rd. Ayld 88 A3
Station Rd. Belv 4 B4
Station Rd. Bexh 19 D4
Station Rd. Bor G 84 A2
Station Rd. Bras 96 B4
Station Rd. Brom 33 D2
Station Rd. Brom 33 E2
Station Rd. Char 130 C2
Station Rd. Cli 27 E4
Station Rd. Cux 58 C3
Station Rd. Dart 20 A3
Station Rd. Dunt 81 D2
Station Rd. E Far 105 E2
Station Rd. Ede 131 F4
Station Rd. Eyn 52 C2
Station Rd. Farn 38 B2
Station Rd. Gou 171 F2
Station Rd. Grave 40 A4
Station Rd. Grave 23 E3
Station Rd. Gree 22 B3
Station Rd. Gro 165 F2
Station Rd. Hals 65 D2
Station Rd. Harr 109 F1
Station Rd. Head 144 C1
Station Rd. Lon 40 A1
Station Rd. Maid 89 D1
Station Rd. Meo 56 B4
Station Rd. Net 121 F3
Station Rd. Norm 195 F2
Station Rd. Orp 50 A2
Station Rd. Orp 35 F1
Station Rd. Otf 81 F4
Station Rd. Padd W 139 D2
Station Rd. Plu 147 F1
Station Rd. Rai (K) 62 B3
Station Rd. Roc 44 C2
Station Rd. Shorn 66 B2
Station Rd. Sid 18 B1
Station Rd. Stapt 143 D1
Station Rd. Swan 37 D1
Station Rd. Ten 186 B2
Station Road N. Belv 4 B4
Station Sq. Orp 35 E1
Station Sq. Orp 49 F4
Steadman Cl. Higham 26 C1
Stede Hill. Harr 110 A3
Stede Hill. Holli 110 A3
Stedman Cl. Bex 20 A1
Steele Ave. Gree 22 B3
Steele St. Roc 44 B2
Steele's La. Meo 56 B1
Steep Cl. Orp 64 A4
Steerforth Cl. Chath 59 F3
Steers Pl. Had 120 A3
Stelling Rd. Eri 4 C2
Stephen Cl. Orp 50 A2
Stephen Rd. Bexh 19 F4
Stephen's Rd. T W 153 E1
Stepneyford La. Ben 184 C2
Steps Hill Rd. Sto 76 C1
Sterling Ave. Maid 88 C1
Sterndale Rd. Dart 21 D2
Stevedale Rd. Well 3 F1
Stevens Cl. Sid 36 C4
Stevens Cl. Snod 72 B2
Stevens Rd. Ayld 73 D1
Stevenson Cl. Eri 5 E2
Stevenson Way. Dit 87 D4
Stewart Rd. Soub 153 F2
Steyning Gr. SE9 34 A4
Steynton Ave. Bex 19 D1
Stickens La. Dit 87 D2
Stickfast La. Head 144 C4
Stickfast La. Ulc 145 D4
Stickland Rd. Belv 4 B3
Stilebridge La. Lint 142 A4
Stilebridge La. Lint 124 B1
Stiles Cl. Brom 49 D4
Stirling Cl. Chath 59 E4
Stirling Cl. Rai (K) 76 A4
Stirling Dr. Orp 50 B1
Stisted Way. Ege 147 D4
Stock La. Dart 37 F4
Stockbury Dr. Maid 88 C2
Stockenbury. E Pec 121 D1
Stockett La. Cox 123 F4
Stockett La. Maid 106 A2
Stockland Green Rd. Spel 152 C2
Stocks Green Rd. Hild 117 F1
Stockton Cl. Maid 89 E2
Stockwell Cl. Brom 33 E2
Stoddards La. Beckl 196 A1
Stofield Gdns. SE9 16 C1
Stoke Rd. All 13 F2
Stoke Rd. Hoo S W 29 E2
Stone Alley. Chath 60 B4
Stone Court La. Pem 155 D2
Stone Hill Rd. Ege 147 D3
Stone Ness Rd. Grays 7 E2
Stone Pit La. Sand 191 D1
Stone Place Rd. Gree 22 A3
Stone Rd. Brom 48 A4
Stone St. Cran 173 F1
Stone St. Grave 24 B3
Stone St. T W 167 E4
Stone Street Rd. Ight 100 B3
Stone Street Rd. Seal 99 F4
Stoneacre Cl. Rai (K) 61 F1
Stoneacre La. Maid 107 E2
Stonebridge Green Rd. Ege 147 D4
Stonebridge Rd. Grave 23 E3
Stonecroft. Meo 70 B2
Stonecroft Rd. Eri 4 C2
Stonecross Rd. Chath 60 C3
Stonefield Cl. Bexh 19 E4
Stonefield Way. SE7 1 C2
Stonegate Cl. Orp 35 F1
Stonehorse La. Cli W 44 B3
Stonehouse La. Grays 7 D3
Stonehouse La. Hals 65 D3
Stonehouse Rd. Dow 64 C3
Stoneings La. Kno P 79 D2
Stoneleigh Rd. Lim C 95 D1
Stones Cross Rd. Swan 51 F4
Stonestile Farm Rd. Char 130 B4
Stonestile Rd. Head 144 B2
Stonewall Park Rd. Spel 166 A4
Stonewood. Dart 22 C1
Stonewood Rd. Eri 5 D3
Stoney Alley. SE18 2 B1
Stoneycroft Cl. SE12 16 A2
Stony Cnr. Ist 41 D1
Stony Cnr. Meo 41 D1
Stony La. Gou 172 A2
Stony La. Wou 59 F1
Stonyfield. Ede 131 F4
Stopford Rd. Gil 60 C4
Store Rd. E16 2 B4
Storey St. E16 2 B4
Stornaway Strand. Grave 42 A4
Stour Cl. Kes 48 C1
Stour Cl. Roc 44 A2
Stour Rd. Dart 20 B4
Stowe Rd. Orp 50 B1
Stowting Rd. Orp 50 A1
Strand Approach Rd. Gil 46 A2
Strand Cl. Meo 56 B3
Strandfield Cl. SE18 3 D3
Stratford Ave. Rai (K) 61 F2
Stratford Rd. W Mal 86 B2
Stratford St. T W 153 F1
Strathaven Rd. SE12 16 B3
Strathede Rd. SE3 1 B2
Stratton Cl. Bexh 19 D4
Stratton Rd. Bexh 19 D4
Stratton Terr. Whm 95 F2
Straw Mill Hill. Maid 106 A3
Strawberry Cl. T W 167 D2
Strawberry Fields. Swan 37 D2
Strawberry Vale. Ton 136 C3
Stream La. Hawkt 189 E2
Stream Side. Ton 118 C1
Stream The. Dit 87 F3
Stream Way. Belv 4 B2
Streamdale. SE2 3 E2
Streampit La. Sand 190 B1
Streamside. Dit 87 E3
Streamside Cl. Brom 33 E1
Streatfield. Ede 131 F3
Street End Rd. Chath 60 B3
Street The. Ben 183 F1
Street The. Birl 86 A4
Street The. Box 89 F4
Street The. Bredh 75 E3
Street The. Cob 42 B1
Street The. Cran 174 B2
Street The. Dod 94 C2
Street The. Ege 147 D4
Street The. H Hals 29 D4
Street The. Hall 58 A1
Street The. Hort 38 C1
Street The. Ight 83 F1
Street The. Meo 56 B3
Street The. Merew 102 C2
Street The. N Ash 55 D1
Street The. New(G) 62 C1
Street The. Plax 101 D2
Street The. Rose 107 F4
Street The. Shor 43 D4
Street The. Tes 104 B2
Street The. Thu 90 B3
Street The. Trot 70 B1
Street The. Ulc 127 D2
Street The. Witt 197 F4
Street The. Worm 93 E2
Streetfield. Ulc 127 D2
Streetfield Mews. SE3 16 B4
Streetfield Rd. Rai (K) 62 A3
Strettitt Gdns. E Pec 121 D1
Strickland Ave. Dart 21 D4
Strickland Way. Orp 50 A1
Strongbow Cres. SE9 17 D3
Strongbow Rd. SE9 17 D3
Strover St. Gil 45 F2
Struttons Ave. Grave 24 A1
Stuart Ave. Brom 48 B3
Stuart Cl. Hex 37 E3
Stuart Cl. Maid 89 E1
Stuart Cl. T W 167 D2
Stuart Evans Cl. Well 18 C4
Stuart Mantle Way. Eri 5 D2
Stuart Rd. Gil 60 C4
Stuart Rd. Grave 24 B3
Stuart Rd. Grays 8 B3
Stuart Rd. Well 3 E1
Stubbs Hill. Kno P 64 C1
Studland Cl. Sid 18 A1
Studley Cres. Lon 40 C2
Studley Ct. Sid 35 E4
Stumble Hill. Ship 100 C1
Sturdee Ave. Gil 61 D4
Sturges Field. Chis 34 C3
Sturla Rd. Chath 60 B4
Sturry Way. Rai (K) 61 F3
Styants Bottom Rd. Ight 83 D1
Style Cl. Rai (K) 76 A4
Styles Cl. Four E 114 B1
Styles Cotts. Four E 114 B1
Sudbury Cres. Brom 33 E4
Suffolk Ave. Rai (K) 62 A3
Suffolk Rd. Dart 21 D3
Suffolk Rd. Grave 24 C3
Suffolk Rd. Maid 106 C2
Suffolk Rd. Sid 35 F3
Suffolk Way. Sev 98 C3
Sugar Loaf Hill. Chath 60 C3
Sullivan Rd. Ton 119 D1
Sultan Rd. Wald 74 C3
Summer Cl. Ten 186 C3
Summer Hill. Chis 34 B2
Summerfield St. SE12 16 A2
Summerhill. Head 144 B1
Summerhill Ave. Soub 153 D3
Summerhill Cl. Orp 50 A2
Summerhill Rd. Dart 20 C2
Summerhill Rd. Mard 142 B3
Summerhouse Dr. Sid 36 C4
Summervale Rd. T W 167 D3
Sumner Cl. Orp 49 F1
Sumner Cl. Rol 192 A4
Sun Ct. Eri 5 D1
Sun Hill. Faw 54 B2
Sun La. Grave 24 C1
Sun La. SE3 1 B2
Sun Rd. Swans 23 D3
Sunbury St. SE18 2 A4
Sunderland Cl. Chath 59 E4
Sunderland Sq. Rai (K) 62 B2
Sundew Ct. Grays 8 C2
Sundorne Rd. SE7 1 C3
Sundridge Ave. Brom 33 F2
Sundridge Ave. Well 17 F4
Sundridge Dr. Wald 74 B4
Sundridge Hill. Cux 58 C4
Sundridge Hill. Sund 79 F2
Sundridge La. Kno P 79 F3
Sundridge Rd. Chev 80 B3
Sundridge Rd. Dart 21 E3
Sunfields Pl. SE3 1 B2
Sunland Ave. Bexh 19 D4
Sunningdale Cl. Rai (K) 61 F1
Sunningdale Dr. Rai (K) 61 F1
Sunningdale Rd. Brom 34 A1
Sunninghill. Grave 24 A1
Sunnydale. Orp 49 E2
Sunnydale Rd. SE12 16 B3
Sunnyfield Rd. Chis 35 E1
Sunnyfields Cl. Rai (K) 62 A2
Sunnymead Ave. Gil 46 A1
Sunnyside. Ede 131 E4
Sunnyside Rd. T W 166 C4
Sunray Ave. Brom 49 D4
Surrenden Rd. Stapt 160 A4
Surrey Cl. T W 167 D2
Surrey Rd. Maid 106 C2
Susan Rd. SE3 1 B1
Susan Wood. Chis 34 B2
Sussex Cl. T W 167 F3
Sussex Dr. Wald 74 B4
Sussex Mews. T W 167 E3
Sussex Rd. Dart 21 E2
Sussex Rd. Eri 4 B2
Sussex Rd. Maid 106 C3
Sussex Rd. Orp 50 C4
Sussex Rd. Sid 35 E4
Sussex Rd. Ton 136 B2
Sutcliffe Rd. SE18 3 D2
Sutcliffe Rd. Well 3 F1
Sutherland Ave. Bigg 78 A3
Sutherland Ave. Orp 50 A4
Sutherland Ave. Well 18 A4
Sutherland Cl. Grave 25 E1
Sutherland Gdns. Rai (K) 62 A1
Sutherland Rd. Belv 4 B4
Sutherland Rd. T W 167 E4
Sutlej Rd. SE7 1 C2
Sutton Rd. Lan H 107 E1
Sutton Rd. Maid 106 C2
Sutton St. Rose 107 F4
Swaffield Rd. Sev 81 F1
Swain Cl. Roc 44 A2
Swain Rd. Rai (K) 61 E1
Swain Rd. Ten 186 C4
Swaisland Rd. Dart 20 B3
Swaislands Dr. Dart 20 A3
Swale Rd. Dart 20 B4
Swale Rd. Roc 43 F2
Swaledale Rd. Dart 21 F2
Swallow Cl. Gree 22 A3
Swallow Dr. T W 154 A1
Swallow Rd. Dit 87 E3
Swallow Rise. Wald 60 B1
Swallowfield Rd. SE7 1 B3
Swallowfields. Grave 24 A1
Swan Cl. Orp 35 E1
Swan Cotts. Witt 197 F4
Swan La. Dart 20 A2
Swan La. Ede 131 E4
Swan La. Gou 172 A4
Swan Rd. SE18 1 C4
Swan Ridge. Ede 131 F4
Swan St. Witt 197 F4
Swan Yd. Grave 24 B3
Swanbridge Rd. Bexh 4 B1
Swanland Dr. Ton 136 A2
Swanley La. Swan 37 D2
Swanley Rd. Well 3 F1
Swanley Village Rd. Hex 37 F2
Swanmead Way. Ton 136 C3
Swanscombe St. Swans 23 D3
Swanton Rd. Eri 4 B2
Swanton Rd. Merew 102 B2
Swanton Rd. W Pec 102 B2
Swanzy Rd. Sev 81 F2
Sward Rd. Orp 50 B4
Swattenden La. Cran 182 B3
Swaylands Rd. Belv 4 B2
Swaynesland Rd. Lim C 113 D3
Sweeps Hill Cl. Pem 154 C2
Sweeps La. Orp 36 A1
Sweetings La. Wad 178 C3
Sweets La. Dit 104 B4
Swetenham Wlk. SE18 2 C3
Sweyn Pl. SE3 1 B1
Sweyne Rd. Swans 23 D3
Swift Cl. Dit 87 E3
Swift Cres. Chath 60 C1
Swifts View. Cran 173 F1
Swiftsden Way. Brom 33 D3
Swiller's La. Shor 43 D4
Swingate Ave. Cli 10 B1
Swingate Cl. Wald 74 B3
Swingate La. SE18 3 D2
Swinton Ave. Hoo S W 28 A1
Swires Shaw. Kes 48 C1
Swithland Gdns. SE9 34 B4
Sycamore Ave. Sid 18 A3
Sycamore Cl. Grave 24 C2
Sycamore Cl. SE9 17 D1
Sycamore Cotts. Pem 154 C1
Sycamore Cres. Maid 88 C1
Sycamore Dr. Dit 88 A3
Sycamore Dr. Swan 37 D2
Sycamore Gdns. Padd W 139 D1
Sycamore Rd. Dart 20 C2
Sycamore Rd. Roc 44 A1
Sychem La. Five O G 138 B1
Sychem Pl. Five O G 138 B2
Sydney Rd. Bexh 18 C4
Sydney Rd. Chath 60 B4
Sydney Rd. SE2 3 F4
Sydney Rd. Sid 35 D4
Sylewood Cl. Chath 59 E2
Sylvan Cl. Grays 8 A3
Sylvan Glade. Wald 74 B2
Sylvan Rd. Rai (K) 61 F2
Sylvan Way. W Wick 48 A1
Sylvester Ave. Chis 34 A3
Symonds Cl. W Kin 54 A1
Symonds La. Yal 122 A1
Symonds Rd. Cli 27 E4
Symons Ave. Chath 60 B3
Syringa Ct. Grays 8 C2

Tadburn Gr. Wald 74 B4
Taddington Wood La. Wald 74 A3
Tail Race The. Maid 106 A3
Tainter Rd. Had 120 A3
Talbot Park. T W 153 F1
Talbot Pl. SE3 1 A1
Talbot Rd. Brom 33 E1
Talbot Rd. Hawkt 189 D2
Talbot Rd. Maid 88 C1
Tall Elms Cl. Brom 48 A4
Tall Trees Cl. Broom (m) 126 C3
Tallents Cl. Sutt H 38 B3
Tallis Gr. SE7 1 B2
Tally Rd. Lim C 113 D4
Tamar Dr. Roc 44 A2
Tamar Rd. Ton 118 B1
Tamar St. SE7 2 A4
Tamarind Cl. Rai (K) 75 E4
Tamesis Strand. Grave 42 A4
Tan Yard La. Bex 19 E2
Tandridge Dr. Orp 49 F3
Tandridge Pl. Orp 49 F3
Tangier La. T W 167 F2
Tanglewood Cl. Rai (K) 61 F1
Tangmere Cl. Gil 46 A1
Tanhurst Wlk. Belv 3 F4
Tank Hill Rd. Pur 6 B3
Tank La. Pur 6 B3
Tanker Hill. Rai (K) 61 F1
Tannery Rd. Ton 136 C3
Tanyard. Sand 190 B1
Tanyard Hill. Shor 43 D3
Tarling Cl. Sid 18 B1
Tarnwood Park. SE9 17 D2
Taswell Rd. Rai (K) 62 B3
Tates. Hawkt 189 E3
Tatler Cl. Wald 74 C3
Tatsfield Cl. Rai (K) 61 E3
Tatsfield La. Whm 78 B1
Tattersall Cl. SE9 17 D3
Tattlebury La. Gou 172 A2
Tattlebury Rd. Head 144 C2
Taunton Cl. Bexh 4 C1
Taunton Rd. SE12 16 A3
Taunton Rd. Swans 23 E3
Taunton Vale. Grave 24 C1
Taverners Rd. Rai (K) 62 A2
Tavistock Cl. Rai (K) 62 A2
Tavistock Cl. Wald 74 A3
Tavistock Rd. Brom 33 E1
Tavistock Rd. Well 3 F1
Tavy Bridge. SE2 3 F4
Tay Cl. Wald 60 B1
Taylor Cl. Orp 50 A1
Taylor Rd. Snod 72 A2
Taylor St. SE18 2 B3
Taylor St. Soub 153 D2
Taylor's Bldgs. SE18 2 B3
Taylor's Cl. Sid 18 A1
Taylor's La. Higham 26 C1
Taylor's La. Roc 44 B2
Taylors La. Trot 70 A1
Tea Garden La. T W 166 C3
Teal Cl. I o G 15 E1
Teapot La. Dit 88 A3
Teasaucer Hill. Maid 106 A2
Teasel Rd. Wald 74 A4
Tebbs Way. Ight 100 C4
Tedder Ave. Chath 60 B2
Tedder Rd. T W 153 E2
Teesdale Rd. Dart 21 F2
Teeswater Ct. Belv 3 F4
Teignmouth Rd. Well 3 F1
Telegraph Hill. Higham 43 F4
Telemann Sq. SE3 16 B4
Telford Rd. SE9 17 F1
Tellson Ave. SE18 1 C1
Telscombe Cl. Orp 50 A2
Telston La. Otf 81 D3
Tempest Rd. Merew 103 D4
Templar Dr. Grave 41 E4
Temple Cl. SE18 2 C4
Temple Hill. Dart 21 D3
Temple Hill Sq. Dart 21 D3
Temple Way. Dit 87 D3
Tenby Rd. Well 3 F1
Tenchley's La. Lim C 113 D3
Tennyson Ave. Cli W 27 E2
Tennyson Ave. Grays 8 C4
Tennyson Cl. Well 3 D1
Tennyson Rd. Dart 21 E3
Tennyson Rd. Gil 60 C4
Tennyson Wlk. Grave 23 F1
Tensing Ave. Grave 24 A1
Tenterden Rd. Bidd 176 B2
Tenterden Rd. Bidd 185 D4
Tenterden Rd. Rol 185 E1
Tenterden Rd. Wald 60 B1
Terence Cl. Chath 60 B3
Terence Cl. Grave 25 D1
Terminus Rd. Maid 105 E3
Tern Cres. Roc 43 F1
Terrace Rd. Maid 106 A4
Terrace St. Grave 24 B3
Terrace The. Chath 44 C1
Terrace The. Chath 45 D2
Terrace The. Grave 24 B3
Terrace The. Grave 24 C3

Terrace The. Sev 80 C1
Terraces The. Dart 21 F2
Terry's Lodge Rd. Stans 68 C1
Terry's Yard. Maid 89 E1
Teston La. Tes 104 C2
Teston La. W Far 104 C2
Teston Rd. Off 85 E2
Teston Rd. W Mal 86 B1
Teston Rd. Waty 104 A3
Tetty Way. Brom 33 E2
Teviot Cl. Well 3 E1
Tewson Rd. SE18 3 D3
Teynham Green. Brom 48 B4
Teynham Green. Rai (K) 61 E4
Thackery Rd. Dit 87 D4
Thames Ave. H Hals 29 D4
Thames Ave. Rai (K) 62 A2
Thames Rd. Dart 20 B4
Thames Rd. Grays 8 B2
Thames Rd. Ton 118 C1
Thames Way. Grave 24 A3
Thamley. Pur 6 B3
Thanet Dr. Brom 48 C2
Thanet Rd. Bex 19 E2
Thanet Rd. Eri 5 D2
Thanet Rd. Rai (K) 75 F4
Thanington Ct. SE9 18 A3
Thatch Barn Rd. Head 144 C1
Thatcher Rd. Stapt 160 A4
Thatchers La. Cli 10 B1
Thaxted Rd. SE9 17 F1
The Common. Chath 44 C1
Thelma Cl. Grave 42 A4
Thelma Gdns. SE3 2 A1
Theobalds. Hawkt 189 D3
Theobalds Ave. Grays 8 C3
Theodore Cl. T W 154 A2
Thicketts. Sev 98 C4
Third Ave. Chath 60 C3
Third Ave. Gil 61 D4
Third Ave. Grays 7 E2
Third St. Spel 166 A4
Thirlmere Cl. Gil 46 B1
Thirlmere Cl. Roc 44 C3
Thirlmere Rd. Bexh 4 C1
Thirlmere Rise. Brom 33 D3
Thirza Rd. Dart 21 D3
Thistle Rd. Grave 25 D2
Thistlebank. Wald 74 B4
Thistlebrook. SE2 3 F4
Thistledown. Grave 41 F3
Thistledown Cl. Rai (K) 75 E4
Thistlemead. Chis 34 B2
Thomas Dr. Grave 24 C1
Thomas St. Chath 59 F4
Thomas St. SE18 2 B3
Thomas St. T W 153 E1
Thomas Wyatt Way. Wro 84 A4
Thomson Cl. Snod 72 B3
Thong La. Bor G 84 A1
Thong La. Shor 42 B3
Thorn Cl. Brom 49 E4
Thorn Cl. Burh 73 F3
Thorn Rd. Mard 159 D4
Thorndale Cl. Wald 73 F4
Thornden La. Rol 192 A2
Thorndon Cl. Orp 35 D2
Thorndon Rd. Orp 35 D2
Thorndyke Way. Wro 84 A4
Thorne Cl. Eri 4 B2
Thorne Estate The. Plu 147 F1
Thornet Wood Rd. Brom 34 B1
Thorneycroft Rd. Stal 112 C1
Thornfield Gdns. T W 154 A1
Thornham Rd. Rai (K) 61 F4
Thornhill Ave. SE18 3 D2
Thornhill Pl. Maid 89 E1
Thorn's Meadow. Bras 96 C4
Thornton Rd. Belv 4 B3
Thornton Rd. Brom 33 E4
Thorntree Rd. SE7 1 C3
Thornwood Rd. SE13 16 A3
Thorold Rd. Chath 60 B4
Thorpe Ave. Ton 118 C1
Thorpe Cl. Orp 50 A2
Thorpe Wlk. Rai (K) 75 F4
Thrale Way. Rai (K) 76 A4
Three Corners. Bexh 4 B1
Three Elm La. Had 120 B1
Three Elm La. Ton 119 F1
Three Gates Rd. Faw 54 B3
Threshers Dr. Thu 90 A1
Thrift The. Dart 22 C1
Throwley Cl. SE2 3 F4
Thrush Cl. Chath 60 B2
Thurloe Wlk. Grays 8 B4
Thurnham La. Thu 90 C1
Thurrock Park Way. Grays 8 C2
Thursland Rd. Sid 36 A4
Thursley Rd. SE9 17 D1
Thwaite Cl. Eri 4 C2
Thyer Cl. Orp 49 F1
Tibb's Court La. Brenc 156 B2
Ticehurst Cl. Orp 35 E3
Tichborne Cl. Maid 88 C1
Tickford Cl. SE2 3 F4
Tidebrook Ct. Orp 35 F1
Tideway The. Chath 59 F3
Tidford Rd. Well 3 D1
Tiepigs La. Brom 48 A3
Tiger La. Brom 33 E1
Tilbrook Rd. SE3 16 C4
Tilbury Cl. Orp 35 E2
Tilbury Gdns. Tilb 24 B4
Tilbury Rd. Rai (K) 62 B3
Tilden Cl. H Hald 177 F2
Tilden La. Mard 141 F3
Tilden Rd. Head 144 C2
Tilden Rd. Ulc 145 D3
Tile Farm Rd. Orp 49 F2
Tile Fields. Lee 108 C3
Tile Kiln La. Bex 19 F1
Tile Kiln La. Dart 20 A1
Tile Lodge Rd. Char 130 A2
Tilebarn Cnr. Ton 137 D4
Till Ave. Farn 53 D3
Tillingbourne Green. Orp 35 E1
Tilmans Mead. Farn 53 E3
Tilsden La. Cran 183 D4
Tilt Yard App. SE9 17 D3
Tilton Rd. Bor G 84 A2
Timber Cl. Chis 34 B2
Timber Tops. Bredh 74 C2
Timberbank. Meo 70 A2
Timbercroft La. SE18 3 D2
Tinker Pot La. W Kin 67 F1
Tinker's Alley. Chath 45 D2
Tinkers La. Tic 187 D3
Tintagel Rd. Orp 50 C3
Tintern Rd. Maid 88 C2
Tippens Cl. Cran 182 C4
Titan Rd. Grays 8 B3
Titchfield Cl. Maid 107 D1
Titchfield Rd. Maid 107 D1
Tithe Yd. Len 110 C1
Tiverton Dr. SE9 17 F2
Tivoli Gdns. SE18 2 A3
Tobruk Way. Chath 60 A1
Toby Gdns. Had 120 A2
Toddington Cres. Burh 73 F3
Toft Ave. Grays 8 C3
Toledo Paddock. Gil 45 F1
Tolgate Way. Ayld 89 D4
Tolhurst Rd. Five O G 138 B2
Tollgate Pl. Head 145 D1
Tollgate Rd. Dart 21 F2
Tolsey Mead. Bor G 84 B2
Tom Coombs Cl. SE9 17 D4
Tom Cribb Rd. SE28 2 C4
Tom Smith Cl. SE10 1 A2
Tomlin Cl. Snod 72 B2
Tomlin Cl. Stapt 160 A4
Tonbridge By-Pass. Hild 117 E2
Tonbridge By-Pass. Lei 135 E3
Tonbridge By-Pass. Ton 136 B1
Tonbridge Chambers. Ton 136 B2
Tonbridge Rd. E Pec 138 C4
Tonbridge Rd. E Pec 121 D1
Tonbridge Rd. Had 119 F2
Tonbridge Rd. Hild 117 F1
Tonbridge Rd. Ight 100 C3
Tonbridge Rd. Maid 105 E3
Tonbridge Rd. Pem 154 B2
Tonbridge Rd. Sev 98 C2
Tonbridge Rd. Tes 104 B2
Tonbridge Rd. Waty 103 F2
Tong La. Brenc 170 B4
Tong La. Lam 170 B4
Tongswood Dr. Hawkt 189 F3
Tooley St. Grave 23 F2
Tootswood Rd. Brom 33 D1
Top Dartford Rd. Hex 37 E3
Top Park. Beck 48 A4
Topcliffe Dr. Orp 49 F1
Topley St. SE9 16 C4
Tor Rd. Well 3 F1
Torbay. E Pec 121 E1
Tormount Rd. SE18 3 D2
Toronto Rd. Gil 46 A1
Torrens Wlk. Grave 42 A4
Torridon Rd. SE13 16 A2
Torrington Cl. Merew 102 C2
Torver Way. Orp 49 F2
Totnes Rd. SE2 3 E2
Tovil Green. Maid 106 A3
Tovil Hill. Maid 106 A3
Tovil Rd. Maid 106 A3
Tower Cl. Grave 42 A4
Tower Cl. Orp 50 A2
Tower Hill. Off 85 F2
Tower La. Rose 107 E4
Tower Rd. Belv 4 C3
Tower Rd. Bexh 19 E4
Tower Rd. Dart 20 C3
Tower Rd. Orp 50 A2
Towercroft. Eyn 53 D2
Towers Rd. Grays 8 C3
Towers Wood. Dart 38 C2
Town Acres. Ton 136 C4
Town Court La. Orp 49 F3
Town Hill. Lam 179 E4
Town Hill. W Mal 86 C3
Town Pier. Grave 24 B3
Town Rd. Cli W 44 B4
Town Sq. Eri 5 D2
Towncourt Cres. Orp 34 C1
Townhill Cl. W Mal 86 C3
Townland Cl. Bidd 176 B3
Townley Rd. Bexh 19 D3
Townsend Rd. Snod 72 A2
Townshend Rd. Chis 34 B4
Toynbec Cl. Chis 34 B4
Toy's Hill. Whm 114 C3
Tradescant Dr. Meo 56 B4
Trafalgar Rd. Dart 21 D1
Trafalgar Rd. Grave 24 B2
Trafalgar Rd. SE10 1 A3
Trafalgar Rd. Wou 72 C4
Trafalgar St. Gil 45 F1
Tranquil Pas. SE3 1 A1
Tranquil Rise. Eri 5 D3
Tranquil Vale. SE3 1 A1
Transfesa Rd. Padd W 139 E2
Transmere Cl. Orp 49 F4
Transmere Rd. Orp 49 F4
Trapfield Cl. Rose 107 F4
Trapfield La. Rose 107 F4
Trapham Rd. Maid 88 C1
Travertine Rd. Wald 74 B3
Trebble Rd. Swans 23 D3
Tredegar Rd. Dart 20 B1
Tredwell Cl. Brom 34 A1
Tree La. Plax 101 D2
Treetops. Grave 41 E4
Treetops. Ton 136 B2
Treetops Cl. SE2 4 A3
Treewall Gdns. Brom 33 E4
Trelawn Cres. Wald 74 B3
Trellyn Cl. Maid 105 D3
Trench Rd. Ton 118 C1
Trent Rd. Wald 60 B1
Trentham Dr. Orp 50 B4
Trenton Cl. Maid 88 B2
Tresco Cl. Brom 33 D3
Trevale Rd. Chath 59 E3
Trevelyan Cl. Dart 21 D4
Trevereux Hill. Lim C 113 E4
Trevino Dr. Wald 74 A3
Trevithick Dr. Dart 21 D4
Trevor Cl. Brom 48 B3
Trevor Dr. Maid 88 B1
Trewin Cl. Dit 87 F3
Trident Cl. Roc 45 D2
Trinity Cl. Brom 49 D3
Trinity Cl. T W 167 F4
Trinity Ct. SE9 17 E3
Trinity Pl. Bexh 19 D4
Trinity Rd. Gil 45 F1
Trinity Rd. Grave 24 C2
Tristan Gdns. T W 166 C4
Tristan Sq. SE3 16 A4
Tristram Rd. Brom 33 D4
Troodos Hill. Maid 89 D2
Trosley Ave. Grave 24 B1
Trosley Rd. Belv 4 B2
Trottiscliffe Rd. WRO H 85 F4
Trotts La. Whm 95 F2
Trotwood Cl. Wald 74 B2
Troughton Rd. SE7 1 B3
Troy La. Ede 131 D4
Troy St. SE18 2 B3
Troys Mead. Holli 108 C3
Trubridge Rd. Hoo S W 29 D1
Truro Cl. Rai (K) 61 F4
Truro Rd. Grave 24 C1
Truro Wlk. Ton 118 C1
Trycewell La. Ight 83 F1
Tuam Rd. SE18 2 C2
Tubbenden Cl. Orp 50 A2
Tubbenden Dr. Orp 49 F1
Tubbenden La. Orp 50 A2
Tubs Hill. Sev 98 B4
Tudeley La. Ton 136 C2
Tudor Ave. Maid 89 E1
Tudor Cl. Chis 34 A2
Tudor Cl. Dart 20 B3
Tudor Cl. Grave 24 A2
Tudor Cres. Otf 81 F4
Tudor Ct. T W 167 D3
Tudor Dr. Otf 81 F4
Tudor Gr. Rai (K) 62 A2
Tudor Way. Orp 49 F4
Tudway Rd. SE3 16 C4
Tufa Cl. Wald 74 B3
Tufnail Rd. Dart 21 D3
Tufton Rd. Rai (K) 62 A3
Tufton St. Maid 106 B4
Tulip Tree Cl. Ton 136 B2
Tumblefield Estate. Stans 69 D2
Tumblefield Rd. Stans 69 D2
Tumblers Hill. Sutt V 126 A2
Tunbury Ave. Wald 74 A3
Tunbury Ave S. Wald 74 A3
Tunnel Ave. SE10 1 A4
Tunnel Rd. T W 167 E4
Tunstall Cl. Orp 50 A1
Tunstock Way. Belv 4 A4
Turgis Cl. Lan H 126 A4
Turnberry Way. Orp 49 F3
Turnbull Cl. Gree 22 A2
Turnden Rd. Cran 182 B4
Turner Ave. Cran 182 C4
Turner Green Rd. Wad 178 A1
Turner Rd. Dart 22 B1
Turner Rd. Ton 119 D1
Turner St. Cli 10 B1
Turners Ave. Ten 186 B2
Turners Gdns. Sev 98 C2
Turners Green La. Wad 178 A1
Turnpike Ct. Bexh 18 C4
Turnpike Dr. Dow 64 C3
Turnstone. Lon 40 B2
Turnstone Rd. Wald 74 C3
Turnstones The. Grave 24 C1
Turp Ave. Grays 8 C4
Turpington Cl. Brom 49 D3
Turpington La. Brom 49 D4
Tuscan Dr. Wald 74 C3
Tuscan Rd. SE18 2 C3
Tutsham Way. Padd W 139 D1
Tuxford Rd. T W 152 B1
Tweed Rd. Ton 118 C1
Tweedy Rd. Brom 33 E2
Twigg Cl. Eri 5 D2
Twisden Rd. Dit 87 D2
Twitton La. Shorn 81 D4
Two Post Alley. Chath 44 C1
Twogates Hill. Higham 27 D1
Twydall Green. Rai (K) 61 E4
Twydall La. Rai (K) 61 E3
Twyford Cl. Rai (K) 62 B3
Twyford Ct. Maid 89 F1
Twyford Rd. Had 120 A3
Tydeman Rd. Rose 107 D3
Tye La. Orp 49 F1
Tyeshurst Cl. SE2 4 A3
Tyland La. Box 89 D4
Tyler Cl. Dit 87 D2
Tyler Dr. Rai (K) 76 A4
Tyler Gr. Dart 21 D4
Tylers Green Rd. Swan 51 F3
Tylney Rd. Brom 33 F2
Tyndall Rd. Well 18 A4
Tyne Cl. Wald 60 B1
Tyne Rd. Ton 118 B1
Tynedale Cl. Dart 21 F2
Typhoon Rd. Merew 103 D4
Tyron Way. Sid 35 D4
Tyrrell Ave. Well 18 B3
Tyrrells Hall Cl. Grays 8 C2

Uckfield La. Hev 149 F4
Ufton Cl. Maid 107 D3
Ulcombe Hill. Ulc 127 D3
Ulcombe Rd. Head 144 C1
Ulcombe Rd. Lan H 126 A4
Ullswater Cl. Brom 33 D3
Ulundi Rd. SE3 1 A2
Undercliff. Maid 106 A4
Underdown Ave. Chath 60 A3
Underling La. Mard 141 F3
Underriver House Rd. Seal 117 F4
Undershaw Rd. Brom 16 A1
Underwood Cl. Maid 106 A3
Underwood The. SE9 17 D1
Unicorn Wlk. Gree 22 A3
Unicumes La. Maid 105 F3
Union Pl. Chath 60 B4
Union Rd. Brom 48 C4
Union St. Chath 60 B4
Union St. Chath 44 C1
Union St. Maid 89 E1
Unity Way. SE18 1 C4
University Pl. Eri 4 B2
Unwin Cl. Ayld 88 B4
Upbury Way. Chath 60 B4
Upchat Rd. Hoo S W 45 D4
Updale Rd. Sid 35 D4
Upland Rd. Bexh 19 D4
Uplands Cl. Roc 43 F1
Uplands Cl. Sev 98 A4
Uplands Rd. Orp 50 B3
Uplands Way. Sev 98 A4
Upnor Rd. Roc 45 D3
Upper Abbey Rd. Belv 4 B3
Upper Austin Lodge Rd. Eyn 52 C1
Upper Ave. Ist 41 D2
Upper Barn Hill. Hunt 123 D4
Upper Britton Pl. Gil 45 E1
Upper Bush Rd. Cux 58 A3
Upper Cumberland Wlk. T W 167 E3
Upper Dunstan Rd. T W 153 E1
Upper East Rd. Gil 45 E2
Upper Fant Rd. Maid 105 F3
Upper Green La. Ship 100 C1
Upper Green Rd. Ship 100 C1
Upper Grosvenor Rd. T W 153 E1
Upper Grove Rd. Belv 4 A2
Upper Haysden La. Ton 136 A2
Upper Holly Hill Rd. Belv 4 B3
Upper Hunton Hill. Hunt 123 E4
Upper Luton Rd. Chath 60 C3
Upper Mill. Waty 103 F2
Upper Nellington. T W 166 B4
Upper Park Rd. Belv 4 B3
Upper Park Rd. Brom 33 F2
Upper Profit. Spel 166 B4
Upper Rd. Maid 106 B3
Upper Sheridan Rd. Belv 4 B3
Upper Spring La. Ight 83 E1
Upper St. Holli 109 D4
Upper St. Lee 108 A1
Upper St. T W 166 C4
Upper Stephens. Spel 166 B4
Upper Stone St. Maid 106 B4
Upper Wickham La. Well 3 E1
Upperton Rd. Sid 35 D4
Upton Cl. Bex 19 D3
Upton Quarry. Spel 166 A4
Upton Rd. Bexh 19 D3
Upton Rd. SE18 2 C2
Upton Rd S. Bex 19 D3
Upwood Rd. SE12 16 B3
Uridge Cres. Ton 136 C4
Uridge Rd. Ton 136 C4
Usborne Cl. Stapt 160 A4

Valan Leas. Brom 33 D1
Vale Ave. Soub 153 D3
Vale Cl. Orp 49 E1
Vale Cotts. Brom 33 E1
Vale Dr. Wald 60 A1
Vale Rd. Brom 34 B2
Vale Rd. Dart 20 B2
Vale Rd. Grave 24 B2
Vale Rd. Hawkt 189 D4
Vale Rd. Loose 106 A1
Vale Rd. Soub 153 D3
Vale Rd. T W 167 E4
Vale Rd. Ton 136 C3
Vale Rise. Ton 136 C3
Valence Rd. Eri 4 C2
Valence View. Frit 161 D2
Valentine Ave. Bex 19 D2
Valentine Cl. Rai (K) 61 E3
Valentine Rd. Maid 107 D2
Valerian Cl. Wald 74 A4
Valeswood Rd. Brom 33 D4
Valiant Rd. Wald 74 C3
Valley Cl. Dart 20 A3
Valley Dr. Grave 24 C1
Valley Dr. Maid 106 A1
Valley Dr. Sev 98 B3
Valley Forge Cl. Ton 137 D4
Valley Gr. SE7 1 C3
Valley La. Meo 70 B3
Valley Rd. Belv 4 C3
Valley Rd. Brom 33 D2
Valley Rd. Dart 20 A3
Valley Rd. Faw 54 B3
Valley Rd. Gil 61 D4
Valley Rd. Orp 35 E3
Valley Rd. T W 166 C4
Valley Rise. Wald 74 A3
Valley The. Cox 123 F4
Valley View. Gree 22 B3
Valley View. Soub 153 E3
Valley View Rd. Chath 59 E3
Valliers Wood Rd. Sid 18 A2
Vambery Rd. SE18 2 C2
Vanbrugh Fields. SE3 1 A2
Vanbrugh Hill. SE3 1 A2
Vanbrugh Park. SE3 1 A2
Vanbrugh Park Rd. SE3 1 A2
Vanbrugh Park Rd W. SE3 1 A2
Vanbrugh Terr. SE3 1 A1
Vanburgh Cl. Orp 50 A3
Vandyke Cross. SE9 17 D3
Vanessa Cl. Belv 4 B3
Vanessa Way. Bex 19 F1
Vanessa Wlk. Grave 42 A4
Vange Cottage Mews. Chath 59 E4
Vanity La. Lint 123 F3
Vanoc Gdns. Brom 33 E4
Vanquisher Wlk. Grave 25 D1
Varnes St. Ayld 73 D1
Varney St. T W 167 E4
Vaughan Ave. Ton 119 D1
Vaughan Rd. Well 3 D1
Vauxhall Cl. Grave 24 A2
Vauxhall Cres. Snod 72 B1
Vauxhall Gdns. Ton 136 C2
Vauxhall La. Soub 153 E4
Vauxhall La. Ton 136 C1
Vauxhall Pl. Dart 21 D2
Veles Rd. Snod 72 A2
Venners Cl. Bexh 5 D1
Ventnor Cl. Chath 60 C2
Venture Cl. Bex 19 D2
Venus Rd. SE18 2 A4
Verdant La. SE6 16 A2
Verdun Rd. SE18 3 E2
Vermont Rd. T W 166 C4
Vernham Rd. SE18 2 C2
Vernon Cl. Orp 35 E1
Vernon Cl. W Kin 21 F1
Vernon Rd. Swans 23 D3
Vernon Rd. T W 153 F1
Veroan Rd. Bexh 4 A1
Verona Gdns. Grave 42 A4
Vesper Ct. Sma 163 E3
Vestry Rd. Otf 81 F2
Via Romana. Grave 25 E2
Vicarage Ave. SE3 1 B2
Vicarage Cl. Ayld 88 A4
Vicarage Cl. Eri 4 C2
Vicarage Cl. Hall 58 B1
Vicarage Cl. Low St 30 B4
Vicarage Dr. Grave 23 F3
Vicarage Hill. Whm 95 F3
Vicarage La. Dunt 80 C2
Vicarage La. E Far 105 E1
Vicarage La. Grave 25 E1
Vicarage La. Hoo S W 46 A4
Vicarage Park. SE18 2 C3
Vicarage Rd. Bex 19 E2
Vicarage Rd. Gil 45 F1
Vicarage Rd. Hall 58 A1
Vicarage Rd. Roc 44 B2
Vicarage Rd. SE18 2 C3
Vicarage Rd. Soub 153 D3
Vicarage Rd. Yal 122 B3
Vicary Way. Maid 88 C1
Vickers Rd. Eri 4 C3
Victoria Ave. Grave 24 B2
Victoria Ave. Grays 8 C4
Victoria Cl. Ede 131 F2
Victoria Cl. Grays 8 C4
Victoria Cl. Wald 73 F3
Victoria Cotts. Ede 131 F2
Victoria Dr. Hort 38 C2
Victoria Hill Rd. Hex 37 E2
Victoria Rd. Bexh 19 E4
Victoria Rd. Brom 48 C4
Victoria Rd. Chath 60 B3
Victoria Rd. Chis 34 B4
Victoria Rd. Dart 21 D3
Victoria Rd. Ede 131 F2
Victoria Rd. Eri 5 D2
Victoria Rd. Grave 24 A2
Victoria Rd. Had 120 A2
Victoria Rd. Sev 98 B3
Victoria Rd. Sid 18 B1
Victoria Rd. Soub 153 D3
Victoria Rd. T W 167 E4
Victoria Rd. Wald 74 A4
Victoria Scott Ct. Dart 20 A4
Victoria St. Ayld 73 D1
Victoria St. Belv 4 A3
Victoria St. Chath 44 C1
Victoria St. Gil 45 F1
Victoria St. Maid 106 A4
Victoria Terr. Chath 59 E3
Victoria Way. SE7 1 B3
Victory Cotts. Sev W 116 C3
Vidgeon Ave. Hoo S W 28 C1
View Rd. Cli W 27 E2
View The. SE2 4 A3
Viewfield Rd. Sid 18 C2
Viewland Rd. SE18 3 D3
Viewlands Ave. Bigg 79 D2
Vigilant Way. Grave 42 A4
Vigo Hill. Trot 70 A1
Vigo Rd. Stans 69 F2
Viking Rd. Grave 23 F1

Viking Way. W Kin 54 A1
Villa Cl. Grave 25 E1
Villa Rd. Higham 43 E4
Villacourt Rd. SE18 3 E2
Village Green Ave. Bigg 78 A3
Village Green Rd. Dart 20 B4
Village Green Way. Bigg 78 A3
Village The. SE7 1 C2
Villas Rd. SE18 2 C3
Vincent Cl. Brom 33 E1
Vincent Cl. Sid 18 A2
Vincent Rd. Ayld 73 F2
Vincent Rd. SE18 2 B3
Vine Ave. Sev 98 B4
Vine Court Rd. Sev 98 C4
Vine Rd. Orp 64 A4
Vine Wlk. Stapt 160 A4
Vineries The. Gil 46 A1
Vines La. Chath 44 C1
Vines La. Hild 117 F3
Vineyard Cres. Rai (K) 62 B3
Vinson Cl. Orp 50 B3
Vintners Rd. Maid 106 B4
Vintners Way. Thu 107 D4
Viola Ave. SE2 3 E3
Violet Cl. Wald 74 B2
Virginia Rd. Gil 45 F2
Virginia Wlk. Grave 42 A3
Vista The. SE9 16 C2
Vixen Cl. Wald 60 C1
Voce Rd. SE18 2 C2
Vulcan Cl. Chath 60 B2
Vyne The. Bexh 19 E4

Wadard Terr. Farn 52 C4
Wade Ave. Orp 50 C3
Wadeville Cl. Belv 4 B3
Wadlands Rd. Cli 10 B1
Waghorn Rd. Snod 72 B2
Waghorn St. Chath 60 B4
Wagon La. Yal 139 F3
Wagoners Cl. Thu 107 D4
Waid Cl. Dart 21 D3
Wainhouse Cl. Ede 131 F4
Wainscott Rd. Roc 44 C3
Wainscott Wlk. Roc 44 C4
Waite Davies Rd. SE12 16 A2
Wake Rd. Chath 59 F2
Wakefield Cl. Roc 43 F1
Wakeley Rd. Rai (K) 62 B3
Waldeck Rd. Dart 21 E3
Waldegrave Rd. Brom 34 A1
Walden Ave. SE9 34 A4
Walden Cl. Belv 4 A3
Walden Rd. Chis 34 A3
Waldenhurst Rd. Orp 50 C3
Waldens Cl. Orp 50 C3
Waldens Rd. Orp 51 D4
Waldens The. Broom (m) 127 D3
Walderslade Rd. Chath 60 A1
Walderslade Rd. Wald 74 A4
Walderslade Woods. Wald 74 A2
Waldo Rd. Brom 33 F1
Waldrist Way. Belv 4 A4
Waldron Dr. Maid 106 A1
Walk The. Broom (m) 127 D3
Walkden Rd. Chis 34 B4
Walker Cl. Dart 20 A4
Walker Cl. SE18 2 C3
Walkhurst Cotts. Ben 184 A2
Walkhurst Rd. Ben 184 A2
Walkley Rd. Dart 20 B3
Wall Cl. Hoo S W 28 C2
Wallace Cl. T W 167 E2
Wallace Gdns. Swans 23 D3
Wallace Rd. Chath 60 A2
Wallace Rd. Grays 8 B3
Wallbridge La. Rai (K) 62 C4
Waller Hill. Frit 160 B1
Wallers. Spel 152 B2
Wallhouse Rd. Eri 5 F2
Wallis Ave. Maid 107 D1
Wallis Cl. Dart 20 A1
Wallis Park. Grave 23 E3
Walmer Ct. Maid 89 E1
Walmer Terr. SE18 2 C3
Walmers Ave. Higham 43 E4
Walnut Cl. Chath 60 B2
Walnut Cl. Padd W 139 E1
Walnut Hill Rd. Ist 41 D1
Walnut Tree Ave. Dart 21 D1
Walnut Tree Ave. Maid 106 B1
Walnut Tree Cl. Chis 34 C2
Walnut Tree Ct. Dit 87 E3
Walnut Tree La. Maid 106 B1
Walnut Tree Rd. Eri 5 D3
Walnut Tree Way. Meo 56 B4
Walnut Way. Swan 36 C2
Walnuts Rd. Orp 50 B3
Walpole Cl. Dit 87 D3
Walpole Cl. Grays 8 C3
Walpole Rd. Brom 48 C4
Walsham Rd. Wald 74 A3
Walsingham Cl. Rai (K) 75 F4
Walsingham Park. Chis 34 C2
Walsingham Rd. Orp 35 E2
Walter Burke Ave. Wou 58 C1
Walter's Farm Rd. Ton 136 C3
Walters Green Rd. Pen 151 D2
Walters Rd. Hoo S W 29 D1
Walters Yd. Brom 33 E2
Waltham Cl. Dart 20 B3
Waltham Cl. Orp 50 C3
Waltham Rd. Rai (K) 61 E4
Walton Rd. Sid 18 C1
Walton Rd. Ton 119 D1
Walwyn Ave. Brom 33 F1
Wanden La. Ege 146 B2
Wansbury Way. Swan 37 E1
Wanstead Cl. Brom 33 F2
Wanstead Rd. Brom 33 F2
Wansunt Rd. Bex 19 F2
Wantage Rd. SE12 16 A3
Warblers Cl. Roc 44 B2
Ward Ave. Grays 8 B3
Ward Cl. Eri 4 C2
Warden Cl. Maid 105 F4
Warden Mill Cl. Waty 104 A2
Warden Rd. Chath 59 F3
Ward's La. Wad 179 D1
Ware St. Thu 90 B1
Warham Rd. Otf 81 E4
Waring Cl. Orp 64 A4
Waring Dr. Orp 64 B4
Waring Rd. Sid 35 F3
Warland Rd. SE18 2 C2
Warland Rd. W Kin 27 F1
Warlingham Cl. Rai (K) 62 B3
Warmlake Estate. Sutt V 126 A3
Warmlake Rd. Chart S 125 F3
Warmlake Rd. Sutt V 125 F3
Warner Rd. Brom 33 D3
Warner St. Chath 60 A4
Warnford Gdns. Maid 106 B2
Warnford Rd. Orp 50 A1
Warren Ave. Brom 33 D3
Warren Ave. Orp 50 A1
Warren Cl. Bexh 19 E3
Warren Ct. Sev 98 C4
Warren Dr. Orp 50 B1
Warren Gdns. Orp 50 B1
Warren La. Grays 7 F3
Warren La. New(G) 76 C4
Warren La. SE18 2 B4
Warren Rd. Ayld 73 F2
Warren Rd. Bexh 19 E3
Warren Rd. Brom 48 B2
Warren Rd. Cob 57 F4
Warren Rd. Cux 58 A4
Warren Rd. Dart 21 D1
Warren Rd. Orp 50 B1
Warren Rd. Sid 18 C1
Warren Rd. Souf 40 B4
Warren St. Char 130 B4
Warren St. Len 111 F2
Warren The. Grave 42 A4
Warren View. Shor 43 D4
Warren Wlk. SE7 1 C2
Warren Wood Cl. Brom 48 B2
Warren Wood Rd. Chath 59 F2
Warrens The. Hart (S) 55 D4
Warrington Rd. Padd W 139 E1
Warrior Ave. Grave 41 F4
Warspite Rd. SE18 2 A4
Warwick Cl. Orp 50 B2
Warwick Cres. Chath 59 D3
Warwick Ct. Sev 98 B3
Warwick Gdns. Meo 56 B2
Warwick Park. T W 167 E3
Warwick Pl. Grave 23 E3
Warwick Pl. Maid 106 A4
Warwick Rd. Sid 35 E4
Warwick Rd. T W 167 E3
Warwick Rd. Well 18 C4
Warwick Terr. SE18 2 C2
Washneys Rd. Kno P 64 B1
Wassall La. Rol 192 A2
Water La. Harr 127 D4
Water La. Harr 109 E1
Water La. Hawkt 182 B1
Water La. Head 161 E4
Water La. Pur 6 B3
Water La. Rose 107 F4
Water La. Shorm 66 A2
Water La. Sid 19 D1
Water La. Sma 163 D3
Water La. Thu 91 D1
Water La. W Mal 86 C2
Water Mill Way. Sutt H 38 B2
Water Slippe. Had 119 F3
Watercress Cl. Sev 81 F2
Watercress Dr. Sev 81 F2
Watercroft Rd. Hals 65 D3
Waterdale Rd. SE2 3 E2
Waterdales. Grave 23 F2
Waterditch La. Len 112 A1
Waterdown Rd. T W 167 D3
Waterfield. T W 167 E2
Waterhead Cl. Eri 5 D2
Wateringbury Rd. Dit 87 E1
Waterlakes. Ede 131 F2
Waterloo Pl. Ton 136 B2
Waterloo Rd. Cran 173 F1
Waterloo Rd. Gil 60 C4
Waterloo Rd. Ton 136 B2
Waterloo St. Grave 24 C2
Waterloo St. Maid 106 B4
Waterlow Rd. Maid 89 E1
Waterlow Rd. Meo 70 A2
Waterman's La. Brenc 156 B4
Watermeadow Cl. Rai (K) 61 D1
Watermill Cl. Roc 44 C2
Waters Pl. Rai (K) 61 E1
Waters Rd. SE6 16 A1
Waterside. Dart 20 A3
Waterside. Maid 89 D1
Waterside La. Gil 46 A2
Waterton Ave. Grave 25 D2
Waterworks Cotts. Chid 133 D4
Watery La. Kemsg 83 D3
Watery La. Seal 82 C2
Watery La. Sid 35 E3
Watkins Cl. Stapt 143 D1
Watling Ave. Chath 60 C3
Watling St. Bexh 19 F4
Watling St. Chath 61 D3
Watling St. Dart 23 E1
Watling St. Dart 21 F2
Watling St. Grave 41 E4
Watling St. Higham 43 E2
Watling St. Roc 44 A2
Watling St. Shor 42 B2
Watson Ave. Wald 59 F1
Watts' Ave. Chath 59 F4
Watts Bridge Rd. Eri 5 D2
Watts Cres. Pur 6 C3
Watt's Cross Rd. Hild 117 E2
Watt's La. Chis 34 C2
Watt's St. Chath 60 A4
Wavell Dr. Sid 18 A3
Waveney Rd. Ton 118 B1
Waverley Cl. Brom 48 C4
Waverley Cl. Cox 123 F4
Waverley Cl. Wald 74 C3
Waverley Cres. SE18 2 C3
Waverley Dr. T W 154 A1
Waverley Gdns. Grays 8 B4
Waverley Rd. SE18 2 C3
Way Volante. Grave 42 A4
Wayfaring Green. Grays 8 A3
Wayfield Rd. Chath 60 B2
Waylands. Swan 37 D1
Waylands Cl. Kno P 80 A4
Wayne Cl. Orp 50 A2
Wayside. Ten 186 B3
Wayside Ave. Ten 186 B4
Wayside Dr. Ede 131 F4
Wayside Gr. SE9 34 A4
Wayville Rd. Dart 21 E2
Weald Cl. Brom 49 D2
Weald Cl. Ist 41 D3
Weald Cl. Maid 106 C1
Weald Cl. Sev W 116 C3
Weald Rd. Sev 98 B2
Weald The. Chis 34 A3
Weald View. Frit 161 D1
Weald View. Wad 178 A1
Weald View Rd. Ton 136 B2
Wealden Ave. Ten 186 B3
Wealden Cl. Hild 118 A1
Wealden Pl. Sev 81 F1
Weardale Ave. Dart 21 F2
Weare Rd. Soub 153 F2
Weavering Cl. Roc 44 C3
Weavering St. Thu 90 A1
Weavers Cl. Grave 24 B2
Weavers Cl. Stapt 160 A4
Weavers La. Sev 81 F1
Weavers The. Bidd 176 B3
Webb Cl. Hoo S W 28 C1
Webb Rd. SE3 1 A2
Webber Cl. Eri 5 E2
Webb's Alley. Sev 98 C3
Webster Rd. Rai (K) 62 A3
Weeds Wood Rd. Wald 74 A4
Week St. Maid 106 B4
Weeks La. Bidd 162 B1
Weigall Rd. SE12 16 B4
Weir Rd. Bex 19 E2
Welbeck Ave. Brom 33 E4
Welbeck Ave. Sid 18 B2
Welbeck Ave. Soub 153 F2
Weld Cl. Stapt 160 A4
Well Cl. Lei 135 D3
Well Field. Hart (S) 40 A1
Well Hall Par. SE9 17 D4
Well Hall Rd. SE9 17 D4
Well Hill. Orp 51 E1
Well Hill. Shorm 51 E1
Well Hill La. Shorm 65 E4
Well Penn Rd. Cli 27 F4
Well Rd. Maid 89 E1
Well Rd. Otf 81 F4
Well St. Dit 87 D1
Well St. Loose 106 A1
Wellan Cl. Well 18 B3
Welland Rd. Ton 136 B4
Wellands Cl. Brom 34 A2
Wellbrook Rd. Orp 49 E1
Wellcome Ave. Dart 21 D4
Weller Ave. Chath 59 F3
Weller Rd. T W 166 C4
Wellers Cl. Whm 95 F2
Welling High St. Well 18 B4
Welling Way. SE9 17 F4
Welling Way. Well 18 A4
Wellington Ave. Sid 18 B3
Wellington Cotts. Hawkt 189 D4
Wellington Gdns. SE7 1 C3
Wellington Pl. Maid 89 D1
Wellington Rd. Belv 4 A3
Wellington Rd. Bex 18 C3
Wellington Rd. Brom 33 F1
Wellington Rd. Dart 20 C3
Wellington Rd. Gil 60 C4
Wellington Rd. Orp 50 C4
Wellington Rd. Tilb 24 B4
Wellington St. Grave 24 C2
Wellington St. SE18 2 B3
Wellmeade Dr. Sev 98 B2
Wellmeadow Rd. SE13 16 A2
Wells Cl. T W 167 E4
Wells Cl. Ten 186 B2
Wells Cl. Ton 136 C4
Wells Rd. Brom 34 A2
Wells Rd. Roc 43 F1
Wellsmoor Gdns. Brom 34 B1
Welton Cl. Ton 136 A2
Welton Rd. SE18 3 D2
Wemmick Cl. Chath 59 F2
Wemyss Rd. SE3 1 A1
Wendover Rd. Brom 33 E1
Wendover Rd. SE9 16 C4
Wendover Way. Orp 50 B4
Wendover Way. Well 18 B4
Wensley Cl. SE9 17 D3
Wentworth Cl. Grave 41 E4
Wentworth Cl. Orp 50 A1
Wentworth Dr. Cli W 27 E2
Wentworth Dr. Dart 20 B3
Wentworth Dr. Rai (K) 62 A2
Wentworth Pl. Grays 8 C4
Wenvoe Ave. Bexh 4 B1
Wernbrook St. SE18 2 C2
Wesley Cl. Maid 105 D4
Wesley Cl. Orp 35 F1
Wessex Dr. Eri 5 D1
West App. Orp 49 F4
West Common Rd. Brom 48 B2
West Crescent Rd. Grave 24 C3
West Cross. Ten 186 A2
West Cross Gdns. Ten 186 A2
West Dr. Sutt V 126 B2
West Dr. Wald 59 F1
West End. Bras 96 B3
West End. Kemsg 82 B3
West End. Mard 141 F1
West Hallowes. SE9 17 D2
West Heath Cl. Dart 20 A3
West Heath La. Sev 98 B2
West Heath Rd. Dart 20 A3
West Heath Rd. SE2 3 F2
West Hill. Dart 20 C3
West Hill. Dow 63 D2
West Hill Dr. Dart 20 C3
West Hill Rise. Dart 20 C3
West Holme. Eri 4 C1
West Kent Ave. Grave 23 F3
West La. I o G 15 E1
West Malling by-pass. W Mal 86 C2
West Mill Rd. Dit 87 F4
West Park. SE9 17 D2
West Park Ave. Soub 153 D3
West Park Rd. Maid 106 B3
West Rd. Chath 45 E2
West Rd. Gil 45 E2
West Rd. Gou 172 A2
West Shaw. Lon 39 F2
West St. Bexh 19 D4
West St. Brom 33 E2
West St. Eri 5 D3
West St. Gil 45 F1
West St. Grave 24 B3
West St. Grays 8 B2
West St. Harr 109 F1
West St. Hunt 122 C2
West St. Len 111 D3
West St. Roc 44 B3
West St. W Mal 86 B2
West St. Wro 84 A4
West Thurrock Way. Grays 7 E3
West View Rd. Dart 21 D3
West View Rd. Swan 37 E1
West View Rd. Swan 51 F4
West Way. Orp 49 F4
West Wlk. Maid 105 E4
West Wood Rd. Sto 76 B2
West Woodside. Bex 19 D2
Westbourne Gr. Bexh 19 E4
Westbourne Rd. Bexh 4 A2
Westbrook Cres. Well 18 C4
Westbrook Dr. Orp 50 C3
Westbrook Rd. SE3 1 B1
Westbrook Terr. T W 167 F3
Westbrooke Cl. Chath 60 B3
Westbrooke Rd. SE9 17 F1
Westbrooke Rd. Well 18 C4
Westbury Rd. Brom 33 F2
Westbury Terr. Whm 95 F2
Westcombe Hill. SE3 1 B2
Westcombe Park Rd. SE3 1 A2
Westcott Ave. Grave 24 B1
Westcourt St. Gil 45 E1
Westdale Pas. SE18 2 B2
Westdale Rd. SE18 2 B2
Westdean Ave. SE12 16 C2
Wested La. Swan 52 B4
Westerdale Rd. SE10 1 B3
Westergate Rd. Roc 44 A3
Westergate Rd. SE2 4 A2
Westerham Cl. Rai (K) 61 E4
Westerham Dr. Sid 18 C3
Westerham Hill. Whm 78 B1
Westerham Rd. Bigg 78 B2
Westerham Rd. Kes 49 D1
Westerham Rd. Lim C 95 E2
Westerham Rd. Sev 97 F4
Westerham Rd. Whm 96 B3
Westerham Rd. Whm 95 E2
Westerhill Rd. Cox 123 F3
Westerhill Rd. Lint 123 F3
Western Ave. Grays 7 D3
Western Ave. Hawkt 189 D3
Western Cross Cl. Gree 22 C3
Western Rd. Bor G 84 A2
Western Rd. Hawkt 189 D3
Western Rd. Maid 105 F3
Western Rd. Soub 153 E3
Western Rd. T W 153 F1
Western Rd. Wad 178 A1
Western Way. SE28 3 D4
Westfield. N Ash 55 D1
Westfield. Sev 81 F1
Westfield Cl. Grave 41 F3
Westfield Cotts. W Kin 68 A4
Westfield Rd. Bexh 19 F4
Westfield Sole Rd. Bredh 74 C2
Westfield St. SE18 1 C4
Westfield Terr. Cran 182 A3
Westgate Rd. Dart 20 C3
Westharold. Swan 36 C1
Westhill Cl. Grave 24 B2
Westholme. Orp 50 A3
Westhorne Ave. SE9 16 C3
Westhurst Dr. Chis 34 B4
Westland Dr. Brom 48 A2
Westleigh Dr. Brom 34 A2
Westmarsh Cl. Maid 107 D2
Westmoor St. SE7 1 C4
Westmoreland Ave. Well 18 A4
Westmoreland Pl. Brom 33 E1
Westmoreland Rd. Brom 33 D1
Westmorland Cl. Maid 107 D2
Westmorland Green. Maid 107 D2
Westmorland Rd. Maid 107 D2
Westmount Ave. Chath 60 A4
Westmount Rd. SE9 17 E4
Weston Gr. Brom 33 D2
Weston Rd. Brom 33 D3
Weston Rd. Roc 44 B2
Westree Rd. Maid 106 A4
Westrise. Ton 136 B2
Westway. Cox 123 F4
Westway. Pem 154 C2
Westways. Ede 131 F3
Westways. Whm 95 F3
Westwell Cl. Orp 50 C3
Westwell Ct. Ten 186 A2
Westwood La. Well 18 A4
Westwood Rd. E Pec 121 D1
Westwood Rd. Grave 40 A3
Westwood Rd. Maid 106 B2
Westwood Rd. T W 152 C1
Westwood Way. Sev 81 D1
Wetheral Dr. Wald 74 B4
Wey Cl. Wald 60 C1
Weybridge Cl. Wald 74 C4
Weyhill Cl. Maid 89 F1
Weyman Rd. SE3 1 C1
Wharf La. Cli 10 B1
Wharf Rd. Gil 45 F2
Wharf Rd. Grave 25 D3
Wharf Rd. Grays 8 A2
Wharf Rd. Maid 106 A3
Wharfedale Rd. Dart 21 F2
Wharton Rd. Brom 33 E2
Whatman Cl. Maid 89 F1
Wheatcroft Gr. Rai (K) 62 A2
Wheatear Way. Chath 60 B2
Wheatfield. Birl 87 D3
Wheatfield Cl. Cran 173 F1
Wheatfield Dr. Cran 173 F1
Wheatfield Lea. Cran 173 F1
Wheatfield Way. Cran 173 F1
Wheatfields. Thu 106 C4
Wheatley Terrace Rd. Eri 5 D2
Wheatsheaf Cl. Maid 106 B2
Wheatsheaf Hill. Orp 65 D3
Wheatsheaf Hill. Sund 115 E4
Wheatsheaf Way. Ton 118 C1
Wheeler Rd. Char 130 C2
Wheeler St. Head 144 C1
Wheeler St. Maid 89 E1
Wheeler Street Hedges. Maid 89 E2
Wheeler's La. Lint 124 A2
Whenman Ave. Bex 19 F1
Whetsted Rd. Five O G 138 C2
Whetsted Rd. Yal 139 E3
Whetstone Rd. SE3 1 C1
Whiffen's Ave. Chath 45 D1
Whimbrel Wlk. Wald 74 C3
Whimbrell Green. Dit 87 D3
Whinchat Rd. SE28 2 C4
Whinfell Way. Grave 42 A4
Whinyates Rd. SE9 17 D4
Whippendell Cl. Orp 35 E2
Whippendell Way. Orp 35 E2
Whistler Rd. Ton 119 D1
Whitby Rd. SE18 2 A3
Whitchurch Cl. Maid 106 A4
Whitcombe Cl. Wald 74 C4
White Ave. Grave 24 A1
White Bear Pas. T W 167 E3
White Cottage Rd. Ton 118 C1
White Gate. Roc 44 A2
White Hart Cl. Sev 98 C2
White Hart Rd. Orp 50 B3
White Hart Rd. SE18 3 D3
White Hart Slip. Brom 33 E2
White Hart Wood. Sev 98 C1
White Hill Rd. Bredh 75 F3
White Horse Hill. Chis 34 B4
White Horse La. Meo 70 C3
White Horse La. Oth 107 E1
White Horse Rd. Birl 71 D3
White Horse Rd. Meo 70 C3
White House La. Sev W 98 A1
White House Rd. Sev 98 A1
White House Rd. Sev W 98 A1
White Oak Cl. Ton 136 B2
White Post Hill. Farn 53 E3
White Post La. Cob 41 F1
White Post La. Meo 41 E1
White Rd. Chath 60 B3
White Rock Pl. Maid 106 A4
Whitebeam Ave. Brom 49 E4
Whitebeam Dr. Cox 123 E4
Whitebine Gdns. E Pec 121 E1
Whitebread La. Beckl 196 B2
Whitebread La. Norm 196 B2
Whitecroft. Swan 37 D2
Whitefield Cl. Orp 35 F1
Whitefield Rd. T W 153 E1
Whitefoot La. SE6 16 A1
Whitefoot Terr. Brom 16 A1
Whitegate Ct. Rai (K) 61 F1
Whitegates Ave. W Kin 68 A4
Whitehall Dr. Broom (m) 126 C4
Whitehall La. Eri 5 E1
Whitehall La. Grays 8 C3
Whitehall Rd. Brom 34 A1
Whitehall Rd. Grays 8 C3
Whitehall Rd. Holli 91 E2
Whitehaven Cl. Brom 33 E1
Whitehead Cl. Dart 20 C1

Whiteheads La. Rose 107 E4
Whitehill. Wro 84 B4
Whitehill La. Grave 41 E4
Whitehill Par. Grave 24 C1
Whitehill Rd. Dart 20 B3
Whitehill Rd. Grave 24 C1
Whitehill Rd. Lon 39 F2
Whitehill Rd. Meo 56 B2
Whitehorse Hill. Chath 60 B4
Whitehouse Cl. Hoo S W 46 A4
Whitehouse Cres. Burh 73 E2
Whitelake Rd. Ton 118 C1
Whiteleaves Rise. Cux 58 B4
Whitepost La. Meo 70 A3
Whites Cl. Gree 22 C3
White's La. Hawkt 189 E3
White's Meadow. Brom 34 B1
Whitewall Rd. Roc 44 C2
Whitewall Way. Roc 45 D2
Whitewebbs Way. Orp 35 D2
Whitfield Rd. Bexh 4 A2
Whitmore St. Maid 105 F3
Whitney Wlk. Sid 36 A3
Whittaker St. Chath 60 B4
Whitworth Rd. SE18 2 B2
Whybourne Crest. T W 167 F3
Whyman Ave. Chath 60 B3
Wichling Cl. Orp 50 C3
Wickenden Rd. Sev 81 F1
Wickens Meadow. Dunt 81 D2
Wickets The. Sev W 116 C3
Wickham Ch. W Wick 48 A3
Wickham Field. Otf 81 D4
Wickham Gdns. T W 152 C1
Wickham La. SE2 3 E2
Wickham St. Chath 59 F4
Wickham St. Well 3 E1
Wickhurst Rd. Sev W 116 B4
Wicks Cl. SE9 33 F4
Wicksteed Cl. Bex 19 F1
Widbury Cl. Spel 166 A4
Widecombe Rd. SE9 17 D1
Widgeon Rd. Roc 43 F1
Widmore Lodge Rd. Brom 33 F2
Widmore Rd. Brom 33 F2
Wierd Wood. Lon 40 C1
Wierton Hill. Bou Mon 124 C2
Wierton La. Bou Mon 125 D3
Wigeon Path. SE28 2 C4
Wigmore Rd. Rai (K) 75 E4
Wilberforce Rd. Cox 123 F4
Wilberforce Way. Grave 41 F4
Wilderness Rd. Chis 34 B3
Wildernesse Ave. Seal 82 A1
Wildernesse Ave. Sev 82 A1
Wildernesse Mount. Sev 81 F1
Wildman Cl. Rai (K) 75 F4
Wildwood Cl. Broom (m) 127 D3
Wildwood Cl. SE12 16 A2
Wildwood Glade. Rai (K) 75 E4
Wilfred St. Grave 24 B3
Wilkinson Cl. Dart 21 D4
Will Adams Way. Rai (K) 61 D3
Will Crooks Gdns. SE9 16 C4
Willechurch Rd. Cli W 27 D2
Willenhall Rd. SE18 2 B3
Willersley Ave. Orp 49 F2
Willersley Ave. Sid 18 A2
Willersley Cl. Sid 18 A2
Willesley Gdns. Cran 173 F1
Willett Cl. Orp 50 A4
Willett Way. Orp 50 A4
William Barefoot Dr. SE9 17 E1
William Luck Cl. E Pec 121 D1
William Rd. Cux 58 C3
William St. Grave 24 B2
William St. Grays 8 C2
William St. Rai (K) 62 B3
William St. T W 153 E1
Willington Green. Maid 107 D2
Willington St. Maid 107 D3
Willington St. Oth 107 D3
Willis Rd. Eri 4 C3
Willow Ave. Hoo S W 46 A4
Willow Ave. Sid 18 B3
Willow Ave. Swan 37 D1
Willow Cl. Bex 19 D3
Willow Cl. Brom 49 D4
Willow Cl. Orp 50 B3
Willow Cres. Five O G 138 B2
Willow Cres. Stapt 143 D1
Willow Gr. Chis 34 B3
Willow La. Padd W 140 A1
Willow Lea. Ton 118 C2
Willow Park. Otf 81 D3
Willow Rd. Dart 20 C2
Willow Rd. Dit 87 D4
Willow Rd. Eri 5 E1
Willow Rd. Roc 44 A1
Willow Tree Rd. T W 167 D3
Willow Vale. Chis 34 B3
Willow Walk. T W 154 A2
Willow Way. Maid 106 B4
Willow Wents. Merew 102 C3
Willow Wlk. Dart 20 C4
Willow Wlk. Meo 70 A4
Willow Wlk. Orp 49 E2
Willow Wood Rd. Meo 70 A3
Willowbank Dr. H Hals 29 D4
Willowby Gdns. Rai (K) 76 A4
Willowmead. Dit 87 D3
Willows The. Grays 8 C2
Willows The. Rai (K) 62 A3
Willrose Cres. SE2 3 E3
Wilman Rd. T W 153 E2
Wilmar Way. Seal 82 A2
Wilmington Ave. Orp 50 C2
Wilmington Court Rd. Dart 20 B1
Wilmington Way. Rai (K) 61 E3
Wilmot Rd. Dart 20 B3
Wilmount St. SE18 2 B3
Wilson Ave. Chath 59 F2
Wilson Cl. Hild 118 A1
Wilson Cl. Maid 107 D2
Wilson Rd. Ton 119 D1
Wilsons La. E Far 105 E1
Wilton Dr. Dit 87 E2
Wilton Rd. SE2 3 F3
Wiltshire Cl. Chath 60 C2
Wiltshire Rd. Orp 50 B3
Wiltshire Way. Maid 107 D2
Wiltshire Way. T W 153 F2
Wimborne Ave. Orp 35 D1
Wimborne Cl. SE12 16 A3
Wimbourne Dr. Rai (K) 61 F1
Winchcomb Gdns. SE9 16 C4
Winchelsea Ave. Bexh 4 A2
Winchelsea Rd. Wald 60 B1
Winchester Ave. Wald 74 A4
Winchester Cl. Brom 33 D1
Winchester Cres. Grave 24 C1
Winchester Ct. Sev 98 B4
Winchester Park. Brom 33 D1
Winchester Rd. Bexh 3 F1
Winchester Rd. Brom 33 D1
Winchester Rd. Hawkt 189 E3
Winchester Rd. Orp 50 C1
Winchester Rd. Ton 118 C1
Winchester Way. Rai (K) 62 B2
Winch's Garth. Stapt 143 D1
Wincliff Rd. Ton 136 B2
Wincrofts Dr. SE9 17 F4
Wind Hill. Char 130 A2
Wind Hill La. Char 130 A2
Windermere Cl. Dart 20 B2
Windermere Cl. Orp 49 E2
Windermere Dr. Rai (K) 61 F2
Windermere Rd. Bexh 4 C1
Windermere Rd. W Wick 48 A2
Windhover Way. Grave 42 A4
Windmill Cl. Roc 44 B3
Windmill Cotts. Low St 13 F1
Windmill Hill. Bor G 84 C1
Windmill Hill. Brenc 156 B3
Windmill Hill. Ulc 127 E2
Windmill Hill. Wro H 85 D2
Windmill La. Kes 48 B1
Windmill La. W Mal 86 C1
Windmill La. Wad 178 C2
Windmill Park. Bor G 85 D2
Windmill Rd. Gil 60 C4
Windmill Rd. Sev 98 B1
Windmill Rd. Sev W 116 B3
Windmill St. Grave 24 B2
Windmill St. Roc 44 B3
Windmill St. T W 167 F4
Windsor Ave. Chath 60 A3
Windsor Ave. Grays 8 B4
Windsor Cl. Chis 34 B4
Windsor Cl. Maid 89 E1
Windsor Dr. Dart 20 B3
Windsor Dr. Orp 64 B4
Windsor Rd. Bexh 19 D4
Windsor Rd. Gil 45 F1
Windsor Rd. Grave 41 E4
Windsor Rd. Sid 35 E3
Windward Rd. Chath 59 F3
Windy Ridge. Brom 34 A2
Windyridge. Chath 61 D3
Winfield La. Plax 101 D4
Wingate Rd. Sid 35 F3
Wingfield. Grays 8 A3
Wingfield Rd. Grave 24 B2
Wingham Cl. Maid 107 D2
Wingham Cl. Rai (K) 61 F4
Wingrove Dr. Thu 90 A1
Wingrove Rd. SE6 16 A1
Winifred Rd. Dart 20 B3
Winifred Rd. Eri 5 D3
Winifred Rd. Rose 107 D4
Winlaton Rd. Brom 33 D4
Winn Common Rd. SE18 3 D3
Winn Rd. SE12 16 B2
Winser Rd. Rol 192 B3
Winston Dr. Roc 44 C3
Winston Rd. Roc 44 A1
Winstone Scott Ave. Spel 166 A4
Winterborne Ave. Orp 49 F2
Winterfield La. Dit 87 D2
Winters Croft. Grave 41 F3
Winton Ct. Swan 37 D1
Winton Rd. Orp 49 E1
Wirrals The. Wald 74 B4
Wise's Lane. Stans 69 D3
Wishart Rd. SE3 1 C1
Wisley Rd. Orp 35 E3
Wistaria Cl. Orp 49 E2
Wisteria Gdns. Swan 36 C2
Witches La. Sev 97 F4
Witham Way. Roc 44 A2
Withens Cl. Orp 35 F1
Witherston Way. SE9 17 E1
Withyham Rd. Gro 165 E1
Wittersham Cl. Wald 60 B1
Wittersham Rd. Brom 33 D4
Wittersham Rd. Rol 192 C1
Wittersham Rd. Witt 193 E1
Wivenhoe Cl. Rai (K) 62 B3
Wodehouse Cl. Dit 87 D4
Woldham Rd. Brom 33 F1
Wolds Dr. Orp 49 E1
Wolfe Cl. Brom 48 B4
Wolfe Cres. SE7 1 C3
Wolfe Rd. Maid 105 E3
Wolfram Cl. SE13 16 A3
Wollaston Cl. Rai (K) 75 F4
Wolseley Rd. Soub 153 F2
Wolsley Cl. Dart 20 A3
Wolvercote Rd. SE2 3 F4
Wood Ave. Pur 6 C3
Wood Cl. Dart 20 A1
Wood Dr. Chis 34 A3
Wood Dr. Sev 98 A3
Wood La. Bidd 184 C4
Wood Lane. Dart 38 C4
Wood Lodge Gdns. Brom 34 A3
Wood Ride. Orp 35 D1
Wood St. Cux 58 B3
Wood St. Gil 45 E1
Wood St. Grays 8 C2
Wood St. Hex 37 F2
Wood St. T W 167 E4
Wood View Cl. W Kin 68 A4
Wood Way. Orp 49 E2
Woodbank Rd. Brom 16 A1
Woodberry Gr. Bex 19 F1
Woodbine Rd. Sid 18 A2
Woodbridge Dr. Maid 106 A3
Woodbrook. Char 130 C2
Woodbrook Rd. SE2 3 E2
Woodbury Cl. Bigg 78 A3
Woodbury Park Gdns. T W 153 E1
Woodbury Park Rd. T W 153 E1
Woodbury Rd. Hawkt 189 E3
Woodbury Rd. Wald 74 A3
Woodchurch Cl. Sid 18 A1
Woodchurch Cl. Wald 60 B1
Woodchurch Cres. Rai (K) 61 F3
Woodchurch Dr. Brom 33 F3
Woodchurch Rd. Ten 186 C2
Woodclyffe Dr. Chis 34 B2
Woodcock La. Ben 191 D4
Woodcock La. Bou Mal 128 A1
Woodcote Dr. Orp 49 F3
Woodcroft. SE9 17 D1
Woodcut. Maid 89 E2
Woodcutters Ave. Grays 8 C4
Woodfall Dr. Dart 20 A4
Woodfield Ave. Grave 24 B1
Woodfield Ave. Hild 118 A1
Woodfield Rd. Ton 136 B2
Woodfield Way. Cli W 45 D4
Woodfields. Sev 97 F4
Woodford Rd. Maid 105 E3
Woodgate La. Bor 77 F3
Woodgate Rd. Birl 85 F4
Woodgers Gr. Swan 37 D2
Woodhayes. Chis 34 B3
Woodhead Dr. Orp 50 A2
Woodhill. SE18 2 A3
Woodhill Park. Pem 154 C1
Woodhurst. Wald 73 F4
Woodhurst Ave. Orp 49 F4
Woodhurst Cl. Cux 58 B3
Woodhurst Rd. SE2 3 E3
Woodington Cl. SE9 17 E3
Woodknoll Dr. Chis 34 A2
Woodland Ave. Hart (S) 55 D4
Woodland Cl. Lon 40 C1
Woodland Cl. T W 153 F2
Woodland Cl. W Mal 86 B2
Woodland Cres. SE10 1 A2
Woodland Dr. Ede 131 F4
Woodland Rd. T W 153 F2
Woodland Rise. Seal 82 A1
Woodland Rise. Sev 99 D4
Woodland Terr. SE7 2 A3
Woodland Way. Bid 152 C4
Woodland Way. Maid 89 E2
Woodland Way. Orp 49 F4
Woodland Way. SE2 3 F3
Woodland Wlk. Brom 33 D4
Woodlands. Bexh 19 E3
Woodlands. Cox 123 E4
Woodlands. Padd W 139 D2
Woodlands. Pem 155 D2
Woodlands. Wald 74 B3
Woodlands Ave. Sid 18 A2
Woodlands Ave. Snod 72 A2
Woodlands Cl. Brom 34 A2
Woodlands Cl. Maid 89 E2
Woodlands Cl. Swan 37 D2
Woodlands Cl. Tes 104 B2
Woodlands La. Shor 43 D3
Woodlands Park. Sid 36 C4
Woodlands Park Rd. SE10 1 A2
Woodlands Rd. Bexh 19 D4
Woodlands Rd. Brom 34 A2
Woodlands Rd. Dit 87 F2
Woodlands Rd. Gil 61 D4
Woodlands Rd. Orp 64 B4
Woodlands Rd. Ton 136 B2
Woodlands Rise. Swan 37 D2
Woodlands The. Orp 64 B4
Woodlands View. Shorm 65 E3
Woodlea. Dit 87 D3
Woodlea Dr. Brom 48 A4
Woodleas. Maid 105 D3
Woodley Rd. Orp 50 C2
Woodmere. SE9 17 D2
Woodmount. Swan 51 F3
Woodpecker Cl. Ede 131 F4
Woodpecker Glade. Rai (K) 61 F1
Woodpecker Rd. Dit 87 D3
Woodrow. SE18 2 A3
Woodsgate Way. Pem 154 B1
Woodside. Meo 70 A2
Woodside. Orp 50 B1
Woodside. Rai (K) 61 F1
Woodside Ave. Chis 34 C4
Woodside Cl. Bexh 19 F4
Woodside Cl. Pem 155 D1
Woodside Cres. Sid 18 A1
Woodside Dr. Bex 37 D4
Woodside Green. Cli W 27 E2
Woodside La. Bex 18 C3
Woodside Rd. Bexh 19 F4
Woodside Rd. Brom 49 D4
Woodside Rd. Maid 106 C2
Woodside Rd. Pem 155 D1
Woodside Rd. Sev 98 B4
Woodside Rd. Sid 18 A1
Woodside Rd. Sund 97 D4
Woodside Rd. T W 166 C4
Woodside Rd. Ton 136 B2
Woodstock Cl. Bex 19 D2
Woodstock Ct. SE12 16 B3
Woodstock Rd. Roc 44 B2
Woodview. Grays 8 C4
Woodview Cres. Hild 118 A1
Woodview Rd. Swan 36 C2
Woodview Rise. Roc 44 A3
Woodville Cl. SE12 16 B3
Woodville Pl. Grave 24 B2
Woodville Rd. Maid 106 B3
Woodville St. SE18 2 A3
Woodward Cl. Grays 8 B3
Woodward Hts. Grays 8 B3
Woodward Terr. Gree 22 A3
Woodyates Rd. SE12 16 B3
Woolacombe Rd. SE3 1 C1
Woolaston Cl. Maid 106 A3
Wooldeys Rd. Rai (K) 62 A3
Woollett St. Maid 89 E1
Woolley Cl. Soub 153 D3
Woolley Rd. Maid 107 D2
Woolley Rd. Soub 153 D3
Woolwich Church St. SE18 2 A4
Woolwich Cl. Chath 60 B2
Woolwich Common. SE18 2 B2
Woolwich High St. SE18 2 B4
Woolwich Manorway. E16 2 B4
Woolwich New Rd. SE18 2 B3
Woolwich Rd. Belv 4 A3
Woolwich Rd. Bexh 19 E4
Woolwich Rd. SE2 4 A2
Woolwich Rd. SE7 1 B3
Wootton Green. Rai (K) 61 F4
Wopsle Cl. Chath 59 F2
Worcester Cl. Grays 22 B4
Worcester Cl. Ist 41 D3
Worcester Cl. Roc 44 A2
Worcester Rd. Maid 106 C2
Wordsworth Cl. Chath 60 C2
Wordsworth Rd. Maid 89 E2
Wordsworth Rd. Well 3 D1
Wordsworth Way. Dart 21 E4
Wordsworth Way. Dit 87 E4
Workhouse La. E Far 105 F1
Workhouse Rd. Birl 71 D1
Workhouse Rd. Sutt V 126 B2
Worlds End La. Orp 64 B4
Wormdale Hill. New(G) 77 E4
Wormdale Rd. New(G) 77 E4
Worships Hill. Sev 98 A4
Worth Cl. Orp 50 A1
Wotton Cl. Maid 107 D1
Wotton Green. Orp 35 F1
Wouldham Rd. Chath 59 D3
Wrangleden Cl. Maid 107 D1
Wrangleden Rd. Maid 107 D1
Wrangling La. Meo 71 D4
Wrekin Rd. SE18 2 C2
Wren Cl. Dit 87 D3
Wren Cl. Orp 35 F1
Wren Industrial Estate. Maid 125 D4
Wren Path. SE28 2 C4
Wren Rd. Sid 18 C1
Wren Way. Wald 60 B1
Wrens Croft. Grave 41 D4
Wren's Cross. Maid 106 B4
Wrenthorpe Rd. Brom 33 D4
Wricklemarsh Rd. SE3 1 C1
Wright Cl. Swans 22 C3
Wrights Cl. Ten 186 B2
Wrotham Hill Rd. Stans 69 E1
Wrotham Rd. Bor G 84 B2
Wrotham Rd. Grave 24 B2
Wrotham Rd. Ist 41 E3
Wrotham Rd. Meo 70 A3
Wrotham Rd. Meo 56 B3
Wrotham Rd. Well 3 F1
Wrotham Water La. Stans 85 D4
Wrotham Water La. Trot 70 A1
Wrotham Water Rd. Stans 85 D4
Wrottesley Rd. SE18 2 C2
Wulfred Way. Kemsg 82 B3
Wyatt Cl. Bor G 84 A2
Wyatt Pl. Roc 44 B2
Wyatt Rd. Dart 20 A4
Wyatt St. Maid 106 B4
Wybourne Rise. T W 167 E2
Wycham Ave. Sid 18 A2
Wycherley Cl. SE3 1 A2
Wycliffe Cl. Well 3 D1
Wycliffe Row. Grave 24 A2
Wydeville Manor Rd. SE12 33 E4
Wye Cl. Orp 50 A3
Wye Rd. Bor G 84 B2
Wye Rd. Grave 24 C1
Wye Rd. Ton 118 C1
Wyke Manor Rd. Maid 106 B4
Wykeham Gr. Lee 108 B2
Wykeham St. Roc 44 B2
Wyles Rd. Chath 60 A3
Wyles St. Gil 45 F2
Wylie Rd. Hoo S W 28 C1
Wyncroft Cl. Brom 34 A1
Wynd The. Char 130 C3
Wyndcliff Rd. SE7 1 B2
Wyndham Ave. Lei 135 D3
Wyndham Cl. Lei 135 D3
Wyndham Cl. Orp 49 F3
Wyndham Rd. Chath 60 A3
Wynford Gr. Orp 35 E1
Wynford Pl. Belv 4 B2
Wynford Way. SE9 17 D1
Wynn's Ave. Sid 18 B3
Wythens Wlk. SE9 17 E3
Wythering Cl. Thu 90 A1
Wythes Cl. Brom 34 A2
Wythfield Rd. SE9 17 D3
Wyvern Cl. Dart 20 C2
Wyvern Cl. Orp 50 B2
Wyvern Cl. Snod 72 B2
Wyvill Cl. Rai (K) 62 A1

Yalding Cl. Orp 35 F1
Yalding Cl. Roc 44 B3
Yalding Hill. Yal 122 B4
Yantlet Dr. Roc 43 F2
Yardley Cl. Ton 136 C4
Yardley Park Rd. Ton 136 C4
Yarnton Way. Belv 4 A4
Yarrow Rd. Wald 74 A4
Yateley St. SE18 1 C4
Yelsted La. Bredh 74 C2
Yelsted La. Sto 76 B3
Yelsted Rd. Sto 76 B2
Yeoman Dr. Chath 61 D3
Yeoman Gdns. Padd W 139 D1
Yeoman La. Rose 107 E4
Yeoman Way. Rose 107 E3
Yeoman's Meadows. Sev 98 B3
Yeovil Cl. Orp 50 A2
Yester Dr. Chis 34 A3
Yester Park. Chis 34 A3
Yester Rd. Chis 34 A3
Yew Rd. Hoo S W 46 A4
Yew Tree Cl. Bredh 74 C3
Yew Tree Cl. Dit 88 A3
Yew Tree Cl. Lon 40 C2
Yew Tree Cl. Sev 97 F4
Yew Tree Cl. Well 3 E1
Yew Tree Green Rd. Brenc 157 E3
Yew Tree Rd. Soub 153 E2
Yewdale Cl. Brom 33 D3
Yews The. Grave 24 C2
Yewtree Industrial Estate. Dit 87 F3
Yolande Gdns. SE9 17 D3
Yopps Green. Plax 101 D3
York Ave. Gil 60 C4
York Ave. Sid 18 A1
York Ave. Wald 74 A4
York Hill. Chath 60 C3
York Par. Ton 118 C1
York Pl. Grays 8 B2
York Rd. Chath 59 F4
York Rd. Dart 21 D2
York Rd. Grave 24 C1
York Rd. Grave 23 F2
York Rd. Maid 106 C3
York Rd. T W 167 E4
York Rd. Ton 118 C1
York Rise. Orp 50 A2
York Terr. Eri 4 C1
Yorkland Ave. Well 18 A4
Yuagher La. New(G) 76 C4

Zambra Way. Seal 82 A2
Zangwill Rd. SE3 1 C1
Zelah Rd. Orp 50 C3
Zetland Ave. Chath 61 D3
Zion Pl. Grave 24 B2
Zion St. Seal 82 A1